Chemical Dependency

SECOND EDITION

Chemical Dependency

A Systems Approach

C. Aaron McNeece
Florida State University

Diana M. DiNitto
University of Texas at Austin

Allyn and Bacon

Boston   London   Toronto   Sydney   Tokyo   Singapore

Series Editor, Social Work and Family Therapy: Judy Fifer
Editor in Chief, Social Sciences: Karen Hanson
Editorial Assistant: Jennifer Muroff
Marketing Manager: Susan E. Brown
Editorial-Production Administrator: Annette Joseph
Editorial-Production Coordinator: Susan Freese
Editorial-Production Service: TKM Productions
Text Design: Denise Hoffman, Glenview Studios
Composition Buyer: Linda Cox
Manufacturing Buyer: Megan Cochran
Cover Administrator: Jenny Hart
Cover Designer: Brian Gogolin

Copyright © 1998, 1994 by Allyn & Bacon
A Viacom Company
160 Gould Street
Needham Heights, MA 02194
Internet: www:abacon.com
American Online: keyword: College Online

Library of Congress Cataloging-in-Publication Data

McNeece, Carl Aaron.
    Chemical dependency : a systems approach / C. Aaron McNeece, Diana
M. DiNitto. — 2nd ed.
      p.   cm.
    Includes bibliographical references and index.
    ISBN 0-205-26485-9
    1. Substance abuse. I. DiNitto, Diana M. II. Title.
HV4998.M46 1998
362.29'18—DC21   97-35141
                                              CIP
                                              Rev.

Printed in the United States of America

10 9 8 7 6 5 4 3 2 1   03 02 01 00 99 98

Text credits: Page 91, footnote 60: "Alcoholism: A Merry-Go-Round Named Denial," copyright © 1969, by Al-Anon Family Group Headquarters, Inc. Reprinted by permission of Al-Anon Family Group Headquarters, Inc. Chapter 11, footnotes 169, 186, 269, 284, and Table 11.1: Reprinted with permission from *Journal of Studies on Alcohol*, vol. 56, pp. 558–565, 1995. Copyright by Alcohol Research Documentation, Inc. Rutgers Center of Alcohol Studies, Piscataway, NJ 08855.

*In loving memory of
my cousin
Stephanie Perry*

D. M. D.

Contents

Preface   xiii

Part One   Theories, Models, and Definitions   1

1   Definitions and Epidemiology of Alcoholism and Drug Addiction   3

Definitions and Myths   4
  Disease, Addiction, or Behavioral Disorder?   4
Epidemiology   8
  Alcohol   8
  Marijuana and Hallucinogens   14
  Nicotine   14
  Cocaine   16
  Other Stimulants and Sedatives   17
  Narcotics   19
Summary   19
Endnotes   20

2   The Etiology of Addiction   23

by Pamela V. Valentine

Etiological Theories   23
  The Moral Model   24
  Psychological Theories   24
  Biological Theories   27
  Sociocultural Theories   29
  Alternative Explanations   31
  A Multicausal Model   32

Summary   33
Endnotes   33

3   Becoming Addicted   36

The Stages of Alcoholism   37
The Course of Cocaine Addiction   39
Becoming a Heroin Addict   40
Marijuana Addiction   41
Summary   43
Endnotes   43

**4   The Physiological and Behavioral Consequences
of Alcohol and Drug Abuse   45**

The Effects of Alcohol   45
The Metabolization of Alcohol   46
Intoxication   46
Withdrawal   47
The Digestive System   47
The Cardiovascular System   48
The Endocrine and Reproductive Systems   48
The Neurologic System   49
Common Neurologic Disorders   49
Alcohol and Other Disorders   50
The Effects of Cannabis   51
The Effects of Stimulants   52
Cocaine   52
Amphetamines   53
MDMA   55
Crystal Methamphetamine   55
The Effects of Sedatives   56
The Effects of Narcotics   57
The Digestive System   58
The Endocrine System   58
Integument   58
The Genitourinary System   58
Other Problems   58
The Effects of Hallucinogens   58
The Effects of Inhalants   60
The Effects of Drugs on Offspring   60
Alcohol   61
Opiates   61
Tobacco   61

Amphetamines and Cocaine   62
    Other Drugs   62
Summary   62
Endnotes   62

Part Two   Intervention, Prevention, and Public Policy   67

5   Screening, Diagnosis, Assessment, and Referral   69

Screening   70
Can Alcoholics and Addicts Be Believed?   75
Diagnosis   77
Assessment   82
    Education   83
    Employment   85
    Military History   86
    Medical History   86
    Legal History   86
    Drinking and Drug History   87
    Psychological or Psychiatric History   88
    Family History   88
    Current Family and Social Relationships   89
    Why the Individual Is Seeking Services   90
Denial, Resistance, and Motivation to Recovery   90
Confidentiality   96
Referrals   98
Summary   100
Endnotes   100

6   Treatment—The System of Care   104

Components of the Treatment System   104
    Detoxification Programs   104
    Intensive Treatment   109
    Residential Programs   115
    Outpatient Services   120
    Pharmacotherapy   131
    Aftercare   136
    Maintenance   137
    Education and Psychoeducation   137
    Adjunctive Services   138
    More Treatment Effectiveness Issues   139
    Nontraditional Treatments   146

Self-Help Groups   151
   Alcoholics Anonymous   151
   Research and Self-Help Groups   154
   Narcotics Anonymous and Other Self-Help Groups   156
Summary   156
Endnotes   157

7   Preventing Alcohol and Drug Problems   166

Overview of Prevention   168
Public Information and Education   168
   Programs Directed at Children and Adolescents   169
Service Measures   170
Technologic Measures   171
Legislative and Regulatory Measures   173
   Advertising and the Media   173
Economic Measures   176
Summary   177
Endnotes   177

8   Regulating Drugs and Their Consequences   180

Sociocultural Influences on Public Drug Policy   180
Economic and Political Factors   181
Changes in Drug Use Patterns   182
The Nature of Drug Control   182
Assumptions Underlying Regulation   183
Regulation of Alcohol   184
   The Lessons of Prohibition   184
   Current U.S. Policies   184
Control of Illicit Drugs   190
   The War on Drugs   192
   The Economics of Drug War/Peace   192
   Issues Regarding Legalization   193
Drugs, Alcohol, and Crime   195
Alcohol and Drug Law Violations   197
Drug Use by Criminals   198
Drug Use by Victims   199
Domestic Violence   199
Drug/Crime Trends in the 1990s   201
   Drug Trafficking   201
   Drugs, Crime, and Prison   202
   Treating Substance-Abusing Offenders   202
Summary   204
Endnotes   205

Part Three   Chemical Dependency in Special Populations   211

9   Treating Chemically Dependent Children and Adolescents   213
by Thomas E. Smith and David W. Springer

Developmental and Contextual Factors   214
    Medical and Psychiatric Context   214
    Legal Context   215
    Social Context   215
    Educational Context   216
Substance Abuse Treatment   216
Managed Care and Dual Diagnoses   217
Prevention   218
    Drug Education   219
Outpatient and Community Self-Help Approaches   219
    Abstinence-Oriented Approaches   221
    Family-Based Treatment   221
Inpatient Treatment   222
Residential Treatment/Treatment Communities   223
Case Example   223
Summary   226
Endnotes   226

10   Family Systems and Chemical Dependency   229
by Catherine A. Hawkins

A Family Perspective in Theory, Research, and Treatment   230
Theories on Alcoholism and the Family   231
Family Systems Theory of Alcoholism and the Family   232
    Rituals and Routines   232
    Shame   234
    Rules and Roles   235
Codependency and Related Constructs   235
    Codependency   235
    Children of Alcoholics   237
    Adult Children of Alcoholics   238
Assessment and Treatment of Alcoholic Families   239
    Behavioral Perspective   240
    Stress-Coping Perspective   241
    Family Therapy Perspective   242
Effectiveness of Family Treatment   244
Case Example   244
Summary   250
Endnotes   251

11   **Ethnicity, Culture, and Substance Abuse   255**

Substance Abuse among Native Americans and Alaskan Natives   257
  *Cultural Issues and Chemical Abuse among Native Americans
    and Alaskan Natives   258*
  Substance Abuse Problems among Native Americans and Alaskan Natives   259
  Prevention and Treatment Services for Native Americans and Alaskan Natives   262
Substance Abuse among African Americans   269
  Contemporary Explanations of Substance Abuse among African Americans   269
  Chemical Dependency Problems among African Americans   271
  Chemical Dependency Treatment for African Americans   275
  Prevention in African American Communities   279
Substance Abuse among Hispanic Americans   280
  Incidence of Substance Use and Abuse among Hispanic Americans   281
  *Historical and Cultural Perspectives on Substance Use and Abuse
    among Hispanic Americans   284*
  Prevention and Treatment Services for Hispanic Americans   287
Substance Abuse among Asian Americans   290
  Alcohol and Drug Use among Asian Americans and Pacific Islanders   291
  Cultural and Genetic Influences in Substance Use among Asian Americans   292
  Prevention and Treatment Services for Asian Americans   295
Substance Abuse among Jewish Americans   297
  Extent of Alcohol and Other Drug Use among Jewish Americans   298
  Explanations of Low Rates of Alcoholism among Jewish Americans   299
  Prevention and Treatment Services for Jewish Americans   300
Summary   301
Endnotes   302

12   **Gay Men, Lesbians, Bisexuals, and Chemical Dependency   318**

Substance Abuse among Lesbians and Gay Men   318
Substance Abuse: Causes and Connections   323
Prevention Issues   327
Treatment Issues   328
  Denial and Defensiveness   328
  Significant Others   331
  Treatment: Together or Apart?   332
Chemical Dependency Professionals   333
The Recovery Movement and Twelve-Step Groups   335
Resources   338
Summary   339
Endnotes   339

13 Compounding the Problem: Substance Abuse and Other Disabilities 347

by Diana M. DiNitto and Deborah K. Webb

Mental Illness and Substance Abuse 349
   Prevalence 349
   Substance Vulnerability 349
   Underdiagnosing 350
   Screening, Assessing, and Making Accurate Diagnoses 350
   Relationships between Abused Drugs and Mental Disorders 351
   Treatment 352
Mental Retardation 359
   Is There a Problem? 360
   Treating Substance Abusers Who Are Mentally Retarded 362
Mobility Impairments 366
Traumatic Head and Brain Injury 370
Sensory Disabilities 373
   Hearing Impairments 373
   Visual Impairments 376
Other Physical Disabilities 377
Resources 379
Summary 379
Endnotes 380

14 Alcohol and Drug Use among the Elderly 391

by Linda Vinton and Kathryn G. Wambach

Prevalence and Patterns 391
Antecedents and Correlates 393
   Sociocultural Models 393
   Psychologic and Psychosocial Models 394
Alcohol and Drug Abuse 396
Assessment and Biopsychosocial Effects 397
   Assessment Strategies and Problems 397
   Effects 398
   Medical Complications 398
   Cognitive Impairment 398
   Depression and Suicide 399
Case Finding and Treatment 399
Summary 402
Endnotes 402

15   **Gender and Drugs: Fact, Fiction, and Unanswered Questions   406**
by Diane R. Davis and Diana M. DiNitto

Susan's Story   406
An Equality Women Don't Want   408
Biological Differences   410
   Genetics and Etiology   410
   Is Biology Destiny?   412
   Sexual Dysfunction   413
   Gynecological and Reproductive Problems   414
Social Differences   417
   Falling from the Pedestal   418
   Social Supports   418
   Crime   420
Psychological Differences   421
   Psychological Distress   421
   Physical and Sexual Abuse   422
Women, Treatment, and Recovery   423
   Treatment Matching   424
   Self-Help Groups   426
Murky Methodological Waters   428
   The Feminist Critique   428
   Alcohol, Drugs, and Measurement   429
   Emerging from Invisibility   430
Susan's Story Revisited   430
Where Do We Go from Here?   431
   Identification   431
   Treatment   431
   The Big Picture   432
Summary   432
Endnotes   433

Part Four   Summary and Conclusions   443

16   **Chemical Dependency: Current Issues and Future Prospects   445**
by Paul R. Raffoul

Research   446
Policy Change   447
Providing Services   448
   Third-Party Coverage   448
   Managed Care   449
Summary and Concluding Thoughts   449
Endnotes   450

Index   451

Preface

Both authors of this text have taught courses titled Alcoholism and Alcohol Abuse, Drug Abuse, Addiction, and Treatment, and Chemical Dependency for a number of years. We also have a number of years of experience working with chemically dependent clients in detoxification centers, halfway houses, outpatient services, juvenile training schools, adult prisons, and probation and parole programs. Additional experiences include participation in volunteer organizations, research efforts, and policymaking bodies regarding drug and alcohol abuse. The other contributors to this book also have valuable experience working with chemically dependent clients. This book grew out of our desire to make available a single textbook providing a comprehensive, systems-based examination of the subjects of alcohol and drug abuse and dependence, as well as the associated problems, policies, and programs. We have included the essential components that social workers and other human service professionals need to understand to work effectively with chemically dependent clients within the system that provides treatment and other services.

Although we believe that this text contains state-of-the-art information regarding theory and practice with people who abuse or are dependent on chemicals, it is in no way intended to serve as a substitute for competent, professional help for anyone with a substance abuse or dependence problem.

Part One of this text, Chapters 1 through 4, deals with theories, models, and definitions of abuse and dependency. In an effort to be as comprehensive as possible, we have included *all* theories that have any credence within the scientific and professional communities. The current level of scientific understanding does not provide definitive answers to such questions as What *causes* chemical dependency? We caution the reader that many practicing professionals adhere to particular etiological models with an ideological fervor. Although our biases may shine through the veneer of scientific objectivity in places, we have tried to present as balanced a perspective as possible. Thus, when discussing consequences of alcoholism such as pancreatitis and cardiomyopathy, we support our belief that alcoholism and drug dependence is a *disease*. At other times, we find it more useful to view drug dependence as an *addiction* or an *addictive behavior* rather than a disease. If there seems to be some uncertainty here in the adoption of the best model, it reflects the state of knowledge in this field.

Part Two concerns intervention, broadly defined. Chapter 5 describes the common processes of screening, diagnosis, and referral. Common treatment approaches and their effectiveness are examined in Chapter 6, as are issues of financing treatment and managed care. Chapter 7 presents prevention theories and describes current programs designed to prevent abuse or dependency. Chapter 8 takes a macroapproach to intervention, dealing with public policies regarding the manufacture, distribution, and use of psychoactive substances, as well as the social, economic, and political consequences of chemical abuse and dependency. The problem of drug-related crime is also covered in this chapter.

Part Three is devoted to substance use, abuse, and dependence among particular populations: children and adolescents; families; ethnic groups; gay men, lesbians, and bisexuals; people with dual diagnoses; older people; and women. We apply some of the etiological theories described earlier in the text in explaining the differential use of addictive substances by various groups, and we discuss some of the special problems that occur in these populations because of alcohol or drug use. In examining these populations, we link them to the larger systems and other subsystems to which they are connected—the community, the state, the church, the political system, the professions, the network of treatment agencies, and so forth. Chapter 9 examines children and adolescents within the context of both family and larger systems, and Chapter 10 takes a careful look at family systems theory. Chapter 11 addresses chemical abuse and dependence from a cultural perspective and describes these problems among particular ethnic groups. Substance abuse in gay, lesbian, and bisexual communities is the focus of Chapter 12. Chapter 13 examines clients with diagnoses in addition to substance abuse or dependence, and Chapter 14 looks at substance abuse and dependence among older people. Gender issues and substance problems are covered in Chapter 15.

Part Four (Chapter 16) summarizes major current issues, such as the decriminalization of some currently proscribed substances, and indicates some areas where research efforts should especially be directed. Chapter 16 also examines trends in service provision for chemically dependent clients.

Acknowledgments

All the material contained in this text has been used with students in our classes. Many thanks to them and to a number of faculty across the country for valuable suggestions. Comments made by the following reviewers were also helpful: Sandra C. Anderson, Portland State University; Edith M. Freeman, University of Kansas; and Paul Raffoul, University of Houston. We also thank our families and Craig Deere for providing the caring environment that allowed this book to be written. Diana especially thanks Dean Barbara White of the School of Social Work at the University of Texas at Austin for her support in completing this manuscript, Mary Margaret Just for her tireless efforts at tracking down reference material, Amy Dolejs for her help with proofreading, Kelly Larson for her assistance with figures and tables, and Louise Warren for her valuable comments and insights. Invaluable editorial assistance was provided by Dr. Marguerite McInnis, Florida State University.

P A R T   O N E

Theories, Models, and Definitions

One of the most puzzling questions in the area of chemical dependency is: Why can one person drink socially for a lifetime and never develop a "drinking problem," while another person may become addicted to alcohol after a very short period of social drinking? Why are most teenagers able to experiment with illicit drugs and then become totally abstinent, while some of their peers will become quickly and perhaps fatally addicted? The complexity of this process is why we devote the first four chapters to theories, models, and definitions.

Chapter 1 covers the most common definitions of terms such as *drug use, drug abuse, addiction, dependency, alcoholism, problem drinking,* and so on. At the heart of these different definitions is the ongoing dispute about whether alcoholism is an addiction, a disease, a behavioral disorder, or something else. In addition, this chapter defines the major classes of drugs and examines the epidemiology of alcohol and drug use.

We take a closer look at the major etiological theories in Chapter 2, including psychologic, biologic, and cultural theories, as well as a moral model. A multicausal model of drug use is examined, in an attempt to link together all the major factors that are thought to influence drug use.

Chapter 3 presents a "user's view" of the process of becoming addicted, and Chapter 4 discusses the physiological and behavioral consequences of alcohol and drug abuse. In both these chapters, we attempt to break down some of the more common myths and stereotypes regarding addiction and addicts.

1

Definitions and Epidemiology of Alcoholism and Drug Addiction

In 1993, the estimated per capita consumption of alcoholic beverages by adults in the United States was 36.8 gallons. This is equal to a per capita consumption of 32.4 gallons of beer, 2.5 gallons of wine, and 1.9 gallons of distilled spirits.[1] Heavy drinkers, about 10 percent of the drinking population, account for half this consumption. (*Heavy drinkers* are defined in this context as those who consume 1 ounce or more of pure alcohol daily; *moderate drinkers* consume 0.22 to 0.99 ounce; and *light drinkers* consume less than 0.22 ounce daily.)[2] It is little wonder that there are 18 million "problem drinkers" and alcoholics in the United States today. Neither is it surprising that half of all accidental deaths, suicides, and homicides are alcohol related. From January to March 1992, there were an estimated 105,378 drug abuse emergency-room episodes in the United States.[3] What is surprising is that despite the pervasiveness of health, social, and economic problems associated with the use of alcohol, experts have yet to agree just what alcoholism really is. Is it a disease, a behavior problem, an addiction, or something completely different?

In recent years, people have become much more concerned with the presence and use of other types of drugs. For example, it was estimated that by the early 1980s, 20 million Americans were spending $18 billion on cocaine.[4] Even though the estimated percentage of high school seniors who have used marijuana dropped in the 1990s according to the Monitoring the Future study, cocaine use has remained disturbingly high. In 1995, 41.7 percent of twelfth-graders had at some time used marijuana and 6.0 percent had at some time used cocaine.[5] Marijuana production in the United States fell from an estimated 5,000 to 6,000 metric tons in 1989 and 1990 to 3,615 to 4,615 metric tons in 1991.[6] Worldwide opium production increased sharply from 2,881 metric tons in 1988 to 3,819 metric tons in 1991.

Generally, attention to other drugs has been focused on illicit mood-altering substances, but there is growing concern with the use of prescription drugs (such as Valium and Darvon), over-the-counter (OTC) drugs, and drugs that have only slight mood-altering properties but present substantial health risks (e.g., tobacco). There are other substances that might not ordinarily be considered as drugs—inhalants and solvents (toluene, paint thinner, glue, etc.) and naturally occurring plants such as mushrooms, morning glory, and yage. Perhaps it might be more technically appropriate to speak of *substances* rather than *drugs*. On the other hand, the reasons that people generally use or abuse a particular substance are related to the specific drug contained in that substance. Tobacco is smoked because of its nicotine; khat is chewed because it contains cathinone; mushrooms are eaten for their psilocybin. Our primary focus in this book is with the most commonly used psychoactive drugs—those that alter mood, cognition, and/or behavior—whether obtained through legal or illegal means.

Definitions and Myths

Alcohol is a chemical compound that, when ingested, has the pharmacological property of altering the functioning of the nervous system. Along with barbiturates and benzodiazepines, alcohol belongs to a class of chemicals called *central nervous system (CNS) depressants*. These drugs are used medically in the induction of anesthesia and the reduction of anxiety. They are often referred to as *sedative-hypnotics*. There are several different types of alcohol, but the two most common types are *methyl alcohol* or *methanol* (the type one uses as fuel for a car) and *ethyl alcohol* or *ethanol* (the type one drinks). Alcoholic beverages generally consist of ethyl alcohol (C_2H_5OH), by-products of fermentation known as congeners, colorings, flavorings, and water.[7] Beverage alcohol has been used by almost every known culture. Since any type of sugary fluid will ferment when exposed to omnipresent yeast spores, spontaneous fermentation is a common occurrence, yielding alcohol as a readily available pharmacological substance.

Technically, *cannabis* is also a CNS depressant, but it is usually treated separately in texts such as this because of the magnitude of the problems associated with it. Americans may spend as much as $100 billion for marijuana by the year 2000.[8]

CNS stimulants are drugs that, in small doses, produce an increased sense of alertness and energy, elevated mood, and decreased appetite. Included in this group are caffeine, cocaine, amphetamines, methamphetamines, and amphetaminelike substances such as Ritalin and Preludin.

Opiates are substances such as heroin, morphine, codeine, opioids, and synthetic morphinelike substances such as pethidine, methadone, and dipipanone. Small doses will produce an effect similar to that of the CNS depressants, but with somewhat less impairment of the motor and intellectual processes.[9]

Hallucinogens have the capacity to induce altered perceptions, thoughts, and feelings. Lysergic acid diethylamide (LSD), mescaline, and "magic mushrooms" (with the ingredient psilocybin) all produce these effects. Volatile solvents such as gasoline, benzene, and trichlorethylene can also produce effects similar to CNS depressants and hallucinogens when their vapor is inhaled.[10]

Disease, Addiction, or Behavioral Disorder?

The major definitional issue concerning chemical dependency is whether it is a bad habit, a disease, or a form of moral turpitude. It has been described as a product of the genes, the culture, the devil, and the body. Disagreements persist among professional groups as well as the public at large. The various definitions of addiction are frequently driven by political motives, ideology, personal interest, and professional training. We will have much more to say about the nature of addiction throughout this chapter. The major reason for concern is that appropriate and effective treatment of addiction must be predicated on a reasonably accurate description of the etiology of the phenomenon. Practitioners cannot effectively diagnose or treat that which they cannot define. The best that they can do is deal with the outward symptoms of the problem.

The reader may have noticed terms in the body of literature on chemical dependency that have not been precisely defined—terms such as *alcoholism*, *addiction, use, misuse, abuse, dependency,* and *problem drinking.* Such terminology is more often used as descriptions of a state of affairs rather than explanations, and there is considerable variation in the meaning attached to each term by different writers. We will do the best we can in the following pages to define these terms; however, there will still be some ambiguity. *Problems* and *abuse* frequently exist only in the eye of the beholder.

We are also concerned that when the term *disease* is used in a metaphorical sense, it may actually make treatment more problematic, especially when the metaphoric aspect is forgotten—as it usually is. Over the years, poverty, pornography, obesity, family violence, and "gangsta rap" have all been portrayed as diseases. It is doubtful that the disease label has helped to facilitate a so-called cure for any of these conditions.

Alcoholism and drug addiction also are frequently regarded as a family disease. The implication is that chemical dependency impacts the *family system.* We will discuss this idea at some length in Chapter 10. Whether it is a disease or not, there is little doubt that chemical dependency dramatically affects not only the family but also all other systems of which the family is a subsystem or with which families interact.

Alcoholism is one of those peculiar phenomena for which every layperson usually has his or her own working definition; many think an alcoholic is "anyone who drinks more than I do." The layperson's definition of *alcoholism* usually does not differentiate *alcohol abuse* and *alcohol dependence.* Professionals working in this field do need to make these distinctions, and perhaps even finer ones. One astute observer has commented that it makes about as much sense to treat all alcoholics alike as to treat all persons having a rash in the same way. Imagine visiting the "rash ward" at your local hospital!

Contemporary scholars of alcoholism owe much to the earlier contributions of Jellinek and Bowman, who insisted that there were important differences between chronic alcoholism and alcohol addiction. The former covered all physical and psychological changes resulting from the prolonged use of alcoholic beverages. The latter was a disorder characterized by an urgent craving for alcohol.[11] According to their model, chronic alcoholism could exist without addiction, and addiction could occur without chronic alcoholism. Jellinek is usually identified as the most important researcher in making the disease concept of alcoholism scientifically respectable, but he also identified five separate types of alcoholism, thus demonstrating that the disease model was not a clear or unitary concept.[12]

According to Jellinek, *alpha* alcoholics use alcohol to relieve physical or emotional pain more frequently and in greater amounts than are allowed under normal social rules. *Beta* alcoholics drink heavily and experience a variety of health and social problems because of their drinking, but they are not addicted to alcohol. *Gamma* alcoholics are characterized by loss of control over the amount consumed and by increased tissue tolerance to alcohol, adaptive cell metabolism, withdrawal symptoms, and craving. *Delta* alcoholics are similar to the gamma type, but they do not lose control over the amount consumed though they cannot abstain from continuous use of alcohol. *Epsilon* alcoholics are similar to gammas, but are binge or periodic drinkers.[13]

It should be noted that Jellinek's research was based on a questionnaire designed by members of Alcoholics Anonymous (AA), distributed in the AA magazine *The Grapevine* and completed by only 98 AA members. It could be very misleading to assume that all alcoholics would fall into the same patterns as these AA members.[14] In his book *The Disease Concept of Alcoholism,* Jellinek also noted that a disease is "simply anything the medical profession agrees to call a disease."

The World Health Organization (WHO) defines *alcoholism* as "a chronic behavioral disorder manifested by repeated drinking of alcoholic beverages in excess of the dietary and social uses of the community and to the extent that it interferes with the drinker's health or his social or economic functioning."[15] This definition, stressing cultural deviance and damage to the drinker, avoids the alcoholism-as-a-disease controversy. The WHO also distinguished between alcohol addicts and symptomatic drinkers. The latter group are similar to Jellinek's beta alcoholics.[16] The WHO committee on alcohol-related disabilities subsequently published a report endorsing the use of the term *alcohol dependence syndrome*. The use of this term suggests that a number of clinical phenomena occur with sufficient frequency to constitute a recognizable pattern, but the different elements are not always expected to appear with the same magnitude or frequency. The following are features of alcohol dependence syndrome:

1. Regularity in the repertoire of drinking behavior
2. Emphasis on drink-seeking behavior
3. Increased tolerance to alcohol
4. Repeated withdrawal symptoms
5. Repeated relief or avoidance of withdrawal symptoms by further drinking
6. Subjective awareness of a compulsion to drink
7. Reinstatement of the syndrome after periods of abstinence[17]

A committee of medical authorities commissioned by the National Council on Alcoholism and Drug Dependence (NCADD) developed a set of guidelines to facilitate the diagnosis and evaluation of alcohol dependence at multiple levels. The criteria that were developed consisted of 86 symptoms grouped into three major diagnostic levels, with each level divided into separate tracks based on physiologic symptoms, behavior, and attitudes.[18] An experimental evaluation of the use of these criteria on 120 male alcoholics concluded that 38 items did not differentiate between alcoholics and nonalcoholics and that only 4 items explained 90 percent of the variance between the two groups. These items were gross tremor, regressive defense mechanisms, morning drinking, and blackouts.[19]

As we mentioned earlier, a major issue in defining chemical dependency is whether it is a *disease*. As one might expect, those persons with medical training who work in this field tend to define both alcoholism and drug addiction as diseases; persons with other types of backgrounds are not so sure. This is not always the case, however. Vaillant points out quite clearly that members of the medical community are not united in their conceptualization of alcoholism. About 85 percent of general practitioners agree that alcoholism is a disease, whereas only 50 percent of medical school faculty consider alcoholism (or coronary thrombosis, hypertension, and epilepsy) to be a disease.[20]

Pattison, Sobell, and Sobell feel that alcoholism is a collection of various symptoms and behaviors related to the inappropriate use of alcohol with harmful consequences.[21] In other words, describing a person as an alcoholic is no more useful than is describing someone as having a rash. Pattison and colleagues argue that there is no single factor that explicitly defines and delineates alcoholism and that there is not a clear dichotomy between alcoholics and nonalcoholics. Furthermore, the sequence of appearance of adverse symptoms associated with drinking is highly variable, and there is no conclusive evidence to support the existence of a specific biologic process that predisposes a person toward alcoholism. Their most controversial assertion, however, is that for many "alcoholics," alcohol problems are reversible. In other words, some alcoholics may safely return to social drinking. This clearly puts Pattison and colleagues at odds with the majority of alcoholism professionals as well as with Alcoholics Anonymous, which regards alcoholism as an incurable illness that can be treated only through total abstinence.[22]

Criteria developed by the American Psychiatric Association in its *Diagnostic and Statistical Manual of Mental Disorders (DSM-III-R)* distinguished between psychoactive substance *dependence* and psychoactive substance *abuse*. The *DSM-III-R* also avoided use of terms such as *illness* or *disease*. It included two major sets of diagnoses related to chemical dependency. One is Psychoactive Substance-Induced Organic Mental Disorders, which includes the problems associated with intoxication, withdrawal, dementia, and so on (i.e., the direct acute or chronic effects of such substances on the central nervous system).[23] The other is Psychoactive Substance Abuse Disorders, which includes both abuse and dependence or "maladaptive behavior associated with more or less regular use of the substances."[24] (The *DSM-IV* and other standards are described and compared in Chapter 5.)

Dependence is defined by any three or more of these criteria:

1. Substance often taken in larger amounts or over a longer period of time than the person intended
2. Persistent desire or one or more unsuccessful efforts to cut down or control substance use
3. A great deal of time spent in activities necessary to get the substance or recover from its effects
4. Frequent intoxication or withdrawal symptoms when expected to fulfill major role obligations at work, school, or home
5. Important social, occupational, or recreational activities given up or reduced because of substance abuse
6. Continued substance use despite knowledge of having a persistent or recurrent social, occupational, psychological, or physical problem that is caused or exacerbated by the use of the substance
7. Marked tolerance (need for markedly increased amounts of the substance)
8. Characteristic withdrawal symptoms
9. Substance often taken to relieve or avoid withdrawal symptoms

Psychoactive substance abuse is defined (where the criteria for dependence have not been met) as:

1. Continued use despite knowledge of having a persistent or recurrent social, occupational, psychological, or physical problem that is caused or exacerbated by use of the psychoactive substance
2. Recurrent use in situations in which use is physically hazardous

3. Some symptoms that persist for at least one month or that occur repeatedly over a longer period of time

Not all use of a drug should be classified as *abuse* or *dependence.* If a person is using a drug without harming himself or herself or others, then it is simply drug *use.* The differentiation between use and abuse has important implications. If one has no moral or religious objections, drug use per se would not seem to be a bad thing. However, if the user is damaging himself or herself or others, drug use becomes *abuse.* (The reader should remember that society has legalized the use of two major drugs, alcohol and tobacco, even though both frequently lead to abuse and dependence.)

If chemical dependency is a disease, is it a physical, emotional, or mental disease? How does one "catch" or "get" it? Is it transmitted by certain genes? Is there a physiological pathology that leads to alcoholism? There is a vast literature devoted to these and similar questions, but it is likely to be more confusing than enlightening to most readers, and the questions are likely to remain unanswered. (A more comprehensive discussion of etiology is found in Chapter 2.) Some of the most interesting and convincing evidence for the disease model comes from the studies of genetically identical (monozygotic) twins.

Kaij studied 174 male twin pairs in Sweden and discovered a 54 percent concordance for alcoholism in one-egg twins versus a 28 percent concordance for alcoholism in two-egg twins. Since both types of twins were raised within the same social environment, it is assumed that any differences in rates of concordance between the two types of twins are the result of genetic factors.[25] On the other hand, a recent longitudinal study of children of alcoholics found a much weaker relationship between their drinking and their parents' drinking problems.[26] This issue is unlikely to be resolved in the near future.

There is no doubt that cirrhosis, pancreatitis, Korsakoff's psychosis, or any other such *effects* that are a result of excessive drinking can properly and indisputably be called diseases. However, these are diseases that *result* from drinking. The debate concerns the etiology of alcoholism, and that is where we turn our attention in the subsequent sections of this chapter as well as Chapter 2.

Is there an identifiable disease called alcoholism that causes a person to engage in excessive and inappropriate drinking? As important a question as this would seem to be, some contemporary scholars of alcoholism see this debate as a rather futile and useless waste of energy. Levin argues that any behavior as dysfunctional and self-destructive as alcoholism is a disease, regardless of etiology. "For an organism to destroy itself is pathological, regardless of the source of the pathology."[27]

The same arguments concerning the disease concept of alcoholism are found in the literature on addiction to other drugs, as well. Psychiatrists hold many different opinions about the relationship between drug abuse and disease/mental illness. The most consistent opinion is that several different forms of physical disease or mental illness may *result* from drug abuse.[28]

The World Health Organization describes drug dependence syndrome with dimensions very similar to those already used for alcohol dependence:

> A cluster of behavioural, cognitive, and physiological phenomena that may develop after repeated substance use. Typically, these phenomena include a strong desire to take the drug, impaired control over its use, persistent use despite harmful consequences, a higher priority given to drug use than to other activities and obligations, increased tolerance, and a physical withdrawal reaction when drug use is discontinued. In ICD-10 (*International Classification of Diseases*), the diagnosis of dependence syndrome is made if three or more of the six specified criteria were experienced within a year.
>
> The dependence syndrome may relate to a specific substance (e.g., tobacco, alcohol, or diazepam), a class of substances (e.g., opioids), or a wider range of pharmacologically different substances.[29]

Drug dependence is not described as an all-or-nothing condition, but one that exists in varying degrees. There is no attempt to weigh or prioritize the syndrome components, and not all of them need to be present for a person to be labeled *drug dependent*.

As with alcoholism, proponents of the disease model of drug addiction can neither demonstrate a clear etiology for addiction nor predict its course or symptoms with any accuracy. It has even been suggested that the disease model is an elaborate and sinister hoax.[30] An important reason for labeling alcoholism and drug addiction as a disease is that it seems to reduce or alleviate the guilt or stigma associated with addiction and to make medical resources available for treatment. The recent decriminalization of alcoholism was undoubtedly related to the acceptance of the disease model. Although most people view these events as improvements, one must allow the possibility that the disease model may also serve as an impediment to *scientific* research and to effective treatment. As we will discuss later in Chapter 6, the track record in providing effective treatment to chemically addicted clients is not impressive.

Epidemiology

Alcohol

There is evidence that alcohol use was widespread by the Neolithic Age. Stone pots dating from the old Stone Age in Clairvoux, Switzerland, have been discovered that once contained beer or wine. Ancient civilizations of the Near East, India, and China made copious use of alcohol. In addition, myths frequently depicted alcohol as a gift from the gods. Some societies even worshipped specific gods of wine: Osiris (Egypt), Dionysius (Greece), and Bacchus (Rome). Priests, too, frequently used alcohol as a part of religious rituals.[31]

Alcohol spread from ritual use to convivial use, and before long, it was a regular part of meals. For example, Assyrians received a daily allotment of bread and barley beer from their masters, and bread and wine were used by the

Hebrews after a successful battle. By the Middle Ages, alcohol was an important staple in the diet and was used to celebrate births, marriages, coronations, diplomatic exchanges, and the signing of treaties.

Beverage alcohol came to the New World with the explorers and colonists. The *Mayflower* landed at Plymouth Rock because, according to the ship's log, "We could not now take time for further search or consideration, our victuals having been much spent, especially our bere."[32] Spanish missionaries brought grapevines to America and were making wine in California before the United States was a nation. In 1640, the Dutch opened the first distillery of the New World (in what is known today as Staten Island, New York). Jamaican rum became the most popular drink in America under British rule, with New England bankers financing the slave trade that was used to produce the molasses needed to make rum. After the American Revolution, rum was eventually superseded by sour-mash bourbon whiskey.[33]

Drinking in America was largely a family affair until the beginning of the nineteenth century. With increasing immigration, industrialization, and greater social freedom, alcohol use (and abuse) became more open and more destructive. The opening of the American West brought the saloon into prominence, with the frontier hero gulping his drinks as his foot rested on the bar rail.[34]

During the 1820s, the founders of the Temperance Movement sought to make Americans into a clean, sober, godly, and decorous people whose values and life-styles would reflect the moral leadership of New England federalism. In the next few decades, abstinence became a symbol of middle-class membership and a way to distinguish the ambitious and aspiring from the ne'er-do-well, the Catholic immigrant from the native Protestant, gradually losing its association with the New England upper classes and becoming democratized. By the 1850s, Temperance was allied with Abolition and Nativism to form a trio of major movements.[35]

Threatened by increasing urbanization, political defeats in both the North and the South, and a steady flow of Catholic immigrants, the Populist wing of the Temperance Movement adopted a theme of coercive reform. With the development of the Anti-Saloon League in 1896, reform pitted the traditional rural Protestant society against urban Catholicism and industrialism, culminating in 1919 in that "grand experiment" known as Prohibition. Since the repeal of the Eighteenth Amendment in 1933, the Temperance Movement generally has been fighting a losing battle. Today, "dry" counties or precincts have become rare, and not even Protestant churches and the respectable, upper-middle-class citizens can safely be counted on to support abstinence.

Estimating the prevalence of alcohol abuse, problem drinking, or whatever else one may choose to call it is very difficult. The first and most obvious difficulty is that there is no widely accepted definition of just what kind of drinking behavior constitutes a problem. Next, as all experienced researchers know, the choice of investigative method may be the overriding factor in arriving at an estimate of this phenomenon. It is widely assumed that most respondents underreport their actual alcohol consumption, either because they do not know or remember how much they drink or because they fear that their admitted use may seem excessive. Highlights of a recent national survey are given in Figure 1.1.

The first national survey of the prevalence of drinking problems was conducted in 1967,[36] and three other nationwide surveys were completed within the next decade.[37] Using Plaut's definition of *problem drinking* as "repetitive use of beverage alcohol causing physical, psychological, or social harm to the drinker or to others,"[38] 15 percent of the men and 4 percent of the women in the samples were judged to have a problem with alcohol. Another interpretation of the data viewed 43 percent of the men and 21 percent of the women as having experienced some degree of problem drinking at some time within the preceding three years.[39] A more recent study reported that 16

FIGURE 1.1   Alcohol Abuse and Dependence

The National Institute on Alcohol Abuse and Alcoholism today released the first report from its National Longitudinal Alcohol Epidemiologic Survey (NLAES), including the most precise estimates to date of alcohol abuse and dependence among U.S. adults.

According to the report, 13,760,00 U.S. adults (7.41 percent of persons aged 18 years and older) met standard diagnostic criteria for alcohol abuse or alcohol dependence during 1992. Although more were classified with alcohol dependence (4.38 percent) than alcohol abuse (3.03 percent), most persons with alcohol dependence also met alcohol abuse criteria.

As in earlier surveys, alcohol use disorder rates were higher among males than females and highest in the youngest age cohort (18–29 years). Gender disparity was least among young nonblacks, suggesting that alcohol use disorders may be gaining ground among young nonblack females.

Age-related role responsibilities and perceived social acceptability of drinking may explain the disparity between male and female rates of alcohol use disorder among young blacks compared with young nonblacks.

Young nonblack males were almost twice as likely as young black males to have an alcohol use disorder. But, while the disorders declined with age among males in both ethnic groups, they increased among black women aged 30–44 years.

Regardless of gender and ethnicity, alcohol use disorders were least prevalent among persons 65 years and older. This may or may not be the result of a true "cohort effect," according to the study: Other possible explanations include faulty recall by older survey respondents and reduced survival rates among alcoholics.

Source: National Institute on Alcoholism and Alcohol Abuse Press Release, March 17, 1995.

percent of males and 6 percent of female drinkers disclosed personal problems associated with alcohol use.[40]

Using the *DSM-III-R* criteria, Grant and colleagues administered the National Health Interview Survey (NHIS) to estimate an alcohol dependence rate within the preceding year of 8.63 percent in the general population, with white males aged 30 to 45 having the highest rate (26.14 percent). For nonwhite males, the rate was 9.29 percent; for nonwhite females, 2.50 percent. The rate for all men was 13.35 percent, and for all women, it was 4.36 percent. The rate for white women was slightly higher, at 4.68 percent.[41]

Another approach is to study morbidity and mortality statistics related to the use of alcohol. Jellinek was one of the first researchers to devise a formula specifying a relationship between liver cirrhosis mortality and alcoholism. Using this approach, Lelbach estimated the proportion of cirrhosis deaths attributed to alcoholism to be 12 percent in Asia, 42 percent in Europe, and 66 percent in the United States.[42]

The most recent national survey[43] indicates that alcohol problems and heavy drinking are more common among young males. There are more abstainers among older people and women, and married people tend to drink less than single, divorced, or separated persons. A later survey that focused on women's drinking patterns confirmed that women had fewer drinking-related problems and fewer dependence symptoms than did men, but it also found higher levels of problem consequences for women who were heavier drinkers.[44] Heavy drinking and adverse consequences were also higher among younger women and among those with depression or a history of obstetric and gynecologic problems.

Problem drinking rates are higher for African Americans than for whites. More than twice as many African Americans as whites report binge drinking and health problems related to drinking. On the other hand, far fewer African American than white women reported alcohol-related problems, and the proportion of abstainers is greater among African Americans than whites.[45]

Surveys of high school students also reveal a higher abstention rate for African American teenagers than for whites, and four times as many heavy drinkers among white youngsters. Some 16 percent of white youth consumed at least five drinks at least once per week, whereas only 4 percent of African American teenagers drank that heavily.[46]

A survey of Hispanic drinkers by Caetano revealed a high abstention rate among women (47 percent) and a high rate of "heavy" drinking among men (36 percent). Among Hispanics, Mexican Americans had the highest rates of both abstention and heavy drinking. There were higher rates of heavy drinking among Hispanics born in the United States to foreign-born parents compared to foreign-born Hispanic drinkers.[47] (As we will explain in Chapter 11, the cultural stress experienced by immigrant groups is frequently associated with heavy drinking.)

Native Americans appear to be particularly susceptible to alcohol-related problems. Native American men between the ages of 25 and 44 have the highest rates of alcohol consumption of any ethnic group. Accidents, liver cirrhosis, homicide, and suicide are among the leading causes of death for this population, and most of these are thought to be alcohol related. For example, it is estimated that 20 percent of all Native American deaths are from accidents, and 75 percent of the accidents are alcohol related.[48]

Although there are significant differences in consumption patterns among Asian Americans, both male and female Asian Americans drink significantly less than Caucasians, African Americans, Hispanics, or Native Americans.[49] A study of native Hawaiians, Japanese, Filipinos, and Chinese living in Hawaii found fewer Asian Americans in alcohol treatment programs and lower rates of cirrhosis among Asian Americans than Caucasians.[50] On the other hand, a study by Helzer and colleagues discovered a high rate of alcoholism among Korean males.[51]

Among other ethnic groups, Americans of Italian descent seem to have both lower abstention and lower problem drinking rates. Americans of British and German stock have intermediate rates, whereas Irish Americans have high rates of problem drinking.[52] Fundamentalist Protestants are more likely to be abstainers, but those who do drink tend to do so more heavily. Catholics, liberal Protestants, and persons with no religious affiliation are less likely to abstain and more likely to be heavy drinkers. Jews have low rates of abstention as well as low rates of problem drinking.[53]

Alcohol consumption is also related to age, education, and location of residence, although the reasons are not clear (see Table 1.1). Some researchers attribute age variations in consumption to physiological changes that occur with aging such as a decrease in tolerance to alcohol.[54] Persons who begin to abuse alcohol earlier in life and continue into old age (early-onset drinkers) account for about two-thirds of elderly problem drinkers. Late-onset drinkers usually seem to begin drinking in response to late-life stresses such as the death of a spouse, retirement, or poor health.[55] Variations due to residence and education may be largely cultural. These variables will be discussed in the next chapter.

Although two-thirds of the adult population drink, actual consumption of alcohol is very unevenly distributed. The 10 percent of drinkers who drink the most heavily account for half of all alcohol consumed, with the other half accounted for by the 90 percent who are infrequent, light, or moderate drinkers.[56] Ledermann has proposed a logarithmic model of alcohol consumption in which a large number of people drink relatively small amounts of alcohol, and a smaller proportion of the population drink larger amounts—accounting for more than their fair share of both alcohol consumption and alcohol problems.[57]

Young adults aged 18 to 25 were most apt to binge or drink heavily, according to the National Household Survey on alcohol use.[58] Binge and heavy drinking were characterized as having five or more drinks on the same occassion at least once in the past month. This includes heavy use, which is defined as five or more drinks on the same occasion on at least five different days in the past month. One-half of these drinkers were

TABLE 1.1   Percentage Reporting Alcohol Use in the Past Year, by Age Group and Demographic Characteristics, 1990

Demographic Characteristic	Age Group (years)				Total
	12–17	18–25	26–34	≥35	
Total	41.0	80.2	78.8	62.5	66.0
Sex					
Male	40.8	86.0	83.1	68.5	71.0
Female	41.1	74.6	74.7	57.2	61.5
Race/Ethnicity[a]					
White	45.6	82.7	81.2	64.3	68.3
Black	24.7	74.4	72.7	50.3	55.6
Hispanic	37.9	74.4	75.3	62.8	64.5
Population Density					
Large metro	42.6	82.0	82.6	68.3	70.9
Small metro	40.4	83.6	80.0	65.9	68.4
Nonmetro	38.9	71.1	69.2	46.1	53.1
Region					
Northeast	41.2	82.8	83.4	74.7	74.1
North Central	42.6	86.6	83.8	66.8	70.9
South	40.2	74.6	72.2	48.8	56.3
West	40.0	79.3	80.2	67.7	69.1
Adult Education[b]					
Less than high school	N/A	70.2	75.4	44.2	52.4
High school graduate	N/A	79.3	75.5	61.3	67.7
Some college	N/A	86.4	81.9	76.7	80.1
College graduate	N/A	86.8	83.9	76.2	79.1
Current Employment[c]					
Full time	N/A	87.2	82.5	72.7	77.8
Part time	N/A	76.8	70.6	77.8	76.2
Unemployed	N/A	75.9	82.1	49.2	65.3
Other[d]	N/A	67.5	64.3	47.4	50.9

Source: National Institute on Drug Abuse, *National Household Survey on Drug Abuse, 1990* (Washington, DC: U.S. Government Printing Office, 1991).

N/A—Not applicable.

[a]The category "other" for race/ethnicity is not included.

[b]Data on adult education are not applicable for persons aged 12 to 17. Total refers to persons aged 18 and older (unweighted $N = 7,082$).

[c]Data on current employment are not applicable for persons aged 12 to 17. Total refers to persons aged 18 and older (unweighted $N = 7,082$).

[d]Retired, disabled, homemaker, student, or "other."

classified as being binge drinkers and one in five were considered heavy drinkers. Also according to this survey, 60 percent of men were past-month alcohol users, compared to 45 percent of women.[59] Men were more likely than women to be binge drinkers (23.8 vs. 8.5 percent, respectively) and heavy drinkers (9.4 vs. 2.0 percent, respectively).[60]

There are also some wide regional variations in alcohol consumption, with the largest proportion of abstainers in the South and the largest proportion of drinkers in the North and West (see Table 1.2). When urbanization, ancestry, and education are held constant, regional differences in alcohol consumption disappear, however.[61] This suggests that differences in alcohol consumption

TABLE 1.2   Percentage Reporting Alcohol Use in the Lifetime, by Age Group and Demographic Characteristics, 1990

Demographic Characteristic	Age Group (years)				
	12–17	18–25	26–34	≥35	Total
Total	48.2	88.2	92.0	85.0	83.2
Sex					
Male	49.5	91.9	94.4	92.3	88.1
Female	46.9	84.7	89.8	78.7	78.7
Race/Ethnicity[a]					
White	52.1	90.9	94.2	86.0	85.2
Black	32.7	81.5	85.4	83.4	76.6
Hispanic	47.8	81.0	90.7	81.0	78.6
Population Density					
Large metro	49.1	88.6	93.7	89.0	86.1
Small metro	49.0	91.6	92.9	85.5	84.2
Nonmetro	45.8	82.3	87.3	77.0	76.2
Region					
Northeast	46.8	86.8	89.6	88.6	84.6
North Central	48.3	91.6	96.0	91.5	87.9
South	48.2	86.3	89.4	76.6	77.7
West	49.6	88.7	93.8	88.6	85.8
Adult Education[b]					
Less than high school	N/A	81.3	88.8	77.4	79.6
High school graduate	N/A	87.4	91.4	84.2	86.4
Some college	N/A	93.4	94.4	93.3	93.6
College graduate	N/A	91.5	93.0	89.5	90.6
Current Employment[c]					
Full time	N/A	92.9	93.8	91.5	92.4
Part time	N/A	86.2	91.7	90.3	89.4
Unemployed	N/A	84.9	88.1	83.1	84.8
Other[d]	N/A	79.9	84.2	76.2	77.3

Source: National Institute on Drug Abuse, *National Household Survey on Drug Abuse, 1990* (Washington, DC: U.S. Government Printing Office, 1991).

N/A—Not applicable.

[a]The category "other" for race/ethnicity is not included.

[b]Data on adult education are not applicable for persons aged 12 to 17. Total refers to persons aged 18 and older (unweighted $N = 7,082$).

[c]Data on current employment are not applicable for persons aged 12 to 17. Total refers to persons aged 18 and older (unweighted $N = 7,082$).

[d]Retired, disabled, homemaker, student, or "other."

among geographic regions occur mainly because of their different sociodemographic compositions.

Marijuana and Hallucinogens

Marijuana was a legal drug and was grown as a cash crop in parts of the United States until its use and possession was prohibited by federal law in 1937. (It is still an important, but illicit, cash crop in many states today.) The plant was probably brought into Texas and California by Mexican immigrants in the early part of the twentieth century. Marijuana smoking was commonly accepted in many Mexican communities as a relaxant, a remedy for headaches, and a mild euphoriant. Cultivation of the plant was a major industry in the area around Mexico City and in several of the provinces, and it extended rapidly to border towns such as Laredo, El Paso, and Nogales. A direct railroad link between Mexico City and San Antonio facilitated marijuana trade between those cities, and for a while, a druggist in Floresville, Texas, established a mail-order marijuana business with customers in Texas, Arizona, New Mexico, Kansas, and Colorado.[62]

Smoking marijuana spread quickly to New Orleans, where it was popular among many African American jazz musicians by the early 1920s.[63] They carried it with them as they immigrated to the urban centers of the North. Anecdotal accounts of its history indicate that marijuana was soon adopted by many so-called deviant groups: professional criminals, prostitutes, and so on. In the 1960s, it became one of the symbols of the hippie movement.[64] Very little hard data exist regarding its use until the mid-1970s, however.

Cannabis is generally regarded as the most commonly used illicit drug. During the 1970s, 16 million Americans used marijuana at least once a month, of whom about 4 million were between 12 and 17 years of age and 8.5 million between 18 and 25 years of age.[65] Marijuana use seems to have peaked between 1979 and 1981, with more than 10 percent of high school seniors being daily users. By 1986, daily use by this group had dropped to 4 percent.[66] By 1988, it had dropped

further to 3.3 percent (4.5 percent for males and 2.2 percent for females).[67] By 1995, 4.6 percent of seniors were using marijuana daily.[68] A 1995 estimate by the National Institute on Drug Abuse puts the total proportion of U.S. population who had ever used marijuana at 31.1 percent. This rate was the highest for the 26- to 34-year-old age group (51.8 percent), and it was higher for males (56.3 percent) than for females (47.5 percent). In the population age 35 and older, 25.3 percent had used this drug.[69] Among high school seniors in the class of 1995, 41.7 percent had used marijuana at some time[70] (see Figure 1.2).

Hallucinogens such as LSD, mescaline, psilocybin, and phencyclidine (PCP or "angel dust") provide the user with effects that are primarily psychological, such as sensory distortion, synesthesia (perceived overlapping of the senses), and a heightened sense of awareness and self-consciousness.[71] With the exception of some Native Americans' traditional use of peyote, the use of these psychedelics is a relatively recent phenomenon. Like marijuana, "acid" and mushrooms are closely connected to the hippie subculture of the 1960s and 1970s.

There are few reliable statistics on the use of these drugs, but they are thought to be used mostly by younger persons. Hallucinogen use is three times more likely among white males than African American males and almost five times more likely among white women than African American women. Although the number of LSD-related arrests is small relative to other drugs, it almost doubled from 125 in 1987 to 230 in 1991.[72] A Monitoring the Future study shows that in 1995, 21.7 percent of twelfth-graders had used hallucinogens in their lives.[73]

Nicotine

The only known natural source of nicotine is tobacco, a plant cultivated in temperate climates all over the world. The origin of *nicotiana tabacum* is America, and it is thought that the first and only users of the drug at the time of the European discovery of the New World were the aboriginal peo-

FIGURE 1.2   Highlights of the 1993 National Household Survey on Drug Abuse

The results of the 1993 National Household Survey on Drug Abuse suggest that the significant declines in the prevalence of illicit drug use that occurred throughout the 1980s did not occur in 1993. The data may reflect a temporary interruption of the trend, a leveling off of prevalence, or the start of an upturn in drug use. Selected findings from the survey are given here.

Illicit Drug Use

In 1993, an estimated 11.7 million Americans were current illicit drug users, meaning they had used an illicit drug in the month prior to interview. This represents no change from 1992, when the estimate was 11.4 million. The number of illicit drug users had been declining since its peak in 1979 at 24 million.

Between 1992 and 1993, there were no significant changes in rates of illicit drug use for any age group, gender, or racial/ethnic group.

In 1993, 28 percent of illicit drug users were age 35 and older, compared with only 10 percent in 1979. Since 1979, rates of current illicit drug use have dropped for 12- to 17-year-olds, 18- to 25-year-olds, and 26- to 34-year-olds, but not for the age group 35 and older. The trend among older adults is affected by the aging of the heavy drug-using cohorts of the 1970s, which has resulted in an overall shift in the age distribution of illicit drug users.

Marijuana is the most commonly used illicit drug, used by 77 percent of current illicit drug users. Approximately 60 percent of current illicit drug users used marijuana only, 16 percent used marijuana and another illicit drug, and the remaining 24 percent used only an illicit drug other than marijuana in the past month.

The number of current cocaine users remained at 1.3 million users in 1993, the same as in 1992. This is down from a peak of 5.3 million in 1985.

There were an estimated one-half million (476,000, or 0.2 percent of the population) frequent cocaine users in 1993. Frequent use, defined as use on a weekly basis during the past year, was not significantly different from that in 1992 (642,000) or 1985 (605,000). However, the estimated number of occasional cocaine users (people who used in the past year but less often than monthly) sharply declined from 8.1 million to 3.0 million in 1993.

Alcohol Use

In 1993, about 11 million Americans were heavy drinkers (drinking five or more drinks per occasion on 5 or more days in the past 30 days). Heavy alcohol use has changed little since 1985 when there were 12 million heavy drinkers. The rate of current alcohol use among 12- to 17-year-olds increased from 16 percent in 1992 to 18 percent in 1993. However, the 1993 rate is lower than it had been in 1985, when it was 31 percent. Of the 11 million heavy drinkers in 1993, 26 percent (3 million) were also current illicit drug users. Rates of illicit drug use were lower for nonheavy drinkers (8 percent) and nondrinkers (2 percent).

Cigarette Use

An estimated 50 million Americans were smokers in 1993. This represents a smoking rate of 24 percent. Cigarette smoking has declined since 1985, when 60 million Americans were smokers and the rate was 31 percent. Among youths age 12 to 17, rates of smoking have stabilized at about 10 percent. Rates were about the same for 12- to 17-year-old males and females in both 1992 and 1993.

Current smokers are more likely to be heavy drinkers and illicit drug users. Among smokers in 1993, 11 percent were heavy drinkers and 12 percent were illicit drug users. Among nonsmokers, 3.4 percent were heavy drinkers and 3.5 percent were illicit drug users.

Source: National Institute on Drug Abuse (NIDA), *National Household Survey on Drug Abuse: 1993 Population Estimates,* Division of Epidemiology and Prevention Research (Washington, DC: U.S. Government Printing Office, 1995).

ples of North and South America. A stone carving in an ancient Mayan temple depicts a priest smoking what appears to be a cigar. Columbus was greeted at San Salvador in 1492 with a gift of dried tobacco leaves.

Native Americans smoked or chewed the tobacco leaf. The practice of smoking soon spread to Europe (along with "snuffing"), but chewing was confined largely to America. Early proponents of tobacco use hailed its medicinal qualities, but almost from the beginning there were vigorous antismoking movements. The Roman Catholic Church forbade smoking in churches on pain of excommunication; Muslim countries defined tobacco as an intoxicant and held that its use was contrary to the Koran; Dr. Benjamin Rush, founder of the Temperance Union, claimed that the use of tobacco created a desire for "strong drink."[74]

Early smoking was practiced by burning the tobacco in pipes or reeds or by wrapping it in the form of a cigar. The discovery of a low-nicotine, sweet flue-cured tobacco in North Carolina in the mid-nineteenth century led to the popularity of cigarette smoking. By the 1880s, machines were mass-producing millions of cigarettes a day. More than 100 years later, cigarettes still constitute the bulk of tobacco usage throughout the world.[75]

Most textbooks of this type do not deal with tobacco as an addictive substance. We think that it deserves special attention for several reasons. First, it is the second most commonly used legal drug, with about 50 million Americans smoking cigarettes on a daily basis. Also, a National Household Survey on tobacco use estimated that 6.9 million Americans were current users of smokeless tobacco. The rate of use was higher among males, particularly white males (6.2 percent), than females (0.6 percent); 90 percent of the smokeless tobacco users were men.[76] Second, it is a powerfully addicting substance, rivaling alcohol and heroin in the strength of its addictive powers. Consider the following:

- Former drug addicts and alcoholics who have been surveyed consider that it is harder to give up tobacco than heroin or alcohol.
- Only 10 to 15 percent of the people alive today who have ever used heroin are still addicted, whereas more than 66 percent of those still living who have ever smoked cigarettes are current daily smokers.
- About 61 million Americans were considered current smokers in 1995.[77]

Third, tobacco constitutes more of a health risk than any of the other drugs—legal or illegal.

More than 400,000 persons will die this year as a result of tobacco use—more than deaths from all other drugs combined, including alcohol! Approximately 37 *million* Americans who are currently smoking tobacco will die premature deaths as a result.[78] Worldwide, 2.5 million deaths are attributed to cigarette smoking each year.[79]

Fourth, although smoking among the general adult population has recently declined, cigarette smoking among women and teenagers is increasing. Among high school seniors, females were smoking as much as males by 1977. Since 1988, smoking rates for female seniors have been slightly higher than for males.[80] Among the class of 1995, 12.4 percent were smoking one-half pack of cigarettes or more a day.[81] It is estimated that 4.5 million youths aged 12 to 17 were current smokers in 1995. The rate of smoking for this age group was 20 percent. This rate is up from 18.9 percent the previous year.[82] This trend is particularly disturbing when one realizes that cigarette smoking is one of the best predictors of other drug use.[83]

Finally, nicotine addiction that results from tobacco smoking is actually *promoted* by a very rich, active, and politically well connected lobby. In some communities in North Carolina and Kentucky, it is considered almost un-American to oppose smoking. This makes the task of prevention and treatment even more difficult in dealing with this drug.

Cocaine

Cocaine made its way into the United States from Latin America, but with a very different history from that of marijuana. Coca leaves have been found in burial middens in Peru that date back to 2500 B.C. Under the Incas, coca became sacred and was used primarily by priests and nobility for special ceremonies. Widespread daily use of the coca leaf did not appear until the Spanish conquest, when it was used to pay for labor in the gold and silver mines in the Andes. The Spanish soon discovered that the Indians could work harder and longer and required less food if they were given coca.[84]

Samples of the plant were sent to Europe in 1749, but the anesthetic effects of cocaine were not discovered until 1862. By 1884, it was in widespread use as a local anesthetic for the eye. In 1885, Sigmund Freud delivered a lecture based on his observations of the effects of cocaine on mood and behavior.[85] The use of cocaine was a common theme in the literature of the day, with such popular heroes as Arthur Conan Doyle's Sherlock Holmes favoring a "seven percent solution." (Holmes once mysteriously disappeared for three years and returned to his Baker Street residence cured of his cocaine addiction.)

In addition to its legitimate medical uses, cocaine was an ingredient in patent medicines and beverages such as Coca-Cola until the passage of the Harrison Tax Act of 1914. Coca-Cola now uses only the decocainized coca leaves as a flavoring agent.[86]

The rediscovery and reintroduction of cocaine to modern American culture is sometimes attributed to the rock musicians of the 1960s. Until recent years, the form of cocaine generally available for illicit use in the United States was the white, bitter-tasting, crystalline powder of cocaine hydrochloride. It could be smoked or injected, but was most commonly snorted (ingested intranasally). More recently, another more dangerous form of cocaine, called *crack,* is made by cooking the powder with baking soda to remove its impurities. The resulting product is smoked and provides a much more rapid and intense "high."[87] Unfortunately, most statistics on cocaine use have only recently distinguished cocaine powder from crack cocaine.

The number of people who had used cocaine rose dramatically from 5.4 million in 1974 to 21.6 million in 1982.[88] In 1976, 9 percent of high school seniors had tried cocaine; in 1985, the percentage rose to 17.3 percent. Fortunately, by 1995, the number dropped to 6 percent.[89] In the 1995 National Household Survey on Drug Abuse, cocaine use appeared to be more common among the 18- to 25-year-old age group, with the 26- to 34-year-old age group a close second. These findings were consistent with previous surveys. The rate of current cocaine use was highest in the South (0.8 percent), followed by the West and North Central regions (0.7 percent), and lowest in the Northeast region (0.5 percent). According to a 1995 estimate, 1.5 million Americans were considered to be current cocaine users; 0.7 percent of the population aged 12 and over are represented in this statistic.[90] In the 1995 Household Survey, the proportion of persons who had ever used cocaine was estimated to be 10.3 percent; an additional 1.8 percent reported using crack at some time during their lives.[91]

Other Stimulants and Sedatives

In general, amphetamines have an effect similar to cocaine, but with a slower and less dramatic action. An amphetamine is a synthetic stimulant synthesized in 1927 as a replacement for ephedrine, a common ingredient in asthma, cold, and hay-fever remedies. Drinamyl, for many years the most widely prescribed drug for symptoms of anxiety and depression, was a combination of amphetamine and barbiturates. Amphetamines were widely used in World War II for keeping the troops alert and overcoming fatigue. During the 1960s, many people unknowingly became addicted to a "Benzedrine inhaler" sold without a prescription for the treatment of colds, allergies, and sinusitis. Until new rules were adopted by the Food and Drug Administration in 1970, many others became addicted while using amphetamine-based diet pills.[92] Amphetamines were also widely used in the 1960s and 1970s in both amateur and professional sports. One report in 1978 revealed that 75 of 87 professional football players interviewed admitted using *speed,* a common name for amphetamines.[93]

Ice, a particularly strong and dangerous form of amphetamine, appeared in Hawaii and California in the early 1990s and rapidly spread to other parts of the country. Although the data are largely anecdotal at this point, ice seems to be responsible for an alarmingly high number of hospital emergency-room admissions.[94] No separate national statistics of use are kept for this particular drug.

The most commonly used stimulant, caffeine, is found in coffee, tea, and certain soft drinks. Although withdrawal effects are not uncommon, caffeine does not ordinarily present a threat to health or an impairment to functioning. For this reason, we will not devote much space to it in this text. Methylphenidate (Ritalin) is still widely sought after by narcotic addicts maintained on methadone injections, since methadone has no antagonist effect on amphetamines. Statistics on its use are not available, but it does not seem to constitute a serious problem.[95] (Ritalin is a drug commonly prescribed to control hyperactivity in children.)

Results of a survey show that 6.0 percent of adults aged 26 and older report using stimulants at some time during their lives.[96] Stimulant drug use during one's lifetime remains highest in western United States (7.1 percent). The North Central region came in second (4.8 percent), then the South (3.9 percent), and the Northeast (3.1 percent). Males are more likely than females to have used stimulants (6.1 percent vs. 3.2 percent, respectively). Males aged 26 to 34 report the greatest percentage of use during their lives (8.9 percent). The percentage of 18- to 25-year-olds who reported using stimulants at some time was 5.3, a decrease from prior years.[97] In a 1995 survey, 15.3 percent of twelfth-graders had tried stimulants in their lifetimes.[98] The percentage of 12- to 17-year-olds who reported using stimulants in their lifetimes was 2.6. In the previous two years, the percentage was reported as being 2.1 percent. This decrease does not reflect a statistically significant difference, however.[99]

Sedative drugs, those that may induce sleep, are usually divided into two categories: barbiturates and nonbarbiturates. Since their synthesis in 1903, over 2,000 different types of barbiturates have been developed. They are used medically as sedatives, short-term anesthetics, and anticonvul-

sants, and to treat psychiatric problems. Nonbarbiturate sedatives such as methaqualone were developed as a safer alternative to barbiturates. They were originally believed to be much safer than barbiturates, but soon proved to be equally dangerous. Marketed in Britain as Mandrax and in the United States as Quaalude, Sopor, and several other names, it soon became a popular drug among polydrug users, especially for "mixing" with alcohol.[100] Unfortunately, alcohol and Quaaludes are frequently a lethal combination. Some readers may remember the tragic case of Karen Ann Quinlan, who went into a coma after using this combination of drugs and lived in a vegetative state for several years. The overall past-month use rate of sedatives in the United States in 1994 was 0.3 percent of youth aged 12 to 17 and 0.3 percent of young adults aged 18 to 25.[101] Males aged 26 to 35 most frequently reported having used sedatives during their lives (6.3 percent). Both the North Central and southern United States reported 2.6 percent as the total for individuals having used sedatives in their lifetimes. In general, males were more likely than females to report having used a sedative at some time during their lives (3.7 percent vs. 1.6 percent, respectively).[102]

Valium is a type of benzodiazepine minor tranquilizer, and during the 1970s, it was the most frequently prescribed legal drug in the United States. Drugs such as Valium came into popular use because, according to Hollister, "The benzodiazepines are virtually suicide proof. Massive overdoses have been taken with very little difficulty in managing patients and with no fatalities in the absence of other drugs."[103] During the 1970s, Valium came to be a sort of folk-medicine in the drug subculture to treat complications of illicit use of other drugs. So-called speedfreaks as well as methadone and LSD users were widely known to maintain their stash of Valium.[104] The past-month use rate of tranquilizers in 1994 estimated by the National Institute on Drug Abuse (NIDA) survey by young adults aged 18 to 25 was 0.4 percent; for the 26 to 34 age group, 0.6 percent; for the age 35 and older group, 0.5 percent; and for 12- to 17-year-olds, 0.2 percent. These percentages reflect decreases from 1993 for the 18- to 25-year-old age group and the age 26 and older group. This survey reported that 0.5 percent of males and 0.4 percent of females reported having used tranquilizers in their lifetimes.[105] There are no reliable statistics on the use of Rohypnol, or *roofies*, a tranquilizer similiar to but much stronger than Valium. (See Chapter 4 for a fuller description of this so-called date-rape drug.)

Narcotics

Opium, morphine, codeine, and heroin are the major drugs included in the category of narcotics. They are derived from the variety of poppy known as *papaver somniferum.* Under federal law, cocaine is classified as a narcotic, but it is actually a stimulant. Narcotics have the effect of depressing the activity of the brain and the central nervous system.

The earliest reference to opium is a Sumerian idiogram dated about 4000 B.C., referring to it as "joy plant." Hippocrates and Pliny both recommended the use of opium for a number of conditions. Since it was not banned in Muslim countries, Arab traders carried it from the Middle East to India, China, and finally Europe. By the early sixteenth century, it was prescribed by physicians throughout Europe. By 1875, the British consumption rate for opium was 10 pounds per 1,000 population.[106]

Before 1900, opium was available in the United States as an ingredient in a number of prescription drugs such as laudanum and "black drop." It was also available in a number of patent medicines. It had a relatively mild psychological effect when taken by mouth, and it was freely prescribed by physicians.

Morphine, an opiate, was found to be an exceptionally effective painkiller, and it came into common medical usage during and after the Civil War. The importation of opium continued to rise and finally peaked in 1896. Smoking opium,

which had no medicinal value, was banned in the United States in 1909.[107] The Harrison Act made it illegal for physicians to prescribe morphine and opium to addicts in 1914, as well as made addiction to opiates a crime. Heroin, which had not been discovered until 1898, soon became a substitute by morphine users. This loophole was closed when Congress finally banned all opiate use, including heroin, in 1924.[108] Heroin addiction continued to climb, however, until 23 of every 10,000 Americans were addicted in 1978.[109]

Both morphine and opium addiction have at times posed serious problems in the United States, but today heroin is regarded as the most dangerous of all existing narcotics. Heroin can be smoked, snorted, injected under the skin ("skin-popping"), or injected directly into a vein ("mainlining"). In the mainlining case, there is an imminent danger of overdosing or contracting the human immunodeficiency virus (HIV) from the use of "dirty needles."[110]

Heroin use has long been associated with deviant groups such as criminals, prostitutes, jazz and rock musicians, as well as poor African Americans living in the ghettos of large urban centers.[111] However, many veterans of the war in Vietnam returned home addicted to heroin.[112] The 1995 NIDA survey reports rates of heroin lifetime use is highest among males, middle-class adults aged 26 to 34, and the unemployed. In general, males are more likely than females to report lifetime use. This statistic switches when looking at youths, where females reported greater lifetime use than males. In the age 35 and older group, blacks reported greater lifetime use than whites. In general, blacks were five times as likely to be past-year heroin users than whites (0.5 percent vs. 0.1 percent, respectively).[113]

Summary

Alcoholism and drug addiction represent substantial problems in U.S. society, however the terms are defined. People abuse both legal and illegal drugs—drugs that were intended primarily for medication and those that have only a "recreational" purpose. There is no doubt that certain groups of people are more prone to abuse drugs, especially young males, but research has yielded no real insights into an alcoholic or addictive personality. Neither have experts settled on a definition of *addiction*. The issue of the *disease model* of addiction is still an open question. If a particular model of addiction is effective in guiding efforts to prevent addiction or to provide treatment to an individual client, we can see no reason not to use it.

Endnotes

1. Department of Agriculture, Economic Research Service, *Food Consumption, Prices, and Expenditures* (Washington, DC: U.S. Government Printing Office, 1994).

2. U.S. Department of Health and Human Services, Public Health Service, Alcohol, Drug Abuse, and Mental Health Administration, National Institute on Alcohol Abuse and Alcoholism, *Sixth Special Report to the U.S. Congress on Alcohol and Health* (Washington, DC: U.S. Government Printing Office, 1987), p. xvi.

3. U.S. House of Representatives, Select Committee on Narcotics Abuse and Control, *Annual Report for the Year 1992* (Washingtion, DC: U.S. Government Printing Office, 1992).

4. U.S. House of Representatives, Select Committee on Narcotics Abuse and Control, *Annual Report for the Year 1984* (Washington, DC: U.S. Government Printing Office, 1985).

5. *Drug Use among 8th, 10th, and 12th Graders (1993–1995)* [Online]. Available: http://www.nida.nih.gov/NIDA/NNVol11Nl/DrugUse.html

6. U.S. House of Representatives, Select Committee on Narcotics Abuse and Control, *Annual Report for the Year 1992*, p. 26.

7. Jerome D. Levin, *Alcoholism: A Bio-Psycho-Social Approach* (New York: Hemisphere, 1989), p. 5.

8. NIJ, *Critical Criminal Justice Issues* (Washington, DC: U.S. Government Printing Office, May 1997).

9. Duncan Raistrick and Robin Davidson, *Alcoholism and Drug Addiction* (New York: Churchill Livingstone, 1985), p. 9.

10. Ibid., p. 11.

11. Karl M. Bowman and Elvin Morton Jellinek, "Alcohol Addiction and Chronic Alcoholism," *Quarterly Journal of Studies on Alcohol*, Vol. 2 (1941).

12. Elvin Morton Jellinek, *The Disease Concept of Alcoholism* (Highland Park, NJ: Hillhouse Press, 1960).

13. Ibid.

14. William A. McKim, *Drugs and Behavior: An Introduction to Behavioral Pharmacology* (Englewood Cliffs, NJ: Prentice Hall, 1991), p. 105.

15. Mark Keller, "Alcoholism: Nature and Extent of the Problem," *Annals of the American Academy of Political and Social Science*, Vol. 315 (1958), pp. 1–11.

16. World Health Organization, Expert Committee on Mental Health, *Report on the First Session of the Alcoholism Subcommittee*, WHO Technical Reporting Service, No. 48 (Geneva: WHO, August 1952).

17. Wallace Mandell, "Types and Phases of Alcohol Dependence Illness," in M. Galanter (Ed.), *Recent Developments in Alcoholism*, Volume 1 (New York: Plenum Press, 1983).

18. National Council on Alcoholism, "Criteria for the Diagnosis of Alcoholism," *American Journal of Psychiatry*, Vol. 129, No. 2 (August 1972).

19. Carol Ringer et al., "The N.C.A. Criteria for the Diagnosis of Alcoholism," *Journal of Studies on Alcohol*, Vol. 38 (1977).

20. George E. Vaillant, *The Natural History of Alcoholism* (Cambridge, MA: Harvard University Press, 1983), p. 15.

21. E. Mansell Pattison, Mark B. Sobell, and Linda C. Sobell, *Emerging Concepts of Alcohol Dependence* (New York: Springer, 1977).

22. Joan Curlee-Salisbury, "Perspectives on Alcoholics Anonymous," in Nada J. Estes and M. Edith Heinemann (Eds.), *Alcoholism: Development, Consequences, and Interventions*, 3rd ed. (St. Louis, MO: C. V. Mosby, 1986).

23. American Psychiatric Association, *Diagnostic and Statistical Manual of Mental Disorders*, 3rd ed., rev. (Washington, DC: APA, 1987), pp. 165–185.

24. Ibid.

25. Lennart Kaij, *Alcoholism in Twins* (Stockholm: Almqvist and Wiksell, 1960).

26. Ernest Harburg, Wayne DiFranceisco, Daniel W. Webster, Llian Gleiberman, and Anthony Schork, "Familial Transmission of Alcohol Use: II. Imitation of and Aversion to Parent Drinking (1960) by Adult Offspring (1977)—Tecumseh, Michigan," *Journal of Studies on Alcohol*, Vol. 51, No. 3 (1990), pp. 245–256.

27. Levin, *Alcoholism*, p. 63.

28. Raistrick and Davidson, *Alcoholism and Drug Addiction*.

29. *Lexicon and Alcohol and Drug Terms*, Geneva World Health Organization, 1994. Reprinted by permission.

30. Jara Krivanek, *Addictions* (Winchester, MA: Allen & Unwin, 1988), pp. 31–38.

31. Levin, *Alcoholism.*

32. Jean Kinney and Gwen Leaton, *Loosening the Grip: A Handbook of Alcohol Information* (St. Louis, MO: Times Mirror/Mosby, 1987), p. 5.

33. W. J. Rorabaugh, *The Alcohol Republic: An American Tradition* (New York: Oxford University Press, 1979).

34. Kinney and Leaton, *Loosening the Grip,* p. 13.

35. Joseph R. Gusfield, "Symbolic Crusade: Status Politics and the American Temperance Movement," in Maureen E. Kelleher, Bruce K. MacMurray, and Thomas M. Shapiro (Eds.), *Drugs and Society: A Critical Reader,* 2nd ed. (Dubuque, IA: Kendall/Hunt, 1988).

36. Don Calahan, *Problem Drinkers* (San Francisco: Jossey-Bass, 1970).

37. Don Calahan and R. Roizen, "Changes in Drinking Problems in a National Sample of Men," paper presented at a meeting of the Alcohol and Drug Problems Association, San Francisco, 1974.

38. T. F. Plaut, *Alcohol Problems: A Report to the Nation by the Cooperative Commission on the Study of Alcoholism* (New York: Oxford University Press, 1967).

39. Don Calahan and Ira H. Cisin, "Epidemiological and Social Factors Associated with Drinking Problems," in Ralph E. Tarter and A. Arthur Sugerman (Eds.), *Alcoholism* (Reading, MA: Addison-Wesley, 1976), p. 541.

40. Henry Malin, R. Wilson, G. Williams, and S. Aitken, "1983 Alcohol/Health Practices Supplement," *Alcohol Health & Research World,* Vol. 8 (1986), pp. 56–57.

41. Bridget F. Grant, Thomas C. Harford, Patricia Chou, Roger Pickering, Deborah A. Dawson, Frederick S. Stinson, and John Noble, "Prevalence of DSM-III-R Alcohol Abuse and Dependence: United States, 1988," *Alcohol Health & Research World,* Vol. 15, No. 1 (1991), pp. 91–96.

42. Werner K. Lelbach, "Cirrhosis in the Alcoholic and Its Relation to the Volume of Alcohol Abuse," *Annals of the New York Academy of Science,* Vol. 252 (1975), pp. 85–105.

43. *Drug Use among 8th, 10th, and 12th Graders (1993–1995)* [Online].

44. Sharon C. Wilsnack, Richard W. Wilsnack, and Albert D. Klassen, "Drinking and Drinking Problems among Women in a U.S. National Survey," *Alcohol Health & Research World,* Vol. 9 (1985), pp. 3–13.

45. Denise Herd, "A Review of Drinking Patterns and Alcohol Problems among U.S. Blacks," in National Institute on Alcohol Abuse and Alcoholism (NIAAA), *Alcohol Use among U.S. Ethnic Minorities,* Research Monograph No. 18 (Washington, DC: U.S. Government Printing Office, 1987).

46. Charles Lowman, Thomas C. Harford, and Charles T. Kaelber, "Alcohol Use among Black Senior High School Students," *Alcohol Health & Research World,* Vol. 7 (1983), pp. 37–46.

47. Raul Caetano, "Drinking Patterns and Alcohol Problems in a National Sample of U.S. Hispanics," in NIAAA, *Alcohol Use among U.S. Ethnic Minorities.*

48. Barbara W. Lex, "Alcohol Problems in Special Populations," in J. H. Mendelson and N. K. Mello (Eds.), *The Diagnosis and Treatment of Alcoholism* (New York: McGraw-Hill, 1985), pp. 89–187.

49. Arthur L. Klatsky, Abraham B. Siegelaub, Cynthia Landy, and Gary D. Friedman, "Racial Patterns of Alcoholic Beverage Use," *Alcoholism: Clinical and Experimental Research,* Vol. 7 (1983), pp. 372–377.

50. Frank M. Ahern, "Alcohol Use and Abuse among Four Ethnic Groups in Hawaii," in NIAAA, *Alcohol Use among U.S. Ethnic Minorities.*

51. John E. Helzer, J. Gloriosa Canino, Eng-kung Yeh, and Roger C. Bland, "Alcoholism: North America and Asia: A Comparison of Population Surveys with the Diagnostic Interview Schedule," *Archives of General Psychiatry,* Vol. 47, No. 4 (April 1990), pp. 313–319.

52. Estes and Heinemann, *Alcoholism,* p. 45.

53. Charles R. Snyder, "Culture and Jewish Sobriety: The Ingroup-Outgroup Factor," in David J. Pittman and Charles R. Snyder (Eds.), *Society, Culture, and Drinking Patterns* (New York: John Wiley and Sons, 1967).

54. Robert Straus, "Alcohol Problems among the Elderly: The Need for a Biobehavioral Perspective," in G. Maddox, L. N. Robins, and N. Rosenberg (Eds.), *Nature and Extent of Alcohol Problems among the Elderly,* National Institute on Alcohol Abuse and Alcoholism, Research Monograph No. 14 (Washington, DC: U.S. Government Printing Office, 1984), pp. 8–9.

55. M. Williams, "Alcohol and the Elderly: An Overview," *Alcohol Health & Research World,* Vol. 8 (1984), pp. 3–9.

56. Henry J. Malin, J. Coakley, C. Kaelber, N. Munch, and W. Holland, "An Epidemiologic Perspective on Alcohol Use and Abuse in the United States," in National Institute on Alcohol Abuse and Alcoholism, *Alcohol Consumption and Related Problems* (Washington, DC: U.S. Government Printing Office, 1982), pp. 99–153.

57. Alcohol Education Centre, *The Ledermann Curve: Report of Symposium* (London: The Centre, 1977).

58. The National Household Survey *Alcohol Use* [On-line]. Available: http://www.health.org/pubs/95hhs/alcohol.html

59. Ibid.

60. Ibid.

61. John W. Welte and Marcia Russell, "Regional Variations in the Consumption of Alcohol in the U.S.A.," *Drug and Alcohol Dependence,* Vol. 10 (1982), pp. 243–249.

62. Richard J. Bonnie and Charles Whitebread II, "The Alien Weed," in Kelleher, MacMurray, and Shapiro, *Drugs and Society*, pp. 256–267.

63. Erich Goode, *Marijuana* (New York: Atherton Press, 1969), p. 7.

64. Maureen E. Kelleher, Bruce K. MacMurray, and Thomas M. Shapirof (Eds.), *Drugs and Society: A Critical Reader* (Dubuque, IA: Kendall/Hunt, 1988), p. 249.

65. Executive Office of the President, *Drug Use, Patterns, Consequences, and the Federal Response: A Policy Review, Office of Drug Abuse Policy*, March 1978.

66. Lloyd D. Johnston, Patrick M. O'Malley, and Jerald G. Bachman, *National Trends in Drug Use and Related Factors among American High School Students and Young Adults, 1975–1986* (Washington, DC: U.S. Government Printing Office, 1987).

67. Johnston et al., *Drug Use*, pp. 176, 210.

68. *Drug Use among 8th, 10th, and 12th Graders (1993–1995)* [On-line].

69. National Institute on Drug Abuse (NIDA), *National Household Survey on Drug Abuse: 1995 Population Estimates*, Division of Epidemiology and Prevention Research (Washington, DC: U.S. Government Printing Office, 1995), p. 23.

70. *Drug Use among 8th, 10th, and 12th Graders (1993–1995)* [On-line].

71. Kelleher, *Drugs and Society*, p. 247.

72. U.S. House of Representatives, Select Committee on Narcotics Abuse and Control, *Annual Report for the Year 1992* (Washington, DC: U.S. Government Printing Office, 1992), p. 41.

73. *Drug Use among 8th, 10th, and 12th Graders (1993–1995)* [On-line].

74. McKim, *Drugs and Behavior*, pp. 160–164.

75. J. E. Brooks, *The Mighty Leaf: Tobacco through the Centuries* (Boston: Little, Brown, 1952).

76. The National Household Survey, *Tobacco Use* [On-line]. Available: http://www.health.org/pubs/95hhs/tobacco.html

77. Ibid.

78. Gwenda Blair, "Why Dick Can't Stop Smoking," in Kelleher et al., *Drugs and Society*, pp. 223–230.

79. Kelleher, *Drugs and Society*, p. 221.

80. Johnston et al., *Drug Use*, p. 81.

81. *Drug Use among 8th, 10th, and 12th Graders (1993–1995)* [On-line].

82. The National Household Survey *Tobacco Use* [On-line].

83. Nada J. Estes and M. Edith Heinemann, "Issues in Identification of Alcoholism," in Estes and Heinemann (Eds.), *Alcoholism*, pp. 317–333.

84. McKim, *Drugs and Behavior*, pp. 202–204.

85. Norman Imlah, *Addiction: Substance Abuse and Dependency* (Winslow, England: Sigma Press, 1989), pp. 56–67.

86. Cohen, *The Substance Abuse Problems*, p. 173.

87. Imlah, *Addiction*, p. 58.

88. Edgar H. Adams and Jack Durell, "Cocaine: A Growing Public Health Problem," in John Grabowski (Ed.), *Cocaine: Pharmacology, Effects, and Treatment of Abuse*, National Institute on Drug Abuse Research Monograph 50 (Rockville, MD: National Institute on Drug Abuse, 1984).

89. *Drug Use among 8th, 10th, and 12th Graders (1993–1995)* [On-line].

90. The National Household Survey *Cocaine Use* [On-line]. Available: http://www.health.org/pubs/95hhs/cocaine.html

91. NIDA, *National Household Survey on Drug Abuse: 1995*.

92. Imlah, *Addiction*, p. 59.

93. G. Rankin Cooter, "Amphetamine Use: Physical Activity and Sport," in Kelleher, *Drugs and Society*, p. 329.

94. Michael A. Lerner, "The Fire of 'Ice,' " *Newsweek*, November 27, 1989, pp. 37–40.

95. Imlah, *Addiction*, p. 63.

96. NIDA, *National Household Survey on Drug Abuse: 1995*.

97. Ibid.

98. *Drug Use among 8th, 10th, and 12th Graders (1993–1995)* [On-line].

99. NIDA, *National Household Survey on Drug Abuse: 1995*.

100. Cohen, *The Substance Abuse Problems*, p. 125.

101. NIDA, *National Household Survey on Drug Abuse: 1995*.

102. Ibid.

103. Leo E. Hollister, *Clinical Use of Psychotherapeutic Drugs* (Springfield, IL: Charles C Thomas, 1973), pp. 129–131.

104. Cohen, *The Substance Abuse Problems*, pp. 130–134.

105. NIDA, *National Household Survey on Drug Abuse: 1995*.

106. McKim, *Drugs and Behavior*, pp. 228–231.

107. David F. Musto, *The American Disease: Narcotics in Nineteenth-Century America* (New Haven, CT: Yale University Press, 1973).

108. McKim, *Drugs and Behavior*, pp. 228–231.

109. A. Wilker, *Opiod Dependence* (New York: Plenum Press, 1980).

110. Don C. Des Jarlais and Samuel R. Friedman, "HIV Infections among IV Drug Users," in Kelleher, *Drugs and Society*, pp. 311–326.

111. Tam Stewart, *The Heroin Users* (London: Pandora Press, 1987).

112. Jara Krivanek, *Heroin: Myths and Realities* (Winchester, MA: Allen & Unwin, 1988).

113. NIDA, *National Household Survey on Drug Abuse: 1995*.

2

The Etiology
of Addiction

Pamela V. Valentine
University of Alabama at Birmingham

As noted in Chapter 1, nearly 1 of every 10 adults in the United States is affected by alcoholism or alcohol abuse. The prevalent use of alcohol (not to mention other addictive substances) "leads to devastating medical and social pathology."[1] Therefore, it is important to understand the origins of alcoholism and drug abuse.

Etiological Theories

There are at least as many explanatory theories of addiction as there are definitions. We will focus on three broad theoretical categories—psychological theories, biological theories, and sociocultural theories—as well as discuss some alternative explanations. These theories are not mutually exclusive, and divisions sometimes seem quite arbitrary. None is presented as the "correct" way of explaining this phenomenon. We do have preferences, and we lean more toward certain models than others, but no single theory adequately describes the etiology of alcoholism.

Before turning to those theories, however, we will briefly define *alcoholism, addict, alcohol abuse,* and *alcohol dependence.* (For a more comprehensive discussion of these and similar terms, see Chapter 5.) Although these definitions focus on alcoholism, they can readily be applied to other forms of substance abuse and/or dependence.

Alcoholism is "the compulsive consumption of and psychophysiological dependence on alcoholic beverages.[2]

An *addict* is one who has become "compulsively and physiologically dependent on a habit-forming substance."[3] (Notice the biological and psychological components to the definition.)

Alcohol abuse precedes alcohol dependence. It is the harmful use of a substance or the "recurrent and significant adverse consequences related to repeated use of substances."[4] Problems related to alcohol abuse are (1) failure to fulfill a major role, (2) using the substance in a physically hazardous situation, (3) related legal problems, and (4) using the substance despite problems. Alcohol abuse is more temporary and less severe than alcohol dependence. It is also a less reliable diagnosis, as it is not consistently defined in different diagnostic systems.[5]

Alcohol dependence, according to the *DSM-IV*, has three or more of the following symptoms at any time in the same 12 months: (1) a need for greatly increased amounts to achieve intoxication and the effect; (2) withdrawal or unpleasant physiological and cognitive symptoms; (3) compulsive behavior aimed at attaining the substance; (4) a persistent desire to cut down or control the use of the substance; (5) a large amount of time spent trying to abstain from the substance; (6) decreased social, recreational, or occupational activities due to the substance; and (7) continued use of the substance despite awareness of substance-related problems.

In summary, addiction is a cluster of cognitive, behavioral, and physiological symptoms. It involves the "continued, self-administered use of a substance despite substance-related problems, and it results in tolerance for the substance, withdrawal from the substance, and compulsive drug-taking behavior due to cravings" or drives to use the substance.[6] The origin of these cravings is the next question at hand.

The Moral Model

One answer to the origin of cravings for mind-altering substances is humankind's sinful nature. Since it is difficult to show empirical evidence of a sinful nature, the *moral model* of addiction has been generally discredited by modern scholars. However, the legacy of treating alcoholism and drug addiction as sin or moral weakness still has an effect on public policies regarding alcohol and drug abuse.

Psychological Theories

Another explanation for the origins of craving alcohol and mind-altering drugs lies in the psychological literature—that is, the literature that deals with one's mind and emotions. Psychological models define addiction as an individual phenomenon but do not necessarily exclude or minimize social factors or other elements in the development of an addiction. There are actually several different psychologic theories of alcoholism and drug addiction; they include cognitive-behavioral, learning, psychodynamic, and personality theories, among others.

Cognitive-Behavioral Theories.   Cognitive-behavioral theories offer a variety of motivations for taking drugs. One such explanation states that humans take drugs to experience variety.[7] The need for variety is demonstrated in cross-cultural expressions such as singing, dancing, running, and joking. Drug use is associated with a variety of activities—for example, religious services, self-exploration, altering moods, escaping boredom or despair, enhancing social interaction, enhancing sensory experience or pleasure, and stimulating creativity and performance. A study on inner-city youths revealed that youths are motivated to take drugs out of a desire for variety, citing curiosity, celebration, getting high, and rebelling as reasons for drug use. (The study pointed out that youths celebrate or explore drugs by using alcohol at home, whereas they choose to use illegal marijuana away from the home.[8]) Assuming that people enjoy variety, it follows that they repeat actions that bring pleasure (positive reinforcement).

The desire to experience pleasure is another cognitive explanation for drug use and abuse. Some animals seek alcohol and even work for it (by pushing a lever) to repeat a pleasant experience. Alcohol and other drugs are *chemical surrogates* of natural reinforcers such as eating, drinking, and reproductive behavior. Social drinkers and alcoholics both report using alcohol to relax, even though tests of actual tension-reducing effects of alcohol have yielded quite different results; scientific observations of persons using alcohol actually show them to become more depressed, anxious, and nervous.[9] The dependent behavior is maintained by the degree of reinforcement the alcohol provides, and this, in turn, depends on the actor's perception of his or her need hierarchy and "the likelihood that this course of action will meet the most important needs better than other available options."[10] Since alcohol and drugs are more powerful and persistent than natural reinforcers to which the human brain is accustomed, they set the stage for addiction.

With time, the brain adapts to the presence of the drug or alcohol. The removal of the substance from the host reveals certain abnormalities experienced by the brain. The host experiences unpleasant withdrawal symptoms such as anxiety, agitation, tremors, increased blood pressure, and, in severe cases, seizures. Naturally, one wants to avoid painful stimuli; by consuming the substance anew, an individual can avoid the unpleasant symptoms of withdrawal. Repetitive action motivated by the avoidance of unpleasant stimuli is called *negative reinforcement*. (In an alcoholic, the need to avoid withdrawal symptoms generally occurs from 6 to 48 hours after the last drink.) Another source of negative reinforcement may lie in the avoidance of unpleasant things other than withdrawal. There is a high correlation between traumatized individuals and substance abuse.[11] The traumatized individual may take drugs to avoid unpleasant memories or heightened physiological states such as startle responses.

Learning Theories.   Closely related to cognitive-behavioral theories is learning, or reinforcement, theory. Learning theory assumes that alcohol or drug use results in a decrease in psychological states such as anxiety, stress, or tension, thus positively reinforcing the user. This learned response continues until physical dependence develops, at which time the aversion of withdrawal symptoms becomes a prime motivation for drug use.[12]

There is a considerable amount of evidence to support that part of learning theory related to al-

cohol use and physiological aversion. Abrupt cessation of drinking will lead to unpleasant symptoms of withdrawal.[13] For the alcoholic, withdrawal could lead to trembling, shaking, hallucinations, and grand mal seizures. Similarly, for the heroin addict, abrupt withdrawal may lead to symptoms much like a case of severe flu. For the social drinker, the symptoms may amount to what is commonly called a hangover. In each case, the addict quickly learns that these symptoms may be avoided by resuming use of the drug.

An interesting view of becoming a heroin addict is provided by Krivanek.[14] Dependencies that involve drug use follow the same basic principles of learning theory, as all other dependencies. Krivanek views drug dependence as a psychological phenomenon that can vary in intensity from a mild involvement to an addiction that seriously restricts the user's other behaviors. This is similar to the idea of alcoholism as a continuum, proposed by Pattison, Sobell, and Sobell: "An individual's use of alcohol can be considered as a point on a continuum from nonuse, to nonproblem drinking, to various degrees of deleterious drinking."[15]

Learning theory is helpful in treatment planning because it addresses the adaptive consequences of drinking. Also, behavioral treatments have incorporated learning theory into a treatment framework based on the premise that what has been learned can be unlearned.[16] Learning theory is also quite adaptable to the systems view, which is followed throughout this book.

Psychodynamic Theories.   Psychodynamic theories are more difficult to substantiate than most other psychological theories because they deal with hard-to-operationalize concepts and with events that may have occurred many years before the onset of addiction. Although Freud never devoted a single paper to the subject of alcoholism, his disciples were not the least bit reluctant to apply psychoanalytic theories to alcohol addiction. The earliest explanations linked alcoholism with the "primal addiction" of masturbation.[17] Most later explanations linked alcoholism to ego deficiencies, with alcohol used to attain a sense of security. This theory assumes that during childhood, inadequate parenting, along with the child's individual constitution, caused the child to form weak attachments to significant others, resulting in a need to compensate for or dull the insecurity. This is accomplished in the consumption of alcoholic beverages.[18] Alcohol abuse has also been explained by psychoanalytic theorists as an expression of hostility and homosexuality. Still others view alcoholics as self-destructive, narcissistic, or orally fixated.[19] Psychoanalytic theory has even blamed the development of alcoholism on the failure of mothers to provide milk![20]

A major problem with psychoanalytic theories is that experiences such as early childhood deprivation are not specific to alcoholism or addiction to other drugs. In fact, they are commonly reported by nonaddicted adults with a variety of other psychological problems. Perhaps the most serious shortcoming is in the psychodynamic theories' implications for the treatment of alcoholism or drug addiction. Many counselors warn that a nondirective approach that focuses solely on the patients' development of insight into their problems neglects the addictive power of alcohol or other drugs.[21]

Personality Theories.   Personality theories, which frequently overlap the psychodynamic theories, assume that certain personality traits predispose an individual to drug use. An individual with a so-called alcoholic personality is often described as dependent, immature, and impulsive.[22] Other personality theorists have described alcoholics as highly emotional, immature in interpersonal relationships, having low frustration tolerance, being unable to express anger adequately, and confused in their sex-role orientation.[23] After reviewing these personality theories, Keller summarized them in *Keller's law:* The investigation of any trait in alcoholics will show that they have either more or less of it.[24] However, the many scales that have been developed in an attempt to identify alcoholic personalities have failed to distinguish consistently the personality traits of alcoholics from those of nonal-

coholics. One of the subscales of the Minnesota Multiphasic Personality Inventory (MMPI) does differentiate alcoholics from the general population, but it may actually detect only the results of years of alcohol abuse, not underlying personality problems.[25]

There is some evidence that individuals with an antisocial personality (as defined in the *DSM-IV*) have a higher incidence of alcoholism than the general population. There is no evidence that this personality disorder caused the alcoholism, but these individuals were more disposed to develop alcohol problems because of their antisocial personality. Apart from this relatively rare occurrence of the antisocial personality, alcoholics have not been found to exhibit a specific cluster of personality traits.[26] Vaillant[27] argues persuasively that personality (as well as psychological) factors are, at most, of minimal consequence as a cause of alcoholism. There have been similar attempts to link a constellation of certain personality traits to drug addiction[28] as well as alcoholism. A consensus seems to have evolved that personality traits are not of much importance in explaining drug dependence. In fact, most of those who work in this field agree that anyone can become dependent irrespective of personality attributes.[29] One book lists *94* personality characteristics that have been attributed to drug addicts by various theorists![30] These include many characteristics that are polar opposites of one another—for example: "poor self-image" and "grandiose self-image," "ego inflation" and "ego contraction," "self-centered" and "externalization," "pleasure-seekers" and "pleasure-avoiders," and several dozen other contradictory pairs.

A report to the National Academy of Sciences concludes that there is no single set of psychological *characteristics* that embraces all addictions. However, there are, according to the report, "significant personality *factors* that can contribute to addiction." These factors number 4 (not 94) and are:

1. Impulsive behavior, difficulty in delaying gratification, an antisocial personality, and a disposition toward sensation seeking.

2. A high value on nonconformity combined with a weak commitment to the goals for achievement valued by the society.

3. A sense of social alienation and a general tolerance for deviance.

4. A sense of heightened stress. (This may help explain why adolescence and other stressful transition periods are often associated with severe drug and alcohol problems.)[31]

Biological Theories

Biophysiological and genetic theories assume that addicts are constitutionally predisposed to develop a dependence on alcohol or drugs. These theories encourage a medical model of addiction. Their advocates apply disease terminology and generally place responsibility for the treatment of addicts in the hands of physicians, nurses, and other medical personnel. In reality, the medical model is generally practiced only during the detoxification phase.

Generally speaking, biological theories branch into one of two explanations: neurochemistry (brain dysfunction and brain chemistry) and genetics. Neurochemistry theories state that abnormal neurochemistry is related to alcohol dependencies. Low neurotransmitter levels, for instance, are strongly related to the preference for alcohol.

Animals can be selectively bred to prefer alcohol.[32] One strain of mice will prefer an alcohol solution in a wide variety of situations, whereas another strain of mice will avoid virtually all ethanol. The genetic selection of animals is based on their propensity to ingest alcohol solutions. Their propensity is called a *phenocopy*, or an "environmentally induced nonhereditary variation in organisms, closely resembling a genetically determined trait."[33] In other words, environment contributed to the risk of alcohol dependence and to phenocopies,[34] but resulted in neurochemical changes in the animals.

Brain Dysfunction Theories. Some scientists believe that the mode of inheritance in alcoholism may be a neurochemical deficiency that manifests itself in childhood as minimal brain damage. Alcoholic parents have children who more frequently exhibit symptoms of minimal brain dysfunction.[35] Others have reported more symptoms of childhood hyperactivity in children of alcoholics than in other children.[36] Such children are more likely to develop addictions.

Biochemical Theories. Two popular theories are that alcoholics have abnormalities in sugar metabolism[37] or a "allergic reaction" to alcohol or congeners.[38] The problem with the former theory is that abnormalities in metabolism are just as likely to develop as a result of years of alcohol abuse. It would require experimental studies of "prealcoholics" to isolate metabolic imbalances as a cause of alcoholism. It also stretches the meaning of *allergy* well beyond the normal use of the term. Allergies usually result in a pathology of one or more organs (such as a skin rash), not a behavior such as loss of control over drinking. No other substance is known to have such an "allergic" effect.

One of the more interesting biochemical theories is that alcohol may produce morphinelike substances such as tetrahydroisoquinolines in the brains of certain users, which are responsible for the development of an alcohol addiction.[39] A similar theory is that as alcohol is metabolized within the body, acetaldehyde reacts with serotonin to form salsolinol, an addicting chemical commonly found in the urine of alcoholics.[40] A difficulty with all these biologic theories lies in the failure of the research to establish cause and effect. Factors that are frequently cited as possible biologic causes of alcoholism could just as easily be viewed as the result of long years of heavy drinking. Nevertheless, these theories do indicate some interesting and perhaps promising areas for future research.

Genetic Theories. Genetic factors have never been established as a definite cause of alcoholism, but the statistical associations between genetic factors and alcohol abuse are very strong. A great volume of research has been amassed in this area over the last several decades, and much of the evidence points toward alcoholism as an inherited trait. It has been observed that (1) adopted children more closely resemble their biological parents than their adoptive parents in their use of alcohol,[41] (2) alcoholism occurs more frequently in some families than in others,[42] and (3) concurrent alcoholism rates are higher in monozygotic twin pairs (53.5 percent) than in dizygotic pairs (28.3 percent).[43] Children of alcoholics are three to seven times more likely to be at risk of alcoholism.[44] Having either parent be an alcoholic, not necessarily both parents, can increase the risk of becoming an alcoholic. Yet, even in the presence of elevated risks, only 33 percent sons and 15 percent daughters of alcoholics demonstrate evidence of the disorder.[45]

Some genetic theorists speculate that an inherited metabolic defect may interact with environmental elements and eventually lead to alcoholism. This genetotrophic theory posits an impaired production of enzymes within the body.[46] Others hypothesize that inherited genetic traits result in a deficiency of vitamins (usually of the vitamin B complex), which leads to a craving for alcohol as well as cellular or metabolic changes.[47]

It is important to remember that despite the impressive statistical relationships in these studies implying a genetic link, no specific genetic marker that predisposes a person toward alcoholism has ever been isolated. The first biological marker established for alcoholism was thought to be color blindness, but a few years later, it was demonstrated that color blindness was actually a result of severe alcohol abuse.[48] Several other genetic discoveries have met a similar fate. A workshop on genetic and biological markers in drug and alcohol abuse suggests promising areas for genetic research, such as polymorphisms in gene products and DNA polymorphisms.[49] A more recent study reports that the so-called dopamine D2 receptor gene, which affects the capacity of cells to absorb dopamine, was present in 77 percent of the brains of alcoholics and only 28 percent of nonalcoholics.[50]

In 1990, the front page of the *New York Times* hailed the discovery of a gene claimed to be directly linked to alcoholism. Two years later, this so-called alcoholism gene, formally known as the dopamine

D2 receptor gene, has become the focus of a bitter controversy. Blum and Noble insist that their finding has been amply documented by subsequent research, and they are taking steps to market a test for genetic susceptibility to alcoholism. Blum suggests that the test could be given to job applicants, children, and perhaps even fetuses.

In Blum and Noble's experiments, the D2 gene was shown to have at least two variants, or alleles, called A1 and A2. They found the A1 allele in the genetic material of 69 percent of the alcoholics studied, compared to only 20 percent of the controls. Blum and Noble theorize that A1 carriers may use alcohol or other drugs excessively to compensate for a reduced ability to absorb pleasure-inducing dopamine.

On the other side are skeptics such as geneticists Kidd and Cloninger. Both contend that Blum and Noble's claim has been contradicted by other studies and "is almost certainly invalid." Bolos and Gelernter also found the incidences of the A1 allele among alcoholics not significantly higher than that among controls.[51]

A study of 862 men and 913 women who had been adopted early in life by nonrelatives identified two types of alcoholism.[52] Type I, or milieu-limited, alcoholism is found in both sexes and is associated with alcoholism in either biological parent, but an environmental factor—low occupational status of the adoptive father—also had to be present as a condition for alcoholism to occur in the offspring. Type II, known as male-limited alcoholism, is more severe but accounts for fewer cases. It is found only in men, and it does not appear to be affected by environmental factors.

Vaillant,[53] however, points out the potential biases in the preceding study. He says that the study failed to control for the environmental effect of parental alcoholism. He continues by pointing out that antisocial personality disorder must be distinguished from alcohol dependence, and that developmental effects of abusing individuals must be controlled. Furthermore, for his studies, Vaillant excludes individuals with other major psychiatric disorders that could, by themselves, directly contribute to alcohol dependence. Such cases (direct and uncomplicated cases) are estimated to represent 60 to 70 percent of the alcohol-dependent population.[54]

The notion of Type I and Type II alcoholics hangs, in part, on the age of the onset of alcoholism. Vaillant[55] found in a study of alcohol-abusing men in inner cities and in college that age of onset and degree of antisocial symptomatology correlated with disturbed family environments but was independent of positive or negative heredity for alcoholism. In other words, this negated the hypothesis that heredity predicts the age of onset. "Alcoholic abuse began 11 years earlier for the socially disadvantaged men with a heredity negative for alcoholism than for the college men with two or more alcoholic relatives."[56] In other words, early-onset alcohol abusers in inner cities had no more alcoholic relatives than did late-onset alcohol abusers in college. Furthermore, inner-city men were 10 times as likely as the college men to come from multiproblem families, to exhibit traits of sociopathy, to have delinquent parents, and to have spent time in jail. These findings lead one to ask: "How do biological factors interact with environment to contribute to heavy enough drinking over long enough periods of time to produce physical and psychological dependence?"[57] Vaillant[58] suggests that rather than there being two kinds of alcoholism, there may be (1) genetic loading (predicting whether one develops alcoholism) and (2) an unstable childhood environment (predicting when one loses control of alcohol). (Late onset is less associated with dependence, substance-related problems, hyperactivity, and dysfunctional families in one's youth.)

Sociocultural Theories

There is little high-quality research regarding the macrovariables that seek to explain addiction.[59] Yet, as we mentioned earlier, almost every known culture has discovered the use of beverage alcohol. "All societies establish a quota of deviance necessary for boundary setting"; rules around alcohol and drug use are a part of boundary set-

ting.[60] The ways in which different societies encourage, permit, or regulate the use of alcohol varies considerably, however.

For the most part, sociocultural theories have been generated by observations of differences or similarities between cultural groups or subgroups. Sociocultural theorists are prone to attribute differences in drinking practices, "problem" drinking, or alcoholism to *environmental factors.* For example, socially disorganized communities often fail to realize the common values of their residents and to maintain effective social controls.[61] Therefore, inner-city drug use is more rampant than in the suburbs.

According to Goode, the social context of drug use strongly influences, perhaps even determines, "four central aspects of drug reality"[62]: drug definitions, drug effects, drug-related behavior, and the drug experience. The sociocultural perspective stands in direct opposition to what is called the *chemicalistic fallacy*—the view that drug A causes behavior X.

Because no object or event has meaning in the abstract, all these central aspects must be interpreted in light of social phenomena surrounding drug use. For example, morphine and heroin are not very different pharmacologically and biochemically. Yet, heroin is regarded as a dangerous drug with no therapeutic value, whereas morphine is defined primarily as a medicine. Definitions are shaped by the social milieu surrounding the use of each substance.

People using morphine as an illegal street drug experience a "rush" or a "high" generally unknown to patients using the same drug in a hospital setting. Psychedelic drugs, such as peyote, which are taken for religious purposes (as in the Native American church), do not typically result in religious or mystical experiences when taken simply to get high. Drugs, according to Goode, only potentiate certain kinds of experiences; they do not produce them. It is important to distinguish between drug effects and the drug experience. Many changes may take place in the body when a chemical is ingested, not all of which are noted and classified by the user. A drug may have a more or less automatic effect of dilating the pupils, causing ataxia or amblyopia, and so on, but the experience is subject to the cognitive system of the user's mind. A person must be attuned to certain drug effects to interpret them, categorize them, and place them within appropriate experiential and conceptual realms.[63] One's propensity to use drugs, the way one behaves when one uses drugs, and one's definitions of *abuse* and *addiction* are all influenced by one's sociocultural system. Why else would someone define heroin and LSD as dangerous drugs, yet almost never perceive social drinkers and smokers as drug users?

Supracultural Theories.   The pioneering work of Bales provides some general hypotheses regarding the relationships among culture, social organization, and the use of alcohol.[64] He proposed that a culture that produces guilt, suppressed aggression, and sexual tension and that condones the use of alcohol to relieve those tensions is likely to have a high rate of alcoholism. Bales also believed that collective attitudes toward alcohol use dramatically influence rates of alcoholism. He classified these attitudes as favoring (1) abstinence, (2) ritual use connected with religious practices, (3) convivial drinking in a social setting, and (4) utilitarian drinking (drinking for personal, self-interested reasons). The utilitarian attitude, especially in a culture that induces much inner tension, is the most likely to lead to problem drinking, whereas the other three mitigate against alcohol problems.

Also important in Bales's theory is the degree to which a society offers alternatives to alcohol use for the release of tension and for providing a substitute means of satisfaction. A social system with a strong emphasis on upward economic or social mobility will excessively frustrate an individual who has no available means of achieving success. In such a system, high rates of alcohol use would be expected.[65]

Unfortunately, few alternatives to alcohol or drugs seem to exist in most modern societies. In traditional societies, such as the hill tribes of Malaysia, a shaman may assist tribesmen in achieving a

trancelike state in which endorphin levels are altered.[67] Also at the supracultural level, Bacon theorized that alcoholism is likely to be a problem in a society that combines a lack of indulgence of children with demanding attitudes toward achievement and negative attitudes regarding dependent behavior in adults.[67] Another important factor in sociocultural theories is the degree of societal consensus regarding alcohol use. In cultures where there is little agreement regarding drinking limits and customs, a higher rate of alcoholism is expected.[68] Cultural ambivalence regarding alcohol use results in weak social controls, allowing the drinker to avoid being labeled as a deviant.

Culture-Specific Theories.   Levin describes two examples of cultural contrast in attitudes toward drinking: the contrast between French and Italian drinking practices and the contrast between Irish and Jewish drinking practices.[69] There are many similarities between the French and Italian cultures; both are heavily Catholic and both produce and consume large quantities of alcohol. The French, however, drink both wine and spirits, both with meals and without, both with and away from the family. The French do not strongly disapprove of drunkenness, and they consider it bad manners to refuse a drink. On the other hand, the Italians drink mostly with meals and mostly with family, and they usually drink wine. They strongly disapprove of drunkenness and they do not pressure people into drinking. As one might expect, France has one of the highest rates of alcoholism in the world, whereas Italy's rate is only one-fifth as great. (Italy, which had the second highest rate of wine consumption in the world in 1952, consumed only half of what was consumed in France.[70]) The strong sanctions against drunkenness and social control imposed by learning to drink low-proof alcoholic beverages in moderation seems to have something to do with the lower rate of Italian alcoholism.

In a fashion, studies of Irish and Jewish drinking practices draw some sharp contrasts. The Irish have a high proportion of both abstainers and problem drinkers, whereas Jews have a low proportion of both.[71] The Irish drink largely outside the home in pubs; Jews drink largely in the home with the family and on ceremonial occasions. The Irish excuse drunkenness as "a good man's fault"; Jews condemn it as something culturally alien. Bales found Irish drinking to be largely convivial on the surface, but purely utilitarian drinking was a frequent and tolerated pattern. Jewish drinking, on the other hand, was mostly ceremonial. Again, it is no surprise that the Irish alcoholism rate is one of the highest in the world, and the Jewish rate is one of the lowest.[72]

Subcultural Theories.   There have been many investigations of sociological and environmental causes of alcoholism at the subcultural level. Within the same culture, a great diversity in alcoholism rates has been related to age, sex, ethnicity, socioeconomic class, religion, and family background.[73] One of the landmark studies of social variables at this level was conducted almost three decades ago by Cahalan.[74] He specified that social environment determines to a large extent whether an individual will drink or not, and that sociopsychological variables also determine the level of drinking. In becoming a problem drinker, variables such as age, sex, ethnicity, and social position influence the probability that a person will learn to drink as a dominant response. Labeling the person as a heavy drinker then reinforces the probability of that response.

Of course, these processes do not occur in isolation from other factors, such as the process of physical addiction. Goode,[75] Laurie,[76] Imlah,[77] and many others have examined the sociocultural context of drug addiction and found there to be many similarities to alcoholism. A major difference is in the outcast nature of certain illicit drug users such as heroin addicts. Users of illegal drugs such as heroin may be more socially isolated than alcoholics because of their addiction. Also, certain types of drug addiction seem to thrive within specific subcultures. Heroin addiction is a persistent problem among jazz musicians. Inner-city youths frequently "huff" spray paint or sniff glue. With three feet of hose and an empty can, Native American youths on certain reservations will always be able to get high on gasoline fumes.

The impact of gender on drug use presents an interesting perspective on sociocultural theories. Either a culture-specific or subcultural model can be used in explaining the differences between male and female drug-related behaviors in the United States. Historically, female drinking has been less accepted than male drinking in the United States, and being intoxicated is clearly more disapproved for women than for men.[78] These double standards may account for the much lower rate of problem drinking noted among women. Social pressure and social stigma may result in less problem drinking by women as a subgroup of the larger U.S. culture.

This phenomenon may be culture specific, however. An early cross-cultural study of sex differences in drinking found that in many societies, men and women do not differ greatly with regard to various aspects of drinking.[79] The fact that men seem to drink more and have more problems because of alcohol in some cultures and not in others fits into a supracultural model of drug use. The degree of female problem drinking appears to be related to cultural norms regarding the overall status of women within different societies. Bear in mind that the vast majority of the research on alcohol and drug abuse has been conducted on men only. Only recently have gender-related issues in this area begun to be systematically examined.

Alternative Explanations

Fingarette sees alcoholism as "neither sin nor disease."[80] Instead, he views it as a life-style. According to Fingarette, proponents of the disease model describe alcoholism as a disease characterized by loss of control over drinking. Recovery is possible only if one voluntarily seeks and enters treatment and voluntarily abstains from drinking. Only then can one be "cured." Cured from what? From a disease that makes voluntary abstention impossible and makes drinking uncontrollable! This, says Fingarette, is an amazing contradiction.[81]

His alternative explanation views the "persistent heavy drinking of the alcoholic as a central activity" of the individual's way of life. Each person develops his or her unique way of life, which consists of a number of central activities. Some will adopt parenting as a central activity, while others will place sex, physical thrills, or their careers at the center. Why do some people choose drinking as a central feature? Fingarette says that there is no general answer, but that the explanation lies not only in motives but also in a person's cultural background, life circumstances, special life crises, or physical abnormalities. No single item will be the reason.

Fingarette believes that it is no harder for the alcoholic to choose to stop drinking than it is for others to abandon activities central to their ways of life. "We should see the alcoholic, not as a sick and defective human being, but as a human being whose way of life is self-destructive. The difficulty we face is stubborn human nature, not disease."[82]

In a similar fashion, Peele has examined the evidence on addiction and concluded that "we have disarmed ourselves in combating the precipitous growth of addictions by discounting the role of values in creating and preventing addiction and by systematically overlooking the immorality of addictive misbehavior."[83] This is not a revival of the *addiction as sin* model, but an argument that addicts and alcoholics do differ from other people in the ways in which they prioritize their values. This fits comfortably with the World Health Organization definitions of both *alcohol* and *drug dependence.* In his book, *Junky,* noted author (and addict) William S. Burroughs attempted to answer the question: Why does a person become a drug addict? "The answer is that he usually does not intend to become an addict. You don't wake up one morning and decide to be a drug addict. . . . You become a narcotics addict because you do not have strong motivations in any other direction."[84]

A Multicausal Model

Which of these etiological models or explanations of drug abuse is "correct"? All are probably help-ful, at least in a heuristic sense, but no single model or theory adequately explains the phenomenon of dependency or addiction. A significant advance in the study of chemical dependency is the realization that it is probably not a unitary disorder. Pattison and Kaufman made a strong case for a multivariate model of alcoholism more than a decade ago.[85] Even though there may be similar behavioral topography in all addicted individuals, the etiology and motivation for drug use may differ widely. Available evidence points strongly to the possibility that addiction may be manifest through different mechanisms. Therefore, a model such as the one in Figure 2.1 may be helpful in understanding this phenomenon.

For some individuals, a genetic predisposition or physiological dysfunction is a necessary condition for drug use, drug abuse, and subsequent addiction. On the other hand, some people with disturbances in their personal development or interpersonal orientation but with no known genetic predisposition or biochemical aberration may become addicted to a drug. This debate over which model is really "best" is valuable only in the sense that it leads one to see the utility in an interdisciplinary, multicausal model.

This model is similar to the public health model, promoted in recent years by health care and other human service professionals. The model conceptualizes the problem of chemical dependency in terms of an interaction among three factors: the agent, the host, and the environment. In most public health areas, the agent is an organism (e.g., a virus), but in this case, it is ethanol. The second factor is the host—the chemically dependent person, including the person's genetic composition, cognitive structure, expectations about drug experiences, and personality. The last factor consists of the social, cultural, political, and economic variables that affect the use of alcohol or drugs and the resulting consequences. The public health approach involves the examination of the complex interaction of the multitude of variables affecting the agent, the host, and the environment.[86]

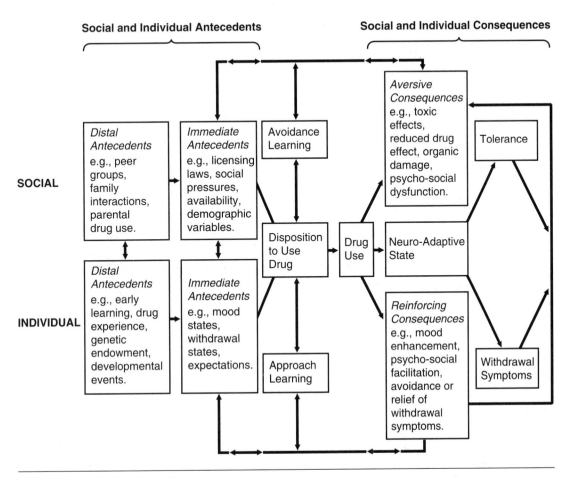

FIGURE 2.1   A Model of Drug Use

Source: Duncan Raistrick and Robin Davidson, *Alcoholism and Drug Addiction* (Edinburgh: Churchill Livingstone, 1985). Reprinted by permission

Summary

The most obvious fact about alcohol and drug addiction is that we have no single theory that explains this phenomenon. Some people may be more genetically predisposed than others to become addicted. Others are more prone to addiction because of their social environment, peer pressure, role models in the family, societal values, and so on. Still others may have one or more personality traits that make them more likely to use or abuse alcohol or drugs. Once use begins, physiological processes such as withdrawal and tolerance make the individual even more prone to continue use.

Endnotes

1. J. C. Crabb, "A Genetic Animal Model of Alcohol Withdrawal," *Alcoholism: Clinical and Experimental Research,* Vol. 20 (1996), pp. 96–100.

2. *The American Heritage Dictionary of the English Language,* 3rd ed. (Boston: Houghton Mifflin, 1996), p. 42.

3. Ibid., p. 20.

4. American Psychiatric Association, *Diagnostic and Statistical Manual of Mental Disorders*, 4th ed. (Washington, DC: Author, 1994), p. 182.

5. M. A. Schuckit, "Advances in Understanding the Vulnerability to Alcoholism," in C. P. O'Brien and J. H. Jaffe (Eds.), *Addiction States* (New York: Raven Press, 1992), pp. 93–108.

6. Ibid., p. 182.

7. Andrew Well and Winifred Rosen, *From Chocolate to Morphine: Everything You Need to Know about Mind-Altering Drugs* (Boston: Houghton Mifflin, 1993).

8. Finn-Agge Esbensen and David Huizinga, "Community Structure and Drug Use: From a Social Disorganization Perspective," *Justice Quarterly*, Vol. 7 (1990), pp. 691–708.

9. National Institute on Alcohol Abuse and Alcoholism, *Alcohol Alert*, Number 33, Ph 366 (1996).

10. Java Krivanek, *Addictions* (Sydney: Allen & Unwin, 1989), p. 96.

11. B. Janoff-Bulman, *Shattered Assumptions* (New York: The Free Press, 1992).

12. Ralph E. Tarter and Dorothea U. Schneider, "Models and Theories of Alcoholism," in Ralph E. Tarter and A. Arthur Sugarmen (Eds.), *Alcoholism: Interdisciplinary Approaches to an Enduring Problem* (Reading, MA: Addison-Wesley, 1976).

13. A & DRCC, *Sci-Mat: Science Matters in the Battle against Alcoholism and Related Diseases* (1995), p. 13.

14. Krivanek, *Addictions*, p. 96.

15. E. Mansell Pattison, Mark B. Sobell, and Linda C. Sobell, *Emerging Concepts of Alcohol Dependence* (New York: Springer, 1977), p. 191.

16. Albert Bandura, *Principles of Behavior Modification* (New York: Holt, Rinehart and Winston, 1969).

17. Marie Bonaparte, Anna Freud, and Ernst Kris (Eds.), *The Origins of Psychoanalysis; Letters to Fliess* (New York: Basic Books, 1954), letter no. 79.

18. B. Chordokoff, "Alcoholism and Ego Function," *Quarterly Journal of Studies on Alcohol*, Vol. 25 (1964), pp. 292–299.

19. Marc A. Schuckit, "Etiological Theories on Alcoholism," in Nada J. Estes and M. Edith Heinemann (Eds.), *Alcoholism: Development, Consequences, and Interventions*, 3rd ed. (St. Louis, MO: C. V. Mosby, 1986), pp. 15–30.

20. Karl Menninger, *The Vital Balance* (New York: Viking Press, 1963).

21. Anne L. Cunynghame, "Some Issues in Successful Alcoholism Treatment," in David Cook, Christine Fewell, and John Riolo (Eds.), *Social Work Treatment of Alcohol Problems* (New Brunswick, NJ: Rutgers Center of Alcohol Studies, 1983), pp. 49–59.

22. Schuckit, "Etiological Theories on Alcoholism."

23. P. Catanzaro, "Psychiatric Aspects of Alcoholism," in D. J. Pittman (Ed.), *Alcoholism* (New York: Harper and Row, 1967).

24. Mark Keller, "The Oddities of Alcoholics," *Quarterly Journal of Studies on Alcohol*, Vol. 33 (1972), pp. 11–20.

25. Craig MacAndrew, "On the Possibility of the Psychometric Detection of Persons Who Are Prone to the Abuse of Alcohol and Other Substances," *Journal of Addictive Behaviors*, Vol. 4 (1979), pp. 11–20.

26. M. Sherfey, "Psychopathology and Character Structure in Chronic Alcoholism," in W. O. Diethelm (Ed.), *The Etiology of Chronic Alcoholism* (Springfield, IL: Charles C Thomas, 1955).

27. George Vaillant, "Evidence That the Type I/Type II Dichotomy in Alcoholism Must Be Re-Examined," *Addiction*, Vol. 89 (1994), pp. 1049–1058.

28. Michael R. Gossop and Sybil Eysenck, "A Further Investigation into the Personality of Drug Addicts in Treatment," *British Journal of Addiction*, Vol. 75 (1980), pp. 305–311.

29. Duncan Raistrick and Robin Davidson, *Alcoholism and Drug Addiction* (New York: Churchill Livingstone, 1985), p. 21.

30. Stanley Einstein, *The Drug User: Personality Factors, Issues, and Theories* (New York: Plenum Press, 1983), pp. 9–11.

31. "The Addictive Personality: Common Traits Are Found," Sec. Y, *New York Times*, January 18, 1983, pp. 11 and 15.

32. R. A. Meisch, "Animal Studies of Alcohol Intake," *British Journal of Psychiatry*, Vol. 141 (1982), pp. 113–130.

33. *The American Heritage Dictionary*, p. 1358.

34. Schuckit, "Advances in Understanding the Vulnerability to Alcoholism."

35. George E. Valliant, *The Natural History of Alcoholism: Causes, Patterns and Paths to Recovery* (Cambridge, MA: Harvard University Press, 1983).

36. Dennis Cantwell, "Psychiatric Illness in the Families of Hyperactive Children," *Archives of General Psychiatry*, Vol. 27 (1972), pp. 414–417.

37. Roger J. Williams, *Alcoholism: The Nutritional Approach* (Austin: University of Texas Press, 1959).

38. Richard Mackarness, "The Allergic Factor in Alcoholism," *International Journal of Social Psychiatry*, Vol. 18 (1972), pp. 194–200.

39. Floyd E. Bloom, "A Summary of Workshop Discussions," in F. Bloom et al. (Eds.), *Beta-carbolines and Tetrahydroisoquinolines* (New York: Alan R. Liss, 1982).

40. Michael A. Collins et al., "Dopamine-Related Tetrahydroisoquinolines: Significant Urinary Excretions by Alcoholics after Alcohol Consumption," *Science*, Vol. 206 (1979), pp. 1184–1186.

41. Donald W. Goodwin, Shirley Hill, Barbara Powell, and Jorge Viamontes, "Effect of Alcohol on Short-Term Memory in Alcoholics," *British Journal of Psychiatry*, Vol. 122 (1973), pp. 93–94.

42. N. A. Cotton, "The Familial Incidence of Alcoholism," *Journal of Studies on Alcohol*, Vol. 40 (1979), pp. 89–116.

43. Lennart Kaij, *Alcoholism in Twins: Studies on the Etiology and Sequels of Abuse of Alcohol* (Stockholm: Almquist & Wiskell, 1960).

44. J. R. Koopmans and D. I. Boomsina, "Familiar Resemblances in Alcohol Use: Genetic or Cultural Transmission," Department of Psychonomics, Vriji Universiteit, De Boelelaan 1111, 1081 HV, Amsterdam, The Netherlands, (1995), p. 19; Schuckit, "Advances in Understanding the Vulnerability to Alcoholism," pp. 93–108.

45. Ibid., 1995; Ibid., 1992.

46. Williams, *Alcoholism: The Nutritional Approach.*

47. Tarter and Schneider, "Models and Theories of Alcoholism," p. 84.

48. A. Valera, L. Rivera, J. Mardones, and R. Cruz-Coke, "Color Vision Defects in Non-Alcoholic Relatives of Alcoholic Patients," *British Journal of the Addictions,* Vol. 64 (1969), pp. 67–71.

49. Warren W. Nichols, *Genetic and Biological Markers in Drug Abuse and Alcoholism: A Summary,* in National Institute on Drug Abuse, Research Monograph Series No. 66, Genetic and Biological Markers in Drug Abuse and Alcoholism (Washington, DC: U.S. Government Printing Office, 1986), pp. 1–4.

50. Kenneth Blum, Ernest Noble, Peter Sheridan, Anne Montgomery, Terry Ritchie, Pudur Jagadeeswaran, Harou Nogami, Arthur Briggs, and Jay Cohen, "Allelic Association of Human Dopamine D2 Receptor Gene in Alcoholism," *Journal of the American Medical Association,* Vol. 263 (1990), pp. 2055–2060.

51. John Horgan, "D2 or not D2," *Scientific American,* Vol. 266, No. 4 (April 1992), pp. 29–32.

52. Michael Boham, C. Robert Cloninger, Anne-Liis von Knorring, and Soren Sigvardsson, "An Adoption Study of Somatoform Disorders. III. Cross-Fostering Analysis and Genetic Relationship to Alcoholism and Criminality," *Archives of General Psychiatry,* Vol. 41 (1984), pp. 872–878.

53. Vaillant, "Evidence That the Type I/Type II Dichotomy in Alcoholism Must Be Re-examined."

54. Schuckit, "Advances in Understanding the Vulnerability to Alcoholism."

55. Vaillant, "Evidence That the Type I/Type II Dichotomy in Alcoholism Must Be Re-Examined."

56. Ibid.

57. Schuckit, "Advances in Understanding the Vulnerability to Alcohol."

58. Vaillant, "Evidence That the Type I/Type II Dichotomy to Alcoholism Must Be Re-Examined."

59. Esbensen, "Community Structure and Drug Use."

60. Ibid., p. 705.

61. Ibid.

62. Erich Goode, *Drugs in American Society* (New York: Alfred A. Knopf, 1972), p. 3.

63. Ibid., p. 8.

64. Robert F. Bales, "Cultural Differences in Rates of Alcoholism," *Quarterly Journal of Studies on Alcohol,* Vol. 6 (1946), pp. 480–499.

65. Tarter and Schneider, "Models and Theories of Alcoholism."

66. Carol Laderman, "Trances That Heal: Rites, Rituals, and Brain Chemicals," in William B. Rucker and Marian E. Rucker (Eds.), *Drugs, Society and Behavior, 87/88* (Guilford, CT: Dushkin, 1987), pp. 233–235.

67. Margaret K. Bacon, "The Dependency-Conflict Hypothesis and the Frequency of Drunkenness," *Quarterly Journal of Studies on Alcohol,* Vol. 35 (1974), pp. 863–876.

68. Harrison Trice, *Alcoholism in America* (New York: McGraw-Hill, 1966).

69. Jerome D. Levin, *Alcoholism: A Bio-psycho-social Approach* (New York: Hemisphere, 1989), p. 59.

70. Jean Kinney and Gwen Leaton, *Loosening the Grip: A Handbook of Alcohol Information* (St. Louis, MO: C. V. Mosby, 1987), p. 85.

71. Levin, *Alcoholism,* p. 59.

72. Bales, "Cultural Differences in Rates of Alcoholism."

73. Tarter and Schneider, "Models and Theories of Alcoholism," p. 95.

74. D. Cahalan, *Problem Drinkers: A National Survey* (San Francisco: Jossey-Bass, 1970).

75. E. Goode, *Drugs in American Society,* 2nd ed. (New York: Alfred A. Knopf, 1984).

76. P. Laurie, *Drugs* (New York: Penguin Books, 1971).

77. N. Imlah, *Drugs in Modern Society* (Princeton, NJ: Averbach Publishers, 1971).

78. Edith S. Gomberg, "Women with Alcohol Problems," in Estes and Heinemann, *Alcoholism,* pp. 241–256.

79. Irving L. Child, Margaret K. Bacon, and Harry Barry, "A Cross-Cultural Study of Drinking: III. Sex Differences," *Quarterly Journal of Studies on Alcohol,* Vol. 3 (1965), pp. 49–61.

80. Herbert Fingarette, "Alcoholism: Neither Sin Nor Disease," *The Center Magazine* (March/April 1985), pp. 56–63.

81. Ibid.

82. Ibid., p. 63

83. Stanton Peele (Ed.), *Visions of Addiction: Major Contemporary Perspectives on Addiction and Alcoholism* (Lexington, MA: D. C. Heath, 1988), p. 224.

84. William S. Burroughs, *Junky* (New York: Penguin Books, 1953), p. xv. Originally published as *Junkie* under the pen name of William Lee, by Ace Books, 1953.

85. E. Mansell Pattison and Edward Kaufman, "The Alcoholism Syndrome: Definitions and Models," in E. Mansell Pattison and Edward Kaufman (Eds.), *Encyclopedic Handbook of Alcoholism* (New York: Gardner Press, 1982), p. 13.

86. Reid K. Hester and Nancy Sheehy, "The Grand Unification Theory of Alcohol Abuse: It's Time to Stop Fighting Each Other and Start Working Together," in Ruth C. Engs (Ed.), *Controversies in the Addictions Field,* Volume I (Dubuque, IA: Kendall/Hunt, 1990), pp. 2–9.

3

Becoming Addicted

Almost everyone has an easy answer to the question: Why do people use drugs? According to Stewart, heroin addicts use "junk" the first time because they are curious. Heroin has a mystique. It is used by pop stars, writers, and glamorous people,[1] and they like its effect. For those who find daily life to be fairly humdrum, heroin can be the ultimate filler of gaps—it can substitute for career, religion, romance, or virtually anything else. Weil and Rosen believe that drug use (and addiction) results from humans' longing for a sense of completeness and wholeness, and searching for satisfaction outside of themselves.[2] As William Burroughs indicated in *Junky*, "Junk wins by default. I tried it as a matter of curiosity. I drifted along taking shots when I could score. I ended up hooked."[3] This notion of *drift* is a recurrent theme in theories of addiction.

People begin using cocaine for some of the same reasons. According to one therapist, his clients provided these excuses for using cocaine:

> "The mystical reputation aroused my curiosity."
> "It's available and being offered all the time."
> "It gave me a sense of well-being, like I was worth something."
> "It felt good to be a part of a group."
> "It was a great way to escape."[4]

One of the major differences between heroin and cocaine is that cocaine has much less stigma attached to it. In fact, it seems to be as commonly accepted as alcohol or tobacco in some circles. Middle-class executives-in-training who are planning a party may be just as embarrassed by forgetting to pick up some "coke" for the guests as by forgetting the hors d'oeuvres. People who refuse to snort "a line" frequently are shunned by friends who do use the drug. Pressure thus becomes much more intense for a person to use cocaine.

Most models of addiction assume that an addiction is an "addictive disease."[5] As such, it continues to exist whether or not the addicted person continues to use the drug. Even if a person who has the disease is abstinent for a long period of time, the symptoms of addiction will appear again from renewed contact with the drug. The disease model of addiction rests on three primary assumptions: predisposition to use a drug, loss of control over use, and progression.[6] Johnson put it somewhat differently in saying, "The most significant characteristics of the disease (*alcoholism*) are that it is primary, progressive, chronic, and fatal."[7] There are others, of course, who question the validity of this model.

The most commonly used (and abused) psychoactive drug, of course, is alcohol. The route to alcohol addiction does vary somewhat from that taken by "junkies," "coke-heads," and "speed freaks." Alcohol is a *legal* drug, and its use is so pervasive in U.S. culture that many people do not ever seriously consider *not* using it. Also, the great majority of people who drink alcohol use it on a fairly regular basis with no apparent negative consequences. These factors lead people to consider alcohol to be a relatively harmless drug. Consider the remarks of the mother of one teenager who discovered that her son was drinking almost on a daily basis: "Thank God it was only alcohol! We were worried that he had gotten involved with the 'wrong crowd' at school and was taking drugs."

Because alcohol is still the most widely abused drug, and because there are many similarities in the addiction process for all drugs, we will begin by describing some widely used models of the stages of alcoholism. After critically examining these models, we will look at similarities and differences between alcoholism and other types of addiction.

The Stages of Alcoholism

Similar to the heroin addicts described earlier by Burroughs, most alcoholics probably "drift" into alcoholism in the sense that very few of them begin drinking with the intention of becoming alcoholic. In many of the models described in this chapter, the journey from experimental drinking to social drinking to addiction (or dependence) generally takes place over the course of several years. Alcoholics Anonymous (AA) meetings are full of middle-aged people who considered themselves to be "social drinkers" for 20 or 30 years before recognizing that they had a "drinking problem."

One of the first attempts to describe the development of alcoholism is found in Jellinek's study of 2,000 male members of Alcoholics Anonymous.[8] He characterized alcoholism as an insidious disease that progresses through well-defined phases, each with symptoms that develop in the majority of persons in an additive, orderly fashion. In Jellinek's model, the drinker progresses through four distinct stages: (1) prealcoholic symptomatic phase, (2) prodromal phase, (3) crucial phase, and (4) chronic phase[9] (see Figure 3.1).

In the *prealcoholic symptomatic phase*, drinking is associated with rewarding relief from tension or stress, something almost all drinkers engage in occasionally. The person who is more predisposed toward alcoholism (whether by chromosomes, culture, or other factors) will tend to increase the frequency of "relief drinking" over a period of time. At the same time, the drinker develops a physical tolerance to alcohol, so that increasingly larger amounts are needed to bring the same degree of relief from stress or tension.

The onset of blackouts marks the beginning of the *prodromal phase.* These are periods of amnesia not associated with the loss of consciousness. The drinker may seem to be acting "normally," but later has no recall of those events that occurred while in a blackout. This phase is also characterized by an increase in the need for alcohol (and attempts to hide the need for alcohol), surreptitious drinking, and increasing guilt.

The primary hallmark of the *crucial phase* is loss of control over drinking, as evidenced by the inability to abstain from drinking or the inability to stop once started. During this stage, the drinker often will drink during the morning, will experience behavior problems in relation to employment and social life, and will frequently seek to avoid family and friends.

The final stage, or *chronic phase*, finds the drinker intoxicated for several days at a time. Drinking becomes obsessive, and both serious physical and emotional problems are evident. According to Jellinek's original model, this is where the alcoholic "hits bottom." Although this work was a pioneering effort in the field of alcoholism research, one must remember that Jellinek's sample were (1) all AA members, (2) all in the latter stages of alcoholism, and (3) all males.

This traditional view of alcohol addiction was supported by many other prominent scholars, however. Mann described alcoholism as a "progressive disease, which, if left untreated, grows more virulent year by year."[10] Others seem to have conveniently ignored available scientific evidence in making assertions such as "the true

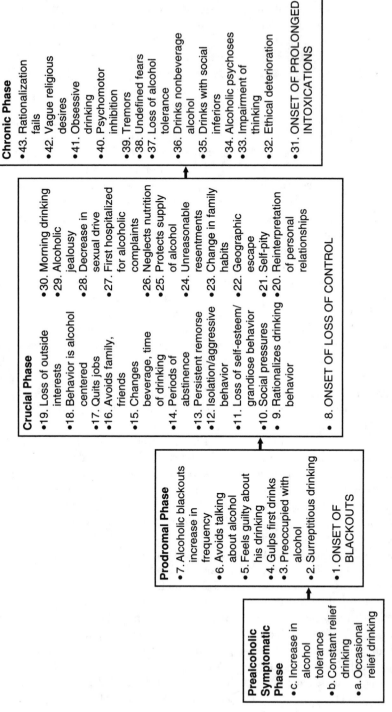

Prealcoholic Symptomatic Phase

- c. Increase in alcohol tolerance
- b. Constant relief drinking
- a. Occasional relief drinking

Prodromal Phase

- 7. Alcoholic blackouts increase in frequency
- 6. Avoids talking about alcohol
- 5. Feels guilty about his drinking
- 4. Gulps first drinks
- 3. Preoccupied with alcohol
- 2. Surreptitious drinking
- 1. ONSET OF BLACKOUTS

Crucial Phase

- 19. Loss of outside interests
- 18. Behavior is alcohol centered
- 17. Quits jobs
- 16. Avoids family, friends
- 15. Changes beverage, time of drinking
- 14. Periods of abstinence
- 13. Persistent remorse
- 12. Isolation/aggressive behavior
- 11. Loss of self-esteem/ grandiose behavior
- 10. Social pressures
- 9. Rationalizes drinking behavior
- 30. Morning drinking
- 29. Alcoholic jealousy
- 28. Decrease in sexual drive
- 27. First hospitalized for alcoholic complaints
- 26. Neglects nutrition
- 25. Protects supply of alcohol
- 24. Unreasonable resentments
- 23. Change in family habits
- 22. Geographic escape
- 21. Self-pity
- 20. Reinterpretation of personal relationships
- 8. ONSET OF LOSS OF CONTROL

Chronic Phase

- 43. Rationalization fails
- 42. Vague religious desires
- 41. Obsessive drinking
- 40. Psychomotor inhibition
- 39. Tremors
- 38. Undefined fears
- 37. Loss of alcohol tolerance
- 36. Drinks nonbeverage alcohol
- 35. Drinks with social inferiors
- 34. Alcoholic psychoses
- 33. Impairment of thinking
- 32. Ethical deterioration
- 31. ONSET OF PROLONGED INTOXICATIONS

PREPATHOGENIC PERIOD   **PERIOD OF PATHOGENESIS**

FIGURE 3.1 The Natural History of Alcoholism According to Jellinek's Model Based on Male Members of AA. Interactions between the host, environment, and agent influence the degree of exposure to alcohol, the response to this exposure, and the likelihood and consequences of further exposures. In some individuals this leads to alcoholism through a series of well-defined phases, as shown.

Source: Nada J. Estes and M. Edith Heinemann (Eds.), *Alcoholism: Development, Consequences, and Interventions,* 3rd ed. (St Louis. MO: C. V. Mosby. 1986). p. 33. Reprinted by permission.

alcoholic is no more able to metabolize ethanol than a diabetic can handle sugar."[11] Others concluded that alcoholism is the result of an allergy and that "one does not become an alcoholic: One is *born* an alcoholic."[12]

Vaillant was involved in one of the most comprehensive studies of alcoholism.[13] Two samples were observed over a 45-year period, and a third group was observed for 8 years. Among the sample of 110 core-city alcohol abusers, Vaillant identified four patterns: (1) progressive alcoholism; (2) return to asymptomatic drinking; (3) stable abstinence; and (4) atypical, nonprogressive alcoholism. Although this study generally supports the developmental or progressive nature of Jellinek's model, it is important to note that Vaillant's study observed both reversibility and nonprogressive alcoholism among a substantial proportion of subjects. Over the period of the study, 18 of the 110 subjects returned to social or asymptomatic drinking.

The traditional concept of the nature and progress of addiction to alcohol was also challenged by Pattison, Sobell, and Sobell. Perhaps the major difference in their view of alcohol *dependence* (a more precise, less value-laden term than *addiction*) are found in the following two assertions:

- The development of alcohol problems follows variable patterns over time and does not necessarily proceed inexorably to severe final stages.
- Recovery from alcohol dependence bears no necessary relation to abstinence, although such a concurrence is frequently the case.[14]

Thus a controversy was launched that continues today. Not only did Pattison, Sobell, and Sobell *not* believe in the disease model, but they also felt that alcohol dependence could be reversed. They pointed to some evidence that certain "alcoholics" had been able to return to social drinking. They also felt that the unproven assumptions that formed the basis for the traditional concept of alcoholism as a disease had been an *impediment* to proper treatment.

The Course of Cocaine Addiction

Other models of drug abuse/addiction reduce the number of stages to three—early, middle, and late. Washton's model of cocaine addiction (see Table 3.1) describes it as a chronic disease that grows progressively worse if it is not treated. (*Chronic* indicates that cocaine addiction is never a single acute attack but is marked by a permanent condition, with a continued vulnerability to recurring symptoms.)[15]

TABLE 3.1   The Course of Cocaine Addiction

Early Stage
Brain chemistry altered
Addictive thinking begins
Obsessive thoughts
Compulsive urges
Conditioned cravings
Life-style changes
Withdrawal from normal activities
Subtle physical and psychological consequences (jitters, irritability, mood swings, etc.)

Middle Stage
Loss of control
Cravings
Inability to stop despite consequences
Denial
Increasing isolation
Increasing physical and psychological consequences—paranoia, panic, seizures, etc.
Impaired work/school performance

Late Stage
Failure of efforts to stop
Severe financial problems
Severe work/school dysfunction
Plummeting self-esteem
Severe relationship problems
Chronic severe depression
Cocaine psychosis
Death

Source: From *Cocaine Addiction: Treatment, Recovery, and Relapse Prevention* by Arnold M. Washton. Copyright © 1989 by Arnold Washton. Reprinted by permission of W. W. Norton & Company, Inc.

According to Washton, cocaine addiction is progressive and predictable in its course.[16] "The disease of cocaine addiction is chronic, never reverses, and grows progressively more severe if left untreated." In the *early* stage of addiction, the user's brain chemistry is altered, withdrawal from normal activities is usually observed, and mood swings occur with increasing frequency.

The *middle* stage of addiction is characterized by loss of control over cocaine use, impaired school or work performance, and denial of the problem. ("I'm not an addict; I just use the stuff a lot!") One can see that this is roughly comparable to the crucial phase in Jellinek's model of alcoholism. The *late* stage of addiction brings serious behavioral and emotional problems to the user, and it can terminate in severe depression, cocaine psychosis, and death.

Becoming a Heroin Addict

As we have mentioned several times earlier, a recurrent theme in heroin addiction is the notion of *drift*. In a 1970 study of addicted inmates in California, Duster asked whether they consciously decided to become addicts. The overwhelming majority knew that heroin was addicting, illegal, and dangerous and could be fatal. They also replied that they neither intended nor believed that they would become addicts when they first began using the drug. The principal ingredient in becoming addicted was the addict's belief in the indestructibility of the self.[17] Two other essential ingredients were the normalcy of the first experience with heroin and the experience itself.

For most addicts, the first venture was an unplanned event. They happened to be in the wrong place at the wrong time, and heroin was available, offered, and accepted. Most users found the first experience fairly neutral, with its duration relatively short and its after-effects minimal. Reasons for the second use are generally as innocuous and as social as for the first. The preaddict gradu-

ally slips into a level of use where dependence develops.[18]

Physical dependence has less of a relationship to heroin addiction than is commonly thought. According to some models, physical dependence has no *direct* relationship to addiction.[19] Becoming physically dependent on heroin requires that the drug be taken at intervals short enough to maintain a minimal level in the body constantly. Given the variable purity of street heroin, between one and two months of daily usage or "two weeks of very heavy daily usage" is required to become physically dependent.[20] The one-shot-and-you're-hooked message that was popular in school drug prevention programs in the 1940s and 1950s was clearly a myth—at least from a physiological standpoint.

One of the more puzzling aspects of heroin addiction is that fewer than half the addicts who have been on the streets for more than a year will have used it daily for that entire period.[21] Addicts frequently withdraw on their own in order to reduce their tolerance, serve a jail or prison sentence, or simply give themselves a rest. One researcher also estimates that 25 to 40 percent of street addicts may have never used heroin with sufficient frequency or in great enough dosages to have developed a true physical dependence. Yet they consider themselves to be "addicted" to heroin, even during periods of abstinence.[22]

An interesting early systems theory approach to heroin addiction was developed by Lindesmith.[23] In this theory, the development of addiction assumes physical dependence, but there are two additional requirements. In order to be addicted, one must have a *craving*, defined as an intense desire and conscious striving for the drug. The positive or euphoric effects of heroin are discounted as being unimportant in this theory. Craving is fixed by "negative rather than positive reinforcement, by relief and avoidance of discomfort and pain rather than by positive pleasure."[24] It is the *interpretation* of the withdrawal experience that is of paramount importance. If it is interpreted as an inevitable physiological process, then no connection is drawn between withdrawal and the consequences of drug use, and people do not become addicts. On the other hand, if withdrawal is interpreted as evidence of a *need* for the drug, addiction does occur.

Either of these interpretations, according to Lindesmith, is imposed on the addict by the social environment and the interaction of the addict with other people, especially other addicts. The heroin user, "when he uses the symbols which society provides him, also assumes the attitudes appropriate to those symbols when he applies them to himself."[25] In other words, the individual's milieu tells whether the heroin user is or is not an addict. Being defined by the social environment as an addict and accepting that definition results in becoming an addict.

> Having joined the fraternity of those who have been hooked, he feels a continuing bond that unites him with others who have had the experience and a communication barrier with others who have not had it. It is in this sense that addiction may be called incurable.[26]

There are others who argue that experts are mistaken in believing that dependence is a property of drugs. According to Peele, dependence is caused neither by drugs nor by their chemical properties. Instead, it has more to do with the experience of an individual using a drug under a specific set of circumstances. Addiction is not "a physical mystery, but rather an organic outgrowth of a person's relationship to the world."[27] What a person experiences from taking a drug is determined in large part by expectations, which are a product of the social environment. Before the heroin user takes that first "hit," he or she will have acquired certain folklore of the community regarding its effects. The relationship between heroin's pharmacological effect and physiological changes is relatively unimportant to the nature of the user's subjective experience. This subjective experience, according to some theories, is the most important aspect of the process of becoming addicted.[28] As we mentioned earlier (Figure 2.1), a person's potential for addiction is a function of susceptibility and exposure. Once the addiction develops, it will continue as long as the activity (drug taking) provides more positive rewards than other available options.

Marijuana Addiction

Unlike the drugs already discussed, the addictive potential of cannabis is still being debated. A decade ago, many people assumed that the debate had been settled and that smoking marijuana would *not* lead to dependence or addiction.[29] Others argued that cannabis (as well as cocaine) produced only "psychic dependence" and little or no physical dependence.[30] In light of more recent studies, there is evidence that this conclusion was not warranted.[31] In fact, many older studies also concluded that cannabis was addictive. Soueif's report on Egyptian hashish users,[32] Chopra's study of Indian "hemp habituation,"[33] and Scher's analysis of American marijuana use[34] all strongly suggest symptoms of dependence. The common symptom was an inability to discontinue using the drug, despite an expressed desire to do so. Experimental studies have also produced withdrawal symptoms (appetite and sleep disturbances, irritability, aggression, tremors, photophobia, etc.) in monkeys[35] and human[36] subjects.

Not everyone relies on the ability of a drug to produce withdrawal symptoms as a definition of addiction. According to Nahas, drug dependence results from "the reproducible interaction between an individual and a pleasure-inducing biologically active molecule."[37] The common denominator of all drug dependence is the reinforcement resulting from reward associated with past individual drug interaction and the subsequent increasing desire for repeated reinforcements.[38] Using either this criterion or the development of tolerance and withdrawal, it is obvious that the popular classification of cannabis as a "soft" drug was greatly misleading.

In an in-depth study of 150 heavy users of marijuana, Hendin and co-workers discovered that they all had begun regular, daily use of the drug within two to five years after smoking their first "joints."[39] The average age for beginning such regular use was about 20. The majority of the group stated that much of their social lives revolved around marijuana, smoking it at their homes and friends' homes and at parties. While three-fourths reported that most or all of their friends were regular users, 89 percent also said that they regularly used marijuana while alone. Their most common reasons for smoking marijuana were:

- To get pleasure, feel good, get high (99 percent)
- To relax, relieve tension (97 percent)
- To use with friends, enjoy effects (88 percent)
- To overcome depression (61 percent)[40]

A sample of this group selected for more intensive study consistently revealed substituting a sensory illusion of life gained by smoking marijuana for the boredom, fear, and "lifelessness" that they perceived surrounding them. Daily heavy marijuana use for these people was closely related to adaptive difficulties in personal relationships and/or work. To the extent that they were aware of their difficulties, they saw marijuana as an escape from their worries. None of them considered marijuana to be the *cause* of their difficulties.[41]

> Marijuana maintained these individuals in a troubled adaptation, reinforcing their tendency not to look at, understand, or attempt to master their difficulties. It served to detach them from their problems and allowed them to regard even serious difficulties as unimportant. Marijuana provided a buffer zone of sensation that functioned as a barrier against self-awareness and closeness to others.[42]

According to Nahas, modern neurophysiology and psychopharmacology support the idea that "soma and psyche are inextricably interwoven."[43] Therefore, a classification of dependence-producing drugs should be based on markers that reflect the biochemical alterations that they induce, primarily in the central nervous system. He suggests the following approach:

1. They produce reversible symptoms of neuropsychological or neurobehavioral toxicity. The effects of such drugs on neurotransmitters in the brain and on specialized function of the limbic structure produce neuropsychological and behavioral anomalies such as adverse effects on arousal, awareness, and psychological and psychomotor performance. These symptoms dissipate when the pharmacological action of the drug has ended.

2. They produce a primary pleasurable reward. Their pleasant effects are associated with the ability to dissipate unpleasant feelings, decrease anxiety, and produce detachment from the world. They are also capable of altering sensory perceptions. Their pleasurable sensations are concurrent with neuropsychological toxicity.

3. They act as "powerful reinforcers" inducing a craving for the drug and causing the user to have a major involvement in securing its use. There is a high tendency toward relapse after continuing use of the drug,

4. Tolerance is associated with frequent use and is closely linked to drug dependence. This is a drug-related adaptive process that allows the brain to function in the presence of xenobiotic substances.

5. Abrupt interruption of long-term use leads to an abstinence syndrome that may be mild or severe, depending on the drug. Withdrawal symptoms may occur independently of tolerance and should not be considered as the major reinforcement for continuing drug use.

6. The long-term use of addictive drugs has been associated with somatic changes and, ultimately, an increased incidence of mental or physical illness.[44]

Summary

Some similarities and differences between various theories of addiction have been discussed and the disease model of addiction was reexamined. Some recurring ideas found in most of these models are (1) the progressive nature of addiction (from early, to middle, and then to late stages or phases), (2) the notion of "drift" from being a casual user to becoming an addict, (3) the development of tolerance and the presence of withdrawal symptoms, and (4) the distinction between physiological or physical dependence and psychological or "psychic" dependence.

Some researchers have used the psychic/physical dependence dichotomy to argue that drugs such as cocaine, cannabis, and nicotine are not truly addictive because cessation of their use is not accompanied by a full-blown withdrawal syndrome of the opiate type. Further claims have been made that the use of cocaine and cannabis could be promptly and readily terminated if the user only exerts enough "psychic" will. These claims, as well as artificial distinctions between mind and body, have become somewhat less defensible with the dramatic increase in crack addiction—an addiction that seems less amenable to treatment than alcoholism or heroin addiction.

Although some somatic changes have been reported for cannabis users, one cannot expect an accurate human pathology of this drug to be written by the dawn of the twenty-first century. By that time, unfortunately, researchers will probably be concerned with the addictive potential and somatic effects of drugs yet to be discovered or manufactured. The damaging physical effects of drugs such as alcohol, cocaine, and heroin will be documented in the next chapter.

Endnotes

1. Tam Stewart, *The Heroin Users* (London: Pandora, 1987), p. 6.

2. Andrew Weil and Winifred Rosen, *From Chocolate to Morphine: Everything You Need to Know about Mind-Altering Drugs* (Boston: Houghton Mifflin, 1993), p. 89.

3. William S. Burroughs, *Junky* (New York: Penguin Books, 1977), p. xv; originally published as *Junkie* under the pen name of William Lee, by Ace Books, 1953.

4. Joanne Baum, *One Step over the Line: A No-Nonsense Guide to Recognizing and Treating Cocaine Dependency* (New York: Harper and Row, 1985), pp. 25–42.

5. Arnold M. Washton, *Cocaine Addiction: Treatment, Recovery, and Relapse Prevention* (New York: W. W. Norton, 1989), p. 55.

6. Jara Krivanek, *Heroin: Myths and Realities* (Sydney: Allen & Unwin, 1988), p. 202.

7. Vernon E. Johnson, *I'll Quit Tomorrow* (New York: Harper and Row, 1973), p. 1.

8. Elvin M. Jellinek, "Phases of Alcohol Addiction," *Quarterly Journal of Studies of Alcohol*, Vol. 13 (1952), pp. 673–684.

9. Elvin M. Jellinek, *The Disease Concept of Alcoholism* (New Haven, CT: Hillhouse Press, 1960).

10. Marty Mann, *New Primer on Alcoholism*, 2nd ed. (New York: Holt, Rinehart and Winston, 1968), p. 3.

11. William Madsen, *The American Alcoholic: The Nature-Nurture Controversies in Alcoholic Research and Therapy* (Springfield, IL: Charles C Thomas, 1974), p. 94.

12. Joseph Kessel, *The Road Back, A Report on Alcoholics Anonymous* (New York: Alfred A. Knopf, 1962), p. 128.

13. George E. Vaillant, *The Natural History of Alcoholism Revisited* (Cambridge, MA: Harvard University Press, 1995).

14. E. Mansell Pattison, Mark B. Sobell, and Linda C. Sobell, *Emerging Concepts of Alcohol Dependence* (New York: Springer, 1977), pp. 4–5.

15. Washton, *Cocaine Addiction*, p. 55.

16. Ibid.

17. T. Duster, *The Legislation of Morality* (New York: The Free Press, 1970).

18. Jara Krivanek, *Addictions* (Sydney: Allen & Unwin, 1989), p. 86.

19. Ibid.

20. Tom Field, *Escaping the Dragon* (London: Allen & Unwin, 1985), p. 53.

21. B. D. Johnson, "Once an Addict, Seldom an Addict," *Contemporary Drug Problems*, Vol. 7, No. 1 (1978), pp. 48–49.

22. Edward Senay, *Drugs, Society, and Behavior* (Guilford, CT: Dushkin, 1986).

23. Alfred R. Lindesmith, *Addiction and Opiates* (Chicago: Aldine, 1968).

24. Ibid., p. 95.

25. Ibid., pp. 192–193.

26. Ibid., p. 52.

27. Stanton Peele, in B. Hafen and B. Peterson (Eds.), *Medicines and Drugs,* 2nd ed. (Philadelphia: Lea & Febiger, 1978), p. 167.

28. Krivanek, *Addictions,* pp. 85–105.

29. J. Griffin-Edwards, "Cannabis and the Question of Dependence," in *Report of the Expert Group on the Effects of Cannabis Use* (London: The Advisory Council on the Misuse of Drugs, 1982).

30. Erich Goode, *Drugs in American Society* (New York: Alfred A. Knopf, 1972), pp. 57–58.

31. Gabriel G., Nahas, *Marijuana in Science and Medicine* (New York: Raven Press, 1984), p. 208.

32. M. I. Soueif, "The Use of Cannabis in Egypt: A Behavioral Study," *Bulletin of Narcotics,* Vol. 4 (1971), pp. 17–18.

33. G. S. Chopra, "Man and Marijuana," *International Journal of Addiction,* Vol. 4 (1969), p. 215,

34. Jordan M. Scher, "The Marijuana Habit," *Journal of the American Medical Association,* Vol. 214 (1970), p. 1120.

35. S. Kaymakcalan, "Tolerance to and Dependence on Cannabis," *Bulletin of Narcotics,* Vol. 25 (1973), pp. 39–47.

36. Reese T. Jones and Neal Benowitz, "The 30-Day Trip: Clinical Studies of Cannabis Tolerance and Dependence," in M. C. Braude and S. Szara (Eds.), *Pharmacology of Marijuana* (New York: Raven Press, 1976), pp. 627–641.

37. Nahas, *Marijuana in Science and Medicine,* p. 208.

38. M. H. Seever, "Drug Dependence and Drug Abuse, A World Problem," *Pharmacologist,* Vol. 12 (1970), pp. 172–181.

39. Herbert Hendin et al., *Living High: Daily Marijuana Use among Adults* (New York: Human Sciences Press, 1987), p. 38.

40. Ibid., p. 42.

41. Ibid., pp. 170–172.

42. Ibid., pp. 171–172.

43. Nahas, *Marijuana,* p. 211.

44. Ibid., pp. 211–212.

4

The Physiological
and Behavioral Consequences
of Alcohol and Drug Abuse

This chapter discusses the major physiological and behavioral consequences of alcohol and drug abuse. We will spare you the more technical details on such disorders as leukopoiesis and thrombopoiesis, which are of somewhat greater interest to the medical professions, but we will outline the more common consequences. Any professional person who has the responsibility of assisting clients with alcohol and drug problems must be able to recognize common symptoms and make appropriate referrals. In fact, it will undoubtedly be advantageous to the practicing social worker or other human service professional to be capable of deciphering a physician's report on an alcoholic or drug-abusing client. We will attempt to keep the medical terminology to a minimum, but it is essential to understand such terms as *cardiomyopathy, hepatic dysfunction,* and *fetal alcohol syndrome.*

Certain classes of drugs, such as CNS depressants, will have common effects on the users' behavior. Individual CNS depressants often will have very different physiological effects, however. In some cases, the same drug will have different physiological effects, depending on the particular method of ingestion. Those who snort cocaine may have very different physical problems than those who inject the same drug with a hypodermic needle. In fact, it is frequently observed that some addicts who inject drugs often seem to be more addicted to the process of "shooting up" than to the effects of a particular drug.

We will pay somewhat more attention to the effects of alcohol in the following pages, since it is the most widely used of all the drugs covered here. Because of its long history, we also know more about the consequences of alcohol abuse. Very little is known about the long-term consequences of abusing some of the newer drugs such as ice.

The Effects of Alcohol

Ethyl alcohol is almost exclusively ingested in the form of a potable beverage. (In relatively rare instances it is used for medical reasons and may be administered intravenously by a physician.) One of the most dangerous and widely used drugs throughout the world, it has the potential for causing deleterious effects on every part of the digestive system as well as every major organ in the human body.

The Metabolization of Alcohol

As soon as alcohol is ingested, the body begins to eliminate or metabolize it, primarily through oxidation. Not long ago, it was thought that approximately 95 percent of all alcohol was eliminated through oxidation and 5 percent through bodily processes such as respiration, urination, and perspiration. It was recently discovered that much of the alcohol that is consumed in small doses is actually metabolized in the stomach.[1] Gastric metabolism acts as a barrier to toxicity with moderate doses of alcohol.

The major organ that metabolizes larger amounts of alcohol is the liver. Small amounts are also eliminated in the feces, and nursing mothers release some alcohol in their milk. The initial step is the conversion of alcohol to acetaldehyde by the enzyme, alcohol dehydrogenase (ADH). Next, the acetaldehyde is converted by another liver enzyme to an active acetate that is further broken down into carbon dioxide and water. The metabolism of alcohol results in significant changes in the ratio of important chemicals within the liver cells—changes that affect the rate of the metabolism.

Depending on the mass of functioning liver that is available, the average adult can oxidize from 10 to 15 grams of alcohol per hour. (This is approximately the amount of pure ethanol in one alcoholic beverage.) An average person could therefore consume about one drink per hour without accumulating alcohol in the body. However, there is tremendous variation in individual rates of metabolism, depending on such factors as other contents of the stomach at the time of ingestion, the body's proportion of fat, and the proportion of healthy versus cirrhotic liver tissue. Alcohol is approximately 30 times more soluble in water than in fat, a fact that accounts for the some of the gender and body weight differences in the rate of metabolism.[2] For example, women tend to metabolize

alcohol at a slower rate than men because of the higher ratio of fat to water content in their bodies.

It is common knowledge that the experienced drinker may show some resistance to the effects of alcohol, a phenomenon known as *tolerance.* Such an individual requires larger and larger doses of alcohol in order to reach a high or a desired state of intoxication. This phenomenon is one of the most reliable physical signs of alcoholism, and it may occur because of (1) altered distribution and/or metabolism of the alcohol, leading to lower concentrations at the receptor site; (2) altered receptor sensitivity to alcohol; and (3) the development of alternative pathways for bypassing the receptor system.[3] Heavy use of alcohol may lead to increased rates of ethanol oxidation up to 100 percent.[4]

Intoxication

The exact mechanism by which alcohol produces its effects on the central nervous system is not known. It is not thought to be like a narcotic, which binds specific receptor systems in certain areas of the brain. It appears that although the actions on specific cells are quite selective, alcohol has a very nonspecific effect on the physiochemical systems that regulate the functions of neurons.[5] The five basic effects of alcohol on the CNS are (1) euphoria, (2) removal of inhibitions, (3) impairment of vision, (4) muscular incoordination, and (5) lengthened reaction time.[6]

Intoxication and alcoholism are two completely different concepts. *Intoxication* will occur whenever alcohol is ingested. In small amounts, it may produce euphoria and a decrease in inhibitions; at a blood-alcohol concentration (BAC) of 0.10 percent, ataxia and dysarthria generally occur.[7] Between 0.20 percent and 0.25 percent, many people cannot sit or stand upright without support. The average person may fall into a coma when the BAC is between 0.3 percent and 0.4 percent, and death normally occurs beyond the 0.5 percent level.[8] These averages may be misleading, however, because of the development of *tolerance* in the chronic user. There have been persons arrested for driving under the influence (DUI) with blood-alcohol levels (BALs) of 0.4 percent—when the so-called average drinker would be in a coma. There also have been reports of persons surviving a BAL of more than 0.7 percent.

Withdrawal

The earliest and most common effects of alcohol withdrawal are anxiety, anorexia, insomnia, and tremor. In the early stages of withdrawal, a person will also be irritable and easily startled and have a subjective feeling of distress, sometimes described as internal shaking. These symptoms peak within 24 to 36 hours and then rapidly disappear. The pulse rate is typically elevated during withdrawal and may reach 120 to 140 beats per minute.

Some people going through withdrawal will experience alcoholic hallucinosis, a generally benign state that is not associated with paranoia or panic. Delirium tremens is the most severe state of withdrawal, characterized by marked tremor, anxiety, insomnia, anorexia, paranoia, and disorientation. The symptoms peak about three days after withdrawal, but may persist for two or three weeks. It may also be accompanied by fever, tachypnea, hyperpnea, diarrhea, diaphoresis, and vomiting. Tachycardia is almost always present.[9]

Grand mal convulsive seizures may also occur during withdrawal, but not usually as a part of delirium tremens. Anticonvulsant therapy should be used with any patient with a past history of seizures. Seizures occurring after more than two weeks of abstinence suggest a dependency on CNS depressants other than alcohol.[10]

The Digestive System

As mentioned earlier, practically every part of the body is adversely affected by the use of alcohol. Cancer occurs with alarming frequency in the mouth, tongue, pharynx, esophagus, stomach, intestines, liver, and pancreas of alcoholics.[11] Alcoholics are also susceptible to inflammation of the esophageal mucosa. This may be caused by increased acid production induced by drinking alcohol, impaired esophageal peristalsis, the direct toxic effects of alcohol on the mucosa, and frequent vomiting.[12] A laceration of the gastroesophageal junction (known as the Mallory-Weiss syndrome) frequently results from alcohol-induced gastritis.[13] Rupture of the lower esophagus, Boerhaave's syndrome, is sometimes caused by vigorous vomiting, coughing, or seizures. This condition is fatal if not promptly treated.[14]

Another common outcome of heavy alcohol use is inflammation of the mucosal lining of the stomach, or *erosive gastritis*. If this condition is severe enough, it may also produce gastric ulcers. Erosive gastritis may be associated with nausea, vomiting, and distention. Occasionally, it may result in upper intestinal bleeding, a potentially life-threatening situation.[15]

One of the most common symptoms experienced by alcoholics is diarrhea. This condition may be caused either by the direct toxic effects of alcohol on the small intestine or by alcohol-related nutritional deficiencies that affect the functioning of the small intestine, most notably a folic acid deficiency.[16] Even moderate amounts of alcohol may cause blisters in the small intestine.[17] A much more serious problem, colon cancer, is also higher than normal among alcoholics.[18]

Alcohol can cause a number of changes in the liver: fatty liver, alcoholic hepatitis, and cirrhosis being the most common. In the United States, cirrhosis is the ninth leading cause of death, and alcohol abuse is the major cause of cirrhosis.[19] A French study showed that as few as three drinks a day for men and one and one-half drinks a day for women could lead to cirrhosis,[20] a condition for which there is only a 50 percent survival rate after five years.[21]

Alcohol consumption can also lead to both acute and chronic pancreatitis. Acute pancreatitis is manifested by upper abdominal pain, nausea, and vomiting. In addition to these symptoms, chronic pancreatitis may be associated with malnutrition, weight loss, diarrhea, and foul-smelling, bulky stools. The chronic condition is so painful that victims often become addicted to analgesics or narcotics.[22] The exact causal mechanism is not clear, but alcohol is thought to have a direct, toxic effect on the pancreas, in addition to causing simultaneously an increase in pancreatic stimulation and obstructing the flow of pancreatic juice to the duodenum.[23] Acute pancreatitis is generally self-limiting, and most people will recover within a few days. Chronic pancreatitis, on the other hand, is thought to be irreversible. Abstinence may reduce the pain, but the inflammation and scarring process continue.[24]

The Cardiovascular System

In nonalcoholic, healthy people, alcohol causes an increase in the heart rate as well as lessened stroke power. In other words, the heart simply functions less efficiently as a pump.[25] In such individuals, alcohol also decreases resistance to blood flow throughout the body, resulting in a reduction in blood pressure.[26] Other studies have found a strong relationship between alcohol use and elevated blood pressure among drinkers with hypertension.[27] Acute alcohol consumption causes dysfunctional changes in heart tissue, even in young, healthy adults.[28] In many chronic alcoholics, there is a form of cardiomyopathy that is characterized by an actual wasting away of the heart muscle.[29]

Congestive heart failure associated with alcoholic cardiomyopathy, diseases involving thromboses (blood clots obstructing blood vessels), and low platelet counts are additional cardiovascular problems encountered in alcoholics. Among men, the average alcoholic has almost *twice* the chance of death from atherosclerotic and degenerative heart disease, compared to nonalcoholics. Women alcoholics are more than *four* times as likely to die from these diseases as nonalcoholics.[30]

The Endocrine and Reproductive Systems

Again, alcohol has both direct and indirect effects on the endocrine and reproductive systems. The spreading of endocrine effects is due in part to the organization of the endocrine glands into functional hierarchies called axes. Every endocrine axis has numerous feedback controls, and changes in one component may affect other components on that axis.[31]

The most common effects of alcohol on the hypothalamic-pituitary-thyroid (H-P-T) axis are a modest decrease in the levels of the hormone thyroxine and a marked decrease in the level of triiodothyronine. These changes are associated with serious liver disease, primarily through an inhibition of liver oxygen consumptions.[32]

Alcohol also has serious consequences on the hypothalamic-pituitary-gonadal (H-P-G) axis in men, impairing the reproductive function and altering physiology.[33] These consequences include testicular atrophy, abnormal morphology of sperm cells, an increase in estrogen levels, and a decrease in testosterone. The relationship between liver disease and sexual dysfunction is extremely complex, but it is widely recognized that alcoholics with cirrhosis are more likely than not to be sexually impotent.[34] Noncirrhotic alcoholics are also likely to lose sexual function for other reasons, such as a decrease in testosterone or psychological impairment.

In women, alcohol-induced endocrinal failure is likely to result in early menopause, heavy menstrual flow, menstrual discomfort, infertility, and a higher frequency of obstetric and gynecologic problems. In both sexes, heavy alcohol consumption is associated with the loss of secondary sex characteristics. Men may develop female hair patterns and gynecomastia (breast enlargement).[35] Another major health problem associated with alcohol use is fetal alcohol syndrome or fetal alcohol effects. Because of the severity and prevalence of the consequences of maternal drug abuse on the newborn, we have a separate section on this problem later in this chapter.

The Neurologic System

Excessive use of alcohol is known to lead to acute and chronic brain damage, as well as peripheral nerve dysfunction. The neuronal membrane is the location where the biochemical effects of alcohol on the central nervous system begin. Alcohol is believed to disrupt normal membrane function by penetrating into the membrane, expanding its volume, and disordering the lipid components. These changes can have profound effects on neurotransmission, the electrical signaling that occurs within and between neurons. This happens because the neurons are no longer capable of transmitting the ions through the neuronal membranes. The overall consequence is a disruption of the flow of information within the brain.[36]

Autopsy studies of alcoholic patients have found both cerebral and cortical atrophy to be quite common. In addition to being atrophied, the brains of alcoholics also have significant cell loss in many regions.[37] Computerized axial tomography (CAT) scans have also revealed that alcoholics have larger brain cavities, wider grooves on the brain's surface, and wider fissures.[38] The exact mechanism by which alcohol damages the brain is not known. One theory is that alcohol triggers a CNS antigen that leads to an autoimmune response that produces brain damage.[39] Another is that higher concentrations of alcohol in the blood leads to occlusion of vessels in the brain. The ensuing edema and hemorrhaging are responsible for the damage to brain tissue.[40] Still another is that brain damage is produced by alcohol-induced interference with protein synthesis.[41]

There are also a number of other secondary factors that may lead to brain damage in alcoholics. Oxygen deprivation related to such things as coma with hypoventilation or vomiting and aspiration of gastric contents can be responsible for

such damage. Alcoholic hypoglycemia may also cause blood glucose levels to fall to dangerous levels. Brain cells (which have no capacity for regeneration) cannot function for long periods of time without both glucose and oxygen. In chronic alcoholics nutritional deficiencies may cause brain damage. Both Wernicke's syndrome and Korsakoff's psychosis are associated with thiamine deficiency. (Thiamine is a primary link in the production of energy for brain cells.[42])

Common Neurologic Disorders

Acute brain syndrome is marked by a rapid onset and a high degree of reversibility. It is manifested simply as acute intoxication or hallucinosis. Chronic brain syndrome is characterized by a generally slow onset and is usually irreversible. Some of the symptoms of both acute and chronic brain syndrome are a decrease in complex intellectual functioning, alteration in memory, impaired judgment, and shallowness of affect.[43] Alcoholics with chronic brain syndrome suffer from recent memory loss, confusion, disorientation (for time, place, and person), and difficulty in concentration.[44] These symptoms may be preceded by months or even years of other symptoms such as fatigue, listlessness, loss of interest, depression, and anxiety or agitation. Unless the brain damage is halted, the person's speech will become monosyllabic and motor controls will fail. Eventually, he or she will be unable to manage even the basic tasks, such as eating or dressing, and sphincter control will fail.[45]

One of the common diseases associated with chronic alcoholism is Wernicke's syndrome. The typical victim is a 40- to 60-year-old chronic alcoholic who becomes easily confused or excited. This person has already experienced peripheral neuropathy and diplopia, the first major clues to the disease. As mentioned earlier, this disease is related to thiamine deficiency, and thiamine replacement is the accepted therapy. With prompt treatment, the prognosis for recovery is generally good.[46]

Korsakoff's psychosis is frequently encountered in patients who are recovering from Wernicke's syndrome. These two conditions are so frequently found together that they are often described simply as the Wernicke-Korsakoff syndrome. The typical victim is a chronic alcoholic, often one with so severe a recent memory deficit that he or she may not be able to remember simple material for even a few moments. The Korsakoff's syndrome patient may show relatively normal retention of nonverbal information however, such as "Jimmie G.," described by Sacks in his fascinating book of "clinical tales."[47] The patient was 49 years old in 1975. He believed that he was still 19 years old and could remember the names of the different submarines on which he had served in World War II, as well as their missions, where he was stationed, and the names of shipmates. He remembered Morse code, was still fluent in touch typing, and could do complex mathematics (including algebra) in his head. On the other hand, after a brief conversation with Dr. Sacks, the doctor left the room for two minutes, reentered the room, and Jimmie did not recognize him. On one occasion, Dr. Sacks laid out his watch, tie, and glasses on the desk, covered them, and asked Jimmie to remember them. "Then after a minute's chat, I asked him what I had put under the cover. He remembered none of them—or indeed that I had even asked him to remember."[48]

Alcoholic pellagra is the result of a thiamine deficiency characterized by a clouding of consciousness, rigidity, and uncontrolled sucking and grasping reflexes. Other symptoms associated with pellagra in nonalcoholics (dementia, dermatitis, and diarrhea) usually do not occur in alcoholics because of the rapid onset of the disease.[49]

Peripheral neuropathy can also occur in alcoholics who do not have Wernicke-Korsakoff's syndrome. Hospital reports indicate that alcoholic peripheral neuropathy is more common than all other forms of peripheral neuropathy combined.[50] Problems occur first in the feet, the most distal parts of the longest peripheral nerves. Initial symptoms are usually burning, tingling, or prickling sensations, along with pain in the calf muscles or feet. Discomfort and numbness begin in the feet and gradually work up the legs, and muscle weakness and wasting occur as the process continues. A treatment consisting of abstinence, a nutritious diet, and supplementary vitamin B will usually allow most patients to recover.[51]

Alcohol and Other Disorders

Alcohol use is a common cause of malnutrition, partly because alcoholic beverages are often substituted for other, more nutritional food, and partly because alcohol disrupts the body's ability to absorb and properly utilize some vitamins.[52] In one study, *all* 41 patients with alcoholic liver disease were also found to suffer from thiamine deficiency.[53] Long-term alcohol intake commonly results in deficiencies in fiber, protein, calcium, iron, vitamins A and C, and thiamine.[54]

People who have not eaten within the past day may experience a drop in blood sugar and hypoglycemia, with a potential for coma and death. Insulin-dependent diabetics are extremely vulnerable to both hypoglycemia and ketoacidosis.[55] Alcohol consumption has also been associated with a reduction in bone mass and with osteoporosis in men.[56]

Chronic alcohol abuse is associated with higher susceptibility to several different types of infectious diseases, due to a suppression of the body's immune system, including tuberculosis, pneumonia, peritonitis, and hepatitis B. Equally disturbing is the fact that alcoholics are at a much higher risk for almost every form of cancer—from the mouth to the rectum! In fact, about one-fourth of all cancer of directly exposed tissue (lip, oral cavity, pharynx, stomach, etc.) is attributed to the effects of alcohol.[57]

From a medical perspective, almost nothing good can be said about the effects of alcohol on the human body. There is some rather inconclusive evidence that moderate drinkers may have slightly lower risks of atherosclerosis and coronary heart disease. This may be because alcohol reduces the oxidizability of low-density lipoprotein

(LDL).[58] Experts in cardiology are recommending against the use of alcohol, however. Even if moderate alcohol intake does provide this benefit, it is far outweighed by other health risks, and it makes more sense to control cholesterol levels by choosing a healthy diet.

The Effects of Cannabis

Compared to alcohol, the purely physiological effects of marijuana and hashish use are relatively few. However, there is still much controversy concerning the scientific evidence on the consequences of using this drug.[59] Most of the proven health risks associated with cannabis come from the common method of ingesting the drug—smoking. Since marijuana smoke also contains carcinogens, regular users are also exposed to an increased risk of lung cancer. Just as in tobacco smoking, there is also an increased risk of heart disease.[60]

A person smoking marijuana will experience a reddening of the eyes (inflammation of the conjunctiva of the eye from the irritant effect of the smoke), slight tachycardia, and a dryness of the mouth. For a long time, it was commonly accepted that dilation of the pupils was a common side effect of marijuana smoking, but that notion has been discredited. Blood sugar levels also seem to be unaffected by marijuana, despite the long-standing impact of this drug on subjective feelings of hunger ("munchies").[61]

No conclusive evidence supports damage to other organs related to marijuana usage.[62] One of the major problems in conducting research in this area, however, is that it is difficult to isolate the effects of marijuana *alone*, apart from other drugs, since marijuana users commonly use other illicit drugs as well as alcohol and tobacco.

There is some evidence (which has been contradicted by other studies) of chromosomal[63] and genetic[64] damage associated with chronic marijuana use. It has long been suspected that heavy marijuana use may result in suppression of the immune system, and studies have confirmed this.[65] Reduced sperm counts and diminished ovulation have also been found among regular users.[66] Mixed results have been derived from studies of brain damage. Several studies have found brain atrophy in regular marijuana users, while others have found no evidence of atrophy.[67]

In experimental animals, marijuana has proven injurious to all phases of gonadal and reproductive functions, through the direct action of the drug on the hypothalamo-pituitary axis as well as the gonads. In male nonhuman primates, cannabis produces decreased testicular size and spermatogenesis. In females, it disrupts ovarian cycles and ovulation.[68]

Cannabis generally produces a state of euphoria in which inhibitions are relaxed and thoughts appear to come more rapidly and to be more profound than normal thoughts. Users often report feeling an exaggerated sense of ability, despite a loss of critical faculties and distorted timing. The primary personality change for regular users has been called the *amotivational syndrome*. The user loses ambition and becomes passive, apathetic, increasingly introspective, and disinterested in anything outside his or her dreamy fantasies.[69]

The psychological effects of cannabis have been studied and reported since the second century, when the use of hashish was reported by a Chinese investigator, Pen-Ts'ao Ching, to produce mental illness.[70] Hashish use was also associated with a certain form of psychosis among the followers (called assassins) of an eleventh-century Moslem leader. Jacques-Joseph Moreau, an officer in Napoleon's army, reported on the similarities between cannabis intoxication and mental illness in 1845. He lists eight cardinal symptoms:

> Unexplainable feeling of bliss and happiness
> Excitement and dissociation of ideas
> Errors of time and space appreciation
> Development of the sense of hearing; influence of music
> Fixed ideas (delusions)
> Damage to the emotions
> Irresistible impulses
> Illusions and hallucinations[71]

Although there may be some debate regarding whether a true cannabis psychosis exists, there is evidence that its use has resulted in temporal disintegration, delusional-type ideation, panic reactions, dysphoric reactions (disorientation, immobility, acute panic, heavy sedation), problems with memory, and inability to follow or to maintain a conversation. Regular use also has been associated with acute brain syndrome and delirium, characterized by confusion prostration, disorientation, derealization, and sometimes auditory or visual hallucinations.[72]

The Effects of Stimulants

Cocaine

Until recently, the most common method for ingesting cocaine in North America was the insulation of refined coca paste, cocaine hydrochloride (otherwise known as coke or snow). This drug is also injected (alone or in combination with heroin) intravenously or intramuscularly. In other parts of the world, users prefer to chew coca leaves or to smoke coca paste.[73] In the United States, the most popular method seems to be smoking a form of solidified cocaine that has been treated with baking soda, known as crack. This form is also known as freebase cocaine, since it is the cocaine alkaloid that has been chemically separated from cocaine hydrochloride. Crack or freebase is more suitable for smoking because more of the cocaine in the freebase form volatizes without decomposing.[74] Different methods of ingestion are frequently associated with different types of physiological problems.

Overdoses from smoking, inhaling, or injecting cocaine may be fatal, a result of ventricular fibrillation, cardiac arrest, apnoea, or hyperthermia. Heavy use may also result in extreme hypertension, cerebrovascular bleeding, stroke, and elliptiform fits.[75] Heart failure is a risk, even among young, otherwise healthy users of cocaine. Chronic use also affects the vision. Users may experience "snow lights," patches or flashes of white light darting in and out of their field of vision. Others may report fuzzy or double vision.

Cocaine's behavioral effects do not differ much from those produced by amphetamines; their duration is simply much shorter.[76] The quality and intensity of the cocaine-induced high vary markedly from one user to the next, depending on the mood, personality, and expectations of the user and the setting and circumstances under which the drug is taken. The acute positive state generally is characterized by euphoria, feelings of increased energy and confidence, mental alertness, and sexual arousal. With continued use, tolerance develops, making it more difficult to achieve a satisfactory high and bringing rebound effects that are dysphoric. When not high, the user feels anxious, confused, depressed, and often paranoid.

Ironically, only a decade ago common wisdom held that cocaine was not an addictive substance. Now it is regarded as being both physically and psychologically addictive, as well as one of the most dangerous of all addictive drugs. Although withdrawal from cocaine does not produce physical symptoms as severe as some other drugs, its psychological hold on the user is one of the strongest. There are also considerable physical risks associated with prolonged use or overdosing.[77]

Although regarded by some to be an aphrodisiac, continued cocaine use generally produces sexual dysfunction. Men suffer from a reduced sexual drive and erectile and ejaculatory functions, while women experience a reduction in sexual desire and lose the ability to produce vaginal lubrication. Weight loss, insomnia, and hallucinations ("cocaine bugs") are also frequently reported.[78]

Since cocaine enters the blood relatively quickly from mucous membranes, the nose is a favorite site for the ingestion or snorting of cocaine hydrochloride. The habit of snorting or sniffing cocaine eventually causes a perforation of the nasal septum, and users are sometimes referred to as "sniffy."[79] When the nasal membrane is beginning to be damaged, the user will appear to have either a stuffy or runny nose, and the mucous will be very watery. As the condition becomes more severe, the user will have difficulty breathing. Eventually, breathing through the nose becomes impossible, and the wall dividing the halves of the nose will disintegrate.

The effects of ingesting cocaine take about three minutes to reach the brain by snorting. Freebasing or smoking crack can deliver the same effects in about six seconds.[80] This form of administration can produce minor lung irritations, sore chest and neck, swollen glands, and a raspy voice. The high produced from smoking crack lasts from two to five minutes and ends as abruptly as it began. After the "crash," the user is irritable, anxious, and depressed and has increasingly severe cravings for more of the drug. Reports from addicts indicate that addiction occurs *much* more quickly from the use of crack than through any other form of cocaine use.[81]

Intravenous injection of cocaine hydrochloride in a water solution delivers a euphoric feeling almost as quickly as smoking crack—about 14 seconds.[82] Some cocaine users prefer injecting a mixture of cocaine and heroin, a combination known as a speedball. (The heroin is said to dampen the unpleasant jitteriness and crash from cocaine.) Taken together, these two drugs sometimes completely halt the user's respiration or cause brain seizures. In one community, two-thirds of cocaine-related deaths were attributed to the injection of speedballs.[83] The danger of cocaine overdoses cannot be overemphasized. Deaths from cocaine or cocaine/heroin combinations have exceeded heroin overdoses at least since 1983.[84]

There are many other risks associated with any type of intravenous drug use—such as hepatitis or HIV infection. Although the new user may begin by scrupulously maintaining sterile needles and syringes ("works"), the chronic user seldom exercises such care. One former user tells about "a day when I drove all the way across Liverpool to borrow a wornout works from an addict who had recently had syphilis."[85] Since bacteria and viruses don't impede the addict's high, they are generally disregarded.

Finally, there is the problem of cocaine babies. A much greater incidence of miscarriages, low-birth-weight infants, premature deliveries, and birth defects have been found to be associated with cocaine use during pregnancy.[86] As these children mature, they have a high incidence of learning disabilities and health problems. The severity and persistence of these problems are frequently perceived to be much greater than the data warrant, however.[87]

Amphetamines

Amphetamines are one of the most preferred drugs of so-called normal Americans—students cramming for exams, truck drivers working 24-hour days, and athletes competing for national or international records. Millions of people have legally used amphetamines for anxiety, depression, and obesity. As mentioned earlier, millions of soldiers were given amphetamines in World War II to enhance combat performance. German Panzer troops used the drug to eliminate fatigue and maintain physical endurance. Because of the aggressive and violent behavior frequently noted in chronic users, some historians believe that many German atrocities were linked to the use of amphetamines.[88] Ten years after the war ended, 200,000 cases of amphetamine psychosis, one of the most extreme side effects of this drug, were reported in Japan.[89] As late as 1969, the U.S. armed forces were still purchasing massive amounts of amphetamines, with the Navy dispensing 21.1 pills per person per year, followed by the Air Force (17.5) and the Army (13.8).[90]

Low dosages of this drug will normally produce the following:

1. Heightened competence in motor skills and mental acuity
2. Increased alertness
3. A feeling of increased energy
4. A stimulation of the need for motor activity (particularly walking or talking)
5. A feeling of euphoria

6. Increased heartbeat
7. Inhibition of appetite
8. Constriction of the blood vessels
9. Dryness of the mouth
10. A feeling of confidence and even grandeur.[91]

Amphetamines are usually taken orally by new users in dosages of 50 to 150 milligrams (mg) daily. Addicts soon discover that highs are obtained faster by snorting or injecting the drug. During a "speed run" a "speed freak" may inject as much as 1,000 mg in one dose and up to 5,000 mg during a 24-hour period. During a run, users will be disinclined to eat or sleep and may lose 10 pounds or more during a week. Some users prefer the "balling" technique, in which a form known as crank is instilled into the vagina prior to intercourse. Low dosages of amphetamine may slightly enhance sexual performance, but higher dosages consistently disrupt sexual function.[92] Orgasm and ejaculation are either delayed or impossible to achieve while using large doses of speed.[93]

After "crashing," the user may experience marked depression, apathy, a variety of aches and pains, and a ravenous appetite. The person may be so exhausted that he or she will sleep for long periods. Some users will begin another speed run as soon as they feel they are beginning to crash. It is not unusual for some users to inject amphetamines in combination with other drugs such as sedatives or heroin. (Although the original speedball was cocaine and heroin, the "poor man's speedball" is methamphetamine and heroin.[94])

Chronic amphetamine use may lead to cerebral hemorrhages, tachycardia, hypertension, cardia arrhythmias, and liver damage. Combining amphetamine use with drinking alcohol has a multiplicative effect that puts the user at a high risk for heart failure.[95] The anorexia produced by chronic use coupled with the high caloric intake required to sustain unusually high levels of motor activity often results in malnutrition. Paranoia inevitably comes with heavy and continued use. Violent behavior, including suicide, may come during or at the end of a run.[96]

As with other drugs, repeated use of amphetamines leads to addiction, tolerance, and the need for increasingly large doses. During the initial phase of withdrawal, the user may sleep almost continuously for up to three days. This is usually followed by a state of depression lasting up to two weeks. During this time, the individual may be irritable and apathetic and experience episodes of anxiety, extreme fear, and obsessions. Sleep disturbances may occur for the next several months. An additional problem for amphetamine users is that they frequently begin using alcohol, barbiturates, or other depressants in order to mitigate the stimulation effects of amphetamine. This is particularly dangerous because of the possibility of drug interaction effects.[97]

Chronic users develop amphetamine toxicity, which is manifested in physical, mental, and behavioral symptoms. General health and personal hygiene deteriorate, and intravenous users may show track marks, infections, and abscesses. Behavioral signs include nervousness, irritability, and restlessness due to the constant overstimulation induced by the drug. This may lead to stereotypic compulsive behavior such as taking an object apart and putting it back together again. They may pace back and forth across a room, and conversation is quite repetitive. The most extreme form of this toxicity is a state of paranoia called amphetamine psychosis. The individual becomes suspicious of everyone, is physically exhausted, and will appear to be quite confused. Delusions or hallucinations may occur, and violent, aggressive behavior is frequently noted. The paranoia of an amphetamine addict may be identical to that observed in schizophrenia.[98]

A unique feature of amphetamine psychosis is the occurrence of tactile hallucinations. Users may feel that they have worms or lice on their bodies (similar to "cocaine bugs"). Constant picking or scratching often results in sores and abrasions. Some users have even used knives or razor blades to remove the imagined organisms from their skin.

Another particular feature of amphetamine psychosis is the quickness with which it can occur.

Studies have shown that it can be induced in human volunteers, who were carefully screened to ensure they did not have a previous history of psychosis, in approximately four days.[99]

MDMA

One of the more popular designer drugs of the 1980s was MDMA (3,4-methylenedioxymethamphetamine), more commonly known as Ecstasy, XTC, or Adam. A *designer drug* is generally defined as a substance tailormade for specific selected effects. It also usually involves the process of chemically engineering existing controlled substances to create a drug that is not currently illegal.[100] MDMA was created to replace its cousin (3,4-methylenedioxyamphetamine), which was a Schedule I drug under the 1970 Controlled Substances Act. It was sold openly, especially in bars in the Dallas, Texas, area until it also became a controlled substance in 1985.[101]

MDMA is described as an aphrodisiac, a "party drug," and a "yuppie psychedelic." It is generally taken orally in doses of 100 to 150 mg. A mild euphoria may appear between 20 and 60 minutes later, and the rush may last from a few minutes to a half hour. The rush levels off to a plateau lasting two to three hours. Users report being in an altered state of consciousness but still in control, having expanded mental perspective and insight into personal problems or patterns.[102] Researchers have noted that the drug tends to enhance the pleasure of touching but interferes with erection in men and inhibits orgasm in both men and women.[103] MDMA produces a distinct hangover with pronounced negative side effects on the second day after use, including sore jaw muscles (from teeth grinding), drowsiness, muscle aches, depression, and difficulty concentrating. Users seem to develop a tolerance quickly to the positive effects of the drug, but not to its negative effects.[104]

There has been recent concern that a large enough dose of MDMA can destroy serotonergic nerve terminals in the brain, thereby disrupting sleep, changing mood, causing sexual dysfunction, and creating hypersensitivity to aversive stimuli.[105] There is also some evidence that MDMA may suppress the immune system, with regular users experiencing more sore throats, colds, influenza, and herpes outbreaks.[106]

Crystal Methamphetamine

"Crystal meth," or ice, has become one of the most popular drugs in Asia and has overtaken cocaine and marijuana as the most commonly used illicit drug in Hawaii.[107] The basic ingredients for this drug can be obtained from almost any chemical company; $100 worth of ingredients will produce a pound of ice in its most highly refined form—worth anywhere from $15,000 to $32,000 on the street.[108] The drug's popularity grew quickly because of the enormous profits, because it can be easily manufactured, and because the high from smoking ice lasts 8 to 24 hours, compared to the 15-minute high from crack.[109]

Ice produces feelings of euphoria followed by severe depression, just as crack does, but the high lasts much longer and the crash is much worse. Addicts call the sensation from smoking ice "amping," for the amplified euphoria it provides them.[110] Ice users may also experience symptoms of acute psychosis that are not normally associated with crack use. Severe paranoia, hallucinations, delusions, and incoherent speech may also make ice addicts indistinguishable from paranoid schizophrenics. Extremely violent and aggressive behavior is common among addicts. One director of a crisis response team in Honolulu reported that "Every person on ice I have seen has to be in restraints."[111]

Other symptoms associated with use of this drug are weight loss, insomnia, irregular heartbeat, convulsions, and body temperatures that can reach 108 degrees—frequently resulting in kidney failure. Devastating effects have been noticed in children born to mothers using ice: They tend to be asocial and incapable of bonding. Some have tremors and cry for 24 hours without stopping. Nurses report that the problems of ice babies are much more severe than the problems of babies born addicted to cocaine.[112]

Crystalline methamphetamine is a relatively new drug to the United States; therefore little research has been conducted on its physiological or psychological effects. Very little is available on the effectiveness of treatment for this addiction.

The Effects of Sedatives

One of the greatest problems associated with abusing either barbiturate or nonbarbiturate sedatives is the danger of overdose. Although some drugs, such as cannabis and amphetamines, have very large "safety zones," an overdose of only one or two seconal or methaqualone pills may cause death. This danger is even further heightened when the sedative is used in combination with alcohol. In the mid-1970s, there were over 10,000 hospital admissions and 2,000 deaths per year attributed to sedative overdoses, many of them in combination with alcohol.[113] Barbiturates are also the most frequent chemical agent used in committing suicide.[114]

Barbiturate intoxication is quite similar to alcohol intoxication: Speech is slurred, thinking is confused, and movements are uncoordinated with a staggering gait. Addicts fall frequently, suffering many injuries and bruises. Barbiturates shift sleep patterns, and many users experience nightmarish, sleep-disrupting dreams upon withdrawal. Many return to using barbiturates or other sedatives in order to deal with insomnia. Barbiturates also depress the respiratory center, and apnea is a common danger to users with marginal pulmonary reserves. A more common problem is the effect of barbiturates on other drugs. Drugs such as phenobarbital induce liver enzymes that cause other drugs to be more rapidly degraded. This can reduce the effectiveness of anticoagulants, or it can speed the effect of drugs such as alcohol. With other drugs, it is simply impossible to predict the effect of the interaction.[115]

Withdrawal from barbiturates can be especially dangerous, much more so than heroin withdrawal. No one who has been using barbiturates over a long period of time should be withdrawn suddenly, and anyone who has taken addictive quantities should withdraw in a hospital. A condition much like delirium tremens occurs within 24 hours in a majority of cases. Three-fourths of people going through abrupt withdrawal will experience major epileptic convulsions between the sixth and eighth day. Without close medical supervision, death is a distinct danger—frequently from exhaustion or pneumonia.[116]

Nonbarbiturate sedatives such as methaqualone (Quaaludes) may produce many of the same respiratory problems as the barbiturates. Other effects of methaqualone may include nausea, weakness, indigestion, numbness and tingling, and rashes. Withdrawal may resemble the symptoms of alcohol or sedative withdrawal, including delirium and convulsions.[117]

One of the most popular sedatives in recent years has been flunitrazepam hydrochloride, a drug legally prescribed in most of the world under the trade name of Rohyphol. It is a benzodiazepam in the same category as Valium. Its abuse in the United States, where it is an illegal drug, was first reported in Florida in 1993. It is commonly known by its street name, "roofies" (also known as rophies, ruffies, rope, rib, R2, roofenol, roche, roachies, and Mexican valium). Much of the publicity about Rohyphol has centered around its use as a date-rape drug, but it apparently has three more common patterns of use:

1. It appears to have a synergistic effect when used with alcohol; it produces disinhibition and amnesia.
2. Heroin users sometimes use it to enhance the effect of low-quality heroin.
3. Cocaine users may take Rohypnol to "come down" from a cocaine high.[118]

Lethal overdoses are rare. Sedation occurs 20 to 30 minutes after ingesting a 2-mg tablet and lasts about eight hours. Like other sedatives, continued use may cause addiction. Withdrawal symptoms include headache, muscle pain and ache, and confusion. Severe withdrawal may result in hallucinations, convulsions, and seizures. (Seizures have been reported up to one week after withdrawal.)[119]

The Effects of Narcotics

True narcotic drugs (which do *not* include marijuana and cocaine) depress the activity of the brain and the central nervous system. Their chief use in medicine is the relief of pain and the inducement of sleep.[120] Narcotics may be divided into two groups: (1) opium and opium derivatives and (2) synthetic substances that produce effects similar to opiates.

Opiates (opium, heroin, morphine, dilaudid, laudanum, paregoric, and codeine) are derived from the opium poppy. The poppy produces a white, milky substance that dries in contact with air. When further dried into a powder, this substance becomes opium. Morphine is the major alkaloid of opium. Heroin is a synthetic derivative of opium produced by exposing morphine to acetic acid. Codeine is a separate alkaloid found in opium. Raw opium contains about 10 percent morphine, and heroin is derived from morphine on roughly a 1-to-5 ratio.[121]

Opium is generally smoked, whereas the preferred method of administration for morphine and heroin is injection. Heroin may also be taken orally, snorted, or smoked.[122] Among U.S. soldiers in Southeast Asia, smoking was the most commonly used method of ingesting heroin.[123] Regular heroin users who shoot (inject) the drug have a characteristic slate-colored line along the veins into which they have been injecting. Frequent injection destroys superficial veins, and it becomes increasingly difficult to find healthy veins. Addicts will inject in sites such as the groin, the temples, and the penis. Gangrene, blood clots, AIDS, hepatitis, and venereal diseases are a common risk among addicts who share needles without paying adequate attention to cleaning their needles and syringes.[124]

Heroin reaches the brain from the bloodstream and is transformed into morphine. Heroin actually has minimal central nervous system effects per se, and it is only after being changed through hydrolysis to 6-mono-acetylmorphine (MAM) and then to morphine that the major CNS effects are produced. Heroin is preferred to morphine by addicts, since it has an analgesic effect two to four times greater.[125] The effect of an injection is described by a former self-described junky:

> The rush is so hard to describe. It's like waiting for a distant thunderstorm to move overhead. A strange foreboding. A bizarre, awesome calm. It's in your blood, moving towards your brain, relentlessly; unstoppable, inevitable. A feeling starts to grow like a rumble from the horizon. The feeling swells, surging, soaring, crashing, screaming to a devastating crescendo. The gear [heroin] smashes against the top of your skull with the power of an uncapped oil well. You won't be able to bear the intense ecstasy. It is all too much. Your body may fall apart. The rock that is your head shatters harmlessly into a million sparkling, tinkling smithereens. They tumble at a thousand miles an hour straight back down over your body, warming, insulating, tingling, denying all pain, fear, and sadness. You are stoned, you are high. You are above and below reality and law.[126]

Morphine and heroin are cleared within six hours, and their subjective effects last four to five hours. With a large dose, the new user "nods out" or enters a dream state moments after an injection. As with other drugs, tolerance develops to a degree that the addict ends up taking the drug simply to avoid the consequences of withdrawal, and increasingly larger doses have to be taken to accomplish this.[127] Other more purely physiological effects also are produced on the body. All opiates act on the gastrointestinal tract, resulting in dehydration of the feces and constipation in the majority of addicts. Contraction of the pupils is also obvious during chronic use.[128] Other major physical problems are common in addicts.

The Digestive System

Both peptic and duodenal ulcers are common in heroin addicts. Obstruction of the intestinal tract and hemorrhoids are also frequently associated with their chronic constipation problems.[129]

The Endocrine System

Morphine and heroin have been demonstrated to decrease the production of hormones and gonadotrophin.[130] Diabetes and hypoglycemic conditions are also frequently found in opiate addicts.[131]

Integument

As mentioned earlier, the "tracks" seen on the bodies of heroin addicts are the result of repeated injections of heroin into the veins. These tracks are most often noticed on the sclerosed veins of the forearms, hands, and feet, but may occur anywhere on the body—including the dorsal vein of the penis and external jugular and sublingual veins.[132] Dark pigmentation may also occur as a result of heating the tip of the "spike" with a match flame in order to supposedly sterilize it. The resulting carbon accumulation is deposited under the skin during injection.[133]

Abscesses and lesions of the skin frequently result from the practice of "skin-popping" (subcutaneous injection). These are usually found on the thighs and back. Another type of lesion commonly found on addicts is a "rosette" of cigarette burns on the chest resulting from nodding out while having a lighted cigarette in the mouth. Tattoos are also frequently found on heroin addicts, usually over the site of tracks they wish to conceal.[134]

The Genitourinary System

There is some evidence of an increased risk of both venereal disease and renal disease associated with heroin addiction, but these problems are not the direct result of the action of the drug. These diseases occur because of the contamination of the heroin or an addict's "works."[135]

Other Problems

Perhaps the greatest risk facing the heroin or morphine addict is the possibility of an overdose. Drugs such as this bought illegally on the street are always cut with some other substance such as quinine, domestic cleaning compounds, or even brick dust![136] It is impossible for the addict to know what the strength of his or her "gear" is, and there is not a large margin of safety for intravenous injection. Death from overdose is a constant risk.

As mentioned earlier, tolerance develops rapidly, especially for the intravenous user. Many addicts purposefully go through withdrawal from time to time in order to reduce their tolerance. A substantial number of overdoses occur when addicts who have abstained for a period of time return to taking their usual dosage. Death or coma can also result from the combined use of opiates with either alcohol or barbiturates. The additive effect of these drugs may depress respiration to life-threatening levels.[137]

The Effects of Hallucinogens

The main property of a hallucinogen is to create an alteration of normal perceptions or to induce abnormal perceptions. These types of drugs are called psychotomimetic, but they also came to be known as psychedelic drugs in the hippie culture of the 1960s.[138] The term *psychedelic* is also applied to the philosophy of that particular generation of the drug culture, generally in a positive manner.

This philosophy is that "man is a creature who has been lied to and blinded by the propaganda socialized into him from infancy."[139] The essential function served by psychedelic drugs, according to this line of thought, is to strip away the impediments that block a direct confrontation with reality and allow the user to see things clearly. Under the influence of mescaline, Aldous Huxley described the awesome "isness" of his trousers, his bookshelf, and the legs of a chair. "This is how things really are; how things really are."[140]

A much different point of view is summed up in the term *hallucinogen*. It brings forth images of something illusory—a deception, a fallacy, or perhaps the ravings of a madman or hallucination of someone in imminent need of treatment. Actually, a true hallucination (a perception without an object) is relatively rare during a drug experience. Much more common is a *distortion* of perception.[141] There is nothing mystical about the action of LSD; it is that of a toxic chemical that disrupts the brain's normal process. It is no more mystical than the hallucinations of an alcoholic, the delusions of a schizophrenic, or the dreams of an opium eater.

Hallucinogens do not cause the physical dependence of alcohol or opiates, and do not have the psychological compulsion of drugs such as cocaine, although a psychological need to repeat the experience of "tripping" is common. In the true sense, these are not drugs of dependence, but they are substances that can as easily result in disaster on the first as on each subsequent use.[142]

The most commonly used hallucinogens are LSD, mescaline (the main alkaloid of the peyote cactus), psilocybin (from a mushroom that flourishes in Mexico), and fly agaric (*amanita muscaria*, a common toadstool). LSD is the strongest of these, having a strength approximately 200 times that of psilocybin and 4,000 times that of mescaline! There are other synthetic hallucinogens such as 2,5-dimethoxy-4-methyl amphetamine (commonly known as STP, for serenity, tranquility, and peace) that have effects in common with both LSD and amphetamines.[143]

D-lysergic acid diethylamide 25 (LSD or "acid") is one of the most commonly used hallucinogens. It is usually taken orally via a pill or capsule, or by chewing and swallowing a "paper" soaked in an LSD solution (frequently decorated with a tattoo or psychedelic design). During the 1960s, it was commonly taken in a sugar cube impregnated with the chemical, but this method is not generally used today. In some areas, LSD is still taken by placing a small amount in an eye dropper and depositing it on the eyes. A quantity as small as 25 micrograms (µg) is psychoactive for most people.[144] (An aspirin tablet is approximately 300,000 µg.)

A "trip" on LSD may last between 5 and 12 hours, although reactions may last for days, and flashbacks may occur indefinitely. During the trip, the user will experience distortions of the senses, especially vision. Loss of a sense of space and distance and the relationship of self to these dimensions is common. The user may describe colors, smells, and sounds as though they are being experienced for the first time. These experiences range from extremely pleasant to nightmarish.[145] A commonly reported effect is called eidetic imagery, or eyeball movies, in which the user (with the eyes closed) "sees" physical objects, usually in motion, as sharply as if he or she were watching a movie. These images are abstract and usually lacking in any dramatic content, and they usually represent repetitions of a pattern or design—such as moving wallpaper—but with the patterns constantly changing.[146]

One of the most common hazards of LSD use is related to the distortion of visual perception. Users frequently fall through windows above ground level, later explaining that they thought they had left through the front door or a ground-level window. Normal physical changes that occur with use are related to overstimulation of the sympathetic nervous system. These include trembling, sweating, dilated pupils, goose bumps, changes in blood pressure and pulse rate, nausea, and bowel problems.[147] Asthma attacks are sometimes precipitated by LSD in the predisposed individual.

Loss of appetite is also common. Convulsions occur rather infrequently, but depression may occur either during or immediately after a trip.[148] A special hazard is the flashback phenomenon, especially when it occurs when victims are in a situation where they are at risk to themselves or others—such as driving an automobile.

The Effects of Inhalants

Most of the inhalants commonly abused today are solvents such as aerosols, paint, gasoline, lacquer thinner, airplane glue, lighter fluid, and trichloroethylene. Most of the users who sniff or "huff" these substances are under the age of 15, possibly because the sources are so much more easily available to children. Glue sniffers will typically empty the contents of a tube into the bottom of a paper bag, hold the bag tightly over the mouth (or mouth and nose), and inhale the vapors until the desired effect is reached. Liquid materials may be inhaled directly from a container or from saturated cloth.[149]

Most materials used in sniffing contain volatile or gaseous substances that are primarily generalized central nervous system depressants. The immediate effects may range from somnolence and dizziness to delusions of unusual strength or supernatural abilities (such as the ability to fly). Visual and auditory hallucinations similar to those associated with the hallucinogens are frequently noted. Other symptoms are slurred speech, ataxia, impaired judgment, and feelings of euphoria.[150] Excessive or prolonged sniffing of high vapor concentrations will ultimately lead to loss of consciousness. Too much solvent can also cause paralysis of the breathing center and death. Other sniffers may die from ventricular fibrillation induced by central respiratory depression. Deaths have also resulted from damage to the liver, kidneys, and bone marrow among chronic sniffers. Occasional deaths from asphyxiation also result from the practice of inhaling a solvent in a closed space or with one's head in a plastic bag.[151]

Amyl nitrite was introduced into medicine over a century ago when it was found to relieve angina pectoris by dilating coronary arteries and temporarily improving the perfusion and oxygenation of heart muscle.[152] It also has the effect of expanding the meningeal arteries over the surface of the brain and producing feelings of suffusion and fullness in the head. The action of amyl nitrite on the brain results in a subjective experience of time being slowed down, and it is this perception that began a modest amount of recreational use of the drug during the 1930s. Taken just before climax, it may extend the sensation of orgasm.

Although some use by heterosexual men and women has been reported, amyl nitrite is more popular as an orgasm expander among homosexual men. Originally available in a capsule or pearl that was crushed and inhaled (called snappers or poppers), it was later sold in aerosol form (either as amyl or isobutyl nitrite) under trade names such as Locker Room, Aroma of Men, Kick, Bullet, Jac, and Rush, ostensibly as room deodorizers![153]

Other symptoms accompanying use of this drug are nausea, dizziness, mild sensory intensification, a diminution of ego controls, and an increase in aggressive behavior. A drop in blood pressure and an increase in the heart rate are usually noted. Pulsating headaches also are frequently mentioned by regular users.[154] Some researchers believe that butyl nitrite depresses the body's immune system and weakens its ability to fight the AIDS virus.[155] The Centers for Disease Control in Atlanta cites evidence that Kaposi's sarcoma is much more common among AIDS victims who use poppers than among AIDS victims who do not use them. Other research indicates that 87 percent of the 290 compounds in the nitrite family have proven to be carcinogenic in tests of laboratory animals.[156]

The Effects of Drugs on Offspring

Offspring may be damaged by drug use by either parent, although the greater risks are generally associated with maternal drug use.[157] Drug use by females may affect offspring when it happens prior to conception, during gestation, and following birth—if the baby is breast fed. The most severe consequence of drugs taken by a pregnant woman is prenatal or perinatal death. Many of the causes of drug-related prenatal death are not well understood, and they may not be noticed if it occurs early in pregnancy. The most commonly identified teratogenic drug is alcohol, but opiates, barbiturates, benzodiazepines, amphetamines, cocaine, tobacco, and marijuana are also frequently implicated in birth defects, pre- and postnatal growth deficiency, and cognitive development.[158]

Alcohol

Although the specific effects of maternal alcohol use on the fetus was not officially recognized and given a label until 1973, alcohol has been suspected as a teratogenic agent at least since biblical times. Judges 13:7 provides the injunction, "Behold thou shalt conceive and bear a son: now drink no wine or strong drink." Other early societies also recognized the danger of alcohol on offspring.[159] It was not until 1973, however, that Jones and colleagues[160] described the children born to chronic alcoholic mothers as having fetal alcohol syndrome (FAS). These children were characterized by prenatal and postnatal growth deficiency, a pattern of physical abnormalities (including short palpebral fissures, epicanthic folds, ear anomalies, and cardiac defects), and mental retardation. In a subsequent review of 245 cases, Clarren and Smith described the three primary characteristics of FAS as growth deficiency, characteristic facial dysmorphology, and central nervous system damage. Cardiac defects occur in 30 to 40 percent of FAS children.[161]

The incidence of FAS varies considerably among various subpopulations, but there is little doubt that the teratogenic effects of alcohol are dose related. One study concluded that between 11 and 13 percent of pregnant women who drink two to three drinks a day will give birth to children with FAS.[162] Careful studies conducted in Göteborg, Sweden, and Roubaix, France, found the rate of FAS to be 1 in 690 births. The rate in Seattle, Washington, is 1 in 750 births, and studies conducted on Native American reservations in southwestern United States indicate a rate of 1 in 100 births.[163]

Children born with FAS are usually not grossly malformed, but they do have a particular cluster of facial characteristics that, along with their small stature and slender build, give them a readily identifiable appearance. Mental handicaps are the most debilitating aspect of FAS, with victims having an average IQ of 65.[164] FAS is one of the few types of mental retardation that is entirely preventable. Since there is no specific treatment for FAS, and its effects are permanent, the primary focus must remain on prevention. No safe level of drinking by pregnant women has ever been established.[165] The only way to eliminate the risk of FAS is to be abstinent during pregnancy.

Opiates

Although it has been difficult to separate the effects of opiates from other factors associated with the living conditions and general life-styles of opiate users, studies indicate that the offspring of heroin-dependent mothers tend to be low in birth weight, more frequently premature, and often suffer from perinatal complications and a range of abnormalities.[166] Neonatal narcotic withdrawal is a common problem of offspring exposed to opiates *in utero.* Hypoxia, hyperactivity, and fetal death have also been noted.[167]

Tobacco

Spontaneous abortion is much higher in pregnant women who smoke than in nonsmokers. Smoking can induce malformations sufficiently severe to cause fetal death at an early stage of pregnancy. Fetuses that do survive are 10 to 15 percent lighter at birth than are those born to nonsmokers.[168] The combination of both smoking and drinking entails a much higher risk to the fetus and its postnatal development.[169]

Amphetamines and Cocaine

A wide range of abnormalities have been associated with maternal amphetamine and cocaine administration, although research on their teratogenic effects is still in its early stages. Among the consequences of maternal use of these stimulants are spontaneous abortion, low birth weight, cleft palate, urogenital anomalies, and an increase in excitability.[170] When a pregnant woman uses crack, it results in a constriction of the blood vessels and a decrease in the flow of oxygen and nutrients to the fetus. Many cocaine-exposed babies suffer physiological and neurological malformations, including deformed hearts, lungs, digestive systems, and limbs. Others may suffer a fatal stroke while still in the womb.[171]

Other Drugs

There is some evidence that maternal *barbiturate* use may result in both morphological and behavioral impairment. This is especially disturbing since many people have to use this drug to keep their epilepsy under control. *Benzodiazepine* use (especially diazepam) by pregnant women is reported to have caused a number of birth defects, including cleft palate. High levels of maternal *caffeine* use may result in higher rates of spontaneous abortion and certain congenital abnormalities. *Hallucinogens* such as LSD are capable of inducing chromosomal damage, but this does not seem to occur at normal human dosage levels. Structural abnormalities, especially of the limbs, have been more frequent in the offspring of LSD users. *Marijuana* also has been observed to induce chromosomal damage at high doses, but there is little evidence that this occurs at normal dosage levels. In animal studies, behavioral differences have been noted in the offspring of marijuana-treated mothers. There is little reliable evidence on the maternal effects of *inhalants*.[172]

Summary

This chapter described the most commonly observed physiological and behavioral consequences of alcohol and drug abuse. The reader must bear in mind that *individuals vary markedly in their reactions to specific doses of particular drugs, and the same reaction cannot be expected even within the same individual over a period of time.* The development of tolerance and chemically induced trauma to organs such as the brain make predictions of behavior somewhat more problematic than the physiological consequences. Except for alcohol, the effects of most drugs on the offspring of users are just beginning to be adequately studied.

Endnotes

1. Risto J. K. Julkunen, Carlo DiPadova, and Charles S. Lieber, "First Pass Metabolism of Ethanol: A Gastrointestinal Barrier against the Systemic Toxicity of Ethanol," *Life Sciences,* Vol. 37 (1985), pp. 567–573.

2. Ted Loomis, "The Pharmacology of Alcohol," in Nada J. Estes and M. Edith Heinemann (Eds.), *Alcoholism: Development, Consequences, and Interventions,* 3rd ed. (St. Louis: C. V. Mosby, 1986), pp. 93–102.

3. Ibid., p. 99.

4. Sujata Tewari and Virginia G. Carson, "Biochemistry of Alcohol and Alcohol Metabolism," in E. Mansell Pattison and Edward Kaufman (Eds.), *Encyclopedic Handbook of Alcoholism* (New York: Gardner Press, 1982), pp. 83–104.

5. Loomis, "The Pharmacology of Alcohol," p. 101.

6. Robert B. Forney and Rolla N. Harger, "The Alcohols," in Joseph R. DiPalma (Ed.), *Drill's Pharmacology in Medicine,* 4th ed. (New York: McGraw-Hill, 1971).

7. Frank A. Seixas, "The Course of Alcoholism," in Estes and Heinemann, *Alcoholism,* pp. 67–77.

8. Loomis, "The Pharmacology of Alcohol," p. 100.

9. Roger H. Butz, "Intoxication and Withdrawal," in Estes and Heinemann, *Alcoholism,* pp. 103–109.

10. C. Brown, "The Alcohol Withdrawal Syndrome," *Annals of Emergency Medicine,* Vol. 11 (1982), p. 276.

11. U.S. Department of Health and Human Services, *Fifth Special Report to the U.S. Congress on Alcohol and Health* (Washington, DC: U.S. Government Printing Office, December 1983).

12. L. Frederick Fenster, "Alcohol and Disorders of the Gastrointestinal System," in Estes and Heinemann, *Alcoholism,* pp. 145–152.

13. C. Michael Knauer, "Mallory-Weiss Syndrome: Characteristics of 75 Mallory-Weiss Lacerations in 528 Patients with Upper Gastrointestinal Hemorrhage," *Gastroenterology*, Vol. 71 (1976), p. 71.

14. R. J. Derbes and R. E. Mitchell, "Rupture of the Esophagus," *Surgery*, Vol. 39 (1956), p. 688.

15. U.S. Department of Health and Human Services (USDHHS), *Sixth Special Report to the US. Congress on Alcohol and Health* (Washington, DC: U.S. Government Printing Office, January 1987), p. 60.

16. John A. Hermos, "Mucosa of the Small Intestine in Folate-Deficient Alcoholics," *Annals of Internal Medicine*, Vol. 76 (1972), p. 957.

17. M. S. Millan, G. P. Morris, Ivan T. Beck, and J. T. Henson, "Villous Damage Induced by Suction Biopsy and by Acute Ethanol Intake in Normal Human Small Intestine," *Digestive Diseases and Sciences*, Vol. 25 (1980), pp. 513–525.

18. Charles S. Lieber, Helmut K. Seitz, Anthony J. Garro, and Theresa M. Worner, "Alcohol-Related Diseases and Carcinogenesis," *Cancer Research*, Vol. 39 (1979), pp. 2863–2886.

19. B. F. Grant, J. Noble, and Henry J. Malin, "Decline in Liver Cirrhosis Mortality and Components of Change: United States, 1973–1983," *Alcohol Health & Research World*, Vol. 10 (1986), pp. 66–69.

20. G. Pequignot and J. J. Tuyns, "Compared Toxicity of Ethanol on Various Organs," in C. Stock and H. Sarles (Eds.), *Alcohol and the Gastrointestinal Tract* (Paris: INSERM, 1980), pp. 17–32.

21. E. Mezey, "Alcoholic Liver Disease," in H. Popper and F. Schaffner (Eds.), *Progress in Liver Diseases*, Volume III (New York: Grune & Stratton, 1982), pp. 555–572.

22. L. Frederick Fenser, "Alcohol and Disorders of the Gastrointestinal System," in Estes and Heinemann, *Alcoholism*, pp. 145–152.

23. H. Kalant, "Alcohol, Pancreatic Secretion, and Pancreatitis," *Gastroenterology*, Vol. 56 (1969), p. 380.

24. R. W. Ammann et al., "Course and Outcome of Chronic Pancreatitis: Longitudinal Study of a Mixed Medical-Surgical Series of 245 Patients," *Gastroenterology*, Vol. 86 (1984), p. 820.

25. Konstanty Markiewi and Marian Cholewa, "The Effect of Alcohol on the Circulatory System Adaptation to Physical Effort," *Journal of Studies on Alcohol*, Vol. 43 (1982), pp. 812–823.

26. H. S. Friedman, S. A. Geller, and C. S. Lieber, "The Effect of Alcohol on the Heart, Skeletal, and Smooth Muscles," in L. H. Smight, Jr. (Ed.), *Medical Disorders of Alcoholism, Pathogenesis, and Treatment*, Volume XXII in *Major Problems in Internal Medicine* (Philadelphia: W. B. Saunders, 1982), pp. 436–479.

27. J. F. Potter and D. G. Beevers, "Pressor Effect of Alcohol in Hypertension," *Lancet*, Vol. I (1984), pp. 119–122.

28. Roberto M. Lang, Kenneth M. Borow, Alexander Neumann, and Ted Feldman, "Adverse Cardia Effects of Acute Alcohol Ingestion in Young Adults," *Annals of Internal Medicine*, Vol. 102 (1985), pp. 742–747.

29. USDHHS, *Sixth Special Report*, p. 63.

30. Wolfgang Schmidt and Jan deLint, "Causes of Death in Alcoholics," *Quarterly Journal of Studies on Alcohol*, Vol. 33 (1972), pp. 171–185.

31. George Fink, "Feedback Actions of Target Hormones on Hypothalamus and Pituitary with Special Reference to Gonadal Steroids," *Annual Review of Physiology*, Vol. 41 (1979), pp. 571–585.

32. Y. Israel, P. G. Walfish, H. Orrego, S. Blake, and H. Kalant, "Thyroid Hormones in Alcoholic Liver Disease," *Gastroenterology*, Vol. 76 (1979), pp. 116–122.

33. Theodore J. Cicero, "Neuroendocrinological Effects of Alcohol," *Annual Review of Medicine*, Vol. 32 (1981), pp. 123–142.

34. C. M. Cornely, R. R. Schade, D. H. Van Thiel, and J. S. Gavaler, "Chronic Advanced Liver Disease and Impotence: Cause and Effect?" *Hepatology*, Vol. 4 (1984), pp. 1227–1230.

35. USDHHS, *Sixth Special Report*, pp. 66–68.

36. Walter A. Hunt, *Alcohol and Biological Membranes* (New York: Guilford Press, 1985).

37. B. Porjesz and Henri Begleiter, "Brain Dysfunction and Alcohol," in Benjamin Kissin and Henri Begleiter (Eds.), *The Biology of Alcoholism, Volume VII of The Pathogenesis of Alcoholism: Biological Factors* (New York: Plenum Press, 1983), pp. 415–483.

38. M. A. Ron, "The Alcoholic Brain: CT Scan and Psychological Findings," *Psychological Medicine, Monograph Supplement No. 3* (Cambridge: Cambridge University Press, 1983).

39. John R. Tkach and Hokama Yoshitsugi, "Autoimmunity in Chronic Brain Syndrome," *Archives of Ceneral Psychiatry*, Vol. 23 (1970), pp. 61–64.

40. H. A. Moskow, R. C. Pennington, and M. H. Knisely, "Alcohol, Sludge, and Hypoxic Areas of Nervous System, Liver and Heart," *Microvascular Research*, Vol. I (1968), pp. 174–185.

41. S. Tewari and E. P. Noble, "Ethanol and Brain Protein Synthesis," *Brain Research*, Vol. 26 (1971), pp. 469–474.

42. James W. Smith, "Neurologic Disorders in Alcoholism," in Estes and Heinemann, *Alcoholism*, pp. 153–175.

43. Ronald D. Page, "Cerebral Dysfunction Associated with Alcohol Consumption," *Substance Alcohol Actions/Misuse*, Vol. 4, No. 6 (1983), pp. 405–421.

44. William R. Miller and J. Orr, "Nature and Sequence of Neuropsychological Deficits in Alcoholics," *Journal of Studies on Alcohol*, Vol. 41 (1980), pp. 325–337.

45. Smith, "Neurologic Disorders," p. 155.

46. Ibid.

47. Oliver Sacks, *The Man Who Mistook His Wife for a Hat* (New York: Summit Books, 1985).

48. Ibid., p. 25.

49. Norman Jolliffe et al., "Nicotinic Acid Deficiency Encephalopathy," *Journal of the American Medical Association*, Vol. 114 (1940), pp. 307–312.

50. Hiram H. Merritt, *A Textbook of Neurology*, 6th ed. (Philadelphia: Lea & Febiger, 1979).

51. Smith, "Neurologic Disorders," p. 163.

52. Charles S. Lieber, "Alcohol-Nutrition Interaction: 1984 Update," *Alcohol*, Vol. 1, No. 2 (1984), pp. 151–157.

53. Ranjit K. Majumdar et al., "Blood Vitamin Status (B1, B2, B6, Folic Acid and B12) in Patients with Alcoholic Liver Disease," *International Journal for Vitamin and Nutrition Research*, Vol. 5 (1982), pp. 266–271.

54. Virginia N. Hillers and L. K. Massey, "Interrelationships of Moderate and High Alcohol Consumption with Diet and Health Status," *American Journal of Clinical Nutrition*, Vol. 41 (1985), pp. 356–362.

55. Ronald A. Arky, "Alcohol Use and the Diabetic Patient," *Alcohol Health and Research World*, Vol. 8 (1984), pp. 8–13.

56. Daniel D. Bikle et al., "Bone Disease in Alcohol Abuse," *Annals of Internal Medicine*, Vol. 103 (1985), pp. 42–48.

57. USDHHS, *Sixth Special Report*, p. 6.

58. Allan Witztum and D. Steinberg, "Role of Oxidized Low Density Lipoprotein in Atherogenesis," *Journal of Clinical Investigation*, Vol. 88 (1991), pp. 1785–1992.

59. Lynn Zimmer and John P. Morgan, *Exposing Marijuana Myths: A Review of the Scientific Evidence* (New York: Open Society Institute, 1995).

60. Norman Imlah, *Addiction: Substance Abuse and Dependency* (Winslow, England: Sigma Press, 1989), p. 87.

61. Erich Goode, *Drugs in American Society* (New York: Alfred A. Knopf, 1972), p. 55.

62. Sidney Cohen, *The Substance Abuse Problems* (New York: Haworth Press, 1981), p. 9.

63. White, *Drug Dependence*, p. 232.

64. Ibid., p. 220.

65. R. Weber, "Immunologic Effects of Drugs of Abuse," in *Problems of Drug Dependence, 1988: Proceedings of the 50th Annual Scientific Meeting, The Committee on Problems of Drug Dependence, Inc.*, DHHS Publication No. (ADM) 89-1605 (Washington, DC: U.S. Government Printing Office, 1988), pp. 99–104.

66. Imlah, *Addiction*, p. 88.

67. Cohen, *The Substance Abuse Problems*, p. 20.

68. Gabriel G. Nahas, *Marihuana in Science and Medicine* (New York: Raven Press, 1984), p. 215.

69. Imlah, *Addictions*, pp. 88–90.

70. Nahas, *Marihuana*, pp. 263–305.

71. Jacques Joseph Moreau, *Du Hashisch et de l'Alienation Mentale* (Paris: Librarie de Fortin, Masson, 1845; English edition: Raven Press, New York, 1972).

72. Nahas, *Marihuana*, pp. 280–285.

73. Awani Arif (Ed.), *Adverse Health Consequences of Cocaine Abuse* (Geneva: World Health Organization, 1987).

74. Kirk J. Brower and M. Douglas Anglin, "Adolescent Cocaine Use: Epidemiology, Risk Factors, and Prevention," *Journal of Drug Education*, Vol. 17 (1987), pp. 163–180.

75. Arif, *Adverse Health Consequences*, p. 21.

76. Hoffman, *Handbook*, p. 242.

77. Arnold M. Washton, *Cocaine Addiction* (New York: W. W. Norton, 1989).

78. Cohen, *The Substance Abuse Problems*, pp. 75–78.

79. Imlah, *Addiction*, pp. 59–60.

80. Joanne Baumm, *One Step over the Line: A No-Nonsense Guide to Recognizing and Treating Cocaine Dependency* (San Francisco: Harper and Row, 1985), p. 67.

81. Arnold M. Washton, *Cocaine Addiction: Treatment, Recovery, and Relapse Prevention* (New York: W. W. Norton, 1989), p. 15.

82. Baum, *One Step over the Line*, p. 67.

83. Washton, *Cocaine Addiction*, p. 17.

84. Baum, *One Step over the Line*, p. 71.

85. Tam Stewart, *The Heroin Users* (London: Pandora Press, 1987), p. 25.

86. Susan Livesay, Saundra Ehrlich, Lynn Ryan, and Lorretta Finnegan, "Cocaine and Pregnancy: Maternal and Infant Outcome," in *Problems of Drug Dependence*, 1988, p. 328.

87. D. E. Hutchings, "The Puzzle of Cocaine's Effects Following Maternal Use during Pregnancy: Are There Reconcilable Differences?" *Neurotoxicology and Teratology*, Vol. 15 (1993), pp. 281–286.

88. Scott E. Lukas (Ed.), *The Encyclopedia of Psychoactive Drugs: Amphetamines* (New York: Chelsea House, 1985), p. 21.

89. Imlah, *Addictions*, pp. 59–61.

90. Lukas, *Amphetamines*, p. 29.

91. I. R. Innes and M. Nickerson, "Amphetamine and Methamphetamine," in L. S. Goodman and A. Gilman (Eds.), *The Pharmacological Basis of Therapeutics*, 3rd ed. (New York: Macmillan, 1970), pp. 501–507.

92. Lukas, *Amphetamines*, p. 43.

93. Cohen, *The Substance Abuse Problems*, p. 147.

94. Ibid., p. 148.

95. Stephen T. Higgins et al., "Behavioral and Cardiovascular Effects of Alcohol and d-Amphetamine Combinations in Normal Volunteers," *Problems of Drug Dependence*, 1988, pp. 35–36.

96. Imlah, *Addictions*, pp. 59–61.

97. Lukas, *Amphetamines*, pp. 54–55.

98. Ibid., pp. 57–58.

99. Ibid., pp. 58–60.

100. Jerome Beck and Patricia A. Morgan, "Designer Drug Confusion: A Focus on MDMA," *Journal of Drug Education*, Vol. 16 (1986), pp. 287–302.

101. "The Trouble with Ecstasy," *Life*, September 1985, pp. 88–94.

102. Beck and Morgan, "Designer Drug Confusion," pp. 292–295.

103. Jerome Beck, "The Popularization and Resultant Implications of a Recently Controlled Psychoactive Substance," *Contemporary Drug Problems*, Vol. 13 (1986), p. 1.

104. Deborah M. Barnes, "New Data Intensify the Agony over Ecstasy," *Science*, Vol. 239 (1988), pp. 864–866.

105. C. Schuster, Statement to Congressional Subcommittee on Bills Relating to Designer Drugs, May 1, 1986.

106. Beck, "The Popularization and Implications."

107. Michael A. Lerner, "The Fire of 'Ice,' " *Newsweek*, November 27, 1989, pp. 37–40.

108. Jane Gross, "Speed's Gain in Use Could Rival Crack, Drug Experts Warn," The *New York Times*, November 27, 1988, Sec. 1, p. 1.

109. Katherine Bishop, "Fear Grows over Effects of a New Smokable Drug," The *New York Times*, September 16, 1989, Sec. 1, p. 1.

110. Lerner, "The Fire of 'Ice,' " p. 40.

111. Bishop, "Fear Grows," p. 8.

112. Lerner, "The Fire of 'Ice,' " p. 40.

113. Imlah, *Addiction*, pp. 64–69.

114. Cohen, *The Substance Abuse Problems*, p. 120.

115. Ibid., p. 120–121.

116. Imlah, *Addiction*, p. 66.

117. Cohen, *The Substance Abuse Problems*, pp. 127–128.

118. National Institute on Drug Abuse, *Epidemiologic Trends in Drug Abuse: Advance Report* (Washington, DC: Community Epidemiology Work Group), June 5, 1995.

119. CESAR FAX, Vol. 4, No. 24, June 19, 1995.

120. Imlah, *Addiction*, p. 40.

121. Erich Goode, *Drugs in American Society* (New York: Alfred A. Knopf, 1972), p. 161.

122. Jerome J. Platt and Christina Labate, *Heroin Addiction* (New York: John Wiley and Sons, 1976), p. 48.

123. Barry J. Rosenbaum, "Heroin: Influence of Method of Use," *New England Journal of Medicine*, Vol. 285 (1971), pp. 299–300.

124. Imlah, *Addiction*, p. 45.

125. Platt and Labate, *Heroin Addiction*, pp. 51–52.

126. Tam Stewart, *The Heroin Users* (London: Pandora Press, 1987), p. 29.

127. Imlah, *Addiction*, p. 45.

128. Krivanek, *Heroin*, pp. 68–70.

129. Platt and Labate, *Heroin Addiction*, p. 91.

130. Anna J. Eisenman, H. F. Fraser, and Janus W. Brooks, "Urinary Excretion and Plasma Levels of 17-Hydroxycorticosteroids During a Cycle of Addiction to Morphine," *Journal of Pharmacology and Experimental Therapeutics*, Vol. 132 (1961), pp. 226–231.

131. Joseph D. Sapira, "The Narcotic Addict as a Medical Patient," *American Journal of Medicine*, Vol. 45 (1968), pp. 555–558.

132. E G. Hofmann, *A Handbook on Drug and Alcohol Abuse* (New York: Oxford, 1975).

133. M. M. Baden, "Pathology of the Addictive States," in Ralph W. Richter (Ed.), *Medical Aspects of Drug Abuse* (Hagerstown, MD: Harper and Row, 1975), pp. 189–211.

134. Sapira, "The Narcotic Addict."

135. Platt and Labate, *Heroin Addiction*, pp. 92–93.

136. Imlah, *Addictions*, p. 45.

137. Krivanek, *Heroin*, p. 83.

138. Imlah, *Addiction*, p. 95.

139. Goode, *Drugs in American Society*, p. 97.

140. Aldous Huxley, *The Doors of Perception and Heaven and Hell* (New York: Harper and Row, 1963), p. 34.

141. Imlah, *Addiction*, p. 95.

142. Ibid., p. 99.

143. Ibid., p. 102.

144. Goode, *Drugs in Modern Society*, p. 99.

145. Imlah, *Addiction*, p. 99.

146. Goode, *Drugs in American Society*, pp. 101–102.

147. Imlah, *Addiction*, p. 99.

148. Cohen, *The Substance Abuse Problems*, pp. 210–213.

149. Hofmann, *Handbook*, pp. 132–135.

150. Ibid., p. 135.

151. Cohen, *The Substance Abuse Problems*, p. 49.

152. Ibid., p. 51.

153. Ibid., p. 52.

154. W. L. Dewey et al., "Some Behavioral and Toxicological Effects of Amyl Nitrite," *Research Communications in Chemical Pathology and Pharmacology*, Vol. 5 (1973), p. 889.

155. Jan P. Vandenbroucke and Veronique P. A. M. Pardoel, "An Autopsy of Epidemiologic Methods: The Case of 'Poppers' in the Early Epidemic of the Acquired Immunodeficiency Syndrome (AIDS)," *American Journal of Epidemiology*, Vol. 129, No. 3 (March 1989), pp. 455–457.

156. "Trendy Chemical, AIDS Tie Feared," The *Miami Herald*, October 12, 1986, Sec. G, p. 14.

157. J. Joffe, "Influence of Drug Exposure of the Father on Perinatal Outcome," *Clinics in Perinatology*, Vol. 6 (1979), pp. 21–36.

158. White, *Drug Dependence*, pp. 227–232.

159. Ann Pytkowicz Streissguth, "Fetal Alcohol Syndrome: An Overview and Implications for Patient Management," in Estes and Heinemann, *Alcoholism*, pp. 195–206.

160. K L. Jones and D. W. Smith, "Recognition of the Fetal Alcohol Syndrome in Early Infancy," *Lancet*, Vol. 2 (1973), pp. 999–1001.

161. S. K. Clarren and D. W. Smith, "Fetal Alcohol Syndrome," *New England Journal of Medicine*, Vol. 298 (1978), pp. 1063–1067.

162. J. W. Hanson, A. P. Streissguth, and D. W. Smith, "The Effects of Moderate Alcohol Consumption During Pregnancy on Fetal Growth and Morphogenesis," *Journal of Pediatrics*, Vol. 92 (1978), pp. 457–460.

163. Streissguth, p. 196.

164. A. P. Streissguth, C. S. Herman, and D. W. Smith, "Intelligence, Behavior, and Dysmorphogenesis in the Fetal Alcohol Syndrome: A Report on 20 Patients," *Journal of Pediatrics*, Vol. 92 (1978), pp. 363–367.

165. Ruth E. Little, John M. Graham, and Herman H. Samson, "Fetal Alcohol Effects in Humans and Animals," in Barry Stimmel (Ed.), *The Effects of Maternal Alcohol and Drug Abuse on the Newborn* (New York: Haworth Press, 1982), pp. 103–125.

166. White, *Drug Dependence*, p. 230.

167. Mary Jeanne Kreek, "Opiod Disposition and Effects During Chronic Exposure in the Perinatal Period in Man," in Stimmel, *Effects of Maternal Alcohol and Drug Abuse*, pp. 21–53.

168. White, *Drug Dependence*, p. 231.

169. Little et al., "Fetal Alcohol Effects," p. 112.

170. White, *Drug Dependence*, p. 231.

171. Besharov, "Children of Crack," p. 7.

172. White, *Drug Dependence*, pp. 229–232.

PART TWO

Intervention, Prevention, and Public Policy

Part One of this book covered many topics: definition of *chemical abuse* and *dependency;* physiological, behavioral, psychological, social, and cultural aspects of chemical abuse and dependency; and the myriad etiological theories that have been offered to explain alcohol and drug problems. It also introduced the reader to the scope of substance abuse problems and to the processes and consequences of addiction. These chapters provide the foundation necessary to move on to Part Two, which presents the systems for preventing and treating chemical abuse and dependency.

Chapter 5 discusses the first steps in assisting individuals who are chemical abusers or who are chemically dependent. These steps are screening, diagnosis, assessment, and referral to appropriate resources. Some commonly used screening instruments and diagnostic tools are described and issues in their use and interpretation are discussed. Helping clients address denial of substance abuse problems and resistance to treatment are included, as are matters of confidentiality, the referral process, and the motivation to change.

Chapter 6 presents the components of the chemical dependency treatment system, including detoxification, intensive treatment, residential services, outpatient services, pharmacotherapy, education, aftercare, and maintenance. Self-help resources for those with alcohol and other drug problems are also discussed. Research on the effectiveness of each of the treatment components and on other aspects of effectiveness such as length of treatment and client-treatment matching is also presented. In addition to financing chemical dependency treatment, some of the most contemporary issues in treatment will be considered, such as the use of brief interventions and what managed care is doing about substance abuse and dependency treatment.

The reader begins to look at the system for regulating or controlling alcohol and drugs in Chapter 7, focusing on prevention. Primary, secondary, and tertiary models of prevention are discussed, but the chapter is organized around five major categories of prevention efforts: public information and education, service measures, technologic measures, legislative and regulatory measures, and economic measures. The effectiveness of prevention efforts, including the popular D.A.R.E. programs, is also examined. The focus of Chapter 8 is on societal regulation of alcohol and drugs, including sociocultural influences on public policies and law enforcement. The war on drugs and issues regarding legalization and decriminalization are also covered.

5

Screening, Diagnosis, Assessment, and Referral

This chapter presents a systems or biopsychosocial approach to determining whether an individual has a chemical abuse or dependency problem. The first steps in this approach are screening and diagnosis. The chapter also considers the extension of this process, called assessment, to examine the client's needs further. A thorough assessment is needed to develop a long-range treatment plan and to make referrals to appropriate resources.

Some individuals with alcohol or drug problems experience medical emergencies (intentional overdoses, accidental alcohol or drug poisoning, pancreatitis, delirium tremens, seizures, etc.) that require immediate attention. Social workers, psychologists, and other human service professionals should know what these emergencies are, but these problems can be diagnosed and treated only by qualified medical personnel. The focus of this chapter is primarily on the work of helping professionals once such medical crises have been resolved or when a client is seen by a helping professional earlier in the addiction process, before these medical complications arise.

We begin by discussing *screening,* which may be defined as the use of brief instruments or other tools to determine the likelihood that an individ-

ual has a chemical abuse or chemical dependency problem. In practice, much screening is informal and is not done with structured or standardized instruments. For example, after reviewing a parolee's "rap sheet" containing repeated alcohol- or drug-related arrests, a parole officer may feel that is all the screening necessary for referring the client to a chemical dependency treatment program or insisting on participation in a self-help group as a condition of parole.

Diagnosis is the confirmation of a chemical abuse or dependency problem, often using more than one source of information. For example, results of a screening instrument may be combined with a client interview or social history and perhaps an interview with others (referred to as collaterals) who know the client well. A medical examination including laboratory tests is often a part of this diagnostic process. Previous medical, psychological or psychiatric, criminal, school, or other records and consultation with other professionals might also be used.

Assessment is sometimes used synonymously with the term *diagnosis,* but we use it to mean an in-depth consideration of the client's chemical abuse or dependency problems as they have affected his or her psychological well-being, social circumstances (including interpersonal relationships), financial status, employment or education, health, and so forth. This process also includes consideration of the individual's strengths and resources that may be assets in treatment and recovery. Going beyond a confirmatory diagnosis, this type of multidimensional or biopsychosocial assessment provides the basis for treatment planning.[1]

The cornerstones of good screening, diagnosis, and assessment in the chemical dependency field are knowledge of alcohol and drug abuse and dependency and interviewing skills, including the ability to establish some level of rapport with clients in a relatively brief period. Denial is a pervasive issue in work with clients who have alcohol and drug problems, and helping professionals must frequently work with clients and their significant others to reduce defensiveness and resistance. The assurance of confidentiality in treatment and research settings can increase the validity of clients' reports of their alcohol and drug problem,[2] but the extent to which confidentiality can be guaranteed varies and should be represented fairly to the client. Denial and confidentiality also warrant attention in this chapter.

In addition to chemical dependency treatment, clients often need the services of other agencies. The final section of this chapter discusses the process of referring clients to other services, including self-help groups.

Screening

Screening for alcohol and drug problems is done in many types of settings in addition to chemical dependency programs, such as in health care facilities, mental health programs, and correctional facilities.

Although much work is being done, there is still no easily used biological testing procedure that can accurately identify people with chemical abuse or dependence problems or those who have the potential to develop these problems.[3] Instead, human service professionals generally inquire about family history of alcohol and drug problems, the quantity and frequency of the individual's own drinking or drug use, and alcohol- and drug-related problems. To do this, they often use one of a number of the paper-and-pencil or verbally administered tests specifically designed to screen for chemical abuse or dependence problems. Some of the many screening instruments available are the CAGE (defined shortly), the Michigan Alcoholism Screening Test (MAST), the Alcohol Use Disorders Identification Test (AUDIT), the Drug Abuse Screening Test (DAST), and the Substance Abuse Subtle Screening Inventory (SASSI). Before these instruments are administered, there is usually some interaction between the client and the treatment professional in order to explain the purpose of the screening, to put the client at ease, to encourage honest responses, and to answer questions the client might have about the procedure.

The CAGE, developed by Ewing and Rouse, is the briefest of the instruments discussed here.[4] It consists of four questions asked directly to the patient:

1. Have you ever felt you should **C**ut down on your drinking?
2. Have people **A**nnoyed you by criticizing your drinking?
3. Have you ever felt bad or **G**uilty about your drinking?
4. Have you ever had a drink first thing in the morning to steady your nerves or get rid of a hangover (**E**ye opener)?

The letters in bold typeface in each question make up the acronym that serves as the instrument's name; the letters also serve as a mnemonic device so that the instrument is easily committed to memory. A positive response to one or more of the questions may indicate the need to explore problems the patient or client may be experiencing with the use of alcohol. Two or more positive responses generally indicate a positive test.[5] This tool has been used by physicians and others who have a need to screen patients or clients quickly for possible alcohol problems. It is easily used in many types of clinical settings. The CAGE is generally reported to be quite effective in correctly identifying adults with alcohol problems.[6]

Since the CAGE inquires only about alcohol, Sciacca has suggested also asking about drugs in each of the four questions.[7] Sciacca has worked extensively with clients dually diagnosed with both substance abuse and mental illness. Like others in the field, she recommends further screening in cases where individuals answer no to all questions yet their behavior or other information indicates that these answers may not be accurate.

A second widely used screening instrument for alcohol problems is the Michigan Alcoholism Screening Test, often referred to as the MAST.[8] It has been shown to have good validity and reliability.[9] The 25-item MAST and its scoring instructions are found in Figure 5.1. The instrument is usually self-administered (i.e., the client is asked to read and complete it). As with most screening instruments, clarifying clients' responses can be helpful. For example, drinkers married to teetotalers may respond positively to question 3 about relatives' worries or complaints even if their drinking is not problematic, or an individual with ties to a religious group that prohibits drinking may respond positively to question 5 about guilt regardless of how much he or she drinks. In question 8, it is possible that an individual has attended an Alcoholics Anonymous meeting, perhaps with a friend who is a member, rather than because of his or her own drinking problem.

Two shorter versions of the MAST are also available. One, called the Short MAST or the SMAST, contains 13 questions.[10] The other is called the Brief MAST (B-MAST); it contains 10 questions.[11] The shorter versions are often used with slower readers. These instruments may also be tape recorded or read to the client or patient by the person administering the test. The MAST has been used as a screening tool in many settings such as in programs for those convicted of driving under the influence (DUI).

The Alcohol Use Disorders Identification Test (AUDIT) is a screening instrument developed by the World Health Organization (WHO) for use by primary health care providers.[12] The core instrument contains 10 items, 3 on the quantity and frequency of drinking, 3 on alcohol dependence, and 4 on alcohol-caused problems. It can be administered by a variety of helping professionals. The WHO developed a second tool, the Clinical Screening Instrument, for use when a patient may not be candid about alcohol use and related problems or when additional information is needed. The Clinical Screening Instrument, which must be conducted by health care professionals, contains 2 questions about traumatic injuries, 5 items pertaining to a clinical health examination, and a blood test called the serum GGT. The AUDIT has been used in a variety of countries and is available in English, Spanish, Slavic, Norwegian, Swahili, and Romanian. Since drinking preferences and customs vary among cultures, these factors must be taken into account when using the first 3 questions on the main instrument concerning quantity and frequency of drinking. There are separate scoring instructions for the main instrument and the Clinical Screening Instrument. A recent study indicates that the core instrument is more useful in detecting harmful drinking (alcohol abuse) and the Clinical Instrument is more useful in detecting alcohol dependence.[13]

Some instruments assess for drug problems in addition to alcohol problems, such as the Drug Abuse Screening Test (DAST).[14] The DAST was patterned after the MAST. Like the CAGE, the MAST, and the AUDIT main instrument, it relies on the client's or patient's self-report. A 28- and a 20-item version of the DAST reportedly have high internal reliability.

Newer on the scene is the Index of Drug Involvement (IDI) developed by Hudson to "measure the severity of problems with drug abuse."[15] This 25-item scale is found in Figure 5.2. Hudson reports that the IDI takes five or fewer minutes to administer and can be read by those with a fourth-grade or higher reading level. Scores range from 0 to 100, with higher scores indicating more problematic use. Using a clinical cutting score of 30, Hudson reports reliability at .90 or greater and validity at .60 or greater. Items 5, 20, and 23 are

FIGURE 5.1   Michigan Alcoholism Screening Test (MAST)

Points	Question	Yes	No
	0. Do you enjoy a drink now and then?	___	___
(2)	*1. Do you feel you are a normal drinker? (By normal we mean you drink less than or as much as most other people.)	___	___
(2)	2. Have you ever awakened the morning after some drinking the night before and found that you could not remember a part of the evening?	___	___
(1)	3. Does your wife, husband, a parent, or other near relative ever worry or complain about your drinking?	___	___
(2)	*4. Can you stop drinking without a struggle after one or two drinks?	___	___
(1)	5. Do you ever feel guilty about your drinking?	___	___
(2)	*6. Do friends or relatives think you are a normal drinker?	___	___
(2)	*7. Are you able to stop drinking when you want to?	___	___
(5)	8. Have you ever attended a meeting of Alcoholics Anonymous (AA)?	___	___
(1)	9. Have you gotten into physical fights when drinking?	___	___
(2)	10. Has your drinking ever created problems between you and your wife, husband, a parent, or other relative?	___	___
(2)	11. Has your wife, husband (or other family members) ever gone to anyone for help about your drinking?	___	___
(2)	12. Have your ever lost friends because of your drinking?	___	___
(2)	13. Have you ever gotten into trouble at work or school because of drinking?	___	___
(2)	14. Have you ever lost a job because of drinking?	___	___
(2)	15. Have you ever neglected your obligations, your family, or your work for two or more days in a row because you were drinking?	___	___
(1)	16. Do you drink before noon fairly often?	___	___
(2)	17. Have you ever been told you have liver trouble? Cirrhosis?	___	___
(2)	**18. After heavy drinking have you ever had delirium tremens (DT's) or severe shaking, or heard voices or seen things that really weren't there?	___	___
(5)	19. Have you ever gone to anyone for help about your drinking?	___	___
(5)	20. Have you ever been in a hospital because of drinking?	___	___
(2)	21. Have you ever been a patient in a psychiatric hospital or on a psychiatric ward of a general hospital where drinking was part of the problem that resulted in hospitalization?	___	___
(2)	22. Have you ever been seen at a psychiatric or mental health clinic or gone to any doctor, social worker, or clergyman for help with any emotional problem, where drinking was part of the problem?	___	___
(2)	***23. Have you ever been arrested for drunk driving, driving while intoxicated, or driving under the influence of alcoholic beverages? (IF YES, How many times? ___)	___	___
(2)	***24. Have you ever been arrested, or taken into custody, even for a few hours, because of other drunk behavior? (IF YES, How many times? ___)	___	___

Source: Reprinted with permission of Melvin L. Selzer, M.D., 6967 Paseo Laredo, La Jolla, CA 92037. See also Dan J. Lettieri, Jack E. Nelson, and Mollie A. Sayers (Eds.), *Alcoholism Treatment Assessment Research Instruments*, Treatment Handbook Series 2 (Rockville, MD: National Institute on Alcohol Abuse and Alcoholism, 1985).

Note: Programs using this scoring system find it very sensitive at the five point level and it tends to find more people alcoholic than anticipated. However, it is a screening test and should be sensitive at its lower levels.

Scoring System: In general, five points or more would place the subject in an "alcoholic" category. Four points would be suggestive of alcoholism, three points or fewer would indicate the subject was not alcoholic.

 *Alcoholic response is negative.

 **Five points for delirium tremens.

***Two points for each arrest.

reverse scored, and total scoring is easily done by applying a simple formula by hand or via computer software.

The Substance Abuse Subtle Screening Inventory (SASSI), another instrument completed by the client, is found in Figure 5.3.[16] The SASSI differs from many instruments available in the field because most of the true/false items on one side of the form do not inquire directly about alcohol or drug use. The reverse side of the SASSI form contains

FIGURE 5.2   Index of Drug Involvement (IDI)

Name: _____   Today's Date: _____

This questionnaire is designed to measure your use of drugs. It is not a test so there are no right or wrong answers. Answer each item as carefully and as accurately as you can by placing a number beside each one as follows.

1 = None of the time	5 = A good part of the time
2 = Very rarely	6 = Most of the time
3 = A little of the time	7 = All of the time
4 = Some of the time	

1. _____ When I do drugs with friends, I usually have more than they do.
2. _____ My family or friends tell me I take too many or too much drugs.
3. _____ I feel that I use too much drugs.
4. _____ After I've begun using drugs, it is difficult for me to stop.
5. _____ I do not use drugs.
6. _____ I feel guilty about my use of drugs.
7. _____ When I do drugs, I get into fights.
8. _____ My drug use causes problems with my family or friends.
9. _____ My drug use causes problems with my work.
10. _____ After I have been using drugs, I cannot remember things that happened.
11. _____ After I have been using drugs, I get the shakes.
12. _____ My friends think I have a drug problem.
13. _____ I do drugs to calm my nerves or make me feel better.
14. _____ I do drugs when I am alone.
15. _____ I do drugs so much that I pass out.
16. _____ My drug use interferes with obligations to my family or friends.
17. _____ I do drugs when things are not going well for me.
18. _____ I can stop using drugs whenever I want to.
19. _____ I do drugs before noon.
20. _____ My friends think my level of drug use is acceptable.
21. _____ I get mean and angry when I do drugs.
22. _____ My friends avoid me when I am using drugs.
23. _____ I avoid excessive use of drugs.
24. _____ My personal life gets very troublesome when I do drugs.
25. _____ I use drugs several times a week.

Source: Copyright © 1994, Walter W. Hudson. Reprinted by permission.
Illegal to Photocopy or Otherwise Reproduce.

FIGURE 5.3 Substance Abuse Subtle Screening Inventory (SASSI)

SASSI-3 Adult Form

If a statement tends to be TRUE for you, fill in the square in the column headed T; that is, ■ ☐ Fill in this way ■
If a statement tends to be FALSE for you, fill in the square in the column headed F; that is, ☐ ■ Not like this ☑
Please try to answer all questions.

T F

1. ☐ ☐ Most people would lie to get what they want.
2. ☐ ☐ Most people make some mistakes in their life.
3. ☐ ☐ I usually "go along" and do what others are doing.
4. ☐ ☐ I have never been in trouble with the police.
5. ☐ ☐ I was always well behaved in school.*
6. ☐ ☐ My troubles are not my fault.*
7. ☐ ☐ I have not lived the way I should.
8. ☐ ☐ I can be friendly with people who do many wrong things.
9. ☐ ☐ I do not like to sit and daydream.*
10. ☐ ☐ No one has ever criticized or punished me.
11. ☐ ☐ Sometimes I have a hard time sitting still.
12. ☐ ☐ People would be better off if they took my advice.
13. ☐ ☐ At times I feel worn out for no special reason.*
14. ☐ ☐ I think I would enjoy moving to an area I've never been before.
15. ☐ ☐ It is better not to talk about personal problems.
16. ☐ ☐ I have had days, weeks or months when I couldn't get much done because I just wasn't up to it.
17. ☐ ☐ I am very respectful of authority.
18. ☐ ☐ I like to obey the law.*
19. ☐ ☐ I have been tempted to leave home.*
20. ☐ ☐ I often feel that strangers look at me with disapproval.
21. ☐ ☐ Other people would fall apart if they had to deal with what I handle.
22. ☐ ☐ I have avoided people I did not wish to speak to.
23. ☐ ☐ Some crooks are so clever that I hope they get away with what they have done.
24. ☐ ☐ My school teachers had some problems with me.*
25. ☐ ☐ I have never done anything dangerous just for fun.
26. ☐ ☐ I need to have something to do so I don't get bored.
27. ☐ ☐ I have sometimes drunk too much.*
28. ☐ ☐ Much of my life is uninteresting.*
29. ☐ ☐ Sometimes I wish I could control myself better.*
30. ☐ ☐ I believe that people sometimes get confused.
31. ☐ ☐ Sometimes I am no good for anything at all.*
32. ☐ ☐ I break more laws than many people.*
33. ☐ ☐ If some friends and I were in trouble together, I would rather take the whole blame than tell on them.
34. ☐ ☐ Crying does not help anything.

35. ☐ ☐ I think there is something wrong with my memory.*
36. ☐ ☐ I have sometimes been tempted to hit people.*
37. ☐ ☐ My most important successes are not a direct result of my effort.
38. ☐ ☐ I always feel sure of myself.
39. ☐ ☐ I have never broken a major law.*
40. ☐ ☐ There have been times when I have done things I couldn't remember later.
41. ☐ ☐ I think carefully about all my actions.*
42. ☐ ☐ I have never used alcohol or "pot" too much or too often.
43. ☐ ☐ Nearly everyone enjoys being picked on and made fun of.
44. ☐ ☐ I know who is to blame for most of my troubles.
45. ☐ ☐ I frequently make lists of things to do.
46. ☐ ☐ I guess I know some pretty undesirable types.*
47. ☐ ☐ Most people will laugh at a joke at times.
48. ☐ ☐ I have rarely been punished.*
49. ☐ ☐ I smoke cigarettes regularly.
50. ☐ ☐ At times I have been so full of energy that I felt I didn't need sleep for days at a time.
51. ☐ ☐ I have sometimes sat about when I should have been working.*
52. ☐ ☐ I am often resentful.
53. ☐ ☐ I take all my responsibilities seriously.*
54. ☐ ☐ I have neglected obligations to family or work because of drinking or using drugs.
55. ☐ ☐ I have had a drink first thing in the morning to steady my nerves or get rid of a hangover.
56. ☐ ☐ While I was a teenager, I began drinking or using other drugs regularly.
57. ☐ ☐ My father was a heavy drinker or drug user.
58. ☐ ☐ When I drink or use drugs I tend to get into trouble.
59. ☐ ☐ My drinking or other drug use causes problems between me and my family.
60. ☐ ☐ I do most of my drinking or drug using away from home.
61. ☐ ☐ At least once a week I use some non-prescription antacid and/or diarrhea medicine.
62. ☐ ☐ I have never felt sad over anything.
63. ☐ ☐ I am rarely at a loss for words.*
64. ☐ ☐ I am usually happy.
65. ☐ ☐ I am a restless person.
66. ☐ ☐ I like doing things on the spur of the moment.
67. ☐ ☐ I am a binge drinker/drug user.

Name _____ Date _____ Sex _____ Age _____

Source: The SASSI Institute. Copyright © June 1997 by Glenn Miller.

Note: It is illegal to reproduce this form.

*These items are taken from the Psychological Screening Inventory. Copyright © 1968 by Richard I. Lanyon, Ph.D., and are used here by permission.

74

another set of questions (formerly called the Risk Prediction Scales)[17] that do inquire directly about alcohol and other drug abuse. The SASSI therefore contains both face-valid items and subtle items that are empirically derived. Administration of the subtle true/false items before the more obvious alcohol- and drug-related questions may help minimize client defensiveness. Since the denial or defensiveness common among many persons with chemical dependency problems may result in failure to provide accurate information on face-valid, self-report measures, there has been interest in less obtrusive measures of substance abuse and dependency such as the SASSI.

The SASSI includes a set of decision rules to determine if the respondent fits the profile of a chemically dependent individual. There are also guidelines that can help identify some substance abusers who are not dependent. Separate profiles are used to score results for men and women. In addition to its basic function as a substance abuse and dependence screening instrument, the SASSI may provide other useful clinical information. Clinical experience indicates that elevations on specific scales that comprise the SASSI reflect such things as defensiveness, willingness to acknowledge problematic behavior, depressed affect, focus on others, and relative likelihood of legal problems. There is a version of the SASSI for use with adolescents. The SASSI is available as a paper-and-pencil test and on computer disk.

The screening instruments discussed thus far are generally reported to have good validity and reliability by their authors, and for most of them, other researchers have also provided evidence of their utility. Other factors to recommend them are that they are easy to administer and they take from about 1 to 15 minutes to complete (depending on the instrument). Except for the AUDIT's Clinical Screening Instrument, they can be administered and scored by most human service professionals who need relatively minimal special training in their use.

Another device included under the category of screening tools is the MacAndrew Alcoholism Scale.[18] It is a subscale of the well-known Minnesota Multiphasic Personality Inventory (MMPI), which is often used by psychologists to detect a wide range of mental disorders. It is unobtrusive and has been used for three decades. Special training and approval are required to interpret the MMPI.

We have presented information on just a few of the instruments that may be useful to human service professionals in screening for substance abuse and dependency. Additional discussion of these and other instruments used primarily with adults is found in Lettieri and associates' text[19] and from the National Institute on Alcohol Abuse and Alcoholism.[20] In doing screenings and assessments, treatment providers often use instruments to detect other problems the client may be experiencing, such as depression, suicidal ideation, or other psychiatric problems.

Can Alcoholics and Addicts Be Believed?

In our section on screening, we mentioned the terms *validity* and *reliability*.[21] These are basic concepts in research and measurement in the social sciences. An instrument is *reliable* if it produces the same results with the same person at different times and under different circumstances. For example, if the MAST or the SASSI were administered to a client today during a visit to an outpatient clinic, one would expect the same or very similar results if it were administered to the client next week at his or her home. If an instrument does not consistently produce the same results, it is not very reliable.

Validity refers to whether an instrument measures what one wants it to measure. In this case, human service professionals want to be sure they are using an instrument that will detect problems with alcohol or drugs, not some other concept such as bipolar disorder or antisocial personality disorder. Professionals may also be interested in these problems, but they clearly want to know which instruments should be used to screen for each of these problems.

An instrument can be reliable but not valid. For example, an instrument may consistently or reliably measure the same concept over and over, but it may not be the concept in which one is interested. To be valid, however, an instrument must be reliable. If an instrument fails to measure consistently the same concept, it is not valid, because one cannot be sure it is measuring what one wants it to measure.

Also of concern is that the instrument have sensitivity and specificity.[22] *Sensitivity* refers to the instrument's ability to identify correctly those with substance abuse problems (called true positives). Clinicians want to avoid instruments that are likely to classify an individual as a substance abuser when he or she does not have such a problem (false positives). The professional also tries to select instruments that have high *specificity.* They maximize the likelihood that people who do not have substance abuse problems will be correctly classified (true negatives), and they minimize the likelihood that people who have substance abuse problems will be misclassified as not having such a problem (false negatives).

Unfortunately, as sensitivity increases, specificity is likely to decrease and vice versa. One key to selecting appropriate instruments is in knowing the prevalence of the problem in the population. For example, sensitivity is greater when there is a greater likelihood of a problem occurring in a given population group. In a study using the Brief MAST to detect alcoholism in three groups (a general population sample, general medical patients, and people in inpatient alcoholism treatment), Chan and colleagues found that sensitivity was lowest for the general population sample, "probably because most of the B-MAST questions deal with severe alcohol problems, and they are not sufficiently sensitive to detect those who drank heavily but who had not yet developed these alcohol problems."[23] Similarly, Heck and Williams found evidence that the CAGE might not be as sensitive in identifying problem drinking among college students, especially women, as it generally is with adults.[24]

To improve sensitivity and specificity of instruments with various populations, changes may be required in cutoff scores or in how items are weighted, or wording changes may provide more valid responses.[25] Additional research is needed to identify appropriate modifications. It may also be that another instrument is better suited to the population of interest. Various studies have compared the utility of the commonly used screening instruments, and some are more easily administered or more accurate with various types of clients in particular types of setting than others.[26] In selecting an instrument, the answer is often not easy. Clinicians are advised to rely on the available research to guide them in their selection. In doing so, they must be mindful of the caveats discussed here, yet staff may be unaware of the psychometric properties of the instruments they routinely use.

Clinicians are concerned about selecting instruments with good psychometric properties, not only in screening and assessment but also in other situations such as measuring client's progress during and after treatment and in evaluating the effectiveness of chemical dependency treatment programs. Factors such as the client's ability to recall past behaviors or events can affect accurate reporting. Questions that are ambiguous or poorly worded also present a problem.

Additionally, professionals want to know if the instrument has been validated on the populations of interest to them. Many instruments have been validated on men. Recent work has been done to develop instruments that may be more sensitive to detecting alcohol problems in women. The TWEAK is one instrument that shows promising results with women.[27] It has largely been developed by using some items from other instruments, eliminating others, and making wording changes that better reflect the situation of women. For example, asking women whether they have had fistfights may not accurately reflect the drinking-related behavior they tend to exhibit. Also, rather than asking women how many drinks it takes to make them feel high, it seems to be more useful to ask how many drinks they can "hold." The TWEAK was developed specifically to screen for problem drinking during pregnancy, but it may also be useful with other groups of women.[28]

Another issue is whether the instrument has been tested with various ethnic groups. Language is a particular concern here. Terms commonly used by one ethnic group may have no meaning or a different meaning for other ethnic groups. Some efforts have been made to develop instruments that are sensitive to various ethnicities, but instruments that are valid across ethnic groups are particularly useful. Language can also be a problem when an instrument is used with individuals from different age cohorts, since words can take on different meanings over time. Some instruments are designed specifically for use with adolescents, others with adults. The types of questions asked differ depending on the client's age. For example, an adult may be asked about job and family responsibilities, whereas a child or adolescent may be asked about school.

Many of the instruments we have discussed so far rely on the client's self-report. Many of them are also face valid, because they clearly ask clients about their alcohol or drug use. When using a face-valid instrument, what confidence does one have that clients are telling the truth about their behavior? When asked about the amount of alcohol or drugs they consume or whether they have had an alcohol-related blackout or lost a job due to drug use, clients can easily lie, but are they likely to do this?

Based on research designed to determine the reliability and validity of clients' self-reports, many think that clinicians can have confidence in them,[29] and some also believe that direct questions about substance use "provide the logical basis for one to evaluate with the assessed person their alcohol and drug consumption and its consequences."[30] A number of studies have correlated clients' self-reports with information from other sources, such as collateral contacts and laboratory (medical) tests, and have found good agreement among them. Fuller agrees that the balance of evidence favors their usefulness.[31] He also notes that some studies raise serious enough questions that self-reports should be used in combination with other evidence to gain the most accurate picture of the client's problems and functioning. Skinner describes the situations or conditions that influence the validity of clients' self-reports.[32] These factors include whether the client is detoxified and psychologically stable at the time of the assessment, the rapport established by the interviewer with the interviewee, the clarity of the questions asked, whether the client knows that his or her responses will be corroborated with other sources of information (particularly laboratory tests[33]), and the degree of confidentiality that can be promised to the individual.

Hesselbrock and colleagues have also suggested that the "demand characteristics of the situation" affect the accuracy of client self-reports.[34] For example, if clients have little to lose from reporting problem behaviors accurately, they are likely to do so. In many situations in which alcohol- and drug-dependent clients are found, such as criminal justice or child welfare settings, this is not the case. A diagnosis of chemical abuse or dependency can have serious consequences for the client. In these cases, it may be particularly important for the clinician to utilize additional sources of information to obtain a complete picture of the individual's alcohol and drug use and any related problems.

There has been an interest in the use of less obtrusive (i.e., nonface-valid) instruments, such as the MacAndrew scale and the SASSI, in situations where demand characteristics might inhibit clients from giving accurate responses to face-valid questions. However, even when less obtrusive measures are used, ethical, professional conduct generally requires that clients be told the purpose of the screening or assessment in which they are participating.

Diagnosis

Once screening has been done, it is necessary to determine if there is sufficient evidence to confirm a diagnosis of chemical abuse or dependency. Ideally, diagnosis is accompanied by a multidimensional, biopsychosocial assessment, which includes not only an in-depth understanding of clients' alcohol- and drug-related problems but also their strengths, support systems, and other factors that may help promote recovery.

The history of attempts to reach agreement on the criteria needed to define and diagnose alcohol and drug problems has been recounted by various authors.[35] Within the last few decades, considerable progress has been made in helping clinicians and researchers grapple with these issues. An important step was the work of the Criteria Committee of the National Council on Alcoholism (NCA), now the National Council on Alcoholism and Drug Dependence (NCADD), which published "Criteria for the Diagnosis and Treatment of Alcoholism" in 1972.[36]

Today, the criteria of the American Psychiatric Association (APA) and the World Health Organization (WHO) are the most widely used diagnostic tools in the field, and both have been influenced by the work of Edwards and Gross.[37] In the last three decades, the APA has revised its criteria several times. The 1994 edition of the *Diagnostic and Statistical Manual of Mental Disorders (DSM-IV)* delineates the current APA criteria for diagnosing substance (alcohol and other drug) use disorders.[38] Substantial changes have been made in these criteria in recent years. For example, tolerance or withdrawal symptoms are no longer required for a diagnosis of dependence. In addition to alcohol and drug disorders, the *DSM-IV* provides a standard set of criteria that professionals, particularly in the United States, use to diagnose a wide range of mental problems. Figure 5.4 contains a portion of the *DSM-IV's* description of cocaine

---

FIGURE 5.4   Abbreviated Descriptions of Cocaine Dependence and Abuse

Cocaine Dependence

Cocaine has extremely potent euphoric effects, and individuals exposed to it can develop dependence after using cocaine for very short periods of time. An early sign of Cocaine Dependence is when the individual finds it increasingly difficult to resist using cocaine whenever it is available. Because of its short half-life, there is a need for frequent dosing to maintain a "high." Persons with Cocaine Dependence can spend extremely large amounts of money on the drug within a very short period of time. As a result, the person using the substance may become involved in theft, prostitution, or drug dealing or may request salary advances to obtain funds. Important responsibilities such as work or child care may be grossly neglected to obtain or use cocaine. Mental or physical complications of chronic use such as paranoid ideation, aggressive behavior, anxiety, depression, and weight loss are common. Regardless of the route of administration, tolerance occurs with repeated use. Withdrawal symptoms, particularly dysphoric mood, can be seen, but are usually transitory and associated with high-dose use.

Cocaine Abuse

The intensity and frequency of cocaine administration is less in Cocaine Abuse as compared with Dependence. Episodes of problematic use, neglect of responsibilities, and interpersonal conflict often occur around paydays or special occasions, resulting in a pattern of brief periods (hours to a few days) of high-dose use followed by much longer periods (weeks to months) of occasional, nonproblematic use or abstinence. Legal difficulties may result from possession or use of the drug. When the problems associated with use are accompanied by evidence of tolerance, withdrawal, or compulsive behavior related to obtaining and administering cocaine, a diagnosis of Cocaine Dependence rather than Cocaine Abuse should be considered.

Source: Reprinted with permission from the *Diagnostic and Statistical Manual of Mental Disorders, Fourth Edition,* pp. 222–223. Copyright 1994 American Psychiatric Association.

abuse and dependence. The *DSM-IV* diagnoses are often used by professionals to request third-party (insurance) payments for treating mental health problems, including substance abuse and dependence. Interview protocols are available to assist in applying the *DSM* diagnostic criteria. Also helpful is a study guide for the *DSM-IV.*[39]

The WHO has also been a leader in the development of diagnostic criteria for alcoholism since the early 1950s.[40] One of its most notable early consultants was E. M. Jellinek. Currently in use is the WHO's tenth edition of the *International Classification of Diseases (ICD-10).* Although the APA and the WHO have not achieved full consensus on their diagnostic criteria for alcohol disorders, there is hope that this might emerge.[41] Such a consensus would help to standardize definitions of alcohol problems for treatment and research purposes. A comparison of the *DSM-IV* criteria for alcohol dependence and alcohol abuse and the *ICD-10* criteria is found in Table 5.1.

A historical controversy in the field of alcoholism centers on whether identifying and treating the underlying causes of alcoholism (such as fear of latent homosexuality or unmet needs for oral gratification) would result in remission of alcohol abuse. This approach has not proven satisfactory for two reasons. First, science has yet to discover the exact etiologies of substance disorders, and second, even if the underlying causes were known, substance abuse often becomes a problem in its own right. Our discussion of diagnosis generally refers to substance abuse or dependence as a major or primary problem presented by the client, requiring specific treatment. The reader may have also encountered the term *secondary* diagnosis. In 1972, the Criteria Committee of the NCA wrote:

> Reactive, secondary, or symptomatic alcohol use should be separated from other forms of alcoholism. Alcohol as a psychoactive drug may be used for varying periods of time to mask or alleviate psychiatric symptoms. This may often mimic a prodromal [early] stage of alcoholism and is difficult to differentiate from it. If the other criteria of alcoholism are not present, this diagnosis must be given. A clear relationship between the psychi-

atric symptom or event must be present; the period of heavy alcohol use should clearly not antedate the precipitating situational event (for example, an object loss). The patient may require treatment as for alcoholism, in addition to treatment for the precipitating psychiatric event.[42]

It may even be that excessive alcohol or drug use that developed following a traumatic event, such as loss of a loved one, may remit without specialized substance abuse treatment once an adjustment is made to the new life circumstance. But this is different from the situation in which alcohol or drug use itself has become a problem for the individual. Take, for example, the case of an individual who blames his diagnosis of alcohol dependence on a divorce that occurred 10 years ago. Although it may be true that his drinking escalated at that time, the alcoholism itself has become a problem, requiring it to be addressed as such. Exploring the issues that caused the client to fixate on his divorce may also be helpful at some point, but this alone is unlikely to resolve his years of alcohol problems. Many practitioners believe that treatment must first focus on arresting the alcohol dependence.

Today, a substantial number of persons with mental disorders also have diagnoses of alcohol or drug disorders. Although their drinking or drug use may have been precipitated by the desire to relieve symptoms of mental disorders (hallucinations, anxiety, etc.), many of them require treatment for substance disorders as well as treatment for mental illness. In fact, the subject of dual or multiple diagnoses has become of such importance that we devote Chapter 13 to it.

Severe mental disorders include psychotic disorders such as schizophrenia and schizoaffective disorder as well as mood disorders such as bipolar disorder, major depression, and anxiety disorders. Other types of mental disorders that also commonly appear in conjunction with psychoactive substance use disorders include borderline, antisocial, dependent, and other personality disorders. In the case of a person who first experiences a severe mental disorder and later psychoactive substance use or dependence, the convention has been to call the mental disorder the *primary*

TABLE 5.1   Comparison of the Diagnostic Criteria for Alcohol Dependence and Alcohol Abuse or Harmful Use in Two Diagnostic Schemes: The *ICD-10*[a] and the *DSM-IV*[b]

ICD-10	DSM-IV
Comparison of Criteria for Alcohol Dependence	
Symptoms of Alcohol Dependence	
Essential: Drinking or a desire to drink; the subjective awareness of compulsion to use is most common during attempts to stop or control drinking.	A maladaptive pattern of alcohol use leading to clinically significant impairment or distress, as manifested by three or more of the following:
At least three of the following:	1. Tolerance defined as (a) a need for markedly increased amounts of alcohol to achieve intoxication or desired effect or (b) markedly diminished effect with continued use of the same amount of alcohol.
1. Evidence of tolerance to the effects of alcohol.	2. Withdrawal, as manifested by (a) the characteristic alcohol withdrawal syndrome or (b) alcohol or a closely related substance taken to relieve or avoid withdrawal symptoms.
2. A physiological withdrawal state (characteristic alcohol withdrawal syndrome or drinking to relieve or avoid withdrawal symptoms).	3. Drinking in larger amounts or over a longer period than intended.
3. Difficulties in controlling drinking behavior in terms of onset, termination, or levels of use.	4. Persistent desire to cut down or control drinking.
4. Progressive neglect of alternative pleasures or interests because of drinking, increased amount of time to obtain or to drink alcohol, or to recover from its effects.	5. A great deal of time spent obtaining alcohol, using alcohol, or recovering from its effects.
5. Persisting in drinking despite clear evidence of harmful consequences which may be physical, psychological, or cognitive.	6. Important social, occupational, or recreational activities given up or reduced because of drinking.
6. A strong desire or compulsion to drink.	7. Continued drinking despite knowledge of a persistent or recurring physical or psychological problem caused or exacerbated by alcohol use.
Also a consideration: a narrowing of the repertoire of drinking patterns (e.g., drinking in the same way, regardless of social constraints that determine appropriate drinking behavior).	
Duration Criteria for Alcohol Dependence	
At least three of the above criteria have been met during previous year.	Three or more symptoms have occurred at any time in the same 12 month period.
Specifiers for Alcohol Dependence	
None.	*With physiological dependence.* Evidence of tolerance or withdrawal (i.e., symptoms 1 or 2 above are present).
	Without physiological dependence. No evidence of tolerance or withdrawal (i.e., neither symptom 1 nor 2 is present).
Course Modifiers or Specifiers for Alcohol Dependence	
Currently abstinent.	Remission Specifiers
Currently abstinent, but in a protected environment.	(Do not apply if individual is on agonist therapy or in a controlled environment.)
Currently on clinically supervised maintenance or replacement regime.	*Early remission.*
Currently abstinent, but receiving aversive or blocking drugs (e.g., disulfiram).	1. *Early full remission.* No criteria for abuse or dependence met in last 1 to 12 months.
Currently drinking.	2. *Early partial remission.* Full criteria for dependence not met in last 1 to 12 months, but at least one criterion for abuse or dependence met, intermittently or continuously.

TABLE 5.1   *(Continued)*

ICD-10	DSM-IV
Course Modifiers or Specifiers for Alcohol Dependence *(continued)*	

ICD-10	DSM-IV
Continuous drinking.	*Sustained remission.*
Episodic drinking.	Twelve months of early remission have passed.
	1. *Sustained full remission.* No criterion for abuse or dependence met at any time in past 12 months or longer.
	2. *Sustained partial remission.* Full criteria for dependence not met in past 12 months or longer, but at least one criterion for abuse or dependence met.
	<u>Additional Specifiers</u>
	No criteria for alcohol dependence or abuse have been met for at least one month.
	On *agonist therapy.*
	In a *controlled environment.*

Comparison of Criteria for *ICD-10* Harmful Use of Alcohol and for *DSM-IV* Alcohol Abuse

Symptoms

Harmful Use of Alcohol	Alcohol Abuse
Clear evidence that a pattern of alcohol use was responsible for:	A maladaptive pattern of alcohol use leading to clinically significant impairment or distress, as manifested by one or more of the following:
1. Actual physical damage to the user. or 2. Actual mental damage to the user.	1. Recurrent drinking resulting in failure to fulfill major role obligations at work, school, or home (e.g., repeated absences or poor work performance). 2. Recurring drinking in situations in which it is physically hazardous (e.g., driving an automobile). 3. Recurrent alcohol-related legal problems (e.g., arrests for alcohol-related disorderly conduct). 4. Continued alcohol use despite persistent or recurrent social or interpersonal problems caused or exacerbated by the effects of alcohol (e.g., arguments, physical fights).

Duration Criteria for Harmful Use and Alcohol Abuse

None.	One or more symptoms have occurred at any time during the same 12-month period.

Exclusionary Criteria Related to Alcohol Dependence

Does not presently meet criteria for alcohol dependence, a psychotic disorder, or other drug- or alcohol-related disorder.	Never met criteria for alcohol dependence.

Source: Adapted from Bridget F. Grant and Leland H. Towle, "A Comparison of Diagnostic Criteria, DSM-III-R, Proposed DSM-IV, and Proposed ICD-10," *Alcohol Health and Research World,* Vol. 15, No. 4 (1991), pp. 284–292.

[a]World Health Organization, *The ICD-10 Classification of Mental and Behavioural Disorders, Clinical Descriptions and Diagnostic Guidelines* (Geneva: WHO, 1992).

[b]Reprinted with permission from the *Diagnostic and Statistical Manual of Mental Disorders, Fourth Edition.* Copyright 1994 American Psychiatric Association.

diagnosis and the substance abuse or dependence the *secondary* diagnosis. It is also quite possible for a substance disorder to predate a severe mental disorder, in which case the substance disorder would technically be called the primary diagnosis and the mental disorder, the secondary diagnosis. However, listing one diagnosis as primary and another as secondary does not necessarily mean that one is more serious than, more important than, or caused by the other. Professionals may define the illness they are currently treating as primary in order to meet the requirements of funding agencies. With the increase in the number of very young people abusing alcohol and drugs at an age before severe mental illnesses are usually expressed, such temporal distinctions can be arbitrary and misleading. Minkoff believes that when two disorders are of major concern, it may be more appropriate to classify both as primary.[43] There is a growing consensus in the field that when clients have two primary disorders, these problems should be treated in an integrated or simultaneous manner (see Chapter 13).

Assessment

The work of the WHO, the APA, and the NCADD has all been important in establishing better ways to diagnose alcohol and drug disorders, but these diagnostic tools do not provide all the information needed to plan for the client's treatment. Various assessment tools such as the Addiction Severity Index (ASI)[44] have been used to gain a better understanding of clients' overall functioning. The ASI is a structured interview accompanied by a numerical scoring system to indicate the severity of the patient's or client's problems in seven life areas: alcohol, drugs, vocational, family and social supports, medical, psychological or psychiatric, and legal. This tool, widely used in the clinical and research fields, can be administered by chemical dependency professionals and other human service professionals who have been trained in its use.

The ASI has a follow-up version that has also contributed to its use in treatment and research to measure client progress and to assess the effectiveness of treatment programs. Training materials and workshops are available to initiate staff in its use. Similar instruments for use with adolescents have also been developed.[45]

A tool recently designed to assess the severity of problems of adolescents and adults on multiple dimensions and to rank these problems is the Drug Use Screening Inventory-Revised (DUSI-R).[46] The 10 domains of the DUSI-R are frequency of and degree of involvement in drug and alcohol use (including drug preference), behavior patterns, health status, psychiatric disorder, social competence, family system, school performance/adjustment, work adjustment, peer relationships, and leisure/recreation. The DUSI-R contains 159 items requiring yes or no answers. Use of the tool progresses in three phases.

First, each domain is assessed using the basic assessment instrument. This instrument is written at a fifth-grade level and takes about 20 minutes to complete as a paper-and-pencil test or by computer, and it can be read to those with lower reading levels. Second, instruments are available to assess further those areas that appear to be problematic in order to provide a more comprehensive evaluation. Third, the information from stages one and two is used to develop an individualized treatment plan for the client.

Versions of the DUSI-R are available to provide information for the past week, past month, and past year. There are no scores that distinguish between types of treatment needed; instead, this is left to clinical judgment once the DUSI-R and other needed assessment information is compiled to give a full picture of the client's needs. Like the ASI, the instrument may be used to chart the client's progress, and client information can be aggregated for program evaluation studies. The developers of the DUSI-R report that it has good ability to classify adults and adolescents with *DSM* substance disorders and that it also has good ability to identify those with no psychiatric disorders.

The information obtained from screening, diagnosis, and assessment is used to determine the type of substance abuse treatment needed by the client. Chapter 6 describes the components of the chemical dependency treatment system, indicating the types of clients that are likely to benefit from each service. Since many alcoholics and addicts initially seek help for marital, family, job, legal, or health problems rather than for alcohol or drug problems, it is incumbent on helping professionals from all disciplines and in various treatment settings to be knowledgeable about screening, diagnosis, and assessment for chemical abuse and dependency problems. Similarly, tools such as the ASI are important to professionals in the chemical dependency field because they are concerned with the client's overall quality of life. Babor and colleagues believe that the jury is still out on whether the unidimensional approach (in which the treatment goal of abstinence is expected to result in improvement in other areas of the client's life) is as useful as the multidimensional approach (which suggests the client's problems in all areas be targeted for treatment since abstinence alone may not resolve them).[47] But the multidimensional or systems view of assessment and treatment seems to have taken precedence over the view that chemical dependency is a unitary phenomenon[48] and that treating alcohol or drug abuse is the only concern of chemical dependency professionals.

Taking a client's social history is particularly important because it is the type of assessment that exemplifies the systems or ecological perspective of this book.* Our discussion is intended to alert the new professional to some of the issues involved in doing a thorough assessment, focusing on the strengths as well as the problems of the client.[49] There are many formats for doing social histories, from checklists to structured interviews to more open-ended formats. The social history outline found in Figure 5.5 can be used to structure an as-

sessment or intake interview with an adult who admits a substance abuse or dependency problem. A skillful interviewer may also be able to use this tool to reduce defensiveness in clients who are less willing to discuss their alcohol or drug use and to begin to engage the client in the treatment process and increase motivation for change.[50] Although not exhaustive of all the avenues that can be explored with a client, the topics and questions suggested in the outline can help the interviewer capture information both about problems in the client's life and about the assets the client brings to the recovery process. The format of the social history is flexible and can be adjusted depending on the client and treatment setting. Sometimes a comprehensive intake interview or social history is done at an initial session. In other cases, the material is obtained over several sessions. Clients may initially give limited answers to questions but reveal more information over time as comfort and trust with the treatment professional increases. Assessment is not a single event; it takes place throughout the treatment process as clients' needs and circumstances change.

In conducting a social history, the interviewer determines which questions to ask at a given time and the order of the questions. In discussing each section of this social history, the interviewer might comment not only on the type of information that might be gathered but also on the reasons for gathering it. Often, the social history starts with information considered to be least threatening to the client. The sections on education and employment may be good starting points. Basic questions about how much education the client has had and whether the client has professional or vocational education are generally considered routine and are usually easily answered by clients without resistance.

Education

School adjustment may be a useful avenue to explore, especially for younger clients, as it may be particularly relevant to their current situations.

---

*I wish to thank William J. McCabe, who taught me about many of the elements in this social history.—D. M. D.

FIGURE 5.5　The Social History As It Relates to Drinking and Drug Use

I. **Education**
   A. How long did the client stay in school?
   B. How did the client like or feel about school?
   C. Did the client do well in school?
   D. What work is the client educated to do?
   E. Did the client have a history of alcohol and/ or other drug use or abuse during the school years?
   F. Did the client have friends and close relationships during the school years? If so, were these individuals alcohol or drug users/abusers?

II. **Employment**
   A. What is the client's current job or when did the client last work?
   B. What other jobs has the client held?
   C. How often has the client changed jobs?
   D. What is the client's favorite type of work?
   E. Has the client experienced job difficulties and what seems to be the causes of these problems?
   F. If the client is not working, is financial support being obtained from other sources?

III. **Military History (if applicable)**
   A. If not currently in the military, what type of discharge did the client receive?
   B. What was the client's last rank in the military?
   C. What were the client's patterns of socialization in the military?
   D. How long did the client remain in the military?
   E. If the client experienced problems in the military, were they related to alcohol, other drug use, or other factors?

IV. **Medical History**
   A. Does the client have current or past medical problems?
   B. Has the client ever been hospitalized for medical problems?
   C. Are past medical records available?
   D. Is the client currently taking medications or has the client taken medications in the past?
   E. Has the client abused prescription or nonprescription drugs?
   F. Are any of the client's medical problems directly related to or exacerbated by the use of alcohol or other drugs?

V. **Drinking and Drug Use History**
   A. What drugs does the client use and what does the client drink (including any technical products)?
   B. How often does the client consume alcohol or other drugs?
   C. How much alcohol and/or drugs does the client use?
   D. What is the client's drinking or drug use pattern (daily, weekend, periodic, etc.)?
   E. When did the client's drinking or drug use begin?
   F. Does the client give a "reason" for his or her drinking or drug use?
   G. Has the client experienced periods of abstinence?
   H. Has the client experienced blackouts or other indications of chemical abuse problems?
   I. Has the client experienced withdrawal symptoms from alcohol or other drugs?
   J. Has the client ever received treatment for a drinking or other drug problem?
   K. Are records of past treatment available?

VI. **Psychological or Psychiatric History**
   A. Does the client express feelings of being tense, lonely, anxious, depressed, etc.?
   B. Has the client ever contemplated, threatened, or attempted suicide?
   C. Has the client received any counseling or psychiatric treatment on an outpatient basis?
   D. Has the client ever had a psychiatric hospitalization?
   E. Are records of past treatment available to determine the exact nature of the problem?

VII. **Legal Involvement (if applicable)**
   A. Is the client currently on probation or parole or incarcerated?
   B. What types of charges or other legal problems has the client had?
   C. Are legal charges related to alcohol or other drug use?
   D. Does the client have any charges pending? If so, does the client believe that chemical dependency treatment will result in reduced legal penalties?
   E. If the client was arrested for DWI, what was his or her blood-alcohol level?

VIII. **Family History**
   A. What are the drinking and drug use habits of members of the client's family of origin (mother, father, grandparents, siblings, aunts, uncles, etc.)?
   B. Are there persons in the client's family of origin who have alcohol or other drug abuse problems?
   C. What were the attitudes toward drinking alcohol and the use of other drugs in the client's family of origin?
   D. How does the client describe his or her relationship with other family of origin members?
   E. Was there a history of psychological or physical (including sexual) abuse in the family?
   F. What is the client's current relationship with family members?

IX. **Relationship with Spouse, Children, and Other Significant Individuals**
   A. What is the client's current marital status and marital history?
   B. If the client has a spouse or other partner, what is the quality of the relationship?
   C. What are the drinking and drug-taking habits of the partner?
   D. If the client has children, what is his or her relationship with them?
   E. What are the drinking and drug-taking habits of the children?
   F. Are the spouse or children experiencing significant problems (psychological or physical abuse, financial problems, etc.)?
   G. What are the client's living arrangements?
   H. What is the extent of the client's other social relationships?

X. **Why Is the Client Seeking Help at This Time (e.g., Are there legal, medical, family, work, or other pressures to do so?)**

For older clients, the interviewer may ask whether he or she liked school, did well, and fit in at school or if school was a frustrating or unsatisfactory experience. Did the client initiate alcohol and/or other drug use or abuse in primary or secondary school or in college? Were his or her friends involved in alcohol and drug use in the same way? These questions may help establish the time frame and circumstances during which alcohol or drug use first became a problem. If the client has no high school diploma or no college or vocational education, and wishes to pursue further education, the chemical dependency professional may note the client's need for a referral to a general equivalency diploma (GED) program or other educational or vocational program. If the client did well in school and has substantial education, these may be noted as assets to recovery.

Employment

Questions about employment often follow logically after questions about education. Is the client currently employed and is the client's job secure or has it been threatened by substance abuse? During assessment interviews, individuals (such as those referred by an employee assistance program or by the correctional system) may deny employment problems related to alcohol or drug use. The pattern of employment—whether it is stable or erratic—is important to note. An erratic employment history is not necessarily the result of a substance abuse problem, but it may be an indication of it or other problems in the client's life. Discussion of employment may provide an opportunity for the assessment specialist to help clients identify how alcohol or drug abuse has negatively affected their work.

Another clue to problems may be the client's employment in a job that is well below his or her educational level. For example, an individual with a graduate degree may be working in a convenience store. Perhaps this work is what the individual prefers, perhaps this is the only work available, or perhaps personal problems such as

chemical dependency have interfered with other employment. Seeming incongruities in the individual's life such as this can be explored to help determine if substance abuse is a problem.

The client may have a job that is an obstacle to recovery. An obvious example is working as a bartender, where constant exposure to alcohol presents a problem for the client. Or perhaps the individual spends long periods on the road alone and is used to going to bars at night to relieve loneliness or boredom. Some clients frequently entertain business associates in settings where the use of alcohol or other drugs is common or expected. For some of these individuals, referrals to outpatient counseling to learn how to engage in alternative activities or to assertiveness training to learn how to refuse drinks or drugs may prove useful; for others, a key to attaining sobriety may include employment changes. A referral to a vocational rehabilitation agency, an employment counselor, or an employment agency may be appropriate. These referrals may be made at the time of the intake or assessment interview or at a later date, depending on the client's circumstances.

Some clients are immediately in need of a job. Professionals who work with skid-row or homeless clients generally know the street corners in town where a client can try to get a day labor job or they know employers who hire and pay individuals by the day. The professional's interest in the whole client, not just the client's substance abuse or dependency problem, is reflected in addressing employment concerns. Productive employment can be a useful tool in maintaining sobriety. For some clients, current employment may be identified as an asset. For example, an individual referred by an employee assistance program may have a job that he or she is anxious to keep. The interviewer may also ask questions about work hours or work habits that may be appropriate in determining whether the client is currently working to the detriment of other aspects of his or her life.

When clients are not working, it may be appropriate to inquire about their current means of support. They may be receiving public assistance or Social Security payments, or they may need a referral to apply for these benefits. Some clients may be getting help from family or friends, or they may be dealing drugs or engaging in other criminal activity to support themselves.

Military History

Questions about military service are often not asked unless the client is currently in the service or is in a Veterans Administration facility. However, these questions may be important, because many young adults are introduced to alcohol and other drugs while in the military. A problematic military history may have been the result of alcohol or drug abuse. Questions that might be asked to probe into this area involve the rank or ranks the client held in the military and the type of discharge the individual received. For example, being demoted in rank or receiving a medical, general, administrative, or dishonorable discharge may have been a consequence of alcohol or drug problems.

Medical History

An obvious reason that questions about medical problems are asked is to determine if they may be related to substance abuse. The client may not have made a connection between his or her medical problems (e.g., sores, gastritis, or neuropathy) and the use of alcohol or other drugs. Some medical problems are not caused by substance use or abuse, but alcohol and drug use may be contraindicated if the client has a particular condition (e.g., diabetes or epilepsy). Another reason to ask these questions is to determine if the client is receiving appropriate care for any current medical problems. If the client does not have personal resources to obtain medical attention, the interviewer may act as a referral source to community clinics, the local health department, or other services, although many communities lack the resources to provide anything but emergency medical care to these individuals.

Also important are any prescribed or over-the-counter medications the client is taking. Some clients are taking medication but do not understand what it is, only that the doctor told them to take it. Many are unaware of the adverse consequences that alcohol can have when combined with medications, such as the synergistic effect of alcohol and minor tranquilizers or of the contraindications of combining illicit drugs with prescribed medications. An important reason that health questions are asked in inpatient and residential programs is for staff to be prepared if the client experiences medical problems. For example, a history of epilepsy would be of concern in order for staff to be prepared for seizures, and it is important to know if a history of seizures is related to epilepsy or to alcohol or drug withdrawal. There is a growing body of literature on those who are dually diagnosed with chemical dependency problems and major physical disabilities (see Chapter 13). A release or consent form signed by the client is generally needed to obtain information about prior health history and medical treatment. It is typical to request this information if it would be useful in assisting the client in the chemical dependency treatment setting.

Legal History

Questions about the client's legal problems are also important. Many referrals to chemical dependency treatment programs are motivated by the legal system. A brush with the law may help the client confront a chemical dependency problem, or a client may seek treatment in the hope of obtaining a lighter or deferred sentence. Probation and parole officers and attorneys frequently refer clients to chemical dependency programs. Those convicted of a driving while intoxicated (DWI) or driving under the influence (DUI) offense may routinely be required by the court to submit to a screening or assessment to determine whether they have an alcohol or drug problem.

Often, a client admits to getting into legal difficulties as a result of using alcohol or drugs but denies an inability to control alcohol or other drug use. An important clue to a drinking problem in these cases may be blood-alcohol level (BAL) or blood-alcohol content (BAC). BAL or BAC are frequently measured by a breathalyzer or intoxilizer, typically following arrest on suspicion of DWI or DUI. A high level may be an indication of tolerance to alcohol or alcohol dependency. For example, a person with a 0.20 percent BAL may deny a problem, but 0.20 is twice what is commonly referred to as the "legal limit" of 0.10 percent in most states (in some states it is 0.08 percent). Most people would be unable to drive at a 0.20 level, yet those with a high tolerance may be able to do so.

Asking how much alcohol was consumed before the arrest may be another clue to the client's candidness in responding to questions. When an individual says she had two cocktails, but her BAL was 0.20, something is amiss. Two cocktails (the type typically served in a bar) would not produce such a high BAL. Sometimes a blood test is used to determine BAL or the presence of other drugs. In accidents where a person is seriously injured and is taken to the hospital, the use of a blood test is common. Previous DWI or DUI arrests or other history of alcohol- or drug-related arrests are also strong clues to consider. Most nonproblem drinkers do not make the mistake of getting a second DWI or DUI, because the consequences are just not worth it. The person with an unrecognized problem is far more likely to make this costly misjudgment.

Other common types of alcohol- and drug-related arrests are public intoxication (in locations where this offense is still a crime), disorderly conduct, and offenses related to the possession and sale of controlled substances. Transient substance abusers are frequently arrested for vagrancy. Arrests for family violence may also be indicative of chemical abuse. Of course, white-collar crime, such as embezzlement and forgery, may also be the result of a drug habit. With the advent of drug screening in the workplace, urinalysis, previously used most by the criminal justice system and in therapeutic communities, has become an increasingly common detection tool.

Clients may bring other legal problems to the attention of the interviewer, such as fears that past behavior may result in prosecution if discovered. Other legal matters worrying clients may be how to deal with an abusive partner or civil matters such as eviction notices and child custody or child support. Referrals to legal services may help clients put these problems in perspective so that they can avail themselves of treatment.

Drinking and Drug History

Naturally, the individual's drinking and drug history are paramount in conducting an assessment for chemical abuse or dependence. What psychoactive drugs has the client used in his or her life? What are the current drugs used, including frequency and amount of use? In some cases, this will also involve asking if the individual has ingested technical products that contain alcohol but are not meant for human consumption (e.g., rubbing alcohol, after-shave lotion, Sterno, etc.). What problems have been experienced as a direct result of the drug use or abuse, such as blackouts or violent behavior or withdrawal symptoms like tremors, seizures, hallucinations, or delirium tremens?

In obtaining information from or about clients who are not detoxified, it is especially helpful to know about previous withdrawal symptoms that the client has experienced. Such information may indicate the need for immediate referral to a detoxification program and can be very helpful to the medical staff assisting the client through withdrawal. Unfortunately, the client may not be in a position to provide this information, and others who know the information may not be available. This is frequently the case when a transient substance abuser is brought to a hospital emergency department or to a community detoxification center (see Chapter 6).

It is also important to know if the individual has made attempts to stop using alcohol or other drugs in the past and if there have been periods of abstinence (no alcohol or drug use, often referred to as "sober time" or being "clean"). These periods may also indicate that the individual is an alcohol or drug abuser, since others usually do not need to make special efforts at abstinence. Periods of abstinence should be considered an asset, and the chemical dependency counselor can discuss with the individual behaviors that may have contributed to the ability to remain alcohol or drug free (also see Chapter 6). Another question is whether the client has had previous treatment for alcohol or other drug problems. The individual's consent is generally requested to obtain treatment records or to talk with previous treatment providers in order to gain a better understanding of the client's progress and setbacks in treatment. Information of this nature may also be helpful in determining whether the client is best served in an inpatient, residential, or outpatient chemical dependency treatment program.

A possible avenue to explore is whether the individual perceives that his or her alcohol or drug problems were precipitated by particular events or circumstances. This may seem like an unusual question since no one really knows the causes of substance disorders. Asking the question is not done to give the client an opportunity to place blame on some internal or external factor. It is done to understand better the client's own perception of the roots of his or her substance abuse or dependence. This is a reflection of the principle of "starting where the client is." Many clients need help in understanding the dynamics of chemical abuse and dependence. Remember the client mentioned earlier who blamed his drinking on a divorce that occurred 10 years ago? He may be correct in identifying that drinking or other drug use escalated at that point, but he is probably incorrect if he thinks that reuniting with his spouse will solve the problem. The professional taking the social history may make note, however, that this will be an important point to which to return with the client. Additionally, knowing events that pre-

cede drinking or drug use may help to establish plans that can avert relapse (see Chapter 6 regarding relapse).

Psychological or Psychiatric History

Psychological or psychiatric history is yet another aspect of the diagnosis and assessment process. Has the client had past mental problems? Of particular concern are current psychological or psychiatric problems the client is experiencing, especially thoughts or plans related to suicide. Substance abusers, particularly those who use depressants such as alcohol, are at high risk for suicide. A referral for psychiatric evaluation or to an inpatient psychiatric unit may be an immediate necessity. Some clients with chemical dependency problems have serious mental disorders such as schizophrenia or they may have personality disorders or other mental problems (also see Chapter 13). If adequate information on mental history is not available and mental health problems are suspected, a psychological or psychiatric evaluation should be obtained. This information will help establish an accurate diagnosis and determine the range of services the client needs and who may best treat the client. A referral to a mental health program or, where available, a program specifically for those with dual diagnoses of chemical dependency and mental disorders may be the best alternative. Dually diagnosed individuals may also be directed to self-help or other support groups designed specifically for them.

Family History

The family history section of the assessment refers to the client's family of origin. These questions should probably be asked after some rapport has been established, because this subject can be particularly emotionally charged for the client. Since many alcoholics have alcoholic parents, it is useful to note whether the parents had entered recovery, and, if so, at what point in the client's life. Did other family members such as siblings, aunts, uncles, or grandparents have drinking or drug problems? Other useful information concerns family attitudes about alcohol and drug use. Was there an intolerant attitude toward any use of alcohol? Was drinking or drug use seen as acceptable, and how was abuse of these substances viewed? To what extent were family attitudes related to particular cultural, ethnic, or religious beliefs (also see Chapter 11)? Checking for a history of psychiatric problems and other problems of family members may also be helpful in understanding the client's situation.

Questions about the client's current relationship with members of his or her family of origin are also important. Is the client in contact with other family members or estranged from them? Are family members seen as potentially supportive of the client's recovery or might they present obstacles by reinforcing or encouraging the client's drug use? It may be appropriate to consider involving family members in the client's treatment. How much the client is asked to reveal about his or her family of origin will depend on the treatment setting and its purpose. In a brief detoxification program, medical history is more important than family history. In an intensive inpatient or extended outpatient treatment setting, the social history may delve further into family matters.

Not so many years ago, chemical dependency professionals were unlikely to ask clients questions about previous physical, sexual, or emotional abuse inflicted on them by family members or others. However, as professionals began hearing about this from clients, particularly women, it could not continue to be overlooked. These problems may surface during treatment and can present serious obstacles to recovery if not addressed appropriately. Physical, sexual, and psychological abuse may or may not be addressed in the initial assessment interview, depending on professional judgment. Unless the client offers this information, it may be premature to broach these problems because they are too distressing to confront so early in the treatment process. These problems may be better addressed once a relationship between client and professional has developed.

Current Family and Social Relationships

Other vital questions concern the client's relationship to any current or former spouse, other partners, or children. If the client's sexual orientation is not clear, the professional should take care not to make an erroneous assumption (also see Chapter 12 on gay men, lesbians, and bisexuals). How do the client's "significant others" perceive his or her drinking or drug use? Are they aware that the client has come for help? Are they similarly engaged in alcohol or drug use, or have they pushed the client to contact the treatment program? Including significant others in the treatment process can be helpful for all parties involved. The interviewer should explore whether significant others are likely to be supportive and inquire as to whether the client wishes to involve them in treatment. Clients are usually encouraged to do so. However, they may be reluctant, especially if there are concerns about retaliation from an abusive partner. Or the client may be threatened with an unwanted separation or divorce, and his or her partner may wish to sever all ties rather than participate in treatment. Occasionally, child abuse or neglect becomes apparent or is suspected, or threats on a partner's life are made and may have to be reported in keeping with state statute or the "duty to warn."

Stable living arrangements make the process of becoming alcohol and drug free easier, but some clients are living with other alcoholics or addicts or have no suitable home. Professionals working in the alcohol and drug rehabilitation fields have always worked with clients who are drifters or who have found themselves with no roof over their heads. Deinstitutionalization of persons with mental illness, unemployment, and lack of affordable housing in addition to alcohol and drug disorders have added to the ranks of people who need housing or residential treatment in order to make rehabilitation a viable option.

Questions about close friends, other social relationships, and involvement with organizations and associations also help to determine the extent of social supports the client has in the community. Religious affiliation or involvement is addressed to determine if it may be an avenue of support and spiritual strength, or if the client's church or religious group holds punitive attitudes toward alcohol and drug abusers that have contributed to the client's guilt or denial. Many clients need assistance in establishing friendships with sober or "clean" individuals and with pursuing activities not centered on alcohol and drug use.

Why the Individual Is Seeking Services

Finally, if it is not clear why the individual is seeking services at this particular time, the interviewer may want to inquire about this. Many clients have abused psychoactive drugs for a long time, but have not previously sought help. Is there some particular concern—threat of job loss, of divorce, of legal consequences, and so on—that has motivated the individual to seek help at this time? Or perhaps as the saying goes, the individual is just "sick and tired of being sick and tired."

Initial appointment or assessment interviews may be done free of charge even by private-for-profit programs as a way of encouraging people to consider some type of treatment or to encourage use of a particular program. For clients who want further services, the initial appointment may also involve obtaining information about insurance or other health care coverage to determine if the individual has a viable method of paying for treatment. If the client does not have the financial resources required by the program or needs services not offered by the program, professionalism generally requires that a referral to another resource be offered.

Denial, Resistance, and Motivation to Recovery

It is probably not possible to work in a substance abuse or dependency treatment program without hearing the terms *denial* and *resistance* during the course of the workday. Tarter and associates describe the ways in which the term *denial* has been used in the field of chemical dependency.

> Denial . . . has frequently been used to explain an alcoholic's failure to recognize the role of his feelings in instigating and sustaining drinking. Denial has also long been believed to reflect a conscious refusal by an alcoholic to recognize the effects of continued and excessive drinking on himself and his environment, thereby contributing to the alcoholic's resistance to initiating treatment, as well as ensuring poor treatment prognosis. Within the rubric of psychodynamic theory, denial has been conceptualized as an ego defense, and as such is considered to be indicative of an unconscious attempt by an alcoholic to protect himself from the threatening or aversive aspects of drinking behavior.[51]

As a largely unconscious process, denial differs from lying or an outright attempt at deceit.[52] Tarter and colleagues propose a biopsychological interpretation of denial, suggesting that some alcoholics have a "disturbed arousal regulation process" in which they fail "to perceive or label internal cues accurately."[53] This causes them to underestimate the severity of stress in their lives, thereby promoting denial.

Everyone employs defense mechanisms to cope with life's stresses and strains. For example, news of the death of a family member or that one has a serious illness may be initially met with denial.[54] In these cases, denial initially serves a protective function until the individual can begin to integrate the event and move along to the next stages of the grief process. Clearly, it is necessary to utilize some level of defenses in order to maintain healthy psychological functioning, but when one is unable to move past denial, well-being can become impaired. This is frequently the case with the individual who has a substance abuse or dependence problem. As Weinberg puts it:

> Denial is a way the human mind often deals with a situation involving incompatible perceptions, thoughts, or behaviors. In the case of drinking problems, the two elements are the powerful reinforcement derived from the drug and the unwanted side effects produced at the same time. The former is comprised of positive reinforcement (euphoria and energy) and/or negative reinforcement (temporary reduction of such unwanted feelings as tension, depression, self-hate, boredom, and sexual inadequacy).[55]

Another function of denial is to shield substance abusers from feelings of hopelessness.[56] Kinney notes that many patients are actually unaware that their problems are a result of substance abuse.[57]

Weinberg as well as Kinney and Leaton recommend helping clients reduce their denial gradually, since it is serving an important, protective function.[58] An important task of the treatment professional is to help clients recognize the relationship between their drug use and its negative consequences. To facilitate this process with cocaine abusers, Washton developed the Cocaine Abuse Assessment Profile (CAAP), which is described as being useful in assessment and in addressing denial.[59] The many questions about drug use and its consequences contained in the profile can help clients understand the magnitude of their substance abuse and the need for treatment.

Family members and other loved ones are also likely to engage in denial. It is equally painful for them to recognize that one of their members is chemically dependent. They may blame themselves for the client's problem or they may just be plain embarrassed that this could be happening to them. Consequently, substance abusers and their loved ones reinforce each other's denial. In a well-known pamphlet published by Al-Anon, Reverend Joseph L. Kellerman likened the process of denial to being on a merry-go-round, but he noted that "the alcoholic cannot keep the merry-go-round going unless the others [family, friends, employers, etc.] ride it with him and help him keep it going."[60] When a couple or more than one member of the family is chemically dependent, denial can be especially strong.

In addition to denial, clients and their significant others may use a variety of other defenses. These include rationalization (attempts to find reasons to explain or excuse the chemical use), projection (blaming or attacking others for problems), avoidance or evasion of discussions of chemical use, recollection of the positive effects and experiences associated with chemical use, minimization of chemical use and its effects, and repression of painful events and feelings.[61] But George says that "denial is a more prominent approach, because it blocks the need for the use of the other defense mechanisms entirely.[62] It is also important to remember that the individual's defensiveness may result in behaving in grandiose, aggressive, and belligerent ways when often their feelings, especially during periods of sobriety, are actually those of remorse, guilt, inferiority, and helplessness.

Just as clients vary in their expression of denial and other defenses, they also vary in the extent to which they enter treatment voluntarily. Individuals who call a 24-hour crisis line asking for help with a drug problem or those who walk into an outpatient alcoholism treatment program are generally considered voluntary referrals. Of course, external factors may have motivated them to request help—for example, fear that their marriage or their work is suffering. Less voluntary clients may be those who have been committed or ordered to treatment through civil procedures. In these cases, family members or others have appealed to the court because the individual has refused to seek help and is in serious danger due to alcohol or drug use. (These laws and procedures vary by state.) Other clients have been referred by their employer because their jobs are at stake or they may have been told by their probation officers to choose treatment or jail. These clients may recognize the problem and may participate willingly in treatment, or they may attend simply to remain employed or to fulfill the terms of their court order.

Resistance to treatment varies with the individual's willingness or ability to terminate substance use and desire to engage in the treatment process. It may take some time for treatment providers to develop rapport with clients and to help them work through their defenses, but clients who come to counseling sessions or stay in halfway houses or therapeutic communities and never engage in the treatment process may be told that there is nothing more that the treatment program can do for them at this time.

When individuals come to a treatment program to satisfy others but are not seeking long-term services, they may be hoping for the "one-session cure." This may sound flip, but the one-session cure happens every day in chemical dependency treatment. It works like this: Following the assessment interview, the individual thanks the interviewer, saying he now understands the problem, and is sure he can quit or control his alcohol or other drug use.

Chapter 6 will present some very brief interventions for use in settings such as primary physicians' offices that are designed to motivate problem drinkers to reduce their drinking. But many individuals are experiencing substance disorders that are more serious than these brief interventions are designed to address. Even so, unless the individual is in an immediate life-threatening situation, it is usually not possible for treatment providers to force or coerce someone into receiving services, even if his or her situation is severe. Some professionals object to the idea that a client would be forced or coerced at all. Treatment providers generally consider their services voluntary. They cannot make someone participate in treatment, even if he or she is under a civil court order or is required to attend by a parole or probation officer. However, the life-threatening nature of alcohol or drug dependency and the problems it poses for other individuals or the community may make some degree of coercion necessary, and there is ample evidence that this can be helpful.[63]

If the individual appears to have an alcohol or drug problem but resists treatment, the assessment specialist may encourage him or her to attend an educational program, a few individual or group counseling sessions, or some meetings of a self-help group before rejecting the notion of treatment entirely. If none of these alternatives is accepted, the professional may be supportive of the individual for his or her willingness to come in at all, being sure to leave the door open should he or she want to return later. Sometimes individuals are willing to make an agreement with the assessment specialist—if they are unable to stay clean or sober, use more than specified amounts of alcohol or drugs during a given time period, or encounter negative consequences of alcohol or drug use, they will concede that they cannot control their use, and they agree to recontact the assessment specialist for treatment. This approach sometimes works in helping individuals identify alcohol and drug problems, especially those who are certain that they are in control of the situation. Some chemical dependency specialists may use more confrontive or direct approaches, depending on the client and the situation, but there is a growing interest today in using less confrontational and more supportive approaches, such as that described in the illustration called The Motivation to Change.

Finally, it may be useful to remember that calling a client unmotivated or resistant to treatment may be unfair or unwarranted. There is a great deal experts do not know about substance abuse and dependency. For example, why is it that some alcoholics or addicts with dozens of admissions to detox are able to maintain sobriety or stay "clean" only after many unsuccessful attempts? The approaches available to treat substance abuse are relatively limited. Professionals rely heavily on psychologically or cognitively based approaches, despite increasing evidence of a genetic component to these problems. There are probably many types of alcoholism and drug addiction with complex etiologies. Clinicians do not yet have the tools to treat all individuals successfully, and this, rather than lack of motivation, may be at the heart of why so many do not recover.

The Motivation to Change

Most people wish to change something about themselves. They might want to study harder, carve out more time to spend with loved ones, lose weight, exercise more, reduce drinking, or stop smoking or using other drugs. Many won't make substantial changes in these areas. They may think about it or they may try, or perhaps some are only marginally aware of a problem. What makes people change is an important question in psychotherapeutic treatment. In the field of alcoholism and drug abuse, some people think that a serious crisis must occur before a person develops sufficient motivation to change. Others contend that professionals can intervene before a client "hits bottom" and help motivate him or her to change.

Stages of Change

Prochaska, DiClemente, and Norcross have devoted a great deal of study to the process of change—the type that comes on one's own and the type that takes place in the psychotherapeutic process—and they believe that a series of stages typifies the change process in both these types of situations, regardless of the behavior the individual wishes to change.[1] Much of their research has been done with smokers, but their work has also been applied to alcohol and drug abuse and other problems. They call their model *transtheoretical* because they believe it is compatible with the wide-range treatments used in the treatment fields. The five stages of change they have identified are:

1. *Precontemplation*, in "which there is no intention to change in the foreseeable future," and people may be "unaware or underaware of their problems" ~~You cause I cant~~
2. *Contemplation*, "in which people are aware that a problem exists and are seriously thinking about overcoming it but have not yet made a commitment to take action" (in this stage, the pros and cons of the problem and solution are weighed) ~~aware but no take action~~
3. *Preparation*, in which individuals intend "to take action in the next month"
4. *Action*, in which individuals have successfully modified their situation "from one day to six months"
5. *Maintenance*, in which people continue to change and prevent relapse.[2]

As Proschaska and colleagues note, change is generally not a linear progression through these five stages, but often involves reverting to an earlier stage before additional progress is made. Although some people may remain stuck at the first or second stage, the researchers note that individuals usually learn something at each point and generally do not regress completely. At any given time, most people are in the precontemplation stage. The techniques that will be successful with clients depend on the stage they are at; therefore, a treatment approach is unlikely to be successful unless it matches the client's stage of change. Generally, the more action the individual takes and the more quickly the client takes it, the more successful he or she will be.

Just how does one move from one stage to the next, and how can treatment providers facilitate this process? Table 1 indicates the processes that seem to facilitate movement between stages.

Two Faces of Confrontation

Miller and Rollnick have also addressed the process of change by developing their work on *motivational interviewing* with problem drinkers.

> Motivational interviewing is a particular way to help people recognize and do something about their present or potential problems. It is particularly useful with people who are reluctant to

(continued)

TABLE 1   Stages of Change in Which Particular Processes of Change Are Emphasized

Precontemplation	Contemplation	Preparation	Action	Maintenance

Consciousness Raising
Increasing information about self and problem: observations, confrontations, interpretations, bibliotherapy (reading materials)

Dramatic Relief
Experiencing and expressing feelings about one's problems and solutions: psychodrama, grieving losses, role playing

Environmental Reevaluation
Assessing how one's problem affects physical environment: empathy training, documentaries

Self-Reevaluation
Assessing how one feels and thinks about oneself with respect to a problem: value clarification, imagery, corrective emotional experience

Self-Liberation
Choosing and commitment to act or belief in ability to change: decision-making therapy, New Year's resolutions, logotherapy techniques, commitment enhancing techniques

Reinforcement Management
Rewarding one's self or being rewarded by others for making changes: contingency contracts, overt and covert reinforcement, self-reward

Helping Relationships
Being open and trusting about problems with someone who cares: therapeutic alliance, social support, self-help groups

Counterconditioning
Substituting alternatives for problem behaviors: relaxation, desensitization, assertion, positive self-statements

Stimulus Control
Avoiding or countering stimuli that elicit problem behaviors: restructuring one's environment (e.g., removing alcohol or fattening foods), avoiding high risk cues, fading techniques

Social Liberation
Increasing alternatives for nonproblem behaviors available in society: advocating for rights of repressed, empowering, policy interventions

Source: Adapted from James O. Prochaska, Carlo C. DiClemente, and John C. Norcross, "In Search of How People Change: Applications to Addictive Behaviors," *American Psychologist,* Vol. 47, No. 9 (1992), pp. 1108 and 1109.

change and ambivalent about changing. It is intended to help resolve ambivalence and to get a person moving along the path to change.[3]

These researchers stress the importance of the therapist's role in the treatment process, saying that therapists have widely varying success rates with clients. They advocate the use of nonpossessive warmth, genuineness, and particularly accurate empathy (reflective listening rather than identification with the client, as defined by the noted psychotherapist Carl Rogers[4]), and they see accurate empathy as much more productive than confrontation.

Miller and Rollnick examine possible reasons that treatment provides in the alcohol and other drug fields have espoused confrontation rather than accurate empathy. Some possibilities they offer are that myths developed that alcoholics and drug abusers are regarded as especially defensive and that confrontation was advocated by leading members of the field. They believe that both ideas are erroneous. Denial, they contend, isn't any more characteristic of alcoholics than of others, but it is a normative reaction in the face of strong confrontation, and neither Vernon Johnson, who developed the technique called *The Intervention* (see Chapter 10), nor the Minnesota Model or Alcoholics Anonymous (see Chapter 6) advocate heavy, aggressive confrontation. These approaches do, however, help people view their alcohol or drug problems more realistically.

Confrontational techniques have been used by some therapeutic communities (see Chapter 6 for further elaboration). Table 2 provides a comparison between confrontation and motivational interviewing. Confrontation also has more than one meaning; it can be a gentle and useful technique or it can be highly threatening and useless. In fact, few professional education programs teach aggressive or authoritarian confrontation. Instead, Miller and Rollnick outline the tasks of the therapist at each stage of change. They suggest eight methods that therapists can use to accomplish these tasks:

> Giving advice
> Removing barriers to change
> Providing choices
> Decreasing desirability of the behavior to be changed
> Practicing accurate empathy
> Providing feedback on how the client is doing
> Helping the client clarify goals
> Active helping rather than passivity (which may result in client failure)

Change and a Systems Approach

Drawing on the work regarding stages of change, particularly that of Prochaska and DiClemente[5] and Kanfer and Grimm,[6] Barber uses a social work approach to develop a holistic or systems model for the treatment of addictions. He believes that this model better captures the

> role of supply-side and demand-side drug prevention policies (mesosystem), or the (sub)cultural (exosystem) factors surrounding the use of certain drugs. [See Chapters 7 and 11, respectively, for a closer look at prevention and the role of culture in drug use.] If only because drug use is not randomly distributed within society, sociocultural factors, such as socioeconomic deprivation, norms, and anomie, must have explanatory and predictive utility for social work practice.[7]

Barber believes his model is also more useful because it focuses more on what can be done to initiate change among precontemplators.

This book will continue to discuss the relationship of many systems to alcohol and drug abuse and dependence, both in promoting and remedying these problems.   *(continued)*

TABLE 2   Contrasts between Confrontation of Denial and Motivational Interviewing

Confrontation-of-Denial Approach	*Motivational Interviewing Approach*
Heavy emphasis on acceptance of self as having a problem; acceptance of diagnosis seen as essential for change	De-emphasis on labels; acceptance of "alcoholism" or other labels seen as unnecessary for change to occur
Emphasis on personality pathology, which reduces personal choice, judgment, and control	Emphasis on personal choice and responsibility for deciding future behavior
Therapist presents perceived evidence of problems in an attempt to convince the client to accept the diagnosis	Therapist conducts objective evaluation, but focuses on eliciting the client's own concerns
Resistance is seen as "denial," a trait characteristic requiring confrontation	Resistance is seen as an interpersonal behavior pattern influenced by the therapist's behavior
Resistance is met with argumentation and correction	Resistance is met with reflection
Goals of treatment and strategies for change are prescribed for the client by the therapist; client is seen "in denial" and incapable of making sound decisions	Treatment goals and change strategies are negotiated between client and therapist, based on data and acceptability; client's involvement in and acceptance of goals are seen as vital

Source: William R. Miller and Stephen Rollnick, *Motivational Interviewing* (New York: Guilford Press, 1991), p. 53. Reprinted by permission.

NOTES

1. James O. Prochaska, Carlo C. DiClemente, and John C. Norcross, "In Search of How People Change: Applications to Addictive Behaviors," *American Psychologist*, Vol. 47, No. 9 (1992), pp. 1102–1114; James O. Prochaska and Carlo C. DiClemente, "Transtheoretical Therapy: Toward a More Integrative Model of Change," *Psychotherapy: Theory, Research, and Practice*, Vol. 19, No. 3 (1982), pp. 276–288.

2. Prochaska, DiClemente, and Norcross, "In Search of How People Change: Applications to Addictive Behaviors," quotes from pp. 1103–1104.

3. William R. Miller and Stephen Rollnick, *Motivational Interviewing* (New York: Guilford Press, 1991), p. 52.

4. Carl R. Rogers, "A Theory of Therapy, Personality, and Interpersonal Relationships as Developed in the Client-Centered Approach." In S. Koch (Ed.), *Psychology: The Study of a Science, Volume 3: Formulations of the Person and the Social Context* (New York: McGraw-Hill, 1959), pp. 184–256.

5. Prochaska and DiClemente, "Transtheoretical Therapy: Toward a More Integrative Model of Change."

6. F. H. Kanfer and L. G. Grimm, "Managing Clinical Change: A Process Model of Therapy," *Behavior Modification*, Vol. 4 (1980), pp. 419–444.

7. James G. Barber, *Social Work with Addictions* (London: Macmillan, 1995), quote from p. 44.

Confidentiality

Respect for client confidences is an important aspect of the codes of ethics of most human service professionals. In addition, professionals working with chemically dependent clients should be aware of the portion of the *Federal Register* called "Confidentiality of Alcohol and Drug Abuse Patient Records" (42 CFR, Part 2). It details information that chemical dependency professionals need to know to protect their clients and themselves. We describe some of its major points and discuss other issues relevant to confidentiality. These comments are no substitute for good legal counsel and are meant only to suggest some of the issues in the field.

Without an individual's permission, treatment providers usually may not reveal whether he or she is a patient or client in a chemical dependency treatment facility or any other information about the individual or his or her treatment. Providing information to those outside the treatment program or requesting information from other sources generally requires the client's written permission. A client's written authorization to release information must state the name of the agency, program, or individual requesting the information; the type of information that the client wishes to be provided; the purpose for which the information will be used; the agency, program, or individual from which the information is requested; the date the release is signed and the date on which the release expires; and the client's signature and a witness's signature as written proof of permission.

As noted earlier, staff may wish to obtain certain types of information, such as medical or psychological information, that may help them better serve the client. A consent or release-of-information form may also be required for the staff to communicate with the client's spouse or other loved ones, since it should not be assumed that these individuals know that the client is receiving treatment or that the client wants the staff to communicate with them. Professional conduct also suggests that information about the client not be shared or discussed with other staff in the facility unless they have a need to know this information to serve the client or in cases where a consultation is needed. Clients should also be informed of the extent to which staff may need to share information with each other.

Sometimes the client requests that the treatment program give information to others. For example, a client may want his employer to know that he is attending treatment, but he may not want any other details of his treatment revealed. In other cases, a client may be anxious for the treatment provider to describe to her probation officer how well she has progressed in treatment.

Exceptions to the right to confidentiality should be explained to the client. For example, under certain circumstances, treatment records of alcohol and drug abuse patients may be subject to subpoenas or court orders. Attempts may be made to subpoena records in cases where there are criminal charges against the client, in child custody cases, or under other circumstances. The issue of what to record in clients' charts or files is an important one. Additionally, many helping professionals do not enjoy privileged communication with their clients; that is, they can be ordered by the courts to provide information even about matters not contained in the client's case record. In situations where the information may be damaging, professionals may be given an opportunity to explain to the court why they think releasing information would not be appropriate, and the court makes a decision on the matter.

In a medical emergency, information necessary to save the client's life may be released. In cases where the client may be harmful to himself or herself, such as in the case of a client with a plan to commit suicide, the professional has a responsibility to seek protection for the client through an appropriate mental health referral. Sometimes this involves asking the local mental health crisis team or law-enforcement agency that handles these problems to intervene. If a client threatens serious harm to another, there may be a duty to warn this person, and the professional may be liable for injury sustained if no warning was issued. Child abuse and neglect must be reported according to state statutes. State laws may also require reporting of elder abuse and other crimes.

Legal issues arise more frequently than ever in the chemical dependency field, as they do in most fields, yet the appropriate responses are not always clear. Questions about what procedures to follow if law-enforcement officers call about a client or arrive at the door with an arrest warrant for a client or a subpoena for a file are not unusual. Good legal counsel is important—so is education about legal matters, since staff may be pressed to respond quickly.

Chemical dependency researchers may be afforded special confidentiality protections by obtaining a "certificate of confidentiality" from a federal agency such as the National Institute on Alcohol Abuse and Alcoholism or the National Institute on Drug Abuse. The certificate covers information obtained for research (not treatment) purposes only. It is particularly useful to obtain this protection when subjects are asked about substance use or illegal activity (e.g., illicit drug use or crimes committed) since it is designed to prevent researchers from having to release information in any type of court (administrative, civil, criminal, etc.). The research must be legitimate, but it need not be funded by the federal government or other external source to qualify for this certificate.

Referrals

Human service professionals of all types and in virtually all settings encounter individuals with substance use disorders and their loved ones. From the elementary school to the child welfare agency to the workplace to the nursing home, chemical dependency problems appear. Although all social workers, psychologists, and other human service professionals should be adept at recognizing these problems, many are not qualified to officially diagnose and treat them. When this is the case, a referral for further assessment or services is indicated. Some agencies—for example, family service agencies—may be able to provide these services in house; in other cases, knowing the local alcohol and drug abuse treatment agencies, their purposes, and their staff members can facilitate a referral.

For example, a child protective services worker suspects that a child neglect case is due to alcohol abuse, but he needs a confirmatory diagnosis to require that the mother seek treatment. Knowing the woman's limited financial resources, he refers her to a community mental health center with a substance abuse treatment component. An adult protective services worker contacts an inpatient chemical dependency treatment to assist with a client whose addiction to minor tranquilizers is preventing her from functioning independently. Or a parole officer makes sure a bed in a therapeutic community for offenders with chemical dependency problems will be available before the release date of a heroin addict on her caseload.

Chemical dependency professionals not only accept referrals but they also frequently make referrals to other agencies. As indicated in the discussion of assessment, chemically dependent clients often need additional services; vocational guidance, parent education, medical care, public assistance, and legal assistance are just a few. Keeping abreast of the services available in the community and developing cooperative working relationships with those who provide them are important professional responsibilities. Some agencies, such as the local offices of the state vocational rehabilitation agency, may have a particular counselor or counselors who work with substance abusers, or counselors may have general caseloads that include substance abusers as well as those with other disabilities. Informal knowledge of staff of other agencies who are most favorably disposed to working with chemically dependent clients can be a big help, and it does not take long to learn who these individuals are.

Making a referral on which the client follows through can involve more than writing a name and a phone number on a piece of paper. No one wants to act as an enabler (in the negative sense of the word) or increase a client's dependency, but calling ahead for a client, letting the client know specifically for whom to ask, and informing the client of the referral's purpose and what the referral source may or may not be able to do can be helpful. Clients with severe mental or physical disabilities may need extra support or assistance. This may mean providing transportation, accompanying them to the referral agency, or helping them complete application forms and compile necessary information. Clients who are desocialized or particularly unassertive may also benefit from someone to accompany them until they can learn to negotiate these situations themselves.

Additional obstacles such as lack of child care or language barriers may also need to be addressed before a client can take advantage of referrals. In making referrals for health care, it is particularly helpful to know if the client has traditional private health insurance; belongs to a health maintenance organization (HMO) or other managed care program; receives Medicaid or Medicare; has another type of coverage, such as CHAMPUS, the coverage for retired military personnel who are younger than age 65; or is entitled to services through the Veteran's Administration.

Many agencies have intake workers whose jobs it is to interview new referrals and see that they are directed to the appropriate staff and services. Appointments may be set in advance or walk-in appointments may be accepted; some agencies allot specific times each day or week for new referrals. Many professionals also refer clients to self-help groups like Alcoholics Anonymous and Narcotics Anonymous (see Chapter 6), but making these referrals is different. These groups are not staffed by professionals, and arrangements for clients generally cannot be made in advance. Anonymity of self-help group members is often stressed, so the client cannot be given the name of an individual to call. The professional can give the client a list of meeting times or encourage the client to call the group for information. Many self-help groups have telephone lines that are staffed 24 hours a day; others have 24-hour answering services. Some have limited hours when telephones are staffed, and they may use a recording to give callers information or allow them to leave messages at other times.

Giving clients a list of meetings is not necessarily the most effective way of making referrals to self-help groups. Many members did get to their first meetings solely on their own, but clients are frequently hesitant to go to a group about which they know very little. Professionals can make the process considerably easier. One way is to educate clients about what to expect in advance.

Facilitating a referral to a self-help group may be easiest for those who "wear two hats." This phrase refers to individuals who are both human service professionals and members of self-help groups. Initially, they might accompany clients to a meeting or two, introduce them to other members, and explain what "working" a self-help program is about. Professionals who are not members of these self-help groups may assist by accompanying the client to an "open" meeting where those who are not alcoholics or addicts are welcome. Perhaps a more useful method is for professionals to become acquainted with self-help group members who do "twelve-step work," which refers to the desire of AA (Alcoholics Anonymous) or NA (Narcotics Anonymous) members to take the message of the self-help program to others.

Many communities have a number of self-help groups. Even professionals who are also recovering alcoholics or drug abusers do not attend all the groups in their community. Some groups are only for men, some are only for women, some are for Spanish speakers, and some are for gays or lesbians. It is not possible for someone who wears two hats to fit in all the groups that his or her clients might need. Neither is it healthy for counselors to fill all these roles for clients. Professionals do not have time to fill this function for all their clients, and clients need to widen their circle of recovering individuals. It may be more effective for professionals to know a number of recovering individuals in the community who are available to assist newcomers to the many self-help groups that have emerged for chemically dependent individuals. It is also more difficult for clients to fail to follow through on a referral when arrangements have been made for someone to pick them up at their home or to greet them at the door of the meeting place. The client is also more likely to stay for the entire meeting and to return when members have made them feel welcome.

There are also self-help groups for loved ones (spouses, partners, children, and other family members and friends) such as Al-Anon and Naranon. Similar procedures can be used to make referrals to these groups. Self-help groups regard themselves as strictly voluntary programs, but many do allow the secretary of the group to sign slips of paper so that attendees can verify their presence at the meeting if this is required by the courts or by probation or parole officers.

Summary

This chapter discussed screening, diagnosis, assessment, and referral, which are the first steps in treating individuals with substance disorders. Many tools are available to assist professionals in determining whether an individual has an alcohol or drug problem. Clients and their loved ones may, however, be resistant to these processes, and helping them overcome denial is often a prerequisite to their accepting help. Engagement of clients during these early stages of treatment requires not only knowledge of substance abuse and dependence but also the skills and talents required to develop rapport and build relationships with clients.

There is much to be learned about an individual before a treatment plan can be developed. A thorough assessment includes knowledge about medical, psychiatric, family, legal, educational, and employment history, as well as other aspects of social functioning. The information obtained will help medical personnel make an immediate determination about whether the client needs medical detoxification and whether this should be done in a hospital, community detoxification center, or on an outpatient basis. It will also help other treatment staff determine whether intensive inpatient treatment, outpatient care, or other chemical dependency services are most appropriate for this individual. The assessment process is also used to identify other needs of the client so that appropriate referrals can be made. The inclusion of family or other individuals in the client's treatment is still another decision to be addressed following assessment. Professionals continue to use their assessment skills throughout the treatment process as the client's needs and circumstances change. The next chapter looks more closely at the components of the treatment system that can benefit clients and their loved ones during recovery.

Endnotes

1. Also see National Institute on Alcohol Abuse and Alcoholism (NIAAA), *Seventh Special Report to the U.S. Congress on Alcohol and Health* (Rockville, MD: U.S. Department of Health and Human Services, 1990), Chapter VIII.

2. See ibid. for a discussion.

3. NIAAA, *Eighth Special Report to the U.S. Congress on Alcohol and Health* (Rockville, MD: U.S. Department of Health and Human Services, 1993), Chapter 13.

4. J. A. Ewing and B. A. Rouse, "Identifying the Hidden Alcoholic," paper presented at the 29th International Congress on Alcohol and Drug Dependence, Sydney, Australia, February 3, 1970, cited in John A. Ewing, "Detecting Alcoholism, The CAGE Questionnaire," *Journal of the American Medical Association*, Vol. 252 (1984), pp. 1905–1907, Copyright 1984, American Medical Association; and Demmie Mayfield, Gail McLeod, and Patricia Hall, "The CAGE Questionnaire: Validation of a New Alcoholism Screening Instrument," *American Journal of Psychiatry*, Vol. 131 (1974), pp. 1121–1123.

5. See NIAAA, *Eighth Special Report to the U.S. Congress on Alcohol and Health;* Barry Liskow, Jan Campbell, Elizabeth J. Nickel, and Barbara J. Powell, "Validity of the CAGE Questionnaire in Screening for Alcohol Dependence in a Walk-in (Triage) Clinic," *Journal of Studies on Alcohol*, Vol. 56, May 1995, pp. 277–281; David G. Buchsbaum, "Quick Effective Screening for Alcohol Abuse," *Patient Care*, Vol. 29, No. 12 (1995), pp. 56–62.

6. Ewing, "Detecting Alcoholism," and Booker Bush, Sheila Shaw, Paul Cleary, Thomas L. Delbanco, and Mark D. Aronson, "Screening for Alcohol Abuse Using the CAGE Questionnaire," *American Journal of Medicine*, Vol. 82 (1987), pp. 231–235; also see Liskow et al., "Validity of the CAGE Questionnaire in Screening for Alcohol Dependence in a Walk-in (Triage) Clinic."

7. Kathleen Sciacca, "An Integrated Treatment Approach for Severely Mentally Ill Individuals with Substance Disorders" in Kenneth Minkoff and Robert E. Drake (Eds.), *Dual Diagnosis of Major Mental Illness and Substance Disorder*, Social and Behavioral Sciences Series, #50 (San Fransisco: Jossey-Bass, Summer 1991), pp. 69–84; and Kathleen Sciacca, Dual Diagnosis Workshop (Austin: Texas Department of Mental Health and Mental Retardation, May 1990).

8. Melvin L. Selzer, "The Michigan Alcoholism Screening Test: The Quest for a New Diagnostic Instrument," *American Journal of Psychiatry*, Vol. 127 (1971), pp. 1653–1658.

9. See Dan J. Lettieri, Jack E. Nelson, and Mollie A. Sayers (Eds.), *Alcoholism Treatment Assessment Research Instruments,* Treatment Handbook Series 2 (Rockville, MD: National Institute on Alcohol Abuse and Alcoholism, 1985); and Harvey A. Skinner, "A Multivariate Evaluation of the MAST," *Journal of Studies on Alcohol,* Vol. 40 (1979), pp. 831–844.

10. Melvin L. Selzer, Amiram Vinokur, and Louis van Rooijen, "A Self-Administered Short Version of the Michigan Alcoholism Screening Test (MAST),"*Journal of Studies on Alcohol,* Vol. 36 (1975), pp. 117–126.

11. Alex D. Pokorny, Byron A. Miller, and Howard B. Kaplan, "The Brief MAST: A Shortened Version of the Michigan Alcoholism Screening Test (MAST)," *American Journal of Psychiatry,* Vol. 129, No. 3 (1972), pp. 342–345.

12. Thomas F. Babor, Juan Ramon de la Fuente, John Saunders, and Marcus Grant, *AUDIT, The Alcohol Use Disorders Identification Test, Guidelines for Use in Primary Health Care* (Geneva: World Health Organization, 1992).

13. Michael J. Bohn, Thomas F. Babor, and Henry R. Kranzler, "The Alcohol Use Disorders Identification Test (AUDIT): Validation of a Screening Instrument for Use in Medical Settings," *Journal of Studies on Alcohol,* Vol. 56 (1995), pp. 423–432.

14. Harvey A. Skinner, "The Drug Abuse Screening Test," *Addictive Behaviors,* Vol. 7 (1982), pp. 363–371.

15. Information on Walter H. Hudson's Index of Drug Involvement can be obtained on the Internet at http://www.syspac.com~walmyr/ or by e-mail at scales@walmyr.com or at WALMYR Publishing Company, P.O. Box 6229, Tallahassee, FL 32314-6229, (850) 656-2787.

16. Glenn A. Miller, *The Substance Abuse Subtle Screening Inventory Manual* (Bloomington, IN: The SASSI Institute, 1985); and Glenn A. Miller, Franklin G. Miller, James Roberts, Marlene K. Brooks, and Linda G. Lazowski, *The SASSI-3* (Bloomington, IN: Baugh Enterprises, 1997).

17. Linda A. Morton, *The Risk Prediction Scales* (Indianapolis, IN: Department of Mental Health, Division of Addiction Services, 1978).

18. Craig MacAndrew, "The Differentiation of Male Alcoholic Outpatients from Nonalcoholic Psychiatric Outpatients by Means of the MMPI," *Quarterly Journal of Studies on Alcohol,* Vol. 26 (1965), pp. 238–246.

19. Lettieri et al., *Alcoholism Treatment Assessment Research.*

20. NIAAA, *Seventh Special Report to the U.S. Congress on Alcohol and Health,* Chapter VIII; NIAAA, *Eighth Special Report to the U.S. Congress on Alcohol and Health,* Chapter 13; National Institute on Alcohol Abuse and Alcoholism, "Alcohol Alert," No. 12, PH294, April 1991; and John P. Allen, "The Interrelationship of Alcoholism Assessment and Treatment," *Alcohol Health and Research World,* Vol. 15, No. 3 (1991), pp. 178–185.

21. Also see Deborah S. Hasin, "Diagnostic Interviews for Assessment: Background, Reliability, Validity," *Alcohol Health & Research World,* Vol. 15, No. 4 (1991), pp. 293–302.

22. *BSW/MSW Curriculum Enhancement Project on Alcohol and Other Drugs,* funded by Center for Substance Abuse Prevention, contract #277-91-2006, July 1991–June 1994.

23. Arthur W. K. Chan, Edward A. Pristach, and John W. Welte, "Detection of Alcoholism in Three Populations by the Brief-MAST," *Alcoholism: Clinical and Experimental Research,* Vol. 18, No. 3 (May/June 1994), pp. 695–701, quote from p. 695; also see Soren Svanum and John McGrew, "Prospective Screening of Substance Dependence: The Advantages of Directness," *Addictive Behaviors,* Vol. 20, No. 2 (1995), pp. 205–213.

24. Edward J. Heck and Michael D. Williams, "Using the CAGE to Screen for Drinking-Related Problems in College Students," *Journal of Studies on Alcohol,* Vol. 56 (1995), pp. 282–286.

25. Michael F. Fleming and Kristen L. Barry, "A Study Examining the Psychometric Properties of the SMAST-13," *Journal of Substance Abuse,* Vol. 1 (1989), pp. 173–182; and Michael F. Fleming and Kristen L. Barry, "The Effectiveness of Alcoholism Screening in an Ambulatory Care Setting," *Journal of Studies on Alcohol,* Vol. 52, No. 1 (1991), pp. 33–36.

26. Ibid.; Ron D. Hays, Laural Hill, James J. Gillogly, Matthew W. Lewis, Robert M. Bell, and Ronald Nicholas, "Response Times for the CAGE, Short-MAST, AUDIT, and JELLINEK Alcohol Scales," *Behavior Research Methods, Instruments, & Computers,* Vol. 25, No. 2 (1993), pp. 304–307; and Lorenzo F. Luckie, Robert E. White, William R. Miller, Milton V. Icenogle, and Milton C. Lasoski, "Prevalence Estimates of Alcohol Problems in a Veterans Administration Outpatient Population: AUDIT vs. MAST," *Journal of Clinical Psychology,* Vol. 51, No. 3 (1995), pp. 422–425.

27. Marcia Russell, "New Assessment Tools for Risk Drinking during Pregnancy: T-ACE, TWEAK, and Others," *Alcohol Health & Research World,* Vol. 18, No. 1 (1994), pp. 55–61.

28. See Arthur W. K. Chan, Edward A. Pristach, John Welte, and Marcia Russell, "Use of the TWEAK Test in Screening for Alcoholism/Heavy Drinking in Three Populations," *Alcoholism: Clinical and Experimental Research,* Vol. 17, No. 6 (1993), pp. 1188–1192.

29. Richard K. Fuller, "Can Treatment Outcome Research Rely on Alcoholics' Self-Reports?" *Alcohol Health & Research World,* Vol. 12, No. 3 (1988), pp. 180–186; NIAAA *Seventh Special Report,* Chapter VIII; and Michie Hesselbrock, Thomas F. Babor, Victor Hesselbrock, Roger E. Meyer, and Kathy Workman, " 'Never Believe an Alcoholic?' On the Validity of Self-Report Measures of Alcohol Dependence and Related Constructs," *The International Journal of the Addictions,* Vol. 18, No. 5 (1983), pp. 593–609.

30. Svanum and McGrew, "Prospective Screening of Substance Dependence: The Advantages of Directness," p. 212.

31. Fuller, "Can Treatment Outcome Research Rely on Alcoholics' Self-Reports?"

32. Harvey A. Skinner, "Assessing Alcohol Use by Patients in Treatment," in Reginald G. Smart, Howard D. Cappell, Frederick B. Glaser et al. (Eds.), *Research Advances in Alcohol and Drug Problems*, Volume 8 (New York: Plenum Press, 1984), pp. 183–207.

33. NIAAA, *Eighth Special Report to the U.S. Congress on Alcohol and Health*, pp. 327–328.

34. Hesselbrock et al., " 'Never Believe an Alcoholic?' " also see Babor et al., *AUDIT*, p. 8.

35. *Alcohol Health & Research World*, Vol. 15, No. 4 (1991) is devoted to definitions and diagnostic criteria of alcoholism, including the history of work in this area.

36. Criteria Committee, National Council on Alcoholism (now National Council on Alcoholism and Drug Dependence), New York, "Criteria for the Diagnosis and Treatment of Alcoholism," *Annals of International Medicine*, Vol. 77 (1972), pp. 249–258, and *American Journal of Psychiatry*, Vol. 129 (1972), pp. 127–135.

37. Griffith Edwards and Milton M. Gross, "Alcohol Dependence: Provisional Description of a Clinical Syndrome," *British Medical Journal*, Vol. 1 (1976), pp. 1058–1061.

38. American Psychiatric Association, *Diagnostic and Statistical Manual of Mental Disorders*, 4th ed. (Washington, DC: American Psychiatric Association, 1994).

39. Michael A. Fauman, *Study Guide to DSM-IV* (Washington, DC: American Psychiatric Association, 1994).

40. NIAAA, *Seventh Special Report*, Chapter VIII.

41. NIAAA, *Seventh Special Report*, p. 186.

42. Criteria Committee, "Criteria for the Diagnosis and Treatment of Alcoholism," p. 256.

43. Kenneth Minkoff, Dual Diagnosis Workshop (Austin: Texas Department of Mental Health and Mental Retardation, May 1990).

44. A. Thomas McLellan, Lester Luborsky, George E. Woody, and Charles P. O'Brien, "An Improved Diagnostic Evaluation Instrument for Substance Abuse Patients: The Addiction Severity Index," *The Journal of Nervous and Mental Disease*, Vol. 168 (1980), pp. 26–33; and A. Thomas McLellan, Lester Luborsky, John Cacciola, Jeffrey Griffith, Frederick Evans, Harriet L. Barr, and Charles P. O'Brien, "New Data from the Addiction Severity Index: Reliability and Validity in Three Centers," *The Journal of Nervous and Mental Disease*, Vol. 173, No. 7 (1985), pp. 412–423.

45. See, for example, Alfred S. Friedman and Arlene Utada, "A Method for Diagnosing and Planning the Treatment of Adolescent Drug Abusers (The Adolescent Drug Abuse Diagnosis [ADAD] Instrument)," *Journal of Drug Education*, Vol. 19, No. 4 (1989), pp. 285–312.

46. Information from The Gordian Group and Dr. Ralph E. Tarter. For information on the original DUSI, see Ralph E. Tarter and Andrea M. Hegedus, "The Drug Use Screening Inventory: Its Application in the Evaluation and Treatment of Alcohol and Other Drug Abuse," *Alcohol Health & Research World*, Vol. 15, No. 1 (1991), pp. 65–75; information on the DUSI-R can be found on the Internet at http://www.pitt.edu/~cedarspr/dusir.html

47. Thomas F. Babor, Zelig Dolinsky, Bruce Rounsaville, and Jerome Jaffe, "Unitary versus Multidimensional Models of Alcoholism Treatment Outcome: An Empirical Study," *Journal of Studies on Alcohol*, Vol. 49, No. 2 (1988), pp. 167–177; also see A. Thomas McLellan, Lester Luborsky, George E. Woody, Charles P. O'Brien, and Ruben Kron, "Are the Addiction-Related Problems of Substance Abusers Really Related?" *The Journal of Nervous and Mental Disease*, Vol. 169 (1981), pp. 232–239.

48. E. Mansell Pattison, Mark B. Sobell, and Linda C. Sobel, *Emerging Concepts of Alcohol Dependence* (New York: Springer, 1977), especially Chapter 1; Babor et al., "Unitary versus Multidimensional Models of Alcoholism Treatment Outcome"; and Edward J. Callahan and Ella H. Pecsok, "Heroin Addiction," in Dennis M. Donovan and G. Alan Marlatt (Eds.), *Assessment of Addictive Behavior* (New York: Guilford Press, 1988), pp. 390–418.

49. NIAAA, *Seventh Special Report*, p. 186.

50. See William R. Miller, "Motivation for Treatment: A Review with Special Emphasis on Alcoholism," *Psychological Bulletin*, Vol. 98, No. 1 (1985), pp. 84–107; also see Dennis M. Donovan, "Assessment of Addictive Behaviors, Implications of an Emerging Biopsychosocial Model," in Donovan and Marlatt, *Assessment of Addictive Behaviors*, especially pp. 26–29.

51. Ralph E. Tarter, Arthur I. Alterman, and Kathleen L. Edwards, "Alcoholic Denial: A Biopsychological Interpretation," *Journal of Studies on Alcohol*, Vol. 45, No. 3 (1984), pp. 214–218.

52. Rickey L. George, *Counseling the Chemically Dependent, Theory and Practice* (Englewood Cliffs, NJ: Prentice Hall, 1990), pp. 36–37.

53. Tarter et al., "Alcoholic Denial," pp. 214–215.

54. Jean Kinney, *Clinical Manual of Substance Abuse* (St. Louis, MO: Mosby Year Book, 1991).

55. Jon R. Weinberg, "Counseling the Person with Alcohol Problems," in Nada J. Estes and M. Edith Heinemann (Eds.), *Alcoholism: Development, Consequences, and Interventions*, 3rd ed. (St. Louis, MO: C. V. Mosby), p. 367.

56. George, *Counseling the Chemically Dependent*.

57. Kinney, *Clinical Manual of Substance Abuse*, p. 2.

58. Weinberg, "Counseling the Person with Alcohol Problems," and Jean Kinney and Gwen Leaton, *Loosening the Grip: A Handbook of Alcohol Information*, 4th ed. (St. Louis, MO: Mosby Year Book, 1991).

59. Arnold M. Washton, Nannette S. Stone, and Edward C. Hendrickson, "Cocaine Abuse," in Donovan and Marlatt, *Assessment of Addictive Behaviors*, p. 372.

60. "Alcoholism: A Merry-Go-Round Named Denial" copyright © 1969, by Al-Anon Family Group Headquarters, Inc. Reprinted by permission of Al-Anon Family Group Headquarters, Inc.

61. See George, *Counseling the Chemically Dependent,* and Vernon E. Johnson, *I'll Quit Tomorrow* (New York: Harper and Row, 1973).

62. George, *Counseling the Chemically Dependent,* p. 36.

63. See, for example, Carl G. Leukefeld and Frank M. Tims (Eds.), *Drug Abuse Treatment in Prisons and Jails,* NIDA Research Monograph 118, DHHS Publication No. (ADM) 92-1884 (Rockville, MD: U.S. Department of Health and Human Services, 1992); Carl G. Leukefeld and Frank M. Tims (Eds.), *Compulsory Treatment of Drug Abuse: Research and Clinical Practice,* NIDA Monograph 86, DHHS Publication No. (ADM) 89-1578 (Rockville, MD: U.S. Department of Health and Human Services, 1988); and Harrison M. Trice and Janice M. Beyer, "Job Based Alcoholism Programs: Motivating Problem Drinkers to Rehabilitation," in E. Mansell Pattison and Edward Kaufman (Eds.), *Encyclopedic Handbook of Alcoholism* (New York: Gardner Press, 1982), pp. 954–978.

6

Treatment— The System of Care

This chapter describes the system of care available to those with substance abuse or dependency problems. Once diagnosis and assessment are complete, the next step in assisting clients is to select the types of treatment and other services that will meet their needs as closely as possible. The phrase *matching clients to treatment* has been used to describe this part of the helping process. To do this, it is necessary to be knowledgeable about all the components of the system of care available to those with substance abuse or dependency, as well as self-help groups. Certainly professionals want to provide clients with the most optimal treatments and services, but many limitations can prevent this from happening. Particular services may not be available in a given locale. Clients may not have the financial resources to obtain services. Clients and the professionals they encounter may not be aware of resources. In many cases, clients get whatever is available without much regard for their particular needs and circumstances. This chapter covers each of these topics and discusses the treatment outcome evaluation literature— just how successful is chemical dependency treatment?

Components of the Treatment System

We have conceptualized the treatment system for chemical abuse and dependency clients using a continuum of care[1] comprised of nine major components that are most commonly offered to clients: (1) detoxification, (2) intensive treatment (provided on an inpatient or outpatient basis), (3) residential programs, (4) outpatient services, (5) pharmacotherapy, (6) aftercare, (7) maintenance, (8) education and psychoeducation, and (9) adjunctive services. Some individuals may require all these services over time, whereas others might need only particular components. The continuum represents a comprehensive service-delivery system designed to meet the biopsychosocial needs of clients. We also discuss some nontraditional methods of treatment that are being used with substance abusers.

Detoxification Programs

Many chemically dependent individuals begin their treatment with detoxification services. These services are needed when an individual has a physical dependence on alcohol or other drugs that results in withdrawal symptoms when drug use is terminated. Although very mild symptoms might not require medical attention, and many individuals withdraw on their own, those with more severe symptoms may require professional care. The individual's medical, psychological, and social situations will help determine whether detoxification is done on an inpatient basis in a hospital, in another inpatient setting, or on an outpatient basis.

Medical, Hospital Detoxification. Medical, hospital detoxification takes place in a general hospital or in a hospital or hospital unit specifically designed for chemical dependency treatment. Hospitals require that a physician admit the patient before services, including detoxification, can be rendered. Some individuals have private physicians who can admit them to a general hospital for detoxification. Physicians who are sensitive to chemical abuse and dependency generally encourage patients to engage in further chemical dependency treatment.

In many cases, those dependent on alcohol and drugs have medical emergencies (e.g., acute withdrawal symptoms, overdoses, or accidents) that cause them to use emergency rooms at local hospitals. These are generally public hospitals that must treat individuals, whether or not they have private physicians or the means to pay for their treatment. Too often, the individual is treated and released without referral to other services. Some general hospitals have medical and counseling staff knowledgeable about the social and medical aspects of chemical dependency. These staff increase the likelihood that patients will be referred to chemical dependency treatment programs following detoxification or emergency treatment.

Hospitals that have chemical dependency treatment units and specialty hospitals devoted to the treatment of chemical dependency often have detoxification programs that also provide assessment for longer-term chemical dependency services as well as referral to other social services. Immediately following detoxification, clients can be transferred to intensive inpatient or outpatient chemical dependency treatment units at these or other appropriate facilities.

State psychiatric hospitals may also have wards for addiction treatment, and some include detoxification services. Although the preference today is to treat chemically dependent individuals in community facilities, involuntary patients with dual diagnoses of substance disorders and mental disorders are still likely to receive treatment in state hospitals.

Medical, Nonhospital Detoxification. Other types of facilities in which withdrawal is done on an inpatient basis are community-based detoxification centers, sometimes referred to as medical, nonhospital (or "social setting") detoxification.[2] Staff include physicians and nurses, as well as other professionals who provide psychosocial services to patients. The bulk of the funding for community detoxification centers comes from the public sector. These detoxification facilities sprang up around the country following passage of the federal Comprehensive Alcohol Abuse and Alcoholism Prevention, Treatment and Rehabilitation Act of 1970 (also known as the Hughes Act after its primary sponsor, Senator Harold Hughes). The act emphasized improved services for alcoholics and decriminalization of public intoxication by states and communities. In the 1970s, these detoxification centers were called *sobering-up stations*[3] for alcoholics and are now formally referred to as *primary care centers*. Most patients and staff simply call them *detox*. Many centers still focus on treating alcohol withdrawal, but some also assist those withdrawing from other types of drugs.

Prior to the establishment of these community detoxification programs, jailers were the detox agents for many public inebriates sent to the local "drunk tank."[4] Jailers often gave these individuals alcohol to ward off withdrawal symptoms and to help them detoxify. The term *revolving door* described public inebriates whose lives consisted of cycles of drinking, public intoxication arrests, and short jail terms (often 30, 60, or 90 days). Community detoxification centers were intended to help alcoholics break this cycle. Community detox centers are not always the finest-looking facilities in town, but they are a vast improvement over the treatment alcoholics generally received while incarcerated.

Patients in community detoxification centers may be self-referred; brought by a relative or friend; or referred by community gate-keepers such as the police, probation or parole officers, health department staff, the clergy, or social agency personnel. Admission procedures vary. Some require screening by a physician before the patient is sent to the center. This is done to prevent inappropriate admissions to the detoxification program. For example, an individual may have ingested some alcohol or another drug, but may actually be experiencing a psychiatric emergency requiring care in a psychiatric hospital, or the individual may be having a medical crisis requiring treatment in a general hospital. Some community detox centers permit nurses to admit patients and provide most of the medical care. There are "standing orders" that provide instructions for how to care for patients with varying degrees of withdrawal symptoms. One or more physicians come daily to examine patients and provide special instructions and are on call for emergencies. Community detoxification centers have been highly successful in helping patients detoxify safely, and their costs are substantially less than hospital care.

There are some limitations to the assistance that can be provided in community centers. For instance, patients needing detoxification who also have another medical emergency, such as a laceration or a broken bone, must generally be attended to in a hospital or emergency medical center before admission to the nonhospital detoxification program. Sometimes patients do not arrive at the detoxification center early enough to receive medical attention that will prevent the most serious withdrawal symptoms such as repeated seizures or delirium tremens (DTs). Medical management of these problems may be beyond the scope of the community center, and the patient may have to be transferred to a hospital.

Since the primary concern of community detoxification programs is chemical dependency treatment, more is usually done to link the client to additional services needed for recovery than in general hospitals where the staff may be overwhelmed with medical emergencies. While at the detoxification program, patients are often provided alcohol and drug education and receive initial counseling and referral services. They are usually expected to participate in educational group sessions just as soon as they are physically able. Loved ones may also be briefly counseled about the need for additional treatment for themselves as well as the patient. Alcoholics Anonymous or other self-help groups may hold meetings at these detox centers in order to introduce patients to these programs and to encourage them to pursue recovery. Members act as role models and give patients hope that recovery is possible.

Patients in community detoxification programs are often of lower socioeconomic status. Many are transients who do not have private health insurance or other coverage. Services are generally charged on a sliding scale based on the patient's ability to pay, but many bills are never collected. Those with very limited resources may not be charged at all. The number of beds in a center usually varies with the size of the city or community served. Rural areas may have no community detox center, and those needing services may have to travel long distances to obtain care.

The day-to-day operation of community detoxification programs differ. In some centers, patients are required to wear hospital gowns, which can deter elopements (patients leaving without the staff's knowledge). In other centers, patients wear their own clothes to help preserve their dignity and to minimize the medical atmosphere, which is thought to prolong physical symptoms of withdrawal. Many indigent patients living on the streets own only the clothes on their backs. Detoxification staff provide services as basic as washing these patients' clothing or offering them clean, donated clothing.

Admissions procedures generally involve a search or check of the individual's possessions. Occasionally, a patient checks in with a weapon (a knife or gun) that must be properly secured or disposed of. More often, the individual arrives with alcohol or other drugs that must be confiscated. Patients are generally allowed visitors, but some friends have been known to smuggle alcohol or drugs to the patient. Like other treatment settings, detoxification centers have developed a culture of their own.

Whether patients are treated in a hospital or in a community detoxification program, medical personnel observe the patient and assess the severity of withdrawal symptoms to determine the medical regimen needed. Often, the medical personnel do not know what drugs the patient has ingested, how much has been ingested, and over what period of time. They may be unaware of the withdrawal

symptoms the patient has experienced in the past. Therefore, they must proceed cautiously before administering any medications for withdrawal (such as Librium for alcohol withdrawal, phenobarbital for barbiturate withdrawal, or methadone for heroin withdrawal).[5] Treatment—including the type and amount of medication, if any, to be administered—will depend on whether the patient's withdrawal symptoms are mild, moderate, or severe. Patients often ask for or demand additional medication to further mitigate physical and psychological discomfort. This is not surprising, given that this is how patients have medicated themselves before entering the detoxification program. When medical staff feel that additional medication is not warranted, they generally respond with verbal encouragement and support that the symptoms will pass.

The stay in detoxification programs is generally brief but depends on the drugs on which the patient is dependent.[6] For example, the acute problems associated with alcohol withdrawal are likely to pass in a few days, whereas the period for barbiturate withdrawal is longer. Sedative-hypnotic withdrawal presents particular dangers

 A Community Detoxification Center Patient

Ed Welch,* a white male in his late forties, was well known at the community detox center. He had been admitted about six times in the last year as a result of his dependence on alcohol. Ed's most prominent withdrawal symptom was severe tremors. His medical history also included several bouts of gastritis. The medical staff was always able to manage his care without referral to the hospital, and it was amazing how much better he looked after a five-day stay. Ed was a cooperative and quiet patient. He worked as a welder and his boss would bring him in when he got drunk. As soon as he was sober, Ed's boss would put him back to work. Ed was divorced, never saw his grown children, and didn't seem to have any friends. He had no trouble downing two fifths of whiskey when he went on a binge. The detox staff was never able to get Ed to enter the halfway house or to attend outpatient groups. It seemed that the thing Ed liked least was talking. He came to AA sometimes but never said much. Ed did get an AA sponsor, a member with a history a lot like Ed's. Ed often managed to put a few months of sobriety together, but his binges, although less frequent, continued, and he returned to the detox center intermittently.

*Clients described in this chapter are fictitious or represent composite cases.

due to the possibility of seizures or DTs. Withdrawal from more than one drug further complicates matters. Patients are detoxified from each drug sequentially, beginning with the drug that produces the most serious withdrawal symptoms. The type of drugs to which the patient is addicted and the severity of symptoms and other complicating medical conditions will also determine the setting in which withdrawal is accomplished.

Since there is usually a high demand for the beds in community detoxification programs, patients are typically not encouraged to stay longer than necessary. As soon as the danger of medical problems has passed, staff may be pressed to refer the patient elsewhere, such as to an inpatient or outpatient treatment center, a halfway house, or the Salvation Army or a mission. Some alcoholics and addicts are reluctant to leave, especially those who are homeless. For them, the detox center is a safe shelter and a temporary home.

Other individuals do not wish to be treated in the detoxification center at all and may leave or try to leave before the dangers of withdrawal have passed. Although some are referred by the courts or are under pressure from other authorities (e.g., probation department or child welfare agency) to enter the center, patients are generally considered voluntary admissions. Voluntary patients cannot be required to stay, but local law enforcement may be called if a patient considered dangerous to himself or herself or to others attempts to leave. Some patients are committed involuntarily under civil procedures. Should these patients elope or otherwise leave against medical advice or without permission, staff may be required to notify the appropriate authorities.

Outpatient Detoxification.   When withdrawal problems can be medically managed without the need for inpatient treatment, outpatient (ambulatory) care may be an economical alternative.[7] The use of outpatient detoxification is contingent on the patient's social and psychological states. Suicidal or severely depressed patients are obviously not good risks for outpatient detoxification, and

outpatient detoxification is not a viable option if the patient lacks the ability or supervision to comply with the treatment protocol. Available emotional supports should also be considered. Although there are advantages of inpatient detoxification, such as continual medical supervision, a study by Hayashida and colleagues indicates that patients requesting detoxification for mild to moderate alcohol withdrawal syndrome can be successfully detoxified on an outpatient basis if they are screened to ensure that they do not have complicating medical and psychiatric problems.[8] These findings are particularly interesting, given the low socioeconomic status of the alcoholic patients who participated in the study and their lack of social supports, including some with unstable living arrangements. Gerstein and Harwood also recommend consideration of alternatives to inpatient hospital detoxification for clients addicted to other types of drugs, and they provide guidelines for making referrals to these settings.[9]

Finally, medical treatment is not always needed to terminate drug use. Some users experience physical discomfort mild enough that medical attention is not required. Others use drugs such as some hallucinogens with no reported physical dependence.[10] These individuals may, however, need emotional support in their efforts to become drug free. Chemical dependency programs offer a number of services to assist in this process, such as outpatient services (described shortly), drop-in centers, and 24-hour crisis lines, that increase the availability of emotional support.

Termination of drug use is the first and usually the briefest step in the recovery process.[11] While some individuals recover spontaneously on their own, many require professional assistance. Following detoxification services, they are likely to need additional components on the continuum of care.

Effectiveness of Detoxification Services.   From a purely medical standpoint, detoxification can be successfully accomplished on an inpatient basis in a hospital, and often in an inpatient nonhospital setting as well as on an outpatient basis in appropriate circumstances.[12] Hayashida and colleagues present initial evidence that alcoholics of low socioeconomic status can comply with outpatient detoxification regimens,[13] but Gerstein and Harwood believe that the jury is still out on which type of detoxification setting may be most effective in ensuring that drug addicts complete detoxification.[14]

Gordis and Sereny[15] and Gerstein and Harwood[16] also note that medically safe withdrawal is only one goal of detoxification programs; more important in the long run is whether participation in a detoxification program promotes further use of treatment and rehabilitation services by clients. In their review of the effectiveness of detoxification programs for illicit drug users, Gerstein and Harwood conclude that "consistently, without subsequent treatment, researchers have found no effects from detoxification that are discernibly superior to those achieved by untreated withdrawal in terms of reducing subsequent drug-taking behavior and especially relapse to dependence."[17] A review by Snair indicates "only small positive effects" from detoxification programs in reducing drug use.[18] Although the literature is scant and reports of success rates vary, reviews often reflect that disappointingly small numbers of alcoholics and addicts continue in treatment following detoxification.[19] Tests of methods that will improve client compliance following detoxification are needed.[20]

Intensive Treatment

The next component on the continuum of care, intensive treatment, has burgeoned since the 1970s. Intensive treatment used to be thought of synonymously with inpatient care, but it is now frequently offered on an outpatient basis.

Intensive Inpatient Care. Intensive inpatient treatment programs originated primarily to assist alcoholics but now also include those with other drug problems. These programs typically lasted for 28 or 30 days, which was the maximum period

that many health insurers would pay for this care. Some programs are longer, such as six weeks, or individual patients may stay longer depending on their treatment needs, including the type and severity of their addiction. Today, the Betty Ford Center is probably the most famous intensive treatment program in the world, although several well-known centers preceded the Ford Center.

Intensive inpatient treatment may be the logical choice when an individual is unlikely to remain alcohol or drug free in his or her current situation. For example, the individual may have suicidal ideation or other psychological or health care needs that are best met in this type of environment. However, it is often those who have the financial resources and can be absent from work or family responsibilities who are able to avail themselves of this type of treatment. In recent years, managed health care has had a major impact on intensive inpatient treatment. Traditional insurance plans and managed care providers such as health maintenance organizations generally have reduced coverage for inpatient care.

Intensive inpatient treatment programs may be located in a special unit of a general hospital or they may be offered by a specialty hospital or other inpatient facility devoted to mental health or chemical dependency treatment. As noted earlier, these programs often have their own detoxification component, and patients can be easily transferred to intensive treatment once the danger of severe withdrawal symptoms has passed.

Many intensive inpatient treatment facilities are privately owned and intended to earn profit; others are private, not-for-profit or public facilities. The number of these programs, especially among the private sector, increased tremendously during the 1980s and 1990s. Several factors accounted for this growth. First was public recognition that chemical dependency can be treated successfully. Second, health insurers succumbed to pressure to cover substance abuse treatment, and third, almost everyone now recognizes the importance of chemical dependency treatment in reducing overall health care costs. Inpatient care is, however,

Managed Health Care and Chemical Dependency Treatment

Managed care refers to methods used to control the use of health care services, with the intent of providing more efficient and effective use of health care resources. Managed care is a response to the rapidly rising costs of health care in the United States. There are several forms of managed care organizations (MCOs) such as preferred provider organizations (PPOs) and health maintenance organizations (HMOs). Various strategies are used to manage care. One is utilization review at the time patients or clients request care and during their treatment. Another is case management, often used to direct the course of care of patients or clients who use a great deal of services. *Managed behavioral health care* is the term currently used to describe the use of managed care for mental and substance use disorders.

Given its ability to control health care costs, managed care has the potential for expanding health care coverage to more Americans; however, as more Americans move from traditional health insurance and fee-for-service plans to managed care, a number of concerns have been raised about what managed care, including managed behavioral health care, is doing to services. For example, HMOs or other MCOs may limit mental health treatment to 20 sessions of outpatient care a year and to 30 to 60 days of inpatient care, and this care may be further limited by *medical necessity*—a term open to interpretation.[1] Other types of health insurance also tend to limit benefits for substance abuse and mental health treatment, but concerns are that HMOs are spending even less on these services.[2] In 1996, the U.S. Congress passed legislation requiring insurers to provide parity for mental health care (benefits equal to those for physical health care) in a limited number of cases, but the law does not cover benefits for substance abuse or dependence services.

Iglehart notes that "the vast majority of corporations now assign (or 'carve out') their behavioral health coverage by contracting with ... specialized companies."[3] An advantage of carve-outs is that the companies that manage them have a vested interest and greater expertise in administering mental health and substance abuse and dependence benefits. A disadvantage is that they may steer away from the comprehensive or biopsychosocial view of patient care. Patients with substance use disorders are known to use large amounts of medical care unless they are treated for their substance disorders. When the primary health care insurer is relieved of responsibility for care of mental and substance disorders, these disorders may be recognized and treated less frequently. In the long run, divorcing health care from mental health and substance abuse care may increase medical care. Substance abuse benefits may also be carved out of mental health benefits, with some fearing that substance abuse benefits will continue to be a stepchild to mental health services.

Studies have shown that those with substance use disorders are less likely than those with mental disorders to get care for their problems.[4] These factors point to the need to get physicians and other primary health care providers involved in screening for mental—especially substance use disorders—problems, despite their historical reluctance to do so. It seems logical that MCOs insist that treatment providers screen for mental illness and substance abuse and dependence and that they find ways to encourage physicians to do this. Fuller suggests random sampling of physicians' cases to see if they are under (or over) diagnosing substance abuse and dependence.[5] He also suggests disenrolling patients who do not comply with their treatment regimen, but this may beg the issue, for people with mental and substance disorders often do not seek treatment until their problems become severe, thereby utilizing more health care resources.

Good assessments are essential to providing good patient care, whether in traditional fee-for-service care or in managed care. The problem is that even with good assessments, diagnosis in mental health and substance abuse care is still more difficult and not as precise as the diagnosis of many physical health problems.[6] Information on the most effective substance abuse treatment for clients is also lacking.

Originally, the hope was that managed care would provide a more individualized approach to treatment, tailored to the client's needs, but evidence indicates that insurance providers of various types are taking a one-approach-fits-all model. Many health care experts are disappointed with the response of MCOs to mental health and substance abuse treatment because most evidence shows that they have not "moved beyond traditional services."[7] Apparently, insurers are approving the same length of stay or outpatient services, regardless of clients' needs. In a study by Wickizer and colleagues of utilization management practices, inpatient psychiatric treatment (including substance abuse treatment) was approved for nearly all (99 percent) of the patients for whom it was requested, but on average, only one-third (6.9) of the 19 days initially requested were authorized, and, on average, a total of 16.8 days were approved, compared with the 23.5 days requested.[8] Wickizer and associates also found more limitations placed on care for alcohol- or drug-dependent patients—for example, compared to patients with other diagnoses, they were more likely to get approvals for outpatient care when inpatient care was requested. These researchers conclude that "the fact that almost all patients were approved for the same initial length of stay implies adherence to strict treatment protocols that do not distinguish among different clinical or patient factors."[9] Practitioners are often heard complaining about the time they spend haggling with MCOs about what treatment will be provided to the client. More discouraging is Mechanic and colleagues' conclusions "that the probability of treatment for substance abuse is certainly no higher and may be significantly lower under prepaid care."[10] For example, in studies they reviewed, outpatient care was not substituted for inpatient care for substance abusers in a number of cases, or insurers were covering detoxification services as the only inpatient service even though detoxification alone is generally viewed as ineffective in the long run.

Shulman points to some other problems that are being encountered in this era of managed care, such as insurers requiring that a patient has "failed" in outpatient treatment as a condition of getting inpatient treatment.[11] Although treatment in the least restrictive environment should be a standard, when an individual clearly needs inpatient care, it should not be denied. Shulman also notes that even if patients do not use the maximum number of inpatient treatment days allotted for a treatment episode, they may not be allowed to use the unused days later. Also, a provider may cover only some of the types of care on the continuum. For example, residential or supported living may not be covered, resulting in use of hospital care when intensive outpatient care with supported living arrangements may be just as helpful or more helpful and less costly.

In terms of how managed care is affecting the lives of substance abusers, a McDonnell Douglas study of mental health and substance abuse services found that more HMO enrollees lost their jobs than those in traditional fee-for-service plans.[12] Of particular concern is the effect of managed care on people with severe problems. After studying treatment services provided to more than 7,000 alcoholics and drug addicts, Miller and Hoffman stress the need for the continuum of care but note that many health care plans do not provide for this; instead, most plans use an acute care model to treat a problem that is chronic for many patients.[13] Those with substance abuse problems often relapse and need recurring care.

Managed care has also raised issues about confidentiality and patient privacy. Payers are now asking more and more questions about the details of patients' lives as they make decisions that were once left between patient and health care provider. Due to stigma and privacy

(continued)

concerns, clients may be paying for substance abuse treatment out of their own pockets rather than asking their insurance carriers to pay.

Pacione and Jaskula suggest three guidelines for helping practitioners provide adequate assistance to clients in this era of cost containment:

1. Use the least-restrictive level of care most likely to initiate abstinence.
2. Assess the likelihood of treatment failure at the level of care chosen and the risks to the client if treatment fails.
3. Identify treatment failure quickly and move the client to a more intensive level of care if significant risks are present.[14]

ENDNOTES

1. Jay M. Pomerantz, Letter to the Editor, *The New England Journal of Medicine*, Vol. 335, No. 1 (1996), p. 57; and John K. Iglehart, "Managed Care and Mental Health," *The New England Journal of Medicine*, Vol. 334, No. 2 (1996), pp. 131–135.

2. Iglehart, "Managed Care and Mental Health."

3. Ibid., quote is from p. 133.

4. David Mechanic, Mark Schlesinger, and Donna D. McAlpine, "Management of Mental Health and Substance Abuse Services: State of the Art and Early Results," *The Milbank Quarterly*, Vol. 73, No. 1 (1995), pp. 19–55; and Deborah W. Garnick, Ann H. Hendricks, Jane D. Dulski, Kenneth E. Thorpe, and Constance Horgan, "Characteristics of Private Sector Managed Care for Mental Health and Substance Abuse Treatment," *Hospital and Community Psychiatry*, Vol. 45, No. 12 (1994), pp. 1201–1205.

5. Mark G. Fuller, "A New Day: Strategies for Managing Psychiatric and Substance Abuse Benefits," *Health Care Management Review*, Vol. 19, No. 4 (1994), pp. 20–24.

6. Mechanic et al., "Management of Mental Health and Substance Abuse Services: State of the Art and Early Results"; Garnick et al., "Characteristics of Private Sector Managed Care for Mental Health and Substance Abuse Treatment."

7. Mechanic et al., "Management of Mental Health and Substance Abuse Services: State of the Art and Early Results," p. 28.

8. Thomas M. Wickizer, Daniel Lessler, and Karn M. Travis, "Controlling Inpatient Psychiatric Utilization through Managed Care," *American Journal of Psychiatry*, Vol. 153, No. 3 (1996), pp. 339–345.

9. Ibid., p. 339.

10. Mechanic et al., "Management of Mental Health and Substance Abuse Services: State of the Art and Early Results," pp. 35–36.

11. Gerald D. Shulman, "Costs: Don't Blame Them All on Providers!" *Behavioral Health Management* (May/June, 1994), pp. 63–65.

12. See Mechanic et al., "Management of Mental Health and Substance Abuse Services: State of the Art and Early Results," pp. 31–32.

13. Norman S. Miller and Norman G. Hoffman, "Addictions Treatment Outcomes," *Alcoholism Treatment Quarterly*, Vol. 12, No. 2 (1995), pp. 41–55; also in Norman S. Miller (Ed.), *Treatment of Addictions: Applications of Outcome Research for Clinical Management* (Binghamton, NY: Haworth Press, 1995), pp. 41–55; and Prezioso, "Preserving Inpatient Care," *Behavioral Health Management* (March/April 1994), pp. 22–23.

14. Tony Pacione and Diane Jaskula, "Quality Chemical Dependency Treatment in an Era of Cost Containment," *Health and Social Work*, Vol. 19, No. 1 (February 1994), pp. 55–61, quote from p. 55.

quite expensive. A fee of $10,000 or more is common for a four-week inpatient stay in a private treatment program. Managed care and other cost constraints have taken their toll on some of the private inpatient programs in recent years, resulting in the closing of some of these programs.

Occasionally, private facilities offer "scholarships" or fee waivers as a community service to clients who do not have health care coverage and cannot afford to pay personally. Private, not-for-profit or public programs often use a sliding scale to assess patient fees. Clients without financial resources may not be charged, but there is often more demand than there are treatment slots available. It is usually possible to get immediate admission to a for-profit program, but not-for-profit and public programs are likely to have waiting lists. Maintaining sobriety while awaiting admission to a public or not-for-profit program can be a challenge for clients.

Although there is some variation in the treatment services offered in these inpatient programs, many are similar to what is called the *Minnesota model.* This model, developed by alcoholism treatment centers in Minnesota during the 1940s and 1950s, "is an abstinence oriented, comprehensive, multi-professional approach to the treatment of the addictions, based upon the principles of Alcoholics Anonymous."[21] The services most commonly offered by these programs are education about chemical dependency, group and individual counseling or therapy, and an introduction to self-help programs. Other services promote general health and well-being. Examples are lectures on adopting good nutritional habits and individual consultation on developing daily menus, exercise periods, plans for incorporating a fitness program into one's daily routine, and social and recreational alternatives to drug use. Improving communication skills, practicing assertiveness, and learning to reduce stress may also be introduced. There are, of course, limits on what can be accomplished in a few weeks. Many clients are only beginning to come to grips with their substance abuse or dependency problem in this early stage of recovery. Only so much information can be processed and retained in a short period of time, especially by those with long-term dependency who are newly detoxified.

Programs vary in the methods used to involve loved ones and the extent of these services. Education is one means, beginning with basic information on alcohol and drugs and definitions of *addiction.* Topics such as chemical dependency as a family disease and codependency generally receive attention (see Chapter 10). Loved ones may also be introduced to self-help groups such as Al-Anon

and Naranon. Therapy sessions may be scheduled for individual families or families may meet in groups. Some family groups are just for spouses or other adult partners; others include children, parents, and others important in the client's life. In some programs, family members, particularly spouses or other adult partners, spend a week or so in residence at the program.

Intensive Outpatient Care. During the last decade, reliance on intensive inpatient treatment for so many chemically dependent individuals has been questioned, not only with regard to costs but also effectiveness. Most of the alcoholism research literature indicates no difference in the effectiveness of inpatient versus outpatient treatment.[22] Professionals directed chemically dependent individuals to inpatient treatment because they assumed it was the best alternative or due to the lack of other treatment alternatives. In addition, insurance policies often limited coverage to inpatient care. Patients were told that inpatient treatment came first, regardless of their personal circumstances. But insistence on inpatient treatment may have alienated potential clients concerned about disruption to their work and family lives. Single parents, those with limited financial resources, and those concerned about explaining a long job absence may see outpatient care as their only viable treatment option. Intensive outpatient treatment is becoming the preferred service for those who can continue to function at home and in the community.

The services provided in intensive outpatient treatment are the same as those provided during inpatient treatment, but clients work at their regular jobs or care for their families during the day and usually attend treatment in the evenings or on weekends. A typical program involves participation four nights a week over a 10- to 12-week period.

In addition to the cost savings and flexibility that intensive outpatient care affords over intensive inpatient services, it also "has clinical advantages by allowing patients to practice relapse prevention and management skills while being in a highly structured treatment setting."[23] However, some clients need relief from the stresses of their current environment to benefit from treatment, and others may have psychiatric disorders that contraindicate outpatient treatment. In all cases, matching clients to the least restrictive treatment suitable to their needs is an appropriate goal of treatment planning.

Day Treatment.   Another type of intensive outpatient treatment is known as day treatment or partial hospitalization. Participation in a day-treatment program often lasts longer than other forms of intensive treatment and is used by clients who are not yet able to function in the community by holding regular jobs or caring for their families. Some of these clients have a combination of psychiatric disorders and substance abuse disorders. Others have substantial physical impairments that may require a longer period of rehabilitation or substantial cognitive impairments from substance abuse and therefore need additional time in learning communication, vocational, or other skills before a complete return to the community can be made. Some clients attend day treatment following intensive inpatient chemical dependency treatment or inpatient psychiatric treatment.

Guydish and colleagues describe a day-treatment program called Walden House for clients with serious alcohol and other drug problems operating in the San Francisco area.[24] It is used either as a stand-alone treatment or to help those awaiting residential treatment. The program was designed to meet the growing demand for substance abuse treatment. Individual, group, and family therapy are provided along with employment, legal, and other services. The staff and clients are regarded as a surrogate family. The program operates from 8:00 A.M. to 8:00 P.M. on weekdays with more limited weekend hours. Alterman and McLellan also discuss a Veterans' Affairs day hospital program for those addicted to alcohol or cocaine.[25] These articles may suggest a growing interest in the use of day treatment in this era of high treatment demand and cost containment.

Effectiveness of Intensive Treatment.   The first studies of Minnesota model intensive treatment programs were conducted in the 1950s.[26] In a review of the effectiveness of these programs, Cook found few significant studies; like criticisms of much chemical dependency research, he noted that "the need [is] for further research incorporating control or comparison treatment groups, longer follow-up, more rigorous assessment procedures, and clearly defined diagnostic/outcome criteria."[27] On a positive note, however, he concluded that "despite exaggerated claims of success, [the Minnesota model] appears to have a genuinely impressive 'track record' with as many as two-thirds of its patients achieving a 'good' outcome at 1 year after discharge."[28] Gerstein and Harwood indicate that those who primarily abuse alcohol appear to have better outcomes in these inpatient programs than do clients who primarily abuse illicit drugs.[29]

Many follow-up studies are based on clients' self-reports of their drinking or other drug use following inpatient or outpatient care. Sometimes clients are also asked to report on their employment, family functioning, illegal activity, and compliance with additional treatment and self-help groups following discharge. The accuracy of self-reports has been debated, but evidence tends to support their usefulness (see Chapter 5).[30] In some cases, collaterals, records, or laboratory tests (e.g., urine toxicologies) are used to validate clients' self-reports at follow-up. These additional sources increase confidence in the information provided about treatment outcomes.

Many questions about intensive treatment remain unanswered. For example, are particular components or combinations of components of these programs the keys to clients' success, or is the total package of services necessary to promote recovery?[31] One question that has been addressed is whether inpatient or outpatient services produce better results. In a review of treatment modalities, the National Institute on Alcohol Abuse and Alcoholism (NIAAA) concluded that almost all studies have found no reported differences in the outcomes associated with inpatient and outpatient care (including partial hospitalization and day treatment) of alcoholics.[32] Even one group of researchers who found that hospital treatment produced better overall results than community treatment wrote that "Noteworthy . . . were the findings that the IC [in community] treatment was effective for some patients and that both IH [in hospital] and IC treatment were relatively ineffective for other patients."[33] A 1991 study of alcoholics treated through an employee assistance program did find that inpatient treatment followed by AA attendance produced better outcomes with regard to drinking and drug use than did AA alone or allowing employees to select their treatment; however, no differences were found on job outcomes.[34]

Goodwin cautions that inpatient programs not be abruptly abandoned, since the studies to date vary greatly in the treatment used, the populations studied, and the evaluation methodologies used.[35] Also, an article in *Psychiatric News* cautioned against abandoning intensive inpatient treatment in an effort to cut costs in this era of mananged care.[36] But given that outpatient treatment for alcoholism seems as effective as inpatient, reluctance to move to outpatient services sooner was probably due to a number of factors. Some of these factors are the heavy investment of private companies in inpatient facilities, large amounts charged to clients receiving inpatient care, and resistance to the changes involved in converting to outpatient services. The rising costs of health care and efforts at health care reform are serving to push providers toward greater use of outpatient options when intensive services are needed.

Residential Programs

Also on the continuum of care are a number of residential services, including halfway houses, therapeutic communities, domiciliaries, and missions. Each serves a different purpose.

Halfway Houses. Halfway houses (sometimes called rehabilitation facilities) are another impor-

tant part of the continuum of care for many alcoholics and addicts. According to Rubington, "The halfway house may be defined as a transitional place of indefinite residence of a community of persons who live together under the rule and discipline of abstinence from alcohol and other drugs."[37] Halfway houses may be publicly subsidized, privately owned, or church sponsored.[38]

Many halfway-house residents have lost their jobs and financial assets, are estranged from family and friends, or lack social and independent living skills. Most halfway houses serve clients who enter more or less voluntarily, but some are solely for those who are mandated to become residents by the criminal justice system.

The term *halfway house* refers to halfway back into the community. Residents sometimes used to progress from a quarterway house to a halfway house and later to a three-quarterway house where they were considered to be close to a complete return to the community. Halfway house is the name primarily used today. As residents move through recovery, they usually earn greater amounts of responsibility and more privileges in the halfway house, similar to the progression from quarterway to three-quarterway houses.

The structure of halfway houses and the services they offer vary considerably.[39] Some are highly structured, with a specific treatment regimen that consumes almost all the residents' time. Others are loosely structured and are more like boarding homes with some supervision or requirements to get a job and attend self-help meetings. The structure of many halfway houses falls in between these two extremes and incorporates treatment and self-help groups along with expectations that residents seek and maintain employment.

The size of the staff and their credentials vary. Many halfway houses are supervised 24 hours a day by managers who are themselves in recovery.[40] Some managers have formal education in the helping professions or in chemical dependency treatment, but this may not be a job requirement. Other halfway-house staff (therapists, vocational counselors, etc.) come from a variety of educational backgrounds. Halfway-house residents may have a case manager or primary therapist who coordinates the various services they need. Other staff may specialize in group treatment or in vocational services.

Some programs require clients to have at least weekly individual counseling or therapy sessions and to participate in group treatment. Seeing that clients get a job is often a priority in halfway-house programs. Other services may include education about independent living skills and communication as well as nutritional counseling, exercise, and instruction on maintaining good health and mental health. Participation in recreational activities and developing social skills is also encouraged because of the desocialization of clients whose problems are severe enough to warrant referral to a halfway house. Attendance at self-help meetings, often several times a week, is a frequent requirement. One of the local AA or NA groups may meet at the halfway house, and residents may also attend meetings in the community. Halfway-house staff often work closely with staff of other community agencies to ensure that their clients receive other services such as vocational rehabilitation and health care. Clients may also be assisted in applying for food stamps, which can help the halfway house defray food costs. Residence in a halfway house provides an opportunity to address many client needs.

Residents may be admitted to the halfway house on the recommendation of an individual staff member, or there may be a client staffing. A *staffing* generally involves the client meeting with a small group of staff members who ask the client questions about his or her motivation to enter the halfway house.[41] The staff members may then vote or come to a consensus on whether to admit the individual. To gain entrance, clients must usually agree to participate in all halfway-house activities and to abide by other rules, which include no drinking of alcohol and no use of drugs except as approved by medical staff. Residents are generally not allowed to keep their own medications but are given access to them by staff. Other rules are no

violence and no sex in the house. Residents are usually obligated to report violations of the rules by other residents.[42] They are also expected to keep their personal living area clean, and general household chores such as cooking and cleaning are shared or rotated. Visitors and personal telephone calls may be restricted to specified times. Passes or leaves of absence are generally limited at first but increase as the client makes progress. Policies regarding readmission after rule violations, especially drinking or drug use, differ among programs, with some more lenient than others.

Some programs have resident or community governments. Residents take turns acting as the chairperson of weekly meetings held to discuss and solve problems in the house such as individuals not doing their chores, knowledge or suspicion of individuals drinking or using drugs, interpersonal conflicts between residents, and so forth. Resident governments are established to help clients learn rational means of problem solving. Staff may participate in all or a portion of these meetings to work out problems, especially conflicts between residents and staff. This gives staff an opportunity to model problem-solving and discussion skills for residents.

The length of time clients may remain in halfway-house programs varies. Some have limits of 30, 60, or 90 days or more. Houses with shorter lengths of stay help clients get back on their feet but are concerned that they not foster dependency. Some houses have such a high demand for services that they cannot accommodate clients longer. In other houses, the stay is open ended and is determined by client needs. The philosophy of open-ended programs is that residents need a period of treatment commensurate with the length and severity of their chemical dependency before they can achieve sufficient stability to live independently.

Clients are generally charged something for their room, board, and treatment while at the halfway house. Fees are usually quite modest, compared to what it would cost to receive treatment and live elsewhere. In addition to the need to defray program costs, reasons commonly used to support charging halfway-house residents are (1) it helps them learn or relearn to accept responsibility, (2) services that involve a fee are more highly valued than those that are free, and (3) those that are not serious about treatment will be deterred from entering the program. Some clients are employed and pay the fees themselves. Others may be sponsored for a period by treatment or rehabilitation agencies such as a state's vocational rehabilitation program. Some residents receive public assistance or disability payments.[43]

Some halfway houses serve men only or women only, but others serve both. Although still very few in number, some innovative programs allow women to bring their children; these programs generally offer the services found in most halfway-house programs while also helping mothers improve their parenting skills (also see Chapter 15). Services are also offered to the children to foster their development and to help them understand chemical dependency.

Effectiveness of Halfway Houses. Attempts have been made to study halfway-house services, but most have used small samples or have other serious methodological flaws.[44] Rubington's review indicates that long-term sobriety remains an illusive goal for most halfway-house residents, that "studies do not give the halfway house high marks when grading their efforts as rehabilitative agencies," and that the construction of most studies makes it "rather hard to arrive at any important theoretical conclusions based on these negative results."[45]

Annis and Liban conducted a study of 35 males who entered halfway houses following detoxification.[46] They matched them (on characteristics such as criminality and employment as well as demographics) with controls who did not enter halfway houses following detoxification. There were no posttreatment differences in the drinking behaviors of the client groups, but clients who had participated in the halfway-house programs were more likely to refer themselves to a detoxification program after drinking. These researchers suggest that clients may need longer-term services, since most did not remain in the halfway house for more than three months. The findings of Van Ryswyk and colleagues using a larger sample of 641 former residents from eight halfway houses are more positive. They conducted a secondary data analysis rather than an experimental study, but compared with preadmission functioning, these individuals had fewer detox admissions, used public assistance less, had fewer encounters with the criminal justice system, had greater abstinence, and had better employment outcomes.[47]

Orford and Velleman reviewed the evaluation literature on halfway-house programs in the United States, Canada, and the United Kingdom.[48] (In the United Kingdom, these programs go by the more generic name of hostels.) Like Annis and Liban, their review indicates that most clients do not achieve the optimal length of stay in a halfway house, which some think is three to nine months. Although there is apparently no empirical evidence validating the most beneficial length of stay in a halfway house, the treatment literature generally associates better outcomes with longer lengths of stay. Reports indicate that most clients leave without staff approval, often after drinking or after a dispute.[49] In a study of 29 residents and staff of a halfway house in England, Velleman found that residents who left prematurely were less liked by staff and that staff spent less time with them; residents who left prematurely felt more negatively about lack of privacy, felt life could be better outside the halfway house, had more negative attitudes about staff, and thought that their expectations about the halfway house were not met.[50] Velleman recommends attention to these factors to prevent clients from leaving prematurely. There are conflicting results on whether clients' length of stay in halfway houses is affected by the degree of structure or institutional atmosphere of these facilities.[51]

Given that many residents stay sober while in halfway houses but have high relapse rates after leaving, we have often wondered whether independent living is a viable goal for some residents.[52] Many clients seen in halfway houses are severely debilitated. For some, this type of communal living may promote sobriety. But regardless of independent living skills that are learned, living alone after discharge can be isolating and may promote drinking or drug use.

Therapeutic Communities.   While halfway houses were originally designed to serve alcoholics, therapeutic communities (TCs) originated to treat addicts who abused heroin or other illegal drugs. TC staff are often addicts with a substantial period of recovery. The first therapeutic community for drug addicts, Synanon, began in 1958. It was based on a combination of ideas from Alcoholics Anonymous and therapeutic communities for those with psychiatric problems.[53] Daytop Village and Odyssey House are also well known TCs. TC residents often began drug involvement at a young age and have not necessarily mastered the developmental tasks of adulthood.[54] As a result, TCs are likely to focus on habilation as well as rehabilitation of residents.[55] These residential programs may be thought of as a combination of intensive treatment and residential care. The recommended stay is often longer than in halfway houses; a year or two is not considered atypical if the resident "works" the entire program.

Therapeutic communities rely on group process and peer pressure to get residents to address their problematic behaviors. Reality therapy[56] is often the underlying treatment philosophy. Confrontation is used to break the denial that is generally a part of chemical dependency. Many professionals are initially quite surprised at the intensity of the confrontation in individual and group counseling sessions, but both TCs and other chemical dependency treatment programs seem to have toned this down in recent years. The dropout rate from TCs is high, due perhaps to the rigors of these programs. Many halfway houses expect clients to obtain jobs quickly, but therapeutic communities tend to believe a longer period of treatment is needed before the resident is capable

of holding an outside job and has earned the privilege of working outside the facility. To teach employment behaviors and skills, some TCs operate cottage industries where residents work in enterprises such as a greenhouse, duplication service, or other small business.

Clients start with few privileges and earn additional privileges as they progress in the TC program. New residents are often assigned the most menial household chores. Progress is measured by abstinence from drugs, active participation in treatment, and adherence to program rules. Urine "drops" may be used to monitor abstinence. Moving up to the next level in the program may be based on a vote of residents and staff. Residents may graduate to become staff of therapeutic communities. Gerstein and Harwood describe today's therapeutic communities as "a remarkable merger of the therapeutic optimism of psychiatric medicine and the disciplinary moralism of the criminal perspective."[57]

Effectiveness of Therapeutic Communities.   Using the Community Oriented Program Environments Scale,[58] Bell studied three therapeutic communities and found that one of the three did not score as highly as the other two on subscales such as practical operation and personal problem solving.[59] More importantly, the lower-scoring TC also had a substantially higher treatment dropout rate, suggesting that program factors can make a substantial difference in the effectiveness of TCs.

Gerstein and Harwood draw these primary conclusions from the treatment effectiveness literature on therapeutic communities serving drug abusers: (1) drug use and criminal activity are reduced and social productivity is increased both during and after treatment; (2) length of stay in treatment is the best predictor of outcome, with at least 3 months of treatment needed and better results indicated for those who spend longer periods (up to 18 months) in treatment; and (3) those who participate in and those who graduate from treatment do better than do those who fail to enter or drop out of treatment, respectively.[60] Snair's re-

A Therapeutic Community Resident

Susan Murphy was 18 when she entered a therapeutic community. She was skinny with long, scraggly black hair and a tattoo of a former boyfriend's name on her left hand. She had run away from home at least a dozen times during her teen years because she and her mother and stepfather never got along. Susan spent many nights on the streets or in runaway shelters. She was a high school dropout and had never had a job for more than a few weeks. Susan was convinced by staff of a criminal justice diversion program to enter the TC after she was picked up on a vagrancy charge and her rap sheet indicated several other infractions. Susan had used many types of drugs. She was particularly fond of amphetamines but did not want to start mainlining drugs like her current boyfriend. Susan hated the TC at first and found it difficult to take the strong feedback from staff and other residents about her attitude of blaming others for her problems. She almost left several times but she did manage to remain for a year and earned a GED along with 12 months of "clean" time. Susan is now a graduate of the TC and is in vocational school learning computer technology. She attends Narcotics Anonymous regularly and likes to sponsor new members.

view also confirms the effectiveness of therapeutic communities in reducing drug use and criminal behavior.[61]

Domiciliaries.   Domiciliaries, another type of residential facility, assist those with severe physical or mental debilitation from alcohol or other drug dependency. Some of these individuals need an extensive period of recovery before they move to a halfway house. For others, the domiciliary will become their long-term home, because their impairments make a successful return to independent living unlikely. Some domiciliaries are referred to as farms because they are on the outskirts of town on large pieces of property with gardening a primary activity of residents. In other cases, they are called this simply because of the pastoral environment.

Domiciliaries usually have 24-hour staff supervision. Residents are given responsibilities or participate in activities commensurate with their abilities. The care provided may be largely custodial but there may be some group treatment, especially to promote socialization. Domiciliaries are generally more lenient in reaccepting a client following alcohol or drug use than halfway houses or therapeutic communities. The Veterans Admin-

istration operates a number of domiciliaries that serve those severely debilitated by alcoholism, drug dependency, or other physical and mental disorders. A number of communities also have publicly supported domiciliary-type facilities. Residents whose conditions deteriorate to the point that they are nonambulatory or in need of psychiatric or nursing home care are referred to appropriate facilities.

Missions.   For years, facilities such as the Salvation Army[62] and rescue missions have assisted those who are homeless, transient, or living on the streets due to a variety of problems such as substance abuse, mental illness, or the inability to secure a job. Some of these facilities are better classified as halfway houses, because residents spend several months at them receiving treatment and working (perhaps in one of their thrift shops). A religious program is generally a component of services.[63] In most cases, the stay at these facilities is brief (a night or two). In street lingo, brief stays are often referred to as "three hots and a cot" (three meals and a bed in which to sleep). Those staying overnight receive an evening meal and may be expected to attend a prayer or spiritual service designed to motivate them to find a new way of life. Following an early breakfast (sometimes toast, coffee, and grits), they are generally expected to leave the premises, and those planning to spend another night usually are not permitted to return until evening check-in time. They may be assisted in finding a few hours or a day's work. The cost of staying overnight might be a few dollars. Some facilities do not charge, or they may give a free night once every month or two.

The staff of public and not-for-profit substance abuse programs frequently refer individuals with alcohol and drug abuse problems who have nowhere else to go or who are not interested in treatment to these facilities. Some substance abuse programs have funds that can be used to pay for a night or two at a mission or shelter for alcoholics and addicts while they try to find a job, make arrangements to get a bus ticket home, or await admission to an inpatient chemical dependency treatment center or a halfway house.

Chemically dependent individuals are also making use of community shelters for homeless persons, which have increased in number in recent years. Missions and shelters generally do not admit those who are intoxicated or who are experiencing serious withdrawal symptoms. Some missions have been criticized for their moralistic approach to substance abuse and for their exploitation of clients' labor; however, they have historically provided a safe haven for those who would otherwise be sleeping on the streets or in the woods.[64]

Effectiveness of Shelters and Missions. Evaluating the effectiveness of shelters and missions is particularly difficult because of the transient nature of the clientele served by these programs. Jacobson reviewed the findings from the few evaluative studies available and concluded that among former clients who could be located, there did seem to be some reduction in drinking.[65] Katz's follow-up study of about 100 residents of two Salvation Army Men's Social Service Centers indicated "that men going through the program were, as a group, 'better off' afterward than before. They showed greater residential stability and reported better health" and "a greater portion . . . showed an improved drinking pattern than showed vocational improvement."[66] Since the bulk of the residents stayed from one to four months and received multiple services, the program functioned more like a halfway house than a transient shelter. Another follow-up study of Salvation Army alcoholism treatment programs showed client improvement in seven of nine areas of client functioning, including abstinence, psychological well-being, and occupational functioning, but not in hospitalization for alcoholism or social functioning.[67] Clients were encouraged to stay six months, but the median stay was 63 days. An important note about this study was that a high proportion (82 percent) of the original 121 participants were located at follow-up.

Jacobson concludes that although the long-term effects of shelter residence are not clear, experience shows that the short-term effects are generally positive—there is interruption of the individual's drinking, meals and safety are provided, and the individual may be referred to other helping resources such as employment services, medical services, halfway houses, self-help and spiritual programs, or other services.[68] Despite recent interest in homelessness, shelters and missions that have traditionally served alcoholics and addicts have not attracted much empirical study as of late.

Outpatient Services

Outpatient services also occupy a place in the system of care. Some clients use outpatient services following detoxification, intensive treatment, or halfway-house services. Those with early stage or less severe problems may begin treatment with this component. For example, a substance abuser who is experiencing early signs of family or other social problems, who is not physically addicted, and who is employed may be well served by an outpatient program.

Outpatient services are usually some type of counseling—individual, couple, family, or group.

The theoretical orientations and treatment philosophies of those who provide these services vary considerably. The frequency with which clients receive outpatient services also varies. Sessions are often weekly but may be more or less frequent.

The content of outpatient treatment sessions is quite similar to topics initiated in intensive and residential treatment. Examples are how to remain alcohol and drug free, dealing with depression or loneliness, fostering positive social relationships, and increasing self-esteem. Other services may involve teaching relaxation or stress-reduction techniques. Obstacles to recovery, such as a previous history of physical or sexual abuse, may also be addressed. Since no single human service professional is equipped to treat all the problems clients may present, referral to other professionals may be needed. For example, clients with sexual dysfunctions may need the assistance of a certified sex therapist.

Today, outpatient chemical dependency services are offered by many types of providers under various auspices. Service providers include psychiatrists, psychologists, nurses, social workers, marriage and family therapists, and various types of counselors (such as rehabilitation and pastoral), as well as chemical dependency counselors (some who have degrees in the helping professions and others who do not). State laws regulating these groups vary, but increasingly human service professionals, including those who treat alcoholics and addicts, are required by state law or by community norms to be licensed or certified. State laws and insurance companies determine which professionals can collect third-party payments for their services.

Outpatient services are provided under four auspices: (1) public; (2) private, not-for-profit; (3) private, for-profit; and (4) church. Some outpatient programs are attached to hospitals; others are part of community mental health centers or community alcohol and drug treatment centers. Private practitioners in the chemical dependency field may also offer their services in individual or group practices. Health maintenance organizations (HMOs) and employee assistance programs (EAPs) may offer outpatient chemical dependency services directly, using their own personnel, or through arrangements with other agencies and individuals who provide chemical dependency services.

Like other services, outpatient chemical dependency treatment may be covered under the individual's health care plan or the client may pay for it directly. In public or not-for-profit programs, a sliding fee scale may be used. Private practitioners usually charge fees based on local market rates; some use sliding scales or provide some treatment on a pro bono basis as a service to the community.

Individual Counseling.   Individual outpatient counseling involves only the client and the human service professional. The preference in chemical dependence treatment has been for group therapy with individual treatment used as an adjunct[69] or to treat specific problems such as sexual dysfunction or other problems not necessarily appropriate for the chemical dependency treatment group. Chemical dependency treatment providers may see clients on an individual basis initially while encouraging them to consider group treatment and self-help groups. Although group treatment may be recommended, clients may opt for individual treatment, because they feel individual treatment will be more effective or because group participation seems too threatening or will not protect their anonymity.

Group Treatment.   Group treatment is frequently offered as the "treatment of choice" to those with alcohol and drug problems on the grounds that they can benefit from the experiences of and interactions with others who are facing the challenges of maintaining sobriety.[70] Levine and Gallogly write that:

> Groups for alcoholics can serve many purposes:
> 1. help reduce the denial and facilitate the acceptance of alcoholism
> 2. increase the motivation for sobriety and other changes

3. treat the emotional conditions that often accompany drinking (i.e., anxiety, depression, hostility)
4. increase the capacity to recognize, anticipate, and cope with situations that may precipitate drinking behavior
5. meet the intense needs of alcoholics for social acceptance and support.[71]

Groups are almost always a component of intensive chemical dependency treatment programs and are also offered by other outpatient programs.

The composition of outpatient chemical dependency treatment groups varies. Groups usually have several members, but more than 12 is generally considered too large to allow everyone to participate actively. Participation may be limited to clients who share certain characteristics. For example, the groups may be composed of only male or only female members, gays or lesbians, those in particular age groups, or white-collar or blue-collar workers. Larger communities or programs that serve many clients tend to offer more groups. There are usually one or two group leaders. Co-ed groups may have male and female leaders, but groups for men or women generally have a leader or leaders of the same gender.

Groups may be closed or open ended. In a closed-ended group, members usually start together and contract for a certain number of sessions. At the end of the sessions, members may be asked if they wish to contract for additional group sessions. An advantage of the closed-ended group is continuity of membership, but if there are many dropouts, those remaining may become discouraged, and the number may dwindle below what is necessary to carry on effective group sessions. In an open-ended group, members may join at different times, and there may be no commitment to attend a specific number of sessions. An advantage of the open-ended group is that more experienced members, especially those who are making progress or who have learned from mis-

 An Outpatient Client

Frank Villa, a 26-year-old Mexican American male, was friendly and cheerful when sober—someone who was always described as a nice guy—but his wife would not put up with his drug use and left him. To make matters worse, he flunked out of college after changing majors three times and got a DWI. He was out of work and had little choice but to move in with his mother and to try to stay away from alcohol, marijuana (his favorite drug), and whatever else came his way. Frank got a part-time job with a moving company and also enrolled part time at the junior college. He joined an outpatient group for young people at the community alcohol and drug treatment program after deciding it was time to "grow up." Frank enjoyed attending the group. The discussions of topics among his peers always seemed relevant to him, and the socialization before and after group helped assuage his loneliness. Frank felt he really fit in with the group members, unlike those at school and at work, who had no idea what it was like to have a drug problem. He also attended AA and NA a few times a week. Frank would stay off alcohol and drugs for a few months and then get high. After his mother became distraught over his behavior and other family members asked him to leave her home, Frank got a girlfriend he met at NA to let him move in with her. With her urging, he went back to his therapy group and to AA and NA. Frank eventually celebrated a year of sobriety. Friends have told him he would make a good counselor. After giving it serious consideration, he is now working on his licensure in chemical dependency treatment.

takes, share their experiences with other members; however, disruptions may occur as members leave and new members are introduced to the group and the group process.

The amount of structure imposed by group leaders varies. In more structured groups, the leader may present topics for discussion and use preplanned exercises. However, in less structured groups, the leader may ask clients to present topics for discussion that are of current concern to them. A great deal has been written on group treatment, some of it specific to substance abusers.[72]

Group treatment is also provided to the loved ones of chemically dependent individuals. Some groups include all types of family members— spouses or other partners, children, parents, and siblings. Membership in other groups may be limited to spouses or other partners, to young children, or to adult children (see Chapters 10 and 12). The goals of these groups are usually to help family members understand the dynamics of chemical dependency, relieve guilt, build self-esteem, avoid enabling, and focus on becoming healthier and happier individuals.

Conjoint Therapy. Conjoint therapy, often called marital therapy, is another outpatient service. (The term *marital* is outmoded for many clients, given the range of relationships that people may experience.) Although couples may participate in conjoint treatment at any time, it is often offered after the client receives initial inpatient or outpatient services for chemical abuse or dependency and has maintained some sobriety. Before participating in conjoint treatment, the nonchemically dependent partner may also have attended educational sessions or group therapy. Initially, conjoint therapy may help the couple explore how chemical dependency or other problems have affected their relationship. Ventilation of hurt and anger may be important at this stage. The topics may then progress to improving communications, working out problems, and reacting to lapses or relapses should they occur. Conjoint treatment

may lead to a strengthening of the relationship, but it may become a forum for determining that the relationship was never satisfactory or that it is not repairable. Some practitioners treating chemically dependent clients and their partners are marriage and family therapists or are otherwise qualified to treat couples and families. Others are not equipped to do extensive work in these areas and refer clients when these services are needed.

Family Therapy. Still another type of outpatient service is family therapy (discussed more fully in Chapter 10). Similar to conjoint therapy, family therapy focuses on the effects of chemical dependency on the particular family, reducing family dysfunction and improving family communications and relationships. Family members may have participated in educational sessions or in family groups before beginning family therapy. All members of the current nuclear family are usually invited to participate, although some may not agree to do so. Members of the extended family such as the parents of an adult chemical abuser may be included, especially if they are directly enabling the client. The client and extended family members may also be seen together if the client is working to resolve family-of-origin issues.

Multiple Approaches. Like intensive inpatient and outpatient treatment programs, other outpatient programs may also combine several treatment approaches or modalities. For example, the community reinforcement approach (CRA) was developed by George Hunt and Nathan Azrin for the treatment of alcoholism.[73] CRA was first used in a hospital setting but has subsequently been used with outpatients. The approach has evolved to include seven components: (1) Antabuse (a medication used with alcoholics; discussed later), (2) assistance in complying with an Antabuse regimen, (3) reciprocity counseling with a significant other (spouse, lover, roommate, etc.) to improve communication, (4) a job club for help with employment, (5) social skills training, (6) social and recreational counseling, and (7) controlling urges to drink through relaxation techniques. Some components may not be needed by clients, such as the job club for stably employed clients. CRA uses a multidimensional approach to chemical dependency treatment—the idea that relevant aspects of the client's life must be addressed in order to promote not only abstinence but general well-being.

Brief Interventions. Brief and very brief interventions are included under outpatient services. Reviews by Bien and colleagues and NIAAA indicate that these interventions take a variety of forms, including counseling or advice by a physician or other professional, medical check-ins, feedback on test results, self-help manuals, and bibliotherapy (reading materials).[74] Some approaches are no longer than a single session, although the number of sessions varies and there is no definition of the maximum number of sessions for brief interventions. There is considerable interest in brief interventions, given issues of cost containment in this era of managed care, but the very briefest interventions are generally considered to be useful with problem drinkers or alcohol abusers rather than those diagnosed alcohol dependent.[75] Perhaps these very brief encounters would not fit a strict definition of *treatment*, although they have often proved effective in reducing patients' drinking.

Effectiveness of Outpatient Services. Snair found outpatient drug-free programs "to be moderately to highly effective in reducing drug use" and also helpful in reducing criminal behavior,[76] but Gerstein and Harwood report that illicit drug abusers have better compliance rates with therapeutic communities and methadone maintenance than with outpatient treatments.[77] One study of military veterans who were cocaine abusers (90 percent were African American) found that inpatients were significantly more likely to complete treatment than were those who participated in a day hospital program.[78]

Although group therapy has been recommended as the treatment of choice for chemical dependency, there are many forms of this type of treatment. Brandsma and Pattison's review of about 30 studies generally indicates positive effects of group therapy as part of a treatment program but also a critical need to more clearly define these treatments, especially in efforts to empirically validate their effectiveness.[79] Solomon adds that the lack of studies comparing group with individual treatment for alcoholics makes it difficult to determine whether one modality is better than the other and that it is not known which types of groups work best with which types of clients.[80]

Marital or conjoint treatment has also shown some promising results for alcohol clients, but the benefits may be more pronounced in the short run.[81] McCrady and colleagues randomly assigned alcohol patients to three treatment conditions: (1) joint hospital admission for the alcoholic and spouse, (2) hospital admission for the alcoholic with the spouse participating in treatment, and (3) hospital admission for the alcoholic and no treatment for the spouse.[82] Initial results indicated that the alcoholics in the first two groups drank less than did those who received treatment by themselves. Four years later, however, there were no statistically significant differences in drinking or other treatment outcomes among the three groups. McCrady then decided to test outpatient treatment for couples. She and her associates randomly assigned couples to three behavioral types of outpatient treatment: minimal spouse involvement, alcohol-focused spouse involvement, or alcohol-focused plus behavioral marital therapy.[83] A six-month follow-up indicated positive benefits for all groups, with the alcohol-focused plus behavioral marital therapy group generally having better outcomes such as a more rapid decline in drinking and greater maintenance of reduced drinking.

Four controlled studies on the community reinforcement approach provide very promising results.[84] For example, Azrin and colleagues found that almost all clients in the CRA groups were totally abstinent at six months; however, the married and cohabitating clients also did very well in a group that received the Antabuse compliance

(text continues on page 131)

Can Matching Enhance Treatment Effectiveness?

Some tools are available to help clinicians identify appropriate types of care for a patient or client. For example, the American Society of Addiction Medicine (ASAM) has developed Patient Placement Criteria for the Treatment of Psychoactive Substance-Related Disorders. An overview of ASAM's Adult Admission Criteria is found in Table 1. The levels range from 0.5, which is early intervention, to IV, which is medically managed, intensive, inpatient treatment. The level of treatment recommended is suggested by the six dimensions in the left-hand column of the table, such as withdrawal potential and other biomedical complications, emotional and behavioral condition, treatment acceptance, relapse potential, and the individual's recovery environment. Rather than conceptualizing treatment as a fixed interval or a fixed length of stay program, there has been a growing recognition in the field that the system of care be flexible, allowing patients or clients to move to more or less intensive levels as their situations change.[1] This requires that tools such as the ASAM criteria be used not only to assess but also to reassess the client during the course of treatment.

Clinical judgments are generally not the only criteria for selecting treatment. These decisions are often determined by clients' preferences. For example, a client may resist the idea of group therapy and prefer to see a counselor for individual treatment, or a client may not see inpatient treatment as a viable alternative given child care, work, or other responsibilities, but he or she may be willing to attend outpatient treatment. Often, the method of care is determined by available financial resources.[2] These are some of the factors that impinge on treatment decisions in the real world.

Evidence indicates that, in general, substance abuse treatment is effective. Although it is difficult to help some clients, many do fare better following treatment, and they often fare better than those who do not receive treatment. NIAAA has provided useful syntheses of information on the effectiveness of alcoholism treatment.[3] Large national studies, including the Drug Abuse Reporting Program (DARP) and the Treatment Outcome Perspective Study (TOPS), provide data on other forms of drug abuse treatment, and a comprehensive analysis by Gerstein and Harwood is also valuable in digesting the information on the effectiveness of treatment for illicit drug use.[4] The review presented in this chapter on the components of care addresses some questions about treatment effectiveness, such as whether outpatient treatment is as useful as inpatient care, but much more knowledge is needed about the effects of treatment setting, treatment modality, duration and intensity of treatment, client characteristics, therapist characteristics, theoretical perspectives, and so forth, on client outcomes.

How can professionals learn more about better matching clients to treatment? One approach is to consider the characteristics of clients and to match them with a theoretical approach to treatment that seems consistent with their needs, as suggested by McLellan and colleagues and others.[5] Litt and colleagues attempted to do this by randomly assigning two types of alcoholics to two different theoretical approaches to treatment.[6] They called the two types of alcoholics Type A and Type B. Type A had "later onset [of alcoholism], fewer indicators of vulnerability, less psychiatric disturbance, a more benign alcohol-related problem profile, and better prognosis," whereas type B had an "early onset of problem drinking, rapid progression [of alcoholism], indicators of childhood and familial vulnerability, more psychiatric disturbance, greater symptom severity, and poor prognosis."[7] The two types of treatment were "more structured coping skills group treatment" and "less structured interactional group therapy." As hypothesized, Type As did better in the interactional therapy and Type Bs did better in the coping skills treatment. Litt and associates believed this would be the case because interactional treatment seemed

(continued)

TABLE 1   Adult Admission Criteria: Crosswalk of Levels 0.5 through IV

	Levels of Service				
Criteria Dimensions	Level 0.5 Early Intervention	OMT Opioid Maintenance Therapy	Level I Outpatient Services	Level II.1 Intensive Outpatient	Level II.5 Partial Hospitalization
DIMENSION 1: Alcohol Intoxication and/or Withdrawal Potential	No withdrawal risk	Patient is physiologically dependent on opiates and requires OMT to prevent withdrawal	I-D, Ambulatory detoxification without extended on-site monitoring<hr>Minimal risk of severe withdrawal	Minimal risk of severe withdrawal	II-D, Ambulatory detoxification with extended on-site monitoring<hr>Moderate risk of severe withdrawal
DIMENSION 2: Biomedical Conditions and Complications	None or very stable	None or manageable with outpatient medical monitoring	None or very stable	None or not a distraction from treatment and manageable in Level II.1	None or not sufficient to distract from treatment and manageable in Level II.5
DIMENSION 3: Emotional/ Behavioral Conditions and Complications	None or very stable	None or manageable in outpatient structured environment	None or very stable	Mild severity, with potential to distract from recovery; needs monitoring	Mild to moderate severity, with potential to distract from recovery; needs stabilization
DIMENSION 4: Treatment Acceptance/ Resistance	Willing to understand how current use may affect personal goals	Resistance high enough to require structured therapy to promote treatment progress but will not render outpatient treatment ineffective	Willing to cooperate but needs motivating and monitoring strategies	Resistance high enough to require structured program but not so high as to render outpatient treatment ineffective	Resistance high enough to require structured program but not so high as to render outpatient treatment ineffective
DIMENSION 5: Relapse/ Continued Use Potential	Needs understanding of, or skills to change, current use patterns	High risk of relapse or continued use without OMT and structured therapy to promote treatment progress	Able to maintain abstinence or control use and pursue recovery goals with minimal support	Intensification of addiction symptoms, despite active participation in Level I, and high likelihood of relapse or continued use without close monitoring and support	Intensification of addition symptoms, despite active participation in Level I or II.1; high likelihood of relapse or continued use without monitoring and support
DIMENSION 6: Recovery Environment	Social support system or significant others increase risk for personal conflict about alcohol/ drug use	Supportive recovery environment and/or patient has skills to cope with outpatient treatment	Supportive recovery environment and/or patient has skills to cope	Environment unsupportive, but with structure and support, the patient can cope	Environment is not supportive but, with structure and support, and relief from the home environment, the patient can cope

TABLE 1   Adult Admission Criteria: Crosswalk of Levels 0.5 through IV *(continued)*

	Levels of Service				
Criteria Dimensions	**Level III.1 Clinically-Managed Low Intensity Residential Services**	**Level III.3 Clinically-Managed Medium Intensity Residential Services**	**Level III.5 Clinically-Managed Medium/High Intensity Residential Services**	**Level III.7 Medically-Monitored Intensive Inpatient Services**	**Level IV Medically-Managed Intensive Inpatient Services**
DIMENSION 1: Alcohol Intoxication and/or Withdrawal Potential	No withdrawal risk	Level III-D, Clinically-Managed Residential Detoxification Services No severe withdrawal risk, moderate withdrawal manageable in III.2-D	Minimal risk of severe withdrawal for Level III.3 and III.5. If withdrawal is present, meets Level III.2-D criteria	III.7-D, Medically-Monitored Inpatient Detoxification Services Severe withdrawal, but manageable in Level III.7-D	IV-D, Medically-Managed Inpatient Detoxification Services Severe withdrawal risk
DIMENSION 2: Biomedical Conditions and Complications	None or stable	None or stable	None or stable; receiving concurrent medical monitoring	Patient requires medical monitoring but not intensive treatment	Patient requires 24-hour medical and nursing care
DIMENSION 3: Emotional/ Behavioral Conditions and Complications	None or minimal; not distracting to recovery	Mild to moderate severity; needs structure to allow focus on recovery	Repeated inability to control impulses; personality disorder requires high structure to shape behavior	Moderate severity; patient needs a 24-hour structured setting	Severe problems require 24-hour psychiatric care with concomitant addiction treatment
DIMENSION 4: Treatment Acceptance/ Resistance	Open to recovery, but needs structured environment to maintain therapeutic gains	Little awareness; patient needs interventions available only in Level III.3 to engage and keep in treatment	Marked difficulty with or opposition to treatment, with dangerous consequences if not engaged in treatment	Resistance high and impulse control poor, despite negative consequences; patient needs motivating strategies available only in 24-hour structured setting	Problems in this dimension do not qualify the patient for Level IV services
DIMENSION 5: Relapse/ Continued Use Potential	Understands relapse but needs structure to maintain therapeutic gains	Little awareness; patient needs interventions available only in Level III.3 to prevent continued use	No recognition of skills needed to prevent continued use, with dangerous consequences	Unable to control use, with dangerous consequences, despite active participation in less intensive care	Problems in this dimension do not qualify the patient for Level IV services
DIMENSION 6: Recovery Environment	Environment is dangerous, but recovery achievable if Level III.1 structure is available.	Environment is dangerous; patient needs 24-hour structure to learn to cope	Environment is dangerous; patient lacks skills to cope outside of a highly structured 24-hour setting	Environment dangerous for recovery; patient lacks skills to cope outside of highly structured 24-hour setting	Problems in this dimension do not qualify the patient for Level IV services

Source: American Society of Addiction Medicine, *Patient Placement Criteria for the Treatment of Substance-Related Disorders,* 2nd ed. (Chevy Chase, MD: American Society of Addiction Medicine, 1996), pp. 46–48 (1-800-844-8948). Reprinted by permission.

Note: This overview of the Adult Admission Criteria is an approximate summary to illustrate the principal concepts and structure of the criteria.

(continued)

to better match the needs and styles of Type A alcoholics, and coping skills treatment seemed better suited to Type B alcoholics.

Other studies have attempted to match clients to treatment based on other personal characteristics—for example, demographic characteristics such as gender, drinking-related characteristics, intrapersonal characteristics, interpersonal characteristics, and other factors—to determine any impacts on client outcomes.[8] Believing that client matching offered a very useful direction to pursue in order to better help people with problems of alcohol abuse or dependence, the National Institute on Alcohol Abuse and Alcoholism invested $25 million to conduct a large, rigorous study of client matching. This five-year study, begun in 1989, is called Project Match. It involved nine clinical sites, including hospital and outpatient facilities run under public and private auspices. The study team was composed of well-known alcoholism researchers throughout the United States. The main hypothesis to be tested was "that more beneficial results can be obtained if treatment is prescribed on the basis of individual patient needs and characteristics as opposed to treating all patients with the same diagnosis in the same manner."[9]

Many decisions must be made about conducting any research study. In making decisions about Project Match, NIAAA decided on psychosocial treatments rather than pharmacological treatments because currently no pharmacological therapy alone has proved to be an effective treatment for alcoholism.[10] A decision was also made to utilize individual rather than group treatments for a number of reasons, some practical (e.g., the advantage of being able to start treatment immediately for each subject) and others methodological (e.g., the interest in matching the characteristics of individual clients rather than groups of clients, despite the wide use of group methods with alcoholic clients). Other considerations were what types of treatment settings to use, evidence of clinical effectiveness of the treatments to be selected, clinical utility, potential for discerning matching effects based on previous research, and distinctiveness among the treatments. Based on these considerations, three approaches were finally chosen: Twelve-Step Facilitation Therapy (TSF), Motivational Enhancement Therapy (MET), and Cognitive-Behavioral Coping Skills Therapy (CBT). Perhaps due to the increased attention on briefer treatments in this era of managed care, the duration of each of the treatments was time limited. The three treatments can be concisely described as follows:

Twelve-Step Facilitation Approach. This therapy is grounded in the concept of alcoholism as a spiritual and medical disease. The content of this intervention is consistent with the 12 steps of Alcoholics Anonymous (AA), with primary emphasis given to steps 1 through 5. In addition to abstinence from alcohol, a major goal of the treatment is to foster the patient's commitment to participation in AA. During the course of the program's 12 sessions, patients are actively encouraged to attend AA meetings and to maintain journals of their AA attendance and participation. Therapy sessions are highly structured, following a similar format each week that includes symptoms inquiry, review and reinforcement for AA participation, introduction and explication of the week's theme, and setting goals for AA participation for the next week. Material introduced during treatment sessions is complemented by reading assignments from AA literature.[11]

Motivational Enhancement Therapy. MET is based on principles of motivational psychology and is designed to produce rapid, internally motivated change. This treatment strategy does not attempt to guide and train the client, step by step, through recovery, but instead employs motivational strategies to mobilize the client's own resources. MET consists of four carefully planned and individualized treatment sessions. The first two sessions focus on structured feedback from the initial assessment, future plans, and motivation for change. The final two sessions, at the midpoint and end of treatment, provide opportunities for the therapist to reinforce progress, encourage reassessment, and provide an objective perspective on the process of change.[12]

Cognitive-Behavioral Therapy. This therapy is based on the principles of social learning theory and views drinking behavior as functionally related to major problems in the person's life. It posits that addressing this broad spectrum of problems will prove more effective than focusing on drinking alone. Emphasis is placed on overcoming skill deficits and increasing the person's ability to cope with high-risk situations that commonly precipitate relapse, including both interpersonal difficulties and intrapersonal discomfort such as anger or depression. The program consists of 12 sessions, with the goal of training the individual to use active behavioral or cognitive coping methods to deal with problems rather than relying on alcohol as a coping strategy. The skills also provide a means of obtaining social support critical to the maintenance of sobriety.[13]

In order to maintain a rigorous design, each treatment was highly structured and guided by a treatment manual. The approximately 80 professionals providing the treatments were carefully selected, trained, and continually supervised to maintain adherence or fidelity to the treatment they were to provide. The study was divided into two parts. One part involved providing each of the three treatments to clients in five different outpatient settings and the other involved providing the three treatments as aftercare to patients at four sites following standard inpatient treatment. Clients were assigned randomly to each of the treatments at each of the sites. Each site included 150 to 200 clients, and to ensure that subjects represented the population seeking alcoholism treatment, 20 percent of the clients were ethnic minorities and 25 percent were women. Extensive pre- and posttreatment data were collected on clients with follow-ups at 3, 6, 9, 12, and 15 months.[14] The goal of all treatments was for the client to remain abstinent from alcohol.

The results seemed encouraging and disappointing at the same time.[15] On the positive side, clients receiving all three treatments generally improved. There were some minor differences across the treatments, but, on average, patients maintained 80 to 90 percent days of abstinence over the follow-up period.[16] However, there were no true controls (subjects who received no treatment) with which to compare the results. In addition, the Hawthorne effect may help to explain the very high rate of treatment success (i.e., patients knew that they were participating in a major, nationally funded study and might have tried harder, especially given the large amount of attention paid to them during initial data collection and follow-up).[17] Perhaps disappointing from a client-treatment matching perspective, there were few matching effects (i.e., client characteristics were not associated with how well they did in each of the three treatments). The only match was that clients in outpatient treatment who had low psychiatric severity drank on fewer days after the 12-step facilitation than after cognitive behavioral therapy. Some furor has been raised about the research methods used in Project MATCH, not to mention the ongoing debate about the utility of alcoholism treatment.[18] But others prefer to interpret the results in a more positive light: that whichever treatment is offered, good results can be expected if the treatment is well delivered with sufficient attention paid to the client.

(continued)

ENDNOTES

1. Frances B. Hamm. "Organizational Change Required for Paradigmatic Shift in Addiction Treatment," *Journal of Substance Abuse Treatment*, Vol. 9 (1992), pp. 257–260.

2. Also see Peter E. Nathan, "Outcomes of Treatment for Alcoholism: Current Data," *Annals of Behavioral Medicine*, Vol. 8, Nos. 2–3 (1986), pp. 40–46.

3. See National Institute on Alcohol Abuse and Alcoholism, *Eighth Special Report to the U.S. Congress on Alcohol and Health* (Rockville, MD: NIAAA, 1993) and earlier editions.

4. Dean R. Gerstein and Henrick J. Harwood (Eds.), *Treating Drug Problems*, Vol. 1 (Washington, DC: National Academy Press, 1990).

5. A. Thomas McLellan, George E. Woody, Lester Luborsky, Charles P. O'Brien, and Keith A. Druley, "Increased Effectiveness of Substance Abuse Treatment: A Prospective Study of Patient-Treatment 'Matching,' " *The Journal of Nervous and Mental Disease*, Vol. 171, No. 10 (1983), pp. 597–605; and A. Thomas McLellan, Lester Luborsky, George E. Woody, Charles P. O'Brien, and Keith A. Druley, "Predicting Response to Alcohol and Drug Abuse Treatments," *Archives of General Psychiatry*, Vol. 40 (1983), pp. 620–625.

6. Mark D. Litt, Thomas F. Babor, Frances K. DelBoca, Ronald M. Kadden, and Ned L. Cooney, "Types of Alcoholics II: Application of an Empirically Derived Typology to Treatment Matching," *Archives of General Psychiatry*, Vol. 49 (August 1992), pp. 609–614.

7. Ibid., p. 610.

8. For reviews of the treatment-matching literature, see Margaret E. Mattson, John P. Allen, Richard Longabaugh, Cynthia J. Nickless, Gerard J. Connors, and Ronald M. Kadden, "A Chronological Review of Empirical Studies Matching Alcoholic Clients to Treatment," *Journal of Studies on Alcohol*, Supplement No. 12 (1994), pp. 16–29; and Margaret E. Mattson, "Patient-Treatment Matching: Rationale and Results, *Alcohol Health and Research World*, Vol. 18, No. 4 (1994), pp. 287–295.

9. Joseph Nowinski, Stuart Baker, and Kathleen Carroll, *Twelve Step Facilitation Therapy Manual: A Clinical Guide for Therapists Treating Individuals with Alcohol Abuse and Dependence* (Rockville, MD: National Institute on Alcohol Abuse and Alcoholism, 1995), p. ix, Project MATCH Monograph Series, Volume 1, NIH Publication 94-3722.

10. Dennis M. Donovan, Ronald M. Kadden, Carlos C. DiClimente, Kathleen M. Carroll, Richard Longabaugh, Allen Zweben, and Robert Rychtarik, "Issues in the Selection and Development of Therapies in Alcoholism Treatment Matching Research," *Journal of Studies on Alcohol*, Supplement No. 12 (1994), pp. 138–148.

11. Nowinski et al., *Twelve Step Facilitation Therapy Manual*, p. x.

12. William R. Miller, Allen Zweben, Carlos C. DiClimente, and Robert Rychtarik, *Motivational Enhancement Therapy Manual: A Clinical Guide for Therapists Treating Individuals with Alcohol Abuse and Dependence* (Rockville, MD: National Institute on Alcohol Abuse and Alcoholism, 1995), p. viii, Project MATCH Monograph Series, Volume 2, NIH Publication No. 94-3723.

13. Ronald Kadden, Kathleen Carroll, Dennis Donovan, Ned Cooney, Peter Monti, David Abrams, Mark Litt, and Reid Hester, *Cognitive-Behavioral Coping Skills Therapy Manual: A Clinical Guide for Therapists Treating Individuals with Alcohol Abuse and Dependence* (Rockville, MD: National Institute on Alcohol Abuse and Alcoholism, 1995), p. viii, Project MATCH Monograph Series, Volume 2, NIH Publication No. 94-3724.

14. For more information on data collection, see William R. Miller and Frances K. Del Boca, "Measurement of Drinking Behavior Using the Form 90 Family of Instruments," *Journal of Studies of Alcohol*, Supplement No. 112 (1994), pp. 112–118; William R. Miller, *Form 90: A Structured Assessment Interview for Drinking and Related Behaviors, Test Manual* (Rockville, MD: National Institute on Alcohol Abuse and Alcoholism, 1996), Project MATCH Monograph Series, Volume 5, NIH Publication No. 96-4004; and William R. Miller and Richard Longabaugh, *The Drinker Inventory of Consequences (DrInC): An Instrument for Assessing Adverse Consequences of Alcohol Abuse, Test Manual* (Rockville, MD: National Institute on Alcohol Abuse and Alcoholism, 1995), Project MATCH Monograph Series, Volume 4, NIH Publication No. 95-3911.

15. Marc A. Schuckit, "Editor's Corner: It Ain't Necessarily So," *Journal of Studies on Alcohol*, Vol. 58 (1997), pp. 5–6.

16. Project MATCH Study Group, "Matching Alcoholism Treatment to Client Heterogeneity: Project MATCH Posttreatment Drinking Outcomes," *Journal of Studies on Alcohol*, Vol. 58 (1997), pp. 7–29.

17. "Project MATCH," *News and Views*, Newsletter of the Texas Research Society on Alcoholism, Vol. 5, Nos. 2 & 3 (1996), p. 2.

18. See, for example, Stanton Peele, "Bait and Switch in Project MATCH: What NIAAA Research Actually Shows about Alcohol Treatment," *PsychNews International*, Vol. 2, Issue 3 (May–June, 1997), PSYCHNEWS@ LISTSERV.NODAK.EDU

regimen only, whereas single clients did much better with the full CRA approach.[85] Although research is needed to replicate these results, this later finding suggests that multimodal treatment may be a greater need for clients without social supports. In general, McCaul and Furst conclude that "there is growing evidence for the effectiveness of outpatient settings for the delivery of treatment services for alcoholics in all stages of recovery."[86]

Reviews of studies of brief interventions show effectiveness with samples composed largely of problem drinkers or alcohol abusers.[87] For example, a WHO study in 10 countries with "1,661 non-dependent heavy drinkers" recruited from a variety of settings used three different approaches: 5 minutes of information on sensible drinking or abstinence, 15 minutes of brief counseling along with a self-help manual, and brief counseling along with three or more monitoring sessions.[88] Overall, the approaches were effective in helping men reduce their drinking. In their review of these types of brief interventions, McKay and Maisto conclude that they are better than no intervention, are often comparable to longer interventions, may increase the utility of subsequent treatment, and are effective across diverse settings.[89]

Pharmacotherapy

Several types of drugs are used to assist alcoholics and addicts in recovery following detoxification. Although no drug is a magic elixir, they may be helpful in maintaining abstinence under appropriate conditions.

Antabuse. Disulfiram, best known by the trade name Antabuse, is used in the treatment of alcoholics.[90] The value of Antabuse is thought to be its ability to deter impulsive drinking. Like other drugs used to treat chemically dependent people, Antabuse is recommended as an adjunct to other treatment services, not as a sole treatment. Antabuse does not reduce the desire to drink. Instead, it is described as "buying time" or as an "insurance policy," because those taking it know they will become violently ill if they drink.

Antabuse interferes with the normal metabolism of alcohol, resulting in a serious physical reaction if even a small amount of alcohol is ingested. Those taking it must avoid all alcohol, including that found in prescription and over-the-counter drugs and other products that may contain alcohol such as mouthwash and skin lotions. Paraldehyde, which is sometimes used to prevent DTs in alcoholics, will also cause a severe reaction. Inhaling alcohol fumes in closed quarters might also result in some reaction. Antabuse-ethanol reactions may involve a variety of symptoms, including flushing, increased pulse and respiration, sweating, weakness, decreased blood pressure, a severe headache, vomiting, and confusion. Reactions may also result in heart failure and other life-threatening problems, and some deaths have been reported. A patient should be completely detoxified from alcohol before beginning Antabuse treatment.

Antabuse is contraindicated for those with certain conditions such as serious mental illness, heart disease, diabetes, epilepsy, or pregnancy. Patients must fully understand the consequences of using alcohol while taking Antabuse before beginning this treatment. It should not be given to those who are intellectually unable to appreciate these consequences. Patients should also be aware that if they do decide to return to drinking, several days must elapse following the last dose of Antabuse to avoid a reaction. Since serious Antabuse-ethanol reactions can occur, it also seems that patients should be screened for their desire to take this drug.

Side effects of Antabuse (not related to the ingestion of alcohol) may include skin eruptions or rashes, drowsiness, headaches, and reduced sexual performance. These symptoms often abate following an initial period of adjustment to the drug, or the dosage may be reduced to prevent these symptoms. More severe effects such as neuritis and psychoses may require discontinuing the drug.

Patients usually take Antabuse once a day. Originally, it was given in larger doses than prescribed today (disulfiram skin implants were used in some countries) and side effects and complications from reactions were more severe. It was then determined that lower doses were safer and effective.

Although this description of Antabuse may sound rather frightening, many clients have used it, apparently with success.[91] Patients generally carry a card with them indicating that they are taking Antabuse. Like a medical alert bracelet, this card helps medical personnel respond if a reaction or other emergency occurs. Some patients do attempt drinking while on Antabuse and usually end up in a hospital emergency room. Ewing recommends the use of contracts with patients taking Antabuse, including having a family member or friend supervise the daily dose.[92]

Originally, it was hoped that Antabuse would provide an answer for many alcoholics. The criminal justice system was enthusiastic about its use and ordered many of its alcoholic charges to take the drug if it was not contraindicated by other medical conditions. Patients reported to the probation and parole office or an alcoholism treatment program to take their Antabuse each day or every other day under supervision. Those who did not wish to comply learned that the drug (which looks like a large aspirin) could be slipped under the tongue and disposed of upon leaving. Those administering Antabuse quickly became aware of this practice and began crushing the pill and mixing it with juice. The patient drank the mixture and then talked with the individual administering it to ensure compliance. Reports of patients ingesting large amounts of ascorbic acid before taking Antabuse to limit reactions[93] or resorting to self-induced vomiting soon followed. Drugs similar to Antabuse have been used in countries other than the United States. Like other forms of treatment, Antabuse may work best for those who want to use it.

Methadone.   Methadone is a synthetic narcotic drug. In addition to its use in narcotic detoxification, it is also used in longer-term chemical dependency treatment as a substitute for the narcotic analgesic drugs. The effectiveness of methadone in treating opioid addiction was demonstrated in the mid-1960s, and it was approved for this purpose by the U.S. Food and Drug Administration in 1972.[94]

Methadone appears to be helpful in deterring addicts from pursuing illegal activities to support their drug habits, but its use remains controversial. Detractors argue that it replaces one drug with another rather than promoting a treatment goal of abstinence. Hanson and Venturelli summarize some advantages and disadvantages of methadone maintenance for the addict:

> The advantages of methadone over other forms of maintenance therapy are (1) It can be administered orally. (2) It acts in the body 24 to 36 hours, compared to heroin's action of 4 to 8 hours. (3) It causes no serious side effects at maintenance doses. (4) At sufficient dose levels, methadone will almost completely block the effects of heroin. (5) When taken orally, it does not produce substantial euphoric effects. Disadvantages of methadone maintenance include (1) The person taking it may develop dependence. (2) It will not prevent the addict from taking other drugs that may interfere with treatment and rehabilitation.[95]

Controversies persist about the safety and health problems of methadone maintenance and how frequently users sell it to obtain illicit drugs. Gerstein and Harwood provide an extensive discussion of these controversies, including the issue of methadone's use as a social control mechanism versus its therapeutic value to the individual client.[96] Despite its cost effectiveness due to factors such as reduced crime,[97] some communities do not have methadone maintenance clinics because they do not wish to attract heroin users to their area.

A 1995 report by the Institute of Medicine questioned whether the very strict federal controls on the administration of methadone to opiate addicts was intended more to "protect the community from methadone" than to protect the society from the problems of illicit drug use.[98] The committee recommended giving more discretion to treatment providers in order to reduce unintended obstacles to treatment, such as eliminating time frames that restrict admission to those with at least a one-year history of addiction in favor of more clinically based criteria that include "intensity, severity, and course of the addiction."[99]

Methadone maintenance is intended only for those with a severe narcotic dependence. Some use methadone for a short period before completely withdrawing, whereas others use it indefinitely. Methadone maintenance treatment can be provided only by approved programs, although some alternatives such as administration to stabilized patients at physicians' offices or medical clinics have been tried on a limited basis.[100] Methadone provides the addict an opportunity for life stabilization and allows the individual to participate in a wide range of habilitative or rehabilitative services.[101] Like Antabuse, methadone maintenance is not recommended as a sole treatment but as an adjunct to other therapeutic services; however, the extent to which methadone clients participate in other services varies.

Patients take methadone orally once a day, typically combined with a sweet drink, at outpatient clinics that also offer other services to clients. Addicts taking methadone may complain about weight gain and insomnia, but these problems have been attributed to factors such as increased alcohol consumption and to personal characteristics of users rather than to the methadone itself.[102] Alcohol and cocaine use can emerge as significant problems for narcotics addicts in methadone maintenance programs and must also be addressed.[103] The drug use of clients on methadone maintenance is usually monitored through urinalyses.

As clients make progress in treatment, they may be allowed to take a Sunday dose of methadone home or to come to the clinic every other day and take a dose home for the intervening day. A team approach to treatment is used in many methadone maintenance programs. Team members may jointly decide on the course of treatment for the client, including decisions to adjust the client's dose of methadone, add or revoke privileges, or conclude the client's treatment.[104] Approximately 750 to 800 methadone clinics are operating in the United States, serving about 100,000 clients.[105]

LAAM. Another promising drug in maintaining narcotic addicts is levo-alpha-acetylmethadol (LAAM), a methadone analog with longer-lasting effects.[106] Patients generally take it three days a week rather than daily.[107] LAAM was approved by the Food and Drug Administration for use in opioid addiction treatment in 1993. Patients may find it more suitable to maintaining a normal lifestyle because they do not have to come to a clinic each day. Studies have generally found LAAM to be about equally effective to methadone on variables such as reduced heroin use, employment rates, arrests, and treatment dropout, and there is some indication that patients feel more normal while taking it than while taking methadone. From a clinical perspective, LAAM is thought to be best used with patients who need fewer clinic visits, whereas methadone may be better for those who can benefit from daily contact with treatment providers. Few programs have made LAAM available, perhaps because of general resistance to new approaches by clients and treatment providers.

Long-term studies of the effectiveness of LAAM are limited; thus, questions about the utility of the drug remain. Prendergast and associates recommend testing the possibility that LAAM may contribute to reduced AIDS transmission more than methadone.[108] They suggest that because of LAAM's longer-lasting effects, a missed appointment day may less likely result in an immediate return to injection drug use, especially if the appointment can be made up the next day. As with other drugs, LAAM has side effects and contraindications. Currently, it is not approved for use by pregnant or nursing women and people under age 18.

Buprenorphine.   Buprenorphine is an FDA-approved analgesic and an investigational opioid antagonist that also seems to have potential in the longer-term treatment of heroin addicts by blocking the effects of opioid drugs. It seems to create low physical dependence and a mild withdrawal syndrome, making it an attractive alternative, especially for patients who wish to become drug free and transfer to naltrexone use (described next).[109] Strain and colleagues generally found it as effective as methadone and point to the need to provide patients with choices in their treatment.[110] Ling and colleagues note that "some patients will have a level of opioid tolerance higher than can be achieved by buprenorphine because of its ceiling effect," suggesting that methadone or LAAM may be a better choice for them.[111]

Naltrexone.   Naltrexone (trade name ReVia) is an improved version of the drug naloxone.[112] Both are synthetic narcotic antagonists. Naltrexone is useful in treating narcotic overdose because it can reverse respiratory depression produced by these drugs. It is also used in the longer-term treatment of narcotic addicts. In long-term treatment, both methadone and naltrexone work to block the effects of narcotics, preventing addicts from experiencing the euphoria these drugs produce. Without this effect, "the recovering opiate addict learns to *not* associate drug use with reward."[113] However, methadone is a substitute for narcotic drugs, whereas naltrexone reverses their effects. Naltrexone is also reportedly nonaddicting.[114] The effects of naltrexone last for a few days. Like Antabuse and methadone, narcotic antagonists are recommended as an adjunct to inpatient or outpatient treatment. In their assessment of the use of narcotic antagonists in treatment, Witters and Venturelli state, "Naltrexone is best suited for adolescent heroin users with relatively short experience with heroin, for recently paroled prisoners who have been abstinent while incarcerated, and for persons who have been on methadone maintenance who wish to go off, but who are afraid of relapsing to heroin."[115] The effective use of narcotic antagonists is dependent on the individual's motivation to remain "clean," since the drug itself does not provide positive effects; monitoring may therefore be necessary to ensure compliance.[116]

Naltrexone has also recently been reported to improve treatment outcomes of alcoholics and cocaine addicts.[117] Naltrexone blocks only the effects of opiates, and it does so by inhibiting the production of endorphins (the brain's natural morphinelike or "endogenous opiate" substances). Although there is still much to be learned about how naltrexone might help alcoholics[118] and those with other drug dependencies, it may also make the effects of these other psychoactive drugs less pleasurable, thereby reducing the amount consumed should a client consume them. The likelihood of a full relapse is therefore reduced.

Clonidine.   Clonidine is an antihypertensive drug that seems promising in treating opiate withdrawal. We include it in our discussion of longer-term drug treatment because it can substantially reduce the rather long period it takes to withdraw from opiates. This may encourage addicts to complete a withdrawal regimen and hopefully to enter inpatient or outpatient treatment. Clonidine is described by Hanson and Venturelli as "the first nonaddictive, noneuphoriagenic prescription medication with demonstrated efficacy in relieving the effects of opiate withdrawal" (such as vomiting and diarrhea).[119] However, not everyone can tolerate this drug since one side effect is lowered blood pressure.

Effectiveness of Pharmacotherapies.   More is known about the effectiveness of methadone maintenance than about other types of treatment for illicit drug users.[120] Snair's review found these programs "to be moderately to highly effective in reducing drug use and criminality."[121] Gerstein and Harwood caution that methadone maintenance is not the answer for all heroin addicts, but in spite of controversies about this treatment, it generally produces favorable results:

There is strong evidence from clinical trials and similar study designs that heroin-dependent individuals have better outcomes on average (in terms of illicit drug consumption and other criminal behavior) when they are maintained on methadone than when they are not treated at all or are simply detoxified and released, or when methadone is tapered down and terminated as a result of unilateral client request, expulsion from treatment, or program closure.[122]

Given individual client differences, higher rather than lower doses of methadone seem to produce more positive results.[123] The benefit-to-cost ratio associated with methadone maintenance is substantial. A study by McLellan and associates continues to support the belief that clients have better treatment outcomes when use of methadone is combined with psychosocial services.[124]

Effects of Antabuse with alcoholics have been modest, and among those who use it successfully, questions arise as to whether it is their desire and motivation to remain sober,[125] fear of becoming sick,[126] or some other corollary that actually promotes positive outcomes. A controlled study by Fuller and colleagues has cast some doubt on Antabuse's usefulness. In the authors' words, "We concluded that disulfiram may help reduce drinking frequency after relapse, but does not enhance counseling in aiding patients to sustain continuous abstinence or delay the resumption of drinking."[127] McNichol and Logsdon seem more optimistic in their review of the research to date; they state that "results have been encouraging but far from definitive" with success rates from 19 to 89 percent.[128] In their view, the benefits of Antabuse far outweigh the few risks associated with its use, particularly in light of the devastating impact of alcoholism. McNichol and Logsdon also make suggestions for improving the research on the effectiveness of this adjunct to treatment by studying supervised rather than unsupervised administration of the drug and by eliminating sampling bias. In fact, the work of Azrin and colleagues shows very good results using an "Antabuse reassurance" approach in which the benefits of Anta-

buse are described, a supportive and helpful (rather than authoritarian and coercive) person is used to help insure compliance, and role rehearsal is used to help address situations in which failure of the client or support person to follow through with the procedure is anticipated.[129] Although these added efforts may be helpful, Antabuse seems to lack a high degree of acceptability among alcoholic clients.

In a review of the effectiveness of treatments for opioid addiction, Landry concludes that naltrexone is especially effective in reducing craving and preventing opioid use in those "who are involved in meaningful relationships with nonaddicted partners, employed full-time or attending school, and living with family members."[130] As also noted, good effects have also been reported to date with opiate addicts using LAAM and buprenorphine.[131]

There has been a particular interest in naltrexone treatment of alcoholics, perhaps because disulfiram is the only other approved and widely used medication with alcoholic patients and because alcoholics are such a large number of the addicted population. Volpicelli and colleagues[132] and O'Malley and colleagues[133] have investigated the use of naltrexone as an adjunct to the short-term (12-week) treatment of alcoholics and have found good results. In a study using alcohol-dependent patients receiving outpatient alcoholism treatment at a Veterans Affairs Medical Center, Volpicelli found less alcohol craving and fewer days on which alcohol was consumed among the experimental group. Although approximately half of both groups consumed some alcohol (what might be called a "lapse"), nearly one-fourth of the experimental group relapsed (defined as "reporting five or more drinks per drinking occasion" or "coming to the treatment appointment with a blood-alcohol concentration above 100 mg/dL") compared with slightly more than half of the control group. The primary benefit of naltrexone seemed to be in preventing subjects from drinking in a particularly harmful way.

O'Malley and associates also found better outcomes for those who received naltrexone with respect to number of days drinking and relapse, as well as lower severity of alcohol-related problems. Of particular interest in O'Malley's study is that 61 percent of patients who received naltrexone in combination with supportive therapy were abstinent for the 12-week period, compared with abstinence rates of 28 percent for those who received naltrexone and coping skills treatment and 21 percent and 19 percent, respectively, for those who received the placebo and coping skills treatment and placebo and supportive treatment. However, both groups of patients receiving naltrexone had relapse rates (defined as five or more drinks on an occasion for men and four for women) that were substantially lower than for the placebo groups. Although many of those in the naltrexone plus skills group consumed some alcohol, they were less likely to proceed to a full-blown relapse. O'Malley suggests that patients may prefer naltrexone to disulfiram, given disulfiram's side effects if alcohol is consumed. Some patients did report side effects from naltrexone, primarily nausea and dizziness. Volpicelli suggests that the combination of naltrexone and alcohol may cause an aversive reaction of nausea in some individuals similar to disulfiram.

Volpicelli also found that naltrexone-treated patients retrospectively reported less subjective experiences of pleasurable effects (a high) from alcohol than did placebo patients.[134] Likewise, members of O'Malley's study group who took naltrexone and drank, retrospectively reported less incentive to continue drinking as a reason for terminating drinking, whereas placebo patients who drank reported that they stopped due to negative consequences of drinking.[135] (The groups did not differ on the pleasantness of the first drinking experience.)

Long-term investigations of naltrexone are needed. Volpicelli suggests further investigations of the mechanisms by which naltrexone works with people who do not have drinking problems. In this way, effects can be studied while patients consume alcohol, yet the ethical issue of giving alcohol to people who are alcohol dependent can be avoided.[136] He also suggests studies to identify the most effective doses and duration of treatment with the drug and to identify patients for whom it seems most beneficial.[137]

Aftercare

Aftercare, the sixth of the treatment system components on the continuum of care, is an extension of intensive treatment, residential, and outpatient programs. Aftercare provides an opportunity for program staff to assist clients in monitoring their progress and to address problems or obstacles to maintaining recovery before they result in serious consequences. Clients participating in aftercare are usually encouraged to continue participation in self-help groups.

Preventing Relapse.   Perhaps the most important part of aftercare is learning and practicing the skills needed to prevent lapses and relapses. An important key to teaching relapse prevention seems to be in increasing clients' perceptions that they can successfully cope with situations that pose risks of drinking or drug use.[138] Marlatt and Gordon,[139] Gorski and Miller,[140] and others[141] have written extensively on relapse prevention and management and recommend the use of a number of behavioral and cognitive techniques. Clients generally identify their behaviors and other factors, referred to as *warning signs* or *triggers*, that usually precede their desire to drink or use drugs or their actual use of alcohol or drugs.[142] Clients then learn techniques to avoid or defuse the particular situations that threaten their sobriety. For example, a trigger may be a fight with a spouse. This trigger may be defused by teaching clients anger-control techniques such as absenting themselves from the situation until they have cooled off and can discuss the problem rationally. Practicing relaxation and stress-reduction techniques or other healthy life-style habits can also be useful in preventing relapses and as essential components of one's aftercare program.[143]

Marlatt and Gordon suggest that clients also develop plans to follow if drinking or drug use does occur.[144] One strategy in this regard is to teach clients that consuming a small amount of alcohol or drugs, which some refer to as a *lapse* or *slip*, need not necessarily result in a full-blown relapse and that it is possible to take measures to avert a relapse. Contracting may be used to accomplish this purpose. For example, a client may develop a written or verbal agreement with a professional or another individual to call for assistance should the client begin to drink or use drugs. Since clients are often embarrassed or ashamed or feel they have let others down once alcohol or drug use commences, they may fail to stop and seek help. The contract can help them acknowledge that there is a way to conclude the episode successfully.

Aftercare services are provided in many ways. Individual sessions may be used but group meetings are more common. Telephone contacts may also be used. Clients may participate weekly, biweekly, monthly, or bimonthly, depending on the program and the clients' needs. Some treatment centers charge a flat fee for services, which includes participation in an aftercare program. The duration of aftercare for alcoholics and addicts may be from a few months to a few years.[145]

Effectiveness of Aftercare.   NIAAA's review of the research literature indicates that "available data do support the traditional view of the importance of aftercare services in alcoholism treatment."[146] Alcoholics who participate in aftercare and who participate longer seem to have better outcomes than do those who do not participate or who participate for shorter periods.[147] With respect to treatment of illicit drug users, Gerstein and Harwood note that "the extended follow-up or aftercare phase is seldom if ever a strong and integrated program element."[148] As a result, the effectiveness of this program component following intensive treatment for drug use has not been well studied.

Maintenance

Maintenance is a particularly important part of the treatment continuum because it lasts throughout

the individual's life. However, it generally receives the least attention. Approaches to maintenance vary, depending on the individual's need and preferences. Perhaps the most popular method of maintenance is the use of self-help groups (discussed at the end of this chapter). Some people drop into aftercare services or contact a professional as they feel the need. Practicing the relapse-prevention techniques learned in intensive treatment, outpatient services, or aftercare components is also an important part of a long-term maintenance program.

Perhaps the most striking statement that can be made about those treated for chemical dependency is that their relapse rates are very high, regardless of the type of treatment they received. In fact, these high rates (perhaps two-thirds or more of alcoholic clients relapse) make the literature on effectiveness of each of the components of treatment difficult to evaluate.[149] Rather than total prevention of relapse, chemical dependency specialists have come to realize that the goals of reduced drug use and longer periods of abstinence are also indicators of success. Studies on the efficacy of teaching relapse prevention to alcoholics as a maintenance strategy have yielded some positive results, but a return to drinking at some level still occurs for many clients.[150]

Alcoholics and addicts frequently use self-help groups (discussed shortly) as aftercare and maintenance programs. Studies of Alcoholics Anonymous (AA) used in this manner generally suggest positive results in helping alcoholics maintain sobriety.[151]

Education and Psychoeducation

Didactic education about chemical abuse and dependency is also part of the treatment continuum. It is an essential element of almost all the components of the service system we have discussed. Whether it is education about the physiological effects of alcohol and other drugs presented to patients during their brief stay in detoxification programs, or education about the effects of chemical dependency on the family presented to clients and their loved ones during intensive treatment, accurate information can address misconceptions, present the controversies in the field, and provide a foundation for rehabilitation and recovery.

Psychoeducation has become increasingly popular in the human service professions. It combines the presentation of didactic information to increase knowledge with a variety of other techniques to help clients make desired changes and to provide support. Among the methods employed as part of psychoeducation are role-plays (e.g., to practice communication or assertiveness skills), structured exercises (e.g., genograms or other family exploration exercises), homework assignments (e.g., reading, charting behaviors, or keeping journals), and group discussion.

Although education or psychoeducation are part of all the components of treatment, they can also be primary services occupying their own place on the continuum of care. For example, in addition to a fine, license suspension, and any jail term, those convicted of driving while intoxicated (DWI) or driving under the influence (DUI) are usually required to attend an educational program. These programs describe the effects of alcohol and other drugs on behavior, allow participants to review the circumstances that led to their arrest and how to avoid such problems in the future, present the signs and symptoms of chemical abuse and dependency, and help participants consider whether they are comfortable with their current use of alcohol or other drugs. Students in DWI or DUI courses may be screened for chemical abuse or dependency and referred to treatment if indicated, but many do not meet the criteria for these problems.

Education and psychoeducation may also be the primary services offered to youths apprehended by law enforcement on minor-in-possession charges or other infractions. The juvenile courts may also require parents to attend educational sessions when their child has been involved in an alcohol- or drug-related incident. High schools, colleges, and universities have established alcohol and drug education courses for those re-ferred for disciplinary action after causing disturbances or damaging property while drunk. These institutions are also using education and psycho-education to help students explore the relationship between alcohol, other drugs, and sexual behavior, including contracting sexually transmitted diseases, and the role that alcohol or other drugs can play in hazing and sexual assault. Education as a tool in preventing chemical abuse and dependency is discussed at length in Chapter 7.

Adjunctive Services

The final component comprising the treatment continuum is adjunctive services, introduced in the previous chapter on screening, diagnosis, assessment, and referral. In addition to chemical abuse or dependence, the systems or multidimensional approach requires the remediation of employment, legal, family, health, and other problems the client is experiencing. A referral is sufficient for some clients to avail themselves of these adjunctive services. Others need additional assistance. For some, this may involve coordinating and monitoring adjunctive services for the client. The terms *case management* and *care management* are used to describe these coordination and monitoring functions. Some state, county, and local agencies have special case-management units to assist clients with multiple problems. Clients served by these units generally (1) have problems that are severe and persistent, (2) have a history of involvement with the chemical dependency or mental health service delivery systems or both, and (3) have had difficulty in utilizing available services. Monitoring is done through contacts with the client, available family members or friends, and service providers. This function can prevent crises through the early identification of new problems and the recognition of recurring problems.[152]

In recent years, case management has gained more attention from substance abuse treatment providers, primarily with populations who may have these multiple and often long-term needs. The National Institute on Drug Abuse published a monograph on a number of case-management models that have been used with various drug-abusing populations: intravenous drug users, methadone clients, HIV-positive drug users, drug-abusing pregnant women, formerly homeless women, youths, and parolees.[153] According to Ridgely and Willenbring, "research to date on case management suggests that it may be an effective intervention," but it has been a particularly difficult treatment modality to study. This is not only due to the difficulty in engaging participants who have been the targets of these services and following up the experimental and control clients, but also due to methodological issues such as how to separate the effects of the case-management technique from other services clients receive.[154] Many creative attempts have been made to use case-management models, such as the approach described by Levy and associates to reach out to active drug abusers in a combined program of case management and peer support.[155] In addition to its use in providing services to clients with multiple needs, case management has a role as a tool used by both private and public providers to control the services used by drug-abusing clients and thereby the costs of assisting them.

Effectiveness of Adjunctive Services. If human service professionals are to continue to support a systems, multidimensional, or biopsychosocial view of substance abuse treatment, it is necessary to demonstrate that treatment of problems in addition to the substance abuse or dependency promotes better outcomes for clients. We can point to some evidence that attention to the client's other problems is also important. For example, a study of supported work demonstration programs indicated that compared to controls, substance abusers participating in these programs had greater employment and less criminal activity, even though drug use did not differ between the two groups.[156] Additional indications that treatment of clients'

problems in addition to chemical dependency may be needed comes from McLellan and colleagues.[157] They followed 742 male veterans after treatment for substance abuse and found "little relation" between the severity of the clients' substance use and functioning in most other life areas, including employment. These findings indicate that substance abuse treatment alone may not be sufficient to improve clients' functioning in other areas. Employment problems and other problems may require specific interventions.

More Treatment Effectiveness Issues

In addition to issues about the effectiveness of each component of the system of care, some concerns cut across components. They include length and intensity or amount of treatment, client and therapist characteristics, theoretical approaches to treatment, and costs.

Length of Stay. In general, Gerstein and Harwood report that improvement among illicit drug users is positively related to length of stay in treatment, whether clients participated in inpatient therapeutic communities, outpatient methadone maintenance programs, or other outpatient services.[158] The evidence on length of stay for alcoholic clients is more equivocal. Some studies show that increased stays did not improve client outcomes, while in other studies longer stays were associated with more positive outcomes.[159]

Amount and Intensity of Services. There is some evidence that the amount of services offered by programs is of importance. For example, McLellan and colleagues studied four private substance abuse treatment programs (two residential and two outpatient) and found that the clients fared better in "the programs that provided the most services directed at a particular treatment problem."[160] They also cite evidence from earlier studies indicating that both "quantity and range of services" are positively related to client outcomes.

However, earlier discussion in this chapter suggests that brief interventions can benefit individuals with less severe alcohol problems.

Client Characteristics.   Some of the clearest evidence from alcoholism treatment outcome studies is that the strongest predictors of outcome are client characteristics rather than the type, length, or intensity of the treatment received.[161] Clients who are "married, stably employed, free of severe psychological impairments, and of higher socioeconomic status" are more likely to have positive outcomes.[162]

Two frequently cited studies by McLellan and colleagues—conducted on all-male samples of veterans with alcohol, drug problems, or both—indicate that treatment is generally effective and that when patients are matched to the appropriate type of treatment based on their personal characteristics, effectiveness can be improved.[163] For example, patients who had low psychiatric severity scores did well in outpatient treatment, whereas those with high scores needed inpatient treatment. Another important finding of this research is that patients with less severe psychiatric symptoms did better than did those with more severe symptoms, regardless of the type of treatment they received. This also indicates the need for special interventions for those with severe mental disorders (also see Chapter 13).

These findings support the need to match clients with appropriate treatment. They also point to the need to develop programs that compensate for factors that appear to inhibit positive outcomes for clients—specifically, marital instability, unstable employment, low incomes, and severe psychiatric symptoms. Progress is being made in addressing some of these issues. For example, some communities now have programs designed specifically for those with dual diagnoses (comorbidity) of substance use and mental disorders. Although vocational rehabilitation has long been an adjunct to substance abuse treatment, some studies indicate that relatively few substance abusers actually get this service, despite its reported effectiveness in helping clients obtain and maintain employment.[164] Services that would improve clients' abilities to develop long-term, stable, personal relationships would also logically be expected to help and should be tested for their usefulness.

Therapist Characteristics.   An area particularly lacking study is the characteristics of treatment providers that might influence the treatment process. The topic has, however, been of interest in the alcoholism literature for some time, with the idea that the therapist can be important in affecting positive outcomes.[165]

McLachlan studied 94 alcoholics and found that those who were similar to their group therapist in terms of conceptual level (defined as interpersonal development) did better in maintaining abstinence than did patients whose therapist did not match their conceptual level.[166] Valle's work indicates that clients who had alcoholism counselors with higher levels of interpersonal functioning (based on an assessment of their empathy, genuineness, concreteness, and respect) had fewer relapse-related outcomes.[167] Other researchers have also investigated the role of the therapist in client improvement. In a study of nine therapists and 78 randomly assigned clients, Luborsky and associates found that "the major agent of effective psychotherapy is the personality of the therapist, particularly the ability to form a warm, supportive relationship."[168] However, the content of the treatment sessions—that is, their concordance with the type of therapy they were assigned to provide—was also an important factor. Miller and colleagues have also shown accurate empathy (see Chapter 5) to be an important factor in predicting client outcome over a two-year period, although the effects of the association deteriorated somewhat over time.[169] Miller and colleagues also found that, in general, clients who received directive feedback (emphasizing drinking problems, giving direct advice, and disagreeing with minimization of problems) or client-centered feedback (emphasizing empathy and reflective listening) did not differ with respect to the drinking outcomes studied. One therapist's behavior deserved special note: "The more the therapist *confronted*, the more the client drank."[170]

Viewing the issue from the perspective of what staff do, rather than how they do it, Costello reviewed 58 studies of the effectiveness of alcoholism treatment programs and found more effective programs to have staff who made home visits and reached out to collaterals.[171] Perhaps researchers should pay as much attention to therapist characteristics and behaviors as they do to that of the clients.

Theoretical Perspectives. A cornucopia of theoretical perspectives have been used to treat substance abusers—reality therapy, rational emotive therapy, rational behavior therapy, transactional analysis, gestalt, several aversion treatments, and a variety of other behavioral, cognitive, and psychodynamic approaches. In a review of just one of the major schools of thought, cognitive-behavioral approaches (broadly defined), Kadden identifies the following techniques currently of interest in alcoholism treatment: coping skills training, relapse prevention, behavioral marital and family therapy, community reinforcement, behavioral self-control training, aversion therapy, cue exposure therapy, and motivation interviewing.[172]

According to NIAAA, "In contrast to classical, dynamic, insight-oriented psychotherapy, alcoholism counseling is directive, supportive, reality centered, focused on the present, short term, and oriented toward real world behavioral changes."[173] This is also true of the treatment of illicit drug abusers. Traditional, insight-oriented treatment has historically been viewed as ineffective in helping clients terminate drug use. Explanations for this perceived ineffectiveness are that the causes or etiology of substance abuse problems are not known, and that even knowing the causes of one's chemical dependency may still not result in abstinence. But in one study using random assignment of 260 male court referrals, Brandsma and colleagues found that those given

rational behavior therapy or insight-oriented treatment did better in reducing drinking than those referred to an AA-focused discussion group.[174] The insight group had the fewest legal problems, and those in all groups did better than controls who pursued their own treatment arrangements. Perhaps insight-oriented psychotherapy or other theoretical perspectives should not be summarily dismissed. At a minimum, substance abusers who wish to address additional concerns following sobriety may benefit from a variety of treatment perspectives.

Interpretation of research studies on the effects of interventions from various theoretical perspectives has been hampered by a lack of specification of what constituted the psychotherapeutic intervention.[175] There also has been little controlled investigation to determine what theoretical perspectives might be most useful—but this is changing as researchers perfect their study designs. One effort in this regard is the use of treatments that have been specified in manual form along with supervision and review of tapes of treatment sessions in order to ensure that therapists are maintaining "fidelity" to the treatment under investigation (see the illustration on pages 125–130). Substantial work is also being done to match clients with treatments from theoretical perspectives that are most likely to meet their needs. For example, a study by Longabaugh and associates found that clients with high support did equally well in both "individually focused cognitive behavioral treatment" (CB) and "relationship enhancement of brief cognitive behavioral treatment" (RE), whereas those with low posttreatment support did better with CB than RE.[176] And in combination with naltrexone, O'Malley found that supportive treatment produced more abstinent patients than coping skills treatment; however, among patients who initiated drinking, those who received coping skills treatment were least likely to relapse. This may suggest that patients with high potential for relapse need the benefit of coping skills approaches.[177]

There is a substantial body of literature on aversion therapies in the treatment of alcoholism.

Studies have shown varying effects with samples of patients exposed to chemical aversion using emetic (nausea-producing) drugs.[178] As with other types of treatment, clients with greater social stability and greater motivation for treatment seem to fare better.[179] Electrical aversion therapy has been less effective, and less is known about the effectiveness of covert sensitization.[180] "Covert sensitization employs imagery of unpleasant stimuli to elicit the aversive responses needed to accomplish . . . counter conditioning," and Shorkey calls it the only aversive conditioning technique that can practically be employed by most human service professionals.[181] Nathan and Briddell add that used alone, none of these aversive conditioning methods has proven effective.[182] Most chemical dependency practitioners do not use these approaches. Cannon and associates report that one corporation "discontinued the use of aversion therapy in all 21 of its hospitals to improve its ability to recruit patients."[183]

It is probably accurate to say that chemical dependency treatment providers bring diverse theoretical perspectives to their work, and that many have developed theoretical perspectives of their own that are a combination of approaches. In many cases, treatment providers try several approaches in an attempt to find everything or anything that might work with a particular client. The results of many studies conducted to date provide encouraging findings about what can be accomplished with chemical dependency treatment, but like most research, it often raises more questions than it answers. Although every chemical dependency treatment program provides a natural laboratory for research, treatment providers and programs rarely conduct any studies besides client follow-up. Most of the research is done by a small core of academic and clinical researchers in a small number of treatment settings. Client demands for services, lack of knowledge of research methods, and lack of funding prevent the conduct of more research, but there is a growing awareness among human service professionals about the need for systematic evaluation of their work.

Although the use of these methods is beyond the scope of this book, more treatment providers should be encouraged to pursue preparation in the use of research techniques that will allow them to contribute to treatment effectiveness studies.

Cost Effectiveness of Treatment.   Finally, the cost effectiveness of treating those with substance abuse and dependence problems should be considered. Research studies consistently show that treating alcohol and drug problems produces favorable cost-benefit ratios. But more information is needed on the costs and benefits of particular treatments for substance disorders. In order to accomplish this task, Holder and colleagues accumulated a large amount of information on treatment effectiveness and service costs for alcohol problems and found an inverse relationship between costs and treatment effectiveness; more specifically, they found:

> None of the modalities with "good evidence of effectiveness" placed in the "medium-high" or "high" cost categories. Therefore, brief intervention in the "minimum" cost category, behavioral self-control training and stress management training in the "low" cost category, and social skills training, marital behavioral therapy and community reinforcement therapy in the "medium-low" cost category are desirable modalities in terms of predicted effectiveness and costs. On the other hand, chemical aversion therapy, residential milieu and insight psychotherapy are in the "high" cost category, while also categorized as having "no evidence of effectiveness." Thus being undesirable on both counts, such extremes provide the basis for encouraging specific minimal to medium-low cost modalities and discouraging specific medium-high to high cost modalities.[184]

The next step is to match clients with the treatments that are most effective for them. As seen in this chapter, however, good information on how to accomplish this goal is often lacking.

Financing Substance Abuse Treatment

In the last few decades, substance abuse treatment has largely been organized in two tiers—"one for the poor under public sponsorship and one for those who can pay with private insurance or out-of-pocket funds."[1] These two tiers have paralleled the general medical delivery systems that serve the affluent and well insured (private medical centers) and the poor and underinsured (public hospitals and clinics), but the differences in the drug treatment systems are even more pronounced. In 1993, President Clinton suggested merging the two tiers of the substance abuse treatment system as part of his proposed Health Security Act, but his rather sweeping plans for national health insurance failed.

Public-tier providers consist primarily of publicly owned programs or private, not-for-profit programs. The bulk of their operating funds come from governmental sources. This system of care includes small outpatient clinics in about 2,000 communities throughout the nation, as well as a number of large residential facilities and methadone maintenance programs. Its origins are found in the federal government's "wars" on crime and poverty beginning in the late 1960s. In many ways, it is still an adjunct to the criminal justice system. The private tier is composed of about 1,275 providers serving clients who have private health insurance or adequate financial resources to pay for their own treatment. This tier developed primarily from private hospital units that originally focused almost exclusively on the medical treatment of alcoholism. Until about 1980, it was an almost invisible component of the treatment system, but it grew rapidly as private insurers increasingly began paying for treatment.[2]

Today, the most important force driving the provision of health, mental health, and substance abuse services is *managed care*. Managed care is causing some blending of the private and public sectors as competition to provide all kinds of health services increases. For example, community mental health centers, some of which operate as public agencies and others as private, not-for-profit agencies, may be competing with private providers for company contracts to provide mental health and substance abuse services. Conversely, some states are turning to private, managed-care providers like health maintenance organizations to handle their Medicaid program benefits. (Also see the illustration on pages 110–112.)

There is less overlap between the two tiers of alcoholism and drug treatment providers than is found within the general medical delivery system.[3] Those with financial resources or private insurance rarely seek services from programs that serve indigent clients, and public subsidies for the less affluent alcoholic or drug abuser are rarely adequate to cover the cost of private treatment. Clients in the public system are generally those with longer histories of drug abuse, and are more likely to be polydrug abusers, be unemployed, be unskilled, and have a criminal record.[4] They also have greater deficits in health, education, and family functioning—characteristics that can mitigate against successful rehabilitation.

Much of the federal funding for substance abuse treatment comes from Medicaid (a federal and state program designed to help certain categories of poor people get medical care), Medicare (a federal program providing health care coverage for virtually all Americans age 65 and older), the Department of Veterans Affairs, and a block grant provided to the states by the federal government (see Figure 1). But state and local governments pay more than half the costs of publicly financed services. Many of the services provided by Medicaid, including coverage for alcohol and drug treatment, are largely determined by the states, and Medicaid is thought to be substantially underutilized as a means of providing care for people with alcohol and drug problems.[5] The federal government does not require that states' Medicaid programs cover specific alcohol and drug abuse treatment services. In 1989, about half of the states limited hospital services for substance

(continued)

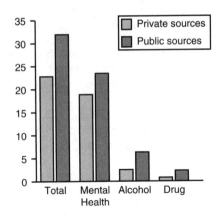

	Dollars (in billions)				Percent ADM by Payer			
	MH	**Alcohol**	**Drug**	**Total**	**MH**	**Alcohol**	**Drug**	**Total**
Private Sources	$18.8	$2.5	$0.9	$23.2	44.3%	29.4%	30.0%	41.1%
Public Sources	23.6	6.0	2.2	31.8	55.7	70.6	70.0	58.9
Medicaid	8.1	1.0	0.3	9.5	19.1	11.8	10.0	17.6
State and local[a]	11.7	3.1	1.1	15.9	27.6	36.5	36.7	29.4
Dept. of Veterans Affairs	1.5	0.6	0.2	2.3	3.6	7.1	6.7	4.3
Other federal[b]	0.8	0.6	0.6	1.9	1.9	7.1	20.0	3.5
Medicare	1.5	0.7	0.0	2.2	3.5	8.2	0.0	4.1
All Sources	42.4	8.5	3.0	54.0	100.0	100.0	100.0	100.0

FIGURE 1   Expenditures for ADM Treatment by Payment Source, 1990 (in Billions of Dollars)

Source: Beatrice A. Rouse (Ed.), *Substance Abuse and Mental Health Statistics Sourcebook* (Washington, DC: Superintendent of Documents, U.S. Government Printing Office, 1995), DHHS Pub. No. (SMA) 95-3064, p. 112.

Source Notes: From Richard G. Frank, Thomas G. McGuire, Darrel A. Regier, Ronald Manderscheid, and Albert Woodard, "Paying for Mental Health and Substance Abuse Care, *Health Affairs,* 13 (1994): 337–342. Published by *Health Affairs,* Copyright 1994, The People-to-People Health Foundation, Inc. Project HOPE, http://www.projhope.org/HA/. Does not include ADM costs for administration, treatment for those age 65 and older in nursing homes or for forensic care in state mental hospitals. Excludes costs for co-existing physical conditions. Client fees are included largely under private insurance and, for public facilities, under State and local. Private sources include total spending, out-of-pocket payments, insurance expenses and philanthropy.

[a]This category includes admissions with no charge because state and local government payers are the ultimate payers.
[b]Includes block grant funds for substance abuse and mental health services, however, does not include prevention and data development under the block grant.

abuse to detoxification only; however, in about half of the states, outpatient substance abuse services were unlimited. Medicaid funds cannot be used to pay for inpatient care for patients ages 22 to 65 in facilities that exclusively treat mental and substance disorders unless these facilities have fewer than 16 beds—a provision designed to restrict the use of Medicaid for long-term care for these individuals. Of course, other public funds are already used to support state psychiatric hospitals and some inpatient substance abuse treatment centers.

Figure 1 shows the sources of funding for alcohol and drug abuse treatment in 1990. A total of $6 billion was spent by the public sector on alcohol treatment, compared to $2.5 billion by the private sector; for drug treatment, the figures were $2.2 billion and $0.9 billion, respectively. Much more is spent for mental health services ($23.6 billion by the public sector and $18.8 billion by private sources in 1990). Public expenditures amounted to about 71 percent of alcohol services and 70 percent of drug services, with the remainder paid for by private sources. This also contrasts with the mental health sector in which public expenditures account for 56 percent of services with private sources paying for 44 percent.

People with higher incomes are more likely to have insurance coverage for alcohol and drug problems, but coverage for mental health and substance abuse services is more restricted than it is for other health problems. Of particular concern is that in 1991, of 36 million workers in medium and large establishments with some type of health care coverage, 23 percent had no coverage for inpatient or outpatient rehabilitation for alcohol or drug problems.[6] Attempts at parity—that is, requiring that coverage for alcohol and drug abuse be equal to that for other physical illnesses—have failed. (Congress did institute a measure calling for parity for mental health coverge in limited cases in 1996.) In addition, federal expenditures on "drug control" largely go toward law enforcement (the supply side of the problem), not to prevention and treatment (the demand side). In 1995, about 36 percent of all federal drug control funds were spent on prevention and treatment.[7] This figure dropped to about 34 percent in 1996 and 1997.

In addition to questions about the appropriate level of public expenditures for law enforcement, prevention, and treatment, there are also important questions to be addressed about the appropriate mix of public and private resources in providing substance abuse treatment. A major concern is how to ensure adequate care for those with chronic substance use disorders who generally do not have private coverage and often do not qualify for public programs like Medicaid. Several authors believe that services for these individuals are rightly the responsibility of state and local government. Paulson, for example, says that "the most cost-effective way of serving chronic populations is through capitated community-based care that emphasizes maintenance and prevention."[8] Similar to the Clinton plan, Paulson advocates integration of mental health and substance abuse services, including parity for these services. This approach could be funded by pooling all the resources that now go to assist people with mental and substance use disorders in order to develop a more integrated approach to care.

A survey done by the Substance Abuse and Mental Health Services Administration (SAMHSA) on one day in 1994 indicated that about 944,000 alcohol and drug abusers were receiving services in approximately 11,500 facilities.[9] The vast majority of clients (823,000) received outpatient care and most were served in free-standing outpatient facilities. In 1994, women were 30 percent of the clients receiving care in facilities specializing in substance abuse treatment. Whites were 59 percent of clients, African Americans were 23 percent, those of Hispanic origin were 15 percent, Native Americans were 2 percent, and Asian Americans were about 1 percent. According to SAMSHA, the "treatment gap" for drug abuse services—that is, the number with severe problems who do not receive treatment—has narrowed, falling from 66 percent in 1989 to 48 percent in 1994.[10]

ENDNOTES

1. Much of this paragraph relies on Dean R. Gerstein and Henrick R. Harwood (Eds.), *Treating Drug Problems*, Vol. 1 (Washington, DC: National Academy Press, 1990), Chapter 6, quote is from pp. 200–201. Reprinted with permission from *Treating Drug Problems, Volume 1.* Copyright 1990 by the National Academy of Sciences. Courtesy of the National Academy Press, Washington, DC.

2. This paragraph relies on ibid.

(continued)

3. This paragraph relies on ibid.

4. Robert L. Hubbard, Mary Ellen Marsden, J. Valley Rachal, Henrick J. Harwood, Elizabeth Cavanaugh, and Harold M. Ginzburg, *Drug Abuse Treatment: A National Study of Effectiveness* (Chapel Hill: University of North Carolina Press, 1989).

5. Constance Horgan, Mary Jo Larson, and Lorna Simon, "Medicaid Funding for Drug Abuse Treatment: A National Perspective," in Gabrielle Denmead and Beatrice A. Rouse (Eds.), *Financing Drug Treatment through State Programs* (Rockville, MD: National Institute on Drug Abuse, 1994), pp. 1–20, Services Research Monograph No. 1, NIH Publication No. 94–3543.

6. Figures are from U.S. Department of Labor, Bureau of Labor Statistics, and are found in Beatrice A. Rouse, *Substance Abuse and Mental Health Statistics Sourcebook* (Washington, DC: Superintendent of Documents, U.S. Government Printing Office, 1995), p. 117, DHS Publication No. 4 (SMA) 95.3064.

7. Office of Drug Control Policy, *The National Drug Control Strategy: 1996* (Washington, DC: Executive Office of the President, 1996).

8. Robert I. Paulson, "Swimming with Sharks or Walking in the Garden of Eden: Two Visions of Managed Care and Mental Health Practice," in Paul R. Raffoul and C. Aaron McNeece (Eds.), *The Future of Social Work Services* (Boston: Allyn and Bacon, 1995), pp. 85–96.

9. Data in this paragraph are from Substance Abuse and Mental Health Services Administration, *National Drug and Alcoholism Treatment Unit Survey (NDATUS): Data from 1994 and 1980–1994* (Rockville, MD: U.S. Department of Health and Human Services, 1996).

10. Substance Abuse and Mental Health Services Administration, "The Need for Delivery of Drug Abuse Services," cited in Office of National Drug Control Policy, *The National Drug Control Strategy: 1996*, p. 91, Table 5–19.

Nontraditional Treatments

Controlled or Moderated Drinking.   The terms *controlled drinking* and *moderated drinking* have been used to describe both the desire of some alcoholics to drink in a socially acceptable manner and the treatment goal of teaching alcoholics to drink in a socially acceptable manner. The idea of teaching alcoholics to drink in a controlled manner has been met with more than spirited debate. Although it is not a new subject, it is included in this section since it is not a routine treatment offered in chemical dependency programs where the goal for clients is usually abstinence.

Many individuals reject total abstinence, and apparently some people who have drunk in an abusive or alcoholic manner may go on to adopt more moderate drinking practices.[185] Some do this following treatment, but surveys also show that many people who report past alcohol-related problems become abstinent or moderate their drinking after minimal contact with detoxification units or information or referral centers or without any assistance from professionals, including clergy, or self-help groups.[186] Humphreys and colleagues "suggest that a potentially useful part of assessment could be determining whether an individual can attain abstinence or moderate drinking without professional help so that limited treatment resources could be more usefully directed to persons who may need them to recover."[187] But one also wonders if treatment might help these clients reach a goal of abstinence or moderated drinking more quickly.

Our discussion of controlled or moderated use is limited to alcohol, since the controlled use controversy has centered on this substance. However, some people apparently use drugs such as marijuana and even heroin or other narcotics (called "chipping") in a controlled manner throughout their lives.[188] The controversy over controlled drinking gained momentum in the 1970s when researchers from the Rand Corporation published an NIAAA-funded study titled *Alcoholism and Treatment.*[189] Similar to reports by Pattison and colleagues,[190] they found that 18 months following contact with an alcoholism treatment program, a number of the male patients in the study sample reported that they were drinking in a so-called controlled (nonproblematic) fashion or were alternating between drinking and abstention, even though they had been treated in traditional, abstinence-oriented programs.

A second follow-up conducted four years after treatment found that 46 percent were in remission (i.e., 28 percent were currently abstinent and 18 percent were "drinking without problems"; the remaining 54 percent were drinking "with problems").[191] There have, of course, been methodological criticisms of the studies, and the studies generated a great deal of controversy among those interested in alcoholism because of the implications that some alcoholics may be able to drink in a controlled manner.

For those who were upset, the work of Mark and Linda Sobell added to their consternation. The Sobells used individualized behavior therapy in an effort to teach some gamma alcoholics to drink in a controlled manner while comparing them with gamma alcoholics who were treated with a goal of abstinence.[192] Patients were selectively assigned to a treatment goal of controlled drinking or abstinence based on factors such as their desire to become abstinent and whether they had social supports available to assist in accomplishing a goal of controlled drinking. The individualized behavior therapy used to teach patients controlled drinking included identification and practice of alternative responses to excessive drinking, electric shocks, education, comparison of videotapes of themselves when drunk and sober, and other procedures. (Another technique that has been used in controlled drinking is teaching clients to discriminate their blood-alcohol levels.)

Following a two-year evaluation, the Sobells concluded from treatment outcomes that *some* alcoholics could successfully pursue controlled drinking as a goal, given treatment by a professional skilled in using this approach; they cautioned that this did not mean that all or a majority of alcoholics would be appropriate for this treatment.[193] Several attacks of this work followed. In an effort to discern what later happened to the original 20 alcoholics taught controlled drinking, Pendery and colleagues conducted a 10-year follow-up.[194] They found that only 1 person had

continued to engage successfully in controlled drinking, 8 continued to drink problematically, 6 had become abstinent, 4 had died from alcoholism, and 1 was missing. How these 20 alcoholics would have fared if treated in an abstinence-oriented program from the outset cannot be determined, and it is not known how they fared over the long run in relation to the comparison group.

Pomerleau and colleagues conducted a similar study in the 1970s and found mixed results when they randomly assigned 32 middle-class volunteers who were problem drinkers to two treatment conditions.[195] They described one treatment as traditional, insight-oriented psychotherapy using confrontation and emphasizing abstinence. The other was behavioral self-control training using positive reinforcement and emphasizing moderation. Substantially more traditional treatment subjects dropped out, but among those remaining in treatment, both groups significantly reduced their drinking.

Note the word *moderation* rather than *controlled* drinking in the previous paragraph. Perhaps the term *moderation* is now being used to avoid the negative connotations associated with the controlled drinking controversy. Connors reviews the chronology of research that indicates "that moderate drinking techniques indeed are a viable treatment approach for some alcohol abusers," and he says that "in fact, moderate drinking interventions with low to moderate severity alcohol abusers may be the treatment of choice."[196] Connors also notes that good outcomes have been less likely with "severely dependent alcoholics," but the hypothesis that achieving moderation is "inversely related to severity of alcohol dependence" has met with mixed results in the research.[197] NIAAA advises alcoholics to abstain, but for those with less severe drinking problems who do not wish to abstain, it has developed a pamphlet titled "How to Cut Down on Your Drinking."[198] The pamphlet suggests (1) making a list of reasons to cut down on drinking; (2) setting a goal, which it suggests should be no more than one standard drink a day for women and two for men (barring other medical complications); and (3) keeping a diary of drinks consumed. The pamphlet also contains other tips for cutting down such as drinking slowly and taking a break from drinking.

Surveys of alcoholism treatment providers in the United States and Canada indicate lower acceptance of moderated drinking as a viable treatment goal than in countries such as Britain and Norway.[199] In a survey of 312 U.S. treatment programs, Rosenberg and Davis found that 77 percent believed that nonabstinence was never an acceptable treatment goal for their clients, although 17 percent of these respondents believed it "was acceptable for patients in other alcohol programs or for their own patients after discharge."[200] Of the 23 percent of the sample who thought that moderate drinking was acceptable for at least some of their clientele, the vast majority worked in outpatient (rather than residential) settings, and they thought that moderation was acceptable for only a minority (1 to 25 percent) of their clients. Nearly one-half of the outpatient program respondents thought that moderation was appropriate for at least some of their clients. A goal of abstinence is an agency policy in many programs.

Interest in moderation led Kishline to develop a self-help program called Moderation Management, based on the ideas that drinking problems fall along a continuum rather than being an all-or-nothing phenomenon and that "brief behavioral self-management approaches" can help people control their behavior.[201] The program contains nine steps which "include information about alcohol, empirically-based moderate drinking limits, self-evaluation strategies, drink monitoring forms, self-management strategies, and goal-setting techniques."[202] Kishline acknowledges that moderation is not for everyone, however, and that some people may need to pursue a goal of abstinence.

Despite the interest of many people in moderated drinking, the topic is likely to remain controversial, at least in certain parts of the world. Treatment providers should, of course, be committed to the highest ethical standards when assisting clients in determining the course of their treatment, but it is also true that emotion can inhibit the pursuit of knowledge in the field. Given the many people who go untreated and the high relapse rates even among those that do seek help, it is critical that professionals remain open to scientific investigation that might lead to improved methods of helping individuals eliminate or moderate their use of chemicals. Connors believes that there "has been an increasing recognition of and appreciation for the varied paths to remission."[203] With this in mind, professionals should be neither too restrictive in their approaches nor too free in their willingness to grasp at new straws.

Acupuncture.   Reports of newer treatments for chemical dependency include the use of acupuncture and alpha-theta brain-wave training (a biofeedback technique). The small number of studies on these methods makes it difficult to draw conclusions about their effectiveness, either as adjuncts to treatment or as alternatives to traditional treatment, but fresh approaches are needed.

In theory, acupuncture, an ancient Chinese approach to treating medical and psychological problems with the use of needles, is said to work in the following way:

> Energy (Chi) from oxygen and food flows through the organs and body where it is transformed and distributed. The acupuncturist assesses (through symptoms, physical examination and pulse diagnosis) the homeostasis of this energy and intervenes with treatment if it is out of balance.[204]

Acupuncture may promote the production of beta-endorphins or other naturally occurring substances in the body, but the precise mechanisms through which it might work are not known.[205]

Brumbaugh enthusiastically discusses the use of auricular (ear) acupuncture with detoxification patients and in treatment following detoxification.[206] He reports that there are over 175 such detoxification programs in the United States. Acupuncture in longer-term chemical dependency treatment has apparently been used most extensively with volunteers from the criminal justice system. Individuals are being treated with the procedure in groups, minimizing the time and the costs of the treatment. Acupuncture has been used with various drug addictions, including alcohol, heroin, and crack cocaine. The procedure has been used for about 20 years at Lincoln Hospital's Substance Abuse Division in New York. A group called the National Acupuncture Detoxification Association has emerged with a suggested protocol for the use of acupuncture in detoxification.

Bullock and colleagues found positive results in two controlled, single-blind studies using acupuncture with severe, chronic alcoholics.[207] Control subjects were less likely to complete treatment, reported a greater desire to drink, and had significantly more episodes of drinking and detoxification admissions than experimental subjects. The experimental groups received acupuncture at points thought to be specific for substance abuse treatment, whereas the controls received it at nonspecific points. The subjects in these studies were given a place to live during the treatment, but other than Alcoholics Anonymous, no traditional chemical dependency treatment was provided. These researchers suggest that acupuncture may not only be an effective adjunct to treatment but may be useful for clients who have not fared well with other treatment approaches.

Worner and associates, on the other hand, found no difference in treatment or control subjects, all of whom were alcoholics of lower socioeconomic status, with respect to attendance at AA or treatment, treatment completion, detox admissions, or relapses.[208] Subjects were randomly assigned to one of three groups: point-specific acupuncture along with standard, outpatient alcoholism treatment; needleless or sham acupuncture with standard treatment; or standard treatment only. They found that many individuals were unwilling to receive acupuncture treatment. Worner reported a much higher dropout rate from the point-specific acupuncture treatment group than did Bullock.

Interest in the use of acupuncture to treat drug addicts continues with researchers working to find better ways of offering placebo acupuncture treatments in "blind" studies.[209] Researchers who have tried using auricular acupuncture at specific and nonspecific sites, as in the Bullock studies, note that needles placed within a certain area of the ear may produce results, even if thought to be in nonspecific points.[210] In using these supposedly nonspecific sites, Avants and colleagues randomly assigned 40 individuals participating in a methadone maintenance program to either a six-week control or experimental group with a hope of controlling their cocaine dependence.[211] Using several outcome measures, they found that patients, in general, tended to improve, but the only statistically significant difference between groups was that the experimentals had less cravings than the controls. Retention rates in both groups were high and the subjects in both groups had similar attitudes to the treatment, with confidence in acupuncture increasing during the course of the study. Given that the two groups may have actually received the active treatment, the authors suggest using sites in other parts of the ear for future control groups.

Lipton and associates used the same auricular acupuncture techniques with people seeking treatment for crack cocaine abuse at Lincoln Hospital.[212] The treatments lasted one month, with sessions available six days a week. No other services were offered. The authors recognize that acupuncture without other services is not recommended, but they conducted the single-blind study in this way in order to remove the confound that other services would introduce. Dropout and attendance rates for the experimental and control groups were similar. Some 55 percent of the experimental group and 53 percent of the control group participated in the treatment for at least 6 days, and 36 percent and 40 percent, respectively, participated at least 10 days with a 9-day mean for both groups. Although the number of subjects in both groups who submitted cocaine-negative urine specimens was not significantly different, subjects who received more than two weeks of acupuncture had lower cocaine metabolites. Subjective ratings to questions such as desire for cocaine did not differ between groups and self-reported cocaine use also did not differ substantially with reduced drug use in both groups.

In another attempt to test auricular acupuncture, Washburn and associates used it with 100 heroin detoxification patients, most of whom were African American.[213] Initial dropout was high in both groups, with a mean attendance of 4.2 days for treatment subjects and 2.1 days for control subjects. Those reporting less drug use attended more than those with more drug use, suggesting that less severe users may find acupuncture more acceptable. Given the high dropout rates, it is difficult to say much about the effectiveness of the treatment in reducing heroin use. The somewhat disappointing results of this controlled study are consistent with another study of acupuncture treatment with substance abusers by a research team headed by Konefal that found less treatment follow-though by cocaine and crack abusers than by alcoholics.[214] As Konefal and Washburn note, heroin addicts may be more receptive to drug replacement than to drug-free treatments (or their expectancies may be for drug treatments). Konefal's study speaks to the many difficulties of attempting to conduct controlled research in community treatment programs. Dropout rates were high in all three treatment conditions in her study (all got standard treatment, another group also got frequent urine tests, and the third got both these treatments plus acupuncture), but Konefal emphasizes that those receiving acupuncture who had clean urine tests achieved this result in a shorter period of time than the standard treatment plus frequent urine-tested group. Given the lack of success and potential medical problems that can arise from acupuncture, Worner and associates "caution against the routine use of this treatment until more randomized control trials demonstrate a beneficial effect."[215]

Biofeedback.   Various stress-reduction or relaxation techniques such as progressive muscle relaxation and relaxation imagery have been used as adjuncts in the treatment of chemical abusers.[216] Other approaches such as hypnosis and meditation have also been tried. The hope is that reducing stress and promoting relaxation will lead to better treatment outcomes for clients. Alpha-theta brain-wave training is a newer relaxation approach being used with alcohol and drug abusers. Like acupuncture, it is administered by those with specialized training. Peniston and Kulkosky have been studying the use of alpha-theta brain-wave training with alcoholics and with veterans with posttraumatic stress disorder.[217] The purpose of this training is to increase alpha and theta brain rhythms, since it is suspected that alcoholics are deficient in these brain activities and that increases in these activities may promote better treatment outcomes. Peniston and Kulkosky explain the procedures they use such as placement of electrodes, audio feedback, and temperature biofeedback. Their controlled study indicated that the experimental group showed improvements (increases) in alpha and theta activity and had less depression and fewer relapses at 13 months following treatment, compared to controls. Hanson and Venturelli note, "Some patients report that they feel biofeedback has helped them. However, carefully controlled studies of addicts going though withdrawal, using muscular relaxation techniques and alpha EEG training, have not demonstrated success."[218] Although interest in biofeedback continues,[219] additional controlled studies would be useful in assessing the benefits of these techniques with alcohol and drug disorders.

Incentives to Improve Treatment Outcomes. Many clients are threatened with negative sanctions for failure to attend treatment and to stay clean and sober; however, positive rather than negative reinforcers may be more useful in treating substance abusers.[220] For example, evidence indicates that offering take-home methadone doses to clients with drug-free urine tests increases abstinence from cocaine.[221] Another approach is the use of material incentives as an adjunct to other forms of treatment to encourage patients to cease illicit drug use.[222] Rather than cash payments, some studies have used vouchers or similar approaches in which methadone clients or cocaine abusers who produce cocaine-free urine specimens earn points or dollar values that can then be applied to the purchase of items that might enhance the clients' treatment goals or quality of life (e.g., household, educational, or recreational items), contingent on the approval of a staff member. Studies to date have used small samples and relatively short follow-up periods, but the results are encouraging when experimental and control subjects are compared. Some may ask whether the public should bear the costs of paying for such incentives, but the benefits to the community in reduced medical, social, and criminal justice spending from helping clients remain drug free may be worth the financial investment.[223]

Self-Help Groups

Self-help groups have been part of the recovery of alcoholics and addicts since the 1930s. They are an important component of the system of care but are not part of the continuum of services provided by professionals. Instead, they are composed of volunteers who both "work the program" and maintain these loosely structured organizations. In most cases, members take turns chairing the meetings or acting as secretary.

Alcoholics Anonymous

The best-known self-help group is Alcoholics Anonymous (AA). AA has been described as everything from a form of psychotherapy[224] to having an "antipsychotherapy attitude."[225] It has also been described in systems terms as "a model for synthesizing biomedical, psychosocial, and environmental approaches to arresting alcoholism and achieving what AA members term 'contented sobriety.'"[226] Alcoholics Anonymous began in 1935, well before most professionals took a serious interest in assisting alcoholics. The founders of AA were two men, a physician and a stockbroker, who shared with each other their prob-

lems with alcohol and supported each other in maintaining sobriety. Alcoholics Anonymous estimates that it now has more than 96,000 groups[227] and about 2 million members.[228] Groups meet throughout the United States and many other countries. A directory is available to help members locate meetings, and almost every phone book in the United States lists a local number for the organization. Local groups operate rather independently, although the General Service Office, located in New York City, provides kits to assist in starting groups and offers a great deal of literature addressed to recovering persons, their friends and family members, and the various professionals who help alcoholics.

AA is referred to as a fellowship. More than meetings, it is a program for the recovering alcoholic to "work" on a daily basis. The program is based on 12 steps (see Figure 6.1) that refer to the individual's powerlessness over alcohol, the need to recognize one's shortcomings and to make amends, and reliance on a higher power. These steps have been adapted by many other self-help groups for chemically dependent individuals, such as Narcotics Anonymous, and a wide variety of other groups concerned about problems ranging from overeating and gambling to sexual behavior. Another important aspect of AA is its 12 traditions, recognizing the group's concerns about anonymity, not taking stands on outside issues, and so forth.

Some alcoholics never seek professional assistance and, instead, have relied on Alcoholics Anonymous to help guide them toward recovery. Others use a combination of professional assistance and self-help groups. The self-help movement does not appeal to all recovering individuals. Some professionals question its utility, believing that it is best reserved for certain types of individuals. However, it is probably accurate to say that most human service professionals concerned about chemical dependency not only refer their clients to self-help groups but strongly encourage them to participate.

The only requirement for membership in AA is a desire to stop drinking. There are no application forms or other requirements for participation.

FIGURE 6.1 The Twelve Steps of Alcoholics Anonymous

1. We admitted we were powerless over alcohol—that our lives had become unmanageable.
2. Came to believe that a Power greater than ourselves could restore us to sanity.
3. Made a decision to turn our will and our lives over to the care of God *as we understood Him.*
4. Made a searching and fearless moral inventory of ourselves.
5. Admitted to God, to ourselves and to another human being the exact nature of our wrongs.
6. Were entirely ready to have God remove all these defects of character.
7. Humbly asked Him to remove our shortcomings.
8. Made a list of all persons we had harmed, and became willing to make amends to them all.
9. Made direct amends to such people wherever possible, except when to do so would injure them or others.
10. Continued to take personal inventory and when we were wrong promptly admitted it.
11. Sought through prayer and meditation to improve our conscious contact with God, *as we understood Him*, praying only for knowledge of His will for us and the power to carry that out.
12. Having had a spiritual awakening as the result of these steps, we tried to carry this message to alcoholics, and to practice these principles in all our affairs.

Source: © Copyright A.A. World Services, Inc. The Twelve Steps are reprinted with permission of Alcoholics Anonymous World Services, Inc. Permission to reprint the Twelve Steps does not mean that A.A. has reviewed or approved the contents of this publication, nor that A.A. agrees with the views expressed herein. A.A. is a program of recovery from alcoholism *only*—use of the Twelve Steps in connection with programs and activities which are patterned after A.A., but which address other problems, or in any other non-A.A. context, does not imply otherwise.

Individuals who come to meetings intoxicated or not completely detoxified are usually allowed to remain unless they cause disruption or appear to need immediate medical attention. There are no dues or fees for membership. The groups are supported by contributions of members, and outside donations are not accepted. Since anonymity is stressed, only first names are used at meetings, and members are reminded to "leave what they hear at the meeting" so as not to violate the confidences of others.

A mainstay of the group is its meetings, which are usually about one hour long. In large cities, it is not surprising to find meetings being conducted around the clock every day of the week. Smaller communities generally having fewer meetings. Some cities have AA clubs where members can drop in whenever they wish.

When AA began, its membership was largely men. Only a few brave women ventured into the meetings, but today women are a sizable portion (33 percent) of members.[229] Some AA groups are designated for women only (see Chapter 15) or men only. Other groups are for young people (although anyone young at heart is usually permitted to attend) or for members of particular ethnic groups with meetings conducted in their native languages (see Chapter 11). Gays and lesbians (see Chapter 12), members of particular professions, and nonsmokers have also organized groups. Again, community size is usually a predictor of the variety of meetings. Sometimes the composition of the group is defined by the location in which the meeting is held—an affluent residential neighborhood, the deteriorating downtown section of a city, or a prison.

Many outsiders think AA is a religious program. The Twelve Steps do include references to God, but AA is better described as a spiritual program.[230] God is considered a "higher power" defined according to individual preference. For some, it is God in the traditional sense of organized religion; for others, it may be the AA group or virtually any other spiritual or physical entity. Religious aspects of meetings seem stronger in some groups than in others, but some atheists and agnostics have successfully recovered through the program.[231] Various ethnic groups have adapted the principles and format of AA according to their beliefs and customs (see Chapter 11). Groups seem to develop their own personalities, depending on their membership. Newcomers may be encouraged to attend the meetings of several different groups and to select those in which they feel most comfortable. They are also encouraged to attend "90 meetings in 90 days" in order to break old patterns, to become fully immersed in the program, and to not give up too quickly.

The overall structure of AA meetings is generally consistent in that they begin and end in the same manner, with readings from the book *Alcoholics Anonymous*[232] and prayers, but there are different meeting formats. A speaker's meeting is devoted to one or more testimonials by members who are from the local community or invited from out of town. Members sometimes call these talks "drunkalogues." Speakers tell their "story," usually beginning with the circumstances surrounding their use and abuse of alcohol and their development of alcoholism. Stories generally contain a number of the negative consequences that the alcoholic experienced while drinking and the way in which the alcoholic was able to recover, including their introduction to and use of AA. The stories assist members, especially newcomers, in realizing that it is possible to recover, no matter how bad one's problems. They are also cathartic for the storytellers. Birthday meetings at which members celebrate each year of their sobriety are often combined with speakers' meetings.

Another format is discussion meetings. At these meetings, the chairperson may offer a topic for discussion (such as guilt, resentments, loneliness, friendships, intimacy) or ask members to suggest a topic. Members may volunteer comments on their personal experiences, or the chairperson may proceed in round-robin fashion. Members who do not wish to speak are usually not pressured to do so and may simply say "I pass" when their turn comes. In this sense, AA differs from group therapy or other forms of group treatment in which members are expected to verbalize their thoughts and interact with other members during sessions.

At step meetings, the chairperson leads a discussion on one of the Twelve Steps. Members comment on points that helped them work the step or the problems they are encountering in working that step. There is no one way, or even recommended ways, to work each step. Members offer their thoughts, but each is free to work the step in a manner suitable to him or her. *Big Book* meetings are another type of meeting. The book *Alcoholics Anonymous*, usually referred to as the *Big Book*, recounts the history of AA and contains the stories of various members. These meetings focus on discussion of passages from the book.

Tokens are among the symbols used in meetings. For example, poker chips of different colors may be given after one, two, three, and six months of continuous sobriety to recognize the progress the individual has made. At birthday meetings, members with one or more years of continuous sobriety are presented with a special memento, such as a silver dollar with a hole drilled in it to commemorate each year of sobriety.

Slogans for living, such as "one day at a time" and "live and let live," are frequently heard at AA and are often displayed on the walls of the meeting room. Meetings generally close with "Keep coming back; it works."

AA conventions are held around the country, and local groups often sponsor social and recreational activities such as dances and family picnics to provide an atmosphere where members can enjoy themselves without exposure to alcohol. For some recovering alcoholics, AA is the focus of their lives. Some have criticized this as an inability to lead a normal life; others call it an individual choice. There are no rules telling a member how often to attend meetings. Many individuals go frequently in the early stages of their sobriety and then less frequently as their length of sobriety increases. In the early stages of sobriety, failing to attend meetings is often considered a "red flag" or a precursor to a slip (a lapse or relapse).

Sponsorship is another aspect of AA and many other self-help programs. Newcomers who wish may ask a member to serve as their sponsor. A sponsor has usually been an AA member for some time and has achieved a substantial period of sobriety, but there are no requirements to serve in this capacity. Newcomers are encouraged to select sponsors whom they feel have "solid sobriety" and with whom they feel comfortable discussing their recovery. They may also be encouraged to select a sponsor of the same gender to avoid confusing issues of recovery and sexual intimacy (issues in AA for gays and lesbians are discussed in Chapter 12). The individual who is asked to be a sponsor is free to accept or decline. Sponsors can be a valuable resource, especially when they are readily available to provide support and encouragement. This is particularly important to members when they experience a crisis such as a strong desire to drink or when they want help with understanding various aspects of the AA program.

Why are so many people attracted to AA? It may well be due to the camaraderie—the idea that there are others who have been there, who have recovered, and who understand. The fellowship of AA and other self-help groups is a strong one. Visitors and newcomers are often struck by the way members introduce themselves and are acknowledged by fellow members. When members speak at the meetings, they usually begin by saying, "I'm so-and-so, and I'm an alcoholic," to which the group responds in chorus, "Hi, so-and-so!" Members and visitors are impressed with the unconditional acceptance of the alcoholic. Visitors sometimes remark that the interaction between members was so positive, they wished they were alcoholics! On the other hand, visitors and newcomers may be concerned about some of the behavior at meetings. For example, members may come and go as they wish during meetings, which can seem disruptive, or they may offer comments but do not always receive responses to their remarks, which can seem uncaring or disrespectful.

AA and similar self-help groups for alcoholics and addicts have closed and open meetings. Closed meetings are only for those who consider themselves alcoholics or addicts. These meetings provide greater assurance to alcoholics or addicts that they are among those who share the same problem and that their anonymity will be re-

spected. Open meetings also serve an important purpose. They allow professionals, family members and friends, those who think they might have a problem, and others to learn more about self-help groups, the problems they address, and the people they help. They are an important resource for every community. Anyone considering a career working with chemically dependent clients should attend these meetings.

Research and Self-Help Groups

AA has been touted as having helped more people recover from alcoholism than any other program.[233] Some have called this aggrandizement "an ill-considered hyperbole,"[234] and others warn that even questioning the effectiveness of AA might cause "surprise, annoyance, anger, exasperation, shock, or perhaps even rage" among some individuals.[235] The informal structure of the organization and its groups[236] and the concern for members' anonymity have deterred researchers from conducting studies on AA in spite of its unique approach and its large following. In 1976, Bebbington wrote that given the nature of AA, "it seems unlikely to be possible to assess its effectiveness in a scientific manner."[237] He noted the bias in studies of AA because members self-select into the program and because samples have been of the convenience types. Using the principles of scientific inquiry, suggestions have been made about how researchers should go about studying AA.[238] Although most studies do not meet these criteria, we consider the efforts that have been made to study AA.

Two types of studies of interest are (1) descriptive studies of members and (2) studies of AA's effectiveness. Descriptive studies include periodic membership surveys of the organization as well as the efforts of other researchers to investigate those most likely to affiliate with AA. In 1981, Ogborne and Glaser summarized the affiliation literature:

Researchers have found that affiliates of AA are more likely to be men, over 40 years of age, white, middle- or upper-class and socially stable. AA affiliation has been associated with binge drinking, physical dependence on alcohol, loss-of-control drinking, and the loss or threatened loss of a valued life-style because of drinking. It has also been associated with an authoritarian personality, strong affiliative needs, proneness to guilt, and external locus of control, field dependence, cognitive simplicity, formistic thinking, a low conceptual level, high autokinesis scores, a religious orientation, existential anxiety and a tendency to conform.[239]

They warned that given the state of the research, these "characteristics should be viewed only as a set of working hypotheses."[240] However, Baekeland suggested that physicians "not blindly recommend AA to patients who are unlikely to accept it (. . . non- or antireligious, uncomfortable in groups) but rather to those likely to profit from it."[241]

Later reviews of the affiliation literature have found considerable variation among AA members.[242] Emrick's conclusion was that

> until specific affiliation characteristics are identified, prudence suggests viewing all alcoholic patients in conventional alcoholism treatment as possible members of AA, while at the same time recognizing that many alcohol-dependent patients recover from their alcohol problems without ever joining the organization.[243]

Keeping the methodological problems of studies in mind, the bulk of literature on the effectiveness of AA generally indicates the positive results of affiliation. Baekeland reported that as a primary treatment, "AA seems to do about as well as alcohol clinics."[244] Vaillant's study of over 600 men found that among some of the study's subgroups, more recovered individuals had begun stable abstinence while participating in AA than other treatment, but those who sought clinic treatment seemed equally as likely to achieve stable abstinence through this form of treatment as they were through AA.[245] In a 1980 review of the literature, Miller and Hester found abstinence rates of AA

members of 26 to 50 percent after one year; although the studies did not use controls, these rates were reportedly similar to other types of treatment.[246] Emrick found abstinence rates of 40 to 50 percent among "long-term, active AA members," which he reported as being higher than rates among "professionally treated alcoholics."[247] When Brandsma and colleagues randomly assigned court referrals to AA-type discussion groups and several other treatments, AA had the highest dropout rate.[248] Since subjects were under coercion to receive help, findings may not generalize to individuals in other circumstances. Walsh and colleagues did find markedly better drinking outcomes (including less need for additional treatment), but not better job-related outcomes, among those assigned to a combination of hospital treatment and mandatory AA attendance, compared to those assigned to mandatory AA only and those allowed to select their own treatment or to forego treatment.[249]

Baekeland suggested that AA might appeal to more individuals when used as an adjunct to other treatment.[250] Studies give credence to his hypothesis. In a four-year follow-up of 225 patients discharged from an addiction treatment program, Pettinati and colleagues found that AA attendance was more likely to be associated with maintaining abstinence than were other posttreatment interventions such as additional inpatient or outpatient treatment.[251] Similarly, in a study of women alcoholics, Corrigan found that prior AA attendance, prior inpatient treatment, and prior outpatient treatment all contributed equally to explaining abstinence as did current AA attendance; however, additional outpatient or inpatient treatment was negatively related to abstinence.[252] In a 1987 review of the literature, Emrick found that those who combined AA and other treatment did as well or better than those whose only involvement was with AA.[253] A 10-year follow-up study of male and female patients who had received intensive inpatient treatment revealed that "involvement in Alcoholics Anonymous (AA) predicted abstinence, suggesting successful outcome for patients who undergo a treatment regimen, which bridges patients into AA involvement."[254]

Like the literature on treatment effectiveness, research is needed on many aspects of self-help groups. Research might help to determine the process through which affiliation with these groups occur, who tends to benefit from this involvement, and the mechanisms of these groups that actually help to produce change.

Narcotics Anonymous and Other Self-Help Groups

Next to AA, Narcotics Anonymous (NA) probably has the greatest name recognition of all the self-help groups for chemically dependent individuals. NA began in the 1950s. Groups were often started by AA members who were also drug addicts; like AA, NA emphasizes taking individual responsibility for problems.[255] The Twelve Steps and Twelve Traditions of NA are almost identical to AA's, with drug terminology substituted for alcohol terminology. Why did NA emerge separately from AA? Before the advent of increased polydrug abuse, there were many more "pure alcoholics." Some alcoholics were uncomfortable with narcotics addicts whom they associated with the criminal element. Alcoholics also abuse a drug, but it can be obtained within the law. Today, however, it is common to hear attendees at AA or NA meetings introduce themselves as alcoholics and addicts.

Cocaine Anonymous is another group that has emerged with the increased use of this drug. Although cocaine abusers would likely be welcome at NA or AA meetings, the unique aspects of preference for a particular drug, such as life-style differences, may have encouraged the emergence of yet another self-help group.

There are a variety of other self-help groups for alcoholics and addicts. Women for Sobriety (WFS) was developed by Jean Kirkpatrick, who feels that AA has a male orientation and that women need alternatives to help them in their so-briety. WFS is discussed further in Chapter 15. Gay Alcoholics Anonymous and Alcoholics Together, for gays and lesbians, are discussed in Chapter 12. Secular Organizations for Sobriety (SOS), also called Save Our Selves, has emerged as a cognitively based group to assist those "uncomfortable with a perceived religious emphasis" in many self-help groups.[256] In 1996, SOS reported 2,000 groups and 100,000 members in the United States, Canada, Europe, and Asia.[257]

Another self-help program is Rational Recovery, which calls itself "a self-help alternative to 12-step groups" and utilizes the principles of rational emotive therapy.[258] The program's literature indicates that it can be used with or without attendance at meetings, although meetings can be useful to accelerate learning.

Other variations of self-help groups have also emerged. Some are run by a combination of volunteers and staff members from chemical dependency, mental health, or other treatment programs. Nurco and colleagues discuss a project using this approach to assist narcotics addicts.[259] Groups now emerging for those with dual diagnoses of substance abuse and mental illness or substance abuse and mental retardation are often organized and led by a professional or they may be led by both a professional and a dually diagnosed, recovering individual (see Chapter 13).

There are also groups for the loved ones of alcoholics and addicts. The first to emerge was Al-Anon, founded by the wife of one of AA's founders (see Chapter 10). Naranon is for the loved ones of narcotic addicts. Alatot and Alateen are for the children of alcoholics.

Summary

This chapter reviewed the components of the treatment system commonly used by those with alcohol or drug problems. A wide range of treatments are available to these individuals and their loved ones. Many of these methods show at least some promising results in helping those who seek professional assistance in their recovery, and chemical dependency professionals try to match clients with the treatments that are most likely to meet their needs. Self-help groups were among the first approaches to aid individuals with chemical dependency problems. They remain an important component of the helping system and have grown in number and in their application to other types of problems. Research has begun to address many of the questions that have been raised about the effectiveness of treatment and self-help approaches. There is still much knowledge to be gained, especially in light of the fact that much of the etiology of chemical abuse and dependency remains a mystery and relapse rates remain high.

Endnotes

1. For other descriptions of the continuum of care, see Benjamin Kissin and Henri Begleiter (Eds.), *The Biology of Alcoholism, Treatment and Rehabilitation of the Chronic Alcoholic* (New York: Plenum Press, 1977); and Daniel John Anderson, "Delivery of Essential Services to Alcoholics Through the 'Continuum of Care,' " *Cancer Research,* Vol. 39 (July 1979), pp. 2855–2858.

2. Also see Kissin and Begleiter, *The Biology of Alcoholism.*

3. Enoch Gordis and George Sereny, "Controversy in Approaches to Alcoholism," in Victor M. Rosenoer and Marcus Rothschild (Eds.), *Controversies in Clinical Care* (New York: Spectrum Publications, 1981), pp. 37–55.

4. Earl Rubington, "Staff Problems in Halfway Houses," *Alcoholism Treatment Quarterly,* Vol. 2, No. 2 (Summer 1985) pp. 29–47.

5. For information on the treatment of withdrawal, see Dennis F. Moore, "Detoxification," in Gerald Bennett, Christine Vourakis, and Donnas S. Woolf (Eds.), *Substance Abuse, Pharmacologic, Developmental, and Clinical Perspectives* (New York: John Wiley and Sons, 1983), pp. 328–340.

6. See Chapter 1 for a description of the various types of drugs and associated withdrawal problems. Also see Bennett et al., *Substance Abuse.*

7. Motoi Hayashida, Arthur I. Alterman, Thomas McLellan, Charles P. O'Brien, James J. Purtill, Joseph R. Volpicelli, Arnold H. Raphaelson, and Charles P. Hall, "Comparative Effectiveness and Costs of Inpatient and Outpatient Detoxification of Patients with Mild-to-Moderate Al-

cohol Withdrawal Syndrome," *The New England Journal of Medicine* (February 9, 1989), pp. 358–365; and Dean R. Gerstein and Henrick J. Harwood (Eds.), *Treating Drug Problems,* Vol. 1 (Washington, DC: National Academy Press, 1990), pp. 125–126.

8. Hayashida et al., "Comparative Effectiveness and Costs."

9. Gerstein and Harwood, *Treating Drug Problems;* also see National Institute on Alcohol Abuse and Alcoholism (NIAAA), *Sixth Special Report to the U.S. Congress on Alcohol and Health* (Rockville, MD: U.S. Department of Health and Human Services, 1987); and National Institute on Alcohol Abuse and Alcoholism (NIAAA), *Seventh Special Report to the U.S. Congress on Alcohol and Health* (Rockville, MD: U.S. Department of Health and Human Services, January 1990).

10. Drug Enforcement Administration, *Drugs of Abuse,* 1989 ed. (Washington, DC: U.S. Department of justice, 1989).

11. Gordis and Sereny, "Controversy in Approaches to Alcoholism."

12. See NIAAA, *Sixth Special Report to the U.S. Congress on Alcohol and Health;* Gerstein and Harwood, *Treating Drug Problems.*

13. Hayashida et al., "Comparative Effectiveness and Costs."

14. Gerstein and Harwood, *Treating Drug Problems.*

15. Gordis and Sereny, "Controversy in Approaches to Alcoholism."

16. Gerstein and Harwood, *Treating Drug Problems.*

17. Ibid., p. 176. Reprinted with permission from *Treating Drug Problems, Volume 1.* Copyright 1990 by the National Academy of Sciences. Courtesy of the National Academy Press, Washington, DC.

18. Joanne R. Snair, *Report on Evaluation Research Review Conducted for the Governor's Study Commission on Crime Prevention and Law Enforcement* (Tallahassee, FL: Florida State University, October 1989, rev.), p. 6.

19. NIAAA, *Sixth Special Report to the U.S. Congress on Alcohol and Health;* Gerstein and Harwood, *Treating Drug Problems.*

20. Gordis and Sereny, "Controversy in Approaches to Alcoholism."

21. Christopher C. H. Cook, "The Minnesota Model in the Management of Drug and Alcohol Dependency: Miracle, Method or Myth? Part I. The Philosophy and the Programme," *British Journal of Addiction,* Vol. 83 (1988), p. 625; also see NIAAA, *Seventh Special Report to the U.S. Congress on Alcohol and Health,* p. 262.

22. NIAAA, *Sixth Special Report to the U.S. Congress on Alcohol and Health.*

23. Mary E. McCaul and Janice Furst, "Alcoholism Treatment in the United States," *Alcohol Health & Research World,* Vol. 18, No. 4 (1994), pp. 253–260, quote from p. 254.

24. Joseph Guydish, David Werdegar, James L. Sorenson, Wayne Clark, and Alfonso Acampora, "A Day Treatment Program in a Therapeutic Community Setting: Six Month Outcomes: The Walden House Day Treatment Program," *Journal of Substance Abuse Treatment*, Vol. 12, No. 6 (1995), pp. 441–447.

25. Arthur I. Alterman and Thomas McLellan, "Inpatient and Day Hospital Treatment Services for Cocaine and Alcohol Dependence," *Journal of Substance Abuse Treatment*, Vol. 10 (1993), pp. 269–275.

26. Cook, "The Minnesota Model in the Management of Drug and Alcohol Dependency: Miracle, Method or Myth? Part I. The Philosophy and the Programme"; and Christopher C. H. Cook, "The Minnesota Model in the Management of Drug and Alcohol Dependency: Miracle, Method or Myth? Part II. Evidence and Conclusions," *British Journal of Addiction*, Vol. 83 (1988), pp. 735–748.

27. Cook, "The Minnesota Model, Part II," p. 735.

28. Ibid., p. 746.

29. Gerstein and Harwood, *Treating Drug Problems*, p. 190.

30. Richard K. Fuller, "Can Treatment Outcome Research Rely on Alcoholics' Self-Reports?" *Alcohol Health and Research World*, Vol. 12, No. 3 (1988), pp. 180–186.

31. John D. Swisher, "Evaluating Professional Counseling in Alcoholism Treatment," *Alcohol Health and Research World*, Vol. 12, No. 3 (1988), pp. 176–179.

32. NIAAA, *Sixth Special Report to the U.S. Congress on Alcohol and Health*; James R. McKay and Stephen A. Maisto, "An Overview and Critique of Advances in the Treatment of Alcohol Use Disorders," *Drugs & Society*, Vol. 8, No. 1 (1993), pp. 1–29; and Gerard K. Conners, *Innovations in Alcoholism Treatment: State of the Art Reviews and Their Implications for Clinical Practice* (Binghamton, NY: Haworth Press, 1993), pp. 1–29.

33. Kenneth W. Wangberg, John L. Horn, and Donald Fairchild, "Hospital versus Community Treatment of Alcoholism Problems," *International Journal of Mental Health*, Vol. 3, Nos. 2–3, pp. 160–176, quote from p. 174.

34. Diana Chapman Walsh et al., "A Randomized Trial of Treatment Options for Alcohol-abusing Workers," *The New England Journal of Medicine*, September 12, 1991, pp. 775–782; and Ron Winslow, "New Study Shows Inpatient Treatment May Be Best Course for Problem Drinkers," *The Wall Street Journal*, September 12, 1991, pp. B–1 and B–4.

35. Donald W. Goodwin, *Alcoholism* (Kalamazoo, MI: The Upjohn Co., 1990).

36. "Efforts to Shift Substance Abuse Treatment to Outpatient Settings Has Patients 'Reeling,' " *Psychiatric News*, March 15, 1991, pp. 2 and 25.

37. Earl Rubington, "The Role of the Halfway House in the Rehabilitation of Alcoholics," in Kissin and Begleiter, *The Biology of Alcoholism*, p. 352; also see Anderson, "Delivery of Essential Services to Alcoholics Through the 'Continuum of Care.' "

38. Rubington, "The Role of the Halfway House in the Rehabilitation of Alcoholics."

39. Allan C. Ogborne, T. R. Ian Wiggins, and Martin Shain, "Variations in Staff Characteristics, Programmes and Recruitment Practices among Halfway Houses for Problem Drinkers," *British Journal of Addiction*, Vol. 75 (1980), pp. 393–403; and Rubington, "Staff Problems in Halfway Houses."

40. Rubington, "Staff Problems in Halfway Houses."

41. Ibid.

42. Ibid.

43. For additional information on halfway houses, see Jim Orford and Richard Velleman, "Alcoholism Halfway Houses," in E. Mansell Pattison and Edward Kaufman (Eds.), *Encyclopedic Handbook of Alcoholism* (New York: Gardner Press, 1982), pp. 907–922; Rubington, "The Role of the Halfway House in the Rehabilitation of Alcoholics"; and Rubington, "Staff Problems in Halfway Houses."

44. H. M. Annis and C. B. Liban, "A Follow-up Study of Male Halfway-House Residents and Matched Nonresident Controls," *Journal of Studies on Alcohol*, Vol. 40, No. 1 (1979), pp. 63–69.

45. Rubington, "The Role of the Halfway House in the Rehabilitation of Alcoholics," p. 363.

46. Annis and Liban, "A Follow-up Study of Male Halfway-House Residents and Matched Nonresident Controls."

47. Carol Van Ryswyk, Margaret Churchill, Joan Velasquez, and Richard McGuire, "Effectiveness of Halfway House Placement for Alcohol and Drug Abusers," *American Journal of Drug and Alcohol Abuse*," Vol. 8, No. 4 (1981–82), pp. 499–512.

48. Some of this paragraph relies on Orford and Velleman, "Alcoholism Halfway Houses."

49. Shirley Otto and Jim Orford, *Not Quite Like Home: Small Hostels for Alcoholics and Others* (New York: John Wiley and Sons, 1978); and Alan C. Ogborne, H. M. Annis, and M. Sanchez-Craig, *Report of the Task Force on Halfway Houses* (Toronto: Addiction Research Foundation, 1978) cited in Orford and Velleman, "Alcoholism Halfway Houses."

50. Richard Velleman, "The Engagement of New Residents: A Missing Dimension in the Evaluation of Halfway Houses for Problem Drinkers," *Journal of Studies on Alcohol*, Vol. 45 (1984), pp. 251–259.

51. See Orford and Velleman, "Alcoholism Halfway Houses"; and Rubington, "Staff Problems in Halfway Houses."

52. Also see Orford and Velleman, "Alcoholism Halfway Houses."

53. Some of this section relies on Weldon Witters and Peter Venturelli, *Drugs and Society*, 2nd ed. (Boston: Jones

and Bartlett, 1988), pp. 332–333. Copyright © 1988 Jones and Bartlett Publishers. Reprinted by permission; and Oakley Ray and Charles Ksir, *Drugs, Society, & Human Behavior,* 5th ed. (St. Louis, MO: C. V. Mosby, 1987), pp. 371–372.

54. Witters and Venturelli, *Drugs and Society.*

55. Gerstein and Harwood, *Treating Drug Problems.* Reprinted with permission from *Treating Drug Problems, Volume 1.* Copyright 1990 by the National Academy of Sciences. Courtesy of the National Academy Press, Washington, DC. See this reference for additional information on therapeutic communities.

56. William Glasser, *Reality Therapy* (New York: Harper Colophon Books, 1965).

57. Gerstein and Harwood, *Treating Drug Problems,* p. 352; for additional information on therapeutic communities, also see Cook, "The Minnesota Model in the Management of Drug and Alcohol Dependency."

58. R. H. Moos, *Evaluating Treatment Environments* (New York: Wiley, 1974); and R. H. Moos, *Community Oriented Program Environments Scale Manual* (Palo Alto, CA: Consulting Psychologists Press, 1974).

59. Morris D. Bell, "Three Therapeutic Communities for Drug Abusers: Differences in Treatment Environments," *The International Journal of the Addictions,* Vol. 20, No. 10 (1985), pp. 1523–1531.

60. Gerstein and Harwood, *Treating Drug Problems.*

61. Snair, *Report on Evaluation Research Review.*

62. Lawrence Katz, "The Salvation Army Men's Social Service Center: II. Results," *Quarterly Journal of Studies on Alcohol,* Vol. 27 (1966), pp. 636–647.

63. Ibid.

64. George R. Jacobson, "The Role of Shelter Facilities in the Treatment of Alcoholics," in Pattison and Kaufman, *Encyclopedic Handbook of Alcoholism,* pp. 894–906.

65. Ibid.

66. Katz, "The Salvation Army Men's Social Service Center," p. 642.

67. Rudolf H. Moos, Barbara Mehren, and Bernice S. Moos, "Evaluation of a Salvation Army Alcoholism Treatment Program," *Journal of Studies on Alcohol,* Vol. 38, No. 7 (1978), pp. 1267–1275.

68. Jacobson, "The Role of Shelter Facilities in the Treatment of Alcoholics."

69. NIAAA, *Seventh Special Report to the U.S. Congress on Alcohol and Health.*

70. Sandra C. Anderson, "Group Therapy with Alcoholic Clients: A Review," *Advances in Alcohol and Substance Abuse,* Vol. 2, No. 2 (1982), pp. 23–40.

71. Baruch Levine and Virginia Gallogly, *Group Therapy with Alcoholics, Outpatient and Inpatient Approaches* (Beverly Hills, CA: Sage, 1985), p. 15.

72. Also see Irving D. Yalom, "Group Therapy and Alcoholism," *Annals of the New York Academy of Sciences,* Vol. 233 (1974), pp. 85–103; David R. Doroff, "Group Psy-

chotherapy in Alcoholism," in Kissin and Begleiter, *The Biology of Alcoholism,* pp. 235–258; and Philip J. Flores, "Modifications of Yalom's Interactional Group Therapy Model as a Mode of Treatment for Alcoholism," *Group,* Vol. 6, No. 1 (1982), pp. 3–16.

73. For a description of this approach and a summary of the research literature on it, see Robert W. Sisson and Nathan H. Azrin, "The Community Reinforcement Approach," in Reid K. Hester and William R. Miller (Eds.), *Handbook of Alcoholism Treatment Approaches: Effective Alternatives* (New York: Pergamon, 1989), pp. 242–258.

74. Thomas H. Bien, William R. Miller, and J. Scott Tonigan, "Brief Interventions for Alcohol Problems: A Review," *Addiction,* Vol. 88 (1993), pp. 315–336; and National Institute on Alcohol Abuse and Alcoholism, *Eighth Special Report to the U.S. Congress on Alcohol and Health* (Rockville, MD: NIAAA, 1993), pp. 307–310.

75. McCaul and Furst, "Alcoholism Treatment in the United States." The illustration on pages 125–130 on NIAAA's patient-treatment matching study highlights some of the time-limited approaches to intervention that have also been used with alcohol-dependent clients.

76. Snair, *Report on Evaluation Research Review,* p. 6.

77. Gerstein and Harwood, *Treating Drug Problems.*

78. Charles P. O'Brien, Arthur Alterman, Dan Walter, Anna Rose Childress, and A. T. McLellan, "Evaluations of Treatment for Cocaine Dependence," in Louis S. Harris (Ed.), *Problems of Drug Dependence 1989: Proceedings of the 51st Annual Scientific Meeting* (Rockville, MD: U.S. Department of Health and Human Services, 1990), pp. 78–84.

79. Jeffrey M. Brandsma and E. Mansell Pattison, "The Outcome of Group Psychotherapy Alcoholics: An Empirical Review," *American Journal of Drug and Alcohol Abuse,* Vol. 11, Nos. 1 & 2 (1985), pp. 151–162; also see Doroff, "Group Psychotherapy in Alcoholism."

80. Susan D. Solomon, "Individual versus Group Therapy: Current Status in the Treatment of Alcoholism," *Advances in Alcohol and Substance Abuse,* Vol. 2, No. 1 (1982), pp. 69–86.

81. NIAAA, *Seventh Special Report to the U.S. Congress on Alcohol and Health.*

82. Barbara S. McCrady, Judith Moreau, Thomas J. Paolino, Jr., and Richard Longabaugh, "Joint Hospitalization and Couples Therapy for Alcoholism: A Four-Year Follow-Up," *Journal of Studies on Alcohol,* Vol. 43, No. 11 (1982), pp. 1244–1250.

83. Barbara S. McCrady, Nora E. Noel, David B. Abrams, Robert L. Stout, Hilary Fisher Nelson, and William M. Hay, "Comparative Effectiveness of Three Types of Spouse Involvement in Outpatient Behavioral Alcoholism Treatment," *Journal of Studies on Alcohol,* Vol. 47, No. 6 (1986), pp. 459–467.

84. Sisson and Azrin, "The Community Reinforcement Approach."

85. N. H. Azrin, R. W. Sisson, R. Meyers, and M. Godley, "Alcoholism Treatment by Disulfiram and Community Reinforcement Therapy," *Journal of Behavior Therapy and Experimental Psychiatry*, Vol. 13 (1982), pp. 105–112.

86. McCaul and Furst, "Alcoholism Treatment in the United States."

87. Bien et al., "Brief Interventions for Alcohol Problems: A Review"; and NIAAA, *Eighth Special Report to the U.S. Congress on Alcohol and Health*, pp. 307–310.

88. NIAAA, *Eighth Special Report to the U.S. Congress on Alcohol and Health*, p. 308.

89. McKay and Maisto, "An Overview and Critique of Advances in the Treatment of Alcohol Use Disorders."

90. Much of this section is based on John A. Ewing, "Disulfiram and Other Deterrent Drugs," in Pattison and Kaufman, *Encyclopedic Handbook of Alcoholism*, pp. 1033–1042; *Antabuse* (Tallahassee, FL: Department of Health and Rehabilitative Services, July 1973); and *Physicians' Desk Reference, 47th ed.* (Medical Economics Data, 1993), pp. 2540–2541.

91. Ronald W. McNichol and Steven A. Logsdon, "Disulfiram: An Evaluation Research Model," *Alcohol Health & Research World*, Vol. 12, No. 3 (1988), pp. 202–209.

92. Ewing, "Disulfiram and Other Deterrent Drugs."

93. Ibid.

94. Richard A Rettig and Adam Yarmolinsky (Eds.), *Federal Regulation of Methadone Treatment* (Washington, DC: National Academy Press, 1995).

95. Glen Hanson and Peter Venturelli, *Drugs and Society*, 4th ed. (Boston: Jones and Bartlett Publishers, 1995), p. 486. Copyright © 1995, Jones and Bartlett Publishers. Reprinted with permission.

96. Gerstein and Harwood, *Treating Drug Problems*; also see Ray and Ksir, *Drugs, Society, & Human Behavior*, pp. 367–369.

97. See Walter Ling, Richard A. Rawson, and Margaret A. Compton, "Substituting Pharmacotherapies for Opioid Addiction: From Methadone to LAAM and Buprenorphine," *Journal of Psychoactive Drugs*, Vol. 26, No. 2 (April–June 1994), pp. 119-128.

98. Rettig and Yarmolinsky, *Federal Regulation of Methadone Treatment*, p. 3.

99. Ibid. p. 191.

100. Michael L. Prendergast, Christine Grella, Susanne M. Perry, and M. Douglas Anglin, "Levo-Alpha-Acetylmethodal (LAAM): Clinical, Research, and Policy Issues of a New Pharmacotherapy for Opioid Addiction," *Journal of Psychoactive Drugs*, Vol. 27, No. 3 (1995), pp. 239–247; and Ling et al., "Substitution Pharmacotherapies for Opioid Addiction: From Methadone to LAAM and Buprenorphine."

101. Much of the remainder of this section relies on Gerstein and Harwood, *Treating Drug Problems*; also see Ray and Ksir, *Drugs, Society, & Human Behavior*.

102. Gerstein and Harwood, *Treating Drug Problems*.

103. See, for example, Warren K. Bickel, Ira Marion, and Joyce H. Lowinson, "The Treatment of Alcoholic Methadone Patients: A Review," *Journal of Substance Abuse Treatment*, Vol. 4 (1987), pp. 15–19; and David S. Metzger, James Cornish, George E. Woody, A. Thomas McLellan, Patrick Druley and Charles P. O'Brien, "Naltrexone in Federal Probationers," in Harris, *Problem of Drug Dependence 1989. Proceedings of the 51st Annual Scientific Meeting*, p. 466.

104. Gerstein and Harwood, *Treating Drug Problems*.

105. Ling et al., "Substitution Pharmacotherapies for Opioid Addiction: From Methadone to LAAM and Buprenorphine."

106. See Gerstein and Harwood, *Treating Drug Problems*; and Witters and Venturelli, *Drugs and Society*.

107. The following description is based on Prendergast et al., "Levo-Alpha-Acetylmethodal (LAAM): Clinical, Research, and Policy Issues of a New Pharmacotherapy for Opioid Addiction"; and Ling et al., "Substitution Pharmacotherapies for Opioid Addiction: From Methadone to LAAM and Buprenorphine."

108. Prendergast et al., "Levo-Alpha-Acetylmethodal (LAAM): Clinical, Research, and Policy Issues of a New Pharmacotherapy for Opioid Addiction."

109. Ling et al., "Substitution Pharmacotherapies for Opioid Addiction: From Methadone to LAAM and Buprenorphine."

110. Eric C. Strain, Maxine L. Stitzer, Ira A. Liebson, and George E. Bigelow, "Comparison of Buprenorphine and Methadone in the Treatment of Opioid Dependence," *American Journal of Psychiatry*, Vol. 151 (July 1994), pp. 1025–1030; also see Ling et al., "Substitution Pharmacotherapies for Opioid Addiction: From Methadone to LAAM and Buprenorphine" for a review of this drug.

111. Ling et al., "Substitution Pharmacotherapies for Opioid Addiction: From Methadone to LAAM and Buprenorphine," p. 126.

112. Some of this paragraph relies on Witters and Venturelli, *Drugs and Society*.

113. "Naltrexone: Breakthrough Treatment for Many Addictions?" *The Facts About Drugs and Alcohol*, Vol. 1, No. 4 (A Publication of the University of Florida College of Medicine) (1992), p. 1.

114. Ibid.

115. Witters and Venturelli, *Drugs and Society*, 2nd ed., p. 331. Copyright © 1988, Jones and Bartlett Publishers. Reprinted by permission.

116. Ibid.

117. This paragraph relies on "Naltrexone: Breakthrough Treatment for Many Addictions?"; also see "New Drug Update," *News & Views* (Newsletter of the Texas Research Society on Alcoholism), Vol. 3, No. 1 (1993).

118. Also see Joseph R. Volpicelli, Karen L. Clay, Nathan T. Watson, and Laura A. Volpicelli, "Naltrexone and the Treatment of Alcohol Dependence," *Alcohol Health & Research World*, Vol. 18, No. 4 (1994), pp. 272–278.

119. This paragraph relies on Hanson and Venturelli, *Drugs and Society*, 4th ed., p. 254. Also see National Institute on Drug Abuse, *Drug Abuse and Drug Abuse Research, The Third Triennial Report to Congress from the Secretary, Department of Health and Human Services* (Rockville, MD: Alcohol, Drug Abuse, and Mental Health Administration, 1991), pp. 56–57 for a discussion of the research on Clonidine.

120. Gerstein and Harwood, *Treating Drug Problems*.

121. Snair, *Report on Evaluation Research Review*, p. 6.

122. Gerstein and Harwood, *Treating Drug Problems*, p. 153. Reprinted with permission from *Treating Drug Problems, Volume 1*. Copyright 1990 by the National Academy of Sciences. Courtesy of the National Academy Press, Washington, DC.

123. Ibid.

124. A. Thomas McLellan, Isabelle O. Arndt, David S. Metzger, George E. Woody, and Charles P. O'Brien, "The Effects of Psychosocial Services in Substance Abuse Treatment," *Journal of the American Medical Association*, Vol. 269, No. 15 (April 21, 1993), pp. 1953–1959.

125. NIAAA, *Sixth Special Report to the U.S. Congress on Alcohol and Health*.

126. Richard K. Fuller, Laure Branchey, Dennis R. Brightwell, Robert M. Derman, Chad D. Emrick, Frank L. Iber, Kenneth E. James, Roy B. Lacoursiere, Kelvin K. Lee, Ilse Lowenstam, Iradj Maany, Dewey Neiderhiser, James J. Nocks, and Spencer Shaw, "Disulfiram Treatment of Alcoholism: A Veterans Administration Cooperative Study," *Journal of the American Medical Association*, Vol. 256, No. 11 (September 19, 1986), pp. 1449–1455.

127. Ibid., p. 1449.

128. McNichol and Logsdon, "Disulfiram: An Evaluation Research Model."

129. Azrin et al., "Alcoholism Treatment by Disulfiram and Community Reinforcement Therapy," pp. 105–112; and Sisson and Azrin, "The Community Reinforcement Approach."

130. Mim J. Landry, *Overview of Addiction Treatment Effectiveness* (Rockville, MD: Substance Abuse and Mental Health Services Administration, 1995), DHS Pub. No. (SMA) 96-3081, p. ix.

131. Ibid.

132. Joseph R. Volpicelli, Arthur I. Alterman, Motoi Hayashida, and Charles P. O'Brien, "Naltrexone in the Treatment of Alcohol Dependence," *Archives of General Pyschiatry*, Vol. 49, No. 11 (1992), pp. 876–880.

133. Stephanie S. O'Malley, Adam J. Jaffe, Grace Chang, Richard S. Schottenfeld, Roger E. Meyer, and Bruce Rounsaville, "Naltrexone and Coping Skills Therapy for Alcohol Dependence: A Controlled Study," *Archives of General Psychiatry*, Vol. 49 (November 1992), pp. 881–887.

134. Joseph R. Volpicelli, Nathan T. Watson, Andrea C. King, Carolyn E. Sherman, and Charles P. O'Brien, "Effect of Naltrexone and Alcohol 'High' in Alcoholics," *American Journal of Psychiatry*, Vol. 152, No. 4 (April 1995), pp. 613–615.

135. Stephanie S. O'Malley, Adam J. Jaffe, Sarah Rode, and Bruce J. Rounsaville, "Experience of a 'Slip' among Alcoholics Treated with Naltrexone or Placebo," *American Journal of Psychiatry*, Vol. 153, No. 2, pp. 281–283.

136. Volpicelli et al., "Naltrexone in the Treatment of Alcohol Dependence."

137. Ibid.

138. Helen M. Annis and Christine S. Davis, "Self-Efficacy and the Prevention of Alcoholic Relapse: Initial Findings from a Treatment Trial," in Timothy B. Baker and Dale S. Cannon (Eds.), *Assessment and Treatment of Addictive Disorders* (New York: Praeger, 1988), pp. 88–112; and NIAAA, *Seventh Special Report to the U.S. Congress on Alcohol and Health*.

139. G. Alan Marlatt and Judith R. Gordon, *Relapse Prevention: Maintenance Strategies in the Treatment of Addictive Behaviors* (New York: Guilford Press, 1985).

140. Terrence T. Gorski and Merlene Miller, *Staying Sober: A Guide for Relapse Prevention* (Independence, MO: Independence Press, 1986).

141. Also see Annis and Davis, "Self-Efficacy and the Prevention of Alcoholic Relapse"; and Dennis C. Daley, *Relapse Prevention Workbook for Recovering Alcoholics and Drug Dependent Persons* (Holmes Beach, FL: Learning Publications, 1986); and Dennis C. Daley, *Relapse Prevention: Treatment Alternatives and Counseling Aids* (Blue Ridge Summit, PA: Tab Books, 1989).

142. Gorski and Miller, *Staying Sober*; and CENAPS Corporation, "The Relapse Dynamic" (Hazel Crest, IL: The CENAPS Corporation, no date).

143. Marlatt and Gordon, *Relapse Prevention*.

144. This paragraph relies on ibid.

145. Gerstein and Harwood, *Treating Drug Problems*.

146. NIAAA, *Sixth Special Report to the U.S. Congress on Alcohol and Health*, p. 130.

147. See, for example, R. Dale Walker, Dennis M. Donovan, Daniel R. Kivlahan, and Michael R. O'Leary, "Length of Stay, Neuropsychological Performance, and Aftercare: Influences on Alcohol Treatment Outcome," *Journal of Consulting and Clinical Psychology*, Vol. 51, No. 6 (1983), pp. 900–911.

148. Gerstein and Harwood, *Treating Drug Problems*, p. 172. Reprinted with permission from *Treating Drug Problems, Volume 1*. Copyright 1990 by the National Academy of Sciences. Courtesy of the National Academy Press, Washington, DC.

149. NIAAA, *Sixth Special Report to the U.S. Congress on Alcohol and Health*.

150. Annis and Davis, "Self-Efficacy and the Prevention of Alcoholic Relapse: Initial Findings from a Treatment Trial"; and NIAAA, *Seventh Special Report to the U.S. Congress on Alcohol and Health*.

151. Chad D. Emrick, "Alcoholics Anonymous: Affiliation Processes and Effectiveness as Treatment," *Alcoholism: Clinical and Experimental Research*, Vol. 11, No. 5 (1987), pp. 416–423, and Ann M. Bradley, "Keep Coming Back:

The Case for a Valuation of Alcoholics Anonymous," *Alcohol Health & Research World*, Vol. 12, No. 3 (1988), p. 198.

152. Marie Weil, James M. Karls, and assoc. (Eds.), *Case Management in Human Service Practice* (San Francisco: Jossey-Bass, 1985); also see Texas Department of Mental Health and Mental Retardation, *Case Management System Components By Mental Health and Mental Retardation Authorities*, June 1984.

153. Rebecca Sager Ashery (Ed.), *Progress and Issues in Case Management*, NIDA Research Monograph 127 (Rockville, MD: National Institute on Drug Abuse, 1992), DHHS Pub. No. (ADM) 92-1946.

154. Susan Ridgely and Mark L. Willenbring, "Application of Case Management to Drug Abuse Treatment: Overview of Models and Research Issues," in Ashery (Ed.), *Progress and Issues in Case Management*, pp. 12–33, quote from p. 30.

155. Judith A. Levy, Charles P. Gallmeier, William W. Weddington, and W. Wayne Wiebel, "Delivering Case Management Using a Community-Based Model of Drug Intervention," in Rebecca Sager Ashery, *Progress and Issues in Case Management*, pp. 12–33; and Judith A. Levy, Charles P. Gallmeier, and W. Wayne Wiebel, "The Outreach Assisted Peer-Support Model for Controlling Drug Dependency," *The Journal of Drug Issues*, Vol. 25, No. 3 (1995), pp. 507–529.

156. Manpower Demonstration Research Corporation, *Summary and Findings of the National Supported Work Demonstration* (Cambridge, MA: Ballinger, 1980).

157. A. Thomas McLellan, Lester Luborsky, George E. Woody, Charles P. O'Brien, and Ruben Kron, "Are the 'Addiction-Related' Problems of Substance Abusers Really Related?" *The Journal of Nervous and Mental Disease*, Vol. 69, No. 4 (1981), pp. 232–239.

158. Gerstein and Harwood, *Treating Drug Problems*.

159. NIAAA, *Sixth Special Report to the U.S. Congress on Alcohol and Health*.

160. A. Thomas McLellan, Grant R. Grissom, Peter Brill, Jack Durell, David S. Metzger, and Charles P. O'Brien, "Private Substance Abuse Treatments: Are Some Programs More Effective Than Others?" *Journal of Substance Abuse Treatment*, Vol. 10 (1993), pp. 243–254.

161. Peter E. Nathan, "Outcomes of Treatment for Alcoholism: Current Data," *Annals of Behavioral Medicine*, Vol. 8, Nos. 2–3 (1986), pp. 40–46.

162. NIAAA, *Seventh Special Report to the U.S. Congress on Alcohol and Health*, p. 130; also see Chad D. Emrick and Joel Hansen, "Assertions Regarding Effectiveness of Treatment for Alcoholism: Fact or Fantasy?" *American Psychologist* (October 1983), pp. 1078–1088.

163. A. Thomas McLellan, George E. Woody, Lester Luborsky, Charles P. O'Brien, and Keith A. Druley, "Increased Effectiveness of Substance Abuse Treatment: A Prospective Study of Patient-Treatment 'Matching,' " *The Journal of Nervous and Mental Disease*, Vol. 171, No. 10 (1983), pp. 597–605; and A. Thomas McLellan, Lester Luborsky, George E. Woody, Charles P. O'Brien, and Keith A. Druley, "Predicting Response to Alcohol and Drug Abuse Treatments," *Archives of General Psychiatry*, Vol. 40 (1983), pp. 620–625.

164. Sherry Deren and Joan Randell, "The Vocational Rehabilitation of Substance Abusers," *Journal of Applied Rehabilitation Counseling*, Vol. 21, No. 2 (1990), pp. 4–6.

165. A. K. J. Cartwright, "Are Different Therapeutic Prespectives Important in the Treatment of Alcoholism?" *British Journal of Addiction*, Vol. 76 (1981), pp. 347–361.

166. John F. C. McLachlan, "Therapy Strategies, Personality Orientation and Recovery from Alcoholism," *Canadian Psychiatric Association Journal*, Vol. 19, No. 1 (February 1974), pp. 25–30.

167. Stephen R Valle, "Interpersonal Functioning of Alcoholism Counselors and Treatment Outcome," *Journal of Studies on Alcohol*, Vol. 42, No. 9 (1981), p. 783–790.

168. Lester Luborsky, A. Thomas McLellan, George E. Woody, Charles P. O'Brien, and Arthur Auerbach, "Therapist Success and Its Determinants," *Archives of General Psychiatry*, Vol. 42 (June 1985), pp. 602–611.

169. William R. Miller and Louise M. Baca, "Two-Year Follow-Up of Bibliotherapy and Therapist-Directed Controlled Drinking Training for Problem Drinkers," *Behavior Therapy*, Vol. 14 (1983), pp. 441–447; also see William R. Miller, Cheryl A. Taylor, and JoAnne Cisneros West, "Focused versus Broad-Spectrum Behavior Therapy for Problem Drinkers," *Journal of Consulting and Clinical Psychiatry*, Vol. 48, No. 5, pp. 590–601.

170. William R. Miller, R. Gayle Benefield, and J. Scott Tonigan, "Enhancing Motivation for Change in Problem Drinking: A Controlled Comparison of Two Therapist Styles," *Journal of Consulting and Clinical Psychology*, Vol. 61, No. 3 (1993), pp. 455–461.

171. Raymond M. Costello, "Alcoholism Treatment and Evaluation: In Search of Methods. II. Collation of Two-Year Follow-Up Studies," *The International Journal of the Addictions*, Vol. 10, No. 5 (1975), pp. 857–867.

172. Ronald M. Kadden, "Cognitive-Behavioral Approaches to Alcoholism Treatment," *Alcohol Health and Research World*, Vol. 18, No. 4 (1994), pp. 279–286.

173. NIAAA, *Sixth Special Report to the U.S. Congress on Alcohol and Health*, p. 127.

174. Jeffrey M. Brandsma, Maxie C. Maultsby, Jr., Richard J. Welsh, *Outpatient Treatment of Alcoholism: A Review and Comparative Study* (Baltimore, MD: University Park Press, 1980).

175. NIAAA, *Sixth Special Report to the U.S. Congress on Alcohol and Health*.

176. Richard Longabaugh, Martha Beattie, Nora Noel, Robert Stout, and Paul Malloy, "The Effect of Social

Investment on Treatment Outcome," *Journal of Studies on Alcohol*, Vol. 54 (July 1993), pp. 465–478.

177. O'Malley et al., "Naltrexone and Coping Skills Therapy for Alcohol Dependence: A Controlled Study."

178. NIAAA, *Sixth Special Report to the U.S. Congress on Alcohol and Health*.

179. Ibid.

180. Ibid.

181. Clayton T. Shorkey, "Use of Behavioral Methods with Individuals Recovering from Psychoactive Substance Dependence," in Donald K. Granvold (Ed.), *Cognitive and Behavioral Treatment: Methods and Applications* (Belmont, CA: Brooks/Cole Publishing, 1993).

182. Peter E. Nathan and D. W. Briddell, "Behavioral Assessment and Treatment of Alcoholism," in Kissin and Begleiter, *The Biology of Alcoholism*, pp. 301-349.

183. Baker and Cannon, *Assessment and Treatment of Addictive Disorders*, p. 205.

184. Harold Holder, Richard Longabaugh, William R. Miller, and Anthony Y. Rubonis, "The Cost Effectiveness of Treatment for Alcoholism: A First Approximation," *Journal of Studies on Alcohol*, Vol. 52, No. 6 (1991), pp. 517–540, quote from pp. 529 and 531.

185. E. Mansell Pattison, Mark B. Sobell, and Linda C. Sobell, *Emerging Concepts of Alcohol Dependence* (New York: Springer, 1977), see Chapter 6; and David J. Armor, J. Michael Polich, and Harriet B. Stambul, *Alcoholism and Treatment* (Publication R-1739-NIAAA) (Santa Monica, CA: Rand Corporation, 1976, also published by John Wiley and Sons, New York, 1978); Gerard J. Connors, "Drinking Moderation Training as a Contemporary Therapeutic Approach," *Drugs & Society*, Vol. 18, No. 1 (1993), pp. 117–134, also published in Gerard J. Connors (Ed.), *Innovations in Alcoholism Treatment: State of the Art Reviews and Their Implications for Clinical Practice* (Binghamton, NY: Haworth, 1993), pp. 117–134.

186. Keith Humphreys, Rudolf H. Moos, and John W. Finney, "Two Pathways out of Drinking Problems without Professional Treatment," *Addictive Behaviors*, Vol. 20, No. 4 (1995), pp. 427–441; and Linda C. Sobell, John A. Cunningham, and Mark B. Sobell, "Recovery from Alcohol Problems with and without Treatment: Prevalence in Two Population Surveys," *American Journal of Public Health*, Vol. 86 (1996), pp. 966–972.

187. Humphreys et al., "Two Pathways out of Drinking Problems without Professional Treatment," p. 439.

188. Edward J. Callahan and Ella H. Pecsok, "Heroin Addiction," in Dennis M. Donovan and G. Alan Marlatt (Eds.), *Assessment of Addictive Behaviors* (New York: Guilford Press, 1988), pp. 390–418.

189. Armor et al., *Alcoholism and Treatment*. Some of this section relies on Ray and Ksir, *Drugs, Society, & Human Behavior*, see pages 363–364.

190. Pattison et al., *Emerging Concepts of Alcohol Dependence*.

191. J. Michael Polich, David J. Armor, and Harriet B. Braiker, *The Course of Alcoholism: Four Years After Treatment* (R-2433-NIAAA) (Santa Monica, CA: Rand Corporation, 1980, also published by John S. Wiley and Sons, 1981).

192. Mark B. Sobell and Linda C. Sobell, "Individualized Behavior Therapy for Alcoholics," *Behavior Therapy*, Vol. 4 (1973), pp. 49–72; and Mark B. Sobell and Linda C. Sobell, "Alcoholics Treated by Individualized Behavior Therapy: One Year Treatment Outcome," *Behaviour Research and Therapy*, Vol. 11 (1973), pp. 599–618.

193. Mark B. Sobell and Linda C. Sobell, "Second-Year Treatment Outcome of Alcoholics Treated by Individualized Behavior Therapy: Results," *Behaviour Research and Therapy*, Vol. 14 (1976), pp. 195–215, reprinted in Pattison et al., *Emerging Concepts of Alcohol Dependence*, pp. 300–335.

194. Mary L. Pendery, Irving M. Maltzman, and L. Jolyon West, "Controlled Drinking by Alcoholics? New Findings and a Reevaluation of a Major Affirmative Study," *Science*, Vol. 217 (July 9, 1982), pp. 169–175.

195. Ovide Pomerleau, Michael Pertschuk, David Adkins, and John Paul Brady, "A Comparison of Behavioral and Traditional Treatment for Middle-Income Problem Drinkers," *Journal of Behavioral Medicine*, Vol. 1, No. 2 (1978), pp. 187–200.

196. Connors, "Drinking Moderation Training as a Contemporary Therapeutic Approach," quotes from pp. 117 and 125.

197. Ibid., pp. 125 and 129.

198. NIAAA, "How to Cut Down on Your Drinking," March 1996, NIH Pub. No. 96-3770.

199. Harold Rosenberg and Leigh-Anne Davis, "Acceptance of Moderate Drinking by Alcohol Treatment Services in the United States," *Journal of Studies on Alcohol*, Vol. 55 (March 1994), pp. 167–172.

200. Ibid., p. 169.

201. Audrey Kishline, "A Toast to Moderation," *Psychology Today* (January/February, 1996), pp. 53–56; and Audrey Kishline, *Moderate Drinking: The Moderation Management Guide for People Who Want to Reduce Their Drinking* (New York: Crown, 1996).

202. Kishline, "A Toast to Moderation," p. 55.

203. Connors, "Drinking Moderation Training as a Contemporary Therapeutic Approach," p. 126.

204. T. M. Worner, B. Zeller, H. Schwarz, F. Zwas, and D. Lyon, "Acupuncture Fails to Improve Treatment Outcome in Alcoholics," *Drug and Alcohol Dependence*, Vol. 30 (1992), pp. 169–173.

205. Alex G. Brumbaugh, "Acupuncture: New Perspectives in Chemical Dependency Treatment," *Journal of Substance Abuse Treatment*, Vol. 10 (1993), pp. 35–43.

206. This paragraph relies on ibid.

207. Milton L. Bullock, Andrew J. Umen, Patricia D. Culliton, and Robert T. Olander, "Acupuncture Treatment of Alcoholic Recidivism: A Pilot Study," *Alcoholism: Clinical and Experimental Research*, Vol. 11, No. 3 (1987), pp. 292–295; and Milton L. Bullock, Patricia D. Culliton, and Robert T. Olander, "Controlled Trial of Acupuncture for Severe Recidivist Alcoholism," *The Lancet*, June 24, 1989, pp. 1435–1439.

208. Worner et al., "Acupuncture Fails to Improve Treatment Outcome in Alcoholics."

209. S. Kelly Avants, Arthur Margolin, Patrick Chang, Thomas R. Kosten, and Stephen Birch, "Acupuncture for the Treatment of Cocaine Addiction: Investigation of a Needle Puncture Control," *Journal of Substance Abuse Treatment*, Vol. 12, No. 3 (1995), pp. 195–205.

210. Avants et al., "Acupuncture for the Treatment of Cocaine Addiction: Investigation of a Needle Puncture Control"; and Douglas S. Lipton, Vincent Brewington, and Michael Smith, "Acupuncture for Crack-Cocaine Detoxification: Experimental Evaluation of Efficacy," *Journal of Substance Abuse Treatment*, Vol. 11, No. 3 (1994), pp. 205–215.

211. Avants et al., "Acupuncture for the Treatment of Cocaine Addiction: Investigation of a Needle Puncture Control."

212. Lipton at el., "Acupuncture for Crack-Cocaine Detoxification: Experimental Evaluation of Efficacy."

213. Allyson M. Washburn, Robert E. Fullilove, Mindy Thompson Fullilove, Patricia A. Keenan, Betty McGee, Kenneth A. Morris, James L. Sorenson, and Wayne W. Clark, "Acupuncture Heroin Detoxification: A Single-Blind Clinical Trial," *Journal of Substance Abuse Treatment*, Vol. 10 (1993), pp. 345–351.

214. Janet Konefal, Robert Duncan, and Cheryl Clemence, "The Impact of the Addition of an Acupuncture Treatment Program to an Existing Metro-Dade Country Outpatient Substance Abuse Treatment Facility," *Journal of Addictive Diseases*, Vol. 13, No. 3 (1994), pp. 71–99; and in Stephen Magura and Andrew Rosenblum, *Experimental Therapies in Addiction Medicine* (Binghamton, NY: Haworth Press, 1994), pp. 71–99.

215. Worner et al., "Acupuncture Fails to Improve Treatment Outcome in Alcoholics," p. 173.

216. Shorkey, "Use of Behavioral Methods with Individuals Recovering from Psychoactive Substance Dependence."

217. Eugene G. Peniston and Paul J. Kulkosky, "α–θ Brainwave Training and β-Endorphin Levels in Alcoholics," *Alcoholism: Clinical and Experimental Research*, Vol. 13, No. 2 (March/April 1989), pp. 271–279; and Eugene G. Peniston and Paul J. Kulkosky, "Alpha-Theta EEG Biofeedback Training in Alcoholism & Post-Traumatic Stress Disorder," *International Society for the Study of Subtle Energies and Energy Medicine*, Vol. 2, No. 4 (1992), pp. 5–7.

218. Hanson and Venturelli, *Drugs and Society*, 4th ed., p. 493.

219. Michael R. Denney and Jarod L. Baugh, "Symptom Reduction and Sobriety in the Male Alcoholic," *The International Journal of the Addictions*, Vol. 27, No. 11 (1992), pp. 1293–1300; Steven L. Fahrion, E. Dale Walters, Lolafaye Coyne, and Thomas Allen, "Alterations in EEG Amplitude, Personality Factors, and Brain Electrical Mapping after Alpha-Theta Brainwave Training: A Controlled Case Study of an Alcoholic in Recovery," *Alcoholism: Clinical and Experimental Research*, Vol. 16, No. 3 (May/June 1992), pp. 547–552.

220. Stephen T. Higgins, Alan J. Budney, Warren K. Bickel, Florian E. Foerg, Robert Donham, and Gary J. Badger, "Incentives Improve Outcome in Outpatient Behavioral Treatment of Cocaine Dependence," *Archives of General Psychiatry*, Vol. 51 (July 1994), pp. 568–576.

221. Maxine L. Stitzer, Martin Y. Iguchi, and Linda J. Felch, "Contingent Take-Home Incentive: Effects on Drug Use of Methadone Maintenance Patients," *Journal of Consulting and Clinical Psychology*, Vol. 60 (1992), pp. 927–934.

222. Higgins et al., "Incentives Improve Outcome in Outpatient Behavioral Treatment of Cocaine Dependence"; and Kenneth Silverman, Stephen T. Higgins, Robert K. Brooner, Ivan D. Montoya, Edward J. Cone, Charles R. Schuster, and Kenzie L. Preston, "Sustained Cocaine Abstinence in Methadone Maintenance Patients through Voucher-Based Reinforcement Therapy," *Archives of General Psychiatry*, Vol. 53 (May 1996), pp. 409–415.

223. Higgins et al., "Incentives Improve Outcome in Outpatient Behavioral Treatment of Cocaine Dependence."

224. Brandsma et al., *Outpatient Treatment of Alcoholism: A Review and Comparative Study*; Nick Kanas, "Alcoholism and Group Psychotherapy," in Pattison and Kaufman, *Encyclopedic Handbook of Alcoholism*, pp. 1011–1021; and Sheldon Zimberg, "Psychotherapy in the Treatment of Alcoholism," also in Pattison and Kaufman, *Encyclopedic Handbook of Alcoholism*, pp. 999–1010.

225. Doroff, "Group Psychotherapy in Alcoholism."

226. Bradley, "Keep Coming Back: The Case for a Valuation of Alcoholics Anonymous," p. 198.

227. Alcoholics Anonymous World Services (AAWS), "Alcoholics Anonymous 1996 Membership Survey" (New York: AAWS, 1997).

228. Figure for 1996 provided by Alcoholics Anonymous General Service Office.

229. AAWS, "Alcoholics Anonymous 1996 Membership Survey."

230. Alcoholics Anonymous World Services, *Forty-four Questions and Answers about the A.A. Program of Recovery from Alcoholism* (New York: AA, 1952).

231. Ibid.

232. Alcoholics Anonymous World Services, *Alcoholics Anonymous: The Story of How Many Thousands of Men*

and Women Have Recovered from Alcoholism, 3rd ed. (New York City: AA World Services, Inc., 1976).

233. Mary Sheeren, "The Relationship between Relapse and Involvement in Alcoholics Anonymous," *Journal of Studies on Alcohol,* Vol. 49, No. 1 (1988), pp. 104–106; and Frederick Baekeland, "Evaluation of Treatment Methods in Chronic Alcoholism," in Kissin and Begleiter, *The Biology of Alcoholism,* p. 406.

234. Paul E. Bebbington, "The Efficacy of Alcoholics Anonymous: The Elusiveness of Hard Data," *British Journal of Psychiatry,* Vol. 128 (1976), pp. 572–580.

235. Frederick B. Glaser and Alan C. Ogborne, "Does A.A. Really Work?" *British Journal of Addiction,* Vol. 77 (1982), pp. 123–129.

236. Ibid.

237. Bebbington, "The Efficacy of Alcoholics Anonymous: The Elusiveness of Hard Data," p. 572; also see Baekeland, "Evaluation of Treatment Methods."

238. Bebbington, "The Efficacy of Alcoholics Anonymous: The Elusiveness of Hard Data"; also see Glaser and Ogborne, "Does A.A. Really Work?"

239. Alan C. Ogborne and Frederick B. Glaser, "Characteristics of Affiliates of Alcoholics Anonymous," *Journal of Studies on Alcohol,* Vol. 42, No. 7 (1981), p. 670.

240. Ibid., p. 670.

241. Baekeland "Evaluation of Treatment Methods," p. 408.

242. Emrick, "Alcoholics Anonymous"; and Bradley, "Keep Coming Back: The Case for a Valuation of Alcoholics Anonymous."

243. Emrick, "Alcoholics Anonymous," p. 418.

244. Baekeland, "Evaluation of Treatment Methods," p. 407.

245. George E. Vaillant, *The Natural History of Alcoholism* (Cambridge, MA: Harvard University Press, 1983).

246. William R. Miller and Reid K. Hester, "Treating the Problem Drinker: Modern Approaches," in William R. Miller (Ed.), *The Addictive Behaviors: Treatment Of Alcoholism, Drug Abuse, Smoking, and Obesity* (Oxford: Pergamon Press, 1980), pp. 11–141.

247. Emrick, "Alcoholics Anonymous," p. 416.

248. Brandsma et al., *Outpatient Treatment of Alcoholism: A Review and Comparative Study.*

249. Walsh et al., "A Randomized Trial of Treatment Options for Alcohol-Abusing Workers."

250. Baekeland, "Evaluation of Treatment Methods," p. 407.

251. Helen M. Pettinati, A. Arthur Sugerman, Nicholas DiDonato, and Helen S. Maurer, "The Natural History of Alcoholism over Four Years After Treatment," *Journal of Studies on Alcohol,* Vol. 43, No. 3 (1982), pp. 201–215.

252. Eileen M. Corrigan, *Alcoholic Women in Treatment* (New York: Oxford University Press, 1980).

253. Emrick, "Alcoholics Anonymous."

254. Gerald M. Cross, Charles W. Morgan, Al J. Mooney, Carolyn A. Martin, and John A. Rafter, "Alcoholism Treatment: A Ten-Year Follow-up Study," *Alcoholism: Clinical and Experimental Research,* Vol. 14, No. 2 (1990), p. 169.

255. Some of this paragraph relies on David N. Nurco, Norma Wegner, Philip Stephenson, Abraham Makofsy, and John W. Shaffer, *Ex-Addicts' Self-Help Groups, Potential and Pitfalls* (New York: Praeger, 1983).

256. G. J. Connors, K. H. Dermen, and M.R. Duerr, "Characteristics of Participants in a Secular Self-Help Organization: Findings from a Survey of S.O.S. Members, " presented at the Research Society on Alcoholism, Annual Scientific Meeting, San Antonio, TX, June 1993.

257. Letter from Ed Batis, Member, National Advisory Board, SOS, 5521 Grosvenor Blvd., Los Angeles, CA 90066.

258. "Rational Recovery, A Self-Help Alternative to 12-Step Groups," pamphlet, no date; books on the approach by Jack Trimpey are *The Small Book* and *The Final Fix;* information is available on the Internet at http://www.rational.org/recovery

259. Nurco et al., *Ex-Addicts' Self-Help Groups.*

7

Preventing Alcohol and Drug Problems

The concept of *prevention* can be operationalized in a number of different ways. Most people seem to equate the term with the prevention of alcohol and other drug abuse, especially among children and adolescents. It is also frequently associated with a specific preventive method used with young people—that is, education. This is a relatively narrow view of prevention. During the last decade, the outlook on prevention has broadened considerably to include new goals, other populations, and additional strategies.

Several factors have contributed to this broader view of prevention. For example, there has been increasing involvement of volunteers and local action-oriented groups such as Mothers Against Drunk Driving (MADD), Students Against Driving Drunk (SADD), the Group Against Smoking Pollution (GASP), and hundreds of parent and community-based antidrug organizations. These groups have succeeded in developing specific *constituencies* for prevention programs, something that has been lacking in earlier efforts focused primarily on school children. It is difficult to disagree with their very specific objectives such as protecting the public from drunk drivers or making the air in office buildings safe to breathe. The groups are

also free of the prior disciplinary and professional constraints that have handicapped many of the professionals working in prevention programs. MADD and SADD have not hesitated to take their concerns directly to the legislative arena to get their point of view across. Neighborhood groups have organized public demonstrations outside the homes of suspected drug dealers. They have also provided surveillance of suspected drug dealers and supplied the police with information on drug transactions.

Community groups have been pushing for broad changes in policies and practices at all levels, from the grass roots to Washington, and they have evolved a national leadership to advocate for reform. There is evidence of the impact of this new movement in such issues as Proposition 99 in California. Despite a $20 million campaign by the tobacco industry to defeat it, voters passed an initiative raising taxes on tobacco products by 25 cents and designating the money for youth-oriented preventive education, research, and health care for people with tobacco-related medical problems.[1]

The recent $11.2 billion settlement of a lawsuit by the state of Florida against the tobacco industry, the plethora of other cases filed by states' attorneys-general, and the current antismoking measures being considered by Congress all foreshadow a new, more militant approach to both preventing tobacco addiction and dealing with the adverse health consequences of smoking.

The new approach is more consistent with a *harm-reduction model* of prevention rather than the *zero tolerance philosophy* that is apparently still favored by the law-enforcement agencies of our federal government (see Chapter 8). The objectives of a harm-reduction approach are to reduce the mortality and morbidity associated with alcohol and drug-related *problems* as well as to reduce the rates of abuse for alcohol and drugs. The new, more comprehensive view includes social, cultural, and legislative aspects of prevention rather than emphasizing individual responsibility.[2] Environmentally and culturally targeted approaches focus on the social and economic aspects of alcohol availability and stress objectives designed to reduce the severity of alcohol-related injuries.[3] Some environmentally oriented programs have specifically targeted young people. Perhaps the best example of the approach was the change in "minimum age of consumption" laws during the early 1980s.[4] The social aspects of prevention are stressed in ad campaigns that repeatedly tell us that "Friends don't let friends drive drunk." At the cultural level, when new legal drugs (cigarettes and alcohol) were recently introduced specifically for young, urban African Americans, organized opposition quickly let the manufacturers and retailers know that this was not an acceptable practice.

This is a utilitarian approach, one that argues for the greatest good for the greatest number of people and one that recognizes that the indirect consequences of abuse and dependency may be far more serious and widespread than is generally believed.[5] Perhaps the best example is the high fatality rate associated with alcohol-related automobile accidents. Another is the high rate of infection (hepatitis, AIDS, etc.) associated with sharing needles among intravenous drug users. Still an-

other is the high crime rates associated with using certain illicit drugs such as heroin. Advocates of harm-reduction approaches assume that certain drugs will always be abused. By recognizing that many college students abuse alcohol, efforts might be turned toward preventing the students from driving while intoxicated. A more realistic approach to intravenous drug use might be able to halt the spread of certain diseases by providing clean needles and syringes to heroin addicts.

Using a traditional public health model, prevention efforts may be classified as primary, secondary, or tertiary. Preventing new cases from occurring, such as convincing a classroom of youngsters not to smoke, is *primary* prevention. Reducing the number of existing cases, generally by identifying and treating those who have a drug or alcohol problem, is *secondary* prevention. The effort to avoid relapse and maintain the health of those who have been treated is *tertiary* prevention.[6]

The Institute of Medicine has developed a prevention paradigm consisting of three completely different categories or levels: *universal* for the general population, *selective* for particularly defined populations at highest risk, and *indicated* for persons already showing problems and requiring intervention to halt progression to more serious problems. This framework may add a more proactive dimension to community-based and individually focused prevention efforts because of its targeting preventive efforts along an operationally applied continuum.[7]

Preventive strategies may be grouped into five major categories: public information and education, service measures, technologic measures, legislative and regulatory measures, and economic measures. Some of these strategies may be directed at preventing or decreasing the use or abuse of alcohol or drugs; others focus on reducing or eliminating the harmful consequences of alcohol and drug use, both to the user and the larger society. All of these will be discussed in the following pages, but first we will present a brief overview of prevention efforts.

Overview of Prevention

Drug problems among U.S. youths became a public concern in the middle to late 1960s. Obviously, young people had been abusing alcohol as long as anyone could remember, but prevention efforts were relatively puny until large numbers of children began experimenting with *illicit* drugs. The majority of prevention programs focused on ways to reduce demand for drugs and alcohol, most often by trying to change individual behavior. Few of these programs have had successful results beyond superficial and transient changes in knowledge and attitudes.[8] One can change both knowledge and attitudes concerning drugs only to discover that it has little effect on behavior.[9] The research and evaluation methodologies used in most of these programs are also quite weak, and few of them have addressed any significant theoretical issues that cut across common areas of concern regarding alcohol, tobacco, and illicit drugs.

Do peer influences operate in the same manner regarding both legal and illegal drugs? Is gender a factor in the success of prevention programs? If a prevention program is assessed a "failure," does one know *why* it failed? Despite the seriousness of polydrug use, programs focusing on alcohol, tobacco, and other drugs have maintained their conceptual distinctness, and professionals working in the prevention field also have tended to focus on differences in their areas of specialization rather than to seek common ground.[10]

Public Information and Education

Information and education are explicit elements in most drug and alcohol prevention programs. Tremendous emphasis has been placed on public information and school-based education as a primary means of prevention throughout the United States. However, these approaches to changing behaviors rooted in deeply held social values have been marginally effective, at best.[11] Nevertheless, it is still widely accepted that informational approaches should be included in programs designed to prevent drug use.[12]

Under highly specific conditions, public information campaigns can sometimes achieve certain limited goals. There is evidence that programs directed at increasing the number of people inoculated for infectious diseases, increasing the response rates for census reports, and getting taxpayers to file by the deadline all have met with a measure of success.[13] Health education in the public schools is another matter, however.[14] This should come as no surprise, since health education has traditionally not been accorded a high priority in the public schools. Teachers often view it as an intrusion and a drain on the so-called legitimate goals of the educational process. Programs are ill conceived, lack clear-cut objectives, and are not designed to engage student interest and involvement. Teachers generally receive little training in how to present the material. Students, perhaps reflecting school and teacher attitudes, typically regard health education as a required bore. It is no wonder that programs are, at best, marginally effective.[15]

Public information and education efforts directed at adults have been much more limited. The primary adult educational programs are "DUI schools." These are designed for persons who generally have long histories of DUI violations and even longer histories of alcohol abuse, but many of their clients are probably not alcoholics. With such a varied group of clients, it is not surprising that their effectiveness is also marginal. Paradoxically, they are probably more successful with the substantial number of students who are not really alcoholic or drug dependent.

There has been a dramatic increase in mass media campaigns dealing with alcohol, drugs, and smoking in recent years. Strategies are aimed at getting children to "just say no" to drugs, at convincing adults to drink in moderation, at convincing drivers not to get behind the wheel after drinking, and at convincing everyone to quit smoking. These strategies appear to have had limited success regarding smoking (not among teenage girls), but the jury is still out on alcohol and drug abuse prevention. Even the modest decrease in alcohol consumption among certain subgroups is very difficult to tie directly to prevention efforts. With few exceptions, the evidence that does exist is no cause for optimism.[16]

Programs Directed at Children and Adolescents

Throughout the 1970s, most drug abuse prevention programs were educational in nature, directed at adolescents, and implemented through the schools. Early programs relied on providing information and using so-called scare tactics. These programs were generally so ineffective that they were denounced by the federal government's Special Office for Drug Abuse Prevention (SODAP). In fact, SODAP was so disillusioned that it imposed a temporary ban on the funding of drug information programs.[17]

Growing evidence of the ineffectiveness of these strategies led to a trend toward use of *affective education* and other alternative approaches.[18] Affective programs assumed that adolescents would be deterred from using drugs if their self-esteem, interpersonal skills, and techniques for decision making and problem solving could be improved. Recreational activities, community service projects, and involvement in the arts were stressed as a way of providing meaningful, fulfilling experiences that would counteract the attractions of drugs. Unfortunately, there is little evidence that this approach has been any more effective than simply providing information.[19] This model was developed as a result of research on the correlates of drug-using behavior primarily among delinquents and addicts.[20] These studies identified drug-abusing youths as less likely to participate in clubs, youth organizations, and religious activities. Generalizing from that population to so-called normal adolescents may have led to a faulty model for prevention efforts.

Early smoking prevention programs were also information oriented and frequently resorted to scare tactics, such as showing students photographs of cancerous and healthy lungs. Like the early alcohol and drug prevention programs, they had little impact on long-term behavior. Confronted with this lack of success, some researchers began to consider ways of addressing the social milieu in which young people begin smoking. This eventually resulted in a new generation of smoking programs that have been somewhat more successful.

Drawing on Evans's "social inoculation" theory[21] and McGuire's concept of "cognitive inoculation,"[22] this approach argues that if adolescents are provided with counterarguments and techniques with which to resist peer pressures to smoke, as well as factual information about smoking, they are more likely to abstain. Most of the new generation of smoking prevention programs focus on the short-term effects of smoking rather than long-term health consequences ("When he kisses you, do you really want your breath to smell like an ashtray?"). The impact of this new approach is well documented in delaying young people's use of tobacco for up to two years.[23] However, longer-term effects have not been demonstrated, and even the short-term effects appear to decay with time.[24]

Many elements from the social inoculation and affective education models were used in developing Project D.A.R.E. (Drug Abuse Resistance Education). This program was originally developed as a joint project of the Los Angeles Police Department and the Los Angeles Unified School District, and it is now operated in several hundred communities across the nation. Project D.A.R.E. is designed to help fifth- and sixth-grade students recognize and resist peer pressure that frequently leads to experimentation with alcohol and drugs. Several lessons focus on building self-esteem, whereas others emphasize the consequences of using alcohol or drugs and identify alternative ways of coping with stress, gaining peer acceptance, or having fun. Most important, students learn and practice specific strategies for responding to peers who offer them drugs. Ways to say "no" include changing the subject, walking away or ignoring the person, or simply saying no and repeating it as often as necessary. The curriculum is organized into 17 classroom sessions conducted by a police officer, coupled with other activities to be taught by the regular classroom teacher.[25]

One of the earliest evaluations of the D.A.R.E. program found that students who received the full-semester D.A.R.E. curriculum during the sixth grade had significantly lower use of alcohol, cigarettes, and other drugs. The impact was much greater for boys (who used more drugs to begin with) than for girls, however.[26] A later longitudinal (three-year) study found significantly lower use rates by D.A.R.E. graduates for all drugs except tobacco.[27] The most recent and comprehensive evolution of D.A.R.E. by the Research Triangle Institute found the program to be ineffective in preventing or reducing drug use.[28] D.A.R.E. officials and the U.S. Department of Justice both disavowed the report.[29]

The most important conclusion to be reached after 20 years of organized prevention programming is that no single strategy has demonstrated a long-term impact, and many of the experts now believe that it may be a mistake to think in terms of a single-strategy solution. In many respects, life has become more complicated for the current generation. Experimentation may be a normal rite of passage for many youths—a phase that most will outgrow. Previous generations of youths experimented mostly with alcohol. The greater availability of illicit drugs provides today's youths with a greater variety of choices. Prevention efforts, therefore, must become more comprehensive. A mixture of public information and education programs with the other measures described shortly may result in a more effective approach to prevention.

Service Measures

Service measures (detoxification, therapeutic communities, 28-day treatment programs, Alco-

holics Anonymous, etc.) are aimed at ameliorating or reversing a condition resulting from alcohol or drug use or reducing the chances of its onset among members of a high-risk population. In traditional community health terms, such measures usually fall into the secondary or tertiary prevention category. Service measures are not generally emphasized in prevention because of their ameliorative or restorative nature. Their lack of popularity among prevention experts is due to the fact that, by definition, they are directed toward the remediation of a problem rather than preventing new cases from occurring.

Service measures are also labor intensive and, therefore, comparatively expensive. They may often require large capital outlays for facilities and personnel, making them not particularly cost effective. In all other fields of public health, a compelling reason for providing prevention services is that it is less expensive to prevent an illness from occurring than it is to "cure" a patient. Service measures also are usually focused on the individual, whereas prevention specialists are more comfortable with strategies that apply to large populations. Finally, when mandated to "do prevention," service providers are inclined to allocate resources to services while neglecting other preventive measures.[30] Faced with dealing with the serious nature of a client's alcohol or drug problem, most counselors or therapists find little time for "prevention work."

Early intervention services—such as those provided in occupational alcoholism programs, "troubled worker" programs, or employee assistance programs—are a common type of secondary prevention. These programs are oriented toward employees whose work performance is impaired by the use of drugs or alcohol. The reported success rates of these programs are impressively high, even though few evaluations actually rely on hard data.[31] (One article states unequivocally that "treatment offered with job retention as leverage generally proves highly effective."[32] No supporting data are provided.) Most referred employees are alcoholics or addicts with long-standing problems, rather than individuals who are at risk for chemical dependency.*

According to a study by Roman and Blum, however, only about 4 percent of the employees in a firm with such a program consult the employee assistance program (EAP) in a given year, and only 1.5 percent specifically present a substance abuse problem.[33] Another report indicates that the employer is mentioned as a primary motivator for treatment admission by only one-sixteenth of inpatients and one-tenth of outpatients.[34]

Chemical dependency manifests itself in the workplace in four ways. First, an employee may be chemically dependent. Second, an employee may be affected by a spouse, child, or other loved one who is chemically dependent. Third, an employee may be an adult child of a chemically dependent parent. Finally, an employee may be selling or using drugs in the workplace.[35] To intervene at the earliest possible stage of dependency, supervisors are taught to be alert for the following common symptoms of alcohol or drug abuse:

> Chronic absenteeism
> Change in behavior
> Physical signs
> Spasmodic work pace
> Lower quantity and quality of work
> Partial absences
> Lying
> Avoiding supervisors and co-workers
> On-the-job drinking or drug use
> On-the-job accidents and lost time from off-the-job accidents[36]

Assuming that early identification and treatment are achieved in a workplace program, the chances of recovery should be increased because:

1. The threat of job loss is a significant motivator.
2. The family may still be present to provide emotional support.

*For a comprehensive treatment of workplace programs, see Gary M. Gould and Michael Lane Smith (Eds.), *Social Work in the Workplace: Practice and Principles* (New York: Springer, 1988).

3. Physical health has not deteriorated seriously.
4. The client's financial resources are not depleted.

Workplace programs use early intervention (service) measures as one component of more comprehensive prevention efforts. Other components include information sessions, substance abuse issue discussions (often at lunch time), posters and pamphlets, use of peer pressure, and financial incentives. Such incentives may take the form of cash awards to employees who quit smoking or reduced insurance rates for healthy lifestyles. Employers are convinced that a healthier work force results in greater organizational efficiency and higher profits.

Although DUI programs were considered earlier as educational prevention, they also could be considered as early intervention. In addition to the educational component, offenders are offered treatment and probation instead of fines, jail, or other punishment. The effectiveness of treatment offered under such compulsion is questionable, however.[37] just as in workplace programs, the clients are also likely to be those with long-standing problems of chemical dependency, so the appropriateness of the "early intervention" label is equally questionable.

A number of pilot early detection, screening, and treatment programs have been funded by the U.S. Department of justice. In Miami, for example, juvenile offenders are routinely screened at detention through urine analysis. Those who test positive for any of five major drugs (about 85 percent) are referred for treatment at local agencies. Because of a lack of follow-up, however, fewer than half the youths referred actually go to treatment, and only about one-third of them complete a treatment program.[38]

Technologic Measures

In the traditional public health prevention model, technologic measures refer to "modifications in the noxious agent or the environment in which it operates that will affect the relationships among the agent, the environment, and members of a population to reduce the rate of occurrence of a disorder."[39] Although relatively new in chemical dependency, technologic measures are commonplace in occupational health and safety, transportation, and water sanitation.

Efforts to alter the noxious agent itself generally have been limited to modifications of alcohol and tobacco products. Cigarette makers produce a variety of "light" brands that are lower in nicotine. Manufacturers of distilled spirits have actually decreased the average amount of absolute alcohol in their products over the past decade, and more brands of low-alcohol beer become available each year. At first, these low-alcohol brands seemed to be socially acceptable only in Europe, but they have now become quite popular in the United States. Biomedical researchers are still searching for a breakthrough that will eliminate the negative physiologic and psychologic effects of alcohol. Some even have hope of developing a practical "sobering-up" pill.

As mentioned in Chapter 6, antagonist therapies have been developed for drugs such as heroin addiction. Drugs such as naloxone, naltrexone, and cyclazocine block the effects of opiate drugs but do not prevent withdrawal symptoms. Patients are withdrawn from heroin before being given these drugs. The addict who then returns to using heroin while taking a narcotic antagonist will find it impossible to get high.[40] Although not technically an antagonist, methadone is a drug used to prevent symptoms of heroin withdrawal, and it also diminishes the effects of heroin. The heroin addict who is taking methadone will not be able to get the same high from using heroin.

Antabuse (disulfiram) is a drug that prevents the normal metabolization of alcohol. A person who ingests alcohol while taking Antabuse will experience an accumulation of acetaldehyde, resulting in severe physical consequences such as difficulty in breathing, nausea, dizziness, vomiting, and blurred vision. In some cases, people are

able to continue drinking despite the symptoms, however.[41]

Other technologic measures are designed to make the environment safer for the person who uses alcohol or drugs. These measures do not prevent the use of alcohol or drugs, but protect both the user and innocent people from the effects of use. Passive restraints and air bags in automobiles are perhaps the best examples. Various devices have also been developed to prevent an intoxicated person from turning on the ignition of his or her automobile, but none are practical for widespread use at this point. Fire-retardant or fireproof clothing, bedding, and furniture also protect users who pass out or fall asleep while smoking.

Many cities have established a "tipsy taxi" service for drivers who have had too much to drink. In Tallahassee, Florida, for example, the city operates a free taxi service available to anyone on major holidays when overdrinking is traditionally a problem. In the same city, Florida State University offers a free chauffeur service to all its students on a year-round basis. Alcohol-related traffic fatalities have fallen since these services were introduced.

Many communities are providing free needles and syringes to intravenous drug users in an attempt to slow the spread of infectious diseases such as AIDS. These programs have spread much faster in European nations, partly because of a more liberal attitude toward such prevention efforts and partly because the laws are more conducive to these approaches. In many communities in the United States, there is a feeling that providing free needles and syringes *encourages* drug use. In many states, needles and syringes are available only through a physician's prescription.

Some communities have attempted to get around this problem by educating intravenous drug users in methods of cleaning their equipment before using it again or sharing it with another user. Both San Francisco and New York City launched efforts to educate these drug users to "bleach their works" before state courts eventually allowed the distribution of needles and syringes.

Legislative and Regulatory Measures

Legislative and regulatory measures regarding drug use can be employed to raise revenue, safeguard public health or morals, provide both political and economic rewards, or *prevent* drug use or abuse. This chapter discusses only the latter purposes. The others will be deferred until the next chapter, where the concept of regulation will be dealt with in considerably greater depth.

Throughout the eighteenth and nineteenth centuries, there were many local and state laws restricting the sale of alcohol, culminating in 1917 in national prohibition. Whatever the failings of this "noble experiment," one of its primary purposes was achieved—a substantial decrease in the consumption of beverage alcohol.[42] Other legislation has controlled the hours and location of sale for alcoholic beverages, and there have been long-standing laws against serving alcohol to minors. These laws are also intended to reduce consumption, frequently among specific populations. Still other laws have placed restrictions on certain activities associated with drinking (gambling; nude dancing; driving a car, boat, or airplane; etc.) as a way of protecting the public from some of the side effects of drinking alcohol. So-called dramshop laws have been revived to make it illegal for bartenders or other servers to serve alcohol to obviously intoxicated persons. Several lawsuits and court decisions upholding server liability laws have impressed on tavern owners the need for better training of their personnel. Perhaps this desire to reduce liability will lead to a reduction of some alcohol problems.[43]

Regulation of other psychoactive drugs is much less complicated. In most cases, there is either no law restricting the use of a drug (e.g., gasoline, glue, and other inhalants) or it is simply illegal to use or possess it (heroin). In relatively few cases (marijuana), a drug may be illegal except for certain limited medical purposes. Regulation of most of these drugs came much later than for alcohol, however. Opiates were not made illegal until the Harrison Act of 1914. Although many states had prohibitions against its use, marijuana was not outlawed nationally until the Marijuana Tax Act of 1937. Recently, there have been many more drugs added to the list of controlled substances, but there is little evidence that these prohibitions have significantly affected drug trade or drug use. In fact, government attempts to limit the supply of drugs may have served mostly to drive up price and increase the profits of drug dealers.[44]

Advertising and the Media

Both legislation and self-regulation have resulted in restrictions on the advertising of alcohol and tobacco products, although there is scant evidence that these restrictions are effective. Industry standards prohibit the advertising of hard liquor on television, and although beer, malt liquor, and wine can be advertised, no one may be shown actually drinking it. There are strong arguments for restricting the advertising of these products in all media, because they frequently appeal to young people who are particularly susceptible to suggestions that wealth, success, or peer approval may be related to using the "right" kind of alcohol or tobacco products. It must be said, however, that the long-term effects of current restrictions on advertising appear to be minimal.[45]

Ads for alcoholic beverages are well researched, slickly produced, and reinforced by well-organized promotions at the local retail level. After the Coca-Cola Company bought Taylor Wines in the late 1970s, it set out to promote the image of wine as a drink to be consumed regularly rather than just on special occasions. Within a short time, the amount of advertising in the wine industry nearly doubled, partly because of Coca-Cola's aggressive marketing techniques.[46]

Although there are restrictions on advertising alcoholic beverages, there are no restrictions on the use of alcohol by actors in television programs. Consumption of alcoholic beverages is frequent in TV programs (the incidence of actors smoking has decreased, however). Attempts to curtail youths from buying alcohol by restricting advertising may be undone by the frequent images of alcohol use in television programs.

The effect of advertising on consumption and the portrayal of alcohol drinking by the mass media are controversial issues on which there is no definitive evidence. A recent review of the literature on advertising concludes that (1) marginal changes in expenditures for alcohol advertising have little or no effect on total alcohol consumption and (2) existing studies shed no light on the relationship between advertising and alcohol abuse.[47] One national survey of 1,200 respondents aged 12 to 22 did find a moderately strong positive correlation between the amount of day-to-day exposure to ads for alcoholic beverages, on the one hand, and alcohol consumption and drinking in dangerous situations, on the other.[48] Both the advertising and the brewing industries recently have come under heavy criticism for directing advertising campaigns at minority groups. A case in point was the advertising of "PowerMaster," a high-alcohol malt liquor, in media targeted toward low-income minorities.[49] The tobacco industry also had developed a new cigarette with plans to market it primarily to African Americans. Fortunately, public opinion and political pressure resulted in the cancellation of both campaigns.

According to Wallack, however, any findings that indicate an association between advertising and increased consumption contradict a larger body of previous research that has failed to substantiate such a relationship.[50] (One must wonder—if advertising doesn't increase consumption, why advertise? The alcoholic beverage industry spends over *$1 billion* yearly advertising its products.[51])

Advertising is not the only way images of alcohol use are disseminated. In his study of Holly-wood's treatment of the alcoholic, Denzin found 664 movies that used alcoholism as a major theme between 1909 and 1991.[52] Many of those, such as *Harvey* and *Arthur*, depict the main characters as "happy alcoholics" with no particular need to deal with their alcohol problems. More recent movies (*Leaving Las Vegas, Trainspotting*) have presented a much more realistic appraisal of both alcoholism and drug abuse. A series of articles in the *Christian Science Monitor* described television's portrayal of alcohol use beginning in 1975. Among prime-time shows in the spring of 1975, scenes involving alcohol use were found in 201 of 249 shows.[53] A study of drinking on daytime soap operas viewed 79 half-hour segments over a five-day period and found 236 events involving alcoholic beverages and only 205 involving soft drinks.[54] In 1980, the top 10 prime-time series and the top soap operas were studied at Michigan State University. The rate of alcohol consumption averaged 8.13 incidents per hour on the top 10 series and 2.25 per hour on the soap operas. Alcohol use was shown in an almost entirely positive context, with no indication of potential risk.[55] This seems strange, indeed, for a medium whose code does not allow the commercial advertising of any "hard" liquor nor the actual drinking of wine or beer during a commercial!

In 1982, one team of researchers developed a strategy for *cooperative consultation* to work with media personnel toward the realistic portrayal of alcohol use on television and in other media.[56] Later that same year, three alcohol-related tragedies rocked Hollywood. Two celebrities, Mary Martin and Janet Gaynor, were critically injured when a drunk driver crashed into their taxi. Next, William Holden died alone in his room because he was too drunk to know that he was bleeding to death. Finally, Natalie Wood, after drinking "a few" glasses of wine, slipped off the side of a boat and drowned. Not long after these events, one of the major networks televised a news series called *The Hollywood Alcoholic*. The result of this new realization of the dangers of alcoholism was an effort by a caucus of producers, writers, and directors to produce guidelines for dealing with alcohol use on television and in the movies.[57]

1. Try not to glamorize the drinking or serving of alcohol as a sophisticated or an adult pursuit.
2. Avoid showing the use of alcohol gratuitously in those cases in which another beverage might be easily and fittingly substituted.
3. Try not to show excessive drinking without consequences or with only pleasant consequences.
4. Try not to show drinking alcohol as an activity that is so "normal" that everyone must indulge. Allow characters a chance to refuse an alcoholic drink by including nonalcoholic alternatives.
5. Demonstrate that there are no miraculous recoveries from alcoholism; normally, it is a most difficult task.
6. Don't associate drinking alcohol with macho pursuits in such a way that heavy drinking is a requirement for proving one's self as a man.
7. Portray the reaction of others to heavy alcohol drinking, especially when it may be a criticism.

There have been some notable efforts by the media since then to incorporate these guidelines into their programming. For example, Detective Andy Sipowicz on *NYPD Blue* is a recovering, sometimes relapsed, alcoholic who regularly attends AA meetings. A made-for-TV movie, *Shattered Spirits*, honestly portrayed the struggle of a family against alcoholism in a realistic manner. The movie *Clean and Sober* not only dealt honestly with the alcoholism and drug addiction of its major characters but it also won rave reviews from the critics. Public service announcements regularly warn young people about the dangers of alcohol and drug abuse and urge them to "just say no." The well-publicized deaths of actors John Belushi and River Phoenix from drug overdoses have also brought a great deal of the entertainment industry's attention to the problem of illicit drugs.

At the same time, however, it is still easy to find the gratuitous portrayal of alcohol use in the media. Although there is little or no evidence that television programming has increased consumption, it is the National Association of Broadcaster's position that alcohol use should be *deemphasized* on television. The truth is that the rate of drinking on television still seems to be much greater than in real life. According to one estimate, a person under the legal drinking age will be exposed to approximately 3,000 acts of drinking during a year of television viewing.[58] Is it any wonder that young peoples' T-shirts sport such popular themes as "Party 'Til You Puke" and "Avoid Hangovers, Stay Drunk"? Obviously, television and the other mass media are not entirely to blame, and they have taken certain steps to improve programming. They generally do not, however, provide the proper messages to young people about the use of alcohol.

All states have legislation prohibiting the sale of both alcohol or tobacco products to underaged youths. While the enforcement of alcohol laws have been a great concern to local and state law enforcement authorities, only recently have they put much efforts into enforcing the tobacco laws. In a study in California, minors aged 14 to 16 years attempted to purchase cigarettes in 412 stores and from 30 vending machines. They were successful in 74 percent of the stores and in 100 percent of the vending machines.[59] The situation may be changing, however. A large Maryland convenience store chain was convicted several years ago of routinely selling cigarettes to underaged youths and fined several million dollars.[60] Today, laws relating to selling cigarettes to underaged youths are being more strictly enforced by store owners because of government's new sensitivity to adolescent substance abuse.

Health warnings also have been mandated for alcohol and tobacco products. Everything from "light" beer to 100-proof vodka must carry a government warning concerning the risk to pregnant women of birth defects and the risk to everyone of impaired driving ability:

Government Warning: (1) According to the Surgeon General, women should not drink alcoholic beverages during pregnancy because of the risk of birth defects. (2) Consumption of alcoholic beverages impairs your ability to drive a car or operate machinery, and may cause health problems.

Tobacco products warn the user of a plethora of possible diseases. (Most of these warnings give new meaning to the term *fine print.* Look closely at the container the next time you purchase an alcoholic beverage.) The impact of the warnings is unknown, but some argue that they may actually serve to protect the manufacturers from liability by providing the consumer with an adequate warning of potential risks involved in using the product.

In addition to restrictions on advertising, some restrictions have been placed on the use of tobacco products. By 1987, there had been restrictions placed on tobacco use in the workplace by 32 states and in other public places such as restaurants in 23 states. In addition, national restrictions were placed on smoking on airlines, and smoking is almost universally prohibited in government buildings, public hospitals, and other health facilities. Tobacco companies have hotly contested these prohibitions, of course.[61] As of 1995, 46 states and Washington, DC, require smoke-free air in some public places. The Center for Disease Control (CDC) and the National Cancer Institute (NCI) identified 1,238 state laws that focus on tobacco-control issues. All states have banned sales of tobacco products to minors.[62]

Drinking-and-driving prevention has been the subject of much legislation since the advent of the automobile. Research in the United States, England, and Scandinavia indicates that no one single approach to preventing driving under the influence (DUI) is preferable, but there is a constellation of measures that seem to be effective under various circumstances. These include vigorous enforcement of DUI laws, rapid application of sanctions, and clear-cut regulations that are widely publicized. Heavy fines appear to be about as effective as the revocation of driving privileges, mandatory "DUI schools," or other treatment.

Some of the more controversial methods, such as roadblocks used to ferret out impaired drivers, have proven less effective.[63] Such methods also have been criticized as infringement on civil liberties, but so far the courts have generally allowed the practice to continue.

Economic Measures

The difference between legislative-regulatory measures and economic measures is primarily one of emphasis. The price of alcohol or tobacco, for example, may be a matter of a producer's competitive strategy to capture a share of the market for its product. On the other hand, price also reflects federal and state legislation governing the rate of taxation for that product. Whether it happens because of company policy or government decree, the impact of a price increase or decrease on the consumer is likely to be much the same. Several recent studies have indicated that the consumption of alcohol is relatively sensitive to price and that everything from cirrhosis to traffic fatalities could be reduced by increasing prices.[64] The increase in prices in the underground market after the passage of Prohibition in 1917 was undoubtedly one of the major factors in the dramatic decrease in consumption. The demand for tobacco products seems to be even more sensitive to price, especially among younger users. Increasing taxes on cigarettes may be the most effective way of convincing novice users, such as adolescents, not to smoke.[65] When it comes to illicit drugs such as marijuana, there is little doubt that consumption increases as prices fall.[66] One of the few successes of the "war on drugs" may be in maintaining prices at a relatively high level, thereby deterring some potential users.

In addition to pricing policies, other economic measures include such items as allocating tax revenues from the sale of drugs to prevention programs (such as Proposition 99, described earlier), reducing insurance premiums for those who abstain from alcohol and tobacco, and tax incentives that discourage drug use. (Recent income tax reforms have disallowed the "three martini" lunch.) It is not uncommon for government to use an economic measure as a subterfuge for prohibiting drugs. For example, the Marijuana Tax Act of 1934 placed a $100 per ounce tax on marijuana. Texas has a drug tax law that requires those who buy or possess illegal drugs to purchase tax stamps for them. Failure to do so results in a tax law violation. These laws are often called *Al Capone laws* because of the prosecution of that notorious gangster, who sold bootleg liquor, under the tax evasion statutes.

Summary

Prevention sounds like a good idea, but how does one measure its effect? To know whether a prevention program *really* works, researchers would have to hold a number of important factors constant while a prevention intervention is implemented. They would probably need to randomize the target population between the program and a control group, and would need to study this cohort over a relatively long period of time. The current state of knowledge regarding prevention programs is largely anecdotal and incomplete. The best information generally comes from correlational studies.

From a logical perspective, one knows that if a population can be prevented from using a drug, morbidity and mortality rates will be reduced. Most indications are that education and public information approaches do not seem to be effective, especially for those people with the most serious problems. Those techniques that do work are relatively limited in their scope. Swift and certain law enforcement for DUI offenses seem to work. Heavy fines are also effective. Price has a strong deterrent effect on the use of certain drugs. Minimum age of purchase legislation keeps many younger drivers alive. The next chapter discusses many other law-enforcement strategies, such as long prison terms, that do not seem to be very effective prevention tools.

The focus of prevention efforts seems to have shifted away from reliance on the traditional educational and public information approaches to a harm-reduction philosophy. Society must try not only to reduce the use and abuse of harmful drugs but also to ameliorate the consequences of those drugs. Preventing the spread of AIDS and decreasing traffic fatalities are just as legitimate prevention goals as reducing intravenous heroin use or the consumption of alcoholic beverages. Guided by this philosophy, there are many other approaches still to be tried. For example, it has been suggested that makers of fortified wines be required to supplement them with vitamins and minerals. The alcoholics who buy these products are especially prone to malnutrition, which is at least partly a result of their alcoholism. Another suggestion is to levy special taxes on products known to be detrimental to people's health (primarily tobacco and alcohol) and dedicate those funds to the provision of additional health care services.

Endnotes

1. Lawrence Wallack and Kitty Corbett, "Illicit Drug, Tobacco, and Alcohol Use among Youth: Trends and Promising Approaches in Prevention," in Hank Resnik, S. E. Gardner, R. P. Lorian, and C. E. Marcus (Eds.), "Youth and Drugs: Society's Mixed Messages," *OSAP Prevention Monograph No. 6*, Alcohol, Drug Abuse, and Mental Health Administration, Office for Substance Abuse Prevention (Rockville, MD: U.S. Department of Health and Human Services, Public Health Service, 1990), p. 16.

2. Ibid., pp. 5–29.

3. Joel M. Moskowitz, "The Primary Prevention of Alcohol Problems: A Critical Review of the Research Literature," *Journal of Studies on Alcohol*, Vol. 50, No. 1 (1989), pp. 54–88.

4. A. C. Wagenaar, "Youth, Alcohol, and Traffic Crashes," paper presented at Prevention Research Center Workshop, Berkeley, 1986.

5. Howard T. Blane, "Preventing Alcohol Problems," in Nada J. Estes and M. Edith Heinemann (Eds.), *Alcoholism: Development, Consequences, and Interventions*, 3rd ed. (St. Louis: C. V. Mosby, 1986), pp. 78–90.

6. Jean Kinney and Gwen Leaton, *Loosening the Grip: A Handbook of Alcohol Information* (St. Louis, MO: Times Mirror/Mosby College Publishing, 1987).

7. P. J. Mrazek and R. J. Haggerty (Eds.), *Reducing Risks for Mental Disorders: Frontiers for Preventive Intervention Research* (Washington, DC: National Academy Press, 1994).

8. M. Klitzner, *Report to Congress on the Nature and Effectiveness of Federal, State, and Local Drug Prevention/ Education Programs—Part 2: An Assessment of the Research on School-Based Prevention Programs,* prepared for the U.S. Department of Education, Office of Planning, Budget and Evaluation (Vienna, VA: Pacific Institute for Research and Evaluation, 1988); also see Nancy S. Tobler, "Meta-Analysis of 143 Adolescent Drug Prevention Programs: Qualitative Outcome Results of Program Participants Compared to a Control or Comparison Group" *Journal of Drug Issues,* Vol. 16, No. 4 (1986), pp. 537–567.

9. Kinney and Leaton, *Loosening the Grip.*

10. Wallack and Corbett, "Illicit Drug, Tobacco, and Alcohol Use among Youth," 1990.

11. Howard T. Blane, "Education and Prevention of Alcoholism," in Benjamin Kissin and Henri Begleiter (Eds.), *The Biology of Alcoholism,* Volume 4 (New York: Plenum Press, 1976); also see Robert L. Bangert-Downs, "The Effects of School-Based Substance Abuse Education—A Meta-Analysis," *Journal of Drug Education,* Vol. 18, No. 3 (1988), pp. 243–265.

12. Wallack and Corbett, "Illicit Drug, Tobacco, and Alcohol Use among Youth," 1990.

13. Blane, "Preventing Alcohol Problems."

14. Howard T. Blane, *Health Education as a Preventive Strategy,* in Tripartite Conference on Prevention (Washington, DC: Alcohol, Drug Abuse, and Mental Health Administration, 1977).

15. Blane, "Preventing Alcohol Problems."

16. Steve Olson and Dean R. Gerstein, *Alcohol in America: Taking Action to Prevent Abuse* (Washington, DC: National Academy Press, 1985), pp. 82–94.

17. Wallack and Corbett, "Illicit Drug, Tobacco, and Alcohol Use among Youth," 1990.

18. Ibid.

19. G. Nicholas Braucht and Barbara Braucht, "Prevention of Problem Drinking among Youth: Evaluation of Educational Strategies," in P. M. Miller and T. D. Nirenberg (Eds.), *Prevention of Alcohol Abuse* (New York: Plenum Press, 1984).

20. Richard Dembo, "Key Issues and Paradigms in Drug Use Research: Focus on Etiology," *Journal of Drug Issues,* Vol. 16, No. 1 (1986), pp. 1–4.

21. Richard I. Evans, R. M. Rozelle, Maurice B. Mittelmark, William B. Hansen, A. L. Bane, and J. Havis, "Deterring the Onset of Smoking in Children: Knowledge of Immediate Physiological Effects and Coping with Peer Pressure, Media Pressure, and Parent Modeling," *Journal of Applied Social Psychology,* Vol. 8, No. 2 (1978), pp. 126–135.

22. William J. McGuire, "The Nature of Attitude and Attitude Change," in G. Lindzay and E. Aronson (Eds.), *Handbook of Social Psychology,* 2nd ed., Volume 3 (Reading, MA: Addison-Wesley, 1969).

23. William J. McCarthy, "The Cognitive Developmental Model and Other Alternatives to the Social Deficit Model of Smoking Onset," in C. S. Bell and R. Battjes (Eds.), *Prevention Research: Deterring Drug Abuse among Children and Adolescents* (Rockville, MD: U.S. Department of Health and Human Services, 1985), pp. 153–169.

24. Wallack and Corbett, "Illicit Drug Use," 1990.

25. William DeJong, "A Short-Term Evaluation of Project DARE (Drug Abuse Resistance Education): Preliminary Indications of Effectiveness," *Journal of Drug Education,* Vol. 17, No. 4 (1987), pp. 279–294.

26. Ibid.

27. The Evaluation and Training Institute, "DARE Longitudinal Evaluation Annual Report: 1987–88," unpublished.

28. Christopher L. Ringwalt, Jody M. Green, Susan T. Ennett, Ronaldo Iachan, Richard R. Clayton, and Carl G. Leukfeld, "Past and Future Directions of the D.A.R.E. Program: Draft Final Report" (Research Triangle Park, NC: Research Triangle Institute, June 1994).

29. *USA Today,* October 11, 1994.

30. Blane, "Health Education."

31. Norman R. Kurtz, Bradley Googins, and William C. Howard, "Measuring the Success of Occupational Alcoholism Programs," *Journal of Studies on Alcohol,* Vol. 45, No. 1 (January 1984), pp. 33–45.

32. Meryl Nadel, Alice W. Petropoulos, and Nelson Feroe, "Alcoholism Treatment Resources: Which One When?" in David Cook, Christine Fewell, and John Riolo (Eds.), *Social Work Treatment of Alcohol Problems* (New Brunswick, NJ: Rutgers Center of Alcohol Studies, 1983), p. 14.

33. Paul M. Roman and T. Blum, "Employee Assistance and Drug Screening Programs," in Dean R. Gerstein and Henrick J. Harwood (Eds.), *Treating Drug Abuse,* Volume 2 (Washington, DC: National Academy Press, 1990).

34. P. A. Harrison and N. G. Hoffman, *Adult Outpatient Treatment: Perspectives on Admission and Outcome* (St. Paul, MN: Chemical Abuse/Addiction Treatment Outcome Registry, Ramsey Clinic, 1988).

35. Diana M. DiNitto, "Drunk, Drugged, and on the Job," in Gary Gould and Michael Lane Smith (Eds.), *Social Work in the Workplace* (New York: Springer, 1988), p. 77.

36. Kinney and Leaton, *Loosening the Grip,* p. 222.

37. Ross Homel, *Policing and Punishing the Drinking Driver: A Study of General and Specific Deterrence* (New York: Springer, 1988).

38. Interview with Miami/Dade County Juvenile Screening, Detection, and Treatment program officials, Miami, FL, June 7, 1991.

39. Blane, "Preventing Alcohol Problems," p. 84.

40. Ibid., pp. 246–247.

41. Jason M. White, *Drug Dependence* (Englewood Cliffs, NJ: Prentice Hall, 1991), pp. 243–244.

42. William A. McKim, *Drugs and Behavior*, 2nd ed. (Englewood Cliffs, NJ: Prentice Hall, 1991), p. 90.

43. Olson and Gerstein, *Alcohol in America*, pp. 62–68.

44. Elliott Currie, *Reckoning: Drugs, the Cities and the American Future* (New York: Hillard Wang, 1993).

45. Kenneth E. Warner, "Clearing the Airwaves: The Cigarette Ad Ban Revisited," *Policy Analysis*, Vol. 4 (1979), pp. 435–450.

46. Olson and Gerstein, *Alcohol in America*, p. 85.

47. Federal Trade Commission, Bureau of Consumer Protection and Economics, "Omnibus Petition for Regulation of Unfair and Deceptive Alcoholic Beverage Advertising and Marketing Practices," Docket No. 209-46, March 1985.

48. Charles Atkin, Kimberly Neuendorf, and Steven McDermott, "The Role of Alcohol Advertising in Excessive and Hazardous Drinking," *Journal of Drug Education*, Vol. 13 (1983), pp. 313–326.

49. "A Real Brew-Haha," *Time*, July 1, 1991, p. 56.

50. Lawrence Wallack, "Practical Issues, Ethical Concerns and Future Directions in the Prevention of Alcohol Related Problems," *Journal of Primary Prevention*, Vol. 4 (1984), pp. 199–224.

51. Steve Olson and Dean R. Gerstein, *Alcohol in America: Taking Action to Prevent Abuse* (Washington, DC: National Academy Press, 1985), p. 94.

52. Norman K. Denzin, *Hollywood Shot by Shot: Alcoholism in American Cinema* (Hawthorne, NY: Aldine De Gruyter, 1991), p. 6.

53. John Dillin, "TV Drinking: How Networks Pour Liquor into Your Living Room," *Christian Science Monitor* Vol. 67, No. 151, pp. 1ff.

54. W. Garlington, "Drinking on Television: A Preliminary Study with Emphasis on Method," *Journal of Studies on Alcohol*, Vol. 38 (1977), pp. 2199–2205.

55. B. Greenberg, C. Fernandez-Collado, D. Graef, F. Dorzenny, and C. Atkin, *Trends in Use of Alcohol and Other Substances on Television* (East Lansing, MI: Department of Communication, Michigan State University, 1981).

56. Warren K. Breed and James R. DeFoe, "Effecting Media Change: The Role of Cooperative Consultation on Alcohol Topics," *Journal of Communication*, Vol. 32 (1982), pp. 100–111.

57. Gerstein, *Toward the Prevention*, p. 97.

58. Greenberg, *Trends in Use of Alcohol*.

59. David Altman, Valodi Foster, Lolly Rasenick-Douss, and Joe Tye, "Reducing the Illegal Sale of Cigarettes to Minors," *Journal of the American Medical Association*, Vol. 261 (1989), pp. 80–83.

60. Tallahassee Democrat, "Chain Fined for Sales to Minors" Sec. C, p. 2, August 18, 1991.

61. Mosher, "Drug Availability," p. 137.

62. Center for Disease Control Surveillance Summaries, Preview/Abstract, *State Laws on Tobacco Control—United States*, 1995, November 3, 1995, vol. 44, no. SS-6.

63. American Bar Association, Criminal Justice Section, *Drunk Driving Laws & Enforcement: An Assessment of Effectiveness* (Washington, DC, American Bar Association, 1986).

64. Olson and Gerstein, *Alcohol in America*, p. 51.

65. James F. Mosher, "Drug Availability in a Public Health Perspective," in Hank Resnik et al. (Eds.). "Youth and Drugs: Society's Mixed Messages," *OSAP Prevention Monograph No. 6*, Alcohol, Drug Abuse, and Mental Health Administration, Office for Substance Abuse Prevention (Rockville, MD: U.S. Department of Health and Human Services, Public Health Service, 1990), p. 152.

66. Ibid., pp. 129–168.

8

Regulating Drugs
and Their Consequences

One of the major obstacles to the successful prevention and treatment of chemical dependency problems is that there is no clear understanding of the etiology of drug abuse or dependence *at the level of individual pathology* (Chapter 2). From a clinical perspective, therefore, it is difficult (some would say impossible) to match an individual's treatment needs with a particular treatment modality that is best suited for those needs. Experts do know, however, that there are a number of social, cultural, and environmental factors that influence an individual's probability of using drugs. Unfortunately, treatment plans are often drawn up for chemical dependency as if it were only an *individual* phenomenon, frequently ignoring important *systemic* causes and consequences. Most of the previous chapters focused more directly on clinical issues; this chapter now turns to some important public policy issues related to drug availability, use, and treatment. We will continue and expand our discussion, begun in Chapter 7, regarding the types of collective action that society may employ in controlling the use of drugs.

We also will continue the debate concerning the deregulation of certain drugs within the context of broad public policy issues. Public policies regarding drug use and addiction include much

more than the *legality* of manufacturing, selling, and using drugs, however. Public policy is concerned with controlling or limiting the use of specific drugs, restricting use to specific segments of the population (such as adults, cancer patients, etc.), avoiding the *misuse* of drugs, enhancing governmental revenues through the collection of taxes on drugs (especially alcohol), and protecting domestic drug producers from foreign competition. Finally, we will turn to one of the most troubling policy issues regarding drug use: what to do about the relationship between drugs and crime. It is clear that the "war on drugs" is being lost, and society is desperate for an alternative course of action.

Sociocultural Influences on Public Drug Policy

Public policies regarding drugs vary widely throughout the world. They have also varied widely within nations during the last few centuries. Until the early part of the twentieth century, very few drugs were strictly regulated by any government.[1] Public policies that are now common in modern Western societies cannot be considered historical norms.[2]

Variations between cultures depend partly on historical accident: Peyote grew in the American Southwest, heroin in Asia, and cannabis from the Middle East to India. Beverage alcohol is the most nearly universal psychoactive drug. As locally produced drugs were spread by international trade, the culture of the importing nation had a profound impact on public policy toward these new drugs. When it was first introduced to Europe, tobacco was used primarily as a medicine in some countries and as a mild stimulant in others. In Russia, it was used as an intoxicant by means of deep and rapid inhalation.[3]

Drugs associated with ceremonial and religious use are generally treated differently from other drugs. Alcohol commonly was used by a great many people in ceremonies and rituals, often to the point of intoxication. But these same people rarely used alcohol outside of these rituals and ceremonies until very recently. The same can be said of marijuana use in some areas of India.[4] Where use of a drug is a very old, traditional practice, such as opium use in Arab countries, it is usually restricted to the adult male population.[5]

Religious beliefs and practices may either inhibit or reinforce the use of particular drugs. Psychoactive drugs were frequently viewed in traditional societies either as a gift from God or as "the devil's brew." The Indians of both North and South America used hallucinogenic drugs as a part of religious rituals. Indeed, Native Americans in the United States are still fighting for the right to use peyote legally in ceremonies sanctioned by the Native American Church. The cactus plant from which the drug is obtained is believed to be a gift from God to man. On the other hand, the strong religious injunctions against the use of alcohol in many Muslim countries severely restricts its use. This ban was decreed by the prophet Mohammed and still carries the force of law in countries such as Saudia Arabia.[6]

Sociocultural differences are also found in conceptions of the role of government regarding the health and welfare of its citizens, and these different conceptions influence public policy responses to the use of drugs.[7] Thus, Sweden, Norway, and Finland have introduced retail liquor monopolies as a way of limiting consumption. The former Soviet Union had a complete state monopoly on the production, distribution, and sale of alcohol. In the United States, several states have adopted a monopoly distribution system for distilled spirits but not for wine and beer. Other states allow competitive retailing but control the hours and location of sales. Some states allow beer and wine sales in supermarkets, convenience stores, and gas stations, whereas other states restrict such sales to "liquor" stores. Communities in states with local option laws may simply prohibit the sale of alcoholic beverages.

Economic and Political Factors

In Ireland—where the giant Guiness brewery is the largest single private employer, is the largest exporter of beer in the world, and operates one of the largest charitable foundations in the nation—legislation controlling or regulating alcohol production or sales is difficult to pass. Private physicians and college professors still relay the message to their patients and students that moderate alcohol use is a healthy practice. Only recently has the prevention of alcohol abuse been placed on the public agenda.[8] Efforts to control the use of other drugs is quite commonplace, however.

Why do societies decide to regulate some drugs, prohibit other drugs, and ignore some drugs altogether? In many cases, the production and supply of the entrenched drugs—such as alcohol, nicotine, and caffeine—are sources of wealth and power in society.[9] Permissive policies toward other drugs may simply have represented a threat to business. Since coffee could not be grown in Europe, it was necessary to import it. The Germans saw this as a threat to their beer industry, and the English imposed heavy taxes on coffee as a way of protecting tea produced in British colonies.

It is easy to understand why U.S. distillers and brewers may oppose the legalization of other drugs. Depending on the degree to which newly legalized drugs could be substituted for alcohol, they stand to lose a great deal of money. On the other hand, some say that the U.S. tobacco industry is prepared to produce marijuana cigarettes in the event that cannabis is legalized.[10] This new market could take up some of the slack resulting from declining cigarette sales.

Economic factors also have an impact on the enforcement of existing drug laws. It would be counterproductive for the tobacco industry to favor strict enforcement of the age limitation for the purchase of cigarettes when *all* their future customers, not to mention the fastest-growing segment of their current market, are under 18 years of age.

The socioeconomic status, political position, and race of drug *users* also must be considered. Heroin and crack cocaine are still regarded as being most common in African American ghettoes. Most experts agree that these are the drugs least likely to be legalized. When marijuana was perceived to be a drug used mostly by African Americans, Hispanics, and a few eccentric literary figures and musicians, there was not much support for its legalization. Now that hundreds of thousands of middle-class college students have used the drug, there is much more support for its "decriminalization"—even in otherwise conservative states such as Nebraska.[11]

Changes in Drug Use Patterns

The types of drugs and the manner of their use within a society vary over time. A society with few or no restrictions in one historical period may have comprehensive regulations of most drugs during another time.[12] Traditional societies tended to have available a rather narrow range of drugs, and they were frequently used in religious rituals or ceremonies. This type of limited use was not viewed as a cause for alarm. Eventually, international trade brought new types of drugs to practically every nation. New drugs presented a threat because they were used recreationally, their effects were not known, and their users were regarded as deviant. This called for regulation.

Changes in the manner of use of a single drug also have resulted in pressures for regulation and control. Oral administration or smoking of drugs such as opium and heroin presented fewer threats to the users' health and safety than did intravenous injection. Little thought was given to the drinking of small amounts of cocaine in soft drinks such as Coca-Cola, since the consequences of this type of use represented no more of a threat to the user than the chewing of coca leaves by South American aborigines. Snorting cocaine brought more immediate results, but it was not regarded as truly dangerous until users began to inject a soluble form with a hypodermic needle. Intravenous use not only makes possible an instantaneous high but it also brings the risk of addiction and the additional hazards of hepatitis, AIDS, and other diseases. Finally, the discovery of a new form of smokable crack cocaine brought even greater risks of addiction. The use of cocaine itself does not seem to be as much an issue as the form of administration.

The Nature of Drug Control

The most obvious function of drug control, and the primary reason cited by lawmakers, is to decrease the amount of a particular drug that is used. In some cases, such as heroin, the goal is complete prohibition. In other cases, such as cocaine, the goal may be to limit use of the drug to medical practice. In still other cases, such as alcohol, government may allow general use by adults, but seek to control the amount used by monitoring price controls, taxes, number of outlets, and the hours of sale.

The Harrison Narcotics Act of 1914 was primarily a labeling and registration act, and its purpose was to restrict the distribution of narcotic drugs to physicians and pharmacists. Prior to this act, access to opium derivatives was not officially restricted. After 1914, distributors had to register with the Treasury Department.

Most legal drugs are taxed. Since they are widely used commodities in any modern economy, governments have discovered that they can be a significant source of tax revenue. In most cases, the tax is imposed primarily for the purpose of raising revenue, but taxes on drugs are also used to regulate trade in one way or another. Such was the case of Britain's tax on Jamaican rum or Indian tea that was destined for other colonies. Alcoholic beverages were first subjected to federal taxation in the United States in 1791, and a liquor excise was the first internal revenue law enacted by Congress under the Constitution. As late as 1907, these revenues constituted 80 percent of all federal internal tax collections![13]

Drug taxes almost always have a dual purpose of decreasing consumption and raising revenue. Sometimes the revenues from taxes on a drug are only incidental to the primary purpose of the tax, restricting *use* of the drug. (The Marijuana Tax Act of 1937 used a tax to outlaw marijuana. Marijuana approved for medical use was taxed at $1.00 per ounce. Marijuana used for other purposes was taxed at $100.00 per ounce.[14]) Both the amount of revenue raised and the success of the tax in curbing consumption depends on the degree of *price elasticity* of the product being taxed. The elasticity of any particular drug depends on a number of factors, such as (1) the degree to which another drug may be substituted for it, (2) the availability of the drug, (3) the addictive power of the drug, and (4) the cost of the drug, including taxes. It is generally agreed that taxes on alcoholic beverages diminish their consumption[15] but that distilled spirits are less price elastic than beer.[16] In other words, a tax on distilled spirits would result in a smaller decrease in consumption than the same tax on beer. The relative elasticity of illicit drugs is less well known.

Assumptions Underlying Regulation

There are a number of important assumptions underlying any government's efforts to control drug use. One is that, whenever drugs are used, there are victims. Victims may be the actual users of drugs or they may be innocent bystanders—those who passively inhale cigarette smoke or who are maimed or killed by drunken drivers. There are those who argue that use of drugs is a "victimless" crime that has no major adverse consequences for the rest of society, but this view is not consistent with governmental regulation.[17]

Closely related to this is a second assumption that governments have the responsibility for enhancing the general welfare. A nation with a large proportion of drug users would be at an economic disadvantage in the world market because of reduced work output by drug users and the need to divert resources to handle the health and welfare needs of users. In regulating drugs as a way of promoting the general welfare, government walks a fine line between benefiting the majority of its citizens and encroaching on the individual liberties of a few. This potential conflict frequently appears when governments declare smoke-free workplaces or prohibit the possession of alcoholic beverages in a public park.

Governments find it just as difficult to distinguish *nonproblem* from *problem* drug use as distinguishing *use* and *misuse* (Chapter 1), but they do it anyway. Those drugs that are perceived not to cause problems (such as caffeine) are subjected to few controls. Those that are deemed to be troublesome but are impossible to prohibit because of widespread public use and acceptance, and because they are easily produced (such as alcohol), are tightly regulated. Those perceived to be the most problematic (heroin, cocaine) are generally banned.

These divisions between problem and nonproblem use are somewhat arbitrary, and the reasons for regarding drugs as acceptable or not are largely historical rather than pharmacological. For example, alcohol produces marked changes in behavior, has dangerous physical effects, and is powerfully addicting. Many experts believe that it is highly unlikely that the United States would ever completely legalize any other drug with such undesirable consequences.[18]

Regulation of Alcohol

Alcohol is tightly regulated in most countries and banned in a few. It remains an extremely popular drug despite its adverse consequences and the problems of addiction associated with its use. Because of its special position in most societies as a historically controlled, but legal, psychoactive drug, it deserves special attention in this chapter.

The Lessons of Prohibition

Although it is widely believed that the Eighteenth Amendment to the U.S. Constitution was a failure and that it demonstrated once and for all the futility of governmental attempts to legislate morality, this is not a completely accurate account of the effects of Prohibition.[19] This legislation was a failure in the sense that it bred contempt and open defiance of law and order, and it also fostered the growth of organized crime. No one denies that the Volstead Act was widely violated and that smuggling, moonshining, and speakeasies all thrived during the Prohibition era. On the other hand, there is considerable evidence that the consumption of alcoholic beverages declined considerably, especially among the working class. The most reliable indicators of heavy consumption—including acute alcohol overdose mortalities, liver cirrhosis, and hospital admissions for alcoholic psychosis—dropped well below their pre-Prohibition levels.[20] These declines were related to the price of alcohol, which tripled or quadrupled in parts of the nation after the Eighteenth Amendment took effect.[21] It can be expensive to deal in the underground economy!

According to Moore and Gerstein, there are three principal lessons of Prohibition that should be remembered in any future attempts to regulate the supply of beverage alcohol:[22]

1. Drinking customs in the United States are strongly held and resistant to frontal assault. It is well beyond the will or capacity of government ever to eradicate the customary demand for alcoholic beverages.

2. A criminal supply network emerges—if not instantly, then within a few years—if production and sale of alcoholic beverages are outlawed. The prices and extent of this criminal supply depend on the degree of public support for the law and the resources devoted to law enforcement.

3. The quantity of alcohol consumption and the rates of problems varying with consumption can, however, be markedly reduced by substantial increases in real prices and reductions in the ease of availability.

One lesson of Prohibition is that an abrupt legislative decree banning beverage alcohol will not work in U.S. society. This seems to be the most well-remembered lesson. In fact, it may be responsible for the tendency of many of those interested in alcohol problems to "disassociate themselves from the taint of temperance."[23] An equally important lesson, but one that seems to have been forgotten, is that regulation *can* reduce consumption and alcohol-related problems.

Current U.S. Policies

Today, all states in the United States set a minimum age for the legal consumption of alcohol and prescribe penalties for retailers who knowingly sell to underage customers. Some states assess penalties even when a retailer mistakenly sells alcohol in good faith to a minor with fake identification. Under pressure from the federal government, including the threat of withholding highway trust funds, the minimum age has shifted back to 21 years. All states also impose special excise taxes on alcoholic beverages, and most have restricted advertising, hours of sale, and credit sales (charge accounts, credit cards, etc.).

Beginning in the 1930s, 18 states chose to create state or county monopolies to control both wholesale distribution and retail sales of distilled spirits. The remaining states adopted licensing systems in which state regulatory agencies are empowered to license wholesalers and retailers and to promulgate and implement other rules and regulations regarding beverage alcohol sales.

Although the Twenty-First Amendment left the "dry" option open to individual states, all of them now permit alcoholic beverage sales in at least part of the state. Only about 3.5 percent of the population still resides in dry counties.[24] In most cases, the dry counties are predominately rural areas, and they tend to be concentrated in the South. Even there, however, drinking usually is allowed in certain lodges, fraternal organizations, and "private" clubs.

Taxes and Price Controls.   A fundamental law of economics is that as the price of something goes up, people will generally buy less of it. Thus, as prices for alcoholic beverages rapidly rose during Prohibition, demand decreased.[25] The same effect, in reverse, may also be partly responsible for the increase in per capita consumption that has occurred since the last major increase in federal taxes in 1951. Between 1967 and 1984, the real price of liquor dropped by almost one-half. One reason for this dramatic decrease in price was the fact that the federal excise taxes were not based on the price of the beverage, but instead were tied directly to the volume. Some critics have argued that the most important feature of federal policy in alcohol abuse prevention during the past several decades is the failure to index excise taxes on liquor to the consumer price index.[26]

In addition to taxes, many state governments had also influenced alcohol prices through fair trade laws and, in monopoly states, by administrative fiat. States with liquor monopolies may still set prices by decree in state-owned liquor stores, but the courts have eliminated price fixing by the liquor industry through fair trade laws. The method used to set prices may make a great difference to the state treasury, but it matters very little to the consumer. A price increase that arrives through taxation, price fixing, or administrative decree is all the same to the customer at the checkout stand. All three methods equally affect demand for the product.

Perhaps the most comprehensive analysis of the connection between alcohol prices, consumption, and alcohol-related problems was accomplished by Philip J. Cook. His examination of changes in liquor tax increases over a 15-year period demonstrated that even relatively small changes in prices influence not only the consumption of alcohol but the most serious health effects as well.[27] Similar decreases in consumption, heavy drinking, and alcohol-related problems due to price increases also have been noted in other countries.[28]

Does a decrease in overall consumption within a population also affect the drinking patterns of heavy drinkers? The pioneering work of Ledermann[29] and subsequent studies by several others confirm that even a significant proportion of problem drinkers in any population will reduce their consumption as overall consumption is reduced.[30] Some have suggested that regulation aimed at prevention of problem drinking might be more effective if specific taxes were levied on particular beverages favored by heavy drinkers, such as cheap brands of fortified wine.[31] However, this may just encourage switching to other alcoholic beverages. This argument also favors keeping the tax tied to the volume of alcohol sold, rather than the purchase price, since the former approach would have a greater impact on alcoholics, especially poor alcoholics who customarily purchase the cheaper types and greater quantities of alcoholic beverages.

Even though taxes on alcohol constitute a relatively small proportion of governmental budgets, governments closely consider the implications of these tax levels on their revenues. This is especially true during the recent past years of serious budget crises. President Bush's promise of "no new taxes" was quickly amended in 1990 to allow consideration of both alcohol and tobacco "sin" tax increases. Governments are most certainly aware of the danger of raising taxes to such a high level that revenues may actually decrease from a reduction in sales. As long as the alcoholic beverage lobby still exerts any influence in legislative circles, taxes are unlikely to rise to such levels. Consider the comments of an Ohio legislator:

> If the main, publicly stated objective from a policy standpoint is to reduce consumption through taxation, I believe it will create substantial problems in building coalitions in the legislature. A lot of folks make a good living selling alcoholic beverages, and they have for years contended that tax policy affects consumption. If a bill goes to a . . . committee, . . . it will have a hard time getting out of that committee because such committees are dominated by people who are generally friendly to the (alcoholic beverage) industry.[32]

Still, if governments have no choice but to raise income taxes or "sin" taxes, and the amount of additional revenue needed is moderate, the latter are politically less volatile.

There are a number of other mechanisms by which government may influence the price and thereby control demand for alcohol. Between 1986 and 1992, tax laws subsidizing alcohol consumption by allowing tax deductions for beverages purchased with business-related meals were gradually changed. Another example is the long-standing practice of selling alcoholic beverages at greatly discounted prices on U.S. military bases, a practice that strongly encouraged drinking by both uniformed and civilian employees and their families. Fortunately, the military establishment has realized that many problems were caused by selling cheap alcohol, and current policies have changed this practice.

Control of Distribution.   In addition to taxation and monopolistic price controls, government can do much to regulate the consumption of alcohol by controlling its distribution. It can do this by adopting and implementing policies regarding the number, size, and location of outlets, hours of business for package stores and bars, advertising practices, and the minimum legal drinking age.

The matter of licensing retail sales is generally a function of state and local governments. A number of earlier studies have attempted to determine the effect of outlet density on alcohol consumption, but there appears to be no relationship.[33] A quasi-experimental study in Ontario compared sales to residents of two cities located some miles apart, both of which were served by a package store located in one of them. Per capita sales were roughly equal for these two cities, despite the considerable differences in accessibility.[34] Outlet density may be more a result than a cause of demand in communities that treat alcohol sales as a proper function of the free market.[35]

Monopoly distribution systems also do not seem to have any appreciable effect on alcohol sales. In the former Soviet Union, for example, consumption is high and alcoholism is a major social problem.[36] A comparison of states in the United States that have monopoly distribution systems with those that allow private competition showed no difference in levels of consumption or indicators of alcohol-related health problems.[37]

There is little evidence that restricting the hours of sale reduces consumption. In fact, a study of changes in the hours of sale over a 25-year period concluded that "Sunday closing" laws (sometimes called *blue laws*) and earlier closing hours had the opposite effect: more sales![38] However, other changes in availability have been related to increased consumption. These include a gradual easing of restrictions on alcohol sales since World War II. Liquor-by-the-drink is now available in almost every large city, wine and beer are routinely sold in grocery stores and convenience stores, mixed drinks are available in restaurants, and sporting events often realize as much profit from the sale of alcohol as from the sale of tickets.

Blose and Holder found a significant increase in alcohol sales and alcohol-related automobile accidents immediately after North Carolina adopted liquor-by-the-drink.[39] When Idaho, Maine, Virginia, and Washington made wine available for sale in grocery stores, wine consumption rose significantly.[40] Anyone who has ever attended a professional baseball or football game where alcoholic beverages are sold can attest to their popularity. Consumption at sporting events has become such a problem in some communities that local officials have imposed beer-free games on the fans. Several major stadiums no longer sell any beer after the seventh inning of major league baseball games—with no significant effect on attendance.

The effect of increased availability on consumption is not peculiar to the U.S. culture. One study of the liberalization of alcohol laws in Finland showed a remarkable *doubling* of consumption in just seven years. The Alcohol Act of 1969 abolished restrictions on sales in rural areas, lowered the drinking age, and permitted retail shops to sell beer with a higher alcohol content. By 1975, the Finns were drinking 156 percent more beer, 96 percent more spirits, and 87 percent more wine. (Another curious fact is that Finnish drivers already had a higher rate of DUI than other Europeans *before* the liberalized liquor laws.[41] This happened despite a lower rate of drinking—indicating, perhaps, that enforcement was more strict in Finland.)

Drinking Age.   Perhaps no other area of alcohol policy has been so emotionally charged as the minimum legal age for purchasing and consuming alcoholic beverages. Minimum age restrictions are based on the assumption that alcohol use is more harmful for young persons than it is for adults. There always has been some variation in this age among the states, but historically most have used the age of 21 as the minimum age for unrestricted purchases. This continues to be a point of contention among the young, since they can now vote and be eligible for military service at age 18. Between 1970 and 1973, 24 states reduced their minimum drinking ages, reasoning that 18- to 21-year-olds should have all the rights and responsibilities of adulthood.[42]

During that period, an enormous amount of research was conducted on the impact of lowering the minimum age of purchase. One conclusion stood out quite clearly: Lower drinking ages were associated with significant increases in the rate of automobile crashes among young people.[43] Estimates of the increase in fatality rates were found to be 7 percent among those states that had dropped their minimum ages from 21 to 18 years of age.[44]

Partly because of this evidence, 15 states raised their minimum drinking ages back to 21 between 1975 and 1982. Among 13 of these states that were studied, automobile crashes were reduced from a minimum of 14 percent to a maximum of 29 percent.[45] Another study of 9 states that raised their minimum drinking age between 1975 and 1979 found a *41 percent* decrease in nighttime single-vehicle fatalities.[46] With such convincing evidence in hand on the effect of minimum age legislation, Congress passed a law in 1984 that would reduce federal highway funds for any state that had not raised its minimum drinking age to 21 years by 1986. Despite the outcry on college campuses and frantic lobbying by the alcohol lobby, most states complied by the deadline. Louisiana held out until its highway system could no longer survive without federal funds.

One of the other arguments against a lower minimum age is that it makes it just that much easier for 16- and 17-year-old students who have 18-year-old friends to obtain alcohol. (Remember, a majority of high school seniors will be 18 years old before their graduation.)

The National Highway Traffic Safety Administration (NHTSA) credits state laws raising the legal drinking age to 21 with preventing about 1,000 traffic deaths annually.[47] Some 29 states have reduced the maximum blood-alcohol concentration (BAC) level for drivers under age 21 to 0.02 percent, and this has reduced nighttime fatal crashes in this age group by 16 percent.[48]

Driving Under the Influence.   In most situations, the possession and use of alcohol by adults is completely legal. However, when a legally intoxicated individual (someone with a BAC of 0.10 percent in most states) attempts to drive an automobile, a *crime* has been committed. Driving under the influence (DUI) or driving while intoxicated

(DWI) is a criminal offense in all 50 states and the District of Columbia. (Most states also have laws against having any kind of open container of alcohol in a moving motor vehicle.) Progress has been made in reducing alcohol-related crash fatalities, falling from 43.6 percent of total crash fatalities in 1986 to 37.4 percent in 1992. Advances in technology (automobile engineering, airbags, etc.) and stricter public policies are thought to be responsible.[49]

All states have laws against driving under the influence of alcohol or driving while intoxicated, with the most common standard for either set at a BAC of 0.10 percent.[50] A few states and a number of other countries have lower levels. Sometimes called the *blood-alcohol level (BAL)*, this figure is determined by the ratio of the weight of alcohol to the volume of blood, grams per 100 milliliters (G/100ml). In states with *per se* laws, it is an offense to drive with a BAC at or above the specified value. A defendant may be convicted on the basis of chemical test evidence alone. Other states use a particular BAC as a "presumptive standard," allowing the defendant to introduce evidence that he or she was not, in fact, impaired at the prescribed limit.[51] The question of how effective these laws are in influencing the rate of drunken driving is still unsettled. Some moderately persuasive evidence does suggest that effectively enforced drunk driving laws deter drunken driving and reduce the accidents and fatalities associated with them.

The most thorough study of drunk driving laws is possibly that of the British Road Safety Act (RSA) of 1967. This act provided a *per se* BAC limit of 0.08 percent, and the first offense was a mandatory one-year suspension of the license. The new law was also preceded by a great deal of publicity. Ross's evaluation of the RSA found a 23 percent decline in auto fatalities, a decline in other auto injuries, and a decline in BAC levels of injured drivers—all within the first few months after implementation. Unfortunately, these improvements gradually flattened out and then began to rise by the end of 1970. The explanation for these

events was that the well-publicized passage of the RSA convinced many drivers that the risk of arrest and punishment would be much higher than it had been. Although they were deterred from drinking before driving and from driving after drinking, law enforcement did not markedly increase the certainty of either detection or punishment, and drivers gradually returned to their old habits as this became known to the public.[52]

In the United States, an evaluation of 35 alcohol safety action programs between 1970 and 1977 concluded that 12 of the programs had produced a decrease in nighttime auto fatalities, an accepted indicator of drunken driving.[53] Nevertheless, there continues to be a great deal of controversy over DUI laws. In most states, a common result of a DUI conviction is the administrative suspension of the driver's license. No one could deny the logic (and perhaps the justice) of this method. However, police report that a very large proportion of DUIs involve drivers whose licenses already have been suspended for previous DUI convictions. Even in states such as Florida, with *mandatory* jail sentences for second offenses, it is not at all uncommon for persons arrested on DUI charges for the second, third, or later offenses to serve no time in jail at all.[54] One reason the courts cite for not strictly enforcing DUI laws is that they impose "new and heavy demands on courts, incarceration facilities, and probation services" at a time when the criminal justice system is already overflowing with more "serious" crimes.[55] Prosecuting attorneys frequently feel that tough mandatory sentences for drunk drivers are ineffective and may actually raise public expectations to unrealistic levels.[56] Organizations such as Mothers Against Drunk Driving (MADD) and Students Against Driving Drunk (SADD) have reacted by bringing even greater pressure for tougher sentences, especially for drunk drivers who kill or injure another person. Such pressure has resulted in much political posturing by state and local politicians, but few effective solutions. Some judges have resorted to bizarre sentences such as mandating a convicted drunken driver to place a

"Drunken Driver" plate or tag on the family automobile. Needless to say, other family members who drive this automobile suffer needless embarrassment.

Another popular approach in dealing with drunken drivers is the *sobriety checkpoint.* The typical procedure is for local police to set up unannounced roadblocks along certain routes and stop vehicles, sometimes at random, to check for indications of alcohol impairment. This strategy provides a highly visible method of approaching the problem that is generally supported by the public, but there is little evidence of its effectiveness.[57] Its chief virtue lies in its symbolic reassurance to the public that something is indeed being done! Sobriety checkpoints are regarded by some motorists as a nuisance, especially in heavy traffic, and have been challenged by others as an unconstitutional invasion of privacy. So far, however, the courts have upheld the legality of this approach in most instances.[58]

Like drug use and possession, drunk driving lacks the usual criminal motives of gaining property or harming another person. DUI offenses are also unique in that a physical test (breathalyzer, blood analysis, etc.) is used and compared against a state standard to determine whether a crime has been committed. Drunk driving offenses are also frequently handled administratively rather than judicially through driver's licensing regulation. This means that one could have a driver's license suspended without any judicial safeguards. In most states, when drivers receive their licenses, they agree to take a breath or blood test if they are stopped on suspicion of driving while intoxicated. Refusal to take a test upon request is a violation of the licensing agreement and can result in automatic suspension or revocation of the license through an administrative process. Forty-two states have such sanctions.[59]

Between 1970 and 1986, arrests for drunk driving increased by 223 percent, while the number of licensed drivers increased by only 42 percent.[60] Although much of this increase can be attributed to concentrated law-enforcement efforts, some increase was almost certainly due to the trend in the early to mid-1970s for the states to lower the minimum age for the purchase of alcoholic beverages, largely in response to the ratification of the Twenty-Sixth Amendment (1971), which extended the right to vote to 18-year-olds. By 1983, 19-year-olds could legally drink in 27 states, and 18-year-olds could legally drink in 13 states.

DUI arrest rates for youths 18 to 19 years old peaked in 1982; for 20-year-olds, they peaked the next year. The number of DUI arrests for 18- to 20-year-olds decreased by 24 percent by 1986. This abrupt reversal of DUI trends among young people may be the result of the states once more raising their minimum legal drinking ages.[61] By 1987, only five states still allowed anyone under the age of 21 to purchase alcohol.[62]

A special survey in 1983 revealed that about three-fourths of all DUI offenders previously had been convicted of a crime. About half had previous DUI convictions. The median age of a DUI offender was 32, and about one-third worked as laborers or in a construction trade. Another one-third were unemployed at the time of their arrest. The typical DUI offender was white (85.6 percent), male (94.7 percent), and had consumed the equivalent of 12 bottles of beer just prior to arrest.[63]

Insurance/Liability Laws. Public policy is sometimes intended to indirectly affect the consumption of alcohol through such measures as the regulation of insurance rates. Drivers with DUI convictions may face higher insurance premiums or, in some cases, they may be unable to purchase automobile insurance. Since many of these drivers will continue to drive without insurance, these laws may actually be harmful to the larger population. There is no evidence indicating that higher insurance premiums have actually reduced consumption.

Another indirect measure involves server liability or *dramshop laws.* In a majority of states, commercial establishments that serve alcoholic beverages are civilly liable to those who suffer harm or injury as the result of an intoxicated or underage person's irresponsible use of alcohol. The typical dramshop law imposes civil liability for damages caused by an establishment's serving alcohol to "visibly intoxicated or underage customers."[64] (Criminal liability may also be attached when a minor is involved.) The courts also have held that even without a dramshop law, civil liability can be imposed on a tavern under common law.[65] One result of these laws has been the provision of better training to servers to help them learn how to recognize and "cut off" a customer who is intoxicated and to see that such a customer gets home safely. Some communities have established training programs for servers on methods of referring problem drinkers to appropriate treatment services.

More recently, decisions in a number of states have extended common law liability from commercial establishments to social hosts who provide alcohol to their intoxicated or underage guests.[66] Even though there are many good reasons to retain these policies, there is no published research indicating that dramshop or server liability laws have affected the use of alcohol.[67] Many feel that the laws have been too vague to persuade servers to change their policies. Also, many establishments buy insurance to cover their liability, and insurance companies have often shortcut the intent of the laws by settling out of court on dubious claims.[68]

Control of Illicit Drugs

Public policies regarding illicit drugs have not reached the degree of specificity that is found in policies regarding alcohol use. The primary debate surrounding illicit drugs is whether it is possible to control their use through law enforcement. The current failure of public policy to deal with the drug problem is the logical outgrowth of policies pursued by the federal government over the past decade. Since the election of Ronald Reagan in

1981, federal policy has been much more concerned with preventing recreational drug use than with helping habitual users. During Reagan's first term, funding for drug treatment fell by almost 40 percent, adjusting for inflation.[69] The budget for the so-called war on drugs continued to rise, however. By 1994, 330,000 Americans were incarcerated for drug offenses, and total criminal justice spending reached $20 billion.[70]

During the 1988 presidential campaign, the drug issue was never far from the political spotlight, and according to most opinion polls, drug problems were the nation's leading concern. At his inauguration, President Bush promised, "This scourge will end," and in September 1989, he devoted an entire speech to the subject.[71]

The approach chosen by the Bush administration was one of "zero tolerance." This approach emphasized law enforcement toward the end of completely eradicating illegal drugs, and it appeared to be based on the following assumptions:

1. If there were no drug abusers, there would be no drug problem.
2. The market for drugs is created not only by availability but also by demand.
3. Drug abuse starts with a willful act.
4. The perception that drug users are powerless to act against the influences of drug availability and peer pressure is an erroneous one.
5. Most illegal drug users can choose to stop their drug-taking behaviors and must be held accountable if they do not.
6. Individual freedom does not include the right to self- and societal destruction.
7. Public tolerance for drug abuse must be reduced to *zero*.[72]

This policy meant that possession of even the smallest amounts of illicit drugs could result in the seizure and confiscation of an individual's automobile, home, or other property. Some saw this as a serious threat to civil liberties.

Although still woefully inadequate, the Bush administration did increase treatment funding by

50 percent, to $1.6 billion. At the same time, the administration continued its preoccupation with casual middle-class drug use, not with addiction or habitual use.

Today, the war on drugs commands relatively little attention. The candidates in the 1992 presidential race seldom mentioned the drug issue, and there would have been little more interest in the 1996 election if there had not been a report indicating an increase in adolescent drug use. The Republican Party seized this issue, despite the fact that this trend had actually started during the Bush administration.[73]

The nation's first "drug czar," William Bennett, developed a strategy of seeking out and punishing casual, nonaddicted users. He also insisted that all drugs were equally pernicious,[74] a somewhat incongruous philosophy for a two-pack-a-day smoker! The next drug czar, former Florida governor Bob Martinez, shied away from the public spotlight and made few changes in Bennett's approach. Barry McCaffrey, the current drug czar, is a retired Army general who seems determined to continue a "zero tolerance" policy. Drug policy during the Clinton administration has changed very little.

Other nations have chosen other strategies. The Netherlands has legalized the use of certain drugs such as marijuana. Although Britain has a reputation for legalization, its approach to controlling illicit drugs really is one of harm reduction through methadone maintenance or needle/syringe exchange programs. Many experts feel that the United States is rather myopic in considering other options. Several states still prohibit the distribution of hypodermic needles or syringes without a prescription, making it impossible to operate a "legal" needle/syringe exchange program.

In the United States, efforts to control illicit drugs have been hampered by the great degree of fragmentation of federal, state, and local drug enforcement programs. A report from the Comptroller General indicated that the supply and demand of illicit drugs have remained relatively constant despite the massive increase in federal drug control efforts. In fact, he seriously questioned the ability of governmental efforts to regulate illegal drugs in the absence of "factual information about which anti-drug programs work best."[75] It is the recognized failure of antidrug enforcement policies that gave rise to the current debate on legalization of illicit drugs.

According to Dale Masi, an expert on employee assistance programs, the legalization of illicit drugs signals "the inevitability that use will increase." Masi testified before Congress that this approach "cannot be reconciled with ethical principles because it would be implemented with recognition of the increased personal and social destruction connected with drug abuse that would result. We, as a civilized society, are responsible for preventing disease and destruction, not spreading them."[76] This view is not accepted by all the experts, however. A New York State Senator, Joseph Caliber, proposed the legalization of *all* drugs. His plan was intended to eliminate criminal drug trafficking by allowing the sales of currently prohibited drugs in the same place and manner as alcohol. Similar restrictions on minimum age for purchase, hours of sale, location of stores, and so on would apply to drugs sales just as to current alcohol sales.[77]

Other testimony favored various compromise proposals, such as the legalization of the "less harmful forms" of illicit drugs. These advocates all favored the legalization of marijuana, and some favored legalizing certain forms of cocaine (coca leaves) and opiates (smokable opium).[78] Compromise proposals frequently advocate some degree of "decriminalization" for particular drugs rather than complete legalization. This approach sometimes suggests a civil rather than a criminal penalty for the use or possession of a controlled substance. On other occasions, it suggests that no penalty be attached to use but that sales be subjected to criminal penalties. This leaves users in the awkward position of being legally entitled to use a drug, but having no legal means to obtain it. The argument for legalization or decriminalization seems to be gaining acceptance, even among conservative politicians and writers. A major portion of a recent issue of the *National Review* was devoted to critiques of the war on drugs,[79] and articles in the *Journal of the American Medical Association* have advocated decriminalization.[80]

The War on Drugs

Richard Nixon was the first president to declare "war" on drugs. He did this in 1971 as he also introduced stronger criminal penalties for drug dealers and proposed a rapid expansion of drug treatment facilities, especially those specializing in heroin addiction.[81] All subsequent presidents have continued this effort, with each promising to increase the war effort against drugs.

The war on drugs was simply a continuation of the policies espoused in the Harrison Act in 1914, in which the federal government relied on a variety of approaches to reduce both the demand for and the supply of illicit drugs. The major changes are seen in the massive amount of funding for law enforcement, the perceived seriousness of the problem of drug abuse, and the advanced technological strategies for controlling drugs. Americans now use Bell 209 assault helicopters, Navy EC-2 and Air Force AWACS "eye-in-the-sky" aircraft, "Fat Albert" surveillance balloons, "Blue Thunder" high-performance Coast Guard vessels, and NASA satellites. The war analogy may seem appropriate in halting the operation of large drug cartels, but it seems inappropriate when it comes to dealing with other aspects of drug abuse. The war analogy seems especially inappropriate regarding efforts to prevent or treat drug abuse by the nation's children.[82]

Critics of the war on drugs have declared it "a losing battle," "almost an afterthought," and "hype from an Administration and Congress eager to justify the expenditure of billions of dollars for law enforcement."[83] These "get-tough" efforts may sound good to the public, but no serious student of drug policy is encouraged by the efforts at law enforcement in the attempt to reduce illegal drug use. Although during the Clinton administration there may have been fewer of the highly publicized drug eradication efforts in nations such as Colombia, the war on drugs has changed little.

The Economics of Drug War/Peace

One of the principal criticisms of the war on drugs is that it simply has not worked. Best estimates indicate that only 10 percent of the major illicit drugs smuggled into the United States are interdicted.[84] Drug-related emergency-room admissions, drug-related arrests, and casual drug use continue to rise.[85] Prison populations are exploding because of drug-related crime. This problem is so severe that even though many penalties for drug-related crimes have been increased, actual sentences served have decreased. Corrections officials are highly critical of this "revolving-door" approach. As new drug offenders are incarcerated, some other prisoners have to be released simply to make room for the new prisoners. Minority offenders are particularly affected by drug law enforcement. In Florida, the majority of all African American adults sentenced to prison are there because of illicit drugs.[86]

Another major criticism is that the nation cannot afford the cost of the war on drugs. From 1981 through 1988, the federal costs alone totaled $16.5 billion.[87] The current cost of the war on drugs for all levels of government is more than $30 billion per year. Former head of the National Drug Control Policy Office, William Bennett, implied that at least $10 billion more per year would be needed just to incarcerate additional drug users.[88]

The present policies on illicit drugs have also amounted to a type of regressive tax: It has dramatically increased the profits of drug dealers and at the same time placed additional economic burdens on the residents of inner cities to provide more law enforcement and to ameliorate the effects of crime. In 1994, U.S. federal law-enforcement agencies seized 120 metric tons of cocaine, and in 1995, they seized 98 metric tons.[89] Politicians as well as police officers often herald such actions as proof not only of the severity of the drug problem but also of the success of the country's interdiction efforts. However, it is questionable whether such raids prevent a single person from using cocaine. Likely no drug lords or street dealers are put out of business, and no additional addicts are driven to seek treatment. These events probably have no perceptible impact on the public's attitudes toward drug use. People who want cocaine are still able to find it.[90]

An article on the costs of the drug war estimated that the legalization and taxation of marijuana and cocaine (powder, not crack) would result in a net savings of about $25.25 billion per year. Legalization of these drugs would save $10 billion a year in federal law enforcement, $10 billion a year in state and local prosecution, $8 billion a year in other law-enforcement costs, $6 billion a year in the value of stolen property associated with drug use, and $3.75 billion a year by eliminating the "match" for Colombians' drug profits. The nation would also receive additional tax revenues of about $12.5 billion. These gains amount to $50.25 billion.

If drug use were to rise by 25 percent because of legalization, it would result in an additional social cost (health costs, stolen property, loss of income, etc.) of about $25 billion. This would leave the net gain of "drug peace" at $25.25 billion per year! Drug peace would be a less costly alternative to the drug war, according to these estimates, unless legalization led to a *doubling* of the number of marijuana and cocaine users. At this point, the net economic benefits of drug peace would be zero.[91] Of course, all these estimates rely on assumptions that are highly speculative, at best. There is no reliable way of predicting how much drug use would increase under a policy of legalization or decriminalization. In Britain, the number of addicts seeking treatment increased after passage of the Dangerous Drugs Act (which decriminalized the use of heroin and other illicit drugs), but it is not known to what extent drug *use* increased or decreased. There is some evidence that marijuana use decreased immediately after the

Dutch government decriminalized its use in 1976, however.[92] Both England and the Netherlands are far different from the United States in culture and economic demographics. One cannot assume that Washington, DC, would react to legalization in the same manner as London or Amsterdam. The Netherlands has a homicide rate only one-eighth that of the United States. Important aspects of its overall drug policy are also very different.

After reviewing hundreds of drug war studies by criminologists, psychologists, sociologists, and economists, Benson and Rasmussen concluded that not only is the United States not winning the drug war, but it is essentially an *unwinnable* war. Furthermore, by engaging in this war, the nation's resources have been stretched to the point where the entire criminal justice system is in a state of crisis. Their conclusion is that the United States will have to learn to coexist with the illicit drug trade and find a rational means of allocating its criminal justice resources. For example, local courts could be assigned a quota of beds for their use. Judges (and voters) would no longer be forced to face decisions that result in a rapist receiving an early release from prison so that a nonviolent crack addict could be incarcerated.[93]

Issues Regarding Legalization

One must remember that in the absence of any convincing empirical data regarding the effectiveness of alternative policies toward illicit drugs, the U.S. political system encourages the use of symbolic values (e.g., increased law enforcement) that become just as important, if not more important, than any tangible outcomes. Thus, the debate over the legalization of illicit drugs has developed very strong moral overtones.

Have Drug Laws Created Problems Worse than the Drugs Themselves?
Is it reasonable to say that present drug policies are responsible for increased corruption, violence, street crime, and disrespect for the law? There is obviously much truth in these assertions. One could easily argue that

present policies have made the sale of illicit drugs a highly profitable enterprise—so profitable that "turf wars" among cartels and neighborhood dealers alike have led to remarkable increases in the homicide rate. One only has to read the headlines in any Washington, DC, newspaper to learn that the great majority of homicides in the nation's capital (also the nation's *murder* capital) are drug related. On the other hand, the evidence suggests that among the majority of street drug users who are involved in crime, their criminal careers were well established prior to the onset of their drug use.[94] As mentioned in the previous chapter, their drug involvement may be due primarily to their involvement in a criminal subculture.

Perhaps more important is that the present laws, coupled with the propaganda fed to children for two generations about the consequences of drugs such as marijuana, have resulted in disbelief and widespread criminal violations. There is a direct parallel between this situation and the consequences of Prohibition, during which the law made criminals of millions of otherwise honest citizens.

Has Law Enforcement Failed in Reducing the Supply and the Demand for Drugs?

A closely related argument often made by advocates of legalization is that the $30 billion a year currently spent for law enforcement could be better used for the treatment and prevention of drug abuse. The use of drugs among U.S. secondary school students has risen consistently since 1991, and the proportion of eighth-graders taking illicit drugs in 1995 doubled since 1991 (from 11 percent to 21 percent). The number of eighth-graders using the most common illicit drug, marijuana, increased two and one-half times between 1991 and 1995.[95] Drug commitments to state prisons increased an astounding 1,055 percent between 1980 and 1992![96] It is obvious that law enforcement has failed as a solution to the problem of illicit drugs.

Can One Stop the Use of Drugs That a Significant Segment of the Population Is Committed to Using?

It is simply impossible to arrest, prose-cute, and punish such large numbers of people, especially in a liberal democracy in which the government must not unduly interfere with personal behavior. Attempting to enforce draconian measures against drug users will not only bankrupt the nation but it will also be an imminent threat to the civil liberties of its citizens.

Is Illicit Drug Use as Great a Threat to Society as the Legally Sanctioned Use of Alcohol and Tobacco?

The surgeon general of the United States estimated that cigarette smoking (the leading preventable cause of death in the United States) alone killed approximately 400,000 people in 1993.[97] Cigarette smoking kills more people each year than all other drugs combined and is virtually always addicting. Sales of tobacco are not just legal—they are actually *subsidized* by government programs providing price supports for tobacco growers! The number of deaths directly caused by alcohol consumption each year is approximately 100,000, and another 100,000 deaths are described as having alcohol consumption as a "contributing factor."[98] These figures are almost certainly conservative estimates of alcohol-related deaths. Compare these numbers with the estimated mortality rate of 20,000 deaths from illicit drug use, and one must wonder why cocaine, marijuana, and heroin are regarded as being so dangerous.[99] To focus on a strong drugs/crime connection, one must remember that more than half of all people convicted of a violent crime were under the influence of alcohol at the time the crime was committed.[100] Alcohol abuse is also involved in a major portion of domestic violence incidents.[101]

What Are the Possible Benefits of Legalization?

Among the expected benefits of legalization are cheaper drug prices, a decrease in drug-related crime, less corruption of governmental officials, and a destruction of the power base of drug lords and criminal syndicates. In addition, the country's legal system would be free to use its resources to provide treatment to those who are addicted, to prosecute and punish "real" criminals, and to eliminate the threat to civil liberties contained in current policies. Finally, government-sanctioned sales outlets could provide "quality control" for drug users and could collect badly needed tax revenues.

Would Legalization Result in Increased Drug Use, Loss of Productivity, and Higher Health Care Costs?

Some people argue that legalization could imply approval and lead to increased use. (If arguing that drug legalization would persuade people that drugs are safe, then the obvious implication is that the country needs to reconsider its policies on alcohol and tobacco!) Even if drug use were to increase with legalization, however, the economic benefits of "drug peace" would in all likelihood pay for the additional costs of increased usage, both socially and economically. As the earlier analysis indicated, the break-even point would be close to a 100 percent increase, and not even the most severe critics of legalization are predicting such dire consequences.

Will Drug Users Seek Greater Quantities and Higher Potencies of Drugs on the Black Market?

If the government legalized drugs but restricted the amount that a person could legally purchase, it is likely that some people would seek greater quantities and higher potencies on the black market. In order to work, legalization must make drugs available at all levels of quantity and potency. Otherwise, a black market in drugs will continue.

Will Legalizing "Soft" Drugs Such as Marijuana Lead Its Users to More Harmful and Addictive Drugs?

If the government wants to restrict "gateway" drugs (drugs that young people use that appear to be precursors of later drug use), then it should place restrictions on alcohol and tobacco, *especially* tobacco. Moreover, keeping marijuana illegal forces buyers into a black market where they are likely to be offered other illegal drugs. Finally, some 60 million Americans have tried marijuana, and the number of co-

caine addicts is estimated at 1 million. Thus, most marijuana smokers did not graduate to stronger drugs. The gateway effect is apparently not very strong.

Proposals for the legalization or decriminalization of drugs are incomplete and imperfect. There are still too many unanswered questions for the country to change course abruptly on these policy issues. Before people can seriously consider radical alternatives to the war on drugs, they need to answer the following questions asked by Paul Stares:

- What is the range of regulatory permutations for each drug?
- What would happen to drug consumption under more permissive policies?
- What would happen to crime under decriminalization? Legalization?
- Would a black market for drugs emerge under legalization?
- Would regulations restricting the purchase of drugs be as difficult to enforce as today's alcohol and tobacco restrictions?
- How would a decision to legalize drugs affect other countries?[102]

Merely asking these questions will anger many people, but the United States must begin to fashion a comprehensive, consistent, and enforceable policy regarding the use of drugs. These questions, and many others, must be answered before the political system is ready to consider an abrupt change in policy. Without a minimum degree of consensus on a number of these issues, the nation is not likely to deviate much from its present course.

Drugs, Alcohol, and Crime

That there is a relationship among alcohol, drugs, and crime is certain. The exact nature of that relationship is quite complex, however, and scholars are still putting the pieces together. David Rasmussen and colleagues argue that the great majority of persons who are arrested for drug of-fenses are *not* participating in other types of more violent criminal activity.[103] On the other hand, re-search shows that the great majority of persons arrested in urban areas for all crimes test positive for illicit drug use.[104] The effects of substance abuse on crime depend on (1) *what* drug is being used, (2) *who* is using the drug, (3) the relation-ship of the user to subcultures tolerant of other forms of social deviance, (4) law-enforcement policies regarding drug use, and, perhaps most im-portant of all, (5) *who* is conducting the research.

People who use drugs (except for alcohol and certain legal prescription drugs) are committing a criminal act. There are some very persuasive ar-guments that because of society's unreasonable definitions of drug use per se as a criminal act, society forces drug users to become criminals. La-beling theorists such as Lemert argue that the sec-ondary deviance that attaches to a person who is arrested or incarcerated for drug offenses can be far more destructive than the consequences of the drug use itself.[105] For the most part, however, so-ciety seems to be more concerned with whether other nondrug crime, particularly street crime, is a direct result of drug-taking behavior. Labeling, stigmatization, and secondary deviance are rather remote issues for citizens facing a crime wave.

Two hypotheses currently dominate the drugs/crime controversy. The first maintains that the "addict of lower socio-economic class is a crim-inal primarily because illicit narcotics are costly and because he can secure his daily requirements only by committing crimes that will pay for them."[106] This hypothesis maintains that crimi-nality is a more or less direct consequence of phys-ical dependence and tolerance, which requires ever-increasing doses of a drug that is economi-cally unavailable to the addict with limited finan-cial means. The other hypothesis maintains that the "principal explanation for the association be-tween drug abuse and crime . . . is likely to be found in the subcultural attachment" of the drug abuser to criminal associations, identifications,

and activities of other persons who are ad-dicted.[107] This hypothesis has more currency with the "hard" drugs such as heroin—a drug that is closely associated with a criminal subculture. It is less fruitful when applied to the "soft" drugs such as marijuana, as most middle-class college stu-dents could eagerly testify. Even cocaine seems to be a favorite drug of some business executives and other middle-class citizens.

There is another category of crime, fre-quently identified as *domestic violence* (spousal abuse, child abuse, etc.) that has been linked to al-cohol or drug abuse so frequently and so consis-tently that one might also hypothesize a direct, causal relationship between drug use and certain crimes of violence.[108] Alcohol, especially, is said to have a "disinhibiting" effect that unleashes emotions such as rage, or at least lessens the abil-ity to control rage.[109] In a study of 234 abusers of women, appearing before the court in Indianapo-lis, 60 percent had been under the influence of al-cohol, and 21.8 percent had been under the influence of other drugs when they physically as-saulted their spouses or partners. The men who were using alcohol or drugs generally displayed greater violence toward the women.[110]

On the other hand, with few exceptions, there is no evidence of a clear cause-and-effect relation-ship between alcohol or drug use and violent be-havior. Drugs such as PCP and amphetamines are known to affect the brain in some way that trig-gers violent behavior.[111] However, CNS depres-sants and marijuana generally alter behavior in the *opposite* direction.[112] There are reasons to sus-pect that much of the domestic violence that oc-curs under the influence of alcohol or drugs is preplanned. According to the *disavowal theory*, the abuser simply gets drunk or gets high so that he will have an excuse for beating his wife or chil-dren. By doing so, both his family and society may treat him less severely.[113]

There is considerable evidence that most of the current problems of the criminal justice sys-tem can be attributed, either directly or indirectly, to drugs—jail and prison overcrowding, court backlogs, increased crime, inmate violence, and the increased costs of incarceration. Strains on the system caused by the increased use of drugs have resulted in frequent crisis management and a "continuing search for more effective ways for the system to absorb the increase in drug arrests and to reduce the cycle of drug use and arrest for these defendants."[114]

The data discussed on the following pages show an undeniable relationship among alcohol, drugs, and crime. One task will be to understand whether the socioeconomic class approach, the subcultural attachment approach, or some other hypothesis best explains the nature of that relationship. First, drug law violations (manufacture, use, and sales) as crimes will be examined. Next will be a discussion about substance abuse and criminal histories of people arrested or incarcerated for nondrug crime. Third will be a review of the research on substance abuse and domestic violence. Finally, current trends in the drugs/crime relationship will be examined, and current policies regarding drugs and crime will be reviewed.

Alcohol and Drug Law Violations

It is no secret that crime statistics are regarded by the experts as seriously flawed. Despite such impressive titles as *Uniform Crime Reports* that fill the basements of university libraries, there is actually very little uniformity in reporting practices. Crime statistics are based on reports taken by thousands of local police officers and county sheriffs. Crime statistics in a community may change dramatically overnight with a change in reporting procedures. Police commissioners arguing for larger budgets have been known to create their own crime waves simply by altering departmental rules for reporting crime.

Anyone doing research on juvenile delinquency certainly has been frustrated by the tremendous variability in state and local reporting procedures. Only about two-thirds of the states regularly report juvenile crime data to a central national registry, and many local jurisdictions are not required to report to a central state agency. There is no way to determine how many juveniles were arrested in Texas or Illinois (or several other states), for example, for drug law violations, except by reviewing records of local police. (Imagine examining the records of 254 county sheriffs and hundreds of city police departments in a state the size of Texas!)

Crime data, although seriously flawed, can be of some help in understanding the drugs/crime relationship, however. Some categories of drug-related offenses, such as adult arrests for drug law violations, are reported with much greater regularity and consistency. Also, one can assume that the direction of error in crime data is toward *underreporting*. On a nationwide basis, one can assume that the degree of underreporting is fairly consistent from one year to the next. Therefore, if dramatic changes occur over a period of years, one may still be able to identify specific trends.

It is obvious from Table 8.1 that there has been a dramatic increase in adult incarcerations for drug violations during the past decade. Between 1980 and 1994, there was more than 1,000 percent increase in drug commitments.[115] Does this mean that there was a comparable increase in illegal drug manufacture, sale, or possession during that period? It's impossible to say. In some communities, there may actually be much smaller increases or possibly even a decrease. Other data indicate that the overall crime rate peaked and began to decrease during this period.[116] Despite this trend, vigorous enforcement of drug laws could still produce an increasing number of arrests and commitments in this category each year.

Juvenile arrest data indicate an increase in juvenile drug arrests of 66 percent between 1985 and 1994, and a disproportionate number of juvenile drug offenders who were waived to adult criminal court were African American (52 percent in 1993).[117]

TABLE 8.1   Estimated Number of Prisoners in Custody of State Correctional Authorities, by the Most Serious Offense, 1980, 1985, 1990–94

	Number of Inmates in State Prison						
Most Serious Offense	**1980**	**1985**	**1990**	**1991**	**1992**	**1993**	**1994**
Total	295,819	451,812	684,544	728,605	778,495	828,566	906,112
Violent Offenses	173,300	246,200	313,600	339,500	370,300	395,700	429,400
Property Offenses	89,300	140,100	173,700	180,700	182,400	191,600	209,800
Drug Offenses	19,000	38,900	148,600	155,200	172,300	183,200	202,100
Public-Order Offenses	12,400	23,000	45,500	49,500	51,100	53,800	58,800
Other/unspecified	1,800	3,200	3,100	2,900	3,100	4,400	6,000

Source: Adapted from Bureau of Justice Statistics, *Correctional Populations in the United States, 1994,* Report No. NCJ-160091 (June 1996), p. 10.

Drug Use by Criminals

In 1986, almost half of all prisoners in state institutions either had been convicted of a drug crime or had been a daily user of an illegal drug in the month preceding the offense for which they were incarcerated.[118] Although comparable data are not available for subsequent years, there is convincing evidence that even more prisoners are drug involved. For example, there was a 478 percent increase in the number of state prisoners sentenced for drug offenses between 1985 and 1995, and a 59.9 percent increase in federal prisoners.[119] Drug offenders accounted for 35 percent of the total growth in state prisoners and 80 percent of the total growth in federal prisoners.[120]

In the 1986 study, 28 percent of prison inmates reported a past drug dependency. The drugs most frequently mentioned were heroin (14 percent), cocaine (10 percent), and marijuana or hashish (9 percent). At the time of the offense, 17 percent were under the influence of drugs only, 19 percent were under the influence of alcohol only, and 18 percent were under the influence of both drugs and alcohol. More than half said they had taken illegal drugs during the month before committing the crime, and 43 percent said that they had used drugs on a daily basis just prior to committing the crime.[121]

The latest drug use forecast for 1996 indicates that a majority of arrestees in 23 major metropolitan areas across the United States tested positive for at least one illicit drug. Cocaine remains the predominant drug among adult male arrestees, although marijuana is a close second and is catching up quickly.[122]

Juveniles accounted for 13 percent of all drug arrests in 1995. Between 1991 and 1995, juvenile arrests for drug abuse violations increased by 138 percent.[123] This seems to represent the continuation of an earlier trend, with juvenile drug arrests increasing by 115 percent between 1986 and 1995.[124]

An analysis of juvenile offenses in Florida reveals a 1,580 percent increase in the number of juvenile drug offenders sentenced to adult prisons on felony charges between 1983 and 1988.[125] During this same period, the number of drug-related delinquency cases increased by about 85 percent.[126] It appears that juveniles arrested for drug offenses are being handled much more severely.

There is ample evidence that both juvenile and adult offenders are more likely than nonoffenders to use alcohol or illegal drugs, but does that mean that the drug use *caused* the crime? Huizinga and associates examined the temporal order of drug and alcohol use and other delinquent behavior and concluded that "other" delinquency generally precedes the use of alcohol or drugs. Therefore, alcohol and drug use cannot be the cause of other delinquent behavior. However, the same study concludes that there may be causal relationships *within* the arena of drug law violations:

1. The onset of alcohol use precedes the onset of either marijuana or polydrug use in 95 percent of all ascertainable cases; among those who never use alcohol, no more than 3 percent initiate marijuana use and no more than 1 percent initiate polydrug use.
2. Marijuana use precedes the onset of polydrug use in 95 percent of ascertainable cases.[127]

It should be stressed that this (and earlier) studies of the drugs/juvenile delinquency relationship were concerned more with alcohol and the "soft" drugs than with "hard" drugs such as heroin. Remember the earlier caveat regarding the nature of the drug having an impact on its connection with criminal behavior. Heroin and cocaine both produce a much more powerful physical craving in the addicted person than drugs such as marijuana, and the price is much more expensive than alcohol. The alcoholic and the regular marijuana user can ordinarily maintain their life-styles through regular employment.

Research in Maryland (Baltimore), California, and New York (Harlem) indicates that criminal activity increases with higher levels of heroin use. Ball, Shaffer, and Nurco found that over a nine-year period, the crime rate of 354 heroin addicts dropped with less narcotics use and rose 400 to 600 percent with increased use.[128] An earlier paper on the Baltimore study estimated that male opiate addicts commit crimes on an average of 178 days per year.[129] Johnson and colleagues revealed in a study of Harlem heroin users that daily users committed about five times as many robberies and burglaries as irregular users, an average of 209 per year.[130] Obviously, they are apprehended for only a tiny fraction of these crimes.

Recent research on the relationship between drugs and crime indicates that the relationship is more complicated than previously thought. For example, groups of individuals with low levels of antisocial personality and self-derogation are most directly affected by the use of drugs during adolescence. They are likely to experience loss of inhibitions and to engage in acts of violence later in life.[131]

Drug Use by Victims

There is evidence that drinking alcohol or using drugs precipitates crime. According to the lifestyle/exposure theory, routines or life-styles involving alcohol or drug use may facilitate the spatial and temporal union of victims and criminals.[132] Ask any police officer about hanging around bars drinking or going into inner-city crack houses to buy and/or use drugs. These are both regarded as very high-risk activities.

A study of over 6,000 cases in England strongly supports the contention that drinking at night away from home greatly increases the prospects of the drinker's suffering a personal attack or injury. For young male respondents, the probability of enduring a serious personal injury as a result of such a life-style was even greater.[133] People who use drugs or alcohol away from home are frequently in an environment unfamiliar to them, surrounded by others who are involved in all types of criminal activities, and suffer from a diminished capacity for flight or self-protection.

Domestic Violence

There is a high degree of family violence in America, as well as an unwillingness to look too closely at the serious incidents of physical abuse that are occurring in many homes. Shame, guilt, fear of reprisal, and lack of appropriate community responses prevent many victims from reporting these crimes. In the 1990s, attitudes of the general public are allowing more and more victims of abuse to take a stand against their abusers, as prison convictions increase and the number of "safe houses" grows. In just a few years, official reports of child abuse and neglect have mushroomed—from over 2 million in 1986[134] to approximately 3,140,000 in 1994.[135] As long ago as 1977, national surveys estimated at least 6 million incidents of *serious* physical abuse of spouses each year.[136] The general picture emerging from the research literature is that women and children are usually the victims of domestic violence, and men are the perpetrators.[137] The one exception is in the case of spousal homicide, in which men are almost as likely as women to be victims. Women who murder their husbands usually cite constant, long-term physical abuse as their motivation, however.[138] It should also be recognized that couples who are not married have rates of domestic violence that are just as high or higher than that of married couples.[139]

Public opinion has long held that the wife beater or child abuser is a "lower class, beer-drinking, undershirt-wearing Stanley Kowalski brute."[140] Family violence is not confined to any social, geographic, economic, or racial group, but it *is* strongly connected to the use of alcohol and drugs. More than two decades ago, Dr. Henry Kempe estimated that alcohol plays a role in about a third of all cases of child abuse.[141] A study conducted at an Arkansas alcoholism treatment center indicated that more than half of the parents being treated were also child abusers.[142] Another study in New York found that the husband's alcohol or drug abuse was an underlying factor in over 80 percent of wife-beating cases.[143] More recently, research in Indianapolis showed that more serious physical abuse is likely to be committed by men with alcohol or drug problems.[144]

According to Cohen, violence among alcohol and drug users may occur because human aggression may be increased through drug use, and this propensity is dose related. Some of the possible explanations for this phenomenon are:

1. The drug might diminish ego controls over comportment, releasing submerged anger that can come forth as directed or diffuse outbursts.
2. It may impair judgment and psychomotor performance, making the individual dangerous to self and to others.
3. It might induce restlessness, irritability, and impulsivity, causing hostile combativeness.
4. The drug could produce a paranoid thought disorder with a misreading of reality. False ideas of suspicion or persecution may bring forth assaultive acts against the imagined tormentors.
5. The craving to obtain and use the drug can result in a variety of criminal behaviors, some of them assaultive.
6. An intoxicated or delirial state may result in combativeness and outbursts of poorly directed hyperactivity and violence.
7. Drug-induced feelings of bravado or omnipotence may obliterate one's ordinary sense of caution and prudence causing harm to one's self or others.
8. An amnesic or fugue state may occur during which unpredictable and irrational assaults may take place.[145]

In the case of certain drugs such as ice, there is an almost certain direct link between drug use and violent or aggressive behavior. With alcohol, however, this relationship is somewhat more indirect. In fact, the most widely accepted viewpoint is that alcohol abuse is a disavowal technique used by abusive husbands. Some men may drink heavily prior to beating their wives or children because they know that by being drunk they will be released from responsibility both by their spouses and by the rest of society. In other words, drunkenness can provide a time-out period when the norms regarding appropriate behavior can be disregarded. Individuals may not become violent because they are drunk, but get drunk so that they may become violent—and be excused.[146]

Drug/Crime Trends in the 1990s

In addition to the dramatic increase in illicit drug use that has been observed during the past decade, some other disturbing trends are developing that merit special attention.

Drug Trafficking

The massive problem of illicit drug use in the United States is not the result of independent manufacturers, growers, and drug dealers. It takes a great deal of *organized* effort to bring cocaine from Peru, heroin from Pakistan, and cannabis from Mexico into this country in a sufficient volume to satisfy current demand. Law-enforcement officials' intelligence on drug distribution networks indicates that a number of well-organized, large, highly competitive regional organizations as well as hundreds of small, independent dealers are involved in the illicit drug trade. Traditional organized crime syndicates, small ethnic groups, street gangs, and motorcycle gangs are all involved in the importation, manufacture, distribution, and sale of illegal drugs.[147]

The growth of nontraditional organized crime is one of the most recent phenomena in illicit drug trafficking. Outlaw motorcycle gangs have been deeply involved in Oklahoma (Outlaws), Texas (Bandidos, Scorpions, Banshees, Ghostriders, Freewheelers, and Conquistadors), and several other states. These groups generally were once synonymous with the manufacture and distribution of amphetamines, but have expanded to include cocaine, heroin, and marijuana.

Los Angeles gangs, primarily the Crips and the Bloods, have developed far-reaching illicit drug networks that operate in Oregon, Washington, Missouri, Maryland, Texas, Colorado, and New York. In some communities such as Seattle, Tacoma, and Denver, they dominate the trade in crack cocaine.

In upstate New York, markets have become more organized along ethnic lines. Jamaican and Hispanic groups seem to be controlling the distribution of larger quantities of drugs and have access to suppliers in the southeastern United States. In southern Florida, Jamaican "posses" have displaced a number of native and other immigrant drug organizations, with occasional violent confrontations taking place.

Maryland reports that the state's supply of illegal drugs is plentiful and the sources varied, with no single group maintaining control over the market. Texas also reports a multitude of organized networks involved both in the manufacture and distribution of drugs. Traditional organized crime, border drug czars, Latin American organized crime, outlaw motorcycle gangs, and ethnic drug gangs are all involved in the Texas drug market.[148]

In California, the Bureau of Organized Crime and Criminal Intelligence reports that criminal activities of street gangs exploded in 1987, with narcotics trafficking contributing heavily to the increased violence. Some of the gangs, especially the Crips and the Bloods, have transformed themselves into well-organized and sophisticated drug distribution networks. Competition between these gangs may explain a large portion of the seemingly random violence that occurs on their turf, and it is undoubtedly a major factor in the uneasy "truce" agreed upon shortly after the 1992 Los Angeles riots. California also has witnessed the involvement of outlaw motorcycle gangs, prison gangs, and three important international drug cartels: the Medellin cartel based in Colombia, the Triads based in Hong Kong, and the Yakuza based in Japan. In addition to heroin and cocaine trafficking, the cartels are also involved in real estate, business investment, and money laundering.[149]

Two New England states have become important links in the drug distribution pipeline. Canadian law-enforcement authorities have verified that large quantities of both heroin and hashish are smuggled through Canada and Vermont to major metropolitan areas in the northeastern United States. Large quantities of cocaine imported through Florida also pass through Vermont on the way to Montreal. Rhode Island has become an important cocaine and heroin distribution center for New England, Canada, and the Midwest. Its proximity to New York and Boston make it a choice distribution center for several Colombian trafficking groups known as clans.[150]

Drugs, Crime, and Prison

In April 1988, the National Council on Crime and Delinquency issued its first national prison population forecast, based on the prison population projections of nine states. At that time, it was estimated that those states would increase their prison populations by 21 percent during the next five years. By December 1989, the estimate for the five-year increase had risen to 68 percent. The earlier forecast had not taken into account the impact of the current war on drugs, which threatens to overwhelm the nation's correctional system.[151]

This expansion of the prison population is due largely to increases in admissions for drug offenses. In 1985, about 15 percent of prison admissions were for drug crimes. By the end of 1988, that percentage had increased to over 35 percent, and over 80 percent of drug prison sentences were for cocaine (43.5 percent for sale and 37.9 percent for possession).[152] As indicated in Table 8.1, admissions to prison for drug offenses increased elevenfold between 1980 and 1994.

One of the reasons for this dramatic growth in drug-related prison admissions is parole failure and revocation. Increased emphasis on drug testing and the intensive surveillance of parolees has resulted in sharp increases in the number of drug offenders who are committed to prison. Approximately one of three prison admissions are people who have failed to complete their parole satisfactorily, and the primary reason for parole failure is the use or possession of drugs.[153] In California, prison admissions for parole violations now exceed prison admissions for new court sentences.[154]

The already high incarceration rate for minorities has exploded with the "get-tough" policies of the war on drugs. Drug enforcement has somewhat narrowly focused on crack, a favorite illicit drug among the poor, who are also disproportionately African American and Hispanic. In Virginia, new drug commitments of whites *fell* from 62 percent of total drug commitments in 1983 to 34 percent in 1989, with minority commitments rising from 38 percent to 66 percent. In Florida, 73.3 percent of all drug offenders committed to prison are African American.[155] There seems to be reasonable evidence that institutional racism has influenced drug law enforcement. Mandatory minimum sentences force judges to incarcerate many drug violators who would not otherwise be sent to prison, and these sentences appear to apply more often to blacks than whites. For example, a conviction in federal court for possessing 5 grams of crack cocaine results in a five-year mandatory sentence, but 500 grams of cocaine powder is required to invoke to same sentence. The U.S. Sentencing Commission's recommendation that sentences for crack (more frequently used by black arrestees) and cocaine powder be equalized was rejected by Congress in 1995.

The projected 68 percent increase in the prison population translates into an additional $35 billion to build and operate new prisons. By 1991, California became the first state to exceed 100,000 inmates; by 1996, it had over 147,000 inmates in prison. It cost California approximately $4 billion annually to operate its prison system in 1994.[156]

Treating Substance-Abusing Offenders

Law-enforcement and corrections administrators have responded to the growing number of alcohol- and drug-involved arrests by increasing the enrollment of offenders in diversion, jail-based, probation, and prison drug treatment programs. In 1979, an estimated 4.4 percent of inmates in state correctional systems were in treatment.[157] By 1987, this figure had grown to 11.1 percent.[158] By 1995, there were 39 special state correctional facilities designed primarily for alcohol or drug treatment.[159] Unfortunately, there were no such special federal facilities.

The most common types of treatment programs in jails and state prisons are Alcoholics Anonymous, Narcotics Anonymous, or other Twelve-Step approaches modeled closely after AA and NA. Over 80 percent of residential programs for noncriminal offenders incorporate family therapy or family counseling, but less than 41 percent of prison programs provide these services. The great majority of residential programs provide referral and aftercare follow-up, but fewer than 65 percent of prison programs provide referral, and less than 27 percent follow-up.[160] Over half of all prison inmates were regularly involved in using drugs before their last arrest but were receiving no programmatic help while incarcerated. When released from prison without effective treatment, a high rate of crime continuation can be expected for these people.

Professionals outside the correctional system might assume that treatment routinely would be provided to chemically dependent inmates. After all, it makes little sense to incarcerate cocaine-abusing offenders for a period of years and then send them back to the community without treatment! However, one must consider the barriers to providing treatment within a prison such as constraints on resources, changes in priorities for specific types of programs, staff resistance, and inmate resistance.[161] Prisons and jails are first and foremost institutions designed for control and punishment of criminal offenders. Rehabilitative programming for inmates never has been a high priority. The U.S. public generally has a punitive, nonrehabilitative approach toward crime, and support for rehabilitation has steadily and precipitously declined since the late 1960s.[162]

The literature on treatment of chemically dependent offenders presents a somewhat confusing picture. Some evaluations of treatment programs sometimes indicate little or no effect,[163] whereas others show that treatment decreased subsequent criminal activity and "normalized" the life-styles

of offenders.[164] Very little of the research followed offenders for a sufficiently long posttreatment phase to generate much confidence in findings of "success."

There is somewhat more optimism regarding the use of civil commitment procedures to require treatment of probationers and parolees. Anglin's 21-year study of the nation's first true civil commitment program, the California Civil Addict Program, resulted in consistently lower posttreatment drug use rates for clients receiving treatment.[165] Other long-term studies of clients of the Lexington, Kentucky, and Ft. Worth, Texas, Public Health Service Hospitals indicated that addicts treated under legal coercion had better outcomes than noncoerced clients.[166]

A typical model of the civil commitment procedure for criminal offenders is the Treatment Alternatives to Street Crime (TASC) Program. TASC programs have been developed with federal funds under local administration to identify drug abusers who come into contact with the criminal justice system, refer those who are eligible for appropriate treatment, monitor their progress in treatment, and return violators to the criminal justice system. A five-year follow-up of both outpatient and residential programs revealed that TASC clients referred from the criminal justice system did as well or better than other clients.[167]

Historically, methadone maintenance programs have been a major treatment modality for drug-involved criminal offenders. Studies of such programs in New York City since the 1950s indicate that methadone maintenance may be the most cost-effective outpatient treatment for the majority of opiate addicts under probation or parole supervision.[168] Unfortunately, many patients maintained on methadone also have serious alcohol and/or cocaine addictions. In such cases, a choice of other treatment alternatives should also be available.

Therapeutic communities (TCs) have a long history of providing treatment to criminally involved drug addicts. Until 1975, drug abusers were sent to TCs under civil commitment procedures by both federal and state courts. Since 1975, the civil commitment procedures have been gradually replaced with "legal referrals," which are equally coercive. Some TCs serve criminal justice clients almost exclusively. Clients in a therapeutic community are isolated from the outside world. Their philosophy is that there is no cure, just control. Addicts are kept away from the neighborhood, friends, and situations that have been a part of their addiction. The aim of TCs sounds surprisingly similar to the early moralistic treatments: to restructure an immature, addiction-prone individual into a strong, self-reliant person who no longer needs a drug.[169] A recent review of the research indicates that TCs are equally effective with legally coerced clients as with other clients.[170]

There are obvious explanations for many of the higher success rates claimed by treatment programs that work with legally coerced clients. First, residential programs such as TCs may require clients to be in residence for a year or more, and they are under constant scrutiny by staff and other residents. The risk of detection under such circumstances is quite high, and more successful outcomes are related to longer periods of treatment.[171] Second, clients in both residential and nonresidential programs may be on long-term parole or probation. Such clients may be routinely monitored either by treatment staff or by probation/parole officers for possible drug use, including unannounced urine analysis. Finally, the threat of legal coercion may simply have a deterrent effect.

Whatever one may think of the appropriateness of the "coerced treatment" approach, since passage of the Anti-Drug Abuse Act of 1988, the majority of illicit drug users in treatment in most communities have been treated through the justice system. Without this approach, there would have been little treatment of any kind for criminal offenders available within the community.[172] Additional funding for treating criminal offenders was provided through the Edward F. Byrne Memorial Fund, which replaced the Anti-Drug Abuse Act.

Summary

Public policy regarding the use of drugs in the United States has been shaped by its culture, historical inheritance, economic forces, and world affairs. Like most other industrialized Western nations, the United States has chosen to sanction, regulate, and tax two major drugs—alcohol and tobacco. Policies regarding the regulation of these drugs are internally inconsistent, however. Millions of dollars are spent on scientific research to show tobacco growers how to increase their yield, and price supports to stabilize the tobacco industry are offered. In the past, the government has been dependent on tax revenues from tobacco and alcohol sales for a major portion of its budget. At the same time, other governmental offices issue periodic reports decrying the dangers of using either alcohol or tobacco, both strongly addicting drugs that together are responsible for approximately one-half million deaths each year in the United States. Policies regarding these drugs seem diametrically opposed to policies regarding illicit drugs.

Since the Harrison Act, national policy toward most other illicit psychoactive drugs has been one of official prohibition. It is a policy that has been, at best, a dismal failure. Some even blame the prohibition approach for the worst of the country's social ills—increasing crime, despair in inner cities, disrespect for law and the political system, and the gradual decline of moral and ethical standards throughout society. For these reasons, as well as the ever-increasing cost of the war on drugs, the nation must face the possibility of changing its policy to allow the legalization or decriminalization of at least some illicit drugs.

That criminals are heavier drug and alcohol users than other citizens is beyond dispute. How much crime is directly attributable to drug and alcohol use is another question. In some cases, the user's physiological response to a drug might be aggressive behavior that results in a criminal act. For some individuals, illicit drug use simply may be another aspect of their criminality that coexists along with certain other criminal activities. Their drug use and their stealing both may be due to the influences of life in an impoverished ghetto, rife with crime. Illicit drug use and other criminal activities may be mutually reinforcing; it is easier to locate and obtain certain drugs if one is already a member of a deviant subculture. If one is a junkie, that status frequently provides easier access to various forms of criminal enterprise.

According to a recovering heroin addict,

You have put yourself on the wrong side of the law and your original framework for interaction becomes shaky. You find that people you know are stealing, kiting cheques, or doing insurance jobs. The process of osmosis into this world is slow and gradual. By the time you realize what is going on, you have ceased to be shocked.[173]

For drugs such as marijuana, perhaps the major connection with crime is the secondary deviance that comes from being caught and officially labeled as a criminal. This is especially important for juveniles, since marijuana is the primary illicit drug used by the nation's children. Official court processing and referral of these cases to agencies of the juvenile justice system are not likely to curtail further delinquent acts. In fact, just the opposite is likely to occur. The deeper a youthful drug offender is immersed in the system, the *more* likely subsequent delinquent behavior is apt to be seen.[174]

It seems obvious that the answer to the nation's drug problem is not law enforcement. Law enforcement should be a vital component of any rational plan to stem the manufacture, sale, and use of illicit drugs, but as a primary strategy, it has failed miserably. At the current rate of imprisonment for drug offenses, it is doubtful that either the economy or the political system can support such high rates of incarceration much longer.

Endnotes

1. Phillip Bean, *The Social Control of Drugs* (London: Martin Robertson, 1974).

2. Jason M. White, *Drug Dependence* (Englewood Cliffs, NJ: Prentice Hall, 1991), p. 166.

3. Ibid., p. 165.

4. Vera Rubin, *Cannabis and Culture* (The Hague: Mouton, 1975).

5. Ibid.

6. White, *Drug Dependence*, p. 167.

7. Mark H. Moore and Dean R. Gerstein (Eds.), *Alcohol and Public Policy: Beyond the Shadow of Prohibition* (Washington, DC: National Academy Press, 1981).

8. This is the author's assessment of the situation after spending a sabbatical in Dublin, teaching at University College and working with the Irish National Council on Alcoholism.

9. White, *Drug Dependence*, p. 185.

10. U.S. Congress, Hearing Before the Select Committee on Narcotics Abuse and Control, House of Representatives, 100th Cong., 2d sess., September 30, 1988, p. 61.

11. John F. Galliher, James L. McCartney, and Barbara E. Baum, "Nebraska's Marijuana Law: A Case of Unexpected Legislative Innovation," *Law and Society Review*, Vol. 8 (1974), pp. 441–455.

12. Howard Wayne Morgan, *Drugs in America: A Social History 1800–1900* (Syracuse, NY: Syracuse University Press), 1981.

13. Moore and Gerstein, *Alcohol and Public Policy: Beyond the Shadow of Prohibition*, p. 68.

14. William A. McKim, *Drugs and Behavior*, 2nd ed. (Englewood Cliffs, NJ: Prentice Hall, 1991), p. 278.

15. Moore and Gerstein, *Alcohol and Public Policy*, pp. 68–73.

16. Stanley I. Ornstein, "The Control of Alcohol Consumption through Price Increases," *Journal of Studies on Alcohol*, Vol. 41 (1980), pp. 807–818.

17. David A. Richards, *Sex, Drugs, Death, and the Law* (Totowa, NJ: Rowman and Littlefield, 1982).

18. White, *Drug Dependence*, p. 191.

19. Harry G. Levine, *The Committee of Fifty and the Origins of Alcohol Control*, Publication #F129. Social Research Group, University of California, Berkeley, 1980.

20. Clark Warburton, *Economic Results of Prohibition* (New York: Columbia University Press, 1932).

21. Steve Olson and Dean R. Gerstein, *Alcohol in America: Taking Action to Prevent Abuse* (Washington, DC: National Academy Press, 1985), p. 49.

22. Moore and Gerstein, *Alcohol and Public Policy*, pp. 63–64.

23. Robin Room and James Mosher, "Out of the Shadow of Treatment: A Role for Regulatory Agencies in the Prevention of Alcohol Problems," *Alcohol Health & Research World*, Vol. 4, No. 2 (1979–80), p. 11.

24. Moore and Gerstein, *Alcohol and Public Policy*, p. 65.

25. Olson and Gerstein, *Alcohol in America*, p. 59.

26. Philip J. Cook, "Increasing the Federal Alcohol Excise Tax," in Dean R. Gerstein (Ed.), *Toward the Prevention of Alcohol Problems: Government, Business, and Community Action* (Washington, DC: National Academy Press, 1984), pp. 24–56.

27. Philip J. Cook, "The Effect of Liquor Taxes on Drinking, Cirrhosis, and Auto Accidents," in Moore and Gerstein, *Alcohol and Public Policy*, pp. 255–285.

28. Robert E. Popham, Wolfgang Schmidt, and Jan DeLint, "The Effects of Legal Restraint on Drinking," in Benjamin Kissin and Henri Begleiter (Eds.), *The Biology of Alcoholism, Volume 4, Social Aspects of Alcoholism* (New York: Plenum Press, 1976), pp. 579–625.

29. Sully Ledermann, *Alcool-Alcoolisme-Alcoolisation, Donnees Scientifiques de caractere physiologique, economique et social*, Institut National d'Etudes Demographiques, Travaux et Documents, Cahier No. 29 (Paris: Presses Universitaires de France, 1956).

30. Ole-Jorgen Skog, *Alkoholkonsumets fordeling i befolkningen.* (Oslo: National Institute for Alcohol Research, 1971).

31. Olson and Gerstein, *Alcohol in America*, pp. 53–54.

32. Gerstein, *Toward the Prevention*, pp. 43–44.

33. Robert E. Popham, W. Schmidt, and J. DeLint, "Government Control Measures to Prevent Hazardous Drinking," in John A. Ewing and Beatrice A. Rouse (Eds.), *Drinking* (Chicago: Nelson-Hall, 1978).

34. Popham et al., "The Effects of Legal Restraint," pp. 579–625.

35. Reginald G. Smart, "The Relationship of Availability of Alcoholic Beverages to Per Capita Consumption and Alcoholism Rates," *Journal of Studies on Alcohol*, Vol. 38, No. 5 (1977), pp. 891–896.

36. White, *Drug Dependence*, p. 186.

37. Popham et al., "The Effects of Legal Restraint," pp. 579–625.

38. J. Hoadley, B. Fuchs, and H. Holder, "The Effect of Alcohol Beverage Restrictions on Consumption: A 25-Year Longitudinal Analysis," *American Journal of Drug and Alcohol Abuse*, Vol. 10 (1984), pp. 375–401.

39. J. Blose and H. Holder, "Liquor-by-the-Drink and Alcohol-Related Traffic Crashes: A Natural Experiment Using Time-Series Analysis," *Journal of Studies on Alcohol*, Vol. 48 (1987), pp. 52–60.

40. S. MacDonald, *The Impact of Increased Availability of Wine in Grocery Stores on Consumption: Four Case Histories* (Toronto: Addiction Research Foundation, 1985).

41. Olson and Gerstein, *Alcohol in America*, p. 57.

42. Ibid., p. 73.

43. Public Health Service, Alcohol, Drug Abuse, and Mental Health Administration, National Institute on Alcohol Abuse and Alcoholism, *Sixth Special Report to the Congress on Alcohol and Health*, DHHS Publication No. (ADM) 87-1519 (Washington, DC: U.S. Department of Health and Human Services, 1987), p. 103.

44. P. Cook and G. Tauchen, "The Effect of Minimum Drinking Age Legislation on Youthful Auto Fatalities, 1970–1977," *Journal of Legal Studies*, Vol. 13 (1984), pp. 169–190.

45. Robert D. Arnold, *Effect of Raising the Legal Drinking Age on Driver Involvement in Fatal Crashes: The Experience of Thirteen States*, NHTSA Technical Report, DOT HS 806 902 (Washington, DC: U.S. Government Printing Office, 1985).

46. A. Williams, P. Zador, and R. Karpf, "The Effect of Raising the Legal Minimum Drinking Age on Involvement in Fatal Crashes," *Journal of Legal Studies*, Vol. 12 (1983), pp. 169–179.

47. National Institute on Alcohol Abuse and Alcoholism, *Alcohol Alert*, No. 31, PH362, January 1996.

48. Ibid.

49. Ibid.

50. Moore and Gerstein, *Alcohol and Public Policy*, p. 83.

51. American Bar Association, Criminal Justice Section, *Drunk Driving Laws & Enforcement: An Assessment of Effectiveness* (New York: Sage Foundation, 1986), p. 31.

52. H. Laurence Ross, "Law, Science, and Accidents: The British Road Safety Act of 1967," *The Journal of Legal Studies*, Vol. 2, No. 1 (1973), pp. 1–78.

53. Paul Levy, Robert Voas, Penelope Johnson, and Terry M. Klein, "An Evaluation of the Department of Transportation's Alcohol Safety Action Projects," *Journal of Safety Research*, Vol. 10, No. 1 (1978), pp. 162–176.

54. Florida Department of Law Enforcement, unpublished report. (Tallahassee, August 1990).

55. ABA, *Drunk Driving Laws*, p. 101.

56. Ibid., p. 105.

57. Ibid., pp. 3–6.

58. *People v. Bartley*, No. 60593 (Ill. Sup. Ct., Nov. 21, 1985); *State v. Deskins*, 234 Kan. 529, 647 P.2d 1174 (1983); and *People v. Scott*, 63 N.Y 2d 518, 473 N.E. 2d 1, 483 N.R.S. 2d 649 (1984).

59. USDOJ, *Report to the Nation*, p. 7.

60. U.S. Department of Justice (USDOJ), Bureau of Justice Statistics, *Special Report: Drunk Driving*, Report NCJ-109945, February 1988.

61. C. Aaron McNeece, "The Impact of Minimum Age Legislation on Alcohol-Related juvenile Offenses," paper presented at the annual meeting of the Academy of Criminal Justice Sciences, San Francisco, 1988.

62. National Highway Traffic Safety Administration, *A Digest of State Alcohol Highway Safety Related Legislation (1983–87)* (Washington, DC: The Administration, 1988).

63. BJS, *Drunk Driving*, pp. 2–3.

64. ABA, *Drunk Driving Laws*, p. 107.

65. *Rappaport v. Nichols*, 31 N.J. 188, 156 A.2d 1 (1959).

66. *Kelly v. Gwinnell*, 96 NJ. 538, 476 A.2d 1219 (1984).

67. ABA, *Drunk Driving Laws*, p. 108.

68. Olson and Gerstein, *Alcohol in America*, p. 67.

69. Michael Massing, "What Ever Happened to the War on Drugs?" *New York Review of Books*, Vol. 39, No. 11 (June 11, 1992), pp. 42–46.

70. Ethan A. Nadelman and Jann S. Werner, "Toward a Sane National Drug Policy" *Rolling Stone*, May 5, 1994, pp. 24–26.

71. Michael Massing, "What Ever Happened to the War on Drugs?" p. 42.

72. Inciardi, "Editor's Instruction," p. 237.

73. University of Michigan News and Information Services Press Release, Monitoring the Future," December 11, 1995.

74. Franklin E. Zimrig and Gordon Hawkins, *The Search for Rational Drug Control* (Cambridge: Cambridge University Press, 1992).

75. U.S. General Accounting Office, *Controlling Drug Abuse: A Status Report*, Special Report from the Comptroller General of the United States (Washington, DC: U.S. Government Printing Office, March 1, 1988), p. 2.

76. U.S. Congress, Hearings, p. 137.

77. Ibid., p. 59.

78. Ibid., p. 27.

79. *National Review*, "The War on Drugs Is Lost." Vol. 48, No. 2 (February 12, 1996).

80. *Journal of the American Medical Association*, "Change of Heart, Perhaps, but Not of Legislation." Vol. 271, No. 21 (June 1, 1994), pp. 1635–1639.

81. Karst J. Besteman, "War Is Not the Answer," *American Behavioral Scientist*, Vol. 32, No. 3 (1989), pp. 290–293.

82. Nora S. Gustavson, "The War Metaphor: A Threat to Vulnerable Populations," *Social Work*, Vol. 36, No. 4 (July 1991), pp. 277–278.

83. Elaine Shannon, "A Losing Battle," *Time*, December 3, 1990, p. 44.

84. Inciardi, "Editor's Introduction," p. 239.

85. Shannon, "A Losing Battle," p. 44.

86. Florida Department of Corrections, unpublished report. Tallahassee, July 1991.

87. Inciardi, "Editor's Introduction," p. 238.

88. Richard J. Dennis, "The Economics of Legalizing Drugs," *The Atlantic Monthly*, November 1990, p. 129.

89. U.S. Department of Justice, Drug Enforcement Administration, National Narcotics Intelligence Consumers Committee 1995, *The Supply of Illicit Drugs to the United States*, August 1996.

90. Dennis, "The Economics of Legalizing Drugs," p. 126.

91. Ibid., p. 130.

92. Ibid.

93. Bruce L. Benson and David W. Rasmussen, *The Economic Anatomy of a Drug War: Criminal Justice in the Commons* (Latham, MD: Rowman & Littlefield), 1994.

94. James A. Inciardi and Duane C. McBride, "Legalization: A High-Risk Alternative in the War on Drugs," *American Behavioral Scientist*, Vol. 32, No. 3 (1989), pp. 259–289.

95. University of Michigan News and Information Services Press Release, "Monitoring the Future." December 11, 1995.

96. Lindesmith Center, "Drug Prohibition and the U.S. Prison System." http://www.lindesmith.org/tlcprfct.html December 13, 1996, p. 2.

97. Cited in *Join Together: A National Resource for Communities Fighting Substance Abuse* (//gopher.igc.apc.org:298810JT-NEWS-DRUG/r.873808357.2188.6) on September 8, 1997.

98. Cited in *National Clearinghouse for Alcohol and Drug Issues.* Homepage (http://www/health.org/pressure/alcart.htm) on September 9, 1997; and E. A. Nadelmann, "The Case for Legalization," *Public Interest*, Vol. 92, No. 3 (1988).

99. *Join Together: A National Resource for Communities Fighting Substance Abuse*, September 8, 1997.

100. A. M. Bradley, "A Capsule Review of the State of the Art: the Sixth Special Report to the U.S. Congress on Alcohol and Health," *Alcohol Health & Research World*, Vol. 4 (Summer 1987).

101. Nannette Lehmann and Steven L. Drupp, "Incidence of Alcohol-Related Domestic Violence," *Alcohol Health and Research World* (Winter 1983/84), pp. 23–27 and 39.

102. Paul B. Stares, "Drug Legalization: Time for a Real Debate," *The Brookings Review* (Spring 1996), pp. 18–20.

103. David W. Rasmussen and Bruce L. Benson, *Drug Offenders in Florida* (Tallahassee: Policy Sciences Program, Florida State University, July 1990), p. 3.

104. U.S. Department of Justice (USDOJ), Office of Justice Programs, National Institute of Justice, 1988 *Drug Use Forecasting Annual Report*, March 1990.

105. Edwin Lemert, *Social Pathology: A Systematic Approach to the Theory of Sociopathic Behavior* (New York: McGraw-Hill, 1966).

106. Paul Tappan, *Crime, Justice, and Correction* (New York: McGraw-Hill, 1960).

107. Fred Goldman, "Drug Abuse, Crime and Economics: The Dismal Limits of Social Choice," in James A. Inciardi (Ed.), *The Drugs-Crime Connection* (Beverly Hills, CA: Sage Publications, 1981), pp. 155–181.

108. Roger Langley and Richard C. Levy, *Wife Beating: The Silent Crisis* (New York: E. P. Dutton, 1977).

109. Natalie Shainess, "Psychological Aspects of Wifebattering," in M. Roy (Ed.), *Battered Women* (New York: Van Nostrand Reinhold, 1977).

110. Albert R. Roberts, "Psychosocial Characteristics of Batterers: A Study of 234 Men Charged with Domestic Violence Offenses," *Journal of Family Violence*, Vol. 2, No. 1 (1987), pp. 81–93.

111. Albert R. Roberts, "Substance Abuse Among Men Who Batter Their Mates," *Journal of Substance Abuse Treatment*, Vol. 5 (1988), pp. 83–87.

112. Jason M. White, *Drug Dependence* (Englewood Cliffs, NJ: Prentice Hall, 1991), p. 143.

113. Janet Wright, "Domestic Violence and Substance Abuse: A Cooperative Approach Toward Working with Dually Affected Families," in Edith M. Freeniati (Ed.), *Social Work Practice with Clients Who Have Alcohol Problems* (Springfield, IL: Charles C Thomas, 1985), pp. 25–39.

114. Steven Belenko, "The Impact of Drug Offenders on the Criminal.justice System," in Ralph Weisheit (Ed.), *Drugs, Crime and the Criminal Justice System* (Cincinnati, OH: Anderson, 1990), p. 27.

115. U.S. Department of Justice (USDOJ), Bureau of Justice Statistics, *Report to the Nation on Crime and Justice* 2nd ed., Report No. NCJ-105506, March 1988, p. 14.

116. Bureau of Justice Statistics, *Correctional Populations in the United States, 1994* (Washington, DC: Government Printing Office) Report No. NCJ-160091, June 1996, p. 10.

117. Office of Juvenile Justice and Delinquency Prevention, *Juvenile Offenders and Victims: 1996 Update on Violence* (Washington, DC: Government Printing Office) Report No. NCJ-15910, February 1996.

118. U.S. Department of Justice, Office of Justice Programs, Bureau of Justice Statistics, *Prisoners in 1996.* NCJ Report 3 NCJ-16419, June 1997.

119. Ibid.

120. Ibid.

121. U.S. Department of Justice, Bureau of Justice Statistics, *Profile of State Prison Inmates*, Report No. NCJ-109926, January 1988.

122. National Institute of Justice, U.S. Department of Justice, Office of Justice Programs, *1995 Drug Use Forecasting Annual Report on Adult and Juvenile Arrestees*, June 1996.

123. U.S. Department of Justice, Office of Justice Programs, OJJDP, *Juvenile Arrests, 1995.* Juvenile Justice Bulletin, February 1997, p. 1.

124. Ibid., p. 2.

125. Florida Department of Health and Rehabilitative Services, Children Youth and Families Program Office, *Preliminary Data Report: Florida Offenders Under the Age of 18 Sentenced to Adult Prisons* (Tallahassee: The Department, 1989).

126. Department of Health and Rehabilitative Services, Children, Youth and Family Services, *Delinquents Charged with Drug Offenses in Florida* (Tallahassee: The Department, 1989).

127. Huizinga et al., "Delinquency and Drug Use," p. 448.

128. John C. Ball, J. W. Shaffer, and D. N. Nurco, "Day to Day Criminality of Heroin Addicts in Baltimore—A Study in the Continuity of Offense Rates," *Drug and Alcohol Dependence*, Vol. 12 (1983), pp. 119–142.

129. John C. Ball, Lawrence Rosen, John A. Flueck, and David N. Nurco, "Lifetime Criminality of Heroin Addicts in the United States," *Journal of Drug Issues* (Summer 1982), pp. 225–238.

130. B. Johnson, P. Goldstein, E. Preble, J. Schmeidler, D. Lipton, B. Spunt, and T. Miller, *Taking Care, of Business: The Economics of Crime by Heroin Abusers* (Lexington, MA: Lexington Books, 1985).

131. Howard B. Kaplan and Kelly R. Damphousse, "Self-Attitudes and Antisocial Personality as Moderators of the Drug Use-Violence Relationship," in Howard B. Kaplan (Ed.), *Drugs, Crime and Other Deviant Adaptations: Longitudinal Studies* (New York: Plenum Press, 1995), pp. 187–210.

132. Michael J. Hindelang, Michael R. Gottfredson, and James Garofalo, *Victims of Personal Crime: An Empirical Foundation for a Theory of Personal Victimization* (Cambridge, MA: Ballinger, 1978).

133. James R. Lasley, "Drinking Routines/Lifestyles and Predatory Victimization: A Causal Analysis," *Justice Quarterly*, Vol. 6, No. 4 (December 1989), pp. 529–542.

134. American Humane Association, *Highlights of Official Child Neglect and Abuse Reporting* (Denver, CO: American Humane Association, 1988).

135. National Committee to Parent-Child Abuse, April 1995.

136. Murray A. Straus, "A Sociological Perspective on the Prevention and Treatment of Wifebeating," in M. Roy (Ed.), *Battered Women* (New York: Van Nostrand Reinhold, 1977).

137. Larry W. Bennett, "Substance Abuse and the Domestic Assult of Women," *Social Work*, Vol. 40, No. 6 (1995), pp. 760–771.

138. C. Y. McCormick, "Battered Women—The Last Resort," survey by Cook County Department of Corrections, Chicago, 1977.

139. Murray A. Straus, "Causes, Treatment and Research Needs," in U.S. Commission on Civil Rights, *Battered*

Women: Issue of Public Policy (Washington, DC: The Commission, 1978).

140. Langley and Levy, *Wife Beating*, 1977.

141. Henry Kempe and Ray E. Helfer, *Helping the Battered Child and His Family* (New York: Lippincott, 1972).

142. Gisela Spieker, "Family Violence and Alcohol Abuse," paper presented at the 24th International Institute on Prevention and Treatment of Alcoholism, Zurich, 1978.

143. Maria Roy, "Current Survey of 150 Cases," in Roy, *Battered Women*.

144. Albert R. Roberts, "Substance Abuse among Men Who Batter Their Mates," *Journal of Substance Abuse Treatment*, Vol. 5 (1988), pp. 83–87.

145. Sidney Cohen, *The Substance Abuse Problems* (New York: Haworth Press, 1981), pp. 358–359.

146. D. H. Coleman and M. A. Straus, "Alcohol Abuse and Family Violence," paper presented at the American Sociological Association Annual Meeting, 1979.

147. USDOJ, *FY 1988 Report*, p. 13.

148. Ibid.

149. Ibid., p. 14.

150. Ibid., p. 15.

151. James Austin and Aaron D. McVey, "The 1989 NCCD Prison Population Forecast: The Impact of the War on Drugs," *NCCD Focus* (December 1989), p. 1.

152. Criminal Justice Estimating Conference, *Final Report of the Florida Consensus*, February 23, 1989.

153. Ibid.

154. James Austin and William Elms, *Parole, Outcome in California: The Consequences of Determinate Sentencing, Punishment, and Incapacitation on Parole Performance* (San Francisco: NCCD, 1989).

155. Criminal Justice Estimating Conference, *Final Report*.

156. U.S. Department of Justice, Office of Justice Programs, Bureau of Justice Statistics, *Correctional Populations in the United States, 1995*. Report NCJ-163916, May 1997.

157. National Institute on Drug Abuse, *Drug Abuse Treatment in Prisons*, Treatment Research Reports (Rockville, MD: The Institute, 1981).

158. Marcia R. Chaiken, "Prison Programs for Drug-Involved Offenders," National Institute of Justice, *Research in Action* (October 1989), p. 1.

159. U.S. Department of Justice, Office of Justice Programs, Bureau of Justice Statistics. *Correctional Populations in the United States, 1995*. Report NCJ-163916, May 1997.

160. Chaiken, "Prison Programs for Drug-Involved Offenders," p. 2.

161. Marcia R. Chaiken, *In-Prison Programs for Drug-Involved Offenders*, U.S. Department of Justice, National Institute of Justice, Office of Communication and Research Utilization (Washington, DC: The Department, July 1989).

162. Francis T. Cullen and Paul Gendreau, "The Effectiveness of Correctional Rehabilitation: Reconsidering the 'Nothing Works' Debate," in Lynne Goodstein and Doris Layton MacKenzie (Eds.), *The American Prison: Issues in Research and Policy* (New York: Plenum Press, 1989), pp. 35–36.

163. Gennaro F. Vito, "The Kentucky Substance Abuse Program: A Private Program to Treat Probationers and Parolees," *Federal Probation*, Vol. 15, No. 1 (March 1989), pp. 65–72.

164. Gary Field, "The Effects of Intensive Treatment on Reducing the Criminal Recidivism of Addicted Offenders," *Federal Probation*, Vol. 53, No. 4 (December 1989), pp. 51–56.

165. M. Douglas Anglin, "The Efficacy of Civil Commitment in Treating Narcotic Addiction," *Compulsory Treatment of Drug Abuse: Research and Clinical Practice*, National Institute on Drug Abuse, Research Monograph Series No. 86 (Rockville, MD: The Institute, 1988), pp. 8–34.

166. James F. Maddux, "Clinical Experience with Civil Commitment," *Compulsory Treatment of Drug Abuse*, pp. 35–56.

167. Robert L. Hubbard, James J. Collins, J. Valley Rachal, and Elizabeth R. Cavanaugh, *Compulsory Treatment of Drug Abuse*, pp. 57–98.

168. Herman Joseph, "The Criminal Justice System and Opiate Addiction: A Historical Perspective," *Compulsory Treatment of Drug Abuse*, pp. 106–125.

169. William A. McKim, *Drugs and Behavior: An Introduction to Behavioral Pharmacology*, 2nd ed. (Englewood Cliffs, NJ: Prentice Hall, 1990), p. 245.

170. George De Leon, "Legal Pressure in Therapeutic Communities," *Compulsory Treatment of Drug Abuse*, pp. 160–177.

171. Gerstein and Harwood, *Treating Drug Problems*.

172. C. Aaron McNeece, *Substance Abuse Treatment Program Evaluation Project* (Tallahassee: Florida State University, Institute for Health and Human Services, December 1991).

173. Tam Stewart, *The Heroin Users* (London: Pandora, 1987), p. 77.

174. Twentieth Century Fund Task Force on Sentencing Policy toward Young Offenders, *Confronting Youth Crime* (New York: Holmes & Meier, 1978).

PART THREE

Chemical Dependency in Special Populations

Part Three addresses chemical dependency in several special population groups. Chapter 9 discusses alcohol and drug problems among children and adolescents. Most young people continue to experiment with alcohol, and the percentages of high school students using other drugs, such as marijuana, has been steadily increasing since 1991. The problem may be even more serious than the data indicate, since drug use among youths who are school dropouts or who are in institutions is not taken into account by most surveys. These young people are not included in the large surveys of drug use, which generally rely on samples of students in regular school classes.

Consistent with the systems approach of this book, Chapter 10 discusses substance abuse from a family systems perspective. Other views of chemical dependency, which focus more on the individual with alcohol or drug problems as part of a family constellation, are also presented. Given the large number of substance abusers in the United States, many family members (both in traditional and nontraditional families) are affected by these problems. Attention is also directed to some of the newer concepts that have emerged in the chemical dependency field such as codependency and adult children of alcoholics.

The focus in Chapters 11, 12, and 13 is on groups that have experienced considerable oppression or isolation, the use of chemicals among these groups, and related problems. Chapter 11 concerns ethnicity. Since it is impossible to describe every ethnic group found in the United States, we consider those that are represented in the greatest numbers. There is considerable ethnic variation in the use of alcohol and other drugs, and ethnic and cultural factors also have implications for prevention, intervention, and treatment. The issue of the rights of gays and lesbians has received increased attention in all sectors of society, from housing and employment to the church and the military. Chapter 12 is devoted to the subject of chemical dependency among these groups, with a particular emphasis on the defenses used by gays and lesbians for psychological protection, and with the issue of whether treatment with or separate from heterosexuals should be promoted. Chapter 13 is concerned with substance abuse and dependency among people with a variety of other physical and mental disabilities. The Americans with Disabilities Act of 1990 has increased awareness of individuals with disabilities. For at least the last decade, chemical dependency professionals and rehabilitation professionals have been concerned with the combination of substance disorders and other disabilities and with efforts to promote integrated treatment of these conditions.

Older persons are the subject of Chapter 14. In general, alcohol and illicit drug use remit with age, and those with serious alcohol and drug problems often fail to live to old age. But a number of alcoholics and addicts defy the odds and live a long life. In other cases, problems with alcohol and drugs can emerge during the later phases of the life cycle due to physical, psychological, or social changes. Finally, Chapter 15 is concerned with gender. Similarities and differences in chemical use and abuse between men and women are discussed, since it cannot be assumed that theory, research, and practice pertaining to persons of one gender can be applied to those of the other gender. Particular attention is paid to the special needs of women, since they have often been ignored.

Each of the seven chapters in Part Three focuses on specific groups, but common threads run through each chapter. First, we address the incidence and prevalence of substance abuse and dependence in each group to the extent that the empirical literature allows. In some cases, such as for men and women, considerable research has been done to identify the extent of alcohol and drug problems. Although methodological problems taint studies of most groups, it has been especially difficult to get a good picture of the substance abuse among some groups, such as gays and lesbians. A second theme is the emphasis we have placed on research about the various aspects of chemical dependency, incidence, prevalence, characteristics of abusers, prevention, treatment, and so forth. Sound theory is the basis of good practice, and theory that has been empirically tested is especially useful. Many topics we have covered, important as they may be, have not been subjected to much empirical testing. We suggest that readers critically evaluate all the material provided, including empirical studies, which frequently suffer from methodological problems such as poor controls for internal validity and limited generalizability.

A third theme that deserves mention is the practical concerns of professionals. Suggestions for prevention, intervention, treatment, aftercare, and follow-up are sprinkled throughout the chapters. Much more creativity is needed, however, and we hope that these pages might spur readers to think about fresh alternatives. Fourth, our concern about the practical has also led us to provide not only extensive lists of references to which readers may wish to refer but also to information on resources in various parts of the country that might prove helpful—that is, places where professionals might call and talk with others, share experiences, and obtain suggestions. Chapters 9 and 10 present case examples. Individual cases are not always easily generalized to the clients or practice situations of readers, but they are an attempt to illustrate the real-life complexities faced by clients and professionals in the chemical dependency field. The case illustrations are also designed to provide better integration of the theoretical and empirical material provided in the chapters.

9

Treating Chemically Dependent Children and Adolescents

Thomas E. Smith
Florida State University

David W. Springer
University of Texas at Austin

There are no simple explanations of why children and adolescents use licit and illicit drugs.[1] Nor is it clear that most drug-using children and adolescents meet diagnostic criteria to justify diagnoses of alcohol dependency and drug dependency. Thus, social workers should guard against the casual acceptance of diagnoses in children and adolescents. In part, the problem is one of definition. As was discussed in earlier chapters, serious definitional problems exist in assessing substance abuse and dependency. However, with children and adolescents, giving and accepting diagnoses may become a prophecy of lifetime difficulties. On the other hand, to ignore symptoms of a child's substance abuse difficulties constitutes negligence. This dilemma is exacerbated by the recent trends in substance abuse found among youths in the United States. The use of drugs among U.S. junior and high school students increased in 1995, continuing a trend dating to 1991 among eighth-grade students and to 1992 among tenth- and twelfth-grade students.[2]

These findings are from the Monitoring the Future study, which is a series of annual surveys of about 50,000 students in over 400 public and private secondary schools nationwide conducted since 1975 by the University of Michigan Survey Research Center. According to the most recent publication of this series,[3] marijuana use has experienced the sharpest increase, and the use of various other illicit drugs such as LSD, hallucinogens other than LSD, amphetamines, stimulants, and inhalants has also continued to increase. In fact, the proportion of eighth-graders taking any illicit drug in the 12 months prior to the survey almost doubled (from 11 to 21 percent) since 1991, and the proportion using any illicit drugs in the prior 12 months rose nearly two-thirds (from 20 to 33 percent) among tenth-grade students and by nearly half (from 27 to 39 percent) among twelfth-graders.[4] Alcohol use among U.S. secondary students generally has remained stable in the past few years, although a small increase has been seen among twelfth-graders over the past two years.[5]

This chapter's intention is to provide a primer on walking the fine line between an uncritical acceptance of unwarranted labels and negligent practice. To accomplish this goal, the chapter will examine chemical dependency treatment for children and adolescents from the perspective of developmental and contextual factors and the perspective of treatment modality.

Developmental and Contextual Factors

Because children and adolescents are experiencing rapid physiological, sociocultural, and psychological development, treatment strategies traditionally designed for adults must be adapted with developmental concerns in mind. There are critical legal, social, psychological, and cultural systems to consider when treating children and adolescents for alcohol and drug problems. Failure to assess any one of the systems accurately can result in ineffective treatment that leaves the child or adolescent vulnerable to increased alcohol and drug use and the family angered by insensitive practice.

Viewing presenting symptoms by a substance-abusing child or adolescent from a developmental framework provides a more inclusive perspective for social workers who are searching for an appropriate treatment strategy. The first developmental question is: What level of medical risk does the substance use have for a child or adolescent? The second developmental question is: What meaning does the child or adolescent ascribe to the substance use? After a discussion of the medical context of substance abuse, the second question is discussed in terms of its legal, social, and educational implications.

Medical and Psychiatric Context

The full extent of medical risk to a child's development caused by substance abuse cannot be easily assessed. Although catastrophic outcomes for children are frequently predicted when they use different addictive substances, conclusive studies for all drugs are not available. For example, Kandel and associates found that different drugs had different constellations of consequences for adolescents.[6] In general, substance abuse represents one of many risk factors that influence a child's physiological development. Other risk factors—such as poor nutrition, lack of sleep, and inadequate exercise—also can adversely affect development.[7] Yet another area of risk factors is in family functioning. For example, having alcoholic parents presents a significant risk factor associated with the offspring's development of alcohol dependency.[8] Balanced against these risk factors is a child's resiliency. Resiliency represents a child's ability to overcome adverse events in his or her life.[9] Although resiliency in children is not well understood, it helps explain why some children can overcome adversity and live seemingly normal lives, while other children succumb.

Among the more serious consequences for chemically dependent children and adolescents is a rise in emotional difficulties.[10] The co-occurrence of severe emotional difficulties and drug abuse is not a coincidence. Some adolescents may use drugs as a means of coping with the tribulations that they experience. For others, drug use exacerbates serious emotional disorders. Studies suggest a prominent role for substance use in the etiology and prognosis of psychiatric disorders, such as affective disorders, conduct disorders and antisocial personality disorders, attention-deficit hyperactivity disorders, and anxiety disorders. Psychiatric disorders also appear to play a crucial role in the etiology of and vulnerability to substance use problems in youths.[11] Thus, the presence of substance abuse and dependency in youths may be a harbinger of serious emotional difficulties; treatment will need to address both conditions concurrently.

A recent ominous risk factor is the possibility of human immunodeficiency virus (HIV) infection and subsequent development of AIDS.[12] Experimentation has always been a defining characteristic in the normative development of children and adolescents. The spread of HIV has made such experimentation increasingly dangerous.

Children and adolescents who use intravenous drugs and who are sexually active place themselves at a high risk to contract the virus. Although drug use and promiscuity have typically been part of what has been labeled as *problem behavior complex* or *syndrome*, the level of medical risk for enacting such behaviors has risen dramatically in the last several decades.[13]

The implication of ideas such as risk factors and resiliency is that no simple formula exists that can predict the effects of drug use on children. Not all drugs will affect all children in any predictable way. However, it cannot be disputed that reducing risk factors and increasing resiliency are beneficial for children. Efforts to ensure that children receive nutritious meals, are fully rested, exercise properly, and avoid harmful substances will assist them to develop to their fullest potential.

Legal Context

The threat of litigation significantly affects practice decisions. The litigious stance of clients is complex and not easily analyzed. It is sufficient to note that social workers today, more so than ever before, must be cognizant of clients' expectations and up-to-date practice wisdom.

When children and adolescents are brought into a social worker's office, parents frequently expect social workers to employ professional methods to remedy the social, psychological, and familial problems brought on by substance abuse. Such an expectation is unfortunate, because social workers do not have any single intervention that can dramatically "cure" children's or adolescents' substance use and abuse. Because alcohol and drug treatments in the United States are heavily influenced by Twelve-Step programs that sometimes make dramatic claims of success, social workers should carefully explain the limitations of available treatment. Otherwise, parents may expect dramatic and lasting results from treatment and may be angered by "failure."[14]

Further, if parents do not understand their role in treatment, it is not surprising that they become increasingly vocal in their complaints about progress. To provide a partial remedy to these legal pitfalls, social workers must avoid endorsing treatment methods that run counter to published literature and practice wisdom. Unfortunately, published literature and practice wisdom do not always provide useful guidance in knowing what interventions to implement with troubled children and adolescents.

In any event, the child's or adolescent's legal standing must be considered when planning treatment. Although the age of consent varies from state to state, parents and guardians must give explicit consent before treatment can begin with minor children. Social workers should examine closely their agencies' guidelines on who can give informed consent for what procedures before undertaking treatment. Drug-abusing children's and adolescents' relationships with parents and/or guardians may be strained, providing fertile grounds for misunderstandings. By remembering that children and adolescents may, in many cases, be unable to give informed consent to proceed with treatment, social workers should from the very start incorporate parents into treatment planning and implementation.[15]

Although homilies about informed consent may seem elementary, such considerations are critical with substance-abusing adolescents. It may not always be clear whether coercion has been used in placing the child or adolescent into treatment. The level of compliance with treatment directives may, in part, hinge on social workers' precise understanding of who initiated and who is maintaining interest in treatment. When parents initiate their children's or adolescents' entry into treatment, social workers will be faced with the unenviable task of gaining a child's or adolescent's cooperation without criticizing his or her parents.

Social Context

The meaning and function of drug use among children and adolescents are important considerations in planning and delivering treatment. Drug use and misuse can be seen as a disease, as a bad habit, as an indication of family dysfunction, or as a symptom of a mental disorder. Depending on how individuals construe drug dependency, reactions will differ for children and adolescents who are experiencing problems associated with drug use and misuse. Social workers must allow the afflicted child or adolescent, parents, friends, teachers, collaterals, and others to voice their understanding of drug abuse.

A child's or adolescent's misperceptions about how others perceive the drug use and misuse may pose a hindrance to successful treatment.[16] If, for example, a child or adolescent believes that others are morally critical of him or her, acrimonious arguments may ensue. On the other hand, if a child or adolescent thinks of the drug use and misuse as a disease, then it might eliminate some of the acrimonious arguments but encourage irresponsible, "I'm-not-responsible-because-I'm-sick" statements. In any event, understanding how the child or adolescent perceives others' evaluations of him or her may provide useful insights. Not surprisingly, treatment that incorporates the child's understanding of others' perceptions is most likely to avoid uncooperative and hostile attitudes.

In addition to assessing accurately the child's or adolescent's understanding of others' perceptions, social workers should examine the meaning of the drug itself. The child's or adolescent's understanding or "relationship" to drugs can frequently assist social workers in planning treatment. Chapter 3 discussed the impact of addicts' expectations regarding the effects of drugs. The reasoning is that using drugs will invariably have a specific effect. Such use eventually creates a relationship between the child or adolescent and the drug. By expecting and receiving a specific effect when using drugs, children and adolescents may come to trust the drug and perceive it as a "friend." As a result, sadness is a natural consequence with the cessation of drug use. A child or adolescent who may not have other friends may consider a drug to be his or her best friend. Treatment that focuses on resolution of the grief that follows a significant loss should be planned.

Educational Context

After homelife, a child's or adolescent's experiences in school help form the attitudes and provide the market that allows drug use. By its nature, the school provides a meeting place for children and adolescents who may engage in drug use as a social activity.[17] During childhood and adolescence, the importance of social activity among peers cannot be overemphasized. Children and adolescents observe, learn, and speak with each other, and by so doing become socialized into the common culture of that school. Such intense activities that include drug use will interfere with educational activities in two ways. First, performance in the classroom will suffer. Documentation of the problems caused by drug use is widespread; attention, memory, and information processing are among the areas adversely affected by drug use.[18] Second, drug use is associated with conflict. Although conflicts are not inevitable with drug use, they occur with alarming frequency. Disputes over payment and extortion to secure payment for drugs can result in violent conflict that reduces confidence in the safety of school settings for all students.

To summarize these last few pages, the foremost rule that cannot be overemphasized is that the child or adolescent should not be viewed out of his or her legal, social, psychological, or cultural context. Such contexts provide social workers with the necessary background in undertaking drug and alcohol interventions. Although drugs have specific physiological effects, their use and meaning derive from their legal, social, and psychological contexts. From this perspective, it is not possible to understand chemical dependency in children and adolescents without considering the contexts in which use takes place.

Substance Abuse Treatment

The treatment modalities that will be discussed in this chapter are by no means the only ones available. In fact, it can be argued that social workers develop their own modalities in accordance with their idiosyncratic abilities. Further, few treatment modalities provide a standard, reliable set of procedures that define their successful implementation. Treatment modalities are generally a loose compilation of interventive techniques, practice beliefs, and ontological assumptions. Because they vary so widely in their implementation, it is difficult to state with any confidence that any one type of treatment will be effective.

In considering what type of treatment modality is best suited for preventing and remediating clients' problems, social workers should consider many issues in addition to reputed effectiveness. Issues such as cost, predicted compliance with treatment procedures, and level of family involvement are also important. The choice of treatment methods must take into account their degree of intrusiveness.

Thus, primary prevention efforts that consist solely of educational efforts are the least intrusive, require the least involvement, and can be implemented in many settings. Outpatient treatment and community self-help groups (e.g., Alcoholics Anonymous) are the next level of treatment. Two forms of outpatient treatment commonly used today are partial hospitalization programs (PHPs) and intensive outpatient programs (IOPs). These approaches are often used as alternatives to inpatient treatment, which is directly related to the growth of managed care over recent years. Inpatient treatment is a third level of treatment, which is usually implemented in a hospital setting. The last and most intrusive level of treatment is residential treatment and treatment communities. These are used less commonly to treat children and adolescents with substance abuse problems than even a few years ago. Again, this is related to the increased presence of the managed care industry, which seeks the least intrusive treatment methods. (In fact, a dual diagnosis is often required to warrant payment of inpatient or residential treatment from third-party payers.) Generally, the least intrusive treatment methods will cost less, demand the least family involvement, and require the least disruption in day-to-day activities. More intrusive treatment methods are much more expensive and typically better suited

when there is a medical risk, danger of suicide or homicide, or uncontrolled behavior that might result in harm to self or others.

The managed care industry has had a significant impact on the treatment of children and adolescents over recent years, and warrants special attention. Therefore, a discussion of managed care and dual diagnoses will be provided before exploring various approaches to treatment.

Managed Care and Dual Diagnoses

"The management of client care is designed to meet two major goals: controlling costs while ensuring the quality of care."[19] In general terms, managed care attempts to regulate services, restrict who is authorized to provide services, determine who truly *needs* treatment, assess whether the treatment is systematic and likely to be successful, and, finally, evaluate the outcome of treatment. These assessments often come in the form of utilization reviews.

There is a reason that a discussion of dual diagnosis is introduced along with one of managed care. It is becoming increasingly difficult to warrant payment from third-party payers to treat substance abuse problems on an inpatient or residential basis. Many third-party payers, such as health maintenance organizations (HMOs), require a client to have a dual diagnosis to justify inpatient or residential treatment. Therefore, in addition to demonstrating that a diagnosis of a substance abuse problem (i.e., polysubstance dependence) is warranted, the practitioner or organization must also be able to identify and justify an Axis I diagnosis in the *Diagnostic and Statistical Manual of Mental Disorders-IV (DSM-IV)*.[20] Thus, the growth of the managed care industry has placed increasing importance on the ability of practitioners and treatment programs to justifiably identify an Axis I diagnosis to be reimbursed for services provided.

Unfortunately, there are circumstances when this exercise is abused when an Axis I diagnosis is attached to a child or adolescent just so inpatient or residential treatment can be justified to the third-party payer, when in fact such a diagnosis may not be warranted. In fact, some Axis I diagnoses receive more attention from some third-party payers than others. For example, a diagnosis of Oppositional Defiant Disorder (ODD) is not given as much concern as it once was by some third-party payers, and a diagnosis of Major Depression often needs to be accompanied by evidence of suicidal or homicidal ideation for some third-party payers to reimburse for inpatient or residential services.

This has led to an increase in the use of intensive outpatient programs and partial hospitalization programs in the field, both of which allow the child or adolescent to return home each night with his or her family rather than "live" at the facility. Otherwise, IOPs and PHPs offer many of the same services as inpatient or residential care at a lower cost. In short, goal-oriented and planned short-term treatment is being favored to longer-term treatment approaches.[21]

Utilizing short-term, outpatient treatment is not the only means of controlling costs. Another way to reduce costs of services is to use less expensive providers, such as master's-level practitioners (MSWs) instead of licensed psychiatrists or other more expensive providers. Currently, the vast majority of treatment is provided by social workers and psychologists, not psychiatrists.[22]

Much of the research on managed care views the industry as cost effective in terms of its ability to decrease hospitalization. The research on managed care effectiveness is marked by a study of inpatient mental health services before and after implementing two managed care programs aimed at cost containment.[23] The effects found seem minimal. Although a decrease in hospitalization was found, those who were admitted evidenced more serious mental illness and often included comorbidity of substance abuse as a secondary diagnosis, which in part contributed to longer lengths of stay. The findings from this study are not encouraging for the managed care industry.[24]

This brief discussion only begins to illustrate how managed care has changed the industry of substance abuse treatment for children and adolescents. Nevertheless, it is a good starting point to invite thoughtful discussion around the complexities of providing the services in the context of a field heavily affected by managed care.

Prevention

The current literature on treatment of drug use, misuse, and dependency emphasizes the complexity of preventing adolescent substance abuse. For example, Arkin discusses the need to differentiate among multiproblem youths, families, and environments in deciding prevention strategies.[25] Such recommendations, however, only highlight the conceptual quagmire of primary, secondary, and tertiary prevention strategies (see Chapter 7). Of the three strategies, only primary prevention is intended to prevent nonusing children and adolescents from beginning substance use. There is an increasing consensus that primary prevention efforts must ameliorate family and school environments to increase children's self-esteem and self-efficacy.[26] Secondary and tertiary prevention address problems of children and adolescents that are caused by varying degrees of drug involvement. Both these types of prevention strategies focus on encouraging a cessation of drug use, remediating problems, and strengthening the children's and adolescents' resiliency.[27] However, prevention works best when there is a clear target for intensive efforts. Unfortunately, there is no clear profile for identifying the neediest children and adolescents at risk for debilitating substance use.[28]

A related form of prevention efforts involves parent-led prevention programs. Such groups recommend four types of change: (1) changes in the home, (2) changes in the peer group, (3) changes in the schools, and (4) changes in the community.[29] These groups are generally formed by grass-roots movements and have modest goals. Their expectations are to raise community awareness and to coordinate with community agencies.

Overall, parent groups remain a small, albeit active, form of prevention programming.[30]

Drug Education

Traditionally, drug education has consisted of school- and districtwide teaching efforts. Drug education has been used with varying degrees of success for the last 40 years.[37] Early drug education consisted of attempts to intimidate children and adolescents from any use of illicit drugs. In general, drug education consisted of didactic presentations that described the drug, its use, and the consequences of its use. Such efforts were generally aimed at public school settings where teachers or other designated school staff were given a packet of materials to present to classes or to assemblies of students.

Both the message and the presenter frequently presented a skewed picture of drug use and misuse. The drug's potency and consequences were described in terms that were often designed to scare students. In many circumstances, older students were well versed in the use of drugs and had not experienced significant consequences. Younger students were intrigued by the presentations and, in some cases, became more interested in drugs as a result of the drug education attempts. In retrospect, one mistake was to rely on a didactic approach in a setting where teachers, in all likelihood, were not perceived as credible role models. Further, some of the teachers might have engaged in recreational use and were undoubtedly ambivalent about presenting materials that seemed incorrect. The lesson that became apparent by the beginning of the 1980s was that pure drug education campaigns needed revision both in terms of their content and their media. The ineffectiveness of such drug education programs resulted in their becoming an object of derision in the 1960s and 1970s, with Congress finally placing a moratorium on prevention.[32]

Thus, one reason for the failure of drug education programs stemmed from promoting patently incorrect information. For example, marijuana was cited as causing psychotic decompensation, juvenile delinquency, and other catastrophic consequences. When children and adolescents experimented with marijuana and failed to experience dire consequences, the credibility of scare-oriented drug education became questionable. Traditional drug education also failed because messages were designed to scare passive participants into compliance.

Differing views regarding the effectiveness of drug education efforts continue to persist in the field. Some drug educators have reported degrees of success when they employed credible information sources, avoided scare tactics, began drug education efforts in primary schools, and involved adolescents through the use of role-plays and problem-solving paradigms.[33] Some studies have shown that students who received the D.A.R.E. (Drug Abuse Resistance Education) curriculum had significantly lower use of alcohol, cigarettes, and other drugs.[34] However, the Research Triangle Institute (1994) conducted a more recent evaluation of Project D.A.R.E. and concluded that the effect of D.A.R.E.'s core curriculum is largely ineffective in preventing drug use among participating groups, and recommended shifting resources to longer-term interactive prevention programs.[35]

Outpatient and Community Self-Help Approaches

As with many aspects of treatment for adolescent chemical dependency, there are sharp disagreements on the usefulness of outpatient and community self-help programs. Although some writers believe that outpatient treatment is ineffective,[36] others argue that it is a viable option for adolescents. For example, Semlitz and Gold outlined seven criteria that they believed would justify a recommendation for outpatient treatment:

1. Absence of acute psychiatric or medical difficulties
2. Absence of chronic medical difficulties

3. Willingness to abstain from all mood-altering drugs
4. Willingness to submit random urine screens
5. A history of successful outpatient treatment
6. Family investment and involvement in the treatment process
7. Evidence of self-motivation[37]

Some examples of outpatient treatment techniques for children and adolescents include cognitive-behavioral skills-training interventions and abstinence-oriented self-help programs. Skills-training models of treatment rely on learning theories to organize practice techniques. These skills-training techniques presuppose that behaviors, whether desired or not, are learned in some social setting. By the same logic, a behavior that is once learned can subsequently be unlearned.

Skills-training models emphasize that children and adolescents learn behaviors that would be incompatible with drug-using behaviors. Skills trainers construct curricula in which skills can be taught. Although some mention is made in passing about personal characteristics and how skills are taught, skills training has traditionally focused on *what* is taught, not *how* it is taught. Skills training typically includes some combination of teaching changes in behavior paired with information about the consequences of drug abuse. Skills-training interventions for drug-abusing adolescents typically consist of several components: drug education, social skills training, and problem solving (i.e., improving "faulty thinking").

Drug education has been discussed earlier. In outpatient settings, drug education is used to heighten a child's or adolescent's awareness of the consequences of prolonged use. However, disseminating information to family members of drug-abusing youths is also a critical element of outpatient treatment. Such information can normalize family members' experiences of stress and help prepare for the erratic behavior that is common among drug-dependent youths.

A second component of cognitive interventions is problem-solving skills. Problem solving has been used in a number of settings in helping children and adolescents make informed decisions. Spivack and associates conducted studies in which problem-solving paradigms were examined.[38] Problem-solving protocols generally consist of a series of intuitively reasonable steps that should be taken in determining the solution to a problem. The first step is for a child or adolescent to slow down his or her decision making to allow the problem-solving sequence to begin. Basically, children and adolescents are taught to *stop* what they're doing. The second step is for a child or adolescent to consider what type of problem is confronting him or her. The third step is to generate alternatives to the problem confronting the child or adolescent. Fourth, the alternatives are evaluated for their viability and their acceptability. Finally, the most promising alternative is chosen and enacted using newly learned social skills. Several investigators have applied variations of this problem-solving interventive method to a variety of drug-abusing populations.[39]

Skills-training interventions are found in inpatient and outpatient settings and are used extensively in prevention approaches. Because skills-training interventions follow a curriculum, they are relatively easy to plan, implement, and evaluate. Unfortunately, such interventions may be difficult for children and adolescents to integrate. First, if children and adolescents are having difficulties at school, the intervention process may be a reminder of a disliked activity. Second, children and adolescents who are actively using drugs and alcohol may have problems learning the materials. Reasons for this difficulty stem from an inability to concentrate, lack of motivation to do well, conflict with authority figures, and an inclination toward thrill-seeking behaviors. However, these difficulties can be avoided, in part, if skills-training interventions comprise a primary prevention strategy aimed at elementary school children. Because these children are not usually experiencing difficulties from drug use, a primary prevention strategy does not encounter the resistance that is common among older children and adolescents.

Skills-training interventions are used in schools, clinics, and hospitals with children and adolescents who have varying degrees of drug and alcohol abuse. It is most effectively implemented in groups; these groups are most readily found in institutional settings such as the public schools.[40] Skills training seeks to identify verbal and behavioral skills that enable children and adolescents to refuse offers of drug and alcohol use and to engage in prosocial behavioral repertoires.[41] Like cognitive-based interventions, skills training is most efficiently conducted within institutional settings. Despite the burgeoning popularity of skills training within institutional settings, its long-term effectiveness is unclear.[42]

One possible reason for the effectiveness of skills-training programs may lie in the use of peer-oriented treatment. Schinke and colleagues conducted an evaluation of the effectiveness of participatory substance abuse prevention programs in Boys and Girls Clubs (BGC) located in selected public housing projects. They found that public housing projects that received such prevention services through BGC had less drug-related activity, less damage to housing units, and increased parental involvement in youth activities.[43] This finding is in concert with school-based programs that have also found children and adolescents are able to benefit from school-based prevention and treatment programs that invite participation in their planning and delivery.[44]

Abstinence-Oriented Approaches

Treatment models that focus on abstinence as a treatment goal dominate programs in the United States. This model, most closely associated with Alcoholics Anonymous (AA), was originally designed for mature male alcoholics and may be difficult for most children and adolescents to understand, let alone embrace. Much as its name suggests, AA requires anonymity from its participants. Although AA is geared toward adults, some communities are making efforts to provide students with support groups.

Abstinence models require that social workers understand the three parts of Twelve-Step programs: surrender steps, integrity steps, and serenity steps.[45] The surrender steps consist of

treatment personnel persuadin[g ado]lescents that they cannot co[ntrol] drugs. Children or adolescents [make] attempts to control drug use to a higher [.] The "higher power" is not always intended to be synonymous with God or any similar deity, and the emphasis is on creating a spiritual defense against drug use. The integrity steps focus on an admission of the harm that has been caused; the direct admission of responsibility to the harmed person enables children and adolescents to accept personal responsibility for conflicts precipitated by tension around drug and alcohol misuse.[46]

Integrity steps allow children and adolescents to apologize for difficulties that were caused by their drug and alcohol use. The last three steps in the Twelve-Step program, serenity steps, are concerned with maintaining a drug-free life-style. The surrender steps assist chemically dependent children and adolescents to cease use, the integrity steps begin the task of rebuilding relationships through apologies, and the serenity steps focus on living a life without the presence of drugs and alcohol.

Despite the enormous popularity of Twelve-Step programs throughout the United States, only one study examined their effectiveness with adolescents (a more thorough discussion of treatment effectiveness is found in Chapter 6). The data suggest that Alcoholics Anonymous benefited those adolescents who were able to understand and accept AA's principles and traditions.[47] Because there was no control group in the research project, however, it would be unwise to generalize the study's findings to all adolescents.

Family-Based Treatment

In treating a chemically dependent person, it is absolutely critical to consider his or her family. It is not surprising that the role of the family system is considered so pivotal. Children's and adolescents' use of drugs often cause and are caused by family conflict.[48] Families are affected heavily by members' drug use and abuse. Not only do use and abuse cause problems but use may also be seen as a method of coping with family conflict.

One caveat, however, should be stressed. Because all families experience conflict, and not all children and adolescents experience drug dependency, social workers must be cautious in concluding that family conflict *caused* children or adolescents to abuse drugs. Severe family conflict creates a context for a child or adolescent in which the likelihood of abusive drug use increases dramatically. However, because of peer influence, children in even the most "normal" families may experiment with or abuse drugs.[49] Adolescents, on the other hand, have begun to pull away from their families in forming their own networks of friends and acquaintances. While a thorough family assessment generally should be conducted, clinical assessments of adolescents may also require that the network of friends be considered when planning treatment.[50]

The most commonly used family treatment approach with substance abuse—structural-strategic family therapy—was developed by Salvador Minuchin and associates.[51] Its popularity was due, in part, to its incorporation of family development and a family systems conceptual framework into its treatment procedures. Minuchin argued that intergenerational "boundaries" should be maintained (i.e., children should respect and obey their parents) and that parents were indigenous allies in the treatment of children and adolescents. Structural approaches stressed that parents should be empowered to parent their children. Minuchin's assertions complement findings from surveys and studies of drug-abusing youths.[52]

Structural family therapy is used primarily with families in which one or more children are identified as having a problem. Although it is desirable to have the entire family involved to implement structural family therapy, some therapists will work with whoever is present.[53] The efficacy of structural family therapy with children and adolescents has been studied and positive results exist regarding its effectiveness with entire drug-abusing families.[54]

Multiple-family group treatment is also being used as a component of treatment approaches for children and adolescents with substance abuse problems. A multiple-family group usually consists of several youths and their family members, including parents, legal guardians, and siblings. In other words, it is a group of several families, with each family viewed as a client system. Family members are able to receive and provide support and learn from one another, which can be accomplished through modeling, role-plays, sharing, and constructive feedback. Techniques of structural family therapy are also often used. Therefore, the facilitator must possess a working understanding of group work and family therapy, and be able to integrate the two in practice.

Inpatient Treatment

There is a common assumption that substance use, abuse, and dependency are progressive in their onset and in their severity, with use as least severe and dependency as most severe. However, as was discussed in Chapter 1, there are significant conceptual and definitional problems in differentiating *abuse* from *dependency*. The problem of measurement and diagnosis is reflected in lax admission policies of hospital wards targeting substance abuse and dependency in youths.[55] To justify admission into an inpatient facility, children and adolescents should have a diagnosis that requires such action. As mentioned earlier in this chapter, children and adolescents should exhibit a high degree of medical risk, suicidal or homicidal threat, or a great likelihood of injury by neglect. Typically, however, diagnoses of substance dependency and conduct disorder are given for admission into inpatient treatment. Unfortunately, there are few hard signs of substance dependency, and it is often easy to misdiagnose to justify admission. Although some children and adolescents undoubtedly benefit from such treatment approaches, the increasing use of these alternatives reflects aggressive marketing by hospitals, parental fatigue, and ineffective school environments.

By contrast, it is much more difficult for social workers to coordinate community resources, provide support to parents, and advocate for better school environments. Community-based treatment that coordinates indigenous treatment resources lacks the glamour of a heroic treatment provider, but may be much more useful to adolescents in the long run. Currently, health care policy and the fragmentation of community-based service networks make inpatient treatment for children and adolescents an expensive and overused form of care.[56]

Inpatient treatment has changed drastically over recent years. The era of 28-day treatment programs is almost extinct. The cost of such programs is too high for most people to pay for personally, and third-party payers overwhelmingly no longer reimburse for such services. Inpatient treatment can average about $1,200 per day, yet some third-party payers only reimburse about $350 per day for these services. This means that inpatient facilities (particularly private-for-profit agencies) are scrambling to increase their populations to compensate for being reimbursed less in order to make a profit, or at least to survive. One hospital administrator in Orlando, Florida, captured this movement in the statement, "Reimbursement drives treatment." Inpatient programs typically provide respite for parents, drug education, group encounters with peers, and individual treatment, which may include a pharmacological component. Although inpatient treatment is prized by some experts for its ability to concentrate services in a short period of time, others point to the inefficiency of using a hospital setting to provide interventions that could be done much more inexpensively.[57]

Residential Treatment/ Treatment Communities

Longer inpatient programs for children and adolescents do exist. Treatment communities are one example of long-term inpatient care. Once admitted into such facilities, adolescents are encouraged to form close emotional ties with other patients. When successful, adolescents will perceive themselves as part of a group of peers who act as a support network.[58] If third-party payers are involved, a dual diagnosis of the child or adolescent is required to warrant payment for such treatment.

There is no evidence to suggest that inpatient treatment is any more effective with most children and adolescents than outpatient treatment.[59] However, for many parents who avail themselves of extended inpatient treatment for their children, the treatment period acts as a respite. Anecdotal reports suggest that the improvement that children and adolescents often demonstrate in inpatient settings is lost when they return to the home settings. For improvements to be maintained, critics of this approach suggest that children and adolescents need changes to occur while in their home settings. Changes that occur within an inpatient setting frequently occur within a vacuum; the typical frustrations and challenges that might encourage alcohol and drug use and abuse are absent in an inpatient setting. Thus, improvements seen in the hospital do not necessarily extend to home settings.[60]

Friedman and Utada found that outpatient settings devoted more staff time to individual and family counseling than residential programs; the latter had a heavier emphasis on art therapy, group counseling, vocational training, and medical services.[61] There is little doubt that extended residential communities are necessary for seriously disturbed children and adolescents. When children or adolescents are chronically endangering themselves with their drug and/or alcohol use, extended residential treatment may be the desired alternative because of its ability to provide 24-hour monitoring of behavior.[62]

Case Example

Family Services of Milwaukee instituted a new program entitled Recovering Families. It was adopted because it allowed family members to receive a peer-group experience coordinated with family therapy. Traditionally, family therapy and peer support/treatment group (e.g., Alcoholics Anonymous) have not always been unified in their treatment philosophy, goals, or methods.[63] Recovering Families allowed all members of a family an opportunity to receive a coordinated treatment experience with their peers and with their family members.

The major difference between this case and the one described in Chapter 10 is that the structure of this time-limited program allowed all members of a family to be entered into groups formed around their peers and to be involved in family therapy. For example, it was common to have five groups: one group for chemically dependent family members, usually one of the parents; one group for spouses of a chemically dependent family member; one group for adolescents; one group for latency-aged children; and one group for young children. All family members agreed to abstain from alcohol use during the duration of treatment. Groups met at the same time, and family therapy was scheduled during other times during the week. In many instances, families had already begun family therapy before entering the Recovering Families program. All group leaders and therapists were either Clinical Members of the American Association for Marriage and Family Therapy (AAMFT) or in training to become AAMFT Clinical Members. The program director was an AAMFT Clinical Member and certified as a drug and alcohol counselor. The family presented here was similar to many who went through the program.

Mr. and Mrs. Wilson had been married for 18 years and had three children: Greg, 15 years, Susan, 10 years, and Betty, 6 years. They had sought treatment for family conflict stemming from Greg's angry behavior in school and at home. During the initial sessions with a family therapist, it was disclosed that Mr. Wilson was a binge drinker whose erratic behavior had become increasingly embarrassing for family members, especially for Greg and Susan. This discussion precipitated a crisis when Greg revealed that he was afraid that his

alcohol use was getting out of control; he cited blackouts, episodes of fighting, and problems with concentrating on schoolwork. After explaining some of the potential health problems that can be caused by excessive drinking, the therapist requested that Mr. Wilson and Greg undergo diagnostic tests to ascertain the level of impairment, especially to their livers, cardiovascular systems, and nervous systems. The therapist believed that it was ethically necessary to rule out organic difficulties by qualified medical professionals before beginning alcohol treatment. This was crucial to understanding which erratic behaviors, if any, were influenced by somatic difficulties.

Further discussion regarding Mr. Wilson's family history revealed that excessive drinking was common in several generations of his family. Mr. Wilson was a vigorous and professionally successful man whose achievements resulted from his competitive drive and understanding of his work environment. Mrs. Wilson worked outside the home as a successful real estate agent. Mrs. Wilson's alcohol use did not appear excessive; typically, she had a glass of wine with dinner, but did not routinely use alcohol. This was confirmed by her husband and the children. Greg was an honors student with extensive extracurricular involvement in sports who had recently begun to do poorly in classes. Susan and Betty were also excellent students and popular among their peers.

During family therapy, family members discussed whether they would commit themselves to abstain from alcohol use for 10 weeks. Strategically, it was important for all family members to agree that they would not use alcohol. The agreement not to use alcohol became a public contract with family members and an impartial witness concerning the family's commitment to sobriety. The therapist did not try to "persuade" the family that their alcohol use could result in death. In keeping with contemporary family therapy treatment philosophies, the decision to cease had to be made by family members.[64] Forceful presentations by therapists on the problems associated with excessive alcohol use seldom persuade alcohol-dependent people to abstain from use.[65] The therapist took an approach in which she linked mishaps from the family's life to family members' use of alcohol, but the ultimate decision to cease use was left to the individual family members.

Mrs. Wilson, Susan, and Betty immediately agreed not to use alcohol; Mr. Wilson and Greg were hesitant about their commitment to abstain. The therapist did not immediately accept their wavering commitment and pressed them to make a firm choice with an understanding that relapse would be a constant temptation. Mr. Wilson and Greg eventually agreed unequivocally to abstain from any alcohol use during the 10 weeks of the program.

Each family member entered into his or her respective peer group, each with two group leaders; Mr. Wilson and Greg both went into the group for chemically dependent family members. Groups typically started with a review of the previous week and what was done to maintain sobriety. Focusing on relapse prevention helped empower family members. Throughout the discussion of what happened during the week, group members would also discuss the influence of alcohol misuse on family dynamics, whether from the perspective of an abuser or a family member. Greg proved to be valuable because he provided both abuser and family member perspectives. Although the group leaders originally were active in structuring the group discussion, group members increasingly assumed responsibility in supporting and challenging each others' statements and beliefs. Because this occurred for all family members, family therapy became a time to share new insights and to challenge each other. Although most Wilson family members found the groups to be stressful, they also stated that they realized the value of the intense 90-minute sessions. Not unexpectedly, family members also sought out and attended psychoeducational presentations on alcohol misuse sponsored by the agency.

The challenge for Greg was to separate his anger toward his father's erratic behavior from his own problems caused by excessive alcohol use. Mr. Wilson was originally resistant to group members' comments but became increasingly willing to listen to his son during group and family therapy sessions. Mrs. Wilson's attitudes toward drinking alcohol in general and binge drinking in particular took on an increasingly firm stance. Although her stance made clear that she was unwilling to subject herself and her family to the vagaries of her husband's alcohol abuse, she also risked demoralizing his uncertain progress toward sobriety. Family therapy sessions were increasingly devoted toward outlining what a drug-free family environment would look like.

At school, Greg's behavior had improved markedly and his grades were improving. Greg received additional counseling from a school social worker who was knowledgeable about teenage drug abuse. The focus of those sessions was to reconsider his peer group. Although Greg received support from some of his friends, other friends heavily used alcohol and other drugs. The latter group of friends were ambivalent about Greg's decision to abstain from alcohol use, but they did not explicitly criticize his choice. However, the school social worker was worried that substance-using friends were not diligent about schoolwork or attending class. In addition, they were often involved in verbal and physical fights with other students. Greg's father proved to be a valuable ally in helping Greg finally decide not to associate with his substance-using friends. Greg was impressed with his father's slow but seemingly successful fight to remain sober; Mr. Wilson's newly found credibility was instrumental in Greg's decision.

Although the groups ended, family therapy continued. The family therapist cautioned against overconfidence; she was emphatic that both Mr. Wilson and Greg were vulnerable to relapses. In addition, family therapy also continued to help Mr. and Mrs. Wilson strengthen their marital relationship. The family therapist encouraged the couple to attend Alcoholics Anonymous and Al-Anon, which provided continued support for both parents. Greg continued meeting informally with the school social worker; she proved invaluable in providing information and daily support.

Mr. and Mrs. Wilson relocated to another state and contact was lost. However, before leaving, the Wilson family expressed their gratitude to staff members in Recovering Families for their able stewardship of the treatment process. Although Wilson family members made all the decisions to become and stay sober, the staff members helped provide opportunities during which those choices could be made.

Summary

Many professionals claim to have developed treatment approaches that will positively affect children's and adolescents' drug and alcohol problems. Unfortunately, no one single treatment has been tested that is consistently effective with children's and adolescents' substance abuse. It can be argued that professionals who rely on only one untested treatment methodology are unethical. However, the research literature does not provide much guidance. It suggests that most treatments are somewhat effective sometimes and that one of the few common features of successful treatment efforts is an empathic relationship with clients. Despite the claims of hospitals and clinics, no "cure" exists for children's and adolescents' drug and alcohol dependency. Social workers, with their tradition of case management, are likely to be more useful in working with these clients than technically proficient therapists.[66]

Because families with drug- and alcohol-dependent children and adolescents encounter a multitude of problems, social workers should strive to empower families and to find community resources. Furthermore, because financial considerations are increasingly critical in planning treatment strategies, social workers must consider the cost of treatment. As Smith argued, social workers should concentrate on clinical case management in assisting chemically dependent clients.[67] Rather than rely on the thin reed of therapy, social workers should also use their knowledge of the community to find more tangible resources for parents and their offspring.

Endnotes

1. Martha A. Morrison and Quentin T. Smith, "Psychiatric Issues of Adolescent Drug Dependence," *Pediatric Clinics of North America*, Vol. 34 (1987), pp. 461–480.

2. L. D. Johnston, P. M. O'Malley, & J. G. Bachman, *National Survey Results on Drug Use from the Monitoring the Future Study, 1975–1995. Volume 1: Secondary School Students.* NIMH Pub. No. 97-4139. Rockville, MD: National Institute on Drug Abuse, 1995.

3. Ibid.

4. Ibid.

5. Ibid.

6. Denise Kandel, M. Davies, D. Karus, and K. Yamaguchi, "The Consequences in Young Adulthood of Adolescent Drug Involvement," *Archives of General Psychiatry*, Vol. 142 (1986), pp. 746–754.

7. George E. Obermeier and Paul B. Henry, "Adolescent Inpatient Treatment," *Journal of Chemical Dependency*, Vol. 2, No. 1 (1988–89), pp. 163–182.

8. Thomas McKenna and Roy Pickens, "Alcoholic Children of Alcoholics," *Journal of Studies on Alcohol*, Vol. 42 (1981), pp. 1021–1029; and Victor J. Callan and Debra Jackson, "Children of Alcoholic Fathers and Recovered Alcoholic Fathers: Personal and Family Functioning," *Journal of Studies on Alcohol*, Vol. 47 (1986), pp. 180–182.

9. Emmy E. Werner, "Resilient Offspring of Alcoholics: A Longitudinal Study," *Journal of Studies on Alcohol*, Vol. 47 (1986), pp. 34–40.

10. Ann M. Downey, "The Impact of Drug Abuse upon Adolescent Suicide," *Omega Journal of Death and Dying*, Vol. 22, No. 4 (1990–91), pp. 261–275.

11. Oscar G. Bukstein, David A. Brent, and Yifrah Kaminar, "Comorbidity of Substance Abuse and Other Psychiatric Disorders in Adolescents," *American Journal of Psychiatry*, Vol. 146 (September 1989), pp. 1131–1141.

12. Harold A. Pincus, "AIDS, Drug Abuse, and Mental Health," *Public Health Reports*, Vol. 99 (1984), pp. 106–108; and James H. Price, "AIDS, the Schools, and Policy Issues," *Journal of School Health*, Vol. 56 (1986), pp. 137–140.

13. J. A. Robertson and H. A. Plant, "Alcohol, Sex and Risks of HIV Infection," *Drug and Alcohol Dependence*, Vol. 22 (1988), pp. 75–78.

14. Benjamin M. Schutz, *Legal Liability in Psychotherapy* (San Francisco: Jossey-Bass, 1982).

15. Douglas J. Besharov, *The Vulnerable Social Worker* (Silver Spring, MD: National Association of Social Workers, 1985).

16. Bruce A. Christiansen, Mark S. Goldman, and Andres Inn, "Development of Alcohol-Related Expectancies in Adolescents: Separating Pharmacological from Social-Learning Influences," *Journal of Consulting and Clinical Psychology*, Vol. 50 (1982), pp. 336–344.

17. Thomas E. Smith, Jeffrey Koob, and Thomas Wirtz, "Ecology of Adolescent Marijuana Abusers," *International Journal of the Addictions*, Vol. 20 (1985), pp. 1421–1428; and Tong Won Kim, *Social Factors and Marijuana Addiction: A Causal Structural Model*, unpublished doctoral dissertation, Florida State University, Tallahassee, 1991.

18. National Institute on Drug Abuse, *Marijuana Research Findings: 1980* (Rockville, MD: U.S. Government Printing Office, 1981); and Alcohol, Drug Abuse, and Mental Health Administration (ADAMHA), *Sixth Special Report to the U.S. Congress on Alcohol and Health* (Rockville, MD: U.S. Government Printing Office, 1987).

19. K. Corcoran and V. Vandiver, *Maneuvering the Maze of Managed Care: Skills for Mental Health Practitioners* (New York: The Free Press).

20. American Psychiatric Association, *Diagnostic and Statistical Manual of Mental Disorders*, 4th ed. (Washington, DC: Author, 1994).

21. R. A. Wells, *Planned Short-Term Treatment* (New York: The Free Press, 1994).

22. American Psychiatric Association, *Economic Fact Book for Psychiatry*, 2nd ed. (Washington, DC: Author, 1987).

23. B. Dickey and H. Azeni, "Impact of Managed Care on Mental Health Services," *Health Affairs*, Vol. 11 (1992), pp. 197–204.

24. K. Corcoran and V. Vandiver, *Maneuvering the Maze of Managed Care: Skills for Mental Health Practitioners* (New York: The Free Press, 1966).

25. E. Arkin (Ed.), *Communicating about Alcohol and Other Drugs: Strategies for Reaching Populations at Risk* (Rockville, MD: Office of Substance Abuse Prevention, 1991).

26. D. Schaffer, I. Phillips, N. B. Enzer, M. M. Silverman, and V. Anthony, "Prevention of Mental Disorders, Alcohol, and Other Drug Use in Children and Adolescents," *OSAP Prevention Monograph No. 2* (Rockville, MD: DHHS Publication No. 89-1646, 1989); and Karol L. Kumpfer and Charles W. Turner, "The Social Ecology Model of Adolescent Substance Abuse: Implications for Prevention," *The International Journal of the Addictions*, Vol. 25, No. 4A (1990–1991), pp. 435–463.

27. D. W. Springer, "Drug Abuse Prevention Programs," in F. Schmalleger (Ed.), *Crime and the Justice System in America: An Encyclopedia* (Westport, CT: Greenwood Publishing Group); and Schaffer et al., *Prevention of Mental Disorders*.

28. Jeannette L. Johnson, "Preventive Interventions for Children at Risk: An Introduction," *The International Journal of the Addictions*, Vol. 25 (1990–1991), pp. 429–434.

29. Marsha Mannatt, *Parents, Peers, and Pot* (National Institute on Drug Abuse, Rockville, MD: U.S. Government Printing Office, 1979).

30. Michael Klitzner and Elizabeth Bamberger, "The Assessment of Parent-Led Prevention Programs: A National Descriptive Study," *Journal of Drug Education*, Vol. 20, No. 2 (1990), pp. 111–125.

31. Bill Kinder, Nancy E. Pape, and Steven Walfish, "Drug and Alcohol Education Programs: A Review of Outcome Studies," *International Journal of the Addictions*, Vol. 15 (1980).

32. Thomas E. Smith, "Reviewing Adolescent Marijuana Abuse," *Social Work*, Vol. 29 (January/February 1984), pp. 17–21.

33. Thomas E. Smith, "Reducing Adolescents' Marijuana Abuse," *Social Work*, Vol. 9 (Fall 1983), pp. 33–44.

34. W. DeJong, "A Short-Term Evaluation of Project D.A.R.E. (Drug Abuse Resistance Education): Preliminary Indication of Effectiveness," *Journal of Drug Education*, Vol. 17, No. 4 (1987), pp. 279–294.

35. S. Monroe, "D.A.R.E. Bedeviled," *Time*, October 17, 1994, p. 49.

36. Kirk Wheeler and Jeffrey Malmquist, "Treatment Approaches in Adolescent Chemical Dependency," *Pediatric Clinics of North America*, Vol. 34 (1987), pp. 437–447.

37. Linda Semlitz and Mark S. Gold, "Adolescent Drug Abuse," *Psychiatric Clinics of North America*, Vol. 9 (1986), pp. 455–473.

38. George Spivack, Jerome J. Platt, and Myrna B. Shure, *The Problem-Solving Approach to Adjustment* (San Francisco: Jossey-Bass, 1976).

39. Steven P. Schinke, Michael S. Moncher, Josephine Palleja, Luis H. Zayas, and Robert F. Schilling, "Hispanic Youth, Substance Abuse, and Stress: Implications for Prevention Research," *The International Journal of the Addictions*, Vol. 23, No. 8 (1988), pp. 809–826.

40. Thomas E. Smith, "Groupwork with Adolescent Drug Abusers," *Social Work with Groups*, Vol. 8 (1985), pp. 55–64.

41. David Smith, Stephen J. Levy, and Diane E. Striar, "Treatment Services for Youthful Drug Users," in George M. Beschner and Alfred S. Friedman (Eds.), *Youth Drug Abuse: Problems, Issues, and Treatment* (Lexington, MA: Lexington Books, 1981).

42. Jeffrey Jenson, Elizabeth Wells, R. D. Plotnick, J. David Hawkins, and Rick Catalano, "The Effects of Skills and Intentions to Use Drugs on Posttreatment Drug Use of Adolescents," *American Journal of Drug and Alcohol Abuse* (in press).

43. Steven P. Schinke, Mario A. Orlandi, and Kristin C. Cole, "Boys & Girls Clubs in Public Housing Developments: Prevention Services for Youth at Risk," *Journal of Community Psychology*, OSAP Special Issue (1992), pp. 118–128.

44. Smith, "Groupwork with Adolescent Drug Abusers."

45. Victoria Brundage, "Gregory Bateson, Alcoholics Anonymous, and Stoicism," *Psychiatry*, Vol. 48 (1985), pp. 40–51.

46. Marcia D. Brown-Standridge, "Creating Therapeutic Realities via Responsibility Messages," *American Journal of Family Therapy*, Vol. 12 (1987), pp. 206–224.

47. G. S. Alford, R. A. Koehler, and J. Leonard, "Alcoholics Anonymous–Narcotics Anonymous Model Inpatient Treatment of Chemically Dependent Adolescents: A Two-Year Outcome Study," *Journal of Studies on Alcohol*, Vol. 52 (1991), pp. 118–126.

48. Murray Bowen, "A Family Systems Approach to Alcoholism," *Addictions*, Vol. 21 (1974), pp. 3–11.

49. Kim, "Social Factors and Marijuana Addiction: A Structural Model."

50. Smith et al., "Groupwork with Adolescent Drug Abusers."

51. Salvador Minuchin, *Families and Family Therapy* (Cambridge, MA: Harvard University Press, 1974); and Salvador Minuchin and H. Charles Fishman, *Family Therapy Techniques* (Cambridge, MA: Harvard University Press, 1981).

52. Denise B. Kandel, "Inter- and Intragenerational Influences on Adolescent Marijuana Use," *Journal of Social Issues*, Vol. 30 (1974), pp. 107–135.

53. Jose Szapocznik, William M. Kurtines, Franklin H. Foote, Angel Perez-Vidal, and Olga Hervis, "Conjoint versus One-Person Family Therapy: Some Evidence for the Effectiveness of Conducting Family Therapy through One Person with Drug-Abusing Adolescents," *Journal of Consulting and Clinical Psychology*, Vol. 51 (1983), pp. 990–999; and Jose Szapocznik, William M. Kurtines, Franklin H. Foote, Angel Perez-Vidal, and Olga Hervis, "Conjoint versus One-Person Family Therapy: Further Evidence for the Effectiveness of Conducting Family Therapy through One Person with Drug-Abusing Adolescents," *Journal of Consulting and Clinical Psychology*, Vol. 54 (1986), pp. 395–397.

54. Ibid. (1983, 1986); and H. Charles Fishman, M. Duncan Stanton, and Bernice Rosman, "Treating Families of Adolescent Drug Abusers," in M. Duncan Stanton, Thomas C. Todd, and Associates (Eds.), *The Family Therapy of Drug Abuse and Addiction* (New York: Guilford Press, 1982).

55. See, for example, the discussion by Ira Strumwasser, Nitin V. Paranjpe, Marianne Udow, and David Share et al., "Appropriateness of Psychiatric and Substance Abuse Hospitalization: Implications for Payment and Utilization Management," *Medical-Care*, Vol. 29, No. 8 (August 1991), pp. 77–90.

56. Ira Schwartz, "Hospitalization of Adolescents for Psychiatric and Substance Abuse Treatment: Legal and Ethical Issues," *Journal of Adolescent Health Care*, Vol. 10, No. 6 (November 1989), pp. 473–478.

57. Strumwasser et al., "Appropriateness of Psychiatric and Substance Abuse Hospitalization"; and William R. Miller and Reid K. Hester, "Inpatient Alcoholism Treatment," *American Psychologist*, Vol. 41 (July 1986), pp. 794–803.

58. George E. Obermeier and Paul B. Henry, "Adolescent Inpatient Treatment," *Journal of Chemical Dependency*, Vol. 2, No. 1 (1988–1989), pp. 163–182.

59. A. Thomas McLellan, Lester Luborsky, Charles O'Brien, George E. Woody, and Keith A. Druley, "Is Treatment for Substance Abuse Effective?" *Journal of the American Medical Association*, Vol. 247 (1982), pp. 1423–1428.

60. Harvey Joanning, B. Gawinski, J. Morris, and William Quinn, "Organizing a Social Ecology to Treat Adolescent Drug Abuse," *Journal of Strategic and Systemic Therapies*, Vol. 5 (1986), pp. 55–66.

61. Alfred S. Friedman, and Arlene Utada, "High School Drug Use," *Clinical Research Notes* (National Institute on Drug Abuse, Washington, DC: U.S. Government Printing Office, 1983).

62. Downey, "The Impact of Drug Abuse upon Adolescent Suicide."

63. For a discussion of some of the tensions between family therapists and Alcoholics Anonymous, and a beginning rapprochement, see Sandra A. Zygarlicki and Thomas Edward Smith, "Alcoholism Treatment and Marriage and Family Therapists: An Empirical Study," *Contemporary Family Therapy*, Vol. 14 (1992), pp. 75–88.

64. Thomas E. Smith, "Alcohol and Misuse: A Systemic Conceptualization for Practitioners," in E. W. Nunnally, C. S. Chilman, and F. M. Cox (Eds.), *Mental Illness, Delinquency, Addictions and Neglect*, Vol. 4 (1988), pp. 69–87.

65. Gregory Bateson argued that individuals who misuse alcohol are caught in an escalatory conflict with people who attempt to mandate sobriety. He argued persuasively that forceful attempts to end someone's alcohol use was similar to an arms race in which both parties vied for primacy; see Gregory Bateson, "The Cybernetics of 'Self': A Theory of Alcoholism," *Psychiatry*, Vol. 34, No. 1 (1971), pp. 1–18.

66. No studies have systematically studied the issue of case management versus therapy. However, the multiple problems encountered by adolescents are not often amenable to a single-treatment provider no matter how skilled that provider may be. For a more thorough discussion, see E. M. Freeman, *The Addiction Process: Effective Social Work Process* (New York: Longman, 1992).

67. See Smith, "Alcohol and Misuse," for a discussion of how alcohol misuse affects family members.

10

Family Systems and Chemical Dependency

Catherine A. Hawkins
Southwest Texas State University

Previous chapters indicate that alcoholism and other drug addictions frequently impair an individual's physical, psychological, and social functioning. There is also recognition and acceptance that alcoholism and other drug addictions adversely affect the individual's marital and family relationships. According to a survey by the Gallup Organization, "alcoholism affects approximately one-third of all American families."[1] A report by the Children of Alcoholics Foundation estimates that one out of every eight Americans is the child or adult child of an alcoholic.[2]

Defining alcoholism at the family level lacks specificity, despite its intuitive appeal. Many terms in the literature attempt to capture this phenomenon, such as *family disease, alcoholic family, addicted or chemically dependent family, alcohol impaired family,* or *family with an alcoholic member.* By necessity, an understanding of the family dynamics associated with alcoholism or other drug addiction cannot be reduced to a single definition but must entail descriptions of interactive processes that occur throughout the life cycle of the family. This chapter

reviews some of the more noteworthy efforts to specify the etiology and treatment of the family processes associated with chemical dependency. Although most literature to date is about alcoholism, it is reasonable to assume that much of it can be generalized to other drug addiction.[3] For the purposes of this chapter, the term *alcoholism* will be used since this is consistent with the literature, but the reader should keep in mind that, theoretically, this may also include other forms of drug addiction. In addition, *family* is a term that is no longer clearly defined in society. The material presented in this chapter applies to all forms of families, including nuclear, extended, single-parent, communal, and gay/lesbian.[4]

This chapter reviews the literature on a family perspective of chemical dependency, including the theory, research, and treatment of alcoholism and other drug addiction in families. Three dominant theoretical approaches—stress coping, behavioral, and family systems—are presented. The constructs of codependency, children of alcoholics, and adult children of alcoholics are also discussed as they relate to family dynamics. The ways in which theory shapes practice with chemically dependent family systems are addressed along with more specific treatment information for working with chemically dependent families. Finally, a case example is presented that illustrates some of the main concepts discussed in this chapter.

A Family Perspective in Theory, Research, and Treatment

During the early decades of this century, a scientific tradition emerged in the social sciences. The study of alcoholism, however, was restrained by the moral overtones attached to the problem, which led to the belief that alcoholism was not amenable to scientific inquiry. The growing Temperance Movement culminated in the Prohibition amendment in 1919. Attempts at treatment of alcoholism (which were almost exclusively directed at men) consisted largely of removing the individual to a residential program for detoxification and some therapy, known euphemistically as "the cure." In *Alcoholics Anonymous*, Bill W., a founder of AA, describes his "rehabilitation" as belladonna treatment, hydrotherapy, and mild exercise.[5]

In the 1930s, the disease or biological model of alcoholism began to gain acceptance. AA, founded in 1935, embraced this model. Although AA was originally oriented toward men, wives would hold meetings modeled after AA to discuss the effects of alcoholism on their lives (Lois W., Bill W.'s wife, is credited with organizing the first meeting). At this same time, psychoanalysis was also growing in popularity, and it explained alcoholism in terms of psychopathology. Both these models were limited to an examination of the etiology of alcoholism in the individual. Psychoanalysts acknowledged the impact of family dynamics on psychopathology, and they had some interest in the family aspects of alcoholism, but they looked at psychopathology in terms of each individual partner rather than their interaction.[6] Psychoanalytic practice wisdom prohibited the involvement of family members in therapy with the alcoholic, as this was believed to contaminate the therapeutic transference. Another development of the 1930s was the emergence of the fields of marital therapy and child guidance, with their focus on interpersonal relationships. However, early practitioners used a collaborative approach in which separate therapists would meet with family members and then the therapists would consult with each other on their treatment sessions.[7]

Theory and research on alcoholism grew through the 1940s and 1950s but continued to be limited to a study of its physiological and emotional effects on the individual (predominantly middle-aged Anglo males), such as the seminal work by Jellinek.[8] Even the conceptualizations of alcoholism in the marital dyad maintained an individual focus.[9] For example, the *distressed personality model*, rooted in psychoanalysis, held that underlying psychopathology in the wife led to the development and maintenance of a drinking problem in the husband.[10] Alternatively, the *stress personality model*, which applied to both genders, viewed personality disturbance in the spouse as resulting from the chronic stress in the home generated by the alcoholic.[11]

In the 1940s, the concurrent approach to marital and family therapy began to emerge. In this model, one counselor would work with a couple but would meet with them separately.[12] One of the first attempts to include families in treatment involved concurrent group therapy for alcoholics and their wives.[13] These early programs demonstrated that involving spouses increased the completion rate of treatment and expanded the criteria of successful outcome to include both partners' psychosocial functioning as well as abstinence by the alcoholic.[14] By 1948, the support groups organized by the wives of AA members had become a formal network called Al-Anon Family Groups (now targeting spouses of both genders), and, in 1957, Alateen was formed for teenage children of alcoholics. Later, Alatot groups were developed for younger children. By the late 1950s, the conjoint approach to marital and family therapy was introduced in which one counselor would meet with couples and families as a unit.[15]

In the 1960s, as social science moved away from a strictly individual perspective and began to consider the influences of the environment, a third model for conceptualizing alcoholism in the marital dyad emerged. The *psychosocial model* integrated the distressed personality and stress personality models.[16] It focused on the consequences of the alcoholic's drinking behavior and the spouse's coping style on *both* the marital partners. Through the 1960s, the rise of systems theory and behavioral theory led to a broader perspective that focused on the interactive, reciprocal nature of family processes. Although conjoint family therapy developed during this time, family treatment for alcoholism continued to consist of a concurrent program for nonalcoholic spouses (i.e., wives). This was attributed to the general ignorance of alcoholism by family therapists, who often failed to identify this problem or considered it secondary to other problems. When alcoholism was recognized as a problem, family therapists frequently referred these families to alcoholism treatment programs, where alcoholism was viewed as an individual disease.[17] Alcoholism counselors reportedly avoided a family perspective due to lack of training or a belief that it was incompatible with the disease model.[18]

This situation gradually changed during the 1970s and 1980s, and today some type of family involvement is part of most alcoholism treatment programs. The current literature includes studies in which the alcoholic is a parent, spouse, or child (although research on female alcoholics and addicts is still limited). In addition, there has been a self-help and clinical movement that has recognized that family members have problems in their own right due to the dynamics of alcoholism. This has led to such concepts as codependency,[19] children of alcoholics,[20] and adult children of alcoholics.[21] According to Seilhamer and Jacob, Western cultures have long recognized the detrimental impact of parental alcoholism on chil-

dren.[22] However, they point out that there was little interest in these children until relatively recently, when the first publications[23] identifying the clinical implications of being reared by an alcoholic parent began to appear. This was soon followed by an awareness of the impact of parental alcoholism on the adult functioning of offspring (the Adult Children of Alcoholics or ACOA movement). There is growing recognition that being the child of an ACOA (i.e., grandchild of an alcoholic), whether the parent is alcoholic or not, can have a potentially negative impact since alcoholism can affect families for several generations.[24] As a result, self-help and advocacy groups (such as the National Association for Children of Alcoholics) have emerged. ACOA support groups originally began in the 1970s under the auspices of Al-Anon. Over the next few years, independent ACOA groups developed,[25] and Co-dependents Anonymous (CODA) groups were also established.

Theories on Alcoholism and the Family

Chapter 2 covered many theories regarding the etiology and treatment of alcoholism. At one extreme is a strict medical model, also known as the disease model, focused on individual biological factors with virtually no consideration of familial, social, or psychological variables. On the other extreme, there is a strict family systems model, focused on the family as a unit, with virtually no recognition of the individual apart from the family. In the middle are theories that address, to varying degrees, both the individual and the familial aspects of dysfunction. The difference between these theories can be quite confusing, even to a person familiar with the chemical dependency field. This section of the chapter is concerned with social and psychological aspects of chemical dependency. It introduces three predominant models that address alcoholism at the family level (behavioral, stress coping, and family systems) with an emphasis on the points that distinguish them. According to the continuum, the behavioral and stress-coping models fall in the midrange, and the family systems model falls toward the extreme.

Family systems theory evolved in the 1950s as an outgrowth of general systems theory, which emerged in biology in the 1940s. This theory represented an epistemological shift from a reductionist, linear (cause and effect) way of thinking to one that formulated circular causality, process orientation, and the interrelatedness of parts. The crux of systems theory, as applied to people, holds that addiction, like any other human behavior, exists in a larger context. However, the family is viewed not merely as the context for an individual's behavior but also as an entity unto itself. Rather than expressing individual pathology, the presence of problematic behavior (such as alcoholism) by a family member is considered a symptom of underlying dysfunction in the system. This alcoholic is referred to as the "identified patient" to indicate that it is the system itself that is dysfunctional. Rather than identifying the effects of alcoholism on the individual members of the family, a family systems approach focuses on the individuals *and* the interactions between them. The structure and dynamics of the family are assessed, and intervention is planned, through applying systems concepts such as homeostasis, boundaries, triangles, and feedback.[26]

The behavioral and stress-coping models first developed as theories of individual behavior but now incorporate a systems perspective, recognizing that relationships among the family members are interrelated and reciprocal and that the individual both influences and is influenced by other family members. In turn, the family exists as part of the larger social system that affects both individual and family functioning. However, these models differ from family systems theory in that the family is generally seen more as a context for individual behavior than as an entity unto itself. Although all three theories share a systems orientation, the term *family systems* will be used here in reference to that particular theoretical orientation, even though the term is often used more broadly in the literature. Further, it should be noted that most family "systems" therapists actually treat the family as a closed system.

Family Systems Theory of Alcoholism and the Family

This section focuses on family systems theory, especially three areas of the current family systems literature on alcoholism: rituals and routines, shame, and rules and roles. A discussion of the behavioral and stress-coping models is presented later in the section on assessment and treatment.

Before proceeding, however, two criticisms of family systems theory should be noted. First, Steinglass noted that it is too descriptive and lacks scientific rigor. Critics claim that it is commonsensical, imprecise, and virtually untestable.[27] However, its defenders consider such criticisms as irrelevant, since the main value of systems theory is not as a traditional scientific model but as a fundamentally different approach to the conceptualization of clinical problems and therapeutic interventions. Second, feminists contend that there is a gender bias in family systems theory. Goldner argues that the central tenet of *context*—defined as a theoretical boundary that can be drawn around a family, thereby making it a distinct entity—disregards the social forces that influence the family.[28] Another central tenet, *circularity*, assumes an equal distribution of power when, in fact, women are often regarded as subordinate to men within families just as they are within the larger society. Goldner warns that ignoring the impact of the social context can lead to theorists and practitioners "blaming the victim" and "rationalizing the status quo" rather than challenging oppressive sex-role arrangements in family life.

Rituals and Routines

Steinglass and colleagues distinguish between an alcoholic family, which is tantamount to an alcoholic system, and a "family with an alcoholic member."[29] This distinction is made by applying three core concepts of family systems theory: (1) organization, (2) morphostasis or internal regulation, and (3) morphogenesis or controlled growth.

In the *alcoholic family*, chronic alcoholism has become its central, organizing theme. "In these families, alcoholism is no longer a condition of an individual family member. Instead, it has become a family condition that has inserted itself into virtually every aspect of family life."[30] In these families, the erratic and unpredictable behavior of the alcoholic, over time, often elicits a characteristic response from other family members. Their behavior becomes impaired and contributes to the perpetuation of the drinking behavior, thus establishing a circular, reciprocal pattern within the family. The functioning of a family organized around alcoholism can be further understood by applying other principles of family systems theory, such as wholeness (the whole is greater than the sum of its parts), boundaries, and hierarchies.[31]

This organization occurs through a process in which the family regulatory behaviors (morphostasis) are altered to make them more compatible with avoiding the stress and conflict associated with alcoholism. The family accommodates to alcohol-related behaviors in an effort to achieve short-term stability (the process of morphostasis is also called *homeostasis*). However, this increases the likelihood that the drinking will continue, because the system has (inadvertently) been organized to maintain it. According to Steinglass and colleagues, family rituals offer the clearest opportunity to investigate this developmental process since they are considered to be the most meaningful shared activity.[32]

Rituals, encompassing cultural traditions, family celebrations, and daily routines are symbolic events repeated in a systematic fashion over time that convey a sense of belonging among family members. Cultural traditions include religious and secular events that are generally observed by the larger society, such as Christmas, Thanksgiving, or Independence Day. Family celebrations, such as birthdays, graduations, weddings, vaca-

tions, and reunions, are special events that, although perhaps shared with the larger society, are practiced in unique ways by each family. Daily routines are the most distinctive form of activity and vary widely across families. Routines reveal how the family relates in terms of time and space—for example, at dinnertime, at bedtime, or during leisure time. "The one construct that more clearly encapsulates the notion of the Alcoholic Family (a family organized around alcoholism) [is the] invasion of family regulatory behaviors by alcoholism."[33] For example, the family may stop having meals together if the mother drinks in the evening and does not prepare them.

The family's long-term growth and development (morphogenesis) entails three major tasks that determine the family's identity: defining boundaries, establishing a family theme, and choosing shared values. Although greatly simplified in the present discussion, families accomplish these tasks as they move through a common developmental pathway encompassing early, middle, and late phases. During each developmental phase, the alcoholic family makes crucial, usually unconscious, decisions either to challenge or accommodate the drinking behavior of a family member and thus shapes family identity. In the early phase, the family initiates its identity. A key variable is how closely a couple links with their respective families of origin (which may also be alcoholic), since this will influence how the family responds to emerging drinking behavior. If the drinking behavior is not resolved, the middle phase for alcoholic families is characterized by maintaining this established identity. For alcoholic families, this means organizing around alcohol-related behaviors (i.e., invasion of rituals by alcoholism). In the later phase, the family consolidates and defends its alcoholic identity and, if the drinking is not successfully confronted, transmits this identity to future generations. Thus, according to this model, the etiology of an alcoholic family is rooted in the sacrifice of morphogenesis (long-term growth) for morphostasis (short-term stability).

Shame

The role of ritual invasion in the development and maintenance of alcoholism in a family has been shown to be important through numerous research studies.[34] Another construct associated with alcoholic systems (which is clinically derived but lacks adequate empirical validation) is shame. Although it is acknowledged that "normative shame" is necessary for an individual to be socially functional, shame-bound families are thought to engage in pathological patterns of communication and interaction that instill a sense of "toxic shame" in their offspring. The theoretical and clinical literature on the relationship between shame and chemical dependency at both the individual and family level is growing rapidly.[35]

Fossom and Mason define *shame* as "an inner sense of being completely diminished or insufficient as a person. . . . [It] is the ongoing premise that one is fundamentally bad, inadequate, defective, unworthy, or not fully valid as a human being."[36] Shame differs from guilt in that the latter comprises a painful feeling of regret for one's actions while the former is an acutely painful feeling about one's self as a person. Guilt offers the opportunity to reaffirm personal values, repair damage, and grow from the experience. Shame, however, is more likely to foreclose the possibility of growth, since it reasserts one's self-identity as unworthy. Although shame is experienced as an intrapsychic process, its development occurs primarily through the interactions of the family. A shame-bound family operates according to a

> set of rules and injunctions demanding control, perfectionism, blame, and denial. The pattern inhibits or defeats the development of authentic intimate relationships, promotes secrets and vague personal boundaries, unconsciously instills shame in the family members, as well as chaos in their lives, and binds them to perpetuate the shame in themselves and their kin. It does so regardless of the good intentions, wishes, and love which may also be a part of the system.[37]

Shame-bound systems can be addictive, compulsive, abusive, or phobic or exhibit some combination of these behaviors. Alcoholic families are susceptible to shame in at least two ways. First, members often construct elaborate networks for hiding the alcoholism from each other and from the community. Second, alcoholism is frequently associated with emotional, physical, or sexual abuse. Such abuse, as well as neglect, is usually cloaked in secrecy. Secrets maintain the equilibrium of the system by inhibiting family members from changing their behaviors. Thus, secrets serve to perpetuate the addiction as well as the shame of the people involved.

Kaufman provides an explanation of how shame is transmitted from the family level to the individual.[38] He theorizes that a single developmental process is involved that takes different pathways, either to a healthy self or to a shame-bound self. The outcome depends on the prevailing affect encountered by the child over time in his or her interactions with adults, primarily the parents. If the child's basic needs (physical and emotional) are understood and acknowledged on a consistent and predictable basis over time, the child acquires an inner sense of trust and competence in his or her ability to get needs met. Ultimately, this child develops healthy self-esteem. However, if the parent fails to meet the child's needs, the child attributes this as personal failure and feels deficient. If this pattern is repeated consistently, the normative experience of shame (which occurs when one's needs are not met) evolves into the person's inner experience or identity. A shame-bound self is governed by feelings of being diminished, lonely, worthless, and alienated. Given the complexity of any family system over time, a child is likely to experience a combination of enhancing and diminishing responses. Parents can replace a shame-inducing reaction in a child with an affirming one by accepting and explaining the parent's own responsibility for the interaction. Thus, they free the child from the sense that he or she failed to elicit the needed response from the parent. Unfortunately, many alcoholic or codependent parents frequently fail to take this corrective step.

Rules and Roles

Wegscheider discusses family interactive processes in terms of "self-worth."[39] Self-worth is reciprocal in that both the alcoholic and other family members suffer from very low self-worth and reinforce it in each other. Thus, the family system does not encourage the health and wholeness of its members, nor do members encourage the health and wholeness of the family. All families, over time, establish rules and roles that determine the values and goals of the family, regulate power and authority, specify how the family will deal with change, and establish patterns of communication. These rules are seldom recognized consciously. "Alcoholic families are governed by rules that are inhuman, rigid, and designed to keep the system closed—unhealthy rules. They grow out of the alcoholic's personal goals, which are to maintain his [sic] access to alcohol, avoid pain, protect his [sic] defenses, and finally deny that any of these goals exist."[40] Wegscheider uses the analogy of a mobile, with family members suspended and held together by strings, which represent rules. An action by the alcoholic reverberates throughout the system. The family's reactions are intended to bring stability, but they actually produce long-term adaptation to alcoholism since "there is no healthy way to adapt to alcoholism."[41]

Families also adjust to alcoholism through the process of establishing roles (i.e., outward behavior patterns). All families function through roles (such as parent, child, etc.), but roles in alcoholic families take on an added dimension. Although there is little empirical study on the subject, it is theorized that these roles are a way of maintaining stability, but they fail to confront the problem of alcoholism, which threatens the system. Thus, the family may preserve its identity, but at a high price of which it is seldom aware. There are six typical family roles: dependent (the alcoholic), enabler (the powerless spouse or partner), hero (the overachieving child), scapegoat (the delinquent child), lost child (the isolated child), and mascot (the immature child).[42] This is only a schema, since, in small families, one person may assume more than one role and, in large families, one role may be played by several people. Further, roles may shift over time. Although these roles may appear in all families at some time, "in alcoholic families the roles are more rigidly fixed and are played with greater intensity, compulsion, and delusion."[43]

Codependency and Related Constructs

As discussed, alcoholism can be viewed at both the individual and familial level: An alcoholic suffers from personal impairment *and* contributes to the impairment of his or her family. Likewise, other family members can develop individual impairment *and* contribute to familial impairment. In turn, family dysfunction can exacerbate each individual family member's problems (i.e., the processes are reciprocal). The impairment of nonalcoholic family members can encompass the three related constructs of codependency, children of alcoholics, and adult children of alcoholics.

Codependency

Several definitional issues need to be considered in a discussion of codependency. It is a ubiquitous concept in the fields of chemical dependency and mental health, yet there is no general agreement as to its meaning. The concept is clinically derived and, to date, has received limited empirical attention. Despite its intuitive appeal, this ambiguity has led to much confusion and controversy in the appropriate use of this concept in assessment and treatment.

The concept originated when chemical dependency counselors first turned their attention to the spouse (i.e., wife) of the alcoholic. They used the term *enabler* since it was observed that the behavior of the spouse often served to support the alcoholic's drinking. Another early term was *coalcoholic*, which implied that the spouse also suffered from the disease through her relationship with the alcoholic. By the late 1970s, the word was replaced by *codependent* as the term *chemically dependent* to describe alcoholics and other addicts gained popularity. Mendenhall notes ongoing confusion over the term *coalcoholic* and contends that it should only refer to any family member who is also alcoholic.[44]

Codependency was a useful framework for explaining some of the dysfunctional behaviors observed in the wives of alcoholics. In their efforts to cope with the stressors brought on by their spouse's drinking, they eventually became a part of the problem by "enabling" it to continue through their own dependence on the relationship with the alcoholic. This concept was also useful in treatment, since it provided a framework for spouses regarding their own "recovery" from the effects of alcoholism. Mendenhall proposes that the term *codependent* can be used in reference to any person living in an ongoing committed relationship with an alcoholic or addict, whether spouse, parent, child, or grandparent.[45] The concept is often applied more broadly to describe individuals who engage in ongoing dysfunctional relationships, whether chemical dependency is present or not. Although these definitions imply that the individual is codependent in relationship to an alcoholic or other person, current use holds that the individual is engaged in a disease process of dependency in his or her own right.[46] Codependent characteristics are thought to emerge from childhood abuse experienced in one's own family of origin.[47] Hence, there is a clinically derived, theoretical relationship between the constructs of shame and codependency.[48]

The concept of codependency seems to defy precision, and various authors have defined it with their own constellation of attitudes and behaviors. Two representative definitions that capture the gist of this concept are offered here. Black

states that codependency can refer to anyone "whose behavior is characterized by the numbing of feelings, by denial, low self-worth, and compulsive behavior. It manifests itself in relationships when you give another person power over your self-esteem."[49] Whitfield defines it as "any suffering and/or dysfunction that is associated with or results from focusing on the needs and behavior of others . . . [so] that they neglect their true self— who they really are."[50] Because the construct is so comprehensive and encompasses such diverse characteristics, Cermack[51] identifies five types of codependency: the martyr, the prosecutor, the co-conspirator, the drinking (or drugging) partner, and the apathetic codependent.[52]

Codependency purportedly develops when individuals learn to "repress their self-awareness, which means that these individuals do not get their needs met or feelings acknowledged."[53] The prevailing explanation is that this first occurs when children grow up in shaming family systems. They lose the ability to distinguish between their needs and the needs of others, and they do not develop a firm sense of self.[54] In adulthood, such individuals have difficulty managing stress, have problems engaging in mature relationships, are at increased risk for alcoholism, and are particularly vulnerable to becoming involved with an alcoholic or prealcoholic partner. Further, in the absence of some sort of treatment, these individuals will likely perpetuate this cycle with their own children. A term often used in the clinical literature to convey this concept is *adult child*, which implies that "within each of these adult-age individuals there is a child who has difficulty experiencing a healthy life until . . . recognition and healing of the past occur."[55] Interestingly, however, the literature on codependency and shame do not necessarily overlap. This is perhaps because codependency originated as a self-help movement, whereas conceptualizations of shame are more theoretically derived; however, knowledgeable practitioners link the two concepts.

Kitchens identifies two contrasting models of codependency.[56] The *addict-centered model* emerged from the chemical dependency field. In this model, the codependent person reacts to the behavior of an addicted person, who is the center of the family. The addiction can be alcoholism, rigid religiosity, workaholism, or other dysfunctional behavior. "Regardless of the problem around which the family is centered, the fundamental element of the model has remained intact: A troubled individual, usually a parent, stands at the center of the problem and the other family members react to that person in self-defeating ways."[57] Alternatively, in the *faulty family model*, which arose from the mental health field, the family itself is viewed as the core problem. In essence, family members are not regarded as reacting to an addicted individual. Rather, the addict, along with other family members, belongs to a system in which all family members have developed dysfunctional patterns of coping with each other. Codependent families "have trouble predominantly in the areas of flexibility, boundaries, parent-child coalitions, blaming, poor communication, discounting, and unhealthy rules."[58] Such patterns have been discussed throughout this chapter, although other authors have used other terms, such as *shame-bound families* and *alcoholic families.*[59]

Although *codependency* is used irrespective of gender, it has been described as more prevalent in women[60] and seems to be used most frequently in reference to women. However, there is a growing critique regarding sexism in this concept. According to this view, codependency implies both individual psychopathology in the woman as well as shared responsibility for dysfunction in a relationship. However, this ignores societal attitudes that foster the oppression of women and patterns of gender socialization that encourage the development of stereotypical female attitudes of passivity, dependence, and self-sacrifice.[61] Still others question the utility of attaching a label to women and assisting them to "recover" from what many view as essentially desirable female (or human) qualities. This debate is related to emerging theories on women's psychological development[62] that critique "male" models of human development as es-

sentially based on separation and autonomy and propose a "female" model based on interdependence. The topic of codependency could certainly benefit from empirical investigation and perhaps reconceptualization.

Children of Alcoholics

A related issue to codependency is the concept of children of alcoholics (COAs). Of the estimated 28.6 million children of alcoholics in the United States, about 6.5 million are under the age of 18 and currently reside in homes where at least one parent is alcoholic.[63] In such alcoholic families, there is not a free flow of emotional expression and open communication. Black coined a phrase that captures the powerful injunctions regarding behavioral and emotional expression in these families: "don't talk, don't trust, don't feel."[64]

There is considerable clinical and empirical literature that indicates the detrimental effects of parental alcoholism on children. Being the child of an alcoholic places an individual at greater risk for alcoholism than children of nonalcoholics.[65] A precise risk has not been established due to methodological differences in prevalence studies, but it is estimated that the child of an alcoholic parent is one and one-half to three times as likely to develop alcoholism as the child of a nonalcoholic.[66] While there may be a genetic component to this risk,[67] several studies indicate that family environment is also a contributing factor.[68]

In addition to elevating the risk for alcoholism, children reared by alcoholic parents are thought to be more vulnerable to psychosocial impairment than other children. Hibbard reports that reviews of the research on COAs indicate that "they are probably at greater risk for conduct disorders, hyperactivity and attention-deficit disorder, somatic problems, substance abuse, truancy and delinquency, lower intelligence, more neuropsychological problems, lower scholastic achievement, and more interpersonal difficulties than other children."[69] Russell and associates,[70] as reported by Seilhamer and Jacob, state that

COAs are "over-represented in the caseloads of medical, psychiatric, and child guidance clinics; in the juvenile justice system; and in cases of child abuse."[71] It should be noted, however, that certain children of alcoholics show remarkable resiliency to the potentially damaging effects of parental alcoholism and often grow into fully functional adults despite these known risk factors. In fact, Seilhamer and Jacob conclude that the research on COA outcome is equivocal.[72]

Adult Children of Alcoholics

The psychosocial difficulties experienced by children and adolescents living with an alcoholic parent do not necessarily end as the individual matures. There is increasing evidence that the vulnerability of many COAs extends into adulthood. Of the estimated 28.6 million children of alcoholics in the United States, about 22 million are adults over the age of 18.[73] Parental alcoholism can be related to adult impairment—in particular, the so-called adult children of alcoholics syndrome proposed by chemical dependency counselors. This syndrome refers to a behavioral and emotional pattern displayed by some individuals from families with a history of parental alcoholism and codependency characterized by a restricted range of affect and extreme distrust of intimacy.[74] Although widely accepted in the chemical dependency field, the ACOA syndrome has not been validated through empirical research. There are only a few studies that have attempted to specify the individual or family characteristics associated with the ACOA syndrome.[75]

There is a lack of specificity in the literature regarding the etiology of the ACOA syndrome. A number of authors assert that an internalized sense of shame is linked to the dysfunctional behaviors of many adults, including those who display the ACOA syndrome (and who may or may not be alcoholic as well). Individuals who grew up in "shame-bound" families, whether characterized by alcoholism or other pathology, are thought to often experience impairment in adulthood.

However, coming from a family with parental alcoholism or other pathology is not sufficient for the development of characteristics of the ACOA syndrome. According to G. Kaufman, current theory on the development of shame does not predict a particular pathogenic family process (i.e., alcoholism, incest, mental illness, etc.).[76] It is surmised that the model of a "shame-based" identity can be applied only to adults since it is presumed that children (less than age 18) have not fully developed a stable identity, healthy or otherwise.

Pathogenic processes in the family of origin are hypothesized to increase the risk of adult offspring establishing pathogenic family processes in their family of procreation. The findings of several studies suggest that the way in which rituals and routines are practiced in the family of origin may have either a detrimental or a protective influence on the development of alcoholism in offspring.[77] In essence, the authors found evidence that families that had a breakdown of rituals were associated with lower levels of functioning in young offspring, higher levels of alcoholism in adult offspring, and lower levels of ritual practices by adult offspring in their family of procreation. Thus, a cross-generational pattern is established that perpetuates alcoholism and its related problems.

To conclude, definitional issues complicate an understanding of the emotional and behavioral patterns of alcoholism, codependency, COA, ACOA, and shame. These terms (and the constructs that they represent) are not only poorly defined but they are also interrelated, and therefore it can be difficult to distinguish them from each other. Some authors contend that all alcoholics are also codependent, although this position is not universally accepted in the chemical dependency field.[78] Others use the terms *adult child, ACOA*, and *codependent* interchangeably. However, not all ACOAs meet the profile of codependency, nor are all codependents from alcoholic families. In an effort to be more inclusive of alcoholism and other forms of chemical dependency, the term *adult children of addicted families* is used by some authors.[79] Yet, since not all people displaying ACOA-like characteristics are from addicted families, the phrase *adult children of dysfunctional families* is becoming more common, especially since the process of recovery that has been helpful to ACOAs appears to be helpful to other people as well.[80] Such a trend is viewed by many practitioners and researchers as *too* inclusive. A phrase often repeated in the increasing overlapping fields of chemical dependency and mental health is that 90 percent of Americans are codependent; if so, this is normative! This phrase illustrates the struggle that exists to establish both compassionate and credible parameters around these concepts.

Assessment and Treatment of Alcoholic Families

There are many reasons for including the family in treating what has traditionally been viewed as an individual problem. Wegscheider identifies several ways that involving the family can benefit the alcoholic in his or her individual treatment: They can provide useful information about the patient, they may be alcoholic or emotionally disturbed themselves (and negatively affect the patient if they are not treated, too), and they are likely to continue to enable the patient's dependency if they do not receive help.[81] Further, "family treatment may be our best hope for preventing alcoholism and drug dependency in the next generation."[82]

There are also reasons for focusing treatment on the family itself. According to Lawson and associates, it is unproductive to treat an individual separate from the system if he or she will be returning to live with the family, family members are also under stress and probably in need of help, and only through participating together in treatment can the family truly understand its dynamics and develop new behaviors.[83] There is some evidence that alcoholics show a better response to treatment when it includes family members (especially the spouse).[84] In addition, such an approach allows the family to share a common goal and, even if problems continue, to perhaps experience some success in nondrinking areas of communication and interaction.[85]

A family may enter treatment through several routes. Lawson and associates classify alcoholic families using five categories.[86]

1. A family may seek therapy with the undesirable behavior of a child as the presenting problem, when there is actually hidden alcoholism or drug addiction in one or both of the parents.
2. A family may acknowledge a problem with parental or spousal drinking, but it is not chronic and seems secondary to other problems in the family, although they probably may be interrelated (as is often the case in abuse or neglect).
3. A family presents with alcoholism as the major problem. These families are organized around the alcoholism, and it is a source of severe conflict.
4. An alcoholic family may seek help after the drinking individual has entered recovery and the family's equilibrium is disturbed.
5. The identified patient may be an adolescent in a family without parental drinking, hidden parental drinking, or parents in recovery.

Elkin contends that alcoholic families usually enter treatment in one of three ways: problems encountered by the children, the wife seeks treatment for herself, or the family experiences a crisis.[87]

Thus, families may enter treatment with or without the goal of directly addressing alcoholism in a spouse, parent, or child. Depending on the nature of the treatment they receive, the alcoholism may or may not be addressed. Since alcoholic families are quite adept at keeping their "secret" hidden, alcoholism may not surface unless the therapist looks for it. If the family acknowledges the problem but the alcoholic or addict does not, a process called *intervention* may help.[88]

Intervention is based on the premise that alcoholics who are in denial will resist any attempt to be engaged in treatment. Therefore, presenting them with the need for help must be done in a way that they can accept. Conducted in conjunction with a specially trained professional, an *intervention* is a carefully planned and rehearsed procedure. In a nonjudgmental tone, significant persons in the alcoholic's life (such as family members, friends, employer, doctor, etc.) confront him or her with firsthand, specific, behavioral feedback regarding how the alcoholic's drinking has affected them. Once the alcoholic's denial has been weakened by the reality of his or her behavior, the interveners present acceptable treatment options to the alcoholic, permitting him or her some input in the decision making. The alcoholic's excuses for avoiding treatment have been anticipated, so they are less likely to be successful. Loneck and colleagues provide a review of the literature on the effectiveness of the Johnson intervention as a therapeutic technique. Although the Johnson intervention (JI) is highly effective for engaging and retaining clients in inpatient treatment, the effectiveness for outpatient treatment and the differential impact of variations of the JI have not been evaluated. This study found that patients receiving JI were more likely to enter treatment than those receiving other methods of referral (coerced, noncoerced, unrehearsed intervention, and unsupervised intervention). Of patients entering treatment, those in the JI and coerced referral were equally likely to complete treatment and were more likely to complete treatment than the other groups.[89]

In family treatment, the goal of therapy is not only sobriety for the identified alcoholic but also improvement in family functioning. Wegscheider identifies three broad goals for treatment: (1) education about alcoholism as a family disease and how each member is contributing to it, (2) assistance in making their system more open and flexible, and (3) fostering each family member's personal growth and self-worth.[90] Elkin identifies five goals: (1) stop the drinking and/or isolate the drinking member, (2) stop life-threatening or destructive behavior of family members, (3) disengage children from parental roles and alter inappropriate parent/child alliances, (4) help re-form the parental alliance and authority, and (5) support members in obtaining necessary resources outside of the family.[91] As noted earlier, Kitchens recommends targeting inflexibility, boundary confusion, parent/child coalitions, scapegoating, inadequate communication, discounting feelings, and unhealthy rules.[92] In a review article, Rotunda and colleagues state that successful family treatment of alcoholism requires addressing relapse prevention and the tendency toward conflict (including violence), and caution against overgeneralizing in the use of empirically invalidated clinical metaphors such as *codependency* and *family roles*.[93]

It should be recognized that a family-oriented perspective in the treatment of alcoholism does not imply that the family *caused* the problem. In fact, as noted throughout this book, there is likely no single cause of chemical abuse or dependency. These problems may arise from and be maintained by a combination of biopsychosocial factors in both the individual and family. A family-oriented approach conceptualizes the problem in terms of family functioning and directs treatment at that level. Although differing theoretically, each of the models presented here recognizes that interactive patterns maintain the drinking and contribute to family dysfunction. Therefore, each advocates including the family in some aspect of treatment and contends that any changes will affect the system, not just individuals.

Behavioral Perspective

A behavioral approach to working with couples or families is based on principles of behavioral theory. Such principles can be used in behavioral therapy of families or as a model of family therapy that utilizes behavioral principles (see the next section). Regardless, according to Goldenberg and Goldenberg, "The unique contribution of the behavioral approach lies not in its conceptualization of psychopathology or adherence to a particular theory or underlying set of principles but in its insistence on a rigorous, data-based set of procedures and a regularly monitored scientific methodology."[94] Briefly stated, behavioral theory argues that virtually all behavior is learned (as opposed to inborn) and maintained (or conditioned) through environmental or social consequences, such as reinforcement. Social learning theory and cognitive-behavioral theory add to the conditioning theories by recognizing that cognitive processes, such as modeling, mediate between the individual and the environment.

How does behavioral therapy apply to chemically dependent families? These families often attempt intuitively to use positive reinforcement (reward drinking behavior through attention or caregiving), negative reinforcement (protect the chemically dependent individual from the negative consequences of drinking or drugging), or punishment (inflict a penalty on the person for drinking or drugging).[95] Unfortunately, each of these responses is considered to increase the likelihood of drinking. Behavioral therapy, on the other hand, attempts to apply the principles of reinforcement to achieve desirable results. "The guiding principle of the application of behavioral techniques in family treatment of alcohol abuse is to increase and reinforce positive behaviors/interactions among family members and to decrease negative behaviors/interactions related to drinking."[96] Another application of behavioral theory to family treatment is modeling. For example, the therapist can model more functional interaction with the alcoholic for family members, and the spouse can model more appropriate drinking behavior for a nonabstinent individual.[97]

Behaviorally oriented family treatment differs from systems-oriented family therapy in several important ways. Treatment begins with a behavioral assessment of family difficulties, which identifies specific areas to target for intervention, as well as a careful analysis of antecedent and consequent events. Assessment is an ongoing process; intervention is modified in response to changing behaviors. Treatment is directed at observable behavior, and there is no effort to address intrapsychic processes or interpersonal patterns (other than those specifically related to the target behavior). The causes and effects of the problem are seen as linear rather than circular, as is common in most family therapy models. Further, the behavioral approach tends to focus on dyadic interactions rather than triads. Families are often educated in the principles of behavior therapy so that they can monitor and modify their own behavior and interactions.[98]

Stress-Coping Perspective

The stress-coping and behavioral models are similar in many respects. Both were first used to address addiction in the individual and both have been expanded to include marital and family relationships. Like the behavioral and systems perspectives, the stress-coping perspective recognizes the reciprocal nature of family interaction. However, this perspective differs from the family system perspective since it does not view the family as a unit unto itself but, rather, the family is viewed as the context for the stress and coping of individual members. The stress-coping model, "which focuses on stressful life circumstances, social resources, and individual coping responses, can shed light on both the processes of remission and relapse for alcoholics in family settings and the processes by which family members adapt to an alcoholic partner or parent."[99]

For the alcoholic, this theory contends that "substance use represents an habitual maladaptive coping response to temporarily decrease life stress and strain."[100] Stressors may or may not precipitate drinking; this depends on a number of factors, including the individual's coping mechanisms, treatment experiences, and life context (including the family). "An alcoholic's life context can provide a supportive milieu for continued improvement, cushion the impact of stressors, or trigger a relapse."[101] For the spouse and children of an alcoholic, other factors in their lives besides the alcoholic's behavior must be considered, such as environmental factors, life stressors, and the functioning of the individual or other family members (for children, this particularly refers to the nonalcoholic parent).[102]

Treatment using the stress-coping approach can vary widely. Al-Anon can be viewed as using this model in that it emphasizes the development of skills for coping with the stress of dealing with an alcoholic loved one. Al-Anon members are encouraged to find satisfaction through their own pursuits. In addition to Al-Anon, family members can learn more adaptive coping through individual therapy. These individual efforts, in turn, can have the added effect of facilitating changes in the alcoholic, since change in one member affects the whole system. Marital or family-oriented treatment assists members in identifying personal and familial stressors that impede the recovery process and shows them how to develop more adaptive cognitive and behavioral coping mechanisms, communication patterns, and problem-solving skills. Wallace identifies five coping mechanisms often employed by the spouses of alcoholics that may actually encourage continued drinking: (1) withdrawal, (2) protection of the alcoholic, (3) attack, (4) safeguarding family interests, and (5) acting out.[103] Identifying more effective strategies can be a complex process, since "the effectiveness of a particular coping skill will vary, in all likelihood, with (1) the situation itself, (2) the individual alcoholic, (3) the characteristics of the spouse, and (4) the strength and cohesiveness of the marital bond."[104]

Family Therapy Perspective

Family therapy is defined as "a variety of different strategies and techniques, based on somewhat different theories, for the ultimate goal of realigning relationships in the family to achieve better adjustment of all individuals in the family."[105] Family therapy (including marital therapy) represents a shift from viewing people as individuals to viewing them through their relationships to others.

There are three broad goals of family therapy: "(1) to facilitate communication of thoughts and feelings between family members, (2) to shift disturbed, inflexible roles and coalitions, and (3) to serve as role models, educators, and demythologizers, showing by example how best to deal with family conflict."[106] Models of family therapy have been classified using several different frameworks. Walsh, for example, typically identifies six models: psychodynamic, Bowenian, experiential, structural, strategic, and behavioral.[107] Other authors use other classifications such as systemic, communication, or existential. Although each model shares a family systems theoretical orientation, they differ in terms of conceptualization of the problem, specific goals of treatment, strategies and techniques, and role of the therapist.[108]

There is no model of family therapy designed specifically to address addiction. Rather, the philosophy, goals, and strategies of each model are applied to alcoholism as the "presenting problem" indicative of underlying dysfunction in the family system. The behavioral or stress-coping perspectives focus directly on the alcohol-related behaviors of family members, whereas family therapy focuses more on the nature of the relationships among family members, which may not be unique to alcoholism. As stated by Collins, research suggests that "the specific nature of the individual's impairment may be a less potent contributor to family dysfunction than is the fact that the family contains an impaired member."[109] Several authors provide guidelines for family therapy with chemically dependent families, although they have not been scientifically validated.[110]

Steinglass and colleagues emphasize that alcoholic families are highly heterogeneous (as are families with an alcoholic member). They believe that "it is no more credible to propose that a single treatment approach will make sense for each and every alcoholic family than it is to assume that all alcoholic families follow comparable developmental courses or manifest the same personality features."[111] However, they do provide some guidelines, briefly highlighted here, for working with these families. It should also be noted that therapists are also heterogeneous. Therefore, as stated by E. Kaufman, "Each therapist should choose those systems of family therapy that best suits his or her personality, making use of those techniques that can be grafted onto one's own individual style and family background."[112]

The Steinglass team has outlined a four-stage sequence for working with alcoholic families.[113] The first stage is a careful assessment in which overall family functioning is evaluated (including the role of alcoholism) and the primary problem is identified and defined at the family level. The assessment, to determine if the system represents an alcoholic family or a family with an alcoholic member, can be accomplished through an interview focused on family rituals to ascertain the extent to which they have been invaded by alcoholism.[114] If the family has become organized around alcoholism,

> a treatment program that leads to a cessation of drinking on the part of the family's alcoholic member will, in such families, have profound implications at almost every level of family life. Thus, in such situations, overall treatment success is likely to depend not only on efforts aimed at alcoholism *per se*, but also on a comprehensive approach to dealing with the family-level implications of the cessation of drinking.[115]

The developmental phase of the family also needs to be ascertained since this has implications in terms of treatment goals and outcome criteria. Alcoholism may or may not be the presenting problem for a family. Families often seek help when they are in the midst of a developmental crisis. It is possible for a family to resolve their developmental crisis without eliminating the drinking. Steinglass and colleagues describe a family making the transition to the later stage of its development.[116] At this stage, one of the family's developmental tasks is to launch adult children into age-appropriate roles. The family successfully achieved this goal even though the parents' drinking pattern remained unchanged.

The outcome of the assessment determines the course of treatment. For an alcoholic family, therapy must target the alcoholism first and then the presenting problem (if it remains after the alcoholism is addressed). For a family with an alcoholic member (i.e., not organized around alcohol), the problem as presented by the family becomes the focus of treatment and alcoholism may be addressed within this context, using traditional family therapy techniques.

If alcoholism is identified as the problem, the second stage is referred to as *family detoxification,* which consists of removing alcohol from the family system. The Steinglass team recommends that the therapist use a problem-solving approach, such as described by Haley.[117] This entails contracting with the alcoholic to stop drinking (including completing a medical detoxification regimen, if necessary) and identifying responsibilities for each family member. The alcoholic may refuse to acknowledge a problem and refuse to detoxify, yet the family may decide to continue treatment. If so, the alcoholic is excluded from the therapy. Examples of tasks in the contract are eliminating alcohol from the home and reinstating family routines. The therapist should anticipate difficulties in negotiating and implementing the contract, since the family is attempting to change instilled patterns.

Following successful completion of the diagnosis and detoxification stages, drinking is no longer considered the major issue. The next two stages address family interactional patterns, using any one of the models of family therapy. The third stage addresses the family's emotional instability that follows when drinking no longer occurs in a family that has been organized around alcohol. The task of this stage is to assist the family in tolerating this shift and in establishing new patterns that are not tied to alcohol. A psychoeducational approach explaining the difficulty of making these changes can be very helpful.

The fourth stage, in which the family consolidates changes, can result in two possible outcomes. In the first, called *family stabilization,* the interactional patterns remain essentially unchanged, but the family no longer relies on drinking to regulate them. Alternatively, *family reorganization* occurs when the family fundamentally alters its interactional patterns.

The foregoing framework is a general guide, since it is possible that a family will drop out of treatment at any stage. Further, a family may slip back into alcohol use at some point. In the latter instance, the therapist can renegotiate a *detox contract* and support the family in continuing to make changes. A family systems approach is not always the treatment of choice, since family members are not always available. In addition, family therapy does not eliminate the need to include individually oriented interventions in the treatment, such as AA or Al-Anon.

Effectiveness of Family Treatment

As discussed in Chapter 6, data on the effectiveness of treatment for alcoholism are often equivocal. This same pattern applies to studies that examine the effectiveness of family therapy of alcoholism. Collins reviewed outcome studies of family treatment for alcoholism using behavioral marital therapy, systems-oriented marital therapy, and Al-Anon groups.[118] She found inconclusive results, mainly attributable to methodological limitations of the studies. Steinglass and associates interpret the literature as more supportive of the positive outcomes of family therapy.[119] Although acknowledging limitations of the data, they point out that no other treatment has been shown to be any more effective in producing desirable changes in behavior.

Steinglass and colleagues "reviewed findings from 21 studies investigating the efficacy of family therapy as a treatment for alcoholism and found evidence to support the potential usefulness of including family members in all three phases of alcoholism treatment—initiation of treatment, primary treatment rehabilitation, and aftercare."[120] No single family therapy approach was

shown to be more effective, and some family variables influenced the findings (i.e., gender of the identified alcoholic, commitment to and/or satisfaction with the marriage, and spousal support for abstinence). Liddle and Dakof examined controlled treatment outcome research of family therapy for drug abuse in both adolescents and adults.[121] They found "family therapy . . . to be more effective than other treatments in engaging and retaining adolescents in treatment and reducing their drug abuse." Only one study provided support in the adult area. While recognizing substantial progress in this clinical research area, they conclude that a blanket endorsement of the family treatment of drug abuse cannot be offered at this time due to the small number of studies and methodological limitations.[121]

Case Example

The following case example illustrates some of the main points emphasized in this chapter, particularly regarding the family therapy perspective. It is a composite of several families with whom I (Hawkins) have worked in my clinical practice. The names and significant characteristics have been altered to protect their identities. The reader should bear in mind that there is considerable variation among families, therapists, and modalities. This case represents only one possible approach and has been simplified for the sake of brevity.[122]

Presenting Problem.   Emily is a white, 18-year-old high school senior. She was admitted to City Psychiatric Hospital in December following a suicide attempt. She had no history of prior psychiatric treatment or difficulties. She presents as an attractive, intelligent, and cooperative adolescent. Behavioral and emotional problems emerged one year ago and escalated rapidly: conflict with her parents over money, studying, household duties, and curfew; school failure and truancy; depression; and social isolation. If these problems persist, she will not graduate in May.

While in the hospital, Emily revealed extensive substance abuse, primarily alcohol, but occasional use of marijuana, cocaine, and "pills." She would use "whatever was available." She began drinking two years ago and reported that she "loved" alcohol, both the taste and the way it made her feel. Typical use consisted of daily drinking and binging on the weekend to the point of intoxication. She successfully hid her drinking from her parents. She described them as "preoccupied with their own problems." Emily feels that her father abuses alcohol. She claims that her suicide attempt, mixing alcohol with barbiturates, was an accident. It occurred after her boyfriend broke up with her and she felt lonely.

After being evaluated in the hospital, Emily was transferred to a 30-day residential treatment program for adolescent substance abusers. She seems to have benefited from this treatment in that she now describes herself as "in recovery." She realizes that she must remain abstinent, and she attends several AA meetings a week. She meets regularly with the high school social worker and participates in a weekly peer support group. Although she feels that she is "turning her life around," conflict has continued with her parents. She and her family were referred to Mental Health Clinic for one hour a week of outpatient family therapy following her discharge from the treatment program.

Family History.   Other family members are the father, Jim, an accountant (age 42); Susan, a homemaker (age 42); and Jason, a high school freshman (age 15). They are a white, middle-class family. Both Jim and Susan described their family of origin as traditionally suburban middle class, with a breadwinner father and homemaker mother. They met in college, married immediately after graduation, and had their first child two years later. Jim described his father as a steady drinker, who was frequently verbally abusive. In retrospect, Jim believes that his father drank heavily throughout his childhood and adolescence, although he believes that his mother protected him

and his older brother from much of their father's alcoholic behavior. Susan reported that there was considerable conflict between her parents, who divorced when she was 16 years old. She rarely saw her father after the divorce. She reports no substance use by her parents.

The couple described their marriage as "average," although closer inspection reveals that they seldom interact. Jim, who is self-employed, has been quite focused on his business over the last few years. The struggling local economy had severely cut his income. Susan is actively involved in several charity organizations and social groups. They acknowledged having "drifted apart." In fact, there is little indication that the family as a whole has much interaction, since they do not eat meals together and spend most of their time in separate rooms. Jim acknowledges that he has three to four drinks a night but does not see this as a problem. Susan confirms this intake and feels that Jim's drinking is a way for him to relax, given his work stress. Susan drinks socially on occasion. Jason denies any drinking or drug use, and his parents believe that this is an accurate report.

Assessment.   According to a family systems perspective, Emily is the "identified patient" in this family. Although she clearly has an alcohol abuse problem in her own right, there appear to be underlying factors in the family that are contributing to her difficulty as well as to that of other family members. One pattern observed in this family is *triangulation*. This concept can refer to the tendency of a marital dyad to maintain stability in their relationship by focusing their attention on a third person, usually a child. When a child experiences difficulties, the parents' attention is diverted away from addressing the problems in their relationship. From a systems perspective, all family members are participating in this pattern with the goal of reducing stress and conflict. Emily's problems could be seen as a way to keep her parents engaged with each other through their mutual concern for her. Thus, they are spared from having to confront the lack of emotional support in their marriage. Developmentally, Emily is at an age when she should be starting to emancipate. This pattern may also serve to keep her in a nonadult role with her parents.

This family presents with at least three generations of active substance abuse. Jim is the adult child of an alcoholic father and a codependent mother and appears to be in denial regarding his own alcohol abuse problem. One could hypothesize that he learned the "don't talk, don't trust, don't feel" rules that are often encountered in these families. It is not surprising that he is having difficulties with intimacy in his marriage and with his children. Susan suffered a severe blow to her sense of security when her parents divorced and her father became distant. She may not recognize the potential for a similar outcome in her own marriage. They have evolved into a classic male alcoholic, female codependent pattern in which both minimize the extent of problems that alcohol is causing in their family. They are locked in behavioral patterns that are self-defeating and are actively training their children into these roles as well. It appears that alcoholism accounts for the lack of shared rituals and routines in their daily life, and therefore they can be described as an "alcoholic family."

Treatment.   From a systems perspective, the focus of therapy will be on improving family functioning (communication and interaction) for the benefit of all family members. (See specific treatment goals discussed on p. 240.) Since there is apparent active alcohol abuse in two family members (Emily and Jim), this will be the initial focus of treatment. Although Emily is engaged in a recovery program, the presence of alcohol in the home, her father's unwillingness to admit to his own alcohol abuse, conflict with her parents, and the general lack of emotional support in the family place her sobriety in jeopardy as well as the well-being of other family members, including Jim. Therefore, the therapy should begin with the immediate goal of cessation of Jim's drinking. Once this is addressed, the goal will become to assist the

family in developing patterns of interaction and communication that foster the growth of all family members. The therapy will be conducted following the four-stage model outlined earlier in the chapter.

The first stage is diagnosing alcoholism and labeling it as a family problem. In the initial session, the therapist assesses the family functioning by questioning each family member. She wants to gain information as well as establish a therapeutic relationship with them. Jim and Susan adamantly insist that Emily's oppositional behavior is the source of their family's current problems. They feel that otherwise they would be "normal" and cite their previous successful functioning (prior to Emily's difficulties) as evidence of their position. Emily remains noticeably sullen throughout the session. Jason seems to make every effort to appear invisible and grudgingly agrees with his parents when asked for his perspective by the therapist.

In the next session, Emily becomes more vocal. She had met with her school social worker who urged her to share her concerns about her father's drinking and her mother's acquiescence in family therapy. She defiantly reports that her father is an alcoholic and that "I should know." She and Jim immediately become entangled in a conflict. He denies that he has a problem and accuses her of trying to shift the blame for her behavior. Susan and Jason watch in silence, with evident discomfort. When questioned by the therapist, Susan expresses concerns for Jim's health, revealing her fear that he will have a heart attack due to the stress of their financial situation. She apparently attempts to deflect the focus back to Emily by adding that their daughter's difficulties have exacerbated his stress. When questioned again about Jim's drinking, she seems to minimize it by stating that he "needs to drink to relax." (Thus, focusing on Emily also serves to avoid having to deal with the pressing economic problems of the family as well as their marital problems.)

The family is in a stand-off, and it is crucial for the therapist to address this issue openly. She presses Jason for his opinion (the "silent" member of a family is often the most valuable source of information). With reluctance, he agrees with both Emily's and Susan's concerns: He thinks his father drinks too much and also worries about his health. With Jason's revelation, Susan's resolve to "protect" Jim in his denial weakens. Although she continues to waver, with further probing by the therapist, she and the children gradually align in their concern about Jim's drinking. They identify the following problems: embarrassment when he is drunk in public, anxiety when he wants to drive while intoxicated, fear of his rageful outbursts, sadness over his emotional unavailability, and concerns regarding his poor health and the financial instability of the family.

Jim becomes increasing defensive and, in an effort to keep him engaged in the therapy, the therapist reframes this feedback in terms of his family's honesty: Although painful, it is an indication of their love for him. She commends him for having developed such a sense of trust with his family that they were willing to be so honest. (It should be noted that the therapist is not labeling Jim as alcoholic at this point. Rather, she is keeping the focus on this topic and facilitating the family members in their efforts to state directly how his drinking is causing problems in their family. This avoids the possibility that the father will "attack" the therapist, be supported by family members, and manage to avoid this issue.) The session concludes by the therapist clearly identifying that's Jim's drinking appears to be a major problem for the family.

On the third session, the family comes in with a crisis: Jason had gotten into a fight at school and was suspended. (Some crisis was almost to be expected, since the family homeostasis had been disrupted last week. One could hypothesize that Jason was assisting Emily in maintaining the family's familiar patterns, particularly in terms of keeping the focus off Jim's drinking.) The therapist quickly moves to counteract this attempt to regain stability by using a psychoeducational approach with the family. She explains the idea of "family system" and how the behavior of each member affects the family as a whole. She observes that the last session

disrupted their usual patterns and notes how distressing this can be. This shows that she is empathic with their situation, places this crisis in a larger context, neutralizes the diversion, and enables her to return the focus to Jim's drinking.

A long silence is broken by Jim's query as to whether the therapist thinks that he has a drinking problem. Aware of the importance of this juncture, she responds that this certainly seems to be the case, based on behavioral indicators, but primarily because she has heard the concerns of his family and cannot disregard them. Since his attendance at this session indicates how strongly he is committed to his family, she is sure that he has heard their concerns as well. (This response puts Jim in a bind, since to disagree with the therapist would suggest that he is disregarding the concerns of his family and would call into question his commitment to them.)

Jim does not respond and is obviously distressed by his predicament. Susan tries to "rescue" him by stating her concern about the problems involving Emily and Jason. The therapist explains that she has not forgotten this, but her experience and the clinical literature indicate that, when present, alcoholism must be addressed first if the family is to resolve other problems successfully. Since Emily is engaged in treatment, Jim's alcoholism must be addressed. Her goal is to keep the topic before the family despite their obvious discomfort. However, they seem reluctant to confront him further. Rather than engage in a power struggle with the family around this reluctance, the therapist wonders aloud at the "power" that alcohol seemed to have over this family. Jim breaks the silence, saying that alcohol has no power over him. She asks why his family is so threatened by the topic (in this way, she highlights the process of alcoholism in the family, not Jim's alcoholism, per se). This provides a less threatening avenue for Susan, Emily, and Jason to once again talk to Jim about his alcohol abuse and the effect it has on them.

In the next session, Jim indicates the effect that his family's disclosure had on him. He was quite withdrawn during the ensuing week. He attempted to prove them wrong by showing that he could quit drinking whenever he wanted. However, in the face of his family's feedback and the unexpected struggle he had in avoiding alcohol, Jim reluctantly agrees that he might have a problem. At this point, several significant events have transpired in the therapy: Jim's denial regarding his alcohol abuse has been broken and his problem has been placed within the larger context of the family. The therapy enters stage 2: removal of alcohol from the family system.

The family and therapist agree to work together to help Jim stop drinking. The next step is to develop a detoxification contract with the entire family, since this is now regarded as a family problem. Since hospitalization is not indicated, the therapist recommends an eight-week outpatient program (only a therapist adequately trained in assessment should make treatment recommendations). Jim will make an appointment with this agency for an evaluation prior to the next session. He will also remove all alcohol from the home (a request made by Emily). Jim asks that the family spend more time together and feels that this will assist him in not drinking. He becomes tearful as he talks about how he feels uninvolved in his children's lives (the therapist notes that he did not include Susan in this sentiment). They decide to have dinner together in the evenings. The therapist praises the family for their courage in confronting this problem together, provides some "reality testing" on the difficulty of their task, but reassures them that they can succeed in making desired changes.

The therapist begins the fifth session by reviewing the family's implementation of the detox contract. Jim has removed all the alcohol from the house, enrolled in an outpatient treatment program, and abstained for the full week. Family members confirm that he has not appeared to drink. However, they did not share any meals together. Susan, although expressing her relief over Jim's adherence to the contract, feels that he has become more "moody." Jim admits to feeling unsupported by the family, particularly since Susan

has not organized any meals. Susan feels that there were too many different schedules among them to plan a specific time for dinner. The therapist anticipated problems with the contract, since the family is attempting to change entrenched patterns. She empathizes regarding the difficulty of their task, commends them for their successes, and assists them to negotiate a better plan. After considerable negotiation, all members agree to adjust their schedule to have dinner together at least three times in the coming week. In addition, they will participate in the family component of Jim's outpatient program. (It is important to recognize that the process of assisting them to develop new skills for problem solving, such as negotiation, is as important to the therapy as the product, the new contract. The therapist also notes the weakness of unity and authority in the parental dyad since they all negotiated equally and independently. Thus, she is continually engaged in assessment, gathering information that will be useful when they begin to address nonalcohol-specific family patterns.)

The next week, Jim enters treatment. In the next six weeks, he indicates that he is clearly engaged in his treatment program. He is feeling a sense of camaraderie with other males that he has not enjoyed since being in the military. Nevertheless, he is finding it difficult not to drink and relies heavily on AA meetings and his sponsor for guidance. The family is actively involved in the family component of his treatment program. Emily is particularly enthusiastic, given her previous positive experience with treatment. She and her father have fewer conflicts as they support each other in their recovery efforts. Jim becomes more involved in Jason's sports activities. The children have developed a habit of "checking in" with Jim at least once a day. Jim frequently expresses a regret that he was not more available to them due to his drinking. The family is managing to have three evening meals together a week and is trying to share one activity together on the weekend.

As Jim continues to maintain sobriety, the therapy shifts into stage 3: the emotional desert.

Jim is six weeks into his treatment and has been sober for two months. The focus of therapy is to support the family as they adjust to the absence of alcohol in the family system and to tolerate these changes. For years, they have slowly altered their behavior to accommodate Jim's drinking. In turn, family members have developed maladaptive behavior, such as Emily's drinking, Susan's codependence, and Jason's social withdrawal. They must learn new patterns of interaction and communication. Since Jim drank excessively for a number of years, the shift from a "wet" to a "dry" state is quite stressful. The therapist expects this transition to be difficult and uses a psychoeducational framework to help them understand the nature of these changes.

Susan appears to experience the most difficult adjustment. She expresses a sense of unfamiliarity with Jim and discomfort with his new behavior. Toward the end of his treatment program, she begins to express anger toward him for now being the "perfect father," despite years of being essentially absent. Although pleased that the family is growing closer, she feels that an unfair burden has been placed on her to prepare meals and provide emotional support while Jim gets to "have fun" with the children or be self-absorbed in his recovery. Susan reveals that she has not been attending Al-Anon meetings or reading about codependency. The therapist discusses with the family, focusing on Susan, how she and Jason, although nonalcoholics, nevertheless must also work on their recovery.

The therapy is now concentrating on non-alcohol-specific areas of family functioning. Susan's concerns have touched on core problems of intimacy in the couple's relationship. To reinforce an appropriate boundary between the parental and child subsystems (i.e., to avoid discussing private marital issues in the presence of the children), the therapist requests a meeting with Susan and Jim alone. (Although marital therapy seems indicated in this case, this change in format is not always necessary.) The goal of this marital therapy is to assist them in sharing their feelings and to problem solve through the use of traditional marital therapy techniques. An early task is to set guidelines for fair fighting as they express mutual feelings of bitterness and regret. The state of "disorganization" in the relationship is punctuated by joint statements regarding the possibility of divorce. Yet both partners indicate their commitment to each other and their desire to improve the marriage. After several conflictual sessions, the therapist is effective in helping each partner to take responsibility for his or her contribution to the breakdown of their marriage and to work toward conflict resolution.

The prospect of divorce is unsettling to both of them. This crisis unveils deep fears in Susan stemming from her parents' divorce, and she gains insight into the origins of her codependency. She realizes that she assumed a childlike position in the marriage and was avoiding many aspects of being a wife and mother, such as giving Jim full authority over financial matters and not monitoring the activities of her children. This appears to be the source of many of her complaints about changes in the family (i.e., being forced into a more mature role). She held the irrational belief that being more assertive and independent would cause him to leave her. For his part, Jim acknowledges that he encouraged her dependence, since this was the model he observed in his family of origin. However, this same upbringing left him with strong unmet needs and weak coping skills. Therefore, he was equally dependent on Susan and fearful of abandonment by her. He was overwhelmed by his perceived sole responsibility for the financial well-being of the family. Rather than turn to his wife for assistance, alcohol became a way of coping with his fears and anxieties. Once they identified these feelings, they were able to view each other's behavior in a more positive light. They began to build trust in their relationship, based on active choices rather than passivity.

The therapist meets with Jim and Susan for six weeks. At the conclusion of the marital sessions, the family had been in therapy for approximately four months. Jim has completed his eight-week treatment and has been participating in the weekly follow-up program for one month. He has been sober for over three months. Emily continues to attend follow-up at her treatment program and has been sober for almost six months. As Jim and Susan address their marital problems directly and change their relational patterns, the family entered stage 4: resolution. The goal of this stage is to help the family in their reorganization, since their basic patterns of functioning have undergone significant change. (If Jim had maintained sobriety but their interactional patterns had gone unchanged, the goal would have been family restabilization.) The role of the therapist is to assist them in developing more functional patterns through the application of traditional family therapy techniques.

A new stability in the marriage leads to overall improved functioning in the family. They remain in family therapy for two more months. As Susan and Jim continue to work on achieving mutuality in their relationship, their parenting improves. They make joint decisions regarding the children and feel more comfortable in asserting their authority. Thus, rules and expectations become more clear, and as a result, Emily and Jason show more age-appropriate behavior. Jason begins to explore an unexpressed artistic ability. In the past, Jim had tried to push him into athletic pursuits, for which he was not temperamentally suited. Now they are looking for areas of common interest. Although problems still arise, they offer opportunities for the family to build and practice skills for problem solving and conflict resolution. The family interacts more and eats together on a regular basis, with Jim sharing parental responsibility with Susan. They continue to develop skills for more effective communication, particularly pertaining to emotional expression. All family members attend support groups to address their individual needs. Jim and Susan jointly sought advice for addressing their financial problems and are implementing a plan.

Breaking old patterns and consolidating new ones is a trial and error process that transpires over the course of therapy. Yet this process will continue even after therapy is completed. One of the last issues discussed is Emily's impending graduation and her plans to attend college in the fall. She wants to begin working this summer so she can save her money and offset some of the expenses, since the family's financial situation remains uncertain. Jim's business has shown slow improvement since he quit drinking, and Susan is considering part-time employment.

At the final session, while reviewing treatment gains and looking forward to the future, the family seems to realize that the end of therapy is really a beginning. Jim voices their commitment to break the cycle of alcoholism and codependence in their family. He states that, although his recovery will take a lifetime, he now understands that, for his family, it will take several generations. From Emily's attempt at death, the family has begun a new life.

Summary

An overview of the history of a family perspective on the theory, research, and treatment of alcoholism indicates that this perspective is widely acknowledged and accepted in the field, although there is no general agreement as to practice. Family treatment can consist of viewing the family as the context for individual behavior as well as viewing the family as a system unto itself (a family systems approach). The related constructs of codependency, children of alcoholics, and adult children of alcoholics have gained a great deal of attention by professionals as well as the public, but these concepts lack empirical investigation that might make them more valuable in affecting positive treatment outcomes for family members. Three predominant models of family assessment and treatment are behavioral, stress coping, and family systems therapies. There is no model of family intervention designed specifically to address addiction. These models share general principles but differ in specific guidelines for intervention. Although outcome studies are inconclusive, it appears that family therapy is equally effective in bringing about desired changes as other treatment modalities.

Endnotes

1. Michael Liepman, Ted Nirenbert, Richard Doolittle, Ann Begin, Thomas Broffman, and Mark Babich, "Family Functioning of Male Alcoholics and Their Female Partners During Periods of Drinking and Abstinence," *Family Process*, Vol. 28, No. 2 (June 1989), pp. 239–249.

2. Migs Woodside, "Research on Children of Alcoholics: Past and Future," *British Journal of Addiction*, Vol. 83, No. 7 (July 1988), pp. 785–792.

3. Saul Shiffman and Thomas Wills, *Coping and Substance Abuse* (Orlando, FL: Academic Press, 1985).

4. Randall Collins, *Sociology of Marriage and the Family: Gender, Love, and Property* (Chicago: Nelson-Hall, 1985).

5. *Alcoholics Anonymous* (New York: Alcoholics Anonymous World Services, 1939), p. 7.

6. Marion Lewis, "Alcoholism and Family Casework," *Social Casework*, Vol. 35, No. 18 (April 1937), pp. 39–44.

7. Irene Goldenberg and Herbert Goldenberg, *Family Therapy: An Overview*, 4th ed. (Pacific Grove, CA: Brooks/Cole, 1996).

8. Elvin Jellinek, *The Disease Concept of Alcoholism* (New Haven, CT: Hill House Press, 1960).

9. Andrew Billings, Marc Kessler, Christopher Gomberg, and Sheldon Weiner, "Marital Conflict Resolution of Alcoholic and Nonalcoholic Couples During Drinking and Nondrinking Sessions," *Journal of Studies on Alcohol*, Vol. 40, No. 3 (March 1979), pp. 183–195; and John Finney, Rudolph Moos, Ruth Cronkite, and Wendy Gamble, "A Conceptual Model of the Functioning of Married Persons with Impaired Partners: Spouses of Alcoholic Partners," *Journal of Marriage and the Family*, Vol. 55, No. 45 (February 1983), pp. 23–34.

10. Samuel Futterman, "Personality Trends in Wives of Alcoholics," *Journal of Psychiatric Social Work*, Vol. 23, No. 1 (October 1953), pp. 37–41; Marion Kalashian, "Working with Wives of Alcoholics in an Outpatient Clinical Setting," *Marriage and the Family*, Vol. 21, No. 2 (May 1959), pp. 130–133; and Gladys Price, "A Study of the Wives of Twenty Alcoholics," *Quarterly Journal of Studies on Alcohol*, Vol. 5 (March 1945), pp. 620–627.

11. Joan Jackson, "The Adjustment of the Family to the Crisis of Alcoholism," *Quarterly Journal of Studies on Alcohol*, Vol. 15, No. 4 (December 1954), pp. 562–568.

12. Goldenberg and Goldenberg, *Family Therapy*.

13. Lester Gliedman, David Rosenthal, Jerome Frank, and Helen Nash, "Group Therapy of Alcoholics with Concurrent Group Meetings of Their Wives," *Quarterly Journal on Studies of Alcoholism*, Vol. 17, No. 4 (December 1956), pp. 655–670; and John Ewing, Virginia Long, and Gustave Wenzel, "Concurrent Group Therapy of Alcoholic Patients and Their Wives," *International Journal of Group Psychotherapy*, Vol. 11, No. 3 (July 1961), pp. 329–338.

14. Peter Steinglass, Linda Bennett, Steven Wolin, and David Reiss, *The Alcoholic Family* (New York: Basic Books, 1987).

15. Goldenberg and Goldenberg, *Family Therapy*.

16. Margaret Bailey, "Alcoholism and Marriage: A Review of Research and Professional Literature," *Quarterly Journal of Studies on Alcohol*, Vol. 22, No. 1 (March 1961), pp. 81–97.

17. Peter Steinglass, "A Systems View of Family Interaction and Psychopathology" in Theodore Jacobs (Ed.), *Family Interaction and Psychopathology: Theories, Methods, and Findings* (New York: Plenum Press, 1987).

18. Gary Lawson, James Peterson, and Ann Lawson, *Alcoholism and the Family* (Rockville, MD: Aspen Publications, 1983).

19. Timmen Cermack, *Diagnosing and Treating Codependency* (Minneapolis: Johnson Institute, 1986).

20. Robert Ackerman, *Children of Alcoholics: Bibliography and Resource Guide* (Pompano Beach, FL: Health Communications Press, 1983); and Robert Ackerman (Ed.), *Growing in the Shadow* (Pompano Beach, FL: Health Communications Press, 1986).

21. Claudia Black, *It Will Never Happen to Me* (Denver: MAC, 1981); and Janet Woititz, *Adult Children of Alcoholics* (Deerfield Beach, FL: Health Communications Press, 1983).

22. Ruth Seilhamer and Theodore Jacob, "Family Factors and Adjustment of Children of Alcoholics," in Michael Windle and John Searles (Eds.), *Children of Alcoholics: Critical Perspectives* (New York: Guilford Press, 1990).

23. Margaret Cork, *The Forgotten Child: A Study of Children with Alcoholic Parents* (Toronto: Alcoholism and Drug Addiction Research Foundation of Ontario, 1969); W. Bosma, "Children of Alcoholics—A Hidden Tragedy," *Maryland State Medical Journal*, Vol. 21, No. 1 (1972), pp. 31–36; and Sharon Slobada, "The Children of Alcoholics: A Neglected Problem," *Hospital and Community Psychiatry*, Vol. 25, No. 9 (September 1974), pp. 605–606.

24. Ann Smith, *Grandchildren of Alcoholics* (Pompano Beach, FL: Health Communications Press, 1988).

25. Claudia Black, *Double Duty* (New York: Ballantine Books, 1990).

26. A discussion of the basic tenets of family therapy can be found in any introductory family therapy text, such as Goldenberg and Goldenberg, *Family Therapy: An Overview*, or Michael Nichols and Richard Schwartz, *Family Therapy: Concepts and Methods* (Englewood Cliffs, NJ: Prentice Hall, 1995).

27. Peter Steinglass, "A Systems View of Family Interaction and Psychopathology," in Theodore Jacobs (Ed.),

Family Interaction and Psychopathology: Theories, Methods, and Findings (New York: Plenum Press, 1987).

28. Virginia Goldner, "Feminism and Family Therapy," *Family Process*, Vol. 24, No. 1 (March 1985), p. 33.

29. Steinglass et al., *The Alcoholic Family*.

30. Ibid., p. xii.

31. Steinglass, "A Systems View of Family Interaction and Psychopathology."

32. Steinglass et al., *The Alcoholic Family*.

33. Ibid., p. 72.

34. Ibid.; and Steven Wolin, Linda Bennett, and Theodore Jacobs, "Assessing Family Rituals in Alcoholic Families," in Evan Imber-Black, Janine Roberts, and Richard Whiting (Eds.), *Rituals in Families and Family Therapy* (New York: W. W. Norton, 1988).

35. Recommended books on shame include Gershen Kaufman, *Shame: The Power of Caring* (Cambridge, MA: Schenkman Books, 1985); Gershen Kaufman, *The Psychology of Shame* (New York: Springer Publishing Company, 1985); Merle Fossom and Marilyn Mason, *Facing the Shame: Families in Recovery* (New York: W. W. Norton, 1986); Ronald Potter-Efron and Patricia Potter-Efron (Eds.), *The Treatment of Shame and Guilt in Alcoholism Counseling* (New York: Haworth Press, 1988); and Ronald Potter-Efron, *Shame, Guilt, and Alcoholism* (New York: Haworth Press, 1989).

36. Fossom and Mason, *Facing the Shame: Families in Recovery*, p. 5.

37. Ibid., p. 8.

38. Kaufman, *The Psychology of Shame*.

39. Sharon Wegscheider, *Another Chance: Hope and Health for the Alcoholic Family* (Palo Alto, CA: Science and Behavior Books, 1981), p. 81. Reprinted by permission of the author and publisher, Virginia Satir, Conjoint Family Therapy Science and Behavior Books, Inc., P.O. Box 60519, Palo Alto, CA 94306 1-800-547-9982.

40. Ibid., p. 81.

41. Ibid., p. 76.

42. Ibid., p. 85.

43. Ibid., p. 85.

44. Warner Mendenhall, "Co-dependency Definitions and Dynamics," in Bruce Carruth and Warner Mendenhall (Eds.), *Co-dependency: Issues in Treatment and Recovery* (New York: Haworth Press, 1989).

45. Ibid.

46. Anne Schaef, *Co-dependence: Misunderstood—Mistreated* (San Francisco: Harper and Row, 1986), and Mendenhall, "Co-dependency Definitions and Dynamics."

47. James Morgan, "What Is Codependency?" *Journal of Clinical Psychology* Vol. 47, No. 5 (September 1991), pp. 720–729.

48. See, for example, Catherine Hawkins, "Pathogenic and Protective Relations in Alcoholic Families (I): De-velopment of the Ritual Invasion Scale," *Journal of Family Social Work*, Vol. 1, No. 4 (1996), pp. 39–49; Catherine Hawkins, "Pathogenic and Protective Relations in Alcoholic Families (II): Ritual Invasion, Shame, ACOA Traits, and Problem Drinking Behavior in Adult Offspring," *Journal of Family Social Work*, Vol. 1, No. (1996), pp. 51–63; and Catherine Hawkins, "Disruption of Family Rituals as a Mediator of Adult Children of Alcoholics' Traits and Problem Drinking," *Addictive Behaviors*, Vol. 22, No. 2 (1997), pp. 219–231.

49. Black, *Double Duty*, p. 6.

50. Charles Whitfield, "Co-dependence: Our Most Common Addiction—Some Physical, Mental, Emotional, and Spiritual Perspectives," in Carruth and Mendenhall (Eds.), *Co-dependency: Issues in Treatment and Recovery*, p. 19.

51. Cermack, *Diagnosing and Treating Co-dependency*.

52. For a more thorough clinical discussion of codependency, see Cermack, *Diagnosing and Treating Co-dependency*; Schaef, *Co-dependence: Misunderstood—Mistreated*; Melodie Beattie, *Codependent No More* (Center City, MN: Hazelden, 1987); Carruth and Mendenhall, *Co-dependency: Issues in Treatment and Recovery*; and James Kitchens, *Understanding and Treating Codependency* (Englewood Cliffs, NJ: Prentice-Hall, 1991).

53. Mendenhall, "Co-dependency Definitions and Dynamics."

54. Kaufman, *Shame: The Power of Caring*.

55. Black, *Double Duty*, p. 3.

56. Kitchens, *Understanding and Treating Co-dependency*.

57. Ibid., p. 5.

58. Ibid., p. 139.

59. See Kitchens, *Understanding and Treating Co-dependency*, for a discussion of intervention techniques for working with individuals and families around the issue of codependency.

60. David Roth and Jeffrey Klein, "Eating Disorder and Addictions: Diagnostic Considerations," *The Counselor* (November/December 1990), pp. 28–33.

61. See, for example, Claudia Bepko, "Disorders of Power: Women and Addiction in the Family," in Monica Mc-Goldrick, Carol Anderson, and Froma Walsh (Eds.), *Women in Families: A Framework for Family Therapy* (New York: W. W. Norton, 1989); and Phyllis Frank and Gail Golden, "Blaming by Naming: Battered Women and the Epidemic of Co-dependence," *Social Work*, Vol. 37, No. 1 (January 1992), pp. 5–6.

62. Carol Gilligan, *In a Different Voice* (Cambridge, MA: Harvard University Press, 1982); and Judith Jordan, Alexandra Kaplan, Jean Miller, Irene Stiver, and Janet Surrey (Eds.), *Women's Growth in Connection* (New York: Guilford Press, 1991).

63. Woodside, "Research on Children of Alcoholics."

64. Black, *It Will Never Happen to Me*.

65. Remi Cadoret, "Genetics of Alcoholism," in Lorraine Collins, Kenneth Leonard, and John Searles (Eds.), *Alcohol and the Family: Research and Clinical Perspectives* (New York: Guilford Press, 1990).

66. Marcia Russell, "Prevalence of Alcoholism Among Children of Alcoholics," in Michael Windle and John Searles (Eds.), *Children of Alcoholics: Critical Perspectives* (New York: Guilford Press, 1990).

67. Cadoret, "Genetics of Alcoholism."

68. Ruth Ann Seilhamer and Theodore Jacob, "Family Factors and Adjustment of Children of Alcoholics," in Windle and Searles, *Children of Alcoholics: Critical Perspectives;* and William Cook and John Goethe, "The Effects of Being Reared with an Alcoholic Half-sibling: A Classic Study Reanalyzed," *Family Process,* Vol. 29, No. 1 (March 1990), pp. 87–93.

69. Stephen Hibbard, "Personality and Object Relational Pathology in Young Adult Children of Alcoholics," *Psychotherapy,* Vol. 26, No. 4 (Winter 1989), p. 504.

70. Marcia Russell, Cynthia Henderson, and Sheila Blume (Eds.), *Children of Alcoholics: A Review of the Literature* (New York: Children of Alcoholics Foundation, 1984).

71. Seilhamer and Jacob, "Family Factors and Adjustment of Children of Alcoholics," p. 169.

72. Ibid.

73. Woodside, "Research of Children of Alcoholics."

74. Black, *It Will Never Happen to Me;* Black, *Double Duty;* Wegscheider, *Another Chance;* and Woititz, *Adult Children of Alcoholics.*

75. Raymond Hawkins II and Catherine Hawkins, "Development and Validation of an 'Adult Children of Alcoholics Tool.' " *Research for Social Work Practice,* Vol. 5, No. 3. (1995), pp. 317–339; Catherine Hawkins, "Alcoholism in the Family of Origin of MSW Students: Estimating the Prevalence of Mental Health Problems," *Journal of Social Work Education,* Vol. 32, No. 1 (1996), pp. 127–143; and Catherine Hawkins and Raymond Hawkins II, "Psychological Type and Adult Children of Alcoholics' Traits," *Journal of Psychological Type,* Vol. 41 (1997), pp. 17–22.

76. Kaufman, *Shame: The Power of Caring.*

77. Linda Bennett, Stephen Wolin, David Reiss, and Martha Teitelbaum, "Couples at Risk for Transmission of Alcoholism: Protective Influences," *Family Process,* Vol. 26, No. 1 (March 1987), pp. 111–129; Linda Bennett, Stephen Wolin, and David Reiss, "Deliberate Family Process: A Strategy for Protecting Children of Alcoholics," *British Journal of Addiction,* Vol. 83, No. 7 (July 1988), pp. 821–829; Stephen Wolin, Linda Bennett, Denise Noonan, and Martha Teitelbaum, "Disrupted Family Rituals: A Factor in the Intergenerational Transmission of Alcoholism," *Journal of Studies on Alcohol,* Vol. 41, No. 3 (March 1980), pp. 200–214; and Stephen Wolin and Linda Bennett, "Family Rituals," *Family Process,* Vol. 23, No. 3 (September 1984), pp. 401–420.

78. Cermack, *Diagnosing and Treating Co-dependency.*

79. Black, *Double Duty.*

80. Ibid.

81. Wegscheider, *Another Chance,* p. 30.

82. Ibid., p. 31.

83. Gary Lawson, James Peterson, and Ann Lawson, *Alcoholism and the Family* (Rockville, MD: Aspen Publications, 1983), p. x.

84. Lorraine Collins, "Family Treatment of Alcohol Abuse: Behavioral and Systems Perspectives," in Collins, Leonard, and Searles, *Alcohol and the Family: Research and Clinical Perspectives,* pp. 285–308.

85. Lawson et al., *Alcoholism and the Family,* p. 286.

86. Ibid.

87. Michael Elkin, *Families Under the Influence: Changing Alcoholic Patterns* (New York: W. W. Norton, 1984).

88. Vernon Johnson, *I'll Quit Tomorrow* (San Francisco: Harper and Row, 1980); and Vernon Johnson, *Intervention: How to Help Someone Who Doesn't Want Help* (Minneapolis: Johnson Institute, 1986).

89. Barry Loneck, James Garrett, and Steven Banks, "The Johnson Intervention and Relapse During Outpatient Treatment," *American Journal of Drug and Alcohol Abuse,* Vol. 22, No. 3 (1996), pp. 363–375.

90. Wegscheider, *Another Chance.*

91. Elkin, *Families Under the Influence,* p. 80.

92. Kitchens, *Understanding and Treating Codependency.*

93. Robert Rotunda, David Scherer, and Pamela Imm, "Family Systems and Alcohol Misuse: Research on the Effects of Alcoholism on Family Functioning and Effective Family Interventions," *Professional Psychology: Research and Practice,* Vol. 26, No. 1 (1995), pp. 95–104.

94. Goldenberg and Goldenberg, *Family Therapy,* p. 252.

95. Barbara McCrady, "The Family in the Change Process," in William Miller and Reid Hester (Eds.), *Treating Addictive Behaviors* (New York: Plenum Press, 1986), p. 310.

96. Collins, "Family Treatment of Alcohol Abuse," p. 288,

97. See Timothy O'Farrell and Kathleen Cowles, "Marital and Family Therapy," in Reid Hester and William Miller (Eds.), *Handbook of Alcoholism Treatment Approaches* (New York: Pergamon Press, 1989).

98. For a framework of a behavioral therapy approach for working with couples and families, see Ray Thomlison, "Behavioral Therapy in Social Work Practice," in Francis Turner (Ed.), *Social Work Treatment: Interlocking Theoretical Approaches* (New York: The Free Press, 1986), p. 142.

99. Ruth Cronkite, John Finney, Jamie Nekich, and Rudolph Moos, "Remission among Alcoholic Patients and

Family Adaptation to Alcoholism: A Stress and Coping Perspective," in Collins, Leonard, and Searles, *Alcohol and the Family: Research and Clinical Perspectives,* p. 309.

100. Raymond Hawkins II, "Substance Abuse and Stress-Coping Resources: A Life Contextual Viewpoint" in Barbara Wallace (Ed.), *The Chemically Dependent: Phases of Treatment and Recovery* (New York: Brunner/Mazel, 1992), p. 161.

101. Cronkite, Finney, Nekich, and Moos, "Remission among Alcoholic Patients and Family Adaptation to Alcoholism," p. 310.

102. For a further discussion of this perspective, see Shiffman and Wills, *Coping and Substance Abuse;* Peter Monti, David Abrams, Ronald Kadden and Ned Cooney, *Treating Alcohol Dependence: A Coping Skills Training Guide* (New York: Guilford Press, 1989); Cronkite, Finney, Nekich and Moos, "Remission Among Alcoholic Patients and Family Adaptation to Alcoholism"; Thomas Wills, "Stress and Coping Factors in the Epidemology of Substance Use," in Lynn Kozlowski (Ed.), *Research Advances in Alcohol and Drug Problems* (New York: Plenum Press, 1990).

103. John Wallace, *Alcoholism: New Light on the Disease* (Newport, RI: Edgehill, 1985).

104. Robert Rychtarik, "Assessment and Implications for Treatment," in Collins, Leonard, and Searles, *Alcohol and the Family: Research and Clinical Perspectives,* p. 357.

105. Vincent Foley, "Family Therapy," in Raymond Corsini (Ed.), *Current Psychotherapies* (Itasca, IL: F. E. Peacock, 1984), pp. 447–490.

106. Irene Goldenberg and Herbert Goldenberg, *Family Therapy: An Overview,* 2nd ed. (Monterey, CA: Brooks/Cole, 1985), p. 250.

107. Froma Walsh, "Family Therapy: A Systemic Orientation to Treatment," in Aaron Rosenblatt and Diana Waldfogel (Eds.), *Handbook of Clinical Social Work* (San Francisco: Jossey-Bass, 1983), pp. 466–489.

108. A more thorough discussion of the different models of family therapy can be found in any basic family therapy text, as noted above.

109. Collins, "Family Treatment of Alcohol Abuse," p. 304.

110. Duncan Stanton and Thomas Todd (Eds.), *The Family Therapy of Drug Abuse and Addiction* (New York: Guilford Press, 1982); Lawson, Peterson, and Lawson, *Alco-*holism and the Family; Elkin, *Families Under the Influence;* Edward Kaufman, "The Application of the Basic Principles of Family Therapy to the Treatment of Drug and Alcohol Abusers," in Edward Kaufman and Pauline Kaufman (Eds.), *Family Therapy of Drug and Alcohol Abuse* (Boston: Allyn and Bacon, 1992); Steinglass, Bennett, Wolin, and Reiss, *The Alcoholic Family;* and O'Farrell and Cowles, "Marital and Family Therapy."

111. Steniglass, Bennett, Wolin, and Reiss, *The Alcoholic Family,* p. 364.

112. E. Kaufman, "The Application of the Basic Principles of Family Therapy to the Treatment of Drug and Alcohol Abusers," p. 287.

113. Steinglass et al., *The Alcoholic Family.*

114. For an example of a family ritual interview, see Wolin, Bennett, and Jacobs, "Assessing Family Rituals in Alcoholic Families," in Imber-Black, Roberts, and Whiting, *Rituals in Families and Family Therapy.*

115. Steinglass et al., *The Alcoholic Family,* p. 333.

116. Ibid.

117. Jay Haley, *Problem-Solving Therapy* (San Francisco: Jossey-Bass, 1976).

118. Collins, "Family Treatment of Alcohol Abuse."

119. Steinglass et al., *The Alcoholic Family.*

120. Martha Edwards and Peter Steinglass, "Family Therapy Treatment Outcomes for Alcoholism," *Journal of Marital and Family Therapy,* Vol. 21, No. 4 (October 1995), pp. 475–509; quote from p. 500.

121. Howard Liddle and Gayle Dakof, "Efficacy of Family Therapy for Drug Abuse: Promising But Not Definitive," *Journal of Marital and Family Therapy,* Vol. 21. No. 4 (1995), pp. 511–543, quote from p. 521.

122. Additional case studies can be found in Peggy Papp (Ed.), *Family Therapy: Full Length Case Studies* (New York: Gardner Press, 1977); Stanton and Todd, *The Family Therapy of Drug Abuse and Addiction;* Elkin, *Families Under the Influence;* Edward Kaufman (Ed.), *Power to Change: Family Case Studies in the Treatment of Alcoholism* (Boston: Allyn and Bacon, 1984); Donald Davis, *Alcoholism Treatment: An Integrative Family and Individual Approach* (New York: Gardner Press, 1987); Steinglass et al., *The Alcoholic Family;* Kitchens, *Understanding and Treating Codependency;* and Kaufman and Kaufman, *Family Therapy of Alcohol and Drug Abuse.*

11

Ethnicity, Culture, and Substance Abuse

Ethnicity and culture are social systems that influence the attitudes and behaviors of individuals and groups with respect to alcohol and drug use.[1] These systems have been called "the strongest determinants of drinking patterns in a society."[2] This chapter addresses the substance use and abuse of Americans whose ethnic roots are in many different countries. We consider Native Americans, African Americans, and Hispanic Americans; like Anglo Americans, they have considerable levels of alcohol and drug use.[3] Anglos, however, are generally less likely than members of these ethnic groups to encounter alcohol- and drug-related health problems (e.g., cirrhosis) and social problems (e.g., arrests).

In addition, we consider Asian Americans and Jewish Americans. They also comprise ethnic groups in the United States. Although many of them use alcohol, they have fewer chemical dependency problems than most other ethnic groups. We also briefly review information on alcohol use among the Irish, Italians, and the French, because many people in the United States are influenced by these cultural heritages.

One outcome of the proliferation of social and economic ties across the globe has been increased awareness of alcohol and drug use almost everywhere. The scholarly literature as well as accounts in the popular media indicate concerns in countries from Asia to the Commonwealth of Independent States (the former Soviet Union) to Mexico.[4]

Historically, there has been considerable interest in the drinking patterns of Europeans, primarily the French and Italians, and among the Irish and the Jews. As described in Chapter 2, the French and Irish have much higher rates of alcoholism than do the Italians and Jews. Various sociocultural explanations may account for these differences, such as the Italians' habit of drinking wine moderately with meals, whereas the French reportedly drink more distilled spirits in addition to wine and do more drinking apart from meals. Jews tend to drink moderately, primarily in conjunction with religious ceremonies and at home, whereas the Irish drink to socialize, frequently outside the home in pubs. The Netherlands, the Scandinavian countries, Great Britain, Germany, the Mediterranean countries, and India all have their unique histories, customs, and laws that govern alcohol and drug use.[5]

Also introduced in Chapter 2 and explored further in this chapter is that cultures with little ambivalence about chemical use and norms that promote moderation and integration of alcohol and even other drug consumption tend to have lower rates of chemical dependency problems than do countries such as the United States in which the norms and attitudes associated with alcohol and drug use differ widely. Most Americans have banded together in their concern about tobacco use, but there is less consensus on many other mind-altering chemicals, particularly alcohol.

In the United States, substance abuse is primarily defined by the majority, because most incidence and prevalence studies have been conducted by whites on samples largely composed of whites.[6] Little attention has been paid to the conceptualizations of these issues by other ethnic groups. As noted in this chapter, accounts of drinking and drug use among ethnic groups and among Americans as a whole can vary considerably, depending on who wrote them.

Although there is controversy about the need for separate, culturally specific, chemical dependency programs,[7] an understanding of human service work with individuals from various cultures is necessary to function adequately in the field. The reported resistance of some clients to chemical dependency services offered by mainstream providers[8] is not surprising, given the previous insensitive treatment of many ethnic groups. The frustrations or lack of efficacy that professionals may feel in working with people from various ethnic backgrounds can be addressed by pursuing education about general models of cultural competence and about specific cultural groups. They can also be addressed through increased contacts with people of different ethnic backgrounds.[9]

A number of volumes have been written on culturally sensitive practice in the human service professions,[10] some specific to substance abuse prevention and treatment.[11] Models of practice with clients of different ethnic backgrounds generally emphasize the need to understand the history of the cultural group, particularly the group's experiences of oppression.[12] In the chemical dependency field, it is important to note the ways in which alcohol and other drugs have (or have not)

been used by the group and the ways in which the group has come to define alcohol and other drug problems. The cultural values of the group, the group's expectations of its members, and the group's use of its native language are also very important in developing relevant prevention, assessment, and treatment strategies. According to Weibel, "The appreciation of alcoholism or problem drinking as a culturally relative concept may prepare alcoholism counselors to deal more empathetically with their clients and allows for a more meaningful exchange of experience and new knowledge."[13] Although it is impossible to cover the many fine points of service provision to members of different ethnic groups in this chapter, we provide an introduction to some of this material.

Before discussing various ethnic groups, three caveats about this chapter deserve mention. First, the material presented is largely illustrative generalizations of what is known about each of the groups discussed. For example, there are several hundred Native American and Alaskan Native tribes, each with many distinctive cultural features, including drinking and drug use, that cannot be captured in a few pages. The same holds true for the many cultural groups that fall under the categories of Hispanic, Asian, and so forth. Second, the cultural experiences of members of an ethnic group or subgroup are not identical.[14] For example, some Americans of German, Mexican, or Japanese background have little connection to their ancestors' heritage, whereas others practice traditions closely tied to their ancestors' homelands. The region of the United States or community in which one lives may also influence ethnic identification and cultural practices. Third, each person's experiences vary, regardless of his or her ethnic background. Even individuals who grew up in the same family may make different choices about how strongly they will identify with their cultural heritage. Furthermore, important demographic characteristics of individuals are often not considered. For example, socioeconomic status is often ignored, even though differences across the major ethnic groups may disappear once this variable is controlled.[15] Collins calls the lumping together of people of a particular group "ethnic glosses," especially when it involves the use of the highly questionable categorization by race.[16]

When human service professionals talk about differential diagnosis and treatment or individual treatment plans, they are reflecting the need to see the client as a unique human being and not to rely on generalizations. As Chapman notes, clinicians want to avoid "treating the alcoholism rather than the client who happens to have alcoholism."[17] Despite these exhortations, clients and professionals continue to be hampered by the lack of programming and research that address important sociocultural factors.[18] This is especially true in regard to differences *within* the major ethnic groups that might lead to improved prevention and treatment outcomes.[19] With these thoughts in mind, we present some information on what is known about chemical dependency among some of the major ethnic groups in the United States.

Substance Abuse among Native Americans and Alaskan Natives

It is common knowledge, mostly as the result of Western movies, that Native Amercans were introduced to alcohol, or "firewater" as it was called, by the "white man."[20] Although use of alcohol is recorded in the Bible and in ancient mythology and has been used by various groups for thousands of years, the history of most Native Americans' use of alcohol is only a few centuries long. A small number of tribes in what is now the southwestern United States had a history of making alcohol for use in ceremonial and religious purposes, but most Native Americans learned of alcohol from contact with explorers in the sixteenth and seventeenth centuries.[21] These early experiences[22] remain important in understanding Native Americans' contemporary use of alcohol, because in addition to learning about alcohol from the white man, they also learned about drunkenness from him.[23] Whites initially offered Native Americans alcohol

to form alliances,[24] but alcohol was also used as a means of getting them drunk and taking advantage of them in trading and other transactions.[25]

It is also written that Native Americans were unprepared for the use of alcohol, and as a result, they experienced negative consequences following its introduction.[26] Such has not been the case with peyote, a hallucinogenic drug that has been used by Native Americans with few negative consequences.[27] According to MacAndrew and Edgerton, it is noteworthy that early accounts of Native American drunkenness were written by white men and "that the facts of the matter require that such talk be taken with a rather large grain of salt, for it is indisputably the case that not all North American Indians were irresistibly drawn to alcohol, nor did they, even if they drank it, always become uncontrollable as a consequence."[28]

Leland studied the "firewater myth," that Native Americans have an inordinate susceptibility to alcohol abuse, and the "reverse firewater myth," that they are less prone to alcohol abuse.[29] Although she came to no definite conclusion about either, alcohol problems became a concern to some Native American leaders. With their encouragement, a federal law was passed in 1832 that prohibited distilled liquor on reservations; later, ale, beer, and wine were included.[30] Excessive drinking continued, however, as bootleggers and smugglers saw to it that alcohol remained available.[31] Native American prohibition may have inadvertently encouraged practices such as gulping and bingeing, since it was illegal to be caught with alcohol. The 1832 law became regarded as discriminatory, but it was not abolished until 20 years after the repeal of national Prohibition.[32] States and tribal councils are now responsible for alcoholic beverage control policies on their lands.[33] May reports that 69 percent of reservations continue to prohibit alcohol, but this practice may continue to exacerbate some alcohol-related problems such as arrests for drunken driving and auto accidents when Native Americans travel to other areas to buy alcohol.[34]

Given both the historical and contemporary oppression of Native Americans, one explanation of their substance use is that the substances are outlets for frustration or ways of coping with poverty; high levels of welfare dependence; lack of access to education, jobs, and other resources; and social alienation as a result of being cut off from reservation and tribal life and trying to reconcile one's own culture with that of the majority.[35] Weibel-Orlando gives one picture of this devastation:

> The Sioux called liquor "mni wakon" or "sacred water" in reference to its power to induce states of euphoria and to reduce pain and sadness. In the late 19th century, when the farms and the railroads of white pioneers displaced the Sioux and drastically altered their nomadic, big game-hunting way of life, they were forced to accept a lifestyle that lacks meaning for them. Alcohol, like the Vision Quest ritual, may help to fill psychological gaps left by the Sioux's loss of cultural integrity, perception of personal worth, and sense of self-esteem.[36]

The Native American population is now about equally divided between those who continue to live on reservations and those who live in urban areas.[37] To escape extreme poverty on the reservations wrought by government intervention (e.g., denial of mineral, oil, and land rights), some Native Americans migrated to cities, but those who have not acculturated have often seen their problems mount, and these problems include alcohol or other forms of drug abuse.[38] Many apparently remain caught between two worlds with conflicting values and expectations, however.[39] Heath has cautioned that the state of research on Native American acculturation is such that the only broad generalization that can currently be made is "to warn against the popular presumption that acculturation invariably results in stress, which in turn prompts heavy drinking."[40] Oetting and colleagues also describe the difficulties of trying to interpret findings from studies on cultural identification, but their research suggests that Native American children who see themselves as bicultural use alcohol and drugs least, and those

who least identify with Native American culture use drugs most.[41]

Cultural Issues and Chemical Abuse among Native Americans and Alaskan Natives

Cultural values that may affect chemical abuse and its treatment among Native Americans include Native Americans' tendencies to avoid interfering in the decisions made by others, and their preference for not giving direct advice or telling others what to do.[42] This is part of the culture's tradition, but it may be perceived as apathy by the majority culture.[43] Lurie says that many whites find it difficult "to keep their noses out of other people's business,"[44] but others suggest that Native Americans' fatalistic views of illness may contribute to a pattern in which chemically dependent individuals get into treatment late.[45] Furthermore, there seems to be an absence of shame attached to drunkenness and a lack of community sanctions against alcohol misuse among some Native Americans.[46] Like others, Native Americans have been accused of enabling: "It appears to have been common experience for family members, for example, grandparents, to excuse unacceptable behavior and even facilitate it by paying bills, including bail, and placing responsibility on others rather than the alcohol abuser themselves."[47]

Among Native Americans (as well as other groups), drinking is a very social activity and "is part of group membership and acceptance."[48] It may be considered discourteous to refuse a drink; in fact, sharing bottles is common.[49] Several authors have described events called "drinking parties" at which cheap alcohol is consumed rapidly until there is none left or the imbibers become unconscious.[50] For many Native Americans, drinking alone is considered aberrant.[51] Lurie describes an interesting view of Native American alcohol use and abuse: "Getting drunk remains a very Indian thing to do when all else fails to maintain the Indian-white boundary."[52] She adds that "thus, before giving vent to aggressive inclinations, you get drunk or convince yourself and others you are drunk, in order that no one mistakes you for acting like a white man."[53] According to Weibel, the picture of the Native American who drinks excessively and behaves aggressively "contrasts with the Indian's typically quiet, low-affect social demeanor when sober."[54] Oetting and colleagues also note that substance abuse is antithetical to the Native American way of life because it destroys harmony and unity: "Recreational drugs destroy this harmony with nature and damage the ability of the mind, body, and spirit to work together. They are clearly counter to the Indian Way."[55] Great Indian leaders such as Tecumseh, Crazy Horse, and Sitting Bull did not condone drinking.[56] As Leland concludes, "Given the widespread use of liquor by the dominant society, a case certainly could be made that the best way for Native Americans to distinguish themselves from Whites would be to leave liquor alone."[57]

Substance Abuse Problems among Native Americans and Alaskan Natives

Alcoholism among Native Americans and Alaskan Natives is a major health and social concern.[58] It is frequently referred to as their number one problem, although using current diagnostic terminology (see Chapter 5), May says it would be more accurate to say that it is alcohol abuse and alcoholism (alcohol dependence) combined that are so devastating to Native Americans as a whole.[59] Interest in the general subject is reflected in an annotated bibliography published in 1980 by Mail and McDonald, which contained 969 references on alcohol use and abuse among Native Americans.[60] May estimates that the literature on Native American alcohol issues "has at least doubled" since then.[61]

In her 1980 bibliography, Mail noted that more than 450 articles suggested explanations for alcoholism among Native Americans.[62] Similar to the etiological categories of alcoholism described in Chapter 2, she divided the theories into three groups and found that 15 articles discussed biological theories (such as possible genetic susceptibility to alcohol), whereas 157 discussed psychological theories and 295 reported on sociocultural theories. Littman believes that there are many reasons for alcoholism among Native Americans but suggests that four explanations typify the literature on this subject: (1) relief from anxiety due to extreme poverty and other hardships, (2) the psychodynamic explanation of the need to release repressed anger (sometimes regarded as an outlet that prevents the development of psychiatric problems), (3) relief from pressures resulting from forced acculturation, and (4) promotion of group solidarity through a shared, social activity.[63]

Littman dismissed biological or genetic explanations specific to Native Americans due to the lack of any convincing evidence, and Lewis describes Native Americans as a social rather than a biological group, because many have a mixed racial background.[64] Lemert also noted little support for "racially induced vulnerability to the effects of alcohol,"[65] even though this explanation was used to justify laws prohibiting Native Americans from drinking.[66] Despite the lack of empirical evidence that Native Americans metabolize alcohol differently than matched controls of other cultures, May notes that even among Native Americans, the belief of biophysiological inability to hold their liquor and a deficit in metabolizing alcohol persists.[67]

As an alternative explanation, Weibel-Orlando notes that alcohol abuse is sometimes blamed on the carryover of historical binge drinking.[68] Ablon earlier suggested that "widespread drinking problems found among Indians in the city appear to be carried from the reservations rather than being any new response to anxieties caused by the urbanization experience."[69]

Lewis adds to the list of possible causative factors, suggesting that Native Americans themselves think they drink as an expression of defiance against whites, and as a response to boredom and despair.[70] In explaining drinking among Native Alaskans in particular, Knisely suggested that "climate, daylight hours, the forceful introduction of modern technology (post–World War II), and the dramatic urbanization, with new leisure time, that replaced a subsistence way of life" might all be factors.[71]

Despite many criticisms of the methodologies that have been used to study substance abuse among native groups (e.g., the bias that may result from participant observation studies) and despite the problems in conducting research in this area (e.g., data collection is difficult due to the large number of tribes),[72] the literature is clear that Native American mortality is closely associated with alcoholism. The rate of deaths attributable to alcoholism has declined substantially for both Native Americans and the general population in recent decades; however, the alcoholism death rate remains much higher for Native Americans as a group. The alcoholism death rate peaked at 66 per 100,000 members of the Native American population in 1973.[73] In 1991, it was 37, still 5.5 times higher than for the entire U.S. population.[74] Although death rates remain substantially higher for this group, there is hope for continued progress with greater emphasis on ethnic-sensitive prevention, intervention, and treatment approaches. Also noteworthy are the differences in alcohol-related mortality rates that have been reported for Native Americans and Native Alaskans by area, ranging from 32.7 in Alaska to 136.9 in Billings, Montana,[75] indicating the considerable variation among tribal groups in alcohol use and its consequences.[76]

Some tribes, like the Cherokee, have lower rates of alcohol consumption than the general population. Lemert notes that there is a smaller proportion of drinkers among Native Americans than in the general population, but while there are more abstainers, there are also more heavy drinkers.[77] Studies also show that drinking prevalence has decreased in some tribes but increased in others.[78] For example, in a 19-year follow-up

study of a small Native American village in the Pacific Northwest, Leung and colleagues found a decline in the prevalence of alcoholism and substantial levels of remission from alcoholism over time.[79] Drinking among Native Americans seems to remit with age; however, this population is young and alcohol-related deaths among Native American young people are high.[80]

Interpretation of the available data on Native American drinking is also complicated by other anomalies. For example, Heath reports that most Hopis do not drink, even though their reservation is surrounded by the Navajo Reservation where heavy drinking is practiced; the Hopis, however, have a much higher cirrhosis death rate than the Navajo.[81] Heath attributes this to Navajo binge drinking which gives the liver time to mend, whereas Hopi drinkers are ostracized and live in their own isolated skid row. (It should be noted, however, that a pattern of binge drinking may also cause serious physical damage.)

Stratton and colleagues suggest a possible historical explanation for the differential rates of alcoholism among various tribes:

> Tribes having a hunting-gathering tradition have more serious drinking problems than do tribes having an agricultural tradition emphasizing communal values and ceremonies. Furthermore, the western tribes that have preserved ceremonies and values reminiscent of their hunting gathering tradition have more serious alcohol problems than do tribes that have been more acculturated.[82]

They note that high rates of alcohol-related problems tend to be found among tribes in western Oklahoma (the Cheyenne-Arapaho, Anadarko, Wichita, and Caddo) compared with much lower rates among eastern tribes (the Chickasaw, Creek, Seminole, and Cherokee). The western tribes were hunters who lost their means of survival when the federal government prevented buffalo hunting. These tribes reportedly had more loosely integrated social structures and were introduced to alcohol much later than members of the eastern tribes, who were primarily farmers and had more developed social and political structures. Although the eastern tribes also suffered displacement, they were able to reestablish their farms and communities.

After studying Navajos in the Denver area, Graves found "no convincing empirical evidence that there is something unique about the way Indians use alcoholic beverages, or that people in similar circumstances would not behave in a similar fashion."[83] Nofz also warns that high rates of alcohol problems are not an indication that an excessively large number of Native Americans drink or have drinking problems, but it does mean that for those who drink, the consequences may be severe.[84]

In addition to liver disease, other major causes of death among Native Americans—accidents, suicides, and homicides—are often alcohol related.[85] High arrest rates for alcohol-related crimes are another concern. These rates may reflect the tendency to drink in public, thereby increasing the likelihood of exposure to arrest.[86] May concluded:

> The mixing of (1) high-risk environments, (2) flamboyant drinking styles, and (3) risky post-drinking behavior combine to elevate Indian rates of alcohol-related death far above those of the general U.S. population. This is true as well with arrest, injury, and other problems for which statistics are recorded.[87]

Figures on drug use among Native American adults are scarce. Unpublished data from the 1991–1993 National Household Survey on Drug Abuse (a survey conducted annually by the Substance Abuse and Mental Health Services Administration) indicate that among those age 12 and older, 11 percent of Native Americans have used an illicit drug in the past month.[88] Also, prior information from the Client Oriented Data Acquisition Process (CODAP) from 23 states, Washington DC, and U.S. territories in 1983 indicated that Native Americans were more likely than whites to report a problem with heroin, marijuana, PCP, and inhalants.[89]

Native Americans are 0.7 percent of the U.S. population. They were 2.4 percent of clients in substance abuse treatment in 1994.[90] Although little is known about Native Americans' drug use based on general population surveys, this figure on treatment admissions may at least reflect the higher rates of alcoholism among this segment of the population. Of all Native Americans admitted to substance abuse treatment programs, 60 percent were admitted for alcoholism, 12 percent for drug abuse, and 28 percent for both diagnoses.[91] Compared with all clients admitted, Native Americans were substantially more likely to be admitted for alcoholism only, and substantially less likely to be admitted for drug abuse only. They were about equally likely to be admitted for both diagnoses.

May's review of the research indicates that drinking is more prevalent among Native American youths than youths in the general population.[92] After 10 years of studying alcohol and other drug use among Native American adolescents on reservations, Oetting and Beauvais concurred that these youths drink more than other youths; the youths who were studied experience their first episode of drunkenness at about the same age, but Native American youths subsequently get drunk more often.[93] They also noted that compared with other youths, Native Americans have "higher use rates for nearly every category of drug," but they initially try drugs about a year later. Weibel-Orlando's review of the literature on alcohol and drug use found that Native American youths drink more beer and use inhalants and marijuana more but have similar usage of other street drugs.[94] She notes that inhalant abuse has been cited as a particular problem among ethnic groups such as Native Americans. This may be due to the accessibility of products such as gasoline, paint, and glue, even if one has little money. Oetting and Beauvais attribute alcohol and drug use on reservations to boredom, and they attribute increased drug use to the lack of availability of alcohol on many reservations.[95]

Dick and colleagues found substantial amounts of alcohol use as well as alcohol problems among 188 students of a boarding high school, an environment, according to the Department of the Interior, that is still used to educate nearly 20 percent of Native American youths.[96] Some 34 percent had consumed alcohol at least three times in the past month, 42 percent had consumed at least six drinks at one time, 45 percent had experienced a blackout, and 9 percent had been treated for alcohol problems. Given the authors' reports of previous studies of problems experienced by Native American youths in boarding schools, one cannot help but wonder if these high levels are associated with characteristics of students who attend boarding schools or of the boarding school environment itself.

Traditional, laissez-faire childrearing practices among some tribes such as the Ogala Sioux have also been suggested to explain Native American youths' substance use.[97] Still other explanations are role models who also abuse drugs and reverence of elders, even if they abuse alcohol.[98] But when Sellers and colleagues compared drinking among Native American and non–Native American youths in the same rural community, they found that the participants' own permissive attitudes towards alcohol and drug use explained more of the variance in the youths' use than did their perception of adults' or peers' permissiveness, regardless of the youths' ethnicity.[99] Although the youths' own permissive attitudes were explained to a substantial degree by peers' permissiveness as well as the youths' own legal attitudes, adults' permissiveness played a less important role in predicting youths' permissive attitudes or their substance use.

As for drinking among Native American women, May says:

> As in the rest of the United States, fewer Indian women drink than Indian men. In some tribes in the Southwest (Pueblo and Navajo) it is rare and quite unacceptable for any woman to drink at all once they have passed their mid-20s and have done some experimentation. In other tribes, such as the Plains and Basin tribes, more women are

drinkers at all ages and drinking is somewhat more acceptable. Women in these tribes are not as prone to negative sanctions.[100]

An analysis of data from several studies, representing several tribes, also showed substantially less drinking among Native American women than men, with Native American women in rural areas reporting more drinking than women in urban areas.[101] Among the Sioux, however, rural women reported *more* frequent drinking than rural men. As explanations for this anomaly among the Sioux, Weibel-Orlando suggests that high unemployment and welfare dependence may be contributing factors. Additionally, children are often cared for by other family members, which may give parents (particularly mothers) more opportunity to drink.

Similar to women in the general population, Native American women drink less than their male counterparts but are at greater risk for alcohol-related health problems. Women account for almost half of cirrhosis-related deaths among Native Americans and Alaska Natives,[102] and the cirrhosis death rate for Native American women is six times higher than that for white women.[103] In general, Native American women have substantially more alcohol-related mortality than women in the general population.[104] High rates of fetal alcohol syndrome have been reported among some tribes but not others (see Chapter 15).

Prevention and Treatment Services for Native Americans and Alaskan Natives

The first major federal government initiative to develop alcoholism treatment services specifically for Native Americans came as a result of the Comprehensive Alcohol Abuse and Alcoholism Prevention, Treatment, and Rehabilitation Act of 1970.[105] In 1978, the NIAAA began the transfer of its 156 alcoholism and drug abuse programs for indigenous groups to the Indian Health Service

(IHS). The IHS is the agency primarily responsible for federal government activities designed to prevent and treat alcohol and other drug problems among Native Americans and Alaskan Natives. A task force on Native American alcoholism was convened in 1986 by the Secretary of the U.S. Department of Health and Human Services, and the Anti-Drug Abuse Act of 1986 also helped to increase the services available to Native Americans, such as special treatment centers for Native American youths. The Western Region Indian Alcoholism Training Center at the University of Utah was established to educate Native Americans to become paraprofessionals in the chemical dependency field.[106] The National Center for American Indian and Alaska Native Mental Health Research at the University of Colorado also addresses alcohol and drug problems among native groups.[107] In 1991, the Substance Abuse and Mental Health Services Administration noted that nationwide, approximately 1,300 treatment units reported providing specialized services for Native Americans, including 71 federal units and 60 tribal units.[108]

What should really be done to remedy alcohol and drug problems among Native Americans? The most pervasive answer is tribal involvement rather than government intervention.[109] Examples of tribal involvement include the Standing Rock Sioux's "over-all program to ameliorate alcoholism and problem drinking on the Reservation."[110] The Council of the Cheyenne River Sioux Tribe declared that it would be alcohol and drug free by the year 2000.[111] Another example comes from the Alkali Lake community in the British Columbia province of Canada. The story of this small community is portrayed in the video "The Honour of All."[112] The group's efforts to eliminate alcoholism came when one couple in the community recovered from alcoholism and patiently waited for others to join them.[113] The community then mobilized to prevent alcohol abuse. Some tribes are requiring that people elected to tribal office are living lives of sobriety.[114]

Willie presents a contrasting view of tribal involvement:

> In the past, many Tribal Councils expected Alcoholism workers to turn out sober Indians as if they were on an assembly line, inputting alcoholics on one end and producing recovered alcoholics on the other; and yet the tribal leaders continued to approve liquor licenses and continued to promote fund raising events that were many times based on liquor sales.[115]

Although the right type of tribal involvement is certainly thought to be important, a survey of 71 Native American alcoholism counselors who were also recovering alcoholics identified factors they thought most important in achieving sobriety.[116] They rated internal factors such as recognition and acceptance of their drinking problem, Alcoholics Anonymous, meaningful activities, spiritual factors, and native pride as more helpful in attaining sobriety than external factors such as involvement with traditional Native American people, tribal activities, and alcoholism programs.

Service providers should recognize that the Native American family model fosters mutual obligation or interdependence among relatives rather than independence from them.[117] Service providers have been advised to utilize this extended family and tribal network,[118] not only by involving families in treatment but also in AA groups, which are usually reserved for alcoholics or addicts.[119] Others note that Native Americans may not have family members on whom to rely[120] and that other family members may also be chemically dependent.[121] Thus, different strategies may be needed to develop social support systems necessary to recovery. The story of the Two Arrows family that follows was written some time ago but remains relevant in describing alcoholism in a Native American family.

Many Native Americans believe that substance abuse is externally caused, and personal responsibility for chemical abuse is often not recognized.[122] The type of intervention that is

Charlie and Rhoda Two Arrows: Turmoil and Withdrawal

Rhoda and Charlie Two Arrows,* both full-blood Teton Dakota, were in their early thirties during their six years in San Francisco. Rhoda was one of four children who grew up in a family where traditional values and discipline were honored. She went to reservation day and boarding schools until the completion of the twelfth grade, after which she moved to a nearby town to live with a sister and work as a waitress. There she first met Charlie Two Arrows.

Charlie grew up on the periphery of the reservation and was exposed to a traditional but disorganized early home life. His mother died when he was young, and his father remarried a woman who joined him in a pattern of continual drinking that soon depleted the money from the lands of his first wife. Charlie attended a public school until the sixth grade and then began the round of hard farm work that has characterized his life to the present.

After their marriage, Rhoda and Charlie lived with Charlie's father. It was a hard life for Rhoda because her father-in-law drank heavily, and she had farm chores to do besides taking care of the household and a growing family of three children. The Two Arrows decided on an impulse to relocate to "sunny California" because they heard there was eternally good weather there and because it was the farthest relocation area from the reservation that they could choose. They planned to save up enough money to buy some land and cattle and then return.

Charlie came to San Francisco with no special skills, but the Bureau of Indian Affairs got him a job in a factory as a machinist. He was reputed to be one of the top workers in the factory, even though he soon initiated a pattern of going on a week's binge every two or three months. He was always careful to call in as ill to cover himself at work and so never got into serious employment difficulties because of his continued drinking. He did, however, lose money for those days missed, since he did not receive sufficient benefits to cover those periods.

The Two Arrows lived in three apartments during their stay in San Francisco. Two years before they returned to the reservation, they moved into the public housing project in which they lived during the twelve months of interviews with them.

Rhoda had two more children in San Francisco and experienced three periods of acute illness during which she was hospitalized. At these times Charlie would often drink heavily, and welfare officials were called in several times, much to Charlie's later chagrin, because of his drunkenness or his "abandoning" the children. On the reservation, grandparents, aunts and uncles, or cousins are ready sources of short- or long-term babysitting, and most Indian women sorely miss such family support.

This couple lived almost completely in an Indian universe despite the immensely diverse population around them and the many cumbersome new rules of white society that dictated their daily life. Rhoda was active for a time in a local Indian Center, but she noticed that the more active her participation the more inclined Charlie was to drink, so she lessened her activities. Charlie did not care to go to Indian gatherings, because he feared that in a group situation pressure to drink would be brought upon him by other Indians.

The Two Arrows' three school-age children had considerable difficulty in the San Francisco school system. They could not understand the teachers' urgings to apply themselves to materials that had little relevance to their lives. . . . They seemed to withdraw almost totally from the situation. They did not read well and, as the years went by and their alienation from the total school experience deepened, found themselves further and further below the class reading level.

*The names used are fictitious.

The Two-Arrows' contacts with the Bureau of Indian Affairs were frequent and involved. The Bureau was called in repeatedly when Rhoda was in the hospital and Charlie was having problems with his drinking and coping with the care of the children. During the last years, Rhoda called the Bureau office only occasionally to say that things were going well and that she would be eternally grateful that the Bureau had brought them out here. Although not liking the bustle and red tape of urban living, she felt it was all worth it to get away from her father-in-law and to have such conveniences as running water, a washing machine, and easy heating.

The facts of personal and family disorganization among the Sioux are well documented in the anthropological literature. Macgregor[1] has noted that the Sioux man particularly has suffered from the loss of the meaningful economic and social roles that he enjoyed in the dramatic Sioux life style of old. The woman now may be thrown into the position of the key family figure, causing additional psychological and social difficulties for the man. Rhoda and Charlie exhibited very different personalities and the general pattern of their family roles and behavior typifies this problem of contemporary Sioux. Rhoda was a handsome woman who bore herself with great pride, was gregarious, and enjoyed many kinds of activities. It was her strength and determination that held her family together throughout their many crises in San Francisco.

Charlie, on the other hand, was a very shy person, sensitive about his Indian identity and quick to take offense at imagined criticisms of Indians. He referred frequently to his lack of education. He was able to support his family; however, he was beset with many insecurities about himself and his worth. Charlie seldom spoke and appeared to loosen up only when in the presence of certain known Sioux or when drunk. Beneath his quiet exterior was the latent drinking problem that could surface any day, usually a Friday payday, when he just would not come home from work.

When Charlie returned from a drinking period, he was very remorseful. Because the Two Arrows were nominal Catholics, Rhoda twice attempted to send Charlie to a priest for counseling after his shamefaced return. On both occasions the priest did not have time to see him until a week or more had passed, and by then Charlie refused to talk to anyone about his problem. Once, in the middle of the night, Rhoda called the well-liked minister of a local Indian Protestant church. He came over immediately and talked to Charlie. This minister once said that every man in his congregation had had at one time a drinking problem, so he was well accustomed to this sort of counseling. He felt that one reason many white ministers are unable to reach Indians is that they are afraid to counsel persons with serious drinking problems, and this sort of interaction is frequently an essential one with Indian parishioners.

Charlie, and, to a lesser degree, Rhoda, held strongly to the important Sioux value placed on sharing and the giving of hospitality, which was difficult, given Charlie's salary. His father came out to stay with them almost every winter, and a variety of other relatives and friends would also drop in and remain for weeks at a time. These houseguests did little but drink and watch television during their prolonged stays, and rarely did any of them contribute to the grocery bill.

Life for the Two Arrows in San Francisco seemed to be an almost continual round of crises caused by unexpected expenses and family illness, by their impulsive, erratic behavior, and by their inability to meet the demands of white society.

Charlie finally found himself seriously involved in what seemed to him to be an incomprehensible maze of traffic offenses. While drunk one night he was picked up and booked on drunk driving and hit-and-run charges. When he sobered up the next day, he did not remember committing any of the crimes with which he was charged. Charlie was released pending trial, and when he got home he informed Rhoda that all this was too much for him; he had decided they would go home. On the federal reservation area he would be safe from state reprisals. In the next few hours they packed the most essential of their belongings, crowded the children into the car,

(continued)

and left. Their flight to San Francisco from the reservation had not freed them from economic or psychological struggles. They had lived in the land of promise six years, and returned without the money they had come to save. Moreover, Charlie was a wanted man. At present they are re-settled with Charlie's father on his lands and Charlie is doing wage labor where he can find it. Rhoda harbors in her heart the hope of another relocation, but it is doubtful that Charlie could be roused to leave the reservation again.

NOTE

1. G. Macgregor, "Community Development and Social Adaptation," *Human Organization*, Vol. 20 (1961–62), p. 238.

Source: Joan Ablon, "Cultural Conflict in Urban Indians," *Mental Hygiene*, Vol. 55, No. 2 (April 1971), pp. 201–203. Reprinted with permission of National Mental Health Association, Inc.

advocated in much of the mainstream writing about substance abuse may be culturally incongruent for many Native Americans. When they are referred to treatment programs, education about confrontation prior to admission is suggested to prevent treatment dropouts.[123] This approach is used at Thunder Child, a chemical dependency treatment program for Native Americans, located in Wyoming. The program is largely based on the Minnesota model, which has come to stand for traditional, inpatient alcoholism treatment comprised of education, group treatment with some individual sessions, and the introduction of the Twelve-Step programs (also see Chapter 6). Such programs have been adapted for Native Americans.

Traditional, Native American concepts of spirituality and religion have also been incorporated into treatment and self-help groups. Tribal spiritual practices are used to gain harmony with the world. Moss and colleagues recommend that treatment programs have medicine men (we assume the use of medicine women or other spiritual advisors is also appropriate) on call and that they should conduct regular spiritual meetings; the sanction of treatment programs by Native leaders is also important.[124] The St. Cloud Minnesota Veterans Hospital has used the traditional sweat lodge, a purification ritual in which Native Americans usually enter a small, tentlike structure heated by rocks. Patients may spend hours in the structure, chanting Native songs, confessing, and seeking spiritual renewal.[125] The vision quest, another ritual which may be helpful with alcohol or drug abuse, is used to find answers to personal problems or to seek the right path. The use of dances, ceremonies, and prayers is also important, but since these may be sacred activities, professionals who are not members of the tribal group may be excluded from participation.[126]

Incorporation of Native spiritual and cultural practices into mainstream chemical dependency programs may be useful, but approaches that are uniquely or solely Native American may deserve more consideration from professionals. Take, for example, the use of peyote in treating alcoholism. Most chemical dependency professionals would probably have a difficult time endorsing the use of an hallucinogenic drug in the treatment of alcoholism or other drug addiction, yet this has been done successfully by the peyote religion or Native American Church (NAC).[127] The peyote ceremony is highly structured. Albaugh and Anderson "do not propose that either the pharmacological effects of peyote or the NAC by itself is a cure for alcoholism," but they do indicate that "others have reported success in the treatment of alcoholism in Indian populations by the NAC alone."[128] According to Menninger:

Peyote is not harmful to these people; it is beneficial, comforting, inspiring, and appears to be spiritually nourishing. It is a better antidote to alcohol than anything the missionaries, the white man, the American Medical Association, and the public health services have come up with. It is understandable that these organizations should be a bit envious of the success of this primitive natural native remedy.[129]

In 1991, the Supreme Court ruled in *Employment Division of Oregon* v. *Smith* that the First Amendment does not protect those using peyote for religious purposes from prosecution under state drug laws. Today, 24 states do permit the use of peyote in religious ceremonies, and the American Civil Liberties Union has supported this aspect of religious freedom.[130]

The traditional, Christian overtones in regular AA groups may be objectionable to Native Americans,[131] but the religious preference of Native Americans should not be presumed. Some have been converted to Christianity by Protestant and Catholic missionaries and espouse these religions.[132] Traditional AA may be more appealing to highly acculturated Native Americans,[133] although this depends on the tribe's customs. Jilek-Aall writes that unlike many other tribes, the Coastal Salish Indians who reside in British Columbia and Washington State have a tradition of confession similar to the personal disclosure that takes place in AA.[134] She points to the usefulness of AA but also to the need for separate Native AA groups due to distrust of whites who have been a source of conflict in Native Americans' lives, Native men's concern about Native women's relationships with white men at AA, the concept of anonymity that may conflict with their principle of openness, and discomfort in speaking in front of whites. In addition, the format of Native American AA meetings may differ from other AA meetings. There is less concern about beginning and ending on time. Cultural customs resembling the potlatch (giveaway) feast are sometimes incorporated at AA "birthday" meetings.

Various helping professionals have attempted to develop treatment modalities specific to Native Americans. In the social work tradition, Nofz[135] describes a task-centered group approach (based on the work of Reid and Epstein[136]) that has proven useful with those who identify with elements of both Native American and non–Native American cultures. In keeping with tribal values, "The group is organized around specific tasks in managing sobriety, with special emphasis on adapting to those situations in which different values impose conflicting behavioral expectations. Thus alcohol abuse is not framed as an 'individual problem' and introspection into group members' personalities is avoided."[137] The group identifies the problems and the tasks to be addressed, since Nofz believes that Native Americans often prefer a "doing" rather than an introspective approach. This approach also emphasizes Native American values of self-determination and of placing group welfare over individual welfare. Nofz suggests that the social worker develop a "'low key,' participatory [leadership] style" and act as a "group facilitator rather than therapist."[138] Treatment may take longer than is typical with the task-centered approach, because more time may be needed to develop rapport with the participants. Confession within the groups and personal stories in AA may be replaced with the tribal tradition of storytelling. These stories "contain metaphorical descriptions of everyday problems, along with practical and moral advice," and they take direct attention off the individual.[139]

According to May, given the youthful age and short life span of many Native Americans, prevention of alcohol and drug problems among young people is critical.[140] He suggests several approaches for prevention and treatment:

1. The need for social and economic roles that are both meaningful and consonant with tribal values and roles
2. Education and other techniques that clarify that problems like chemical dependency can be reduced
3. More programs to limit alcohol morbidity and mortality among younger people
4. Innovative programs for chronic abusers that reflect contemporary and traditional Native cultural approaches[141]

The approach to prevention among youths suggested by Oetting and Beauvais focuses on peer resistance, strengthening family relationships and cultural identification, improving economic well-being, and encouraging school success.[142]

LeMaster and Connell's 1994 review of health education interventions for Native Americans contains three small-scale studies of programs to assist youths that used various techniques, including controlled drinking, skills enhancement, and decision-making skills, as well as culturally relevant material.[143] All indicated evidence of reduced substance use, but apparently no particular models have emerged as especially useful.

Parker describes the prevention program of the Rhode Island Indian Council that is based on Project CHARLIE (CHemical Abuse Resolution Lies in Education) developed in Edina, Minnesota.[144] The approach, which is designed to build self-esteem and can be adapted to meet cultural needs, includes four major components: self-awareness, relationships, decision making, and chemical use. Although the evaluation of the Rhode Island project involved only a small number of participants, the cultural component seemed to be what attracted youths to it. In fact, Parker says that culture is the missing component in most substance abuse prevention efforts.

Cultural and community themes continue to appear in the literature, with Stivers describing drug prevention efforts on the Zuni Reservation through involvement of the community in attempts to establish a teen center.[145] Stivers describes the Zuni community as having experienced its share of alcohol- and drug-related problems, but explains that as a small and close-knit community, it was not difficult to involve nearly everyone in the teen center effort. Like Parker, Stivers reports that young Native Americans did not have substantial knowledge of their people's history, despite practicing many traditions and ceremonies. The teen center was meant to address one of the problems on isolated reservations—few organized or meaningful activities to engage youths as alternatives to activities such as alcohol and drug experimentation. The Indian Health Service's efforts to prevent chemical abuse and dependency begin early with children in Head Start programs.[146]

A number of programs have been used to promote prevention and recognition of fetal alcohol syndrome (FAS) and fetal alcohol effects among Native Americans (see Chapter 15). Streissguth's review of some of these programs not only suggests the importance of cultural relevance but also the necessity to educate and involve the entire community, since drinking does not occur in a vacuum.[147] For example, among the strategies used by the Fort Belknap Service Unit in Montana are encouraging bars to offer pregnant women free nonalcoholic drinks and to post information on the effects of alcohol on the fetus. Streissguth notes that lower rates of FAS are a "natural consequence of reducing community alcoholism."[148] Community residents are staff members and are apparently key to the effectiveness of such programs as the Tuba City FAS Prevention Project. The Lummi Reservation in Washington State uses an Indian Aunt program and includes support groups for sobriety as well as individual approaches with highest-risk women. Indian Head Start programs have also been involved in FAS awareness.

Weibel found that "events that are urban, sacred, indoors, public, of short duration, and include many non-Indians exhibit lower levels of drinking and aberrant subsequent behavior than do events that are rural, secular, outdoors, private, Indian, and not time bound."[149] To prevent excessive drinking among adults in social contexts, these factors may need to be taken into account. This fits with suggestions that alcohol abuse (as well as chronic alcohol problems) must be addressed in reducing alcohol-related morbidity and mortality among Native Americans.[150] It also complements views that public health[151] and harm-reduction strategies are necessary tools in attempts in preventing alcohol- and drug-related problems, especially when other approaches to changing attitudes and behaviors are unsuccessful.

Substance Abuse among African Americans

Africans have a long history of alcohol consumption dating to the use of beer and palm wine in precolonial West Africa; use was ceremonial, medicinal, and social.[152]

> In traditional African cultures, as in most of the rest of the world, alcohol was widely used. Palm wine was a regular part of the diet, an important part of community celebrations, and a medicinal substance believed to be particularly effective against measles and dysentery. It was used as a medium of exchange as well. Natural substances such as Kola nuts or guinea corn were used as intoxicants or stimulants.[153]

Intoxication, however, was disapproved of, and excessive drinking and related problems were apparently uncommon.[154]

Harper and others have described the history of alcohol use by African Americans dating to the seventeenth century, when alcohol was provided to slaves to promote compliance and to prevent escapes; permission to imbibe heavily on weekends and holidays supposedly pacified the slaves and provided a respite from their oppressive existence.[155] Genovese's account is that even though slaves had easy access to cheap liquor, alcohol excess was less common among them than among the slaveholders and that "the general sobriety of the slaves speaks well for their community strength and resistance to demoralization."[156]

Some accounts indicate that once slavery ended, African Americans were anxious to test their new-found freedoms, including drinking alcohol at will.[157] Similar to the situation with Native Americans, many whites tried to prevent African Americans from drinking, which they blamed for inciting problems such as violence and crime.[158] Herd's analysis is that drunkenness and alcohol-related mortality among African Americans in the nineteenth century were insignificant.[159] The early American Temperance Movement was closely associated with the Antislavery Movement, and abstinence was thought to be important to freedom and equality.[160] But African Americans withdrew from the Temperance Movement when southern prohibitionists were joined by groups such as the Ku Klux Klan and adopted their racist attitudes. As African Americans migrated from the South to northern cities to seek employment and other opportunities, they became familiar with nightclubs, speakeasies, and other sources of alcohol. Bootlegging became a ready source of income, and alcohol abuse eventually became a problem. During the 1950s, cirrhosis among African Americans grew to epidemic proportions. Herd questions whether urbanization alone would have led to such high rates of alcohol-related problems among African Americans if the prohibitionists had not gone to such efforts to thwart black equality.

Contemporary Explanations of Substance Abuse among African Americans

With the preceding information as background, Harper offers four explanations for contemporary drinking patterns among African Americans:[161]

1. *"The historical patterns of alcohol use and nonuse by Blacks have played a significant part in influencing their current drinking practices and their current attitudes toward drinking."* According to this explanation, some African Americans drink heavily on weekends after a hard week's work, reminiscent of the days when slaves were rewarded with alcohol and of the early days of freedom. Others, primarily women, do not drink at all due to early prohibitions against African Americans' drinking and to religious beliefs, role expectations, and family responsibilities. There are substantially different attitudes toward drinking among African Americans.

2. *"Many Blacks choose to drink because (a) liquor stores and liquor dealers are readily accessible and*

(b) Black peer groups often expect one to drink and at times to drink heavily." In white communities, liquor stores and bars are generally located in commercial areas; these establishments are more prevalent in African American residential neighborhoods. There is easy access to alcohol, and drinking is highly visible. Especially among men, there may be pressure to drink. There is also a lack of sanctions against chemical abuse in some African American communities.[162]

3. *"Many Blacks, especially men, drink heavily due to the economic frustration of not being able to get a job or not being able to fulfill financial responsibilities."* Unemployment and economic deprivation may contribute to excessive drinking among African Americans. Although this chapter does not allow for a discussion of the complex issues surrounding the position of African American men in the United States or of the issues surrounding the relationships between African American men and women, Harper writes that the inability to fulfill the role of breadwinner is particularly problematic for men.

4. *"Numerous emotions and motivations influence heavy drinking among Black Americans in their attempt to escape unpleasant feelings or to fulfill psychological needs."* The pain associated with the African American experience may be mitigated, at least temporarily, by using alcohol for social and recreational purposes. Dozier also notes that "alcoholism is often tolerated as a stress reducer for many African Americans."[163]

In a similar vein, Moore applied three theoretical perspectives to explain drug addiction and trafficking among African American male adolescents.[164] Using Emile Durkheim's work on suicide, she notes that drug addiction and trafficking may occur when an individual feels little control over his or her life circumstances and sees few choices or options.[165] Life becomes increasingly meaningless as self-worth diminishes. From Karl Marx's theory of capitalism, Moore views drug dealers as the capitalists and addicts as the downtrodden

proletariat.[166] The addict is dependent on the dealer for his or her means of survival, and low-level street dealers are readily replaced if they balk at their working conditions. Moore also states that Molefi Asante's theory of Afrocentricity leads one to view drug problems as arising from a lack of connection with African history and community.[167] The self-worth of those who do not feel this connection is weakened.

Herd, however, believes that factors such as stress and racism fail to explain the relatively recent increase of problems such as cirrhosis among African Americans.[168] These problems may be due to longer periods of heavy drinking and frequency of alcohol consumption, although black men are not more often classified as frequent heavy drinkers compared to white men.[169] Herd also discusses explanations for drinking among African Americans based on social disorganization (i.e., individual and family pathology) and on structural interpretations (i.e., social and economic marginality) that include the roles of political, legal, and economic institutions.[170] She is critical of the social disorganization literature that takes African American drinking out of its social context and that is often based on studies with small samples of individuals that are not representative of larger African American communities. Instead, she calls for greater study of social and economic conditions such as unemployment and discrimination in the criminal justice system that might contribute to substance abuse.

Watts and Wright say that of all the possible physiological, psychological, sociocultural, environmental, and ecological contributors, it remains unclear which "specific factors, at what times, contribute to the development of alcoholism" among African Americans.[171] African Americans are diverse in socioeconomic status and have origins in many countries (Africa, the West Indies, South and Central America, the Caribbean, etc.). Each area has a unique history of alcohol and drug use. Even within the United States, the experiences of African Americans vary based on the region of the country in which they reside, but some experiences such as slavery and racism are pervasive influences for virtually all African American individuals.[172]

Racism in the current drug scene continues to affect African Americans. When 400 people in the Washington, DC, area were asked to visualize a drug user and a drug trafficker, most, including African Americans, pictured an African American individual.[173] Burston and associates say such stereotypes are reinforced by the marginal status of African Americans, including the perception that drug use is a means of dealing with environmental stressors, despite the fact that in absolute numbers and often by percentage of ethnic group, more drug users and drug traffickers are white. Media coverage further reinforces this perception. Despite the adverse effects of all illicit drugs as well as alcohol, the authors note that crack cocaine and heroin use get the most public attention. The repercussions of this for African Americans are severe, given the higher arrest rates for blacks and the harsher penalties for crack rather than powdered cocaine.

Chemical Dependency Problems among African Americans

African Americans suffer from poorer health than whites. Although the life expectancies for all Americans have increased, African Americans continue to die earlier than whites. The Task Force on Black and Minority Health appointed by the Secretary of Health and Human Services in 1984 reported that chemical dependency was one of the six leading contributors to the lower life expectancies of ethnic minorities.[174] The other five major contributors were cancer, heart disease and stroke, diabetes, homicides and accidents, and infant mortality. Many deaths associated with these causes are also related to alcohol and other drug consumption. The task force was particularly alarmed that rates of alcohol-related problems (e.g., fatty liver, cirrhosis, heart disease, cancers of the mouth and esophagus, accidents, and homicide) among African Americans, which had been

lower than or similar to rates for whites, have increased dramatically since World War II. African American death rates for cirrhosis are now twice the rate for whites. Robins, however, found no overall difference in rates of lifetime or current alcohol-related psychiatric disorders between blacks and whites based on data from the Epidemiological Catchment Area (ECA) program, even after controlling for age and gender.[175] Based on the National Comorbidity Survey, Kessler and colleagues found lower rates of substance use disorders among blacks than white, even after controlling for income and education.[176]

The representative sampling methodologies of the ECA program and the National Comorbidity Survey are impressive and are cause for confidence in the data. Studies of clinical populations, although often less generalizable given the particular demographic characteristics of the population served, are also of interest. Pavkov and colleagues report that research shows an inconsistent picture of the psychiatric symptomatology of African American substance abusers.[177] Using assessments by clinicians and patient self-reports, they studied 86 African American and 244 Caucasian patients seen at "a comprehensive university-affiliated hospital-based substance misuse treatment program in a large Midwestern city." Their study paints a picture of substantially more impaired functioning among African American subjects who "had a higher overall severity of substance misuse and . . . higher levels of somatization, interpersonal problems, depression, hostility, obsessive/compulsive disorder, phobia, paranoia, and psychoticism, . . . higher levels of psychosocial stress and lower levels of global functioning than did Caucasians." The authors speculate that these findings may be due to the use of more illicit substances among the African American subjects and lack of exposure to information on the early warning signs of problems. Another possible explanation is that these subjects may rely on informal resources, and may not go to treatment facilities until their substance abuse problems are more severe than that of Caucasian subjects, especially when they perceive treatment facilities as not being receptive to them.

The 1984 National Alcohol Survey (NAS), funded by the National Institute on Alcohol Abuse and Alcoholism, was the first major study of drinking that incorporated a representative (multistage area probability) sample of African Americans.[178] Earlier studies of African Americans have more serious methodological problems but have provided information consistent with at least some of the findings of the 1984 study.[179] Herd analyzed data from the 1984 NAS, and, combined with other information, she found the following:[180]

1. What might be considered an epidemic level of alcohol-related health problems for African Americans may be associated with a later onset of heavy drinking and more prolonged heavy drinking compared with whites.

2. African Americans' arrest rates for drunkenness are still higher than those for whites, but have decreased faster than those for whites' since the 1960s. Current levels of arrests for liquor law violations and driving under the influence (DUI) are similar, perhaps due to more equitable application of drunk driving laws.

3. The drinking patterns of African American and white men are generally similar (proportions of abstainers, infrequent drinkers, heavy drinkers, etc.), but African American men have more alcohol-related problems of all types. Among white men, there is more heavy drinking and more alcohol-related problems in the 18- to 29-year age group; among African Americans, these problems are more likely to occur in the 30- to 39-year-old group. Heavy drinking increases as income increases for white men, but heavy drinking decreases as income increases for African American men. White men drink more heavily in the North, Midwest, and in urban areas than in other parts of the country. This pattern was also true of African American men, but the 1984 study indicates they now drink more heavily in the South and nonurban areas.[181] This may indicate an increase in alcohol consumption by African American men in some areas of the country, especially the South. African American males report more problematic drinking patterns, including binge drinking, and more alcohol-related health problems than do white men. There are fewer differences with respect to the social and interpersonal problems reported.[182]

4. Compared with white women, the 1984 study showed that African American women abstain more, drink less frequently, and report fewer alcohol-related problems, except health problems. These findings conflict with earlier studies that indicated more frequent heavy drinking as well as more abstention among African American women. This may be due to the inclusion of more southern women in the 1984 study and more northern women in earlier studies (the South has traditionally been known as a "drier" area than the North). Among younger women, African Americans are considerably less likely to drink than whites, but heavy frequent drinkers are represented in nearly equal proportions in both groups. For both groups, increased income is associated with less abstention and more frequent drinking.[183]

In the 1984 NAS, 7 percent of black women reported at least one alcohol-related problem, compared to 12 percent of white women.[184] In the ECA study, 2 percent of black women had a 12-month prevalence rate for alcohol abuse or dependence, compared with 1 percent of white women.[185]

A group of individuals from the 1984 NAS was recontacted in 1992. Changes in drinking patterns between 1984 and 1992 among blacks, whites, and Hispanics are found in Table 11.1. Caetano and Kaskutas identify increased abstention as an important change among black men; however, the rate of frequent heavy drinking was stable.[186] These patterns were the same for Hispanic men, but among white men, there was increased abstention and decreased frequent heavy drinking. Abstention also increased among white and black women, but it was stable among Hispanics, thus

TABLE 11.1   Drinking Patterns among Whites, Blacks, and Hispanics, 1984–1992 (in percent based on the National Alcohol Survey)

	Whites (n = 389)		Blacks (n = 321)		Hispanics (n = 329)	
Men	*1984*	*1992*	*1984*	*1992*	*1984*	*1992*
Abstention	23	28	29	35	16	22
Infrequent	13	9	13	6	15	11
Less frequent	16	21	12	19	22	21
Frequent	27	29	30	25	25	24
Frequent heavy drinker	19	12	16	15	21	23
	Whites (n = 399)		Blacks (n = 409)		Hispanics (n = 374)	
Women						
Abstention	31	36	46	51	47	48
Infrequent	23	22	18	24	27	34
Less frequent	19	24	19	12	15	12
Frequent	23	15	13	8	11	5
Frequent heavy drinker	4	3	4	5	1	3

Source: Raul Caetano and Lee Ann Kaskutas, "Changes in Drinking Patterns among Whites, Blacks, and Hispanics, 1984–1992." Reprinted with permission from *Journal of Studies on Alcohol,* vol. 56, pp. 558–565, 1995. Copyright by Alcohol Research Documentation, Inc., Rutgers Center of Alcohol Studies, Piscataway, NJ 08855.

reducing the disparity in abstention rates between Hispanic and white women during the eight-year interval. Except for Hispanic women, changes in overall drinking patterns were statistically significant in all the ethnic/gender groups.

Although black women continued to abstain more frequently than white women, the 5 percent of black women classified as frequent heavy drinkers in 1992 consumed an average of 148 drinks a month, compared to 104 drinks for the 3 percent of white women in this category. This compared with 120 and 117 drinks, respectively, in 1984.[187] The incidence of new cases of frequent heavy drinking was highest for Hispanic men followed by blacks and then whites. The 1992 data continue to support different maturational patterns of drinking among men, depending on their ethnic group, with white men more likely to reduce their drinking as they age than is the case for blacks or Hispanics.

After controlling for sociodemographic variables, blacks were twice as likely as whites to remain frequent heavy drinkers; however, Caetano and Kaskutas note that the variables tested explain only a small percentage of the variance in drinking patterns, especially for women. They also note that sociocultural changes in the eight-year interval were not included in the analysis but may well account for the changes that were found across ethnic groups. In general, there was less reduction in drinking among blacks and Hispanics than whites, especially among frequent heavy drinkers, and they conclude that these ethnic groups apparently remain at higher risk for alcohol-related harm, constituting a significant public health concern.

The 1994 National Household Survey on Drug Abuse indicates that among those ages 12 and older, 30 percent of African Americans had ever used an illicit drug, compared with 25 percent of Hispanics and 37 percent of whites.[188] For use within the past year, the figures were 12 percent, 9 percent, and 11 percent, respectively; and within the past month, they were 7 percent, 5 percent, and 6 percent, respectively. Looking more closely at young people, African American adolescents drink and use drugs less than their white peers,[189] but caution should be used in interpreting the data because samples often exclude school dropouts and institutionalized youths. The 1994 National Household Survey showed that 12 percent of African American adolescents (ages 12 to 17 years) have tried marijuana, compared with 14 percent of both whites and Hispanics (see Table 11.2), and that among young adults (ages 18 to 25 years), 33 percent of blacks have tried marijuana, compared with 48 percent of whites and 28 percent of Hispanics. Crack, thought to be especially prevalent in poor, inner-city neighborhoods, has been tried by 0.4 percent of black adolescents, compared with 0.7 percent of whites and 0.8 percent of Hispanics. Also of note is that 4 percent of black young adults have tried cocaine, compared to 11 percent of Hispanics and 14 percent of whites, and that whites in this age group are much more likely to report having tried

inhalants than black or Hispanic youths; the same is true for hallucinogens.

One possible explanation for lower levels of alcohol and drug use among African American youths is that many have fundamentalist Protestant upbringings.[190] They are also likely to grow up in female-headed households, with greater exposure to female relatives who have high levels of abstention.[191]

In a follow-up to the National Collaborative Perinatal Project, a major longitudinal study conducted in Philadelphia, 318 female and 322 male African Americans, who had originally been studied from birth to 7 years of age, participated.[192] The study looked at a large set of early-life variables to determine whether any predicted later substance use or abuse. The mean age of subjects at follow-up was 24 years. "High activity and intensity of response in infancy was a predictor for both genders," suggesting a possible temperamental disposition to substance use or abuse. The number of fetal deaths experienced by their mothers was also predictive of substance abuse for subjects of both genders. Fewer of the factors studied predicted drug use among the men than the

TABLE 11.2   Percent Surveyed Reporting That They Ever Used Drugs, 1994, by Ethnicity (Race): U.S. Civilian Noninstitutionalized Population

	White		Black		Hispanic	
	12–17 Years	18–25 Years	12–17 Years	18–25 Years	12–17 Years	18–25 Years
Alcohol	45.3	91.6	32.9	74.8	39.1	76.7
Illicit Drugs						
Marijuana	14.5	47.5	11.8	32.7	14.4	28.4
Cocaine	1.8	14.3	.7	3.8	2.7	11.1
Crack	.7	3.2	.4	1.8	.8	1.9
Inhalants	8.1	13.0	3.9	3.0	5.4	4.8
Hallucinogens	5.0	18.7	1.0	2.3	2.9	8.7
Stimulants	2.2	4.0	1.9	1.4	1.0	2.4
Tranquilizers	2.0	5.8	2.0	1.4	1.4	2.5
Any	21.7	52.4	18.8	35.5	19.8	33.4

Source: Substance Abuse and Mental Health Services Administration, *National Household Survey on Drug Abuse: Population Estimates 1994,* Department of Health and Human Services Pub. No. (SMA)95-3063 (Rockville, MD: SAMHSA, 1995).

women, and many other predictive factors differed between the men and women. Residing in an intact family mitigated against substance abuse more for women than for men, which the authors suggest may be because boys, even at a very young age, tend to engage in outside activities. Among women, drug use and abuse was also more strongly related to poor intellectual and academic functioning and abnormal mental status and behavior. Male use and abuse seemed more related to factors at delivery, which may also suggest greater biological vulnerability. However, the factors studied were more predictive of alcohol abuse for women than they were for men and they were not particularly predictive of other drug abuse for either gender. Given the lack of identification of strong models among the many individual-level variables considered, it may be that sociocultural or environmental influences are more predictive of use and abuse, especially among the young men studied.

Another study found that the following factors were related to increased drinking among a sample of 1,177 African American youths in grades 6, 8, 10, and 12: living with both parents; having parents who drink, but more important, having peers who drink; having greater knowledge about alcohol; and having more liberal attitudes toward alcohol use.[193] Urban or rural residence and mother's work status were not related to youths' drinking. Studies published in 1993,[194] 1994,[195] and 1995[196] of students ranging from sixth- to twelfth-graders support some of these findings. The most consistent finding is that peer-related variables such as friends' substance use and susceptibility to peer pressure are substantial predictors of substance use among the black, Hispanic, and white students studied. This finding suggests a common focus for prevention efforts for youths, regardless of ethnic group. The influence of parents varied across the studies.

Also of importance in considering chemical dependency problems among African Americans and other ethnic groups is the risk of contracting AIDS through use of dirty needles. Of AIDS cases among male injecting drug users (adolescents and

adults) that were reported through 1996 in the United States, 50 percent were African American, 29 percent were Hispanic, and 20 percent were white. The corresponding figures for adolescent and adult women were 58 percent black, 20 percent Hispanic, and 22 percent white. Among pediatric cases of AIDS associated with mothers' injecting drug use, 60 percent were black, 24 percent were Hispanic, and 15 percent were white. Of all AIDS cases among black men, injecting drug use accounts for 36 percent, compared with 37 percent for Hispanic men and 9 percent for white men. Of all AIDS cases among black women, injecting drug use accounts for 47 percent, compared with 44 percent for Hispanic women and 43 percent for white women. And of all pediatric AIDS cases among blacks and among Hispanics, mothers' injecting drug use is associated with 38 percent of cases, compared with 31 percent for whites.[197]

Some of the important questions now being asked in the chemical dependency field are why African Americans, primarily men, experience much more serious consequences from drinking, especially health risks, when their drinking patterns are similar to whites; why African American men's drinking- and alcohol-related problems increase later in life when they drink less in adolescence and early adulthood; and why African American men and women in alcoholism treatment are much younger than whites when they drink less in younger age groups.[198] There are similar concerns about the increased risks of drug-related problems for African Americans. Unemployment, poverty, and other factors related to deprived living environments likely exacerbate the effects of alcohol and drug use among this ethnic group.[199]

Chemical Dependency Treatment for African Americans

According to 1992 data from the Drug Abuse Warning Network, blacks are overrepresented in emergency-room visits for drug-related episodes.[200] They constituted 28 percent of such visits but are only 12 percent of the U.S. population. Although blacks are much more likely than whites to go to an emergency room for drug dependency and to seek detoxification services, they are much less likely than whites to end up in an emergency room for an attempted suicide or as the result of an overdose. In 1994, blacks were 23 percent of all clients in substance abuse treatment programs, somewhat higher than the 19 percent of clients they constituted in 1987.[201] More detailed data on black clients are available from the 1991 NDATUS.[202] In that year, of all black clients treated, 44 percent were admitted for a drug diagnosis only, 30 percent for an alcoholism diagnosis only, and 27 percent for both diagnoses. This compares with 29 percent, 45 percent, and 26 percent, respectively, for all clients. Thus, African Americans are more likely to be treated for drug abuse and less likely to be treated for alcoholism. In 1991, about 32 percent of treatment units reporting having specialized services for African Americans. Additional sources suggest that blacks are disproportionately represented among narcotics users[203] and that these figures are reflected in the proportion of black clients among all those treated for heroin addiction.[204]

Although the importance of ethnic-specific services in gaining sobriety has been debated,[205] Beverly has argued that African Americans need these services because their life experiences differ from those of whites, and social service agencies controlled by whites are by definition racist.[206] Burks and Johnson also note that treatment theories that emphasize the here and now deny African Americans' historical experiences of discrimination.[207] They emphasize that African Americans know what is best for them, and they resent the idea that they should conform to white society rather than change it. As with other ethnic groups, a sense of ownership of services is important.

Although chemical dependency services originated to meet the needs of white males, individuals who blame racism alone for inadequate services or who reject the idea that those of other ethnic backgrounds can help them in recovery may also be shortsighted.[208] Bell and Evans have discussed ways to make the therapeutic relationship between clients and counselors of differing ethnic backgrounds more productive in the field of chemical dependency.[209] This includes an understanding of the different personal experiences and counseling styles that black and white treatment providers may bring to their work, especially their views of their own ethnicity and that of others. African American clients may prefer different counseling styles, depending on their experiences and identity.[210] For example, black clients described by Bell and Evans as "traditional" may be uncomfortable with the self-disclosure typically expected in chemical dependency treatment programs; black clients whose lives are largely separate from those of whites may prefer or insist on a counselor of the same ethnic background, whereas those who function more comfortably in both cultures may accept a black or white counselor.[211]

There is a lack of research-tested models for assisting black alcoholics,[212] but Ziter[213] believes that empowerment (techniques to prevent societal victimization and to increase self-esteem),[214] bicultural counseling (helping clients to negotiate the majority culture while supporting the positives of their own culture),[215] and the dual perspective (a method for comparing clients' values and behaviors and those relevant to their immediate social systems with that of the larger society)[216] are important elements in the effective treatment of African Americans.

The literature on African Americans also emphasizes the need for a strengths rather than a deficit perspective in treatment, capitalizing on the positive attributes of clients and their significant others rather than "blaming the victim" by focusing on presumed weaknesses or deficiencies.[217] In addition, use of an ecological systems perspective, focusing not only on the individual but also on relationships with family and other social systems that might reinforce sobriety, has been recommended.[218] In addition to the nuclear family, the extended family of African Americans may include nonblood relatives such as close neighbors and friends who are referred to as "auntie" or "uncle"; these individuals can be sources of material as well as emotional support and may be helpful in treatment.[219]

According to McGee and Johnson, the "superwoman myth" is very strong among African Americans, as is the idea that women can endure inordinate amounts of pain when other family members are chemically dependent.[220] They stress the need for codependency services as well as chemical dependency services in promoting recovery of the family.

Additional suggestions to increase the effectiveness of services for African Americans include addressing "racial pain," low self-concept and expectations, perceptions of physical unattractiveness, negative stereotypes, stereotypical role expectations, the necessity of operating in black and white cultures, and views of whites as being more competent professionals than blacks.[221] Bell has also addressed the need to assist African American clients in addressing racial pain, noting that in many treatment programs, the issue of race is not addressed because staff do not want it to become an excuse for addiction and because staff encourage discussions of similarities rather than differences among alcoholics and addicts.[222] Bell notes staff discomfort and feelings of inadequacy in discussing this important topic. Although there are no easy answers, he encourages African Americans pursuing programs of recovery to take time to "distinguish between cultural ignorance, insensitivity, and racism."[223] At the same time, staff members should be increasing their skill at cultural sensitivity and competence since the responsibility for improving the treatment environment rests with the treatment providers.

In addition to focusing on self-esteem, Moore suggests encouraging a sense of community or collectivity, perhaps through Afrocentric materials and approaches, and she suggests addressing environmental factors such as limited options for earning a living.[224] Other suggestions for improving treatment are more concrete. They are to "reduce social distance between staff and clients, reduce paperwork required of clients, ask fewer questions unrelated to treatment, and do a better job to inform the black community of the purpose of the agency."[225]

Attempts have been made to identify differences between black and white women alcoholics that might improve treatment.[226] In one study, black women entering treatment reported fewer financial resources but higher self-esteem and more supportive social networks.[227] Afrocentricity is a theory that has been applied to treatment for African American women as well as men and adolescents. Jackson describes a residential and continuing care chemical dependency treatment program for African women and their children called *Iwo San*, a Swahili term meaning "house of healing."[228] Afrocentric values that undergird the program are spirituality, community, tradition, wisdom of elders, and self-identity and dignity. The length of stay is open ended, and although a period of "atonement" away from the program may be required if a client acts contrary to program norms, she is always welcomed back.

Cooperation with churches, core institutions in African American communities, is repeatedly acknowledged as necessary for reaching many alcoholics and addicts.[229] Spiritual and religious convictions can be a "well-spring of hope and strength" in recovery.[230] The African Methodist Episcopal (AME) church in particular has taken an active role in addressing alcoholism, including recognition of the disease concept.[231] McGee and Johnson note that although churches in African American communities can be very helpful, some deny the problems of alcohol and other drug abuse and oppose nonreligious treatment approaches.[232] Bell concurs that for some clergy, the sin rather than disease explanation of chemical dependency prevails.[233] Developing a relationship with church elders, deacons, and ministers and helping to educate them and other church members about chemical dependency are important steps in gaining allies in prevention and treatment. Such education may be necessary to avoid moralistic explanations of alcohol and other drug abuse,[234] as well as ideas that accepting Jesus

Christ and prayer are the only requirements for the faithful to overcome these problems.

Other resources that can help address chemical dependency problems are physicians, other health care providers, and members of the business community, as well as civic groups and fraternities and sororities to which many African Americans belong. A resource for identifying problems and making referrals that appears unique to the chemical dependency literature on African Americans is barbers and beauticians.[235] Some innovative approaches have included showing films on chemical dependency in barber and beauty shops. Spiritualists, an indigenous resource used by some African Americans, might also be helpful.[236]

Self-help groups to address alcohol and drug problems have had an impact in African American communities, although there has been debate about their usefulness and sensitivity. Hudson traced the beginning of Alcoholics Anonymous in African American communities to 1945 when Dr. Jim S., a black physician recovering from alcoholism, began a group in Washington, DC.[237] According to Hudson's research, Dr. Jim's sobriety came when Ms. Ella G., a black friend of Dr. Jim's family, asked a white AA member to help him. Ms. Ella G. had learned about AA as a result of her church work and her brother's alcoholism. Alcoholics Anonymous received many requests for information from African Americans, and other early groups were formed by blacks in St. Louis, Greenwich Village, and Harlem. The AA office in New York, citing the policy that it took no political stands, left it to local groups to address African Americans seeking help. Rather than discriminatory or racist, Hudson defends this position as consistent with AA's view that the only requirement for membership is a desire to stop drinking and that the Twelve Steps and Twelve Traditions provide the guidance necessary to help others in need, regardless of their ethnic background.

Hudson also rejects claims that AA is not effective with African Americans because it reflects primarily white, middle-class values and it fails to address the deprivation and discrimination incurred by African Americans. He believes that Alcoholics Anonymous has been successful in African American communities because its spiritual base is familiar, its fellowship is needed, and its traditional values appeal to members of most ethnic groups. Caldwell also believes that AA is well suited to African Americans because it is consonant with the value they place on interpersonal relationships and also with their appreciation of language, metaphors, and imagery.[238] He believes that there is nothing in the program itself that makes it inherently unsuitable for blacks.

The question does arise as to whether certain aspects of self-help groups such as admitting one's powerlessness might conflict with empowerment and strength approaches and avoidance of the deficits perspective suggested by other authors. Humphreys and Woods reject such criticisms of the self-help movement, noting that mutual-help organizations are democratic in nature and respect members as competent and intelligent. They also believe that individuals can still take responsibility for their own situations such as alcoholism or drug addiction, even when structural and political forces are at the root of many problems in African American communities.[239]

Few empirical analyses have been done of African Americans' participation in self-help groups, but based on Epidemiologic Catchment Area data, Snowden and Lieberman found that, in general, few people used self-help groups.[240] Only 2 percent of African Americans and only 8 percent of whites with a lifetime alcohol, drug, or mental disorder had ever used self-help groups. More surprising, given the literature on the importance of African American churches, was that whites were more likely than African Americans to seek help from a religious figure, and there was no evidence that African Americans used nontraditional healers more.

Humphreys and Woods studied 233 African Americans and 267 whites who had received alcoholism treatment in the state of Michigan.[241] They found that similar percentages of whites (32 percent) and African Americans (34 percent) were attending Twelve-Step programs one year later, but substantially different factors predicted their self-help group use. Among whites, the factor most predictive of Twelve-Step group attendance was having been treated in an inpatient program. Living in a white area and longer length of stay in treatment also predicted their attendance. Other factors were negatively associated with whites' Twelve-Step group attendance. In descending order, these were being referred to treatment by the criminal justice system, having more legal problems, having greater substance abuse problems at intake, and attending a program with staff who more strongly support the AA program. The variables combined explained 36 percent of the variance in Twelve-Step group attendance for whites. The model for blacks was quite different. The factors most predictive of attending Twelve-Step groups were living in an African American area and longer length of stay in treatment. The only factor that had a significant negative association with attending treatment was having greater psychological problems at intake. These variables predicted 43 percent of the variance in attendance. Involvement with the criminal justice system did not negatively affect Twelve-Step group attendance as it did for whites, which the authors suggest may indicate that treatment rather than punishment is seen as a relief by African American clients. Although living in an African American or white community was crudely measured, it is noteworthy that this variable showed up so strongly in the findings, suggesting that when a person sees more people like himself or herself, that person may be more willing to participate in self-help groups.

Prevention in African American Communities

McRoy and Shorkey once noted that "just as the problem and consequences of black alcoholism have been largely ignored in the research literature, historically black Americans and the black community have also tended to ignore this issue."[242] This situation is changing. To prevent alcohol and drug problems among African Americans, the Chemical Dependency Subcommittee of the Task Force on Black and Minority Health made the following recommendations:

1. Improve data collection on alcohol and other drug abuse among ethnic minority groups.
2. Promote positive coping skills among youth.
3. Use school-based peer groups to encourage resistance to drug use.
4. Conduct research to learn how cirrhosis develops in minority populations.
5. Conduct research to better understand the role of alcohol use as a contributor to other causes of excess mortality such as the use of alcohol by those with hypertension and the role of alcohol in infant mortality.
6. Develop programs to prevent deaths and accidents related to chemical dependency.
7. Educate health care professionals about alcohol and other drug abuse.[243]

The task force also encouraged the private sector to educate minority researchers and health care providers about chemical dependency. The Cork Institute on Black Alcohol and Drug Abuse at the Morehouse School of Medicine in Atlanta has a program to incorporate more elective chemical dependency education into the clinical education of third- and fourth-year medical students.[244]

Some culturally relevant guidance for people working in substance abuse prevention and treatment has emerged in the recent literature. For example, Brinson writes about group work with black male adolescents, recommending the group approach as a way to reduce isolation and increase connectedness.[245] He recommends the use of closed groups of 6 to 8 members that meet twice weekly during 50-minute sessions over a 12-week period. Members are encouraged to interact socially outside the group. Physical posturing (e.g., shadow boxing), attire of the individual's choice, spontaneous participation during group sessions (rather than each person taking a turn), and cultural language (e.g., hip-hop expressions) are allowed or encouraged, and making direct eye contact is not demanded, since the belief is that the member will do this once respect or trust is established. Brinson considers these practices important to the expression and identity formation of the group participants. Many of these suggestions require that group leaders be versed in the cultural meaning of these elements. He also encourages use of a male and female coleader for purposes of modeling appropriate male/female interactions for the young men. Other features are naming of the group, opening and closing rituals, lack of admonishment for coming late, democratic leadership style, and incorporation of each member's unique talents. A graduation ceremony along with a certificate or plaque of recognition are suggested.

Also recommended are broad strategies that not only focus on substance abuse but also include "a large-scale ecological, environmental, systems-oriented approach" addressing social problems such as unemployment, failure to complete schooling,[246] crime, health, and welfare.[247] There should be an emphasis on the "will to" address the problem of chemical abuses[248] and on the collective responsibility of African American communities to act.[249] Among African Americans, there has been a renewed call to use mutual self-help efforts to address social problems.[250] Bell has emphasized the need for African American communities to communicate rules, values, and sanctions regarding chemical use,[251] and Amuleru-Marshall urges "blacks to develop a stronger sense of community and a consensus on acceptable versus unacceptable behavior based on 'Afro-centric' values."[252]

Gray summarizes an evaluation of prevention programs targeted at African American youths, funded by the Center for Sustance Abuse Prevention.[253] Whether the programs were identified as Afrocentric or not, the effective ones seemed to share common themes that she "identified as aspects of African-American experiences: values of the traditional African-American community, emphasis on extended community involvement, and emphasis on spirituality."[254]

Rites of passage programs emphasizing positive achievements are currently being used as alternatives to the rites of drug use and incarcera-

tion.[255] Instilling black pride appears as an important theme in prevention and treatment. Special attention has been paid to alcohol advertising (billboards, magazines, etc.) directed toward African Americans (see also Chapter 8).[256] Blacks apparently prefer Scotch and cognac (more expensive liquors) and advertising has taken advantage of this.[257] Rather than alcohol advertising using African Americans, more emphasis is needed on African American role models who promote sobriety and recovery. There has also been an outcry against alcoholic beverages, particularly malt liquor with high alcohol content, marketed to youths. Herd notes that messages about alcohol use in popular rap music and the hip-hop culture are inconsistent, though the antidrug message is clearer.[258] The targeting of high-alcohol content beverages has caused African American communities to mobilize against this threat to youths.[259]

An important resource in the prevention and treatment of chemical abuse among African Americans has been the Institute on Black Chemical Abuse with offices in Minneapolis and St. Paul, Minnesota. According to a pamphlet published by the Institute:

> The black community must itself determine under what circumstances and at what times alcohol or other drug use is appropriate. Black people must set their *own* agenda on this issue. That means, for instance, formal and regulatory control on beverage control boards and zoning commissions that determine the hours, places, and location for alcohol sale. Community residents must challenge current zoning practices allowing a high density of liquor stores and advertisements in their neighborhoods.[260]

Substance Abuse among Hispanic Americans

So many different cultural and ethnic groups fall under the term *Hispanic* that discussions of substance use and abuse frequently obscure important differences between those whose roots are in Mexico, Cuba, Puerto Rico, Central America, South America, Spain, and other areas. McQuade notes that "there is no 'typical Hispanic.' Representing combinations of European, African and Native American blood, each of these racial and national backgrounds influence a particular temperament and pre-disposition towards the use of alcohol and drugs."[261] Hispanic Americans are also quite diverse with respect to important factors such as education and living environment,[262] but they are younger than the U.S. population, in general, and are the nation's fastest-growing ethnic group[263] (now about 10 percent of the population). Mexican Americans are the largest segment of the Hispanic population in the United States. Other important demographic factors about Hispanics are that their poverty rate is substantially higher than that of Anglos, and compared to the general population, they have fewer married couples and more female-headed, single-parent households.[264] Given that McQuade also notes that "however diversified, common language, religion and tradition have molded certain recurring patterns [among Hispanics],"[265] both similarities and differences among Hispanic groups are considered as they relate to substance use and abuse.

Incidence of Substance Use and Abuse among Hispanic Americans

Heavy drinking and alcohol-related problems among Hispanic American men, *in general*, seem to be at levels higher than for the population overall,[266] although some studies indicate that white men and Latin men report similar levels of abstainers as well as those consuming three or more drinks per day.[267] The most comprehensive look at Hispanic drinking in the United States is the 1984 National Alcohol Survey (NAS), which was followed by a study of a smaller group of the same participants in 1992. The 1984 wave contained a probability sample of 1,453 Hispanics. From the 1984 study, Caetano found that the rate of frequent, heavy drinkers among Hispanic men (those who consumed the most and did so most

frequently in this study) was approximately 17 percent for those 18 to 29 years of age, 26 percent for those 30 to 39, 11 percent for those 40 to 49, 12 percent for those 50 to 59, and 3 percent for those age 60 and over, indicating the need for particular attention to those in the 30- to 39-year-old group.[268] This pattern was similar to that reported by African American men in 1984 and discussed in the previous section of this chapter, and it was different from the general population where the proportion of heavy drinkers continues to decline from younger to older age groups.

In 1992, both Hispanic and black men responding to the NAS had increased rates of abstainers and stable rates of frequent heavy drinkers, but the pattern of more heavy drinking after youth among Hispanic and black men remained.[269] Hispanic men were more likely than white men to become frequent heavy drinkers during the eight-year interval between the NAS studies. Among Hispanic men who drank at higher levels in 1984 than in 1992, lower acculturation and higher education were the variables associated with lower consumption. Data from the 1992 wave of the NAS are still being analyzed in more detail, but some of the information available thus far on Hispanic men as a whole is found in Table 11.1. As can be seen, more Hispanic than white or black men fall into the frequent heavy drinking category. Information on drinking-related problems from the 1992 wave remains to be published.

Previously, Caetano analyzed the 1984 data in greater detail. He combined the frequent, heavy drinkers with the frequent high maximum drinkers (the two heaviest drinking categories) in the 1984 survey and found that 44 percent of Mexican American men fell into these categories compared with 24 percent of Puerto Rican Americans and 6 percent of Cuban Americans.[270]

More Mexican American men (22 percent) reported having at least one alcohol-related problem compared with 8 percent of Puerto Ricans and 4 percent of Cubans, but using a more stringent criteria of four or more problems, the rates were 7 percent, 5 percent, and 2 percent, respectively.[271]

These figures can be slippery. As Caetano and others have noted, the numbers reported can change, depending on how drinking categories and drinking problems are defined.[272] Other reports also indicate fewer problems among Cuban Americans, although there have been reports of Cuban immigrants abusing substances to cope with the stresses of acculturation.[273] Alcocer also suggests that information on Cuban Americans may be incomplete, since they have not been studied as thoroughly as some other Hispanic groups.[274]

A small, clinical study found that some alcoholic men of Puerto Rican origin had more cognitive impairment than did blacks or whites and that they drank more often, consumed more alcohol, and were of lower socioeconomic status.[275] A literature review by Gordon also raises concerns about the severity of alcoholism and drug use problems among Puerto Ricans in the United States.[276]

Caetano reports that compared with Puerto Rican and Cuban Americans, Mexican American men and women fall more frequently into both the categories of abstainers and heavy drinkers.[277] He found more Mexican American women (14 percent) in the two heaviest drinking categories than Cubans (7 percent) or Puerto Ricans (5 percent). Gordon found no more than isolated reports of drinking problems among Puerto Rican women, and he says that Dominican men in the United States drink moderately and Dominican women drink very little.[278] Burnam found that Mexican American men had a higher prevalence of alcohol disorders than white men based on data from the Los Angeles ECA study, but Mexican American women had lower rates than white women.[279] Among Hispanics as a whole, Kessler and colleagues found that the National Comorbidity Survey "does not replicate the ECA finding that Hispanics have elevated rates of alcohol use disorders compared with whites."[280]

Hispanic American women are more likely to be abstainers, and they apparently have fewer alcohol problems than do other U.S. women, in general. Klatsky and associates previously reported that twice as many Latin as white women were abstainers and that half as many Latin as white women consumed three or more drinks per day.[281] Caetano and Kaskutas's analyses (see Table 11.1) show the difference in abstention rates to be much smaller. For example, in 1992, the rate was 48 percent for Hispanics and 36 percent for whites. However, when abstainers are combined with infrequent drinkers, the percentages are 82 and 58, respectively. At the other end of the spectrum, frequent drinkers were 5 percent among Hispanics and 15 percent among whites, whereas both groups were composed of 3 percent of frequent heavy drinkers in 1992. In comparison with the larger 1984 study, abstention rates for Hispanic women in 1992 remained nearly the same, whereas frequent drinking declined by more than half (from 11 percent to 5 percent) and frequent heavy drinking increased from 1 percent to 3 percent. (Since the number of Hispanic women in the frequent heavy drinking category in the 1992 study is small, these data should be used cautiously.) In comparison to black and white women, Hispanic women were the only group that did not have a significant increase in abstainers; however, they were already more likely to be abstainers. The 1984 data also reveal that white women (12 percent) report one or more alcohol-related problems more frequently than black women (7 percent) and Hispanic women (6 percent).[282]

In the 1984 NAS, factors associated with Hispanic women reporting alcohol problems were being married, young, acculturated and born in the United States, and having one or both U.S.-born parents.[283] The 1992 wave of the NAS raises a caveat with respect to the affect of education on Hispanic men's drinking.[284] Prior to this study, the data have shown that both greater acculturation and higher education among Hispanic men were associated with more drinking. Effects of acculturation were the same in 1992 and have been supported in a number of studies;[285] however, the 1992 data show that those with higher drinking and higher education levels in 1984 drank less in 1992, suggesting that increased education may be an important factor leading Hispanic men to moderate their drinking. This trend has previously been noted for the United States as a whole but not for Hispanics. Since this finding for Hispanics is contrary to other studies, future research will be necessary to see if it can be supported.

The 1994 National Household Survey on Drug Abuse indicates that 9.8 percent of Hispanics age 12 and older reported some use of an illicit drug in the past year, compared with 12.5 percent of blacks and 11 percent of whites.[286] Figures for any cocaine use in the last year were 2.4 percent for Hispanics, 2.9 percent for blacks, and 1.5 percent for whites. For lifetime heroin use, figures were 1.1 percent for Hispanics, compared with 1.5 percent for blacks and .09 percent for whites. Unpublished survey data for 1991 to 1993 indicate that illicit drug use in the past month was 6.7 percent among Puerto Ricans, 6.2 percent among Mexican Americans, 5.1 percent among Cuban Americans, 4.7 percent among South Americans, and 2.5 percent among Cuban Americans.[287]

In an early study of 1,509 Spanish (Hispanic) American adolescents, more of the Hispanic male and female youths reported being abstainers and slightly more reported being infrequent drinkers than Anglo youths, while more Anglo youths reported being low-, medium-, or high-level drinkers.[288] Hispanic girls reported the lowest levels of consumption. Alcocer reviewed literature on the alcohol use of Hispanic American youths in 1982 and found that they used less or that their use did not differ from white youths.[289] The 1994 Household Survey on Drug Abuse also shows that among Hispanic youth ages 12 to 17, 39 percent had ever used alcohol, 33 percent had used it in the past year, and 18 percent had used it in the past month.[290] This was somewhat lower than the figures of 45 percent, 40 percent, and 24 percent, respectively, for white youths, and somewhat higher than the figures of 33 percent, 28 percent, and 18 percent, respectively, for black youths. Percentages of Hispanic, black, and white youths ever reporting use of various illicit drugs are found in Table 11.2. Wallace and Bachman's review indicates that youths' use by ethnic group is highest to

lowest in the following order: Native American, white and Hispanic, black and Asian, and "that drug use [cigarette, alcohol, marijuana, and cocaine] is not disproportionately high among youth in most racial/ethnic minority groups."[291] Their analysis also indicates that differences between ethnic groups that were found can be explained primarily by background (parents' education, family structure, etc.) and life-style factors (religious views, college plans, etc.).

Studies of alcohol and drug use among youths tend to rely on school surveys, which exclude youths who have dropped out, or on household surveys, which omit institutionalized youths. If these youths have higher rates of alcohol and drug use, then such surveys may underestimate young people's use. Some recent surveys have attempted to study use by youths younger than the age normally associated with dropping out of school. One study was of more than 2,000 Mexican American children attending grades 4, 5, and 6 in a relatively low-income area in Texas.[292] Some 44 percent of the children had used at least one "minor substance" in their lifetimes and 27 percent had used two or more. Of the minor substances, 31 percent had tried cigarettes, 26 percent had tried beer, 24 percent had tried wine and liquor, and 8 percent had tried marijuana. "Major substance" use was 13 percent for inhalants, 8 percent for pills, 5 percent for hallucinogens, 5 percent for cocaine, and 4 percent for crack. Boys had more lifetime use of minor drugs than girls, but differences for use of minor substances in the last year and use of major substances were not significant. Demographic and environmental variables (such as peer influences) were more highly correlated with substance use than were psychological variables (such as interpersonal stressors, locus of control, self-esteem, and school satisfaction). The lifetime use of minor substances was predicted by more deviant behavior, peer substance use, being offered these substances, higher grade level in school, increased peer influence, greater depression, and predominant use of the Spanish language, accounting for 53 percent of the variance in the model. Although

greater use of Spanish (a proxy for less acculturation) is generally associated with less use, the authors speculate that more use of Spanish may
make these young students feel disconnected at
school where the majority of personnel are white,
thus leading to drug experimentation.

Few students had used major substances, but
lifetime major substance use (pills, cocaine, crack,
inhalants, and hallucinogens) was predicted by
more lifetime use of minor drugs, more deviant
behavior, being offered major substances, and
more peer substance use, accounting for 36 percent of the variance in the model. Predictors were
similar for boys and girls, but for lifetime minor
use, being offered minor substances and peer influence was significant for girls, whereas depression was significant for boys. The number of
predictor or risk factors was higher for boys, and
half of the students reported three or more risk
factors. The likelihood of using substances increased with the number of risk factors, especially
for use of major substances, and girls with a high
number of risk factors used more minor substances than boys with equal numbers of risk factors. The authors emphasize the need to reduce
risk factors. This seemed particularly necessary
for the Mexican American girls in light of their
heightened susceptibility to risk.

Another study, this one conducted in New
York City, examined differences in alcohol use
among more than 2,000 sixth- and seventh-
graders who comprised four groups of Latino
youths: Puerto Ricans, Dominicans, Colombians,
and Ecuadorians.[293] Many were from low-income
families. As expected, boys drank more than girls.
Dominican and Colombian boys had higher rates
of drinking at least monthly (14 percent for both
groups), compared to 8 percent for Puerto Ricans
and 7 percent for Ecuadorians. Colombian girls
had the highest rate of drinking at 7 percent, compared to 6 percent for Dominicans, 4 percent for
Puerto Ricans, and 2 percent for Ecuadorians. For
the entire sample, having friends who drink was
an especially strong predictor of a student's own
drinking. Students' reports of neutral or favorable

parental attitudes toward their child's drinking
were also correlated with students' drinking. The
same affect was true for students who reported
that their friends were neutral about or favored
the student's drinking. There were adequate sample sizes to conduct the same multivariate analyses for Puerto Rican and Dominican youths. The
same predictive factors emerged for both groups
except that peers' attitudes toward the respondent's drinking was not significant for Dominican
youths. The findings of similar risk factors for
these two groups suggest that similar types of interventions may be suitable for them. As in other
studies, the importance of social influences in this
analysis suggests that this area should be targeted,
such as helping students deal with peer influences. In fact, there is considerable evidence that
predictive factors are similar across ethnic groups,
despite any differences in rates of use.[294]

Historical and Cultural Perspectives on Substance Use and Abuse among Hispanic Americans

In addition to the possible influences of acculturation,[295] poverty and discrimination may contribute to alcohol consumption. According to
Caetano, "Heavy drinking and alcohol problems do
not appear in a contextual vacuum, but are linked
to the status of Hispanics as an underprivileged
ethnic minority in the U.S."[296] Poverty is associated with less political power and may help explain
reports of the large numbers of alcohol outlets
in Hispanic[297] and African American residential
communities.[298] Yet Caetano also writes that
"many of these explanations do not actually assess
levels of stress among minorities but assume that
processes such as acculturation or discrimination
increase stress, which then leads to drinking."[299]

What beliefs do Hispanics hold about chemical
use and abuse? Some suggest that Hispanics often
do not see chemical dependency as an illness. Instead, they may view it as moral weakness and rely
on God or divine intervention rather than professional help to solve the problem.[300] But a study

comparing a sizable number of Hispanics and non-Hispanics in Texas contradicts the strength of the moral explanation among Hispanics.[301] When respondents who "had never tried *any* illicit drug and were not willing to use if they had the opportunity" were asked why they felt this way, health concerns were the most frequently endorsed reason among the two groups, with 46 percent of Hispanics and 43 percent of non-Hispanics endorsing this reason. Family and peer disapproval was next for Hispanics (18 percent), followed by moral reasons (16 percent), whereas for non-Hispanic whites, 30 percent cited moral reasons and 10 percent cited family and peer disapproval.

Marin surveyed a random sample of Mexican Americans and non-Hispanic whites residing in San Antonio and San Jose and found that the two groups did not differ on their endorsement of a number of indicators of excessive drinking.[302] For example, 79 percent of the non-Hispanics and 88 percent of the Mexican Americans thought that becoming sick was an outcome of excessive drinking, and 11 percent of the non-Hispanics and 9 percent of the Mexican Americans thought that excessive drinking would help people forget their problems. However, there were statistically significant differences on 12 of 35 items. As examples, 74 percent of the Mexican Americans thought that excessive drinking would make one nervous, compared to 51 percent of the non-Hispanics; 44 percent and 23 percent, respectively, thought that it would result in fights; and 79 percent and 48 percent, respectively, thought it would result in problems with police. Furthermore, there were some statistically significant differences between low- and high-acculturated Mexican American respondents. For example, low-acculturated Mexican Americans were significantly more likely to believe that excessive drinking would lead to becoming sick, depressed, angry, and guilty. Low-acculturated Hispanics were also significantly more likely than high-acculturated Hispanics to endorse nervousness, fights, and police problems as outcomes of excessive drinking. Such endorsements might have a sound basis in reality, given

the likelihood of certain cultural and socioeconomic groups to encounter police intervention.

Comas-Díaz discusses Puerto Rican "folk beliefs encouraging externalization, passivity and fatalism regarding the problem of drinking" with alcoholism among Puerto Ricans sometimes thought to be caused by bad spirits, reinforcing denial of these problems.[303] Some authors take exception to the idea that denial of substance abuse problems among Hispanics is especially strong. In writing about Mexican Americans in particular, Gilbert and Cervantes say that the little data available suggest that they are as likely as others to be referred to treatment by themselves or by family members,[304] and González-Ramos has called resistance to services by Hispanics a myth.[305]

La familia (the family) is of central importance to Hispanics, but ethnic families can be a source of conflict as well as strength.[306] Since *confianza* (interdependence and trust) is an important value held by Hispanic families, both nuclear and extended, several authors have discussed the necessity of treating the family as a unit rather than treating members individually.[307] Among specific Hispanic cultures, familial relationship patterns differ. "For example, the relationship between mother and son is exceptionally close and dependent among Mexicans and Cubans. And Peruvians and Bolivians experience a stronger commitment to parents and siblings than to their spouses and children."[308] Maternal and sibling relationships are also very important in Puerto Rican families.[309] Traditional chemical dependency treatment programs have been known to stress getting into treatment for one's self, but other approaches might be more successful with Hispanic clients.

Hispanic families often prefer to solve problems within their own boundaries. For many families, this is culturally normative and adaptive[310] but is sometimes misconstrued by professionals as dysfunctional. As with Native Americans, "Concepts like assertiveness, detachment, and independence, commonly effective tools when working with many alcoholics and their families, will rarely, if ever, be understood, much less accepted, by Hispanic clients, because those concepts are seen as a direct threat to the family."[311]

The shame (*verguenza*) that results from drug use may isolate Hispanic alcoholics and addicts (particularly women) from their families. Melus recommends appealing to Hispanics to enter treatment because family unity is threatened,[312] and Gilbert recommends appealing to chemically dependent Hispanic mothers based on improving the lives of their children.[313]

McQuade discusses the extremes of female and male behavior among Hispanics.[314] The man may wish to be thought of as the *parrandero* (carefree reveler), but it is disgraceful to be the *borrachero* (staggering drunk). Public disclosure of personal problems is generally unacceptable for Hispanic men and can result in feelings of emasculation or powerlessness.[315] Women may take a passive role and not dare to seek outside help.[316] Melus says that "attitudes and perceptions must be changed in the community to make treatment and prevention of alcoholism more successful."[317]

Differences in gender norms or the "double drinking standard"[318] in Hispanic cultures also contribute to a lack of recognition of substance abuse problems. Heavy drinking may be an acceptable practice among men, and it may even be justified as part of *machismo*. However, there is confusion about the meaning of this term. Machismo has been used to describe male virility, but it has also been defined as honor, respect, and fulfilling family obligations.[319] There is a notion that if a man "works hard and is a good family provider one then has the 'right' to drink without criticism from others."[320] As a result, men may excuse their heavy drinking, and women may also deny that men drink excessively. Women may view their partner's substance abuse as a behavior to be tolerated rather than changed.[321]

Gordon, however, denies any empirical support for the "widely accepted popular belief that Hispanic drinking is characterized by macho, aggressive drinking (more so than in other ethnic groups)."[322] Neff and colleagues actually developed a scale to measure machismo and used it

with a probability sample of 481 men in San Antonio, Texas.[323] Although Mexican Americans and blacks had higher scores than Anglos, multivariate analysis failed to show that the heavier drinking reported by Mexican American than Anglo or black males was due to machismo.

The cultural mandate for Hispanic women is that they should avoid any appearance of intoxication or other drug-related problems. Like women in general (see Chapter 15), Hispanic women who are substance abusers reportedly face more stigmatization and rejection than their male counterparts.[324] A study of Anglo and Chicano (Mexican American) narcotics addicts demonstrated that the women, particularly the Chicanas, were more likely to be living with an addicted partner and that the men, particularly the Chicanos, were less likely to reside with an addicted partner.[325]

Perhaps Hispanic women's relatively low rates of alcoholism can be explained by the culture value of "'marianismo,' which sees women as the center of family life, a vision that demands chastity, purity, and abstention from alcohol."[326] This should not, however, obscure the needs of those who do have problems. Comas-Díaz speculates that "Hispanic women cope with specific stresses that may lead to drinking. Such stresses include alcoholic significant others, cultural values discouraging direct expression of assertiveness and aggressiveness, [and] a subordinated role in their society."[327] Caetano suggests,

> It is possible that abstention and light drinking are more determined by cultural, social, and historical characteristics than are heavier patterns of drinking, which lead to alcohol abuse and dependence. Personality characteristics and women's personal and family histories may be of importance in the development of these pathological forms of drinking.[328]

The strongly held belief among many Hispanics that women should not drink much or exhibit substance abuse problems may prompt families to deny even the possibility of chemical abuse among their female members (see also Chapter 5 regarding denial). Anglin and colleagues refer to Chicana narcotics addicts as "more deviant" than their Anglo counterparts and as individuals marginal to both the Chicano community and the larger society.[329] They reported that although the Chicanas entered addiction later than the Anglo women, used fewer drugs, and engaged in less prostitution, they experienced more unemployment and more arrests (for all types of crimes). From this description, one may conclude that although narcotics addicts, in general, are marginalized, being a member of an ethnic minority group as well as being a woman further adds to the marginal status of these individuals.

Prevention and Treatment Services for Hispanic Americans

Hispanic Americans are reported to underutilize health and mental health services.[330] Although the same has apparently been assumed about alcoholism services, Gilbert and Cervantes's analysis indicates that Mexican Americans utilize alcoholism services at rates higher than their representation in the population, but that more of their admissions to treatment are involuntary than is the case for the general population.[331] In 1994, Hispanic Americans were 14.6 percent of all clients in substance abuse treatment, indicating that they remain somewhat overrepresented among treatment clients, compared with their representation in the general population.[332] Hispanic American clients are more likely to be treated for drug abuse and less likely to be treated for a combined diagnosis of alcoholism and drug abuse than the total population of clients.[333] Their treatment rates for alcoholism were very similar to the general treatment population. Some 29 percent of treatment units in the United States report that they have specialized services for Hispanic clients.

Quinones and Doyle describe efforts to develop a culturally relevant therapeutic community (TC) and outpatient treatment program for drug addicts in Newark, New Jersey, called CURA. The program utilizes Hispanic staff and encourages cultural values of *dignidad* (dignity), *respeto* (respect), and *machismo* rather than traditional TC methods of punishment (such as haircuts and wearing signs).[334] Other recommendations for making services more useful to Hispanics are to target specific age groups and to use interventions appropriate to each of the groups that comprise the Hispanic population.[335] Advice about how to use social services[336] and client advocacy[337] may also increase service utilization. Concrete services, such as transportation to appointments, have also been suggested and can be especially important for low-income individuals from all ethnic groups.[338]

Since cultural norms regarding women's alcohol and drug use differ from men's, women are likely to require some different treatment strategies. Melus has recommended "more sensitive and cautious" treatment approaches as a result of the physical and verbal abuse that Hispanic women may incur from their families.[339] Comas-Díaz describes a group treatment approach with Puerto Rican women who are alcoholics based on literature that suggests that Hispanic women may feel isolated and alienated and on literature that recommends women-only groups as a forum for expressing anger and other feelings that cannot be vented directly toward family members.[340] However, she notes that the women enrolled in the group did not attend sessions regularly and had difficulty maintaining abstinence.

Aguilar and colleagues suggest using psychoeducational groups with Hispanics, particularly women, to address chemical dependency and codependency.[341] The groups they describe are for adult family members and are open to men and women, making them less suspect than women-only groups, which men may perceive as threats to family cohesion. Education, group discussion, experiential exercises, and "homework" are used to educate members about chemical dependency. The majority of participants have been women.

In a study that used treatment programs as the unit of analysis, researchers found that "units with higher concentrations of Latinos treat clients who are significantly poorer, more prone to abuse drugs than alcohol, more prone to turn to crime to support their habit, more likely to be ordered to treatment by the courts, and at a higher risk for HIV/AIDS."[342] Compared to the programs with lower concentrations of Latino clients, those with higher concentrations reported similar percentages of clients who completed treatment, met the goals of treatment, terminated involuntarily, and injected drugs during the treatment period, but they reported lower percentages of clients remaining clean and sober. The seemingly more severe problems of the clients entering programs that serve higher percentages of Latinos may account for the lower rates remaining alcohol or drug free; however, the analysis does not allow for an examination of individual client characteristics. The mix of services received by the clients in the two types of programs differed, with units serving higher percentages of Latino clients offering more of their clients employment, financial, and legal services. This seems appropriate, given the nature of the problems experienced by the clients in these treatment units. As the authors note, it may be something about these programs that accounts for the differences in alcohol and drug use outcomes. One factor that naturally comes to mind is whether the budget and other resources of the two types of programs differed, given the socioeconomic differences in clientele.

Many Hispanics are Catholic, and often the first person outside the family to whom they turn for help with a problem is a priest or nun. The clergy's support of chemical dependency treatment can facilitate recovery, as can holding self-help group meetings at churches. The spiritual aspects of recovery for Hispanic substance abusers and their family members must also be addressed. Hispanic women are encouraged to emulate the Virgin Mary through self-sacrifice and acceptance of suffering, but this can cause one's own well-being to suffer. With careful reframing, Mary can be discussed in a more feminist light that emphasizes her strengths and independent characteristics.[343] Membership in fundamentalist churches

has grown in Hispanic communities, and some of these churches have developed their own alcohol recovery programs.[344]

Hispanics may consult indigenous folk healers such as *curanderos* and *curanderas* for help with chemical dependency problems, and this should not be summarily dismissed by professionals. The extent to which folk healers are used in recovery is not known,[345] but there are some indications that they are consulted frequently about such problems.[346]

> Other indigenous Hispanic recovery models are based on spiritual systems that date back to the Native American and African roots of many of the Latin American subcultures. These traditions incorporate a long cultural history of attempting to help alcoholics through a combination of herbal medicine, enlisting the aid of spirits, and faith healing.[347]

One treatment, *haba de San Ignacio*, is prepared from a seed and results in nausea and vomiting if taken with alcohol.[348]

Although many AA groups in the United States are conducted in Spanish, little has been written about self-help groups with respect to Hispanic populations. Hoffman noted that "it is unclear whether transcultural adaptation of A.A. involves simple translation of A.A. doctrine or actual changes in content and emphasis of the A.A. program itself."[349] Aguilar and colleagues recommend preparation to participate in groups such as Alcoholics Anonymous and Al-Anon, particularly when there are few other Hispanic members.[350] One of their suggestions is to describe "working the steps" of these programs as taking on responsibilities and as a means of gaining respect for one's self and from others.

Although detailed descriptions of culturally relevant treatment programs are few in the literature, there is some helpful information about culturally relevant prevention approaches. An important aspect of prevention for many Hispanics is *la comunidad* (community), since "Hispanics tend to live together, work together, and spend free time together."[351] Celebrations or fiestas are important in many Hispanic communities, and the use of alcohol during these occasions is common. McQuade describes fiestas as "compensation for life's suffering."[352] Fiestas without the use of alcohol are being incorporated into the prevention and treatment of alcoholism among Hispanics.[353]

Contact with gatekeepers in ethnic, social, civic, religious, neighborhood, and church organizations, as well as PTAs and other community groups, is recommended if prevention efforts are to be successful in Hispanic American communities.[354] Gordon emphasizes community health centers or clinics as an important point of identification of substance abuse problems, especially for Hispanic women and children (although in many cases the medical personnel either do not have the time or do not take the time to intervene).[355] These suggestions are similar for most communities. The key is in developing relationships with those in the target communities of interest and learning about the cultural norms that guide their work. Unfortunately, lack of coordination of community services often presents an obstacle in intervening in substance abuse problems.[356] Mutual education in which professionals learn about the community from its leaders and residents and, in turn, educate community leaders and groups about the dynamics of chemical abuse are necessary steps in initiating all types of chemical dependency services.[357]

The need for culturally appropriate prevention, education, and treatment in both English and Spanish continues to be stressed.[358] For those whose first language is Spanish, their "native tongue is needed to express the deepest feelings and longings endemic to the recovery process."[359] Santiago-Rivera's review of the importance of the use of language in counseling Spanish-speaking clients suggests taking into account whether the client prefers to use Spanish at some times and English at others, and that this may depend on the nature of the material being discussed.[360] She also notes Sciarra and Ponterotto's suggestion that in working with families, some members may prefer to use Spanish while others may prefer English,[361] and Zuniga's work on the use of *dichos* (Spanish proverbs or metaphors) such as "*Dime con quién andas y te diré quién eres* (Tell me who your friends are and I will tell you who you are)."[362] Such sayings may resemble those commonly heard in Alcoholics Anonymous and other Twelve-Step groups.

In reaching out to children of alcoholics, one community health center in Washington, DC, has used *tardes infantil* (afternoons for children) to educate them about alcohol abuse.[363] Painting, movies, and dramatizations are used to help the children express their feelings about family issues; local theater groups have assisted with these activities. The Los Niños program in San Antonio, Texas, utilizes various prevention approaches with children, including puppets.[364] An *abuelita* (grandmother) puppet is a central figure in this approach, because grandmothers are very important in Mexican American life.

With regard to prevention efforts for adults, the idea of the right to drink among men may require emphasis on responsible drinking.[365] One California prevention program featured the family with the mother as the central figure, as it often is in Hispanic family life. Use of the Spanish language media (newspapers, magazines, TV, etc.), developing community newsletters, and designing "foto-novelas" to prevent alcohol and drug abuse and to promote recovery are other suggestions.

Studies of the drinking expectancies of Mexican Americans provide information that may be useful in targeting prevention efforts. For example, Marin found that Mexican Americans were significantly less likely than non-Hispanics to say that alcohol increases enjoyment, clear thinking, and relaxation, and they were less likely to say that alcohol decreases nervousness and tastes good.[366] However, they were more likely to say that alcohol use increases loss of self-control, violence, problems at work, aggression, family problems, depression, and carelessness, and that it increases independence and gives a bad example to children. Level of acculturation among the Mexican Americans also influenced responses. For instance, low-acculturated respondents were more likely to believe that drinking makes one lose self-control, and high-acculturated respondents were more likely to believe that alcohol results in enjoyment. Such information is useful in determining which prevention messages may be most important in influencing reduced consumption among particular segments of the population. Given the growth of the Hispanic population in the United States, it is likely that considerably more attention will be devoted to their integration into U.S. society, including addressing problems associated with alcohol and drug use.

Substance Abuse among Asian Americans

According to Kitano there are more than 20 Asian nationalities.[367] The largest groups of Asians in the United States are of Chinese and Filipino origin, but there are also Japanese, Asian Indians, Koreans, Vietnamese, Laotians, Cambodians, Thais, Hmong, and those of many other Asian nationalities.[368] Pacific Islanders are often included as part of the Asian population, but many take exception to placing so many diverse groups under a single classification. Asian Americans and Pacific Islanders constitute about 3 percent of the total U.S. population, and many reside in Hawaii and on the Pacific Coast.[369]

Alcohol has been used for centuries in the Far East. Stoil traced references to *sake,* Japan's traditional alcoholic drink, to the fifth century; to wine in the Chinese literature of the eighth century; and to social drinking in the classical literature of Vietnam and Korea.[370] There are few references to problematic use of alcohol in most Asian countries.[371] Singer's description of drinking in Hong Kong gives clues to possible explanations for the low prevalence of alcohol-related problems:

The Chinese in Hong Kong traditionally drink at meals and banquets and not without food. Drinking is incidental to eating and drinking-centered

institutions [e.g., bars] and groups are absent. The main aims of drinking are to promote conviviality and improve health. Moderate drinking is sanctioned on defined occasions, drunkenness especially in public strongly disapproved.[372]

Singer notes that although alcoholism may not be common among the Chinese people, it may be more prevalent than thought, with alcoholic psychosis having accounted for an increased proportion of first admissions to psychiatric hospitals in Hong Kong.[373] In China and some other Asian countries, the more significant problem has been narcotic addiction as a result of opium's availability.[374]

Differences in the cultural and social backgrounds of Asian groups reportedly affect attitudes toward alcohol use. The Moslem background of Indonesians and Malaysians prohibits drinking; the Confucianist and Taoist backgrounds of the Chinese emphasize that moderation (the "golden mean") be practiced in all aspects of life, including the use of alcohol; Buddhist, Shintoi, and Chinese philosophies influence the Japanese, but today's Japanese drinking practices reflect a more permissive, business-oriented, urban style; Filipinos' drinking has been influenced by Moslem, Spanish, American, and Japanese colonists.[375]

Hsu wrote that the Chinese prefer opium to other types of drugs because it promotes withdrawal or retreatist behavior and is more consistent with the concept of harmony with the environment (an important component of Taoism).[376] He also wrote that Americans are attracted to drugs such as marijuana and alcohol that disinhibit behavior and result in acting out and conflict with the environment, which is more typical of Americans' self-centered, aggressive nature. Although everyone will not agree with Hsu's depiction, Singer adds that the Chinese abhor loss of self-control and value intellectual control.[377] However, Singer and Hsu also note that even when intoxicated, Asians do not tend to act out (such as becoming violent or engaging in behavior that might prompt an arrest). This suggests the strong influence of cultural mores on behavior, even when consuming alcohol.[378] Other sociocultural factors offered as possible explanations for narcotics use in China are the high degree of social disorganization typified by political upheaval, modernization, illiteracy, poverty, and poor health care, with opium rather than alcohol offering the cheapest, most readily available means of escape.[379]

Alcohol and Drug Use among Asian Americans and Pacific Islanders

Like Asians, Asian Americans apparently have relatively low levels of alcohol use, other drug use, and substance abuse problems, compared to the general U.S. population, but consider the following:

1. Few epidemiological studies of alcohol and other drug use have included Asian Americans.
2. The use of probability samples in identifying substance use and abuse among Asians has been limited.
3. Few studies have identified Asian Americans by subgroup.[380]

These observations led Matsushima and colleagues to suggest that it may be the *perception* rather than the *reality* that Asians Americans have few alcohol problems,[381] and Sue and colleagues refer to alcoholism as "a problem of growing concern among Asian-Americans."[382] The 1977 Health Interview Survey (a household survey conducted by the National Center for Health Statistics) showed relatively low alcohol use in the 256 Asian/Pacific American subjects who participated.[383] Klatsky and colleagues studied records of nearly 60,000 individuals who had routine health examinations from 1978 to 1980 in Oakland, California, and found that both Oriental men and Oriental women reported much less drinking than those of other ethnic groups.[384] The study included 1,960 Chinese, 1,151 Filipinos, 702 Japanese, and 364 members of other oriental groups. In each of the ethnic groups they studied, men drank more than women, but the gender differences were least pronounced in whites and blacks, and, in as-

cending order, were more pronounced in Filipinos, Japanese, Latinos, and Chinese.

A study, reported by Kitano and Chi in the late 1980s, compared 298 Chinese, 295 Japanese, 280 Koreans, and 230 Filipinos from the Los Angeles area and found variation between the groups.[385] Most subjects were identified using Asian surnames from telephone directories, but Filipinos, who often have names similar to Hispanics, were identified through community agencies and snowball sampling techniques. Of men in the study, Koreans were most likely to be abstainers (46 percent), whereas about one-third of men in the other ethnic groups abstained. Chinese men were the most likely to be moderate drinkers (55 percent) and Korean men the least likely to fall in this category (28 percent), whereas slightly more than one-third of Japanese and Filipino men drank moderately. The Chinese men were least likely to be heavy drinkers (14 percent), whereas reports for Japanese and Filipino men were both 29 percent and for Korean men, 26 percent.

The women in the study were substantially more likely than men to be abstainers in every ethnic group except the Japanese, where the proportion of male and female abstainers was nearly identical at about 33 percent. Japanese women were the least likely to abstain. The highest proportions of female abstainers were among the Koreans (82 percent) and the Filipinos (80 percent), whereas 69 percent of Chinese women abstained. Moderate drinking among the women was lowest among Filipinos (16 percent), followed by Koreans (18 percent), Chinese (31 percent), and Japanese (55 percent). Japanese women had the highest proportion of heavy drinkers (12 percent); rates for all the other groups of women were lower (4 percent of the Filipino, 1 percent of the Korean, and none of the Chinese women).

Despite differences in drinking patterns among the groups, few instances of alcohol-related problems were reported. Those most likely to drink were men under age 45 of higher socioeconomic status who had permissive attitudes toward alcohol use.[386]

Ahern surveyed the literature on alcohol use among ethnic groups in Hawaii.[387] There are some differences in estimates, but, in general, Caucasians and Native Hawaiians' use is highest, followed by the Japanese; Filipinos and Chinese drink the least. A 1984 study of 2,503 households in Hawaii presents a somewhat different picture.[388] The Japanese reported the highest rate of abstention (58.5 percent), followed by Filipinos (53.0 percent), Native Hawaiians (40.7 percent), and Caucasians (31.0 percent). Conversely, the highest percentage of heavy drinkers were Caucasians (13.6 percent), followed by Native Hawaiians (11.0 percent), Filipinos (6.7 percent), and Japanese (5.2 percent). Caucasians also reported the highest rates of lifetime prevalence of drug use followed by Native Hawaiians with fewer Japanese and Filipinos reporting drug use.

In a study of 141 patients 50 years and older receiving services through the Chinese-American Service League in Chicago, the number who abstained from alcohol decreased with age (as compared with the general population in which abstinence increases with age).[389] The authors suggest that some Chinese begin drinking later in life because it is viewed as acceptable for health reasons. (Chinese herb medicines may contain substantial amounts of alcohol.)[390] However, health reasons were also cited as reasons for abstaining from alcohol.

In terms of problem indicators, data from the National Center for Health Statistics show that Chinese Americans have much lower age-adjusted death rates from cirrhosis than do whites or African Americans—1.2, 4.7, and 10.5 per 100,000 members of the population, respectively.[391] Although arrests rates of Japanese and Chinese Americans are lower than those for other groups, Kitano noted that a substantial portion of arrests among these ethnic groups are alcohol related.[392]

Data on drug use among Asian Americans are limited, but a study of 1,337 Asian Americans who received drug abuse treatment indicated that the primary drug of abuse was heroin (similar to the whites in the study) but that twice as many

Anglo Americans as Asian Americans received methadone maintenance.[393] The Asian Americans had considerably more primary and secondary barbiturate abuse, but the whites had more secondary use of all other drugs.

Unpublished data for 1991 to 1993 from the National Household Survey on Drug Abuse show that within the past month, about 1 percent of Asian Americans and Pacific Islanders drank heavily and that about 3 percent had used an illicit drug.[394] A small study of two nonrandom samples of Cambodian refugee women residing in the United States raised concerns about both prescription drug use and drinking among these individuals who have endured severe trauma.[395] Whereas most used prescription drugs, 58 percent of the West Coast sample reported use for purposes other than the condition they were prescribed, such as altering mood; the East Coast sample did not report use for nonprescribed purposes. On the other hand, more of the East Coast sample reported using alcohol, and they often reported use for nervousness, stress, insomnia, or pain. Also of interest was that Cambodian women reported that men's drinking is social, whereas women's drinking was to deal with emotional or physical pain, and that some women are encouraged to drink in the months prior to or after child birth as a means of "strengthening the blood."

Studies are generally consistent in their reports that Asian American youths drink and use other drugs less frequently than other youths. Although Asian American youths are more likely to abstain, some findings indicate that those who drink consume more than their counterparts of other ethnic backgrounds.[396]

Cultural and Genetic Influences in Substance Use among Asian Americans

Discussions of Asian American drinking and drug use have largely been concerned with explaining why the incidence of chemical abuse is lower than among other population groups. Genetic and sociocultural explanations have both received attention. There is evidence on both sides, with many more questions to be answered. We begin by discussing sociocultural factors, then genetic factors, and summarizing with a synthesis of evidence on these perspectives.

Sociocultural Influences. In addition to the various philosophical and religious traditions that influence Asian Americans (Confucianist, Taoist, Moslem, etc.), acculturation may also play a part in Asian American drinking.[397] Phin and Phillips note that "peripheral studies of Chinese who have sought treatment for narcotic abuse and Japanese who have sought treatment for barbiturate abuse have linked abuse to problems with acculturation."[398] Wang predicted that alcoholism among Chinese Americans would increase as they move "from the old pattern of domination by father and husband to the new pattern of the increasing power for mother and wife, and from the Chinese pattern of loyalty to personal and familial authority figures, to the American pattern of allegiance to impersonal and abstract ideals."[399] Matsushima and colleagues also believe that as with other immigrant groups facing the pressures of acculturation, "an increase in alcohol consumption, alcohol abuse and alcoholism is something to be expected rather than to be speculated about."[400] The Japanese American and Chinese American students studied by Sue and colleagues at the University of Washington in Seattle drank less than their Caucasian American counterparts, but greater acculturation (as measured by less fluency in Japanese or Chinese and a greater number of generations of family that had resided in the United States) was related to increased alcohol consumption.[401] The researchers reported that the Asian American students had more negative attitudes toward alcohol, as did their parents, but they were less likely than Caucasian students to report that alcohol harms the body.

A study conducted in Canada by Li and Rosenblood also found that college students of Chinese background drank less than Caucasian students. Although there was no difference in the number of physical symptoms the two groups reported after drinking, the Chinese tended to report symptoms after fewer drinks.[402] The Chinese students endorsed abstinence more than the Caucasians. Chinese students born in Canada were more likely to be drinkers than Chinese students born in Asia, and the Chinese students' drinking was positively associated with the number of Caucasian friends they had and their Caucasian friends' approval of alcohol use.

However, analyses by Clark and Hesselbrock of data from a joint U.S. and Japanese research endeavor indicate that the effects of acculturation are not clear.[403] For example, they found that Japanese men in Japan consumed more alcohol and had more alcohol-related problems than did Japanese Americans residing in California and Hawaii and Caucasians residing in California. Sue concluded that among Asians both in Asia and in America, frequency and amount of drinking are on the rise.[404]

Further information confounding interpretation of the acculturation explanation comes from Lubben and colleagues.[405] They found only partial support for acculturation as a current explanation of drinking practices among Filipino American men and women. Their nonprobability sample of 230 Filipinos may not be representative of the population (for example, 90 percent reported having at least some college education and men reported attending church somewhat more often than women). Male drinking was interpreted to be influenced more by Western practices and female drinking by traditional Asian practices, giving support to an acculturation explanation for men but not for women. The best predictor of women's drinking was church attendance (more frequent attendance was associated with less drinking); education was also important (greater education was associated with more drinking). Women who were younger and who were Catholic drank more, but age and religion were less important predictors of their drinking than church attendance and education. Predictors of male drinking were different from those for the females. For men, the most important predictors of increased drinking were lower income and having friends who drank, followed by less frequent church attendance. Neither age, education, nor Catholicism were significant for men but were for women. In addition to acculturation, gender-role explanations are likely to account for a substantial amount of the variance in men's and women's drinking.

Other cultural factors also reportedly affect drinking and drug use and identification of substance abuse problems. Asians attach considerable shame to these problems and families generally try to conceal them. For example, Coleman reported that Asian American "families had a tendency to be permissive about allowing junkies to be high or to crash at home," apparently to prevent embarrassment.[406] The desire to "save face" and to show respect to family members, particularly elders, may also result in concealing a problem until it escalates.

Genetic Influences.   Evidence that Asians may metabolize alcohol more rapidly than whites led to speculation about the role of the *flushing response* (also called the flushing reflex or reaction) in inhibiting alcohol use among this population.[407] "This physiological reaction is characterized by facial flushing, which is often accompanied by headaches, dizziness, rapid heart rate, itching, or other symptoms of discomfort."[408] Both Stoil and Sue discuss the scientific literature on the flushing response beginning with Wolff's work in 1972.[409] Shortly after, Goedde and colleagues found that the Japanese subjects they studied tended to lack an enzyme called aldehyde dehydrogenase (ALDH) 1, but they had ALDH 2, whereas nearly all Japanese alcoholics and all the German subjects studied had both ALDH 1 and 2.[410] Additional research also suggests that flushing may help protect against drinking. As described by Stoil, a by-product of alcohol metabolism, acetaldehyde, is a highly toxic substance. If not converted into a nontoxic form, it causes the discomfort associated with the flushing response (which has been likened to an Antabuse

reaction). Without ALDH 1, the body does not dispose of acetaldehyde quickly enough to prevent flushing.

The flushing response may help protect against alcohol abuse and alcoholism, but apparently it does not fully explain why Asians have a lower rate of alcoholism. Kitano concluded,

> The results of research comparing Asians with whites generally support the hypothesis that there are racial differences in toxic responses to alcohol. However, it should be noted that not all Asians exhibit the flushing response and that there may not necessarily be a cause-effect relationship between the toxic response, the consumption of alcohol, and problem behavior.[411]

Towle, for example, reported that about three-quarters of the Japanese Americans he studied who flushed could continue to drink after the onset of this response.[412] Johnson's extensive study of the subject indicates that "contrary to popular beliefs, flushing is only marginally related to reduced alcohol use."[413] Ewing has noted that contemporary social, cultural, and psychological factors may also limit the ability of the flushing response to continue to act as a protective factor.[414] Although groups such as Alaskan Natives and Native Americans have some Asian ancestry, a substantial number have serious alcohol problems, also failing to support flushing as a sufficient, protective factor.[415]

Sue and colleagues suggest that the flushing response alone may be insufficient to prevent excessive drinking. However, interaction effects may be present in which cultural prohibitions against drunkenness arise as a result of adverse physiological responses to alcohol consumption, and cultural taboos on drinking may cause individuals to report negative physical consequences from drinking.[416] In other words, cultural and genetic influences may have reciprocal effects, and it is difficult to separate the effects of one set of factors from the other in explaining chemical use by Asians and Asian Americans.

In an attempt to test the competing explanations of physical symptoms and cultural norms by using three proposed path models, Li and Rosenblood compared samples of Canadian Chinese and Caucasian Canadian college students.[417] They found no support in either sample for any direct or indirect path testing physical symptoms in the three models as a predictor of alcohol consumption. With regard to cultural norms, they found the same pattern of results for both samples. Cultural norms were found to be a direct predictor of alcohol consumption but not an indirect predictor (i.e., in the model that suggested that cultural norms influence physical symptoms, which in turn influences alcohol consumption, neither of the paths was significant). The authors recognize methodological problems in the study such as reliance on self-report data only. Rather than settle the issue, the study keeps alive the debate over explanations of drinking among those of Asian background.

Prevention and Treatment Services for Asian Americans

The lack of special chemical dependency services for Asian Americans is likely related to two factors: Asians comprise only a small percentage of the U.S. population and they apparently have a low incidence of chemical dependency problems. Asians' preference for not attracting attention to themselves may also inhibit the development of special services to meet their needs.[418] Asian Americans reportedly underutilize chemical dependency treatment services.[419] Although they are 3 percent of the U.S. population, they were just under 1 percent of clients in substance abuse treatment in 1994.[420] Kitano reported that Asian Americans say that they would prefer to receive services from an ethnic agency, but specialized services for problems may not be available, causing them to turn to religious leaders, doctors, or family and friends for help.[421]

Underutilization of substance abuse treatment services by Asian Americans has been blamed on inaccessibility and cultural values.[422] Inaccessibility may be due to language barriers, insensitivity to or lack of understanding of Asian

cultures, Asians' distrust of other cultures, and limited outreach to Asian Americans.[423] Cultural factors that may inhibit treatment use are lack of identification of substance abuse as a problem, lack of familiarity with social service agencies, pride in handling one's problems alone, preference for handling problems within the family or one's immediate community, and the stigma associated with drinking problems that would bring shame on one's self and on one's family.[424] To improve treatment and prevention, Matsushima and colleagues recommend extensive outreach efforts, education about substance abuse, and bilingual and bicultural services.[425]

A statewide survey in Hawaii attempted to identify barriers to seeking professional help among Caucasians, Native Hawaiians, Japanese, and Filipinos.[426] "Personal embarrassment" was rated slightly higher by Japanese than Native Hawaiians or Filipinos and was rated lowest by Caucasians, but most individuals said they would not be embarrassed to seek treatment. Likewise, among all ethnic groups, most said that they would not "be ashamed or embarrassed if my family or friends knew." However, of all the items on the list, personal and family embarrassment were identified as the most substantial, potential barriers to seeking treatment. More Filipinos than Japanese and Native Hawaiians did not know where to go for help, whereas Caucasians were most likely to report knowing where to seek assistance.

Coleman indicated that despite family interconnectedness, therapists tend to treat Asian American family members separately from addicts in order to "sever unhealthy supports."[427] The suggestions that Phin and Phillip describe for treating Asian American drug abusers include support of traditional values and cultural identification; use of Asian American staff; emphasis on commonalties among Asian groups rather than on unique cultural factors; involvement with the larger Asian community; family therapy; and, for women, consciousness raising and identity building.[428] Little has been written on self-help groups with Asians. Some groups in the United States conduct their meetings in Japanese, and there is a version of Alcoholics Anonymous in Japan called *Danshukai*.[429]

Some general suggestions from the literature on the help-seeking behavior of Asian Americans are also in order.[430] The multiservice model, in which agencies locate together, or a single agency offers multiple services, may make services more appealing. Asian Americans who are hesitant to seek mental health services may be more willing to go to an agency that also offers other social services. As is true for all ethnic and cultural groups, sanction from respected members of the ethnic community is useful in encouraging service utilization. Agencies may garner support by including board members who are representative of the Asian American groups to be served and by gaining the backing of Asian American organizations and churches. Chemical dependency professionals can also make individual attempts to better serve Asian American clients. For example, those who are aware of values such as filial piety (respect of children for their parents) will likely be more effective in helping clients develop solutions to problems that are consistent with their culture.

Likewise, social service providers can better assist clients if they understand how Asian Americans view problems. The most frequent explanations of personal or behavioral problems are organic.[431] Holistic medicine views the mind and body as functioning together, not separately, as is often the case in Western cultures. A Westerner may consider a particular problem as purely psychological, but those from Asian and Pacific cultures may view the problem as having a biological basis, thus relieving the individual and family of personal blame. In fact, Cho and Faulkner found that Korean students attending U.S. universities are more likely than their American counterparts to define alcoholism as a physiological rather than a behavioral or social problem.[432] These authors suggest that the definition of alcoholism is culture bound. Americans are taught to look for social and behavioral signs that are part of the disease

concept of alcoholism in the United States, and Koreans are taught to look for physiological signs.

Cho and Faulkner presented their subjects with a vignette of a man who would qualify as an alcoholic based on the Michigan Alcoholism Screening Test. Although 75 percent of Korean and 88 percent of U.S. respondents believed that alcoholism is a disease, 96 percent of Americans thought the man in the vignette was an alcoholic, and 71 percent of Koreans thought he was not. Inability to control drinking and daily drinking were most often endorsed as the reasons that both groups thought the man was an alcoholic. However, reasons such as work absence due to a hangover and a drunk driving arrest were endorsed by substantial numbers of Americans but not by Koreans as reasons to believe the man is an alcoholic. Although the Koreans favored a physiological explanation of alcoholism, they more often saw alcoholics as weak-willed, whereas Americans more often saw the problem as hereditary. Americans more often believed that abstinence was required for recovery, and Koreans were less likely to feel that alcoholics experience guilt over drinking. One possible explanation of the findings is that Americans recognize signs of alcoholism earlier than Koreans; nevertheless, this study indicates different cultural conceptions of alcoholism and raises the question of whether U.S. conceptions are appropriate to other cultures.

Kitano's study of mental illness among Japanese and Japanese Americans also found that families tended to see these problems as moral issues, such as laziness, indicating the need for education about these problems and for preparing families to utilize services.[433]

Like many Native Americans, Asian Americans may have great hesitation about self-disclosure because they have been taught to be stoic and endure problems without complaining.[434] Suggestions for making Asian and Asian American clients feel more comfortable in service settings include taking a personal approach, since they may construe professional demeanor as disinterest. Other suggestions are to speak to the client in a quiet, respectful tone of voice and to use indirect rather than direct questions. Older clients should be shown special respect. Treatment providers should also be aware that Asian American clients may say what they think the professional would like to hear as a sign of respect.

With regard to prevention strategies, Kuramoto reviewed results of forums held in various Asian American communities (Chinese, Japanese, Korean, Filipino, Vietnamese, Cambodian, Laotian, Hmong, and Thai heritages) in California.[435] A few of the issues and suggestions that arose were unique to particular ethnic communities. For example, in the Laotian American community, an identified need was education about drug laws due to the dissimilarity between laws in Laos and the United States. The various communities differed somewhat in the drugs they saw as most problematic. For example, the Hmong American community saw alcohol, tobacco, and opiates as most problematic, whereas the Thai American community identified alcohol, tobacco, marijuana, and amphetamines. Most of the concerns that emerged were common across the groups, such as lack of bilingual and bicultural materials and culturally competent services. Other barriers often identified were stigma and lack of recreational opportunities. Family-oriented approaches were also emphasized, as was the need for better referral systems.

Kuramoto also reviewed the limited literature on prevention programs that have been used with Asian American groups. A review of 18 programs assessed by the National Asian Pacific American Families Against Substance Abuse indicated themes that seemed to make the programs successful, such as sponsorship by established and credible community agencies, bilingual and bicultural staff, youth involvement, pride in culture, emphasis on group activities, and a comprehensive approach to addressing the needs of youths.[436] Kuramoto's review also suggests the need to assist parents and children with accultur-

ation and intergenerational conflicts as they adapt to life in the United States. Mokuau discussed prevention strategies with respect to Pacific Islanders, referring to programs such as the Kamehameha Schools/Bishop Estate Native Hawaiian Drug-Free Schools and Community Program, which incorporates cultural themes including messages such as *He Hawai'i au;'ai 'ole i ka la 'au 'ino*—Hawaiian and drug free.[437]

Substance Abuse among Jewish Americans

Jews may be considered a cultural and ethnic as well as a religious group. Cultural factors associated with low rates of alcohol problems among Jews were noted by Immanuel Kant 200 years ago.[438] Keller notes that the Bible contains a number of accounts of Jewish drinking and drunkenness, but he suggests three reasons why alcoholism did not become a problem for the Jews: (1) they denounced pagan gods who had been worshiped with orgiastic drinking, (2) they developed a religious culture with a focus on the Torah and with worship and education taking place at synagogues, and (3) they confined drinking to rituals practiced at the synagogue and at home.[439] Weiss calls Judaism "permissive in matters concerning alcohol use."[440] In Israel, alcohol is readily available and its use in rituals remains common. But in recent years, the country's concerns about alcoholism have begun to mount.[441] The 1980s marked the first time that Israel had enough alcoholics to be included in international rankings on rates of alcoholism.[442] Two percent of the Israeli adult population is reported to have alcoholism.[443] Drinking and alcohol-related problems have been blamed on "adoption of foreign norms" that encourage drinking "for pleasure and fun."[444] Other explanations concern the adjustment problems of Holocaust survivors and the difficulties that immigrants have experienced earning a living and finding a place in the society.[445]

The literature on alcohol use, alcohol problems, and prevention and treatment efforts in Israel has grown rapidly.[446] Concern about the need to prevent excessive drinking in Israel resulted in the establishment of organizations such as the Israeli Department of Prevention and Treatment of Alcoholism and the Israeli Society for the Prevention of Alcoholism.[447] Israel's official state policy is that alcoholism is a disease, and the number of treatment centers in the country has increased.[448] But Jews live in many places besides Israel. We now focus on Jews in the United States.

Extent of Alcohol and Other Drug Use among Jewish Americans

A major U.S. study published in 1968 reported that 92 percent of adult Jews, a greater proportion than any other major religious group, drank alcohol.[449] A 1984 study also showed that a large percentage of Jews drink alcohol.[450] But despite high rates of drinkers, Jews continue to be known for their low rates of alcoholism.[451] Glatt noted that it is curious that Jews, who have been exposed to many strains and stressors and who exhibit at least as much neuroticism as the rest of the population, tend not to develop alcohol problems.[452] In contrast, he mentioned some anecdotal reports of overrepresentation of Jews among drug abusers and noted that, unlike alcohol, there were no proscriptions against drug use in the Jewish culture.[453] A more recent article in the *Jewish Exponent* indicated an acceptance of medication use among Jews and "heavy use . . . of diet pills, tranquilizers and mood-altering drugs."[454] Teller noted information in *Psychiatric News* indicating substantial numbers of Jewish alcoholics and addicts and the possibility of cross-addiction among this group.[455]

Among the few investigations of drug use among Jewish college students is one study, published in 1980, based on a sample of 278 undergraduate psychology students, about equally divided between men and women, 84 of whom were Jewish.[456] The researchers found support for earlier studies that indicated that Jews, rather than

Catholics or Protestants, and that men, rather than women, use marijuana more frequently, but length of marijuana use was not related to religious affiliation or gender. Among the males, Jews used marijuana an average of 5.77 times per month, compared with 2.50 for Catholics, and 0.91 for Protestants; among females, use was 1.20 for Jews, compared with 1.71 for Catholics and 0.97 for Protestants. Students who rated highest on measures of creativity, adventuresomeness, and some aspects of novelty seeking used marijuana more frequently. Although not statistically significant, there was a trend for more frequent marijuana users to be less authoritarian. The authors attributed their findings about marijuana use to explanations that "traditionally in our society, adventuresomeness has been encouraged in the male and discouraged in the female, and Jews repeatedly have been found to be less authoritarian than Catholics or Protestants."[457]

Another survey, using data collected in 1980, based on 704 male students and staff ages 18 to 25 at the University of California at San Diego, 110 of whom were Jewish and the remainder Christian (i.e., Catholic or Protestant), indicated no differences in average quantity and frequency of alcohol consumption.[458] The Christian men did report more heavy drinking and more drinking problems and had more first-degree relatives and some second-degree relatives with histories of alcoholism. The authors say these findings support descriptions of Jews as nonproblem drinkers. The same study found no statistically significant differences in lifetime drug use or related problems and no substantial pattern of differences in drug use between the two groups. Although random sampling was used and there was a 70 percent response rate, the relatively small number of Jews and the fact that all subjects were males at a college limits the study's generalizability.

Jews apparently have low rates of alcoholism, but Flasher and Maisto emphasize that being Jewish does not provide total immunity from alcoholism or other drug abuse, and they question whether rates of alcoholism among Jews are really so low.[459] In 1958, Snyder found that Jews may underreport their drinking, perhaps due to the need to maintain their image as sober people,[460] although in 1980, researchers studying Jewish alcoholics indicated that they had no problem in identifying subjects.[461] Given the current state of research on Jews, it is not possible to report with confidence the extent of their substance abuse or whether substance abuse has increased among this group.[462]

Explanations of Low Rates of Alcoholism among Jewish Americans

Jews reportedly have much lower rates of alcoholism than many other religious groups, but Jews are also a cultural group. Many individuals have a strong Jewish identity but do not participate in Judaism on a religious level.[463] The reportedly lower rates of alcoholism among those who identify themselves as Jewish (in the religious sense, the cultural sense, or both), combined with information that many Jews use alcohol, has resulted in a good deal of attention paid to what might be viewed as these contradictory circumstances. Various authors have noted cultural norms that suggest that drunkenness is a behavior of Gentiles (Christians or other non-Jews), not Jews, and that drunkenness, especially among Jewish women, is strongly condemned.[464] Disapproval of drunkenness, along with factors such as the well-defined role of alcohol in religious ceremonies and holidays[465] and "the importance of moderation in all life activities,"[466] may provide Jews with a degree of insularity from alcoholism.

Notable studies of differences in drinking between Jewish Americans and other groups were conducted by Glad[467] and by Snyder.[468] Glad reviewed the state of knowledge at the time and found six potential explanations for these differences. First were biological determinants. Despite interest in this topic,[469] Glad discounted this explanation because Jews do not constitute a separate race. In his own research, Glad defined Jews as those who had a "Jewish self-consciousness." A

second explanation Glad encountered was that of "group protection"—the idea that Jews are sober because this behavior protects them from further endangerment and further condemnation by others, a position espoused by Immanuel Kant in the 1700s.[470] This is also referred to as the "in-group, out-group factor." The third hypothesis Glad encountered was religious sanctions against alcohol use, often expressed in the "drunkenness is not Jewish" idea. The fourth hypothesis he discerned was that drinking among Jews was ritualized or sacred. Bales also suggested this explanation in his frequently cited article on cultural factors affecting drinking.[471] Snyder emphasized these third and fourth points as well as the importance of adherence to Jewish religious orthodoxy in encouraging sobriety. In Snyder's words, "Through the ceremonial use of beverage alcohol religious Jews learn how to drink in a controlled manner; but through constant reference to the hedonism of outsiders, in association with a broader pattern of religious and ethnocentric ideas and sentiments, Jews also learn how not to drink."[472]

A fifth hypothesis Glad considered concerned family solidarity, the idea that a strong and secure family life among Jews provided insulation from alcoholism. Many years earlier, Emile Durkheim, in his classic work on suicide, described the protection that social solidarity offers against deviant behavior.[473] The final hypothesis Glad outlined was that a preference for wine, rather than distilled spirits, resulted in less inebriety among Jews.

Glad's empirical investigation concerned 49 male adolescents from each of three groups: American Jews, American Irish-Catholics, and a "control group" of third-generation Americans of central and northern European descent. He did not find support for the group protection hypothesis, and he found evidence about familial (parental) influences on drinking inconclusive. He did find that Jewish adolescents drank in a more matter-of-fact manner, but contrary to expectations, Jewish adolescents were more likely to associate drinking with independence and maturity. Jews did prefer wine, but he thought this evidence insufficient to provide an explanation for lower rates of inebriety. Like Bales and Snyder, Glad concluded "that the rates of inebriety in the adult Jewish and Irish cultures in America are explainable in terms of (a) the Jewish tendency to drink for socially and symbolically instrumental results, and (b) the Irish tendency to use alcohol for personally and socially affective consequences."[474]

Snyder's comparison of Jewish subgroups found the lowest to highest frequency of intoxication in the following order: Orthodox, Conservative, Reform, and secular Jews.[475] (Later work by Snyder and colleagues in Israel also indicates that the more Orthodox Ashkenasi Jews experience less alcoholism than the Sephardi and Oriental Jews but that other factors such as economic status and cultural stress might also influence these rates.[476]) After reviewing subsequent studies related to Snyder's belief that religious Orthodoxy promotes sobriety, Flasher and Maisto concluded that some studies support this view and others do not. They suggest investigating whether members of other religious groups who had moved away from their religious traditions also have higher rates of drinking and alcoholism.[477] However, increased acculturation with a concomitant move away from traditional Jewish life and religious practices continues to be offered as one possible explanation for increased alcohol problems among Jews.[478]

In a continuation of efforts to investigate religious and cultural issues in alcoholism among Jews, Glassner and Berg conducted a qualitative study of 88 Jews in central New York state using a randomly selected stratified sample.[479] They found that Orthodox Jews drank as part of rituals, did not know heavy drinkers, defined alcoholism as a disease, and were fearful of alcoholics. Reform and "nonpracticing" Jews more closely resembled each other. They drank more as part of regular socialization, were more likely to know alcoholics, defined alcoholism as a psychological dependence, and were more likely to view alcoholism with condemnation and blame. Conservative Jews (who incorporate both aspects of Orthodoxy and Reformism) were less clear in their views of alcoholism, but many considered it a habit. Conservatives were more likely than Orthodox Jews, but less likely than Reform and nonpracticing Jews, to know alcoholics.

Glassner and Berg identified four factors which they believe taken together continue to help Jews avoid alcohol problems: (1) Jews continue to believe that they are not susceptible to alcohol problems; (2) even with a trend away from religious Orthodoxy, Jews continue to practice ritualistic drinking during events like religious observances; they drink moderately, mostly while eating, and they continue to teach these practices to their children; (3) the bulk of Jews' social relationships are with others (primarily Jews) who drink moderately and do not have alcohol problems; (4) rather than rationalize excessive drinking, Jews avoid drinking too much by practices such as nursing a single drink at a party.[480] These explanations are in keeping with Ullman's earlier discussion of the protective nature of drinking customs that are well integrated within the cultures of Orthodox Jews, Italians, and Chinese.[481]

The literature may give the impression of homogeneity among Jews in the United States, but Sanua says that Jews are heterogeneous with respect to sociodemographic characteristics and religious differences.[482] He suggests that the available studies are inadequate to provide a comprehensive picture of alcoholism and drug abuse among this population. Weiss and Eldar call for cross-cultural studies comparing Jews in Israel and in other countries to isolate factors in the development of alcoholism among Jews.[483]

Prevention and Treatment Services for Jewish Americans

There are indications that Jews voluntarily use mental health services more than others,[484] but the same has not been said of chemical dependency treatment. Denial and lack of recognition of alcoholism (and perhaps other drug abuse) by substance abusers, their families, and professionals are considered significant barriers to chemical dependency treatment among Jews.[485] Or as one rabbi put it, "The general impression is that there are no Jewish alcoholics, so in addition to the low self-esteem that is often attached to alcoholism, there is the additional feeling of failure as a Jew. The way you deal with that is to deny your Jewishness. 'If I were really Jewish, I wouldn't be an alcoholic.' "[486] Thus, there is concern that "the failure to seek treatment may be especially common among Jewish alcoholics."[487] Rabbis' understanding of the problem is considered particularly important, but they have been known to accept the stereotype that Jews do not become alcoholics.[488] One suggestion for assisting Jews with chemical dependency problems is to hold self-help group meetings in synagogue facilities.[489]

Two organizations of particular interest to Jews are the JACS Foundation, whose central office is in New York City, and the Alcohol and Drug Action Program (ADAP) of the Jewish Family Services of Los Angeles.[490] JACS assists Jews with chemical dependency problems and their significant others and incorporates Jewish content in recovery. In addition to offering mainstream or traditional alcoholism services, ADAP also helps Jews who would benefit from the incorporation of their religious beliefs in their recovery. Rabbinic counseling and L'Chaim workshops are some of ADAP's innovative services. L'Chaim (the Yiddish word for health) workshops emphasize the compatibility of Twelve-Step programs with Judaism and act as a bridge to participation in these groups. The workshops also help participants with issues such as maintaining sobriety during September, the time of the major Jewish religious holidays (just as when other groups help Christians in December).[491] Although Alcoholics Anonymous might be viewed as having a Christian orientation, the literature indicates that Jews have successfully used the program.[492] Master notes that Rabbi Daniel Grossman emphasizes that powerlessness in AA need not be associated with the Holocaust and that surrender is to God and to one's self.[493] Other suggestions for better serving Jews include such obvious but often overlooked practices as

making Kosher food available during inpatient treatment.[494]

Summary

We close our discussion by reviewing a number of themes that have emerged from our consideration of ethnic systems and substance abuse:

1. There is considerable variation in alcohol and drug use and related problems both among and within the major ethnic groups in the United States. For example, Native Americans are much more likely than whites to die from alcohol-related causes, but among Native American tribes, rates of drinking vary widely.

2. There are similarities in alcohol and drug use among the major ethnic groups. For example, the importance of peer influences in the use of alcohol and other drugs among youths, regardless of ethnicity, suggests a common pathway for prevention.

3. The research on ethnicity and substance abuse is inadequate. The methodology of epidemiological studies has improved in many cases, but few studies have tested culturally specific treatment approaches or the effects of special prevention programs for ethnic minority groups.

4. Acculturation is often mentioned as a factor that tends to increase alcohol and drug consumption. Definitions of acculturation vary, as do the research findings on this topic. Studies are needed to clarify the relationship of acculturation to substance use and abuse.

5. Among all ethnic groups, women use alcohol and drugs less than men, but as discussed in Chapter 15, whether this will remain the case is uncertain. Women substance abusers are more stigmatized among all ethnic groups than men.

6. Discrimination and deprivation are thought to be related to substance abuse problems, particularly to the more severe health and social consequences experienced by members of

certain ethnic groups, even when their patterns of use are similar to the majority.

7. Genetic factors have thus far not explained the differences in alcohol consumption and its consequences among ethnic groups.

8. Ethnic minority youths often report less alcohol and drug use than white youths, but methodological problems in studies of youths (such as exclusion of school dropouts and institutionalized youths) may cloud the true picture of use across groups.

9. Strong family ties are important among most ethnic groups, but even well-meaning families can present obstacles to recovery. Education of family members and incorporation of them in treatment are universally suggested.

10. A consistent theme in the prevention literature is that ethnic communities must take an active role in defining social norms and promoting responsibility in alcohol and drug use.

11. Community gatekeepers (such as members of ethnic, religious, business, and educational organizations and institutions) should be recruited and educated to provide pathways to prevention and treatment (also see Chapter 7).

12. Indigenous helpers (medicine men, curanderas, etc.) should be considered potentially viable helping resources by professionals.

13. Some progress has been made, but further development of model programs is needed for prevention and treatment of substance abuse among ethnic groups along with funding to support their implementation.

14. There is a need for greater understanding of those factors that protect members of ethnic groups from alcohol and drug problems.

15. Ethnic sensitivity and competence are necessary to function effectively as a professional in the field of chemical dependency.

16. Differences in rates of alcohol and other drug problems among the various ethnic groups should not obscure the need to provide appropriate treatment to members of each ethnic group and to provide individualized treatment to any person in need.

Endnotes

1. The terms *ethnicity* and *culture* are used in this chapter rather than *race*. Race is thought to be a politically divisive term, whereas ethnicity and culture are thought to better reflect the richness of the experience of the groups discussed here. See James W. Green, *Cultural Awareness in the Human Services* (Englewood Cliffs, NJ: Prentice Hall, 1982).

2. Arthur L. Klatsky, Abraham B. Siegelaub, Cynthia Landy, and Gary B. Friedman, "Racial Patterns of Alcoholic Beverage Use," *Alcoholism: Clinical and Experimental Research*, Vol. 7, No. 4 (Fall 1983), p. 372.

3. The terms *Native American, American Indian*, and *Indian* are used interchangeably in this chapter, as are the terms *African American* and *black*, and *Hispanic American* and *Latino*.

4. Leslie Brody, "Asia's Drug Problems Appear to Be Getting Worse," *Honolulu Star-Bulletin*, September 18, 1986, p. F–4; Laura Castaneda, "Mexicans Turn to Inhalants; Nation Fears Rise in Addiction," *Austin American-Statesman*, October 13, 1990, p. A32; and Oleg Romaniouk, "Vodka's Stranglehold on Russia," *Cape Cod Times*, June 30, 1992, p. A11.

5. Information on the history of alcohol use and policies regarding alcoholic beverages in over two dozen countries is found in Gunno Armyr, Åke Elmér, and Ulrich Herz, *Alcohol in the World of the 80s* (Stockholm: Sober Förlags AB, 1982); more recent information concerning drinking patterns and alcoholism is found in John E. Helzer and Glorisa Canino, *Alcoholism in North America, Europe, and Asia* (New York: Oxford University Press, 1992).

6. James M. Schaefer, "Ethnic and Racial Variations in Alcohol Use and Abuse," *Alcohol and Health Monograph 4, Special Population Issues*, DHHS Publication No. (ADM) 82-1193 (Rockville, MD: National Institute on Alcohol Abuse and Alcoholism, 1982), pp. 293–294.

7. Donald E. Maypole and Ruth E. Anderson, "Alcoholism Programs Serving Minorities," *Alcohol Health & Research World* (Winter 1986–87), pp. 62–65.

8. See Arleen Rogan, "Recovery from Alcoholism, Issues for Black and Native American Alcoholics," *Alcohol Health & Research World* (Fall 1986), pp. 42–44.

9. See, for example, Peter Finn, "Addressing the Needs of Cultural Minorities in Drug Treatment," *Journal of Substance Abuse Treatment*, Vol. 44, No. 4 (1994), pp. 325–337.

10. Some of them are Wynetta Devote and Elfriede Schlesinger, *Ethnic-Sensitive Social Work Practice*, 3rd ed. (New York: Charles E. Merrill, 1991); James W. Green, *Cultural Awareness in the Human Services: A Multi-Ethnic Approach*, 2nd ed. (Boston: Allyn and Bacon, 1995); Sadye M. L. Logan, Edith M. Freeman, and Ruth G. McRoy, *Social Work Practice with Black Families, A Culturally Specific Perspective* (New York: Longman, 1990); and Derald

Wing Sue and David Sue, *Counseling the Culturally Different: Theory and Practice*, 2nd ed. (New York: Wiley, 1990).

11. See, for example, Frederick D. Harper (Ed.), *Alcohol Abuse and Black America* (Alexandria, VA: Douglass Publishers, 1976); National Institute on Alcohol Abuse and Alcoholism (NIAAA), *Alcohol and Health Monograph No. 4, Special Population Issues*; M. Jean Gilbert and Richard C. Cervantes, *Mexican Americans and Alcohol*, Monograph 11 (Los Angeles: Spanish Speaking Mental Health Research Center, University of California, 1987); Thomas D. Watts and Roosevelt Wright, Jr. (Eds.), *Black Alcoholism: Toward A Comprehensive Understanding* (Springfield, IL: Charles C Thomas, 1983); and S. G. Levy and Sheila B. Blume (Eds.), *Addictions in the Jewish Community* (New York: Commission on Synagogue Relations, 1986).

12. Devote and Schlesinger, *Ethnic Sensitive Social Work Practice*.

13. Joan Crofut Weibel, "American Indians, Urbanization and Alcohol: A Developing Urban Indian Drinking Ethos," in NIAAA, *Alcohol and Health Monograph 4, Special Population Issues*, pp. 331–358.

14. See Green, *Cultural Awareness in the Human Services*, for an elaboration of points in the remainder of this paragraph.

15. Lorraine Collins, "Sociocultural Aspects of Alcohol Use and Abuse: Ethnicity and Gender," *Drugs & Society*, Vol. 18, No. 1 (1993), pp. 89–116; and Gerard J. Connors (Ed.), *Innovations in Alcoholism Treatment: State of the Art Reviews and Their Implications for Clinical Practice* (Binghamton, NY: Haworth Press, 1993), pp. 89–116.

16. Collins, "Sociocultural Aspects of Alcohol Use and Abuse: Ethnicity and Gender."

17. Robert Jacque Chapman, "Cultural Bias in Alcoholism Counseling," *Alcoholism Treatment Quarterly*, Vol. 5, Nos. 1/2, (1988), p. 106; also see Finn, "Addressing the Needs of Cultural Minorities in Drug Treatment."

18. See, for example, Finn, "Addressing the Needs of Cultural Minorities in Drug Treatment."

19. Collins, "Sociocultural Aspects of Alcohol Use and Abuse: Ethnicity and Gender."

20. See Allan M. Winkler, "Drinking on the American Frontier," *Quarterly Journal of Studies on Alcohol*, Vol. 29 (1968), pp. 413–445.

21. Indian Health Service, *Alcoholism: A High Priority Health Problem, A Report of the Indian Health Service Task Force on Alcoholism*, Department of Health Education and Welfare, Pub. No. (HSA) 77-1001 (Washington, DC: Indian Health Service, 1977); Edwin M. Lemert, "Drinking among American Indians," in Edith Lisansky Gomberg, Helene Raskin White, and John A. Carpenter (Eds.), *Alcohol, Science and Society Revisited* (Ann Arbor: University of Michigan Press, and New Jersey: Rutgers Center for Alcohol Studies, 1982), pp. 80–95; and Terry Beartusk cited in Kathy Brown Ramsperger, "Salvation for an Invisible People," *The Counselor* (May/June 1989), pp. 21–23.

22. For some interesting early accounts of Native American drinking, see R. C. Dailey, "The Role of Alcohol among North American Indian Tribes as Reprinted in *The Jesuit Relations*," in Mac Marshall (Ed.), *Beliefs, Behaviors, & Alcoholic Beverages, A Cross-Cultural Survey* (Ann Arbor: University of Michigan Press, 1979), pp. 116–127.

23. Craig MacAndrew and Robert B. Edgerton, *Drunken Comportment: A Social Explanation* (Chicago: Aldine, 1969), see especially Chapter 7; also see Dennis Kelso and William Dubay, "Alaskan Natives and Alcohol: A Sociocultural and Epidemiological Review," in National Institute on Alcohol Abuse and Alcoholism, *Alcohol Use among U.S. Ethnic Minorities, Research Monograph No. 18* (Rockville, MD: U.S. Department of Health and Human Services, 1989), pp. 223–238.

24. Indian Health Service, *Alcoholism: A High Priority Health Problem*.

25. Winkler, "Drinking on the American Frontier."

26. Ibid.; Ramsperger, "Salvation for an Invisible People"; and Lemert, "Drinking among American Indians."

27. Robert L. Bergman, "Navajo Peyote Use: Its Apparent Safety," *American Journal of Psychiatry*, Vol. 128, No. 6 (December 1971), pp. 695–699.

28. MacAndrew and Edgerton, *Drunken Comportment*, p. 123.

29. Joy Leland, *Firewater Myths, North American Indian Drinking and Alcohol Addiction* (New Brunswick, NJ: Rutgers Center of Alcohol Studies, 1976).

30. Indian Health Service, *Alcoholism: A High Priority Health Problem*; also see Winkler, "Drinking on the American Frontier."

31. Indian Health Service, *Alcoholism: A High Priority Health Problem*.

32. Ibid.

33. Philip A. May, "Substance Abuse and American Indians: Prevalence and Susceptibility," *The International Journal of the Addictions*, Vol. 17, No. 7 (1982), pp. 1185–1209; also see Weibel, "American Indians, Urbanization and Alcohol."

34. May, "Substance Abuse and American Indians."

35. See Gerard Littman, "Alcoholism, Illness, and Social Pathology among American Indians in Transition," *American Journal of Public Health*, Vol. 60, No. 9 (1970), pp. 1769–1787, © American Public Health Association; and Weibel, "American Indians, Urbanization and Alcohol."

36. Joan C. Weibel-Orlando, "Drinking Patterns of Urban and Rural American Indians," *Alcohol Health & Research World* (Winter 1986/87), p. 8.

37. Ibid.

38. Weibel, "American Indians, Urbanization and Alcohol."

39. Michael P. Nofz, "Alcohol Abuse and Culturally Marginal American Indians," *Social Casework* (February 1988), p. 68; and Littman, "Alcoholism, Illness, and Social Pathology."

40. Dwight B. Heath, "American Indians and Alcohol: Epidemiological and Sociocultural Relevance," in National Institute on Alcohol Abuse and Alcoholism, *Alcohol Use among U.S. Ethnic Minorities*, p. 216.

41. E. R. Oetting, Fred Beauvais, and George S. Goldstein, *Drug Abuse among Native American Youth: Summary of Findings (1975–1981)* (Fort Collins: Colorado State University, 1982).

42. Littman, "Alcoholism, Illness, and Social Pathology"; Everett R. Rhoades, Russell D. Mason, Phyllis Eddy, Eva M. Smith, and Thomas R. Burns, "The Indian Health Service Approach to Alcoholism among American Indians and Alaska Natives," *Public Health Reports*, Vol. 103, No. 6 (November–December 1988), pp. 621–627; and Audry Hill, "Treatment and Prevention of Alcoholism in the Native American Family," in Gary W. Lawson and Ann W. Lawson (Eds.), *Alcoholism & Substance Abuse in Special Populations* (Rockville, MD: Aspen Publishers, 1989), see pp. 262–265, 268.

43. Rhoades et al., "The Indian Health Service Approach."

44. Nancy Oestreich Lurie, "The World's Oldest On-Going Protest Demonstration: North American Indian Drinking Patterns," in Marshall, *Beliefs, Behaviors, & Alcoholic Beverages*, p. 135.

45. See Littman, "Alcoholism, Illness, and Social Pathology."

46. Ibid.; also see Rhoades et al., "The Indian Health Service Approach," p. 626.

47. Rhoades et al., "The Indian Health Service Approach," p. 626.

48. Weibel, "American Indians, Urbanization and Alcohol," p. 337; also see Merwyn S. Garbarino, "Life in the City: Chicago," in Jack O. Waddell and O. Michael Watson (Eds.), *The American Indian in Urban Society* (Boston: Little, Brown, 1971), pp. 193–196; and Peter Z. Snyder, "The Social Environment of the Urban Indian," p. 237, in the same book. Much of the literature in this paragraph is also cited in National Institute on Alcohol Abuse and Alcoholism, "Alcohol Topics: Research Review, Alcohol and Native Americans" (Rockville MD: NIAAA, 1985).

49. M. Burns, J. M. Daily, and H. Moskowitz, *Drinking Practices and Problems of Urban American Indians in Los Angeles, Part 1, Study Description and Findings. Preliminary Report* (Santa Monica, CA: Planning Analysis and Research Institute, 1974), cited in Weibel, "American Indians, Urbanization and Alcohol."

50. See, for example, Weibel-Orlando, "Drinking Patterns of Urban and Rural American Indians"; and Lemert, "Drinking among American Indians."

51. J. C. Weibel and T. Weisner, *An Ethnography of Urban Indian Drinking Patterns in California* (Los Angeles: The Alcohol Research Center, The Neuropsychiatric Institute,

University of California, 1980), cited in Weibel, "American Indians, Urbanization and Alcohol."

52. Lurie, "The World's Oldest On-going Protest Demonstration," p. 138; also see Ronald G. Lewis, "Alcoholism and the Native Americans—A Review of the Literature," in National Institute on Alcohol Abuse and Alcoholism, *Alcohol and Health Monograph 4, Special Population Issues*, p. 320.

53. Lurie, "The World's Oldest On-going Protest Demonstration," p. 133.

54. Weibel, "American Indians, Urbanization and Alcohol," p. 338.

55. Oetting et al., *Drug Abuse among Native American Youth*, p. 35.

56. Lewis, "Alcoholism and the Native Americans," p. 320.

57. Joy H. Leland, "Native American Alcohol Use: A Review of the Literature," in Patricia D. Mail and David R. McDonald (Eds.), *Tulapai to Tokay: A Bibliography of Alcohol Use and Abuse among Native Americans of North America,* (New Haven: HRAF Press, 1980), p. 38.

58. See, for example, Theodore G. Graves, "Drinking and Drunkenness among Urban Indians," in Waddell and Watson, *The American Indian in Urban Society*, pp. 274–311; and Heath, "American Indians and Alcohol."

59. Philip A. May, "The Epidemiology of Alcohol Abuse among American Indians: The Mythical and Real Properties," *American Indian Culture and Research Journal*, Vol. 18, No. 2 (1994), pp. 121–143; and Philip A. May, "Alcohol Abuse and Alcoholism among American Indians: An Overview," in Thomas D. Watts and Roosevelt Wright (Eds.), *Alcoholism in Minority Populations* (Springfield, IL: Charles C Thomas, 1989), pp. 95–119.

60. Mail and McDonald, *Tulapai to Tokay.*

61. May, "The Epidemiology of Alcohol Abuse among American Indians: The Mythical and Real Properties."

62. P. Mail, "American Indian Alcoholism: What Is Not Being Done?" *The IHS Primary Care Provider*, Vol. 9, No. 3 (March 1984), pp. 1–5, cited in NIAAA, "Alcohol Topics: Research Review, Alcohol and Native Americans," p. 3.

63. Littman, "Alcoholism, Illness, and Social Pathology."

64. Lewis, "Alcoholism and the Native Americans," p. 319; May, "Substance Abuse and American Indians."

65. Lemert, "Drinking among American Indians," p. 87.

66. Kelso and Dubay, "Alaskan Natives and Alcohol," pp. 223–238.

67. May, "The Epidemiology of Alcohol Abuse among American Indians: The Mythical and Real Properties."

68. Weibel-Orlando, "Drinking Patterns of Urban and Rural American Indians."

69. Joan Ablon, "Cultural Conflict in Urban Indians," *Mental Hygiene*, Vol. 55, No. 2 (April 1971), p. 204.

70. Lewis, "Alcoholism and the Native Americans," pp. 319–320.

71. E. R. Knisley, "Native Alaskan Indians, Eskimos and Aleuts and Their Drinking Habits," paper presented at the 30th International Congress on Alcoholism and Drug Dependence, 1972, cited in Lewis, "Alcoholism and the Native American," p. 324.

72. Lewis, "Alcoholism and the Native Americans," pp. 315–328; Nofz, "Alcohol Abuse and Culturally Marginal American Indians"; and Heath, "American Indians and Alcohol."

73. Indian Health Service, *Trends in Indian Health, 1991* (Rockville, MD: Indian Health Service, 1992), cited in National Institute on Alcohol Abuse and Alcoholism, *Eighth Special Report to the U.S. Congress on Alcohol and Health* (Rockville, MD: U.S. Department of Health and Human Services, 1993), p. 28.

74. Indian Health Service, *Trends in Indian Health— 1995* (Washington, DC: U.S. Department of Health and Human Services, 1996) p. 68.

75. Rhoades et al., "The Indian Health Service Approach"; these figures are based on data from 1981 to 1983.

76. Heath, "American Indians and Alcohol."

77. Lemert, "Drinking among American Indians."

78. May, "The Epidemiology of Alcohol Abuse among American Indians: The Mythical and Real Properties."

79. Paul K. Leung, J. David Kinzie, James K. Boehnlein, and James H. Shore, "A Prospective Study of the Natural Course of Alcoholism in a Native American Village," *Journal of Studies on Alcohol*, Vol. 54 (1993), pp. 733–738.

80. May, "The Epidemiology of Alcohol Abuse among American Indians: The Mythical and Real Properties."

81. Heath, "American Indians and Alcohol."

82. Ray Stratton, Arthur Zeiner, and Alfonso Paredes, "Tribal Affiliation and Prevalence of Alcohol Problems," *Journal of Studies on Alcohol*, Vol. 39, No. 7 (1978), p. 1175.

83. Graves, "Drinking and Drunkenness among Urban Indians," pp. 305–306.

84. Nofz, "Alcohol Abuse and Culturally Marginal American Indians"; also see Weibel, "American Indians, Urbanization and Alcohol," p. 339.

85. Rhoades et al., "The Indian Health Service Approach," p. 622.

86. Littman, "Alcoholism, Illness, and Social Pathology"; Lewis, "Alcoholism and the Native Americans"; and Weibel, "American Indians, Urbanization and Alcohol."

87. May, "The Epidemiology of Alcohol Abuse among American Indians: The Mythical and Real Properties," p. 130.

88. Beatrice A. Rouse (Ed.), *Substance Abuse and Mental Health Statistics Sourcebook* (Washington, DC: Department of Health and Human Services, 1995), p. 64, DHHS Pub. No (SMA) 95-3064.

89. U.S. Department of Health and Human Services, *Report of the Secretary's Task Force on Black & Minority Health, Volume 1, Executive Summary* (Washington, DC: Department of Health and Human Services, 1985), p. 138.

90. Substance Abuse and Mental Health Services Administration, *National Drug and Alcoholism Treatment Unit Survey (NDATUS): Data for 1994 and 1980–1994*, Advance Report Number 13 (Rockville, MD: U.S. Department of Health and Human Services, 1996), p. 17.

91. Substance Abuse and Mental Health Services Administration, *National Drug and Alcoholism Treatment Unit Survey (NDATUS): 1991 Main Findings Report* (Rockville, MD: U.S. Department of Health and Human Services, 1993), DHHS Pub. No. (SMA) 93-2007.

92. May, "Substance Abuse and American Indians."

93. E. R. Oetting and Fred Beauvais, "Epidemiology and Correlates of Alcohol Use among Indian Adolescents Living on Reservations," in National Institute on Alcohol Abuse and Alcoholism, *Alcohol Use among U.S. Ethnic Minorities*, pp. 239–267.

94. Joan C. Weibel-Orlando, "Pass the Bottle, Bro!: A Comparison of Urban and Rural Indian Drinking Patterns," in National Institute on Alcohol and Alcoholism, *Alcohol Use among U.S. Ethnic Minorities*, pp. 269–289.

95. Oetting and Beauvais, "Epidemiology and Correlates of Alcohol Use."

96. Rhonda Wiegman Dick, Spero M. Manson, and Janette Beals, "Alcohol Use among Male and Female Native American Adolescents: Patterns and Correlates of Student Drinking in a Boarding School," *Journal of Studies on Alcohol*, Vol. 54 (1993), pp. 172–177.

97. R. Wax, "The Warrior Dropouts," *Transactions*, Vol. 4, pp. 40–46, cited in Joan Weibel-Orlando, "Substance Abuse among American Indian Youth: A Continuing Crisis," *Journal of Drug Issues*, Vol. 14 (1984), pp. 313–335.

98. G. Trimble, "Drug Abuse Prevention Research Needs among American Indians and Alaska Natives," *White Cloud Journal of American Indian Mental Health*, Vol. 3, No. 3 (1984), pp. 32–34, cited in NIAAA, "Alcohol Topics: Research Review, Alcohol and Native Americans."

99. Christine S. Sellers, L. Thomas Winfree, Jr., and Curt T. Griffiths, "Legal Attitudes, Permissive Norm Qualities, and Substance Use: A Comparison of American Indian and Non-Indian Youth," *The Journal of Drug Issues*, Vol. 23, No. 3 (1993), pp. 493–513.

100. May, "Substance Abuse and American Indians," p. 1191.

101. Weibel-Orlando, "Drinking Patterns of Rural and Urban American Indians"; and Weibel-Orlando, "Pass the Bottle, Bro!"

102. Indian Health Service, *Indian Health Service Chart Series Book*, DHHS Pub. No. 1988 0-218-547: QL3 (Washington, DC: Superintendent of Documents, U.S. Government

Printing Office, 1988), cited in National Institute on Alcohol Abuse and Alcoholism, *Seventh Special Report to the U.S. Congress on Alcohol and Health* (Rockville, MD: U.S. Department of Health and Human Services, January 1990), p. 36.

103. NIAAA, *Alcohol Use among U.S. Ethnic Minorities*, p. xxi.

104. May, "The Epidemiology of Alcohol Abuse among American Indians: The Mythical and Real Properties."

105. Much of this paragraph relies on Rhoades et al., "The Indian Health Service Approach."

106. E. Daniel Edwards, "A Description and Evaluation of American Indian Social Work Training Programs," unpublished doctoral dissertation, University of Utah, 1976, cited in Fenton Moss, E. Daniel Edwards, Margie E. Edwards, Fred V. Janzen, and George Howell, "Sobriety and American Indian Problem Drinkers," *Alcoholism Treatment Quarterly*, Vol. 2, No. 2 (Summer 1985), pp. 81–96.

107. Deborah Goodman, "Mental and Addictive Disorders in American Indians/Alaska Natives Studied," *ADAMHA News*, Vol. 18, No. 2 (March–April 1992), pp. 14–15.

108. Substance Abuse and Mental Health Services Administration, *National Drug and Alcoholism Treatment Unit Survey (NDATUS): 1991 Main Findings Report.*

109. Lewis, "Alcoholism and the Native Americans," p. 323; also see Rhoades et al., "The Indian Health Service Approach"; NIAAA, "Alcohol Topics: Research Review, Alcohol and Native Americans"; Littman, "Alcoholism, Illness, and Social Pathology"; and Louise Jilek-Aall, "Acculturation, Alcoholism, and Indian-Style Alcoholics Anonymous," *Journal of Studies on Alcohol*, Supplement No. 9 (1981), pp. 143–158.

110. James O. Whittaker, "Alcohol and the Standing Rock Sioux Tribe, II. Psychodynamic and Cultural Factors in Drinking," *Quarterly Journal of Studies on Alcohol*, Vol. 24 (1963), pp. 80–90.

111. Rhoades et al., "The Indian Health Service Approach."

112. The film is available from Alkali Lake Indian Band, P.O. Box 4479, Williams Lake, B.C., Canada V2G 2V5 or contact the Bureau of Indian Affairs.

113. Elvin Willie, "The Story of Alkali Lake: Anomaly of Community Recovery or National Trend in Indian Country?" *Alcoholism Treatment Quarterly*, Vol. 6, Nos. 3/4 (1989), pp. 167–173; and Veronica Taylor, "The Triumph of the Alkali Lake Indian Band," *Alcohol Health & Research World*, Vol. 12, No. 1 (Fall 1987), p. 57.

114. Rhoades et al., "The Indian Health Service Approach."

115. Willie, "The Story of Alkali Lake," p. 168.

116. Moss et al., "Sobriety and American Indian Problem Drinkers."

117. See, for example, John G. Red Horse, "Family Structure and Value Orientation in American Indians," *Social Casework*, Vol. 61, No. 8 (October 1980), pp. 462–467.

118. Ramsperger, "Salvation for an Invisible People."

119. Littman, "Alcoholism, Illness, and Social Pathology," p. 1782; also see Jilek-Aall, "Acculturation, Alcoholism, and Indian-Style Alcoholics Anonymous."

120. J. F. Merker, "Indians of the Great Plains: Issues in Counseling and Family Therapy," paper presented at the National Council on Alcoholism Forum, New Orleans, LA, April 1981, cited in NIAAA, "Alcohol Topics: Research Review, Alcohol and Native Americans."

121. A. Whiting, personal communication, June 1985, cited in NIAAA, "Alcohol Topics: Research Review, Alcohol and Native Americans."

122. Nofz, "Alcohol Abuse and Culturally Marginal American Indians," p. 70.

123. The remainder of this paragraph relies on Ramsperger, "Salvation for an Invisible People."

124. Moss et al., "Sobriety and American Indian Problem Drinkers."

125. "VA Hospital Calls in 'Medicine Man' to Help Indians Beat Alcoholism," *Austin American-Statesman*, August 25, 1991, p. D28.

126. Nofz, "Alcohol Abuse and Culturally Marginal American Indians."

127. Bergman, "Navajo Peyote Use"; and Bernard J. Albaugh and Philip O. Anderson, "Peyote in the Treatment of Alcoholism among American Indians," *American Journal of Psychiatry*, Vol. 131, No. 11 (November 1974), pp. 1247–1250.

128. Albaugh and Anderson, "Treatment of Alcoholism among Native Americans," p. 1249.

129. Karl A. Menninger, "Discussion," following Bergman, "Navajo Peyote Use," p. 699.

130. David Fidanque, "Religious Freedom Makes Comeback in Oregon, with Passage of Peyote Bill," *Civil Liberties*, 1992, p. 5.

131. Littman, "Alcoholism, Illness, and Social Pathology."

132. Jilek-Aall, "Acculturation, Alcoholism, and Indian-Style Alcoholics Anonymous."

133. Lewis, "Alcoholism and the Native Americans," p. 323.

134. The remainder of this paragraph relies on Jilek-Aall, "Acculturation, Alcoholism, and Indian Style Alcoholics Anonymous."

135. This paragraph relies on Nofz, "Alcohol Abuse and Culturally Marginal American Indians."

136. See William J. Reid and Laura Epstein, *Task-Centered Casework* (New York: Columbia Press, 1972); and Laura Epstein, *Helping People: The Task-Centered Approach* (St. Louis, MO: C. V. Mosby, 1980).

137. Nofz, "Alcohol Abuse and Culturally Marginal American Indians," p. 70.

138. Ibid., p. 71.

139. Ibid.

140. May, "Substance Abuse and American Indians."

141. For additional information on primary, secondary, and tertiary prevention among Native Americans, also see James R. Moran and Philip A. May, "American Indians," in Joanne Philleo and Frances Larry Brisbane (Eds.), *Cultural Competence for Social Workers: A Guide for Alcohol and Other Drug Abuse Prevention Professionals Working with Ethnic/Racial Communities*, CSAP Cultural Competence Series 4 (Washington, DC: U.S. Government Printing Office, 1995), pp. 1–39, DHHS Pub. No. (SMA)95-3075.

142. Oetting and Beauvais, "Epidemiology and Correlates of Alcohol Use."

143. Pamela L. LeMaster and Cathleen M. Connell, "Health Education Interventions among Native Americans: A Review and Analysis," *Health Education Quarterly*, Vol. 21, No. 4 (1994), pp. 521–538.

144. Linda Parker, "The Missing Component in Substance Abuse Prevention Efforts: A Native American Example," *Contemporary Drug Problems* (Summer 1990), pp. 251–270.

145. Cathie Stivers, "Drug Prevention in Zuni, New Mexico: Creation of a Teen Center as an Alternative to Alcohol and Drug Use," *Journal of Community Health*, Vol. 19, No. 5 (1994), pp. 343–359.

146. "Indian Health Service School/Community-Based Alcoholism Substance Abuse Prevention Survey" (Rockville, MD: Indian Health Service, 1987), cited in Rhoades et al., "The Indian Health Service Approach," pp. 625–626.

147. Ann P. Streissguth, "Fetal Alcohol Syndrome: Understanding the Problem; Understanding the Solution; What Indian Communities Can Do," *American Indian Culture and Research Journal*, Vol. 18, No. 3 (1994), pp. 45–83.

148. Ibid., p. 64.

149. Weibel, "American Indians, Urbanization and Alcohol," p. 344.

150. May, "The Epidemiology of Alcohol Abuse among American Indians: The Mythical and Real Properties."

151. Collins, "Sociocultural Aspects of Alcohol Use and Abuse: Ethnicity and Gender."

152. For an account, see Denise Herd, "Ambiguity in Black Drinking Norms, An Ethnohistorical Interpretation," in Linda A. Bennett and Genevieve M. Ames (Eds.), *The American Experience with Alcohol: Contrasting Cultural Perspectives* (New York: Plenum Press, 1985), pp. 149–170.

153. Vivian Rouson Gossett, *Alcohol and Drug Abuse in Black America, A Guide for Community Action* (Minneapolis: Institute on Black Chemical Abuse, 1988), p. 2.

154. Herd, "Ambiguity in Black Drinking Norms"; and Gossett, *Alcohol and Drug Abuse in Black America*.

155. Frederick D. Harper, "Research and Treatment with Black Alcoholics," *Alcohol Health & Research World*, Vol. 4, No. 4 (Summer 1980), pp. 10–16; Frederick D. Harper, "Etiology: Why Do Blacks Drink?" in Harper, *Alcohol Abuse and Black America*, pp. 27–37; also see Eugene D. Genovese, *Roll, Jordan, Roll, The World the Slaves Made* (New York: Pantheon Books, 1974).

156. Genovese, *Roll, Jordan, Roll*, p. 644; also see Gossett, *Alcohol and Drug Use in Black America*.

157. Gossett, *Alcohol and Drug Use in Black America*.

158. Denise Herd, "Migration, Cultural Transformation and the Rise of Black Liver Cirrhosis Mortality," *British Journal of Addiction*, Vol. 80 (1985), pp. 397–410.

159. John Koren, *Economic Aspects of the Liquor Problem* (Boston: Houghton Mifflin, 1899), and U.S. Census Bureau Office, *Tenth Census: 1880, Volume II, Vital Statistics of the United States* (Washington, DC: U.S. Government Printing Office, 1886), cited in Herd, "Migration, Cultural Transformation and the Rise of Black Liver Cirrhosis Mortality"; also see Denise Herd, "The Epidemiology of Drinking Patterns and Alcohol-Related Problems among U.S. Blacks," in National Institute on Alcohol Abuse and Alcoholism, *Alcohol Use among U.S. Ethnic Minorities*, pp. 3–50.

160. The remainder of this paragraph relies primarily on Herd, "Migration, Cultural Transformation and the Rise of Black Liver Cirrhosis Mortality"; Herd, "Ambiguity in Black Drinking Norms"; also see the account in Gossett, *Alcohol and Drug Abuse in Black America*.

161. Harper, "Etiology: Why Do Blacks Drink?"; italicized material is quoted verbatim.

162. Also see Gossett, *Alcohol and Drug Abuse in Black America*, p. 18.

163. Cheryl Davenport Dozier, "The African-American and Alcoholism, Roadblocks to Treatment," *The Counselor* (May/June 1989), p. 33.

164. Sharon E. Moore, "Adolescent Black Males' Drug Trafficking and Addiction," *Journal of Black Studies*, Vol. 26, No. 2 (1995), pp. 99–116.

165. Emile Durkheim, *Suicide: A Study in Sociology* (New York: The Free Press, 1951).

166. Karl Marx, *The Communist Manifesto* (New York: Monthly Review Press, 1964).

167. Molefi K. Asante, *Afrocentricity* (Buffalo: Amulefi, 1980).

168. Herd, "Ambiguity in Black Drinking Norms."

169. Raul Caetano and Lee Ann Kaskutas, "Changes in Drinking Patterns among Whites, Blacks and Hispanics, 1984–1992," *Journal of Studies on Alcohol*, Vol. 56 (1995), pp. 558–565.

170. Herd, "Editorial, Rethinking Black Drinking," *British Journal of Addiction*, Vol. 82 (1987), pp. 219–223.

171. "Prevention of Alcohol Abuse among Black Americans," an interview with Thomas D. Watts and Roosevelt Wright, Jr., *Alcohol Health & Research World* (Winter 1986/87), pp. 40–41, 65.

172. Ibid.; see also Dozier, "The African-American and Alcoholism."

173. This paragraph relies on Betty Watson Burston, Dionne Jones, and Pat Roberson-Saunders, "Drug Use and African Americans: Myth versus Reality," *Journal of Alcohol and Drug Education*, Vol. 40, No. 2 (1995), pp. 19–39. Information on the Washington, DC, survey is from B. Watson and D. Jones, "Drug Use and African Americans," Runtafac sheet of the National Urban League, Vol. 2 (1989).

174. U.S. Department of Health and Human Services, *Report of the Secretary's Task Force on Black and Minority Health*, p. 138.

175. Lee N. Robins, "Alcohol Abuse in Blacks and Whites as Indicated in the Epidemiological Catchment Area Program," in National Institute on Alcohol Abuse and Alcoholism, *Alcohol Use among U.S. Ethnic Minorities*, pp. 63–73.

176. Ronald C. Kessler et al., "Lifetime and 12-month Prevalence of DSM-III-R Psychiatric Disorders in the United States," *Archives of General Psychiatry*, Vol. 51 (1994), pp. 8–19.

177. Much of the remainder of this paragraph relies on Thomas W. Pavkov, Mark P. McGovern, and Eric S. Geffner, "Problem Severity and Symptomatology among Substance Misusers: Differences between African-Americans and Caucasians," *The International Journal of the Addictions*, Vol. 28, No. 9 (1993), pp. 909–922, quotes from p. 909.

178. Denise Herd, "Drinking Patterns in the Black Population," in Walter B. Clark and Michael E. Hilton (Eds.), *Alcohol in America, Drinking Practices and Problems* (Albany: State University of New York Press, 1991), pp. 308–328, adapted from Herd, "The Epidemiology of Drinking Patterns and Alcohol-Related Problems among U.S. Blacks."

179. For discussions of earlier studies, see Klatsky et al., "Racial Patterns of Alcoholic Beverage Use"; also see Barbara W. Lex, "Review of Alcohol Problems in Ethnic Minority Groups," *Journal of Consulting and Clinical Psychology*, Vol. 55, No. 3 (1987), pp. 293–300.

180. Herd, "Drinking Patterns in the Black Population"; also see Herd, "The Epidemiology of Drinking Patterns and Alcohol-Related Problems among U.S. Blacks."

181. Additional analyses of the effects of region, urbanization, and migration on the drinking patterns of African American respondents to the 1984 NAS are found in Denise Herd, "The Impact of Region and Urbanization on African American Drinking Patterns: Results from a National Survey," *Contemporary Drug Problems*, Vol. 22 (Fall 1995), pp. 453–481.

182. For another analysis of these data comparing African American and white men, see Denise Herd, "Subgroup Differences in Drinking Patterns among Black and White Men: Results from a National Survey," *Journal of Studies on Alcohol*, Vol. 51, No. 3 (1990), pp. 221–232.

183. Also see Marsha Lillie-Blanton, Ellen MacKenzie, and James C. Anthony, "Black-White Differences in Alcohol Use by Women: Baltimore Survey Findings," *Public Health Reports*, Vol. 106, No. 2 (1991), pp. 124–133. They report that their findings based on data collected in 1981 from the Baltimore Epidemiologic Catchment Area household survey are similar to the 1984 national survey. Lillie-Blanton and colleagues concluded that "after controlling for differences in sociodemographic characteristics, black women were found to be at no greater risk than whites for heavy drinking or for suffering from alcohol abuse or dependence" (p. 124).

184. D. Herd and R. Caetano, "Drinking Patterns and Problems among White, Black and Hispanic Women in the U.S.: Results from a National Survey," Paper presented at the Alcohol and Drug Problems Association of North America Conference on Women's Issues, Denver, CO, May 3–6, 1987, cited in Raul Caetano, "Drinking and Alcohol-Related Problems among Minority Women," *Alcohol Health & Research World*, Vol. 18, No. 3 (1994), pp. 233–241.

185. Lee N. Robins, "Alcohol Abuse in Blacks and Whites as Indicated in the Epidemiological Catchment Area Program," in D. Spiegler, D. Tate, S. Aitken, and C. Christian (Eds.), *Alcohol Use among U.S. Ethnic Minorities* (Washington, DC: U.S. Government Printing Office, 1989), pp. 63–73, DHHS Pub. No. (ADM) 89-1435; cited in Caetano, "Drinking and Alcohol-Related Problems among Minority Women."

186. Caetano and Kaskutas, "Changes in Drinking Patterns among Whites, Blacks and Hispanics, 1984–1992."

187. Caetano, "Drinking and Alcohol-Related Problems among Minority Women."

188. Substance Abuse and Mental Health Services Administration, *National Household Survey on Drug Abuse: Population Estimates 1994* (Rockville, MD: Department of Health and Human Services, 1995), DHHS Pub. No. (SMA) 95-3063.

189. Laura Ronan, "Alcohol-Related Health Risks among Black Americans, Highlights of the Secretary's Task Force Report on Black and Minority Health," *Alcohol Health & Research World* (Winter 1986/87), pp. 36–39, 65; also see Denise Herd, "Editorial, Rethinking Black Drinking"; Herd, "The Epidemiology of Drinking Patterns and Alcohol-Related Problems among U.S. Blacks"; and Thomas Harford and Cherry Lowman, "Alcohol Use among Black and White Teenagers," in National Institute on Alcohol Abuse and Alcoholism, *Alcohol Use among U.S. Ethnic Minorities*, pp. 51–61. Results of surveys are also summarized in Office for Substance Abuse Prevention, "The Fact Is Alcohol and Other Drug Use Is a Special Concern for African American Families and Communities" (Rockville, MD: August 1990).

190. Thomas C. Harford, "Drinking Patterns among Black and Nonblack Adolescents: Results of a National Survey," in Roosevelt Wright, Jr., and Thomas D. Watts (Eds), *Prevention of Black Alcoholism, Issues and Strategies* (Springfield, IL: Charles C Thomas, 1985), pp. 122–139.

191. Herd, "Subgroup Differences in Drinking Patterns among Black and White Men."

192. Alfred S. Friedman, Samuel Granick, Shirley Bransfield, Cheryl Kreisher, and Jag Khalsa, "Gender Differences in Early Life Risk Factors for Substance Use/Abuse: A Study of an African-American Sample," *American Journal of Drug and Alcohol Abuse*, Vol. 21, No. 4 (1995), pp. 511–531.

193. Mary Ann Forney, Paul D. Forney, and William K. Ripley, "Alcohol Use Among Black Adolescents: Parental and Peer Influences," *Journal of Alcohol and Drug Education*, Vol. 36, No. 3 (1991), p. 36–45.

194. Heather J. Walter, Roger D. Vaughan, and Alwyn T. Cohall, "Comparison of Three Theoretical Models of Substance Use among Urban Minority High School Students," *Journal of the American Academy of Child and Adolescent Psychiatry*, Vol. 32, No. 5 (1993), pp. 975–981.

195. Daniel J. Flannery, Alexander T. Vazsonyi, Julia Torquati, and Angela Fridrich, "Ethnic and Gender Differences in Risk for Early Adolescent Substance Use," *Journal of Youth and Adolescence*, Vol. 23, No. 2 (1994), pp. 195–213.

196. Jennifer A. Epstein, Gilbert J. Botvin, Tracy Diaz, and Steven P. Schinke, "The Role of Social Factors and Individual Characteristics in Promoting Alcohol Use among Inner-City Minority Youths," *Journal of Studies on Alcohol*, Vol. 56 (1995), pp. 39–46.

197. Data in this paragraph rely on *HIV/AIDS Surveillance Report*, year-end edition, Vol. 8, No. 2 (1997).

198. Herd, "Drinking Patterns in the Black Population"; and Lillie-Blanton et al., "Black-White Differences in Alcohol Use by Women."

199. See "An Interview with Peter Bell," *Alcohol Health & Research World* (Winter 1986/87), pp. 24, 50–51; and Julia A. Lee, Brian E. Mavis, and Bertram E. Stoffelmayr, "A Comparison of Problems-of-Life for Blacks and Whites Entering Substance Abuse Treatment Programs," *Journal of Psychoactive Drugs*, Vol. 23, No. 3 (1991), pp. 233–239.

200. Substance Abuse and Mental Health Services Administration, *Annual Emergency Room Data 1992: Data from the Drug Abuse Warning Network* (Rockville, MD: U.S. Department of Health and Human Services, 1994), DHHS Pub. No. (SMA) 94-2080.

201. Substance Abuse and Mental Health Services Administration, *National Drug and Alcoholism Treatment Unit Survey (NDATUS): Data for 1994 and 1980–1994*, Advance Report 13.

202. Substance Abuse and Mental Health Services Administration, *National Drug and Alcoholism Treatment Unit Survey (NDATUS): 1991 Main Findings Report.*

203. Gossett, *Alcohol and Drug Abuse in Black America.*

204. National Institute on Drug Abuse, "SMSA Statistics 1981: Data from the Client Oriented Data Acquisition Process (CODAP): Statistical Series E, Administrative Report" (Rockville, MD: National Institute on Drug Abuse, 1983), cited in Richard M. Selik, Kenneth G. Castro, and Marguerite Pappaioanou, "Distribution of AIDS Cases, by Racial/Ethnic Group and Exposure Category, United States, June 1, 1981–July 4, 1988," *MMWR Surveillance Summaries*, Vol. 37, No. SS-3, pp. 29–37.

205. See, for example, Moss et al., "Sobriety and American Indian Problem Drinkers."

206. Creigs C. Beverly, "Toward a Model for Counseling Black Alcoholics," *Journal of Non-White Concerns* (July 1975), pp. 169–176.

207. Ethel B. Burks and Tyron S. Johnson, "The Black Drug Abuser: The Lack of Utilization of Treatment Services," in Arnold G. Schecter (Ed.), *Drug Dependence and Alcoholism, Vol. 2, Social and Behavioral Issues* (New York: Plenum Press, 1981), pp. 113–120.

208. For a discussion of this issue, also see Peter Bell and Jimmy Evans, "Counseling the Black Alcoholic Client," in Watts and Wright, *Black Alcoholism*, pp. 100–121, and Gossett, *Alcohol and Drug Abuse in Black America.*

209. See, for example, Bell and Evans, "Counseling the Black Alcoholic Client."

210. Bell and Evans, "Counseling the Black Alcoholic Client"; also see William H. Wheeler, *Counseling from a Cultural Perspective* (Atlanta, GA: A. L. Nellums and Associates, 1977).

211. Bell and Evans, "Counseling the Black Alcoholic Client."

212. Beverly, "Toward a Model for Counseling Black Alcoholics"; see also Raymond A. Winbush and Pamela S. Henderson, " 'We May as Well Try This': Some Reflections on Alcoholism Services Research in the African-American Community," in Watts and Wright, *Black Alcoholism*, pp. 198–205.

213. Mary Lou Politi Ziter, "Culturally Sensitive Treatment of Black Alcoholic Families," *Social Work* (March–April 1987), pp. 130–135.

214. Barbara Bryant Solomon, *Black Empowerment: Social Work in Oppressed Communities* (New York: Columbia University Press, 1976).

215. Beverly, "Toward a Model for Counseling Black Alcoholics."

216. Delores G. Norton, *The Dual Perspective: Inclusion of Ethnic Minority Content in the Social Work Curriculum* (New York: Council on Social Work Education, 1978).

217. Roosevelt Wright, Jr., Barbara Lynn Kail, and Robert F. Creecy, "Culturally Sensitive Social Work Practice with Black Alcoholics and Their Families," in Sadye M. L. Logan, Edith M. Freeman, and Ruth G. McRoy (Eds.), *Social Work Practice with Black Families* (New York: Longman, 1990), pp. 203–222; Mary S. Jackson, "Afrocentric

Treatment of African Women and Their Children in a Residential Chemical Dependency Program," *Journal of Black Studies*, Vol. 26 No. 1 (1995), pp. 17–30.

218. Ibid.

219. Frieda Brown and Joan Tooley, "Alcoholism in the Black Community," in Lawson and Lawson, *Alcoholism & Substance Abuse in Special Populations*, pp. 115–130.

220. Gloria McGee and Leola Johnson, *Black, Beautiful and Recovering* (Center City, MN: Hazelden, 1985).

221. Ibid.

222. Peter Bell, *Cultural Pain and African Americans: Unspoken Issues in Early Recovery* (Center City, MN: Hazelden, 1992).

223. Ibid., p. 23.

224. Moore, "Adolescent Black Males' Drug Trafficking and Addiction."

225. John Nickens, "Black Outreach Alcoholism Program of Brevard County, Results and Evaluations," 1972, cited in Burks and Johnson, "The Black Drug Abuser," p. 117.

226. Marvin P. Dawkins and Frederick D. Harper, "Alcoholism among Women: A Comparison of Black and White Problem Drinkers," *The International Journal of the Addictions*, Vol. 18, No. 3 (1983), pp. 333–349.

227. Hortensia Amaro, Linda J. Beckman, and Vickie M. Mays, "A Comparison of Black and White Women Entering Alcoholism Treatment," *Journal of Studies on Alcohol*, Vol. 48, No. 3 (1987), pp. 220–228.

228. Jackson, "Afrocentric Treatment of African American Women and Their Children in a Residential Chemical Dependency Program."

229. See, for example, Carolyn F. Swift and Sethard Beverly, "The Utilization of Ministers as Alcohol Counselors and Educators: Increasing Prevention and Treatment Resources in the Black Community," in Wright and Watts, *Prevention of Black Alcoholism*, pp. 182–198.

230. Thomas Prugh, "The Black Church: A Foundation of Recovery," *Alcohol Health and Research World* (Winter 1986/87), pp. 52–54; also see Dorothy Headley Knox, "Spirituality: A Tool in the Assessment and Treatment of Black Alcoholics and Their Families," *Alcoholism Treatment Quarterly*, Vol. 2, Nos. 3/4 (Fall 1985/Winter 1985–86), pp. 31–44.

231. Prugh, "The Black Church: A Foundation of Recovery."

232. McGee and Johnson, *Black, Beautiful and Recovering*.

233. Bell, *Cultural Pain and African Americans*.

234. Prugh, "The Black Church: A Foundation of Recovery."

235. Dozier, "The African-American and Alcoholism"; and Wright et al., "Culturally Sensitive Social Work Practice."

236. Prugh, "The Black Church: A Foundation of Recovery."

237. This paragraph relies on Henry L. Hudson, "How and Why Alcoholics Anonymous Works for Blacks," *Alcoholism Treatment Quarterly*, Vol. 2, Nos. 3–4 (Fall 1985–Winter 1985/86), pp. 11–30.

238. Fulton J. Caldwell, "Alcoholics Anonymous as a Viable Treatment Resource for Black Alcoholics," in Watts and Wright, *Black Alcoholism, Toward a Comprehensive Understanding*, pp. 85–99.

239. Keith Humphreys and Michael D. Woods, "Researching Mutual-Help Group Participation in a Segregated Society," in Thomas J. Powell (Ed.), *Understanding the Self-Help Organization: Frameworks and Findings* (Thousand Oaks, CA: Sage, 1994) pp. 62–87.

240. Lonnie R. Snowden and Morton A. Lieberman, "African-American Participation in Self-Help Groups," in Powell, *Understanding the Self-Help Organization*, pp. 50–61.

241. Humphreys and Woods, "Researching Mutual-Help Group Participation in a Segregated Society."

242. Ruth G. McRoy and Clayton T. Shorkey, "Alcohol Use and Abuse Among Blacks," in Edith Freeman (Ed.), *Social Work Practice with Clients with Alcohol Problems* (Springfield, IL: Charles C Thomas, 1985), pp. 202–213.

243. Ronan, "Alcohol-Related Health Risks among Black Americans."

244. "An Interview with O. Amuleru-Marshall," *Alcohol Health & Research World* (Winter 1986/87), pp. 25, 51.

245. Jesse A. Brinson, "Group Work for Black Adolescent Substance Users: Some Issues and Recommendations," *Journal of Child and Adolescent Substance Abuse*, Vol. 24, No. 2 (1995), pp. 49–59.

246. "Prevention of Alcohol Abuse among Black Americans."

247. David Grant and BoisSan Moore, "MIBCA-Sponsored Conference, Groundwork for Future Action," *Alcohol Health & Research World* (Winter 1986/87), pp. 18–23.

248. "Prevention of Alcohol Abuse among Black Americans."

249. Grant and Moore, "MIBCA-Sponsored Conference."

250. See, for example, Glenn C. Loury, "The Moral Quandry of the Black Community," *Public Interest*, No. 79 (Spring 1985), pp. 9–22.

251. "An Interview with Peter Bell."

252. Cited in Grant and Moore, "MIBCA-Sponsored Conference," p. 18.

253. Muriel Gray, "African Americans," in Joanne Philleo and Frances Larry Brisbane (Eds.), *Cultural Competence for Social Workers: A Guide for Alcohol and Other Drug Abuse Prevention Professionals Working with Ethnic/Racial Communities*, CSAP Cultural Competence Series 4 (Washington, DC: U.S. Government Printing Office, 1995), pp. 71–101, DHHS Pub. No. (SMA) 95-3075.

254. Ibid, p. 92.

255. Gossett, *Alcohol and Drug Use in Black America*.

256. Herd, "Editorial, Rethinking Black Drinking."

257. See, for example, Gossett, *Alcohol Abuse in Black America*; and Harper, "Research and Treatment with Black Alcoholics."

258. Denise A. Herd, "Contesting Culture: Alcohol-Related Identity Movements in Contemporary African-American Communities," *Contemporary Drug Problems* (Winter 1993), pp. 739–758.

259. Ibid.

260. Gossett, *Alcohol and Drug Abuse in Black America*, p. 6.

261. Francis X. McQuade, "Treatment and Recovery Issues for the Addicted Hispanic," *The Counselor* (May/June 1989), p. 29.

262. Anthony M. Alcocer, "Alcohol Use and Abuse among the Hispanic American Population," in NIAAA, *Alcohol and Health Monograph No. 4, Special Population Issues*, pp. 361–382; and Raul Caetano, "Responding to Alcohol-Related Problems among Hispanics," *Contemporary Drug Problems* (Fall 1988), pp. 335–363.

263. Also see Elaine Bratic Arkin and Judith E. Funkhouser, "Reaching Hispanic/Latino Youth," in Elaine Bratic Arkin and Judith E. Funkhouser (Eds.), *Communicating about Alcohol and Other Drugs: Strategies for Reaching Populations at Risk, OSAP Prevention Monograph 5* (Rockville, MD: Office for Substance Abuse Prevention, 1990), Chapter 3.

264. See U.S. Bureau of the Census, *Statistical Abstract of the United States, 1995* (Washington, DC: U.S. Government Printing Office, 1995) for demographic information.

265. McQuade, "Treatment and Recovery Issues," p. 29.

266. See Alcocer, "Alcohol Use and Abuse among the Hispanic American Population"; Lex, "Review of Alcohol Problems in Ethnic Minority Groups"; and M. Jean Gilbert and Richard C. Cervantes, *Mexican Americans and Alcohol, Monograph 11* (Los Angeles: Spanish Speaking Mental Health Research Center, 1987).

267. Arthur L. Klatsky, Abraham Siegelaub, Cynthia Landy, and Gary D. Friedman, "Racial Patterns of Alcoholic Beverage Use," *Alcoholism Clinical and Experimental Research* (Fall 1983), pp. 372–377.

268. Raul Caetano, "Drinking Patterns and Alcohol Problems in a National Sample of U.S. Hispanics," in NIAAA, *Alcohol Use among U.S. Ethnic Minorities*, pp. 147–162; Raul Caetano, "Findings from the 1984 National Survey of Alcohol Use among U.S. Hispanics," in Clark and Hilton, *Alcohol in America*, pp. 293–307; and Caetano, "Responding to Alcohol-Related Problems Among Hispanics."

269. Caetano and Kaskutas, "Changes in Drinking Patterns among Whites, Blacks and Hispanics, 1984–1992."

270. Caetano, "Responding to Alcohol-Related Problems among Hispanics."

271. Caetano, "Findings from the 1984 National Survey of Alcohol Use among U.S. Hispanics."

272. Caetano, "Responding to Alcohol-Related Problems Among Hispanics."

273. See J. Bryan Page, Lucy Rio, Jacqueline Sweeney, and Carolyn McKay, "Alcohol and Adaption to Exile in Miami's Cuban Population," in Bennett and Ames, *The American Experience with Alcohol*, pp. 315–332, and M. A. Scopetta, O. E. King, and J. Szapocnick, "Relationship of Acculturation, Incidence of Drug Abuse and Effective Treatment for Cuban Americans" (Washington, DC: National Institute on Drug Abuse, 1977), Research Contract No. 271-75-4136, cited in Lillian Comas-Díaz, "Puerto Rican Alcoholic Women: Treatment Considerations," *Alcoholism Treatment Quarterly*, Vol. 3, No. 1 (Spring 1986), pp. 47–57.

274. Alcocer, "Alcohol Use and Abuse among the Hispanic American Population."

275. Ricardo Castaneda and Marc Galanter, "Ethnic Differences in Drinking Practices and Cognitive Impairment among Detoxifying Alcoholics," *Journal of Studies on Alcohol*, Vol. 49, No. 4 (1988), pp. 335–339.

276. Andrew J. Gordon, "State-of-the-Art Review: Caribbean Hispanics and Their Alcohol Use," in NIAAA, *Alcohol Use among U.S. among U.S. Ethnic Minorities*, pp. 135–146.

277. Caetano, "Drinking Patterns and Alcohol Problems in a National Sample of U.S. Hispanics."

278. Gordon, "State-of-the-Art Review."

279. M. Audrey Burnam, "Prevalence of Alcohol Abuse and Dependence Among Mexican Americans and Non-Hispanic Whites in the Community," in NIAAA, *Alcohol Use among U.S. Ethnic Minorities*, pp. 163–177; also see Caetano, "Drinking and Alcohol-Related Problems Among Minority Women."

280. Kessler et al., "Lifetime and 12-Month Prevalence of DSM-III-R Psychiatric Disorders in the United States, Results from the National Comorbidity Survey," p. 13.

281. Klatsky et al., "Racial Patterns of Alcoholic Beverage Use."

282. Denise Herd and Raul Caetano, "Drinking Patterns and Problems among White, Black and Hispanic Women in the U.S.: Results from a National Survey," paper presented at the Alcohol and Drug Problems Association of North America Conference on Women's Issues, Denver, CO, May 3–6, 1987, cited in Caetano, "Drinking and Alcohol-Related Problems among Minority Women."

283. Herd and Caetano, "Drinking Patterns and Problems among White, Black and Hispanic Women in the U.S.: Results from a National Survey"; and Caetano, "Drinking and Alcohol-Related Problems among Minority Women."

284. Caetano and Kaskutas, "Changes in Drinking Patterns among Whites, Blacks and Hispanics, 1984–1992."

285. See, for example, David Farabee, Lynn Wallisch, and Jane Carlisle Maxwell, "Substance Abuse among Texas

Hispanics and Non-Hispanics: Who's Using, Who's Not, and Why," *Hispanic Journal of Behavioral Sciences*, Vol. 17, No. 4 (1995), pp. 523–536; and Charles M. Christian, Terry S. Zobeck, Henry J. Malin, and Dale C. Hitchcock, "Self-Reported Alcohol Use and Abuse among Mexican Americans: Preliminary Findings from the Hispanic Health and Nutrition Examination Survey Adult Sample Person Supplement," in NIAAA, *Alcohol Use among U.S. Ethnic Minorities*, pp. 425–438.

286. Substance Abuse and Mental Health Services Administration, *National Household Survey on Drug Abuse, Population Estimates, 1994.*

287. Rouse, *Substance Abuse and Mental Health Statistics Sourcebook*, p. 64.

288. Ruth Sanchez-Dirks, "Drinking Practices among Hispanic Youth," *Alcohol Health & Research World* (Winter 1978), pp. 21–27.

289. Alcocer, "Alcohol Use and Abuse among the Hispanic American Population."

290. Substance Abuse and Mental Health Services Administration, *National Household Survey on Drug Abuse, Population Estimates, 1994.*

291. John M. Wallace and Jerald G. Bachman, "Explaining Racial/Ethnic Differences in Adolescent Drug Use: The Impact of Background and Lifestyle," *Social Problems*, Vol. 38, No. 3 (August 1991), pp. 333–357.

292. Jesse T. Zapata and David S. Katims, "Antecedents of Substance Use among Mexican American School-Age Children," *Journal of Drug Education*, Vol. 24, No. 3 (1994), pp. 233–251; Zenong Yin, Jesse T. Zapata, and David S. Katims, "Risk Factors for Substance Use among Mexican American School-Age Youth," *Hispanic Journal of Behavioral Sciences*, Vol. 17, No. 1 (1995), pp. 61–76.

293. Lina Dusenbury, Jennifer A. Epstein, Gilbert J. Botvin, and Tracy Diaz, "Social Influence Predictors of Alcohol Use among New York Latino Youth," *Addictive Behaviors*, Vol. 19, No. 4 (1994), pp. 363–372.

294. Yin et al., "Risk Factors for Substance Use among Mexican American School-Age Youth"; and Zapata and Katims, "Antecedents of Substance Use among Mexican American School-Age Children."

295. See M. Jean Gilbert, "Alcohol-Related Practices, Problems, and Norms among Mexican Americans: An Overview" in *Alcohol Use among U.S. Ethnic Minorities*, pp. 115–134 for a discussion of studies on acculturation and the complexity of studying the issue.

296. Caetano, "Responding to Alcohol-Related Problems among Hispanics," p. 356.

297. Marcelline Burns, "The Alcohol Problem in Los Angeles," *Abstracts and Reviews in Alcohol and Driving*, Vol. 4 (1983), pp. 9–15.

298. For a discussion see Harper, "Research and Treatment with Black Alcoholics."

299. Caetano, "Drinking and Alcohol-Related Problems among Minority Women," p. 240.

300. McQuade, "Treatment and Recovery Issues"; also see Marian A. Aguilar, Diana M. DiNitto, Cynthia Franklin, and Becky Lopez-Pilkinton, "Mexican-American Families: A Psychoeducational Approach for Addressing Chemical Dependency and Codependency," *Child and Adolescent Social Work Journal*, Vol. 8, No. 4 (1991), pp. 309–326.

301. Farabee et al., "Substance Use among Texas Hispanics and Non-Hispanics: Who's Using, Who's Not, and Why."

302. Gerardo Marin, "Expectancies for Drinking and Excessive Drinking among Mexican Americans and Non-Hispanic Whites," *Addictive Behaviors*, Vol. 21, No. 4 (1996), pp. 491–507.

303. Comas-Díaz, "Puerto Rican Alcoholic Women."

304. M. Jean Gilbert and Richard C. Cervantes, "Alcohol Services for Mexican Americans: A Review of Utilization Patterns, Treatment Considerations and Prevention Activities," in Gilbert and Cervantes, *Mexican Americans and Alcohol*, pp. 61–93.

305. Gladys González-Ramos, "Examining the Myth of Hispanic Families' Resistance to Treatment: Using the School as a Site for Services," *Social Work in Education*, Vol. 12, No. 4 (1990), pp. 261–274.

306. Devore and Schlesinger, *Ethnic-Sensitive Social Work Practice*; and McQuade, "Treatment and Recovery Issues."

307. Antonio Melus, "Culture and Language in the Treatment of Alcoholism," *Alcohol Health & Research World* (Summer 1980), pp. 19–20; Aguilar et al., "Mexican-American Families"; and Comas-Díaz, "Puerto Rican Women."

308. Melus, "Culture and Language," pp. 19–20.

309. Comas-Díaz, "Puerto Rican Alcoholic Women."

310. Robert B. Hampson, W. Robert Beavers, and Yosaf Hulgus, "Cross-Ethnic Family Differences: Interactional Assessment of White, Black, and Mexican-American Families," *Journal of Marital and Family Therapy*, Vol. 16, No. 3 (1990), pp. 307–319.

311. Melus, "Culture and Language," p. 20.

312. Ibid.

313. M. Jean Gilbert, "Programmatic Approaches to the Alcohol-Related Needs of Mexican Americans," in Gilbert and Cervantes, *Mexican Americans and Alcohol*, pp. 95–107.

314. McQuade, "Treatment and Recovery Issues."

315. Ronald Figueroa and Philip Oliver-Diaz, "Hispanic Alcoholics' Children Need Extra Help," *Alcohol Health & Research World* (Winter 1986/87), pp. 66–67.

316. McQuade, "Treatment and Recovery Issues"; also see Aguilar et al., "Mexican American Families."

317. Melus, "Culture and Language," p. 20.

318. Gilbert, "Alcohol-Related Practices, Problems, and Norms among Mexican Americans: An Overview."

319. Gordon, "State-of-the-Art Review."

320. Caetano, "Responding to Alcohol-Related Problems Among Hispanics," p. 343, refers to M. Jean Gilbert, "Mexican-Americans in California: Intracultural Variation in Attitudes and Behavior Related to Alcohol," in Bennett and Ames, *The American Experience with Alcohol*, p. 268.

321. Aguilar et al., "Mexican-American Families"; and McQuade, "Treatment and Recovery Issues."

322. Gordon, "State-of-the-Art Review."

323. James Alan Neff, Thomas J. Prihoda, and Sue Keir Hoppe, "'Machismo,' Self-Esteem, Education and High Maximum Drinking among Anglo, Black and Mexican-American Male Drinkers," *Journal of Studies on Alcohol*, Vol. 52, No. 5 (1991), pp. 458–463.

324. Melus, "Culture and Language."

325. M. Douglas Anglin, May W. Booth, Timothy M. Ryan, and Yih-Ing Hser, "Ethnic Differences in Narcotics Addiction. II. Chicano and Anglo Addiction Career Patterns," *The International Journal of the Addictions*, Vol. 23, No. 10 (1988), pp. 1011–1027.

326. Caetano, "Drinking and Alcohol-Related Problems among Minority Women," p. 240.

327. Comas-Díaz, "Puerto Rican Women," p. 48.

328. Caetano, "Drinking and Alcohol-Related Problems among Minority Women," p. 240.

329. Anglin et al., "Ethnic Differences in Narcotics Addiction, II."

330. See Alcocer, "Alcohol Use and Abuse among the Hispanic American Population."

331. Gilbert and Cervantes, "Alcohol Services for Mexican-Americans."

332. Substance Abuse and Mental Health Services Administration, *National Drug and Alcoholism Treatment Unit Survey (NDATUS): Data for 1994 and 1980–1994*, Advance Report 13.

333. The remainder of this paragraph relies on Substance Abuse and Mental Health Services Administration, *National Drug and Alcoholism Treatment Unit Survey (NDATUS): 1991 Main Findings Report.*

334. Mark A. Quinones and Kathleen M. Doyle, "Cultural Variables and the Hispanic Drug Abuser," in Schecter, *Drug Dependence and Alcoholism*, Vol. 2, pp. 1–9.

335. Caetano, "Responding to Alcohol-Related Problems among Hispanics."

336. Comas-Díaz, "Puerto Rican Alcoholic Women."

337. Melus, "Culture and Language."

338. Comas-Díaz, "Puerto Rican Alcoholic Women"; and Aguilar et al., "Mexican-American Families."

339. Melus, "Culture and Language."

340. Comas-Díaz, "Puerto Rican Alcoholic Women."

341. Aguilar et al., "Mexican-American Families."

342. William C. McCaughrin and Daniel L. Howard, "Variation in Outpatient Substance Abuse Treatment Units with High Concentrations of Latino versus White Clients: Client Factors, Treatment Experiences, and Treatment Outcomes," *Hispanic Journal of Behavioral Sciences*, Vol. 17, No. 4 (1995), pp. 509–522.

343. Aguilar et al., "Mexican-American Families."

344. Figueroa and Oliver-Diaz, "Hispanic Alcoholics' Children"; and Andrew J. Gordon, "Alcoholism Treatment Services to Hispanics: An Ethnographic Examination of a Community's Services," *Family and Community Health*, Vol. 13, No. 4 (1991), pp. 12–24.

345. Caetano, "Responding to Alcohol-Related Problems among Hispanics."

346. R. C. Trotter and J. A. Chavira, "Discovering New Models for Alcohol Counseling in Minority Groups," in B. Velimirov (Ed.), *Modern Medicine and Medical Anthropology in the United States-Mexico Border Population* (Washington, DC: Pan American Health Organization, 1978), pp. 164–171, cited in Gilbert and Cervantes, "Alcohol Services for Mexican Americans," pp. 78–79.

347. Figueroa and Oliver-Diaz, "Hispanic Alcoholics' Children," p. 66.

348. Trotter and Chavira, "Discovering New Models," cited in Gilbert and Cervantes, *Alcohol Services for Mexican Americans*, p. 79.

349. F. A. Hoffman, "Mexican American Participation in Alcoholics Anonymous," unpublished proposal submitted to the National Institute on Alcohol Abuse and Alcoholism, 1984, referred to in Gilbert and Cervantes, *Alcohol Services for Mexican Americans*, p. 76.

350. Aguilar et al., "Mexican-American Families."

351. Melus, "Culture and Language"; also see Comas-Díaz, "Puerto Rican Alcoholic Women."

352. McQuade, "Treatment and Recovery Issues," p. 30.

353. Aguilar et al., "Mexican-American Families"; McQuade, "Treatment and Recovery Issues"; and Comas-Díaz, "Puerto Rican Alcoholic Women."

354. Caetano, "Responding to Alcohol-Related Problems among Hispanics."

355. Gordon, "Alcoholism Treatment Services to Hispanics."

356. Ibid.

357. Caetano, "Responding to Alcohol-Related Problems among Hispanics."

358. McQuade, "Treatment and Recovery Issues"; Azara L. Santiago-Rivera, "Developing a Culturally Sensitive Treatment Modality for Bilingual Spanish-Speaking Clients: Incorporating Language and Culture in Counseling," *Journal of Counseling & Development*, Vol. 76 (1995), pp. 12–17; also see Melvin Delgado, "Hispanics/Latinos," in Joanne Philleo and Frances Larry Brisbane (Eds.), *Cultural Competence for Social Workers: A Guide for Alcohol and Other Drug Abuse Prevention Professionals Working with Ethnic/Racial Communities*, CSAP Cultural Competence Series 4 (Washington, DC: U.S. Government Printing Office, 1995), pp. 41–67, DHHS Pub. No. (SMA) 95-3075.

359. McQuade, "Treatment and Recovery Issues," p. 30; also see Santiago-Rivera, "Developing a Culturally Sensitive Treatment Modality for Bilingual Spanish-Speaking Clients."

360. See Santiago-Rivera, "Developing a Culturally Sensitive Treatment Modality for Bilingual Spanish-Speaking Clients."

361. Daniel T. Sciarra and Joseph G. Ponterotto, "Counseling the Hispanic Bilingual Family: Challenges to the Therapeutic Process," *Psychotherapy*, Vol. 28 (1991), pp. 473–479.

362. Maria E. Zuniga, "Dichos as Metaphorical Tools for Latino Clients," *Psychotherapy*, Vol. 28 (1991), pp. 480–483.

363. Melus, "Culture and Language."

364. Sylvia Rodriguez-Andrew, "Los Niños: Intervention Efforts with Mexican-American Families," *Focus on Family and Chemical Dependency* (March/April 1984), pp. 8, 20.

365. The remainder of this paragraph relies on Caetano, "Responding to Alcohol-Related Problems."

366. Marin, "Expectancies for Drinking and Excessive Drinking among Mexican Americans and Non-Hispanic Whites."

367. Harry H. L. Kitano, "Alcohol Drinking Patterns: The Asian Americans," in NIAAA, *Alcohol and Health Monograph 4, Special Population Issues*, pp. 411–430.

368. U.S. Bureau of the Census, press release CB91-216 cited in U.S. Bureau of the Census, *Statistical Abstract of the United States, 1992*, 112th edition (Washington DC: U.S. Government Printing Office, 1992), p. 17.

369. U.S. Bureau of the Census, *Statistical Abstract of the United States: 1995*, Table 31.

370. Michael J. Stoil, "The Case of the Missing Gene, Hereditary Protection against Alcoholism," *Alcohol Health & Research World* (Winter 1987/88), pp. 130–136.

371. Ibid.; Richard P. Wang, "A Study of Alcoholism in Chinatown," *International Journal of Social Psychiatry*, Vol. 14 (1968), pp. 260–267; and David Sue, "Use and Abuse of Alcohol by Asian Americans," *Journal of Psychoactive Drugs*, Vol. 19, No. 1 (January–March 1987), pp. 57–66.

372. K. Singer, "Drinking Patterns and Alcoholism in the Chinese," *British Journal of Addiction*, Vol. 67 (1972), p. 13.

373. Ibid.

374. Ibid.; and K. Singer, "The Choice of Intoxicant Among the Chinese," *British Journal of Addiction*, Vol. 69 (1974), pp. 257–268.

375. Kitano, "Alcohol Drinking Patterns: The Asian Americans"; also see " 'Old Country' Values Influence Asian-American Drinking," *Alcohol Health and Research World* (Winter 1986/87), p. 47; see Singer, "Drinking Patterns and Alcoholism in the Chinese," on the subject of alcoholism and Confucian philosophy; on Confucianism and Taoism, see Wang, "A Study of Alcoholism in Chinatown,"

and Singer, "The Choice of Intoxicant among the Chinese"; and on Western influences on Filipinos, see James E. Lubben, Iris Chi, and Harry H. L. Kitano, "Exploring Filipino American Drinking Behavior," *Journal of Studies on Alcohol*, Vol. 49, No. 1 (1988), pp. 26–29.

376. See Francis L. K. Hsu, *Americans and Chinese* (London: Cresset Press, 1955); for additional discussion of Hsu's work and this point, see Singer, "The Choice of Intoxicant among the Chinese"; Wang, "A Study of Alcoholism in Chinatown"; and Sue, "Use and Abuse of Alcohol by Asian Americans."

377. Singer, "The Choice of Intoxicant among the Chinese."

378. Sue, "Use and Abuse of Alcohol by Asian Americans."

379. Singer, "The Choice of Intoxicant among the Chinese."

380. Bob Matsushima, Carlos Gonzalez, Curtiss Brown, and Emily Gibson, "Do Pacific/Asians Have Alcohol Problems? A Preliminary Report," in Schecter, *Drug Dependence and Alcoholism*, Vol. 2, pp. 39–46.

381. Ibid.

382. Stanley Sue, Nolan Zane, and Joanne Ito, "Alcohol Drinking Patterns among Asian and Caucasian Americans," *Journal of Cross-Cultural Psychology*, Vol. 10, No. 1 (March 1979), p. 54.

383. E. K. Yu, W. T. Liu, and P. Kurzeja, "Physical and Mental Health Status Indicators for Asian/Pacific Americans, Report to the Task Force on Black and Minority Health" (Bethesda, MD: National Institutes of Health, 1984), cited in Elena S. H. Yu and William T. Liu, "Alcohol Use and Abuse among Chinese-Americans, Epidemiologic Data," *Alcohol Health & Research World* (Winter 1986/87), pp. 14–17, 60–61.

384. Klatsky et al., "Racial Patterns of Alcoholic Beverage Use."

385. Harry H. L. Kitano and Iris Chi, "Asian-Americans and Alcohol Use: Exploring Cultural Differences in Los Angeles," *Alcohol Health & Research World* (Winter 1986/87), pp. 42–47; and Harry H. L. Kitano and Iris Chi, "Asian-Americans and Alcohol: The Chinese, Japanese, Koreans, and Filipinos in Los Angeles," in NIAAA, *Alcohol Use among U.S. Ethnic Minorties*, pp. 373–382.

386. For a broader review of prevalence and incidence studies on alcohol and other drug use in various communities, see Ford H. Kuramoto, "Asian Americans," in Joanne Philleo and Frances Larry Brisbane (Eds.), *Cultural Competence for Social Workers: A Guide for Alcohol and Other Drug Abuse Prevention Professionals Working with Ethnic/Racial Communities*, CSAP Cultural Competence Series 4 (Washington, DC: U.S. Government Printing Office, 1995), pp. 103–155, DHHS Pub. No. (SMA) 95-3075.

387. Frank M. Ahern, "Alcohol Use and Abuse among Four Ethnic Groups in Hawaii: Native Hawaiians,

Japanese, Filipinos, and Caucasians," in NIAAA, *Alcohol Use among U.S. Ethnic Minorities*, pp. 315–328.

388. Sharon R. Murakami, "An Epidemiological Survey of Alcohol, Drug, and Mental Health Problems in Hawaii: A Comparison of Four Ethnic Groups," in NIAAA, *Alcohol Use among U.S. Ethnic Minorities*, pp. 343–353.

389. Yu and Liu, "Alcohol Use and Abuse among Chinese-Americans."

390. Wang, "A Study of Alcoholism in Chinatown."

391. Yu and Liu, "Alcohol Use and Abuse among Chinese-Americans."

392. Kitano, "Alcohol Drinking Patterns: The Asian Americans."

393. Matsushima et al., "Do Pacific/Asians Have Alcohol Problems?"; also see John G. Phin and Paul Phillips, "Drug Treatment Entry Patterns and Socioeconomic Characteristics of Asian American, Native American, and Puerto Rican Clients," in Schecter, *Drug Dependence and Alcoholism*, Vol. 2, pp. 803–818.

394. Rouse, *Substance Abuse and Mental Health Statistics Sourcebook*, p. 64.

395. Carolyn E. D'Avanzo and Barbara Frye, "Culture, Stress and Substance Use in Cambodian Refugee Women," *Journal of Studies on Alcohol*, Vol. 55 (1994), pp. 420–426.

396. For a discussion, see Sue, "Use and Abuse of Alcohol by Asian Americans."

397. Matsushima et al., "Do Pacific/Asians Have Alcohol Problems?"; also see Kitano, "Alcohol Drinking Patterns: The Asian Americans"; Kitano and Chi, "Asian-Americans and Alcohol Use, Exploring Cultural Differences in Los Angeles"; Han Z. Li and Lorne Rosenblood, "Exploring Factors Influencing Alcohol Consumption Patterns among Chinese and Caucasians." *Journal of Studies on Alcohol*, Vol. 55 (1994), pp. 427–433.

398. Phin and Phillips, "Drug Treatment Entry Patterns," p. 808.

399. Wang, "A Study of Alcoholism in Chinatown," p. 26.

400. Matsushima, "Do Pacific/Asians Have Alcohol Problems?" p. 45; also see Kitano, "Alcohol Drinking Patterns: The Asian Americans"; and Wang, "A Study of Alcoholism in Chinatown."

401. Sue et al., "Alcohol Drinking Patterns among Asian and Caucasian Americans."

402. Li and Rosenblood, "Exploring Factors Influencing Alcohol Consumption Patterns among Chinese and Caucasians."

403. Walter B. Clark and Michie Hesselbrock, "A Comparative Analysis of U.S. and Japanese Drinking Patterns," in National Institute on Alcohol Abuse and Alcoholism, *Alcohol Use Patterns Among Populations of Different Cultures* (Washington, DC: U.S. Government Printing Office, 1988), pp. 79–98.

404. Sue, "Use and Abuse of Alcohol by Asian Americans."

405. Lubben et al., "Exploring Filipino American Drinking Behavior"; this is apparently the same Filipino American sample discussed in Kitano and Chi, "Asian-Americans and Alcohol Use."

406. Sandra B. Coleman, "Cross-Cultural Approaches to Working with Addict Families," in Schecter, *Drug Dependence and Alcoholism*, Vol. 2, pp. 941–948.

407. Sue, "Use and Abuse of Alcohol by Asian Americans."

408. National Institute on Alcohol Abuse and Alcoholism, *Seventh Special Report to the U.S. Congress on Alcohol and Health* (Rockville, MD: U.S. Department of Health and Human Services, January 1990), p. 35.

409. Peter H. Wolff, "Ethnic Differences in Alcohol Sensitivity," *Science*, Vol. 175 (1972), pp. 449–450; see Stoil, "The Case of the Missing Gene" and Sue, "Use and Abuse of Alcohol by Asian Americans" for a discussion of research on flushing.

410. The work of H. W. Goedde, S. Harada, and D. P. Agarwal, "Racial Differences in Alcohol Sensitivity: A New Hypothesis," *Human Genetics*, Vol. 51 (1979), pp. 331–334 and later research developments on flushing are also traced in Stoil, "The Case of the Missing Gene."

411. Kitano, "Alcohol Drinking Patterns: The Asian Americans," p. 414; also see Stoil, "The Case of the Missing Gene"; and Sue, "Use and Abuse of Alcohol by Asian Americans."

412. Leland H. Towle, "Japanese-American Drinking, Some Results from the Joint Japanese-U.S. Alcohol Epidemiology Project," *Alcohol Health & Research World*, Vol. 12, No. 3 (1988), pp. 216–223 and Vol. 12, No. 4 (1988), pp. 314–315.

413. Ronald C. Johnson, "The Flushing Response and Alcohol Use," in NIAAA, *Alcohol Use among U.S. Ethnic Minorities*, p. 383.

414. J. A. Ewing, "Explaining Alcoholism: What Does Research Tell Us and Where Does It Need to Go?" *Japanese Journal of Studies on Alcohol*, Vol. 15 (1980), pp. 268–283, cited in Stoil, "The Case of the Missing Gene."

415. See Sue, "Use and Abuse of Alcohol by Asian Americans"; and Shaefer, "Ethnic and Racial Variations" for a discussion of this point and related research.

416. Sue et al., "Alcohol Drinking Patterns among Asian and Caucasian Americans."

417. Li and Rosenblood, "Exploring Factors Influencing Alcohol Consumption Patterns among Chinese and Caucasians."

418. Kitano, "Alcohol Drinking Patterns: The Asian Americans."

419. Sue, "Use and Abuse of Alcohol by Asian Americans"; and Matsushima et al., "Do Pacific/Asians Have Alcohol Problems?"

420. Substance Abuse and Mental Health Services Administration, *National Drug and Alcoholism Treatment Unit Survey (NDATUS): Data for 1994 and 1980–1994*, Advance Report 13, p. 17.

421. H. H. Kitano, "Social Service Needs of Asian Americans in the West Los Angeles Area," paper presented to the United Way of Los Angeles, 1980, cited in Kitano, "Alcohol Drinking Patterns: The Asian Americans."

422. Kitano, "Alcohol Drinking Patterns: The Asian Americans."

423. Phin and Phillips, "Drug Treatment Entry Patterns."

424. Ibid.

425. Matsushima et al., "Do Pacific/Asians Have Alcohol Problems?"

426. Murakami, "An Epidemiological Survey of Alcohol, Drug, and Mental Health Problems in Hawaii."

427. Coleman, "Cross Cultural Approaches to Working with Addict Families."

428. Phin and Phillips, "Drug Treatment Entry Patterns."

429. Kitano, "Alcohol Drinking Patterns: The Asian Americans."

430. This paragraph relies on Hideki A. Ishisaka and Calvin Y. Takagi, "Social Work with Asian and Pacific Americans," in Green, *Cultural Awareness in the Human Services*, pp. 122–156.

431. This explanation relies on ibid.

432. Young Ik Cho and William R. Faulkner, "Conceptions of Alcoholism among Koreans and Americans," *The International Journal of the Addictions*, Vol. 28, No. 8 (1993), pp. 681–694.

433. Harry H. Kitano, "Mental Illness in Four Cultures," *Journal of Social Psychology*, Vol. 80 (1970), pp. 112–134, cited in Kitano, "Alcohol Drinking Patterns: The Asian Americans."

434. This paragraph relies on Ishisaka and Takagi, "Social Work with Asian and Pacific Americans."

435. Kuramoto, "Asian Americans," based on T. Sasao, *Statewide Asian Drug Service Needs Assessment* (Sacramento: California Department of Alcohol and Drug Prevention, 1991).

436. National Asian Pacific American Families Against Substance Abuse, "Programs of National Significance: Asian and Pacific Islander Demonstration Project," unpublished manuscript, 1993, cited in Kuramoto, "Asian Americans."

437. Noreen Mokuau, "Pacific Islanders," in Joanne Philleo and Frances Larry Brisbane (Eds.), *Cultural Competence for Social Workers: A Guide for Alcohol and Other Drug Abuse Prevention Professionals Working with Ethnic/Racial Communities*, CSAP Cultural Competence Series 4 (Washington, DC: U.S. Government Printing Office, 1995), pp. 157–188, DHHS Pub. No. (SMA) 95-3075.

438. E. M. Jellinek, "Immanuel Kant on Drinking," *Quarterly Journal of Studies on Alcohol*, Vol. 1 (1941), pp. 777–778.

439. Mark Keller, "The Great Jewish Drink Mystery," in Marshall, *Beliefs, Behaviors, & Alcoholic Beverages*, pp. 404–414.

440. Shoshana Weiss, "Primary Prevention of Excessive Drinking and the Jewish Culture—Preventive Efforts in Israel 1984–1985," *Journal of Primary Prevention*, Vol. 8, No. 4 (1988), p. 218.

441. Weiss, "Primary Prevention of Excessive Drinking and the Jewish Culture"; Shoshana Weiss and Penina Eldar, "Alcohol and Alcohol Problems Research 14: Israel," *British Journal of Addiction*, Vol. 82 (1987), pp. 227–235; Charles R. Snyder, Phyllis Palgi, Pnina Eldar, and Beatrice Elian, "Alcoholism among the Jews in Israel: A Pilot Study, I. Research Rationale and a Look at the Ethnic Factor," *Journal of Studies on Alcohol*, Vol. 43, No. 7 (1982), pp. 623–654; and Marinel Sagiv, "The Problem of Alcohol in Israel," *Archives of International Medicine*, Vol. 139 (March 1979), pp. 280–281.

442. Weiss, "Primary Prevention of Excessive Drinking and the Jewish Culture"; and Weiss and Eldar, "Alcohol and Alcohol Problems Research 14: Israel."

443. H. Bar, "Drinking Patterns of the Israeli Public" (second research) [Hebrew-text] (Jerusalem, The Israel Institute of Applied Social Research, 1984), cited in Weiss, "Primary Prevention of Excessive Drinking and the Jewish Culture," and Weiss and Eldar, "Alcohol and Alcohol Problems Research 14: Israel."

444. Weiss, "Primary Prevention of Excessive Drinking and the Jewish Culture," p. 220; also see Weiss and Eldar, "Alcohol and Alcohol Problems Research 14: Israel."

445. Weiss and Eldar, "Alcohol and Alcohol Problems Research 14: Israel."

446. Ibid.

447. Weiss, "Primary Prevention of Excessive Drinking and the Jewish Culture."

448. Weiss and Eldar, "Alcohol and Alcohol Problems Research 14: Israel."

449. Donald Cahalan and Ira Cisin, "American Drinking Practices: Summary of Findings from a National Probability Sample. I. Extent of Drinking by Population Subgroups," *Quarterly Journal of Studies on Alcohol*, Vol. 29 (1968), pp. 130–151.

450. Michael E. Hilton, "The Demographic Distribution of Drinking Patterns in 1984," in Clark and Hilton (Eds.), *Alcohol in America*, pp. 73–86, reprinted from *Drug and Alcohol Dependence*, Vol. 22 (1988), pp. 37–47.

451. M. M. Glatt, "Alcoholism and Drug Dependence amongst Jews," *British Journal of Addiction*, Vol. 64 (1970), pp. 297–304; and Barry Glassner and Bruce Berg, "How Jews Avoid Alcohol Problems," *American Sociological Review*, Vol. 45 (August 1980), pp. 647–664.

452. Glatt, "Alcoholism and Drug Dependence amongst Jews."

453. Ibid.

454. Sissy Carpey, "Alcoholism, New Expressions of Jewish Concern Create Climate of Hope," *Jewish Exponent* (June 7, 1985), p. 48.

455. Barbara Teller, "Chemical Dependency in the Jewish Community," *The Counselor* (May/June 1989), pp. 27–28.

456. Russell Eisenman, Jan Carl Grossman, and Ronald Goldstein, "Undergraduate Marijuana Use as Related to Internal Sensation Novelty Seeking and Openness to Experience," *Journal of Clinical Psychology*, Vol. 36, No. 4 (October 1980), pp. 1013–1019.

457. Ibid., p. 1018.

458. Maristela G. Monteiro and Marc A. Schuckit, "Alcohol, Drug, and Mental Health Problems among Jewish and Christian Men at a University," *American Journal of Drug and Alcohol Abuse*, Vol. 15, No. 4 (1989), pp. 403–412.

459. Lydia V. Flasher and Stephen A. Maisto, "A Review of Theory and Research on Drinking Patterns among Jews," *The Journal of Nervous and Mental Disease*, Vol. 172, No. 10 (1984), pp. 596–603.

460. Charles R. Snyder, *Alcohol and the Jews, A Cultural Study of Drinking and Sobriety* (Glencoe, IL: The Free Press, 1958).

461. Sheila Blume, Dee Dropkin, and Lloyd Sokolow, "The Jewish Alcoholic: A Descriptive Study," *Alcohol Health and Research World* (Summer 1980), pp. 21–26.

462. Flasher and Maisto, "A Review of Theory and Research on Drinking Patterns among Jews"; and Monteiro and Schuckit, "Alcohol, Drug, and Mental Health Problems among Jewish and Christian Men at a University."

463. Teller, "Chemical Dependency in the Jewish Community."

464. See, for example, Blume et al., "The Jewish Alcoholic: A Descriptive Study."

465. Robert Freed Bales, "Cultural Differences in Rates of Alcoholism," *Quarterly Journal of Studies on Alcoholism*, Vol. 6 (1946), pp. 480–499.

466. Teller, "Chemical Dependency in the Jewish Community."

467. Donald Davison Glad, "Attitudes and Experiences of American-Jewish and American-Irish Male Youth as Related to Differences in Adult Rates of Inebriety," *Quarterly Journal of Studies on Alcohol*, Vol. 8 (1947), pp. 406–472.

468. Snyder, *Alcohol and the Jews.*

469. Mark Keller, "The Great Jewish Drink Mystery"; and L. Cheinisse, "La Race Juive Jouit-elle d'une Immunité a l'égard de l'alcoolisme," *Semaine Medicale*, Vol. 28 (1908), pp. 613–615, cited in Snyder et al., "Alcoholism among the Jews in Israel."

470. See Jellinek, "Immanuel Kant on Drinking."

471. Bales, "Cultural Differences in Rates of Alcoholism."

472. Snyder, *Alcohol and the Jews*, p. 182.

473. Emile Durkheim, *Le Suicide* (Paris: Felix Alcan, 1897).

474. Glad, "Attitudes and Experiences of American-Jewish and American-Irish Male Youth," p. 462.

475. Snyder, *Alcohol and the Jews*, p. 101.

476. Snyder et al., "Alcoholism among the Jews in Israel."

477. Flasher and Maisto, "A Review of Theory and Research on Drinking Patterns among Jews," p. 599.

478. Blume et al., "The Jewish Alcoholic"; and Teller, "Chemical Dependency in the Jewish Community."

479. Barry Glassner and Bruce Berg, "Social Locations and Interpretations: How Jews Define Alcoholism," *Journal of Studies on Alcohol*, Vol. 45, No. 1 (1984), pp. 16–25.

480. Glassner and Berg, "How Jews Avoid Alcohol Problems."

481. Albert D. Ullman, "Sociocultural Backgrounds of Alcoholism," *Annals of the American Academy of Political and Social Science*, Vol. 315 (1958), pp. 48–54.

482. Victor D. Sanua, "Psychopathology and Social Deviance among Jews," *Journal of Jewish Communal Service*, Vol. 58, No. 1 (1981), pp. 12–23.

483. Weiss and Eldar, "Alcohol and Alcohol Problems Research 14: Israel."

484. See Montiero and Schuckit, "Alcohol, Drug, and Mental Health Problems."

485. Flasher and Maisto, "A Review of Theory and Research on Drinking Patterns among Jews," p. 601.

486. Carpey, "Alcoholism," p. 47.

487. Flasher and Maisto, "A Review of Theory and Research on Drinking Patterns among Jews," p. 601.

488. Blume et al., "The Jewish Alcoholic"; and Teller, "Chemical Dependency in the Jewish Community."

489. Blume et al., "The Jewish Alcoholic"; and Carpey, "Alcoholism."

490. Some of this paragraph relies on Teller, "Chemical Dependency in the Jewish Community"; also see Carpey, "Alcoholism."

491. Teller, "Chemical Dependency in the Jewish Community."

492. Lisa Master, "Jewish Experience of Alcoholics Anonymous," *Smith College Studies in Social Work*, Vol. 59, No. 2 (1989), pp. 183–199.

493. Master, "Jewish Experience of Alcoholics Anonymous."

494. Teller, "Chemical Dependency in the Jewish Community."

12

Gay Men, Lesbians, Bisexuals, and Chemical Dependency

L ike alcoholism and other forms of drug abuse, homosexuality[1] has variously been called a crime, a sin, and an illness or disease.[2] Human service professionals generally refer to neither chemical dependency nor homosexuality as a crime or as a sin. Many individuals have, however, fought for the treatment of chemical dependency using a disease or illness perspective, while also fighting to eliminate the definition of homosexuality as a crime or disease. In 1973, the American Psychiatric Association removed homosexuality from its *Diagnostic and Statistical Manual of Mental Disorders.* The American Psychological Association concurred with this decision. However, certain acts between members of the same gender remain crimes in some states. Ziebold comments that many still view alcoholics and homosexuals with disdain.[3] As a result, gay men, lesbians, and bisexuals with chemical dependency problems may face stigmas that compound their lack of access to good health and mental health care.[4]

This chapter explores alcohol and drug use among gay men, lesbians, and bisexuals. The focus is largely on alcohol abuse, since it is discussed more widely in the literature on these populations. We primarily discuss gay men and lesbians, since

bisexual individuals are often not referred to separately in the literature. Gay men, lesbians, and bisexuals function in the social systems of the majority culture, but many are also integrally involved in the social systems or subcultures of gay and lesbian communities. Although it is beyond the scope of this book to discuss many aspects of the life-styles of lesbians, gay men, and bisexuals, the diversity among them, and the many myths surrounding them, such knowledge is important in helping the reader integrate the material presented here. Finnegan and McNally have written a basic book about gay men and lesbians addressed to professionals in the chemically dependency field,[5] and there is a considerable clinical literature addressing mental health issues with gay men and lesbians of value to chemical dependency professionals.

Substance Abuse among Lesbians and Gay Men

Since Kinsey's research in the 1940s, many have assumed that the incidence of homosexuality in the general population is 10 percent and that a higher percentage of individuals have had some homosexual experience.[6] Although more recent reports suggest that these figures may be overestimates,[7] the literature generally indicates similar levels of social adjustment and similar incidences of social or psychological problems for gay men and lesbians compared with heterosexual men and women.[8] The incidences of substance abuse and of suicide *may*, however, be higher for gay men and lesbians,[9] and a strong association between alcohol use, alcoholism, and suicide in the general population has been documented.[10] People with substance use disorders have a higher propensity for psychiatric disorders than the general population (see Chapter 13). If the incidence of substance use disorders is indeed greater among gay men and lesbians than in the general population, Hellman raises the question as to whether psychiatric disorders may also be more common in these groups.[11] However, adequate studies of co-occurring substance and mental disorders are lacking among gay, lesbian, and bisexual populations.

In 1978, the President's Commission on Mental Health recognized gay male and lesbian alcoholics as an at-risk group "that has been inadequately or inappropriately served."[12] Many gay men and lesbians shared this concern. The advent of the human immunodeficiency virus (HIV) has further raised concerns about substance abuse among gay men and lesbians, as it did among most segments of the population. There is concern not only about the transmission of HIV through sexual activity and through injecting drug use but also about alcohol's deleterious effect on the immune system and on judgment that may play a part in the transmission of the virus.[13]

Several studies suggest higher rates of substance abuse among gay men and particularly lesbians, compared with men and women in the general population. A study by Fifield conducted in Los Angeles and published in 1975 has been cited frequently.[14] She estimated that nearly one-third of the gay and lesbian population drank excessively. Weinberg and Williams conducted a study of gay men that included a question on alcohol.[15] Of the 1,057 U.S. respondents, 29.4 percent said they "drank more than they should many times" and another 31.3 percent said they did so "sometimes." Lohrenz and colleagues found that 29 percent of the 145 gay men in their study recruited from four urban areas in Kansas scored as alcoholics on the Michigan Alcoholism Screening Test.[16]

In an in-depth study of gay men and lesbians, Saghir and Robins generally found more heavy drinking, alcohol-related problems, and nonprescription drug use in a gay and lesbian sample compared with heterosexual men and women, but their nonprobability sample was also relatively small (89 gay men, 57 lesbians, 35 heterosexual men, and 44 heterosexual women).[17] The differences they found between the heterosexual and lesbian women were substantial, whereas the differences between the gay and straight men were much smaller. The lesbians drank considerably more than the heterosexual women; their drinking was more similar to that of the gay and heterosexual men. In a further analysis of these data, 28 percent of the lesbians met the criteria the authors described for alcoholism, compared with 5 percent of the heterosexual women; another 33 percent of the lesbians were considered heavy drinkers or "questionable" alcoholics, compared with 7 percent of the heterosexuals.[18]

The National Lesbian Health Care Survey, conducted from 1984 to 1985, is based on information provided by about 1,900 respondents to surveys distributed in a number of cities through various means.[19] Some 6 percent of the lesbian respondents reported drinking daily, and an additional 25 percent reported drinking more than once a week. The percent drinking daily increased with age, with 3 percent of women in the 17–24 and 25–34 age groups reporting daily use, compared with 21 percent in the 55 and older age group. Of the respondents, 14 percent were worried about their alcohol use. Younger lesbians used marijuana more frequently than older lesbians. Some 5 percent of respondents used marijuana daily, 9 percent more than once a week, and

8 percent more than monthly, with 7 percent worried about their use. Cocaine was used more than once a week by 1 percent of respondents and by another 2 percent more than once monthly. Tranquilizers were used primarily by those age 45 and older, with 1 percent of respondents using them daily, 1 percent more than once a week, and 2 percent more than once a month. Use of other drugs was less frequent. Substance abuse counseling had been sought by 16 percent of the responents.

In his review of incidence studies, Bickelhaupt describes two other studies of note here.[20] One study, by Morales and Graves, is based on a sample of 453 individuals in San Francisco who completed questionnaires distributed through various channels, such as on the street, in the county jail, and through community agencies and organizations.[21] Of the respondents, 59 percent were gay men, 28 percent were lesbians, and 13 percent were bisexuals (this small group of bisexuals was excluded from the tabulation of results). The authors concluded that using conservative estimates, 18 percent of the gay men and almost 25 percent of the lesbians "presented an 'at risk' substance abuse pattern." Alcohol was most commonly used, with slightly fewer respondents using marijuana. Over 50 percent had used cocaine in the prior year. The gay men generally reported more drug use than the women.

The other study, by Kelly, included a sample of 748 gay men, lesbians, and bisexuals.[22] Most were white, employed, and had some college education; 44 percent were women. Data were also collected in San Francisco over a two-month period using surveys and interviews. According to the author's criteria, 31 percent of the men reported use indicative of chemical dependency and another 11 percent suggested problematic use. Some 10 percent of the gay male respondents used alcohol daily, compared with 5.5 percent of the lesbians. Alcohol was the drug used most often by men and women. Within the past year, 50 percent of the men and 38 percent of the women had used marijuana.

Despite similarities in many of the findings, especially with regard to alcohol, most of these studies have serious methodological limitations, such as the use of convenience samples rather than general population surveys.[23] Some samples have been obtained from gay and lesbian organizations, and others have included subjects identified in gay bars or other social settings where those with drinking problems may be overrepresented. We do not know how well these samples represent the gay, lesbian, and bisexual population in the United States.

McKirnan and Peterson tried to obtain a broader sample by widely dispersing 21,000 surveys through various channels in Chicago's gay community, including newspapers, community organizations, bars, and so forth.[24] About 16 percent (3,400) were returned. They compared their results for alcohol use with the widely cited Clark and Midanik general population survey[25] and for other drug use with a study by Clayton and associates.[26] Comparisons indicated that gay men and lesbians were less likely to abstain from alcohol (14 percent of the respondents were abstainers, compared to 29 percent of the general population), more likely to be moderate drinkers (71 percent and 57 percent, respectively), and were similar in terms of the percentage of heavy drinkers (15 percent and 14 percent, respectively). Some 13 percent of the gay male respondents and 14 percent of the lesbians were abstainers. Abstention rates among the general population are not only higher but are also more disparate between genders (23 percent for men and 34 percent for women). Some 17 percent of the gay men and 9 percent of the lesbians were heavy drinkers, compared with 21 percent of men and 7 percent of women in the general population.

Despite similar rates of heavy drinking between the gay and straight men and between the lesbian and straight women, higher rates of alcohol problems were reported for lesbians and gay men than for the general population (23 percent and 12 percent, respectively). Similar to Saghir and

Robins's study, the gay men and lesbians were relatively similar in terms of drinking problems, yet in the general population, men report substantially higher rates of problems than women. In the younger age groups, the level of alcohol-related problems among gay men and men in the general population was about the same. After age 30, however, problems declined for heterosexual men, but remained relatively constant for gay men. Among the gay men and lesbians, 56 percent had used marijuana in the previous year, compared with 20 percent of men and women in the general population. The figures for cocaine use in the past year were 23 percent and 8.5 percent, respectively, and for frequent cocaine use 2.3 percent and 0.7 percent, respectively. Figures for frequent marijuana users were more alike at 11 percent and 9 percent, respectively. Like the findings for alcohol, there was less of a difference in drug use between lesbians and gay men than between men and women in the general population. There was also more drug use among older gay men and lesbians than their counterparts in the general population. McKirnan and Peterson conclude that "there is . . . some cause for concern about substance abuse among homosexuals, although we did not find the very heavy alcohol and drug use that has often been ascribed to homosexual populations."[27]

Stall and Wiley were able to obtain information on the drinking and drug use of 1,034 gay and heterosexual men in San Francisco as part of a larger epidemiological study of AIDS.[28] This study did use random sampling (multistage cluster), although participation was, of course, voluntary. After controlling for age, the researchers found few differences in the quantity and frequency of alcohol consumption between the two groups of men. Like some of McKirnan and Peterson's findings, the gay men's drinking tended to be consistent across age groups, whereas it declined with age among the heterosexuals. However, the gay men, particularly the younger ones, were more likely to be abstainers than their heterosexual counterparts, but they were also more likely to be heavier drinkers.

The gay men were more apt to use marijuana, MDA, psychedelics, barbiturates, ethyl chloride, and amphetamines, but the greatest difference was in the use of "poppers." Most of the drug use was among the younger gay men, but in general, drug use for the gay sample was not frequent.

The most recent major study of drinking and drug use among gay men and lesbians is the Trilogy Project, a five-year longitudinal study funded by the National Institute on Drug Abuse (NIDA).[29] (Trilogy is a symbolic reference to the popular movie and play *Torch Song Trilogy* about the gay culture.) Subjects were from two metropolitan areas of a southern state. The study used a variety of sampling techniques yielding 1,067 respondents (a response rate of 53.3 percent). Most respondents were white, with an average age of 34 years and 15 years of education, currently employed, and living in cities or suburbs; 53 percent were gay men and 47 percent were lesbians. The substance use of Trilogy Project subjects was compared with NIDA's 1988 National Household Survey of Drug Abuse (NHSDA).[30]

With regard to alcohol, Trilogy Project participants were less likely to have abstained in the last month and they drank more than the general population. Consumption of five or more drinks on 20 to 30 days was 1.3 percent for the Trilogy participants and 1.0 percent for NHSDA participants; of five or more drinks on 5 to 19 days was 9.2 percent for Trilogy participants and 5.7 percent for NHSDA participants; and of five or more drinks on 1 to 4 days was 18.1 percent for Trilogy participants and 9.9 percent for NHSDA participants. If problematic consumption is defined as having five or more drinks on 1 to 30 days in the past month, the rates of problematic use are 29 percent for Trilogy participants and 17 percent for NHSDA participants. However, the studies' authors have defined use that "could be considered problematic" as five or more drinks on 5 to 30 days, which constitutes 10.5 percent of Trilogy and 6.7 percent of NHSDA respondents. The authors further analyzed the data by eliminating from both study samples those who had not consumed five or more drinks on any one day during the past month, and found that 36.8 percent of Trilogy and 40.6 percent of NHSDA participants had consumed five or more drinks on 5 to 30 days.

Clearly, data can be interpreted in different ways, and we leave it to readers to determine the definition of problematic use that they believe is more appropriate. When one includes all respondents in the sample, the Trilogy respondents consumed more; however, if one excludes abstainers or those who have not consumed five or more drinks on one day during the month, then the results are more comparable for the two samples. Again, differences in drinking among the lesbians in the Trilogy Project and women in the NHSDA were generally more pronounced than for gay and heterosexual men in the two studies.

In summarizing findings about use of other drugs, marijuana use was significantly higher among Trilogy than NHSDA participants, especially when comparing the female samples in both studies. Inhalant use was also higher for the Trilogy compared to the NHSDA participants. Inhalant use among women was low in both studies; as expected, it was much higher among men in the Trilogy compared with the NHSDA study. Cocaine use was higher for Trilogy participants but relatively small percentages of participants in both studies had used this substance in the past year. Similarly, less than 10 percent of gay men and lesbians in the Trilogy Project reported use of crack, hallucinogens, heroin, and nonmedical use of stimulants, sedatives, tranquilizers, and analgesics in the past month or year. In general, drug use findings for gay men and lesbians were more similar than for men and women in the general population. Finally, cigarette smoking was higher for Trilogy Project subjects than has been found in studies of the general population, especially when comparing lesbians with women in the general population.

A few recent studies have not found statistically significant differences between lesbian and heterosexual women in alcohol or other drug consumption or substance-related problem measures.[31] The small numbers of subjects make these results tentative, even though a study by Bloomfield relies on a randomly selected sample.[32] In summarizing the literature on lesbian alcohol use, Hughes and Wilsnack contend that with a few exceptions, the following patterns emerge:

> First, fewer lesbians than heterosexual women abstain from alcohol. Second, the rates of alcohol problems are higher among lesbians than among heterosexual women, even when the rates of heavy drinking are comparable. Third, the relationships between demographic characteristics, such as age, and drinking behaviors may differ for lesbians and heterosexual women.[33]

Some studies paint a picture of alcohol use and alcohol problems among gay men and lesbians that is two or three times greater than in the general population,[34] but more recent and larger studies suggest that these differences may not be as dramatic as thought. The McKirnan and Peterson and the Stall and Wiley studies were conducted about 15 years after the Fifield and Saghir and Robins studies, and the Trilogy Project is even more recent. Much has changed during the last few decades. AIDS has arrived; there is a greater awareness of health-risk factors, and chemical dependence has become known as a treatable disease. Hastings suggests that the gay rights and women's rights movements, greater openness about gay or lesbian identity, greater opportunities for socialization outside bars, and specialized substance abuse education and treatment for gay men and lesbians may have helped to mitigate drinking.[35] Due to the number of other available drugs and the problems in quantifying them by amount and frequency of use, it is especially difficult to interpret findings about this aspect of substance use.[36] Studies suggest greater drug use, but much of it may be experimental.

It may be tempting for some groups to emphasize data that support similarities in alcohol and drug among gay and straight populations and equally tempting for others whose agenda may be served by emphasizing the differences that have been reported. We urge caution in the use of findings on alcohol and drug use until more conclusive work is done to determine the extent of alcohol and drug-related problems among gay men and lesbians. Regardless of whether substance abuse problems are more frequent among gay men, lesbians, and bisexuals, professionals working with these populations must be prepared to recognize substance abuse and dependence when it does occur and to treat or refer clients with these problems.

In addition to concerns about substance abuse among gay men, lesbians, and bisexuals, Small and Leach noted that nearly one-third of the men they saw in their clinical alcoholism practice were "concerned about homosexuality."[37] This suggests that not only is knowledge of substance abuse among helping professionals working with gay men, lesbians, and bisexuals a prerequisite but also that chemical dependency professionals need knowledge of gay, lesbian, and bisexual populations.

Substance Abuse: Causes and Connections

At one time, the excessive use of alcohol to cope with fears of homosexuality or latent homosexuality was advanced as a cause of alcoholism.[38] In discussing this literature, Small and Leach noted that "it might be inferred that overt homosexuality averts alcoholism, or that no one can manifest both alcoholism and overt homosexuality."[39] Presumably this suggested that when one stops covering up his or her gayness, there is no need to drink excessively. But others saw the situation quite differently. They espoused the position that by "treating" homosexuality and converting the client to heterosexism, substance abuse problems would remit.[40]

Recent literature takes the position that chemical abuse and homosexuality are not causally linked, despite evidence of potentially higher rates of alcohol and other drug use among lesbians and gay men.[41] As Israelstam states,

Present day authors working with the alcohol problems of homosexuals believe it is not homosexuality (physical acts or emotional attachments), but rather homophobia (guilt and/or negative attitudes) in both homosexuals and heterosexuals that causes the stress and denial that may lead to alcohol and drug problems in the homosexual group.[42]

This position appears consistent with the view of lesbian feminists. They offer a political explanation of alcohol and other drug abuse in which the majority group sees that alcohol and drugs are available as a means of rendering minority groups more powerless[43] (also see Chapter 11 on substance abuse in ethnic minority communities). Saulnier says that "a focus on the structural etiological factors is as vital to the understanding of lesbian alcoholism as it was to the study of internalized homophobia."[44]

Brandsma and Pattison summarized four explanations for alcohol abuse problems among lesbians and gay men:

1. Alcohol may assist members of these oppressed groups in coping with feelings of shame, isolation, guilt, and other negative feelings.
2. The view of homosexuality as deviant may contribute to the development of other socially identified forms of deviance such as alcoholism.
3. Gay men and lesbians have had few outlets for socialization except gay bars and parties where drinking is a part of the environment.
4. Alcohol can reduce anxieties associated with identifying and accepting one's self as a gay man or as a lesbian, including initiation of intimate relationships with persons of the same gender.[45]

Another description from the literature on substance abuse among gay men and lesbians affirms these views:

Gay people drink and party to hide from the world, to escape their feelings of being different, and all too many never manage to take off the mask. Shallowness and narcissistic self-indulgence are then interpreted and given public currency as the evidence of the "homosexual personality," not as evidence of societal confinement. Accepting this view of themselves, the victims accumulate more guilt and more of an urge to escape into drinking.[46]

Others believe that lack of access to roles in marriage, childrearing, and mainstream occupations may exacerbate drinking and drug use.[47]

McKirnan and Peterson provide some empirical evidence that gay men who are vulnerable to substance abuse (e.g., have more positive attitudes about the benefits of alcohol) and who report more negative affect (e.g., depression and low self-esteem) and discrimination, and therefore experience more stress, encounter more alcohol- and drug-related problems.[48] They also found some indication that the degree to which gay men were "out" and their role status (e.g., underemployment) were related to substance use; however, the correlations were generally weak, and these relationships did not hold up as well for women. Stronger correlations were found between alcohol and drug use to reduce stress and alcohol- and drug-related problems for the entire sample of gay men and lesbians, but this finding may not be exclusive to these groups. In cross-sectional, correlational research of this nature, it is often difficult to separate causes from effects. After studying a group of gay men, Weinberg contends that alienation is a result, not a cause, of problem drinking, but that drinking among gay men is related to social pressures to drink among peers.[49]

Some attempts have been made to apply various theoretical perspectives or frameworks such as symbolic interaction to the development of alcoholism in lesbians and gay men.[50] Reference group theory has also been applied to explain gay men's drinking,[51] and developmental theory[52] and identity transformation[53] have been used to explain alcoholism among lesbians. Much remains to be done in the area of theory development.[54] As in the general population, there are probably many explanations of chemical abuse and dependency among gay men, lesbians, and bisexuals.

Kus has challenged some of the more popularly espoused explanations for substance abuse among gay men and lesbians, especially what he terms "gay bar ethnotheory."[55] Ziebold earlier reviewed evidence that "most homosexuals do not spend much time in bars"; however, the literature contains many discussions of these bars.[56] D'Emilio, for example, traces the development of gay bars during the twentieth century, identifying them not only as opportunities for socialization for gay men and lesbians but also as places where consciousness raising began and the solidarity necessary to organize politically to fight oppression developed.[57] The bars continue to play a role in the initial socialization to gay life-styles.[58]

Kus, however, offers a "gay non-acceptance theory," attributing substance abuse to unresolved issues at each stage of the "coming out" process.[59] The various stages of this process (the stages of acknowledging one's homosexual identity) and the labels given to them have been discussed by many authors.[60] As described by Kus, during the first stage, which he calls *identification*, the individual recognizes that he or she is homosexual. In the second stage, which Kus calls *cognitive changes*, the individual addresses homophobia by learning about gay and lesbian life-styles. In stage 3, *acceptance*, individuals free themselves from the shame and guilt that society attaches to homosexuality. The fourth stage, *action*, involves positive acceptance of a gay life-style and often involves disclosure to others. According to Kus, homosexual-oriented individuals may develop substance abuse problems because they are unable to acknowledge and accept their homosexuality in a positive light.

Kus attempted to validate his theory by studying 20 homosexual men in recovery from substance abuse. Based on their recall, all the men had developed drinking problems before they began going to gay bars—evidence that Kus cites as discrediting the gay bar ethnotheory. One of Kus's hypotheses was that accepting being gay would lead to sobriety, but evidence showed that it was becoming sober that led the respondents to accept themselves as gay. This seems logical, given that clarity of thinking and the ability to address problems rationally comes after one is sober.

McKirnan and Peterson did not find that "outness" was related to substance use or related problems among lesbians.[61] However, in a study with a small sample of lesbians, McNally and Finnegan found that a stage or phase model captured the recovery and identity transformation of lesbian alcoholics: "There was a powerful circular interaction between the women's transformation of their alcoholic and lesbian identities. Accepting and internalizing their alcoholic identities enabled them to explore, accept, and internalize their lesbian identities which, in turn, enabled them to continue to transform and strengthen their alcoholic identities."[62]

The clinical literature also addresses the need to make sobriety the first step in assisting gay men and lesbians who are chemically dependent.[63] Small and Leach indicated that in 7 of 10 cases they reported, the alcoholic men "who were able to accept and live comfortably with the need for abstinence seemed also most likely to achieve relatively successful sexual function"; however, the other three "patients who had come to terms with their homosexuality seemed to find it easier to accept the diagnosis of alcoholism and the need for abstinence."[64] Small and Leach also concluded that "recovery from pathological drinking seemed to be within reach almost as soon as the patient could view alcoholism as a condition independent of homosexuality."[65]

An analysis by Lewis and colleagues provides equivocal information on whether gay bar ethnotheory may explain the drinking behavior of lesbians.[66] The lesbians in their study described as "nonsocial drinkers" began having "homosexual psychological responses" at an average age of 13, followed by their "first significant homosexual experiences" at an average age of 21. Heavy drinking started somewhat later, at an average age of 24. Although the age at which the lesbians began

going to gay bars was not indicated, after controlling for frequency of bar attendance, there was still a higher rate of alcoholism and heavy drinking among the lesbians than the heterosexual women they studied. However, half the lesbians did not go to gay bars, and the drinking of the lesbians who did and did not go to bars was similar.

Do lesbians and gay men believe that their sexual orientation influences their drinking? Hawkins interviewed 30 lesbians who were also alcoholics, 22 of whom "clearly" believed that their lesbianism had not contributed to their alcoholism.[67] In their sample containing gay men and lesbians with a range of drinking behaviors, Saghir and Robins reported that 90 percent of the lesbians they interviewed saw no connection between their drinking behavior and their sexual orientation, compared with 62 percent of the gay men. The remaining lesbians and gay men saw a connection between their affectional preference and their drinking, largely as a result of socialization in gay bars.[68]

Some additional studies of lesbians are of interest, but the empirical literature remains sparse. Diamond and Wilsnack interviewed 10 lesbians who drank excessively and suggested that factors such as a high level of dependency needs might be investigated further as a correlate of drinking behavior.[69] Schilit and colleagues compared 15 lesbians who were alcoholic with 15 lesbians who were not alcoholic; the alcoholics reported more unhappiness in childhood, more loneliness, and fewer individuals in whom they could currently confide.[70] Although differences were not found in their relationships with their mothers, the alcoholics were more likely to report poor relationships with their fathers and to indicate that their fathers also had drinking problems. The only significant difference with respect to involvement in group activities was that the alcoholic women were more involved with religious groups. The authors conclude that the lesbian alcoholics had more social supports than anticipated, but this may have been due to the fact that these women were in recovery and were participating in groups such as Alcoholics Anonymous.

Hughes and Wilsnack identify some themes from the empirical literature on women and alcoholism to identify factors that may put lesbians at risk for drinking, heavy drinking, alcoholism, or alcohol-related problems.[71] These risk factors include paid employment outside the home, cohabitation, having a partner with a drinking problem, and the role of drinking in abusive relationships (also see Chapter 15). However, Rothblum says that "many of the factors that are presumed to place women and men at risk for mental health disorders may not be true for lesbians and gay men."[72] She notes that factors that may protect lesbians are less likelihood of being married to a man, which may lower the propensity for sexual abuse, and less likelihood of having children, which may lower stress in trying to balance multiple roles and cope with financial demands; in addition, lesbians tend to share more household tasks, including child care. Ideas on which factors constitute risks and which serve as protections remain speculative.

The issue of genetic transmission of chemical dependency has been given minimal consideration in the literature on gay men and lesbians. Lewis and associates found no statistically significant difference in the proportion of lesbian and heterosexual women with alcoholic parents in their small sample, suggesting that there may be equal genetic risk of alcoholism between the groups.[73] Kus notes that little is known about whether there are general biological differences between gay men and men with other affectional preferences.[74] In a study Kus conducted, most alcoholic men reported drinking "abusively" from their first drink.[75] This may indicate that a genetic predisposition is a precursor of alcoholism in at least some gay men, as it may be in the general population. Family social history and other environmental factors have also only been touched on in the substance abuse research literature on gay men and lesbians. The oppression or unresolved coming-out issues faced by gay men and lesbians may interact with genetic and environmental factors to produce higher rates of substance abuse among them.

A neglected population in the substance abuse literature is gay male and lesbian adolescents. Wellisch and colleagues matched 14 gay male and lesbian adolescents who were substance abusers with 14 adolescent, heterosexual substance abusers.[76] All were clients of the same treatment program. They found that both groups received the same number of therapy sessions; however, sexuality was more often discussed in the therapy sessions of the gay and lesbian than heterosexual adolescents. The gay and lesbian adolescents were more likely to discuss sexual identity in their individual than group sessions. In fact, for the gay, lesbian, and heterosexual adolescents, there was more focus on substantive issues in individual rather than group sessions, suggesting that further study be done to determine the most effective treatment modalities for these young clients.

Shifrin and Solis report on a group of 266 gay and lesbian adolescents served by the Hetrick-Martin Institute, a multiservice agency offering an outreach program and counseling to gay and lesbian youths.[77] They note substantial levels of problematic alcohol and drug use and call for intervention on many levels to assist gay and lesbian young people who are often ignored, perhaps because professionals believe that both sexual experimentation and experimentation with alcohol and drugs are phases that will pass. The recent development of community programs for gay and lesbian youths may help these young people adopt more positive self-images and healthier life-styles, including less substance abuse.

Gay men and lesbians from African American, Hispanic American, and other cultural backgrounds are also overlooked in the literature. Icard and Traunstein have discussed black, gay, alcoholic men, the multiple sources of discrimination they face, and the need for attention to the interactions of substance abuse, ethnicity and culture, sexual preference, and reference groups in developing treatment plans for them.[78]

In a cross-cultural review, Ross and associates found "that homosexuality is present in the vast majority of cultures, and is generally stigmatized in only about one-third of them."[79] Since the United States is among the cultures that stigmatize homosexuality, Greene addresses mental health treatment issues for lesbians and gay men of several ethnic backgrounds, including the views of homosexuality expressed by different cultural groups in the United States and countertransference issues that therapists may experience in working with gay and lesbian clients.[80] As Greene concludes, "Aside from being culturally literate, the practitioner must develop a sense of the unique experience of the client with respect to the importance of their ethnic identity and sexual orientation and the need to establish priorities in an often confusing conflict of loyalties [among their group memberships]."[81] (Ethnic issues related to substance abuse are discussed in Chapter 11.) The relationships among gay and lesbian identity, cultural and ethnic background, and substance abuse and dependence need a great deal more exploration.

Prevention Issues

Opportunities for socialization and other activities—political, civic, religious, and so on—have proliferated in gay and lesbian communities. These activities, which raise awareness of issues affecting gay men, lesbians, and bisexuals and promote "gay pride," provide alternatives to the bars and may help avert substance abuse.[82] In the early 1980s, Mongeon and Ziebold offered a model for preventing alcohol abuse in gay communities.[83] Given distrust of traditional or mainstream society, they asserted that prevention can be successful only if it is a self-help effort among gay men and lesbians. Their optimism about such an approach is based on the success of similar strategies that have been used to control the spread of venereal diseases (they have also been used to contain the spread of HIV). Although it has been suggested that a contributing factor to alcoholism in gay and lesbian communities may

be greater tolerance and encouragement of excessive drinking,[84] Mongeon and Ziebold believe that the gay community is acutely aware of its drinking and drug problems.

Like many prevention models, Mongeon and Ziebold's model focuses on both change in the individual and change in the environment. The focus on the individual would involve an early intervention program "to increase self-esteem and coping skills."[85] (Similar approaches have been used with women and other oppressed groups.) There would also be an outreach program to change the environmental context in which drinking takes place. In bars, they recommend alcohol-free areas, alcohol-free hours of operation, and promotion of nonalcoholic beverages (that also produce a good profit for the bar owner), but Israelstam points out that gay bar owners may be more supportive of antidrug campaigns than alcohol prevention and education on their premises.[86] Some bars are permitting substance abuse screenings on their premises,[87] as has been done with testing for venereal disease and the human immunodeficiency virus.

Since the gay bars remain a place of socialization and political activity, Finnegan and Cook believe that "to flatly tell gay/lesbian clients to stay out of bars is not always the most therapeutic move."[88] They agree that changing socialization in bars may be a reasonable alternative, and Kus and Smith suggest that it is possible for recovering gays and lesbians to return to the bar scene.[89]

As socialization in bars gives way to other alternatives, knowledgeable professionals are helping clients identify other social outlets.[90] The development of community centers for gay and lesbian adults and youths may help further the emphasis on alternative means of socialization.[91] But an overarching concern in the literature is that, ultimately, it is reduction of both culturally reinforced and internalized homophobia and the integration of gay men, lesbians, and bisexuals into the broader society that will help prevent recourse to negative behaviors such as substance abuse.[92]

Treatment Issues

The empirical literature on chemical dependency treatment of gay men and lesbians is scarce, but a number of issues are raised in the clinical literature. They include denial and defensiveness, inclusion of significant others, and whether gay and lesbian clients are better treated in separate programs.

Denial and Defensiveness

Denial is the defense mechanism most often discussed in the chemical dependency literature (see Chapter 5). It also operates in the process of identifying as a gay man or lesbian. According to Finnegan and Cook, since being raised in a homophobic culture virtually ensures that gay men and lesbians will learn to be homophobic, the excessive use of alcohol and other drugs to cope with the self-hatred that arises from internalized homophobia is not surprising.[93] It has also been noted that gay men, lesbians, and bisexuals may use their sexual orientation and oppressed status as an excuse or rationalization for drug or alcohol use or as a means of diverting attention away from sobriety.[94] But it should not be assumed that clients are using this as a rationalization.[95] Hall, for example, notes that "providing that the alcohol [or drug] problem itself continues to be acknowledged, . . . concerns about sexual trauma, social control, heterosexism and male dominance should not be dismissed as avoidance or denial of the real alcohol [or drug] problem in lesbian clients."[96] Other suggestions have also been made for addressing a client's sexual orientation in the context of chemical dependency treatment. Finnegan and Cook believe that

> in order to treat their gay and lesbian clients in constructive and health-enhancing ways, counselors must be able to determine when to focus on their clients' alcoholism and basically ignore their sexual orientation and when to attend closely to client's sexual orientation and the interplay between it and the alcoholism. Although the

counselor needs always to be sensitive to sexual orientation, there are times when it must be directly addressed if it is creating problems for the client.[97]

Authors vary in the amount of attention they think should be given to sexual orientation, especially very early in the recovery process. Ziebold believes that "for the homosexual alcoholic, sexual identity will be paramount among his or her concerns and must be handled openly and without bias,"[98] although other professionals note that the lesbian clients they have served are more comfortable discussing their sexual orientation than their chemical dependency.[99] Although a confrontational style is not appropriate, exploration of a client's relationships and sexual history is often important.[100] In fact, Hellman recommends "direct and specific questioning" about the various issues that the client may present, such as substance abuse, psychiatric problems, and sexual orientation because it "helps to overcome the secretiveness and denial that are associated with stigmatizing issues."[101] Hellman suggests that the therapist set the stage for discusing such matters by acknowledging the discomfort they may elicit in the client. Colcher advises professionals to approach sexual orientation as they would other client characteristics such as age or ethnicity and to present themselves "in a warm, nonjudgmental way regarding homosexuality."[102]

The professional should be mindful of the stage of the coming-out process of the client in determining the focus on sexual orientation. In any case, good clinical judgment, including proceeding cautiously, should guide the therapist's work when there is uncertainty about the best course of treatment. Obtaining consultation may also be necessary. The illustration titled "Lesbian Chemical Dependency—A Composite Case" shows the importance of the professional's recognition and acceptance of a client's sexual identity.

Chemical dependency can be as stigmatizing in gay communities as it is in straight communities,[103] and some believe that treating alcoholics

Lesbian Chemical Dependency—A Composite Case

Louise Warren, MSSW, LMSW-ACP

Leslie was 23 the first time she sought help for her dual addiction to alcohol and amphetamines. She began drinking at age 16. Leslie was living in a midsized Texas city with her parents and two older brothers. She knew at age 14 that she was attracted to girls. When her friends at school talked about boys, she felt vaguely disinterested. She knew that her relationships with girl friends were emotionally very important to her, and she began to feel sexually drawn to girls as well.

In her midteens Leslie would surreptitiously read lesbian literature, which was not difficult to obtain in her city. What *was* difficult was finding a person with whom to talk about her feelings or a place to do this. At age 16, she built up her courage and asked a sales clerk at a woman's book store where she might find "someone like me" to talk to. The woman suggested a popular lesbian bar.

Leslie described herself as "incredibly nervous" when she went to her first lesbian bar. Easily passing for 18, alcohol quickly addressed her anxiety. Leslie's father and grandfather also drank heavily. Within two weeks, Leslie met her first girlfriend, Paula. Paula and Leslie had a social life that revolved around meeting at the bar, shooting pool, and getting drunk. The relationship quickly became sexual. Although spending more and more time around lesbians and in environments heavily populated by lesbians felt rather comfortable for Leslie, becoming sexual was much more difficult. Paula, who was 20, noticed how difficult it was for Leslie to relax, and suggested that they do a line of cocaine on top of the alcohol. This created a pleasant psychological mixture of arousal and relaxation.

A pattern was thus created for Leslie. As with many lesbians, her social life revolved around the bar. Sexual experiences were accompanied by use of alcohol or alcohol and some type of stimulant.

Leslie finished high school with poor grades, made half-hearted attempts at going to a local community college, and eventually began working full-time for the family business.

Between the ages of 20 and 23, several significant events happened that underscored Leslie's worsening addictive disease. She received two DWIs and incurred serious financial debt in a effort to pay the consequent fines. Leslie had also begun shooting speed regularly, and as a result she developed three serious infections, one of which required hospitalization. Leslie also watched her brother go to prison on several drug charges.

Leslie first sought help after her brother's conviction. John had been both her closest ally in her family, as well as her primary drug source. She sought help at a women's addiction referral agency. Through the use of the Johns Hopkins Questionnaire, as well as information gathered through her social history, Leslie was told that she showed signs of being dually addicted to alcohol and speed. She was not particularly surprised and accepted several referrals for help. Leslie never told her counselor that she was lesbian, and the counselor never asked any questions that might have elicited this information. Leslie felt "it was none of her [the counselor's] business," and did not see any connection between her sexual identity and her chemical dependency.

She attempted to follow through on the suggested referrals, which included attending self-help meetings and seeing a counselor who specialized in alcohol and drug abuse issues. Roadblocks quickly presented themselves—all her lesbian friends drank heavily, and she had no idea where to meet other women. She did not feel comfortable in self-help meetings. Anything she might have shared seemed to include coming out as a lesbian, and she thought she would be laughed at and not taken seriously. Besides, she thought, how were these straight people going to

(continued)

understand *her?* For the first time in her life, during these first few sober days, she began to feel ashamed of her sexuality.

Leslie got drunk seventy-two hours after seeking help, and stayed drunk for another two years. During this time, her brother was released from jail, and then returned on new drug-related offenses. After visiting him in prison, she once again sought help from the women's addiction referral agency.

Leslie saw a new counselor, who utilized the same assessment tools as before, but who also picked up on subtle cues provided by the client. Leslie talked about "them" in reference to significant others. She also talked about "the bar" in ways that indicated it was at least equally a social club as it was a place to drink alcohol. The counselor used the same pronouns as Leslie, thereby not assuming that Leslie was heterosexual, and asked Leslie if she knew of places to meet people in addition to the bar. After a few moments of silence, Leslie told the counselor she was lesbian. The counselor told Leslie that she, too, was lesbian, and was a recovering alcoholic.

With this barrier down, Leslie was able for the first time to fully discuss her chemical dependency. She stated she knew she needed help, she just had no idea how to be sober and still be able to have a fulfilling social, emotional, and sexual life. The counselor used appropriate self-disclosure to provide Leslie with enough hope so that she could begin to seriously consider sobriety. This time Leslie was referred to gay and lesbian self-help meetings and to a treatment center with an openly lesbian counselor. Treatment lectures included content on internal and social homophobia.

At this writing, Leslie has nine years of sobriety, is in a seven-year relationship, and runs the family business. She states that had she remained closeted, she would have died from her addiction.

who are gay or lesbian is a particularly difficult challenge because of their strong defense systems. According to Finnegan and Cook, "Every gay and lesbian person develops defenses to deal with the forces and stresses of oppression" and "the gay/lesbian alcoholic's defenses attain extra strength because the defenses against the disease of alcoholism and the disease of homophobia intertwine."[104] For gay men who are chemically dependent, there is a double stigma.[105] For lesbians, there may be a triple stigma, since chemically dependent women generally face more social disapproval than their male counterparts.[106] Members of ethnic minority groups may face added stigma.[107] Finnegan and Cook caution that chemical dependency professionals "need to be mindful of distinguishing between confronting defenses that protect alcoholism and respecting defenses that serve as survival mechanisms."[108]

Finnegan and McNally encourage professionals to develop a good understanding of diagnoses such as severe depression and posttraumatic stress disorder, since these problems may continue to plague those who are working recovery programs for chemical dependency even if they have a positive gay or lesbian identity.[109]

In addition to denial, other defenses may subvert treatment. When the professional treating the chemically dependent gay male or lesbian is heterosexual, the client may complain that he or she cannot relate to a straight counselor or that the counselor cannot effectively assist someone whose sexual orientation he or she does not share.[110] Similar scenarios occur when clients complain that a professional who has not recovered from addiction cannot understand their problems. Well-educated professionals anticipate these behaviors and usually address them by refocusing on the client's chemical dependency and restating their desire to assist the client. However, a client's desire for another counselor is not always resistance. It may be an accurate perception that the counselor is not accepting of gay, lesbian, and bisexual clients and is uncomfortable working with them.[111] Of the 145 gay men surveyed by Lohrenz and colleagues, 55 percent said they would prefer a therapist of the same sexual orientation if they needed assistance, and 42 percent said the therapist's sexual orientation was not a concern.[112] Israelstam describes a "bill of rights" for clients developed by San Francisco's Department of Health that includes the right to be treated by a professional sensitive to gay life-styles, including a professional of the same sexual preference.[113]

Significant Others

Scant attention has been given to including the partners of gay men and lesbians in substance abuse treatment.[114] Correcting these oversights includes changing policies such as "permitting visits from lovers in a detoxification hospital if the policy is 'family' only,"[115] but the issue can be far more complex. As has been noted, "given the limited size and scope of the lesbian community, it would not be surprising that the nonalcoholic lesbian might be reticent to alienate a friend or lover by confronting that person about her substance abuse."[116] A study by Weinberg indicates that gay men who drink excessively rarely report attempts to intervene by their friends, and that their friends do not support them in their attempts at sobriety.[117]

Whitney writes that gay or lesbian coalcoholics may be particularly prone to adopt the victim role because they are already demeaned in a homophobic society,[118] and Finnegan and McNally say that "being gay or lesbian . . . is perfect training for codependence."[119] (Codependency is also discussed in Chapter 10.) The term *codependency* is highly charged. As Hall comments, "Mutual reliance, which has historically meant survival for lesbians, may be unfairly pathologized as codependence."[120] However, among straights, gay men,

lesbians, and bisexuals, some individuals are desperately trying to hold on to their partners as a result of low self-esteem. Whitney recommends group treatment in this situation.[121]

The lack of role models for gay men and lesbians makes it difficult to know what a healthy and happy intimate relationship is, and the disruption caused by chemical abuse makes it more difficult to achieve a fulfilling relationship.[122] Gay Al-Anon can be very helpful to gay and lesbian partners of chemically dependent individuals. Anderson and Henderson call "couples and family therapy . . . the treatment of choice when significant others are aiding in the maintenance of alcoholic drinking" by lesbians (and they suggest group treatment for substance abusers when significant others are not involved in their recovery).[123]

Taking a careful family history is essential to developing a meaningful treatment program, especially when clients have grown up in dysfunctional families, including families in which one or both parents were alcoholics or drug abusers[124] (also see Chapter 5). The gay and lesbian children of alcoholics face the stresses of adolescent development coupled with those of growing up in a dysfunctional family and homophobic society.[125] Shame, denial, secrecy, isolation, and other destructive behaviors may become the themes that pervade their lives.[126] Such problems make the development of healthy adult relationships extremely difficult and may result in fused or enmeshed relationships in adult life. Adult Children of Alcoholics (ACOA) groups and lesbian and gay ACOA groups can be important resources for these individuals. Warren believes that lesbians and gay men from alcoholic families may be at greater risk for developing chemical dependency because of their exposure to the bar culture and drinking in lesbian and gay communities.[127]

The inclusion of parents and siblings in the chemical dependency treatment of gay men and lesbians has also received little attention, even though this is an area well worth exploring. Exposing one's chemical abuse is generally difficult enough, but if "coming out" to family members is also involved, the process can be especially stressful for everyone concerned. According to Nardi, the client is likely to be concerned about being rejected on both counts, and parents may "focus on their own perceived failures in raising not only an alcoholic [or drug abuser] but also a homosexual."[128] At the Pride Institute, an inpatient chemical dependency treatment facility for gay men and lesbians, "some patients invite their families to participate in the [family portion of the] program specifically so they can come out."[129] In other cases, reunification with family or making amends when alcohol or drug use have caused family problems comes later in sobriety.[130]

Intervention can be an important step in getting substance abusers into treatment, but Ziebold notes that gays may not have family or even close friends to intervene; gays also reportedly have less job stability than other alcoholics, and therefore are less likely to have an employer to do this.[131] In the absence of other supports, acquaintances in the gay community may be the only ones available to intervene.[132] Unfortunately, there is a lack of programs and facilities designed to treat gay male and lesbian alcoholics, especially halfway houses,[133] which can be critical when family or significant others are not available.[134]

Treatment: Together or Apart?

Considerable debate exists as to whether chemical dependency treatment programs should be established for gay and lesbian clients separate from heterosexual clients.[135] Similar questions arise over whether women should be treated separately from men, and the logical extension is whether lesbians should be treated separately from gay men. Hawkins reported that of 30 lesbians that were alcoholic, 21 responded "not necessarily" or "no" when asked "Should alcoholism programs be solely operated by, for, and within the lesbian community."[136] Although some chemical dependency treatment programs provide special services for women, most do not provide any special accommodations for gay male and lesbian clients.[137]

There are apparently no studies comparing the effectiveness of separate programs for gay men and lesbians with programs in which these clients are treated with heterosexual clients.

There have been reports of over 100 specialized chemical dependency programs for gay men and lesbians in the United States.[138] According to Vourakis, many gay and lesbian clients do well in separate programs because the staff at these programs may be particularly adept at addressing chemical dependency and helping clients with concerns they may have about their sexual identity.[139] In this type of program, clients need not fear ostracism if they reveal their affectional preference. In fact, a goal of these programs is to affirm gay and lesbian life-styles and to foster gay pride.[140] Gay men and lesbians have a longstanding distrust of traditional social service agencies due to misdiagnosis of their problems or well-founded fears that providers were more interested in helping them change their sexual preference than treating their presenting problem.[141] Warren notes that a gay or lesbian counselor may be helpful, as can a recovering gay or lesbian counselor, but just because the therapist is gay or lesbian or the program is gay oriented does not mean that the therapist or program is good.[142] She also notes that a negative experience with a gay or lesbian service provider may be even more devastating for a gay or lesbian client because their expectations may be so high.

One drawback of separate programs is that they may reinforce homophobia in heterosexual professionals and contribute to alienation of gay men and lesbians from the rest of society.[143] Hellman and colleagues also note that programs that treat clients sensitively, regardless of their sexual preference, are needed by those unsure of their sexual identity and for those who are concerned about exposure of their gay or lesbian identity.[144] Several authors have commented on the usefulness of gay clients receiving social approval from straight as well as gay treatment providers.[145] Additional arguments for "integrated" treatment are that it "offers a richness of experience, maintains a proper focus on alcoholism as the primary disease, and facilitates adjustment to the real world after treatment."[146] If treatment programs were more sensitive to the needs of gays and lesbians, separate programs may not be needed.[147] Blume believes that rather than separate programs, "the solution really lies in changing existing agencies so that everyone can be served."[148]

Vourakis recommends the use of heterosexual and openly homosexual staff in treatment programs and adds that gay treatment staff, both recovering and nonalcoholic, can serve as important role models for gay men and lesbians who are newly "clean" and sober.[149] However, she notes that gay and lesbian counselors often do not come out to the professional community, because they are unsure of their colleagues' views on homosexuality, or because they have reason to believe their colleagues would not be accepting. This deprives gay male and lesbian clients of important role models.[150] Clearly, closer association between gay, lesbian, and bisexual communities and the chemical dependency treatment community would be beneficial.

Vourakis also believes that clients should not necessarily be in the same treatment group solely because they are gay or lesbian; there is a great deal of diversity among gay men and lesbians requiring that individual characteristics and preferences be taken into account. The difficulty in identifying enough gay, lesbian, or bisexual clients in some areas to form a group is also an obstacle to separate treatment, and adequate funding to support separate programs is another. Nicoloff and Stiglitz suggest offering special services for gay and lesbian clients within alcohol and drug abuse programs, but they acknowledge that administrators may fear that client referrals and funding might be jeopardized if the agency becomes "gay identified."[151] Colcher recommends incorporating alcoholism professionals in agencies that specialize in providing health care services to gay men and lesbians.[152] Ziebold urges gay communities to offer substance abuse intervention services through gay-identified agencies.[153] Kus also en-

courages the gay community to reach out and assist alcohol treatment centers.[154] Conversely, substance abuse programs could do more outreach in gay, lesbian, and bisexual communities.

When mainstream programs reach out to gay, lesbian, bisexual, and heterosexual clients, the homophobia of heterosexual clients often needs to be addressed. For example, heterosexual clients may misinterpret a gay man or lesbian's social interaction with them as "coming on."[155] Although the question of separate or mutual services remains unresolved, the principle of client self-determination indicates that the professional's responsibility is to help the client explore all the treatment options, and the client's responsibility is to select from among the available options. As Hall states about lesbians, in particular, "Recognizing the historical, social, and political ramifications of lesbians' alcohol problems, providers ought to offer supportive flexibility rather than directiveness."[156]

Chemical Dependency Professionals

Individuals working in the field of chemical dependency may harbor their own prejudices toward gay men and lesbians. Finnegan and McNally say that "don't ask, don't tell" has typified the relationship between treatment professionals and clients in the chemical dependency field.[157] And Blume believes that paraprofessionals in the field "sometimes hold very traditional values, values that have not been challenged through professional training or supervision."[158] Many authors have described the abominable treatment that gay and lesbian clients have received from health, mental health, and substance abuse service providers.[159] Consciousness-raising groups and staff education have been recommended as necessary to encourage better treatment.[160]

Gaining credibility in gay and lesbian communities requires that chemical dependency professionals, especially those who are heterosexual, network with individuals serving gay male, lesbian, and bisexual clients in health care, counseling, and other agencies. Building relationships with civic groups and other organizations in the gay community such as the Metropolitan Community Church, social clubs, and political groups is also necessary. Developing contacts within Gay AA and attending meetings of Gay AA (as appropriate) is recommended, as is displaying gay- and lesbian-sensitive literature in one's office.[161] Clinicians who find that they are unable to overcome their discomfort with homosexuality have an obligation to refer gay male, lesbian, and bisexual clients to therapists who can better treat them.[162] In addition to addressing one's own homophobia, professionals need to become comfortable with discussing sexuality with clients, regardless of their own affectional preference.[163] Ubell and Sumberg state that the client may express "anger towards the therapist's heterosexuality, as a representation of the injustices that the client has experienced."[164] They recommend that therapists appreciate this anger, examine their own beliefs about homosexuality (this may take more introspection than initially presumed), and demonstrate their acceptance of a gay or lesbian life-style.

Hellman and colleagues[165] and Israelstam[166] have studied the attitudes and knowledge of chemical dependency service providers concerning lesbians and gay men. The 164 professionals in New York City who responded to the Hellman survey felt that their education about gay male and lesbian life-styles was inadequate, that clinical supervision in this area was lacking, and that they had limited knowledge about referral resources for these clients. The therapists' academic degrees and years of practice were not related to their knowledge of working with gay male and lesbian alcoholics, but as might be expected, gay male and lesbian professionals reported being most prepared to work with this clientele. There was an awareness among most respondents that gay men and lesbians have unique treatment needs, and many also thought that achieving so-

briety was as difficult, if not more difficult, for them compared with heterosexuals. In spite of their reported lack of knowledge, 82 percent of the professionals indicated that they were comfortable working with gay men and lesbians, and 79 percent said they would treat them rather than refer them elsewhere.

Israelstam's study included responses from 85 substance abuse professionals in Ontario, Canada. Respondents indicated that they were most comfortable working with heterosexual clients and least comfortable with clients trying to hide their homosexuality; comfort level with openly gay men or lesbians fell in between. Three-quarters of the respondents believed that it was important to take sexual orientation into account when treating alcoholism, but they were divided on the issue of whether gay men and lesbians needed specialized treatment for their drinking problems. Few of the respondents had any specialized education in working with gay men or lesbians.

In an attempt to look at the sensitivity issue from the client's perspective, MacEwan conducted a study in New Zealand of 25 gays, 25 lesbians, 25 heterosexual men, and 25 heterosexual women, all of whom who had been treated for alcohol problems (53 different alcohol and drug treatment providers were represented).[167] He found that at the time intake was completed, 96 percent of the heterosexual men and 88 percent of the heterosexual women, but only 36 percent of the gay men and 12 percent of the lesbians, thought that the treatment provider "was clear about their sexual orientation." By the end of treatment, all the heterosexuals, 92 percent of the gay men, but only 52 percent of the lesbians thought their sexual orientation was clear to the provider. All the heterosexuals "felt their sexual orientation was included in their treatment plan," but only 43 percent of the gay men and 46 percent of the lesbians who had disclosed their sexual orientation felt that it was included in their treatment plan. When those whose sexual orientation was unclear to the provider were added, 60 percent of the gay men and 70 percent of the lesbians thought their sexual orientation was not taken into account. Only 4 percent of the straight men and 12 percent of the heterosexual women felt that the treatment provider thought their sexual orientation was a causative factor in the substance abuse, compared with 62 percent of lesbians and 74 percent of the gay men.

Among those receiving group therapy in this study, 95 percent of the straight women, 90 percent of the straight men, and 63 percent of the lesbians felt positively about this treatment modality, compared to only 14 percent of gay men. The gay men and lesbians who felt negatively about group treatment frequently mentioned feeling unsafe and feeling stereotyped. Some 40 percent of the straight women, 20 percent of the straight men, 8 percent of the lesbians, and 4 percent of the gay men said that their partner or significant other was asked to participate in treatment. Although the time since treatment was rather short in this study, slightly more than three-quarters of the straight subjects felt that treatment had helped improve their substance abuse problem, compared to slightly less than half of the gay men and lesbians.

The Recovery Movement and Twelve-Step Groups

Although there is really no way of knowing, Bittle believes that gay men and lesbians are underrepresented in AA,[168] but there is substantial support for the position that Twelve-Step programs such as Alcoholics Anonymous can be important resources for gay men and lesbians.[169] Kominars indicates that the program helps both gay and straight people because it addresses four obstacles blocking the way to recovery—"anger, fear, guilt, and isolation."[170] In an effort to encourage participation in self-help programs and to help explore aspects of chemical dependency specific to them, "special interest" groups for gays and lesbians have emerged.[171] Gay Alcoholics Anonymous is the best known, and Israelstam calls it "the largest

of A.A.'s splinter groups."[172] Sometimes they are called Lambda groups for the 11th letter of the Greek alphabet, which stands for liberation.[173] Some groups are for gay men only or lesbians only. There is also Alcoholics Together, which began in Los Angeles in 1970 to meet the needs of gay men and lesbian alcoholics.[174] Israelstam believes that the self-help movement has been more responsive to drinking problems among gays than professionals have been.

Although the only requirement for membership in AA is a desire for sobriety, some members may hold stereotypical beliefs about gay men and lesbians.[175] Bittle offers a number of other reasons for his perception that Alcoholics Anonymous may be "experienced by gay people as hostile or unattractive:"[176]

1. AA emphasizes the similarities rather than the differences among members, but gay men and lesbian members are likely to feel that their sexual or affectional preference is a difference that cannot be ignored.

2. The feeling that many members are not comfortable with issues of homosexuality causes gay men and lesbians to hide their sexual or affectional preference, which is harmful to their well-being. This conflicts with AA's emphasis on honesty.[177]

3. Although the fellowship of AA encourages members to develop a program of recovery unique to one's life-style, individual members may offer their own approach as the preferred method. As a result, the program often appears to be orthodox and rigid to gay men and lesbians (as it can to heterosexuals).

4. In the early stages of recovery, the idea of sexual abstinence is often promoted to members, as is putting sexuality issues on the "back burner" until more stable sobriety is achieved, yet the issues of sexuality and alcohol abuse are often inextricably linked for the gay man or lesbian and likely need to be addressed together. (This is often also true for heterosexuals.)

5. Gay men and lesbian members (as well as heterosexuals) often encounter difficulty with the concepts of God, a higher power, and spirituality, since traditional religious groups have often condemned their sexual orientation and practices (and perhaps their alcoholism). However, the spiritual dimension of recovery, which may be interpreted quite broadly, can be important and should not be overlooked.[178]

There is some disagreement over the role AA and NA might play in the life of a recovering gay man or lesbian. Ziebold writes that in spite of their usefulness, AA and Gay AA "do not provide a social setting to substitute for gay bar life, nor do they offer the more intense short-term therapy required by many alcoholics to get firmly started into successful recovery."[179] But Warren notes that many lesbians do find social fulfillment in these groups.[180] According to Saulnier, "The lesbian Twelve Step movement has functioned as a way of defining oneself within a community of similar others, as a means of finding a lesbian place in a heterosexual world and a feminist place in AA, and, not to be underestimated, an alternative source of socializing and perhaps a place to meet a life partner."[181]

Obstacles to utilizing self-help groups may reflect the individual's interpretation of these programs. They are not an answer for everyone, but professionals as well as AA, Gay AA, and NA members can help gay, lesbian, and bisexual newcomers appreciate their usefulness.

To use AA more effectively, Bittle encourages gay men and lesbians to obtain a gay or lesbian sponsor or one who is knowledgeable about and comfortable with these life-styles, and he recommends they use additional support groups to address issues not regularly discussed in AA meetings.[182] He also encourages them to foster education within AA about gay men and lesbians once they have achieved solid sobriety and comfort with their sexual or affectional preference.

In his study of the etiology of chemical dependency in homosexual men, Kus discovered

four elements of participation in AA that were important in helping the respondents accept their homosexuality:[183]

1. Just as AA members accept that they are powerless over alcohol, it may be helpful to accept that individuals are powerless over their affectional preference or sexual orientation (i.e., it cannot be changed).
2. In making one's moral inventory during the fourth step of the AA program, acknowledging anger and resentment about being gay can help eliminate these feelings. In working on this step, homophobia, self-hatred, and other negative feelings can also be addressed. The sixth and seventh steps addressing character defects and shortcomings can also be used to help remove these self-defeating feelings.
3. Recognizing that continued sobriety requires coming to peace with other issues (such as sexual identity and family issues) may result in acceptance of one's self as gay.
4. Associating with gays in AA and attending other self-help groups for gay alcoholics and addicts can also facilitate acceptance through positive role models.

Kus urges urban AA groups to provide a "loner" network for rural gays who do not have the benefit of Gay AA, which can be done with letters, phone calls, and visits.[184] He also reminds gays in rural areas that it only takes two to make a meeting, and he encourages travel to communities with Gay AA whenever possible.

Israelstam discusses the various perspectives on whether AA or Gay AA is best suited for gay men and lesbians.[185] The opinions vary, with some saying that Gay AA allows more freedom in discussing gay issues[186] and others indicating that at AA there is less "sex talk" and that members generally have longer sobriety and help more with the spiritual aspects of the program.[187] Among the advantages of attending meetings for gay men and lesbians are that trust may be more readily established when everyone is gay or lesbian and there is a shared gay or lesbian experience; there is little need to teach others about the gay or lesbian experience, as there is in other meetings; it is easier to work on reducing internalized homophobia; and it can provide a source of new supportive gay or lesbian peers.[188] However, in discussing gay men, Kus and Latcovich note that as a result of internalized homophobia, regular meetings may be preferable until a period of sobriety is established, followed by attendance at meetings for gays.[189]

In his study of 28 gay men and 1 lesbian who were recovering alcoholics, Saunders found that most currently attended AA, and most attended both general and gay meetings.[190] Kus and Latcovich believe "that attending gay men's groups is most often seen by gay men as an important *adjunct* to attending regular groups; attending gay groups is *in addition to*, rather than *instead of*, attending regular groups."[191] Hall notes that "not all lesbians in recovery prefer lesbian AA meetings, which may reflect needs characterizing particular periods of recovery, demographic differences or dynamics of lesbian groups in general."[192] Some observers encourage attendance at AA as well as Gay AA, since AA helps gay men and lesbians recognize the similarities that they do share with other alcoholics,[193] and it helps broaden one's perspective.[194] Lesbians may also benefit from women's AA groups and from Women for Sobriety (see Chapter 15).

As in the literature on women, the literature on the use of AA by lesbians as well as gay men suggests that the concept of powerlessness in the program may be contrary to the needs of members of already oppressed groups.[195] In addition, some self-help groups for gay men or lesbians take a separatist attitude, "reinforcing members' views of the world-at-large as hostile to gays, and increasing feelings of alienation and isolation."[196] Some clients may wish to hear this message, but others will likely prefer a more integrationist approach.

Twelve-Step programs such as AA may serve to meet the spiritual needs of gay men and lesbians. In fact, AA has been described as a spiritual program of recovery. Spirituality is a highly personal concept, but Kus interviewed 50 gay men who participated in AA and found that they

> practiced spirituality by maintaining sobriety, ridding themselves of internalized homophobia, communicating with their Higher Power (who was defined as God by the overwhelming majority of the study's participants), turning their lives and wills to the care of God as they understood Him, performing good works . . . , meeting adult social roles, engaging in self-examination, applying AA slogans to everyday life, sharing themselves with others, attending AA meetings, seeking forgiveness, reading positive gay, alcoholic, and other literature, engaging in rituals, engaging in sacrifice and discipline, and doing everyday tasks as well as they possibly could.[197]

This very broad description leaves room for nearly everyone to identify elements of spirituality in their lives if they wish to do so.

Chemical dependency professionals may assist clients in meeting spiritual needs by making referrals to clergy or religious groups who are known to be sensitive to gays and lesbians.[198] Addressing spiritual and religious conflicts is a frequent part of the recovery process for alcoholics and addicts, and gay men and lesbians may need additional assistance with these issues due to the negative messages they have received from clergy and religious groups about both their drug use and their sexual orientation.[199] Heyward notes that substance abuse often proceeds to isolation, and as a result of heterosexism, homosexuality can also result in isolation; she believes that "the Christian religious tradition in the modern West has done much to shape a *theology of loneliness and autonomy* to undergird this alienation" (italics hers).[200] She also blames the institution of psychiatry for its overemphasis on individuation and autonomy. However, she notes the potential of the church and of therapy to provide for empowerment and the important role that sensitive clergy and therapists can play in gay men and lesbians' recovery from chemical dependency. Heyward also believes that AA promotes connection with others, calling recovery a "relational adventure" in which "*We* discover that our healing is *with* one another" (italics hers).[201]

Although there is apparently very little literature on it, Saulnier says that "lesbian involvement in Al-Anon seems to have followed on the heels of lesbians' concern with the place of alcohol in their lives."[202] Saulnier used a small sample to study a lesbian Al-Anon group. She found that many of the attendees reported that their lives had not been directly affected by alcoholism, perhaps indicating the lack of other support groups available for lesbian women. She also noted that the group she attended sometimes tried to conform to traditional Al-Anon (a program originally designed for wives of alcoholic men) and sometimes tried to adapt to meet lesbian or feminist concerns.

Finally, a comment should be made about the controversies over the recovery movement—an issue that seems to be of more concern among lesbians rather than gay men, perhaps due to greater powerlessness experienced by women. Some relate lesbians' embrace of the recovery movement to a concern with "healthy self-development,"[203] whereas others believe that the focus on personal deficits or intrapsychic work comes at the expense of political activism.[204] Apparently, Twelve-Step programs have become such a part of the lesbian culture that some lesbian comedians incorporate them into their acts.[205] Hall believes that the controversy over the place of the recovery movement in lesbian communities is best resolved by moving from a single-approach perspective to one that allows for many options.[206]

Resources

We conclude this chapter with information on some of the resources that can be helpful in serving lesbians, gay men, and bisexuals who have chemical abuse and dependency problems. The National Association of Lesbian and Gay Alco-

holism Professionals (NALGAP, 440 Grand Avenue, Suite 401, Oakland, CA 94610-5085, 510-465-0547), formerly the National Association of Gay Alcoholism Professionals, was established in 1979 to address chemical dependency among gay men and lesbians and homophobia among treatment providers.[207] NALGAP was established with four major goals: (1) to encourage support and communication among professionals in the field, (2) to educate those working with gay men or lesbians who are chemically dependent, (3) to raise the consciousness about alcoholism and other drug abuse in gay and lesbian communities in order to overcome denial, and (4) to advocate for improved treatment of alcoholics and other drug abusers who are gay or lesbian.[208] The organization maintains a directory of chemical dependency services and educational materials for gay men, lesbians, bisexuals, and transgendered individuals. NALGAP works with others concerned about these groups and with those concerned about chemical dependency.

The National Lesbian and Gay Health Foundation (1407 S Street NW, Washington, DC 20009, 202-797-3536) provides information on substance abuse and other health issues. Gay Alcoholics Anonymous World Service Office can be reached at 475 Riverside Drive, New York, NY 10115 (212-777-1800), and Gay Al-Anon Intergroup Referral at 220 Park Avenue South, New York, NY 10003 (212-254-7230). The Center for Substance Abuse Prevention produces *Alcohol, Tobacco, and Other Drugs Resource Guide: Lesbians, Gay Men, and Bisexuals*, which contains a listing of useful resources as well as a bibliography.[209] The Gayellow Pages (P.O. Box 292, Village Station, New York, NY 10014, 212-674-0120) also lists services and resources of many types.

A number of outpatient and inpatient programs that specialize in treating gay men and lesbians with substance abuse problems have assisted professionals interested in working with this clientele. Two of them are the Whitman-Walker Clinic located in Washington, DC, and the Pride Institute in Waltham, Massachusetts.

Summary

Although additional evidence is needed to determine whether chemical dependency is more prevalent among lesbians and gay men than among heterosexuals, the use of alcohol and drugs to excess remains an issue for gay, lesbian, and bisexual communities. The specific etiologies of substance abuse in the general population remain unclear, but there is concern that the oppression faced by gay men, lesbians, and bisexuals may contribute to increased use of alcohol and other drugs. Many human service professionals lack the depth of understanding of gay, lesbian, and bisexual life-styles that may improve services to these groups. Prominent among the treatment issues raised by substance abuse among lesbians, gay men, and bisexuals are the strong defense mechanisms used to protect both their sexual identity and their substance abuse.

Another issue is the inclusion of family members in the chemical dependency treatment of gay men, lesbians, and bisexuals, which can be difficult because family members may not recognize the individual's sexual orientation. Although it should go without saying, it is also essential that the partners of gay men and lesbians be included in treatment, especially because many of these individuals have not had the opportunity to observe healthy relationships among gay or lesbian couples. There is considerable debate about whether the preferred method of treating gay men, lesbians, and bisexuals is within mainstream treatment programs or whether they should be treated separately. Some believe that societal homophobia requires that treatment be separate, because professional service providers as well as heterosexual clients may also harbor these negative feelings. Others believe that such separatism reinforces homophobia and fails to contribute to a more just society.

The self-help movement also figures prominently in the recovery of lesbians, gay men, and bisexuals who are chemically dependent. Gay AA and Alcoholics Together typify the self-help groups addressed to these populations. Other organizations, especially the National Association of Lesbian and Gay Alcoholism Professionals, are also important resources in helping to serve this clientele better.

Endnotes

1. Language is an important aspect of all cultures; so too is it important among gay men, lesbians, and bisexuals. The word *homosexual* means a preference for sexual and affectional partners of the same gender; see Raymond M. Berger, "Homosexuality: Gay Men," in Anne Minahan (Ed.), *Encyclopedia of Social Work*, Volume 1, 18th ed. (Silver Spring, MD: National Association of Social Workers, 1987), pp. 795–805; and A. Elfin Moses and Robert O. Hawkins, Jr., *Counseling Lesbian Women and Gay Men: A Life-Issues Approach* (St. Louis, MO: C. V. Mosby, 1982). Although the term *homosexual* continues to be used in the literature, many consider it not only passe but unacceptable; see Robert J. Kus, "Alcoholism and Non-Acceptance of Gay Self: The Critical Link," *Journal of Homosexuality*, Vol. 15, Nos. 1–2 (1988), note 1, p. 39; also see Sophie Freud Loewenstein, "Understanding Lesbian Women," *Social Casework*, Vol. 61, No. 1 (January 1980), p. 29. Some individuals reject any labeling at all; see James L. Hawkins, "Lesbianism and Alcoholism," in Milton Greenblatt and Marc A. Schuckit (Eds.), *Alcoholism Problems in Women and Children* (New York: Grune & Stratton, 1976), pp. 137–153. In this chapter, we generally use the terms *lesbian, gay man,* and *bisexual,* except in some references to other authors' works that utilize the term *homosexual*.

2. Sandra C. Anderson and Donna C. Henderson, "Working with Lesbian Alcoholics," *Social Work*, Vol. 30, No. 6 (1985), pp. 518–525; and Lowenstein, "Understanding Lesbian Women."

3. Thomas O. Ziebold, "Alcoholism and Recovery: Gays Helping Gays," *Christopher Street*, Vol. 3, No. 6 (January 1979), p. 36.

4. Thomas O. Ziebold and John E. Mongeon, "Introduction: Alcoholism and the Homosexual Community," *Journal of Homosexuality*, Vol. 7, No. 4 (1982), pp. 3–7; Herbert J. Freudenberger, "The Gay Addict in a Drug and Alcohol Abuse Therapeutic Community," *Homosexual Counseling Journal*, Vol. 3, No. 1 (1976), pp. 34–45; and Sandee Potter, "Social Work, Traditional Health Care Systems and Lesbian Invisibility," *Journal of Social Work and Human Sexuality*, Vol. 3, No. 2–3 (1984–1985), pp. 59–68.

5. Dana G. Finnegan and Emily B. McNally, *Dual Identities: Counseling Chemically Dependent Gay Men and Lesbians* (Chicago: Hazelden, 1987).

6. Alfred C. Kinsey, Wardell B. Pomeroy, and Clyde E. Martin, *Sexual Behavior in the Human Male* (Philadelphia: W. B. Saunders, 1948); and Alan P. Bell and Martin S. Weinberg, *Homosexualities: A Study of Diversity among Men and Women* (New York: Simon & Schuster, 1978).

7. John O. G. Billy, Koray Tanfer, William R. Grady, and Daniel H. Klepinger, "The Sexual Behavior of Men in the United States," *Family Planning Perspectives*, Vol. 25, No. 2 (1993), pp. 52–60.

8. See, for example, Marcel T. Saghir and Eli Robins, *Male and Female Homosexuality: A Comprehensive Investigation* (Baltimore: Williams and Wilkins, 1973); Edward J. Small, Jr. and Barry Leach, "Counseling Homosexual Alcoholics: Ten Case Histories," *Journal of Studies on Alcohol*, Vol. 38, No. 11 (1977), pp. 2077–2086; Anderson and Henderson, "Working with Lesbian Alcoholics"; Michael W. Ross, James A. Paulsen, and Olli W. Stålström, "Homosexuality and Mental Health: A Cross-Cultural Review," *Journal of Homosexuality*, Vol. 15 (1988), pp. 131–152.

9. Judith M. Saunders and S. M. Valente, "Suicide Risk among Gay Men and Lesbians: A Review," *Death Studies*, Vol. 11 (1987), pp. 1–23; Marcel T. Saghir, Eli Robins, Bonnie Walbran, and Kathye A. Gentry, "Homosexuality. IV. Psychiatric Disorders and Disability in the Female Homosexual," *American Journal of Psychiatry*, Vol. 127, No. 2 (August 1970), pp. 147–154; and Marcel T. Saghir, Eli Robins, Bonnie Walbran, and Kathye A. Gentry, "Homosexuality: III. Psychiatric Disorders and Disability in the Male Homosexual," *American Journal of Psychiatry*, Vol. 126, No. 8 (February 1970), pp. 1079–1086.

10. See National Institute on Alcohol Abuse and Alcoholism, *Sixth Special Report to the U.S. Congress on Alcohol and Health* (Rockville, MD: U.S. Department of Health and Human Services, 1987), pp. 11–12; also see Saunders and Valente, "Suicide Risk among Gay Men and Lesbians: A Review."

11. Ronald E. Hellman, "Dual Diagnosis Issues with Homosexual Persons," *Journal of Chemical Dependency Treatment*, Vol. 5, No. 1 (1992), pp. 105–117.

12. See Ziebold and Mongeon, "Introduction: Alcoholism and the Homosexual Community."

13. See, for example, Craig A. Molgaard, Chester Nakamura, Melbourne Hovell, and John P. Elder, "Assessing Alcoholism as a Risk Factor for Acquired Immunodeficiency Syndrome (AIDS)," *Social Science & Medicine*, Vol. 27, No. 11 (1988), pp. 1147–1152; and Ron Stall and James Wiley, "A Comparison of Alcohol and Drug Use Patterns of Homosexual and Heterosexual Men: The San Francisco Men's Health Study," *Drug and Alcohol Dependence*, Vol. 22 (1988), pp. 63–73.

14. Lillene Fifield, *On My Way to Nowhere: Alienated, Isolated, Drunk* (Los Angeles: Gay Community Services Center & Department of Health Services, 1975), cited in Kus, "Alcoholism and Non-Acceptance of Gay Self"; Hawkins,

"Lesbianism and Alcoholism"; Molgaard et al., "Assessing Alcoholism as a Risk Factor"; Ethan E. Bickelhaupt, "Alcoholism and Drug Abuse in Gay and Lesbian Persons: A Review of Incidence Studies," *Journal of Gay & Lesbian Social Services*, Vol. 2, No. 1 (1995), pp. 5–14, also published in Robert J. Kus (Ed.), *Addiction and Recovery in Gay and Lesbian Persons* (Binghamton, NY: Haworth Press, 1995), pp. 5–14.

15. Martin S. Weinberg and Colin J. Williams, *Male Homosexuals: Their Problems and Adaptations* (New York: Oxford University Press, 1974), p. 116.

16. Leander J. Lohrenz, John C. Connelly, Lolafaye Coyne, and Keith E. Spare, "Alcohol Problems in Several Midwestern Homosexual Communities," *Journal of Studies on Alcohol*, Vol. 39, No. 11 (1978), pp. 1959–1963.

17. Saghir and Robins, *Male and Female Homosexuality*; also see Saghir et al., "Homosexuality IV. Psychiatric Disorders and Disability in the Female Homosexual"; and Saghir et al., "Homosexuality III. Psychiatric Disorders and Disability in the Male Homosexual."

18. Collins E. Lewis, Marcel T. Saghir, and Eli Robins, "Drinking Patterns in Homosexual and Heterosexual Women," *Journal of Clinical Psychiatry*, Vol. 43, No. 7 (1982), pp. 277–279.

19. Judith Bradford, Caitlin Ryan, and Esther D. Rothblum, "National Lesbian Health Care Survey: Implications for Mental Health Care," *Journal of Consulting and Clinical Psychology*, Vol. 62, No. 2 (1994), pp. 228–242.

20. Bickelhaupt, "Alcoholism and Drug Abuse in Gay and Lesbian Persons: A Review of Incidence Studies."

21. E. S. Morales and M. A. Graves, *Substance Abuse: Patterns and Barriers to Treatment for Gay Men and Lesbians in San Francisco* (San Francisco: San Francisco Prevention and Resources Center, 1983).

22. J. Kelly (Ed.), *San Francisco Lesbian, Gay, and Bisexual Alcohol and Other Drugs Needs Assessment Study*, Vol. 1 (Sacramento, CA: EMT Associates, 1991).

23. Joseph H. Neisen and Hilary Sandall, "Alcohol and Other Drug Abuse in a Gay/Lesbian Population: Related to Victimization?" *Journal of Psychological and Human Sexuality*, Vol. 3, No. 1 (1990), pp. 151–168; also see David J. McKirnan and Peggy L. Peterson, "Alcohol and Drug Use among Homosexual Men and Women: Epidemiology and Population Characteristics," *Addictive Behaviors*, Vol. 14 (1989), pp. 545–553; Stall and Wiley, "A Comparison of Alcohol and Drug Use Patterns of Homosexual and Heterosexual Men"; Potter, "Social Work, Traditional Health Care Systems and Lesbian Invisibility," p. 62.

24. Reprinted from *Addictive Behaviors*, Volume 14, David J. McKirnan and Peggy L. Peterson, "Alcohol and Drug Use among Homosexual Men and Women: Epidemiology and Population Characteristics," pp. 545–553, Copyright 1989, with kind permission from Pergamon Press Ltd, Headington Hill Hall, Oxford OX3 OBW, UK.

25. Walter B. Clark and Lorraine Midanik, "Alcohol Use and Alcohol Problems among U.S. Adults: Results of the 1979 National Survey," in National Institute on Alcohol Abuse and Alcoholism, *Alcohol and Health: Alcohol Consumption and Related Problems*, Monograph No. 1 (Rockville, MD: U.S. Dept. of Health and Human Services, 1982).

26. Richard R. Clayton, Harwin L. Voss, Cynthia Robbins, and William F. Skinner, "Gender Differences in Drug Use: An Epidemiological Perspective," in Barbara A. Ray and Monique C. Braude (Eds.), *Women and Drugs: A New Era for Research, NIDA Research Monograph 65* (Washington, DC: U.S. Government Printing Office, 1986), pp. 80–99.

27. McKirnan and Peterson, "Alcohol and Drug Use among Homosexual Men and Women," p. 552.

28. Stall and Wiley, "A Comparison of Alcohol and Drug Use Patterns."

29. William F. Skinner and Melanie D. Otis, "Drug and Alcohol Use among Lesbian and Gay People in a Southern U.S. Sample: Epidemiological, Comparative, and Methodological Findings from the Trilogy Project," *Journal of Homosexuality*, Vol. 30, No. 3 (1996), pp. 59–92, © 1996 by Haworth Press, Binghamton, NY; and William F. Skinner, "The Prevalence and Demographic Predictors of Illicit and Licit Drug Use among Lesbians and Gay Men," *American Journal of Public Health*, Vol. 84, No. 8 (1994), pp. 1307–1310.

30. National Institute on Drug Abuse, *National Household Survey on Drug Abuse: Main Findings 1988* (Rockville, MD: U.S. Government Printing Office, 1990).

31. For a discussion, see Christine Flynn Saulnier and Brenda A. Miller, "Alcohol and Drug Problems: Heterosexual versus Lesbian and Bisexual Women," *Canadian Journal of Human Sexuality*, in press, 1997.

32. Kim Bloomfield, "A Comparison of Alcohol Consumption between Lesbians and Heterosexual Women in an Urban Population," *Drug and Alcohol Dependence*, Vol. 3, No. 3 (1993), pp. 257–269.

33. Tonda L. Hughes and Sharon C. Wilsnack, "Research on Lesbians and Alcohol: Gaps and Implications," *Alcohol Health & Research World*, Vol. 18, No. 3 (1994), pp. 202–205, quote from p. 202.

34. Ziebold and Mongeon, "Introduction: Alcoholism and the Homosexual Community"; and William E. Bittle, "Alcoholics Anonymous and the Gay Alcoholic," *Journal of Homosexuality*, Vol. 7, No. 4 (1982), pp. 81–88.

35. P. Hastings, "Alcohol and the Lesbian Community: Changing Patterns of Awareness," *Surveyor*, Vol. 18 (1982), pp. 3–7, cited in Stephen Israelstam and Sylvia Lambert, "Homosexuals Who Indulge in Excessive Use of Alcohol and Drugs: Psychosocial Factors to Be Taken into Account by Community and Intervention Workers," *Journal of Alcohol and Drug Education*, Vol. 34, No. 3 (1989), pp. 54–69.

36. Stall and Wiley, "A Comparison of Alcohol and Drug Use Patterns."

37. Small and Leach, "Counseling Homosexual Alcoholics," p. 2077.

38. For a review of the literature supporting and refuting a causal relationship between alcoholism and homosexuality, see S. Israelstam and S. Lambert, "Homosexuality as a Cause of Alcoholism: A Historical Review," *The International Journal of the Addictions*, Vol. 18, No. 8 (1983), pp. 1085–1107; also see Joanne M. Hall, "Lesbians and Alcohol: Patterns and Paradoxes in Medical Notions and Lesbians' Beliefs," *Journal of Psychoactive Drugs*, Vol. 25, No. 2 (June 1993), pp. 109–119.

39. Small and Leach, "Counseling Homosexual Alcoholics," p. 2078.

40. See Stephen Israelstam, "Alcohol and Drug Problems of Gay Males and Lesbians: Therapy, Counselling and Prevention Issues," *The Journal of Drug Issues*, Vol. 16, No. 3 (1986), pp. 443–461.

41. Small and Leach, "Counseling Homosexual Alcoholics"; Peter M. Nardi, "Alcoholism and Homosexuality: A Theoretical Perspective," *Journal of Homosexuality*, Vol. 7, No. 4 (1982), pp. 9–25; and Ziebold and Mongeon, "Introduction."

42. Israelstam, "Alcohol and Drug Problems of Gay Males and Lesbians," p. 455; also see Sheppard B. Kominars, "Homophobia: The Heart of Darkness," *Journal of Gay & Lesbian Social Services*, Vol. 2, No. 1 (1995), pp. 29–39, also published in Kus, *Addiction and Recovery in Gay and Lesbian Persons*, pp. 29–39.

43. Lee K. Nicoloff and Eloise A. Stiglitz, "Lesbian Alcoholism: Etiology, Treatment, and Recovery," in Boston Lesbian Psychologies Collective (Ed.), *Lesbian Psychologies* (Urbana and Chicago: University of Illinois Press, 1987), pp. 283–293; also see Hall, "Lesbians and Alcohol: Patterns and Paradoxes in Medical Notions and Lesbians' Beliefs."

44. Christine L. Saulnier, "Lesbian Alcoholism: Development of a Construct," *Affilia*, Vol. 6, No. 3 (Fall 1991), pp. 66–84, quote from p. 77.

45. Jeffrey M. Brandsma and E. Mansell Pattison, "Homosexuality and Alcoholism," in E. Mansell Pattison and Edward Kaufman (Eds.), *Encyclopedic Handbook of Alcoholism* (New York: Gardner Press, 1982), pp. 736–741.

46. Ziebold and Mongeon, "Introduction," pp. 5–6, offer this comment referring to Merle Miller, *On Being Different* (New York: Random House, 1971).

47. McKirnan and Peterson, "Alcohol and Drug Use among Homosexual Men and Women," p. 552.

48. David J. McKirnan and Peggy L. Peterson, "Psychosocial and Cultural Factors in Alcohol and Drug Abuse: An Analysis of a Homosexual Community," *Addictive Behavior*, Vol. 14 (1989), pp. 555–563.

49. Thomas S. Weinberg, *Gay Men, Drinking, and Alcoholism* (Carbondale and Evansville, IL: Southern Illinois University Press, 1994).

50. Emily B. McNally and Dana G. Finnegan, "Lesbian Recovering Alcoholics: A Qualitative Study of Identity Transformation—A Report on Research Applications to Treatment," *Journal of Chemical Dependency Treatment,* Vol. 5, No. 1 (1992), pp. 93–103; Joanne M. Hall, "Alcoholism in Lesbians: Developmental, Symbolic Interactionist, and Critical Perspectives," *Health Care for Women International,* Vol. 11 (1990), pp. 89–107; and Weinberg, *Gay Men, Drinking, and Alcoholism.*

51. Weinberg, *Gay Men, Drinking, and Alcoholism.*

52. Hall, "Alcoholism in Lesbians: Developmental, Symbolic Interactionist, and Critical Perspectives."

53. McNally and Finnegan, "Lesbian Recovering Alcoholics: A Qualitative Study of Identity Transformation—A Report on Research Applications to Treatment."

54. Joanne M. Hall, "Alcoholism Recovery in Lesbian Women: A Theory in Development," *Scholarly Inquiry for Nursing Practice: An International Journal,* Vol. 4, No. 2 (1990), pp. 107–125.

55. Kus, "Alcoholism and Non-Acceptance of Gay Self."

56. See Ziebold, "Alcoholism and Recovery," p. 38, for a discussion.

57. John D'Emilio, *Sexual Politics, Sexual Communities: The Making of a Homosexual Minority in the United States 1940–1970* (Chicago: University of Chicago Press, 1983).

58. Ziebold, "Alcoholism and Recovery."

59. Kus, "Alcoholism and Non-Acceptance of Gay Self," copyright 1988, Haworth Press, Binghamton, NY; also see Robert J. Kus and George Byron Smith, "Referrals and Resources for Chemically Dependent Gay and Lesbian Clients," *Journal of Gay & Lesbian Social Services,* Vol. 2, No. 1 (1995), pp. 91–107, also published in Kus, *Addiction and Recovery in Gay and Lesbian Persons,* pp. 91–107.

60. See, for example, Moses and Hawkins, *Counseling Lesbian Women and Gay Men: A Life-Issues Approach;* Marta Ann Zehner and Joyce Lewis, "Homosexuality and Alcoholism: Social and Developmental Perspectives," in Robert Schoenberg and Richard S. Goldberg (Eds.), *With Compassion Toward Some, Homosexuality and Social Work in America* (New York: Harrington Park Press, 1985), pp. 75–89; and Cassandra Diamond-Friedman, "A Multivariant Model of Alcoholism Specific to Gay–Lesbian Populations," *Alcoholism Treatment Quarterly,* Vol. 7, No. 2 (1990), pp. 111–117.

61. McKirnan and Peterson, "Psychosocial and Cultural Factors in Alcohol and Drug Abuse: An Analysis of a Homosexual Community."

62. McNally and Finnegan, "Lesbian Recovering Alcoholics: A Qualitative Study of Identity Transformation—A Report on Research Applications to Treatment," p. 96.

63. Zehner and Lewis, "Homosexuality and Alcoholism: Social and Developmental Perspectives"; Kathleen O'Halleran Glaus, "Alcoholism, Chemical Dependency and

the Lesbian Client," *Women and Therapy,* Vol. 8, Nos. 1–2 (1988), pp. 131–144; and Vivian Ubell and David Sumberg, "Heterosexual Therapists Treating Homosexual Addicted Clients," *Journal of Chemical Treatment,* Vol. 5, No. 1 (1992), pp. 19–33.

64. Small and Leach, "Counseling Homosexual Alcoholics," p. 2084.

65. Ibid.

66. Lewis et al., "Drinking Patterns in Homosexual and Heterosexual Women."

67. Hawkins, "Lesbianism and Alcoholism."

68. Saghir and Robins, *Male and Female Homosexuality.*

69. Deborah L. Diamond and Sharon C. Wilsnack, "Alcohol Abuse among Lesbians: A Descriptive Study," *Journal of Homosexuality,* Vol. 4, No. 2 (Winter 1978), pp. 123–142.

70. Rebecca Schilit, W. Mark Clark, and Elizabeth Ann Shallenberger, "Social Supports and Lesbian Alcoholics," *Affilia,* Vol. 3, No. 2 (Summer 1988), p. 37.

71. Hughes and Wilsnack, "Research on Lesbians and Alcohol: Gaps and Implications."

72. Esther D. Rothblum, " 'I Only Read About Myself on Bathroom Walls': The Need for Research on the Mental Health of Lesbians and Gay Men," *Journal of Consulting and Clinical Psychology,* Vol. 62, No. 2 (1994), pp. 213–220, quote from p. 218.

73. Lewis et al., "Drinking Patterns in Homosexual and Heterosexual Women."

74. Robert J. Kus, "Alcoholics Anonymous and Gay American Men," *Journal of Homosexuality,* Vol. 14, Nos. 1–2 (1987), pp. 253–276; also see Nardi, "Alcoholism and Homosexuality: A Theoretical Perspective."

75. Kus, "Alcoholism and Non-Acceptance of Gay Self," pp. 31–32.

76. David K. Wellisch, G. G. DeAngelis, and Carl Paternite, "A Study of Therapy of Homosexual Adolescent Drug Users in a Residential Treatment Setting," *Adolescence,* Vol. 16, No. 63 (Fall 1981), pp. 689–700.

77. Francine Shifrin and Mirtha Solis, "Chemical Dependency in Gay and Lesbian Youth," *Journal of Chemical Dependency Treatment,* Vol. 5, No. 1 (1992), pp. 67–76.

78. Larry Icard and Donald M. Traunstein, "Black, Gay, Alcoholic Men: Their Character and Treatment," *Social Casework,* Vol. 68 (May 1987), pp. 267–272.

79. Ross et al., "Homosexuality and Mental Health: A Cross-Cultural Review," p. 142, copyright 1988, Haworth Press, Binghamton, NY.

80. Beverly Greene, "Ethnic–Minority Lesbians and Gay Men: Mental Health and Treatment Issues," *Journal of Consulting and Clinical Psychology,* Vol. 62, No. 2 (1994), pp. 243–251.

81. Ibid., pp. 249–250.

82. Ziebold, "Alcoholism and Recovery."

83. John E. Mongeon and Thomas O. Ziebold, "Preventing Alcohol Abuse in the Gay Community: Toward a Theory and Model," *Journal of Homosexuality*, Vol. 7, No. 4 (1982), pp. 89–99.

84. Peter M. Nardi, "Alcohol Treatment and the Non-Traditional 'Family' Structures of Gays and Lesbians," *Journal of Alcohol and Drug Education*, Vol. 27 (Winter 1982), pp. 83–89; also see Diamond and Wilsnack, "Alcohol Abuse among Lesbians."

85. Mongeon and Ziebold, "Preventing Alcohol Abuse in the Gay Community," p. 94; also see Kus, "Alcoholism and Non-Acceptance of Gay Self," for a discussion of the need to increase self-esteem.

86. Israelstam, "Alcohol and Drug Problems of Gay Males and Lesbians," p. 454.

87. Personal communication with Louise Warren.

88. Dana G. Finnegan and David Cook, "Special Issues Affecting the Treatment of Gay Male and Lesbian Alcoholics," *Alcoholism Treatment Quarterly*, Vol. 3 (1984), p. 97, copyright 1984, Haworth Press, Binghamton, NY; and Kus and Smith, "Referrals and Resources for Chemically Dependent Gay and Lesbian Clients."

89. Kus and Smith, "Referrals and Resources for Chemically Dependent Gay and Lesbian Clients."

90. Personal communication with Louise Warren; and Glaus, "Alcoholism, Chemical Dependency and the Lesbian Client."

91. Personal communication with Louise Warren.

92. Israelstam, "Alcohol and Drug Problems of Gay Males and Lesbians," p. 455; also see Kus, "Alcoholism and Non-Acceptance of Gay Self."

93. Finnegan and Cook, "Special Issues."

94. Small and Leach, "Counseling Homosexual Alcoholics"; also see Anderson and Henderson, "Working with Lesbian Alcoholics"; and Tom Mills Smith, "Specific Approaches and Techniques in the Treatment of Gay Male Alcohol Abusers," *Journal of Homosexuality*, Vol. 7, No. 4 (1982), pp. 53–69.

95. Anderson and Henderson, "Working with Lesbian Alcoholics," p. 521.

96. Hall, "Lesbians and Alcohol: Patterns and Paradoxes in Medical Notions and Lesbians' Beliefs," p. 116.

97. Finnegan and Cook, "Special Issues," p. 85, copyright 1984, Haworth Press, Binghamton, NY; also see Smith, "Specific Approaches."

98. Ziebold, "Alcoholism and Recovery," p. 41.

99. Personal communication with Louise Warren.

100. Finnegan and Cook, "Special Issues," p. 90; also see Smith, "Specific Approaches."

101. Hellman, "Dual Diagnosis Issues with Homosexual Persons," p. 111, copyright 1992, Haworth Press, Binghamton, NY.

102. Ronnie W. Colcher, "Counseling the Homosexual Alcoholic," *Journal of Homosexuality*, Vol. 7, No. 4 (1982), p. 48, copyright 1982, Haworth Press, Binghamton, NY; also see Hellman, "Dual Diagnosis Issues with Homosexual Persons."

103. Colcher, "Counseling the Homosexual Alcoholic," p. 49; also see C. A. Polo, "Common Sense Approach to Working with Gay Alcoholics," Alcohol and Drug Problems Association Meeting, New Orleans, LA, 1976, cited in Israelstam, "Alcohol and Drug Problems of Gay Males and Lesbians," p. 452.

104. Finnegan and Cook, "Special Issues," p. 89, copyright 1984, Haworth Press, Binghamton, NY.

105. Christine Vourakis, "Homosexuals in Substance Abuse Treatment," in Gerald Bennett, Christine Vourakis, and Donna S. Woolf (Eds.), *Substance Abuse: Pharmacologic, Developmental and Clinical Perspectives* (New York: John Wiley and Sons, 1983), pp. 400–419; also see Finnegan and Cook, "Special Issues."

106. Anderson and Henderson, "Working with Lesbian Alcoholics."

107. Finnegan and Cook, "Special Issues," p. 89.

108. Ibid.

109. Dana G. Finnegan and Emily B. McNally, "Chemical Dependency and Depression in Lesbians and Gay Men: What Helps?" *Journal of Gay & Lesbian Social Services*, Vol. 2, No. 1 (1995), pp. 115–129, also published in Kus, *Addiction and Recovery in Gay and Lesbian Persons*, pp. 115–129.

110. E. Sue Blume, "Substance Abuse (Of Being Queer, Magic Pills, and Social Lubricants)," in Hilda Hidalgo, Travis L. Peterson, and Natalie Jane Woodman (Eds.), *Lesbian and Gay Issues: A Resource Manual for Social Workers* (Silver Spring, MD: National Association of Social Workers, 1985), pp. 79–87.

111. Personal communication with Louise Warren.

112. Lohrenz et al., "Alcohol Problems in Several Midwestern Communities."

113. Israelstam, "Alcohol and Drug Problems of Gay Males and Lesbians"; also see Raymond M. Berger, "Health Care for Lesbians and Gays: What Social Workers Should Know," *Journal of Social Work & Human Sexuality*, Vol. 1, No. 3 (Spring 1983), pp. 59–73.

114. Nardi, "Alcohol Treatment and the Non-Traditional 'Family' Structures of Gays and Lesbians"; Ziebold and Mongeon, "Introduction"; Blume, "Substance Abuse"; Scott Whitney, "The Ties That Bind: Strategies for Counseling the Gay Male Co-Alcoholic," *Journal of Homosexuality*, Vol. 7, No. 4 (Summer 1982), pp. 37–41; and Ian MacEwan, "Differences in Assessment and Treatment Approaches for Homosexual Clients," *Drug and Alcohol Review*, Vol. 13 (1994), pp. 57–62.

115. Blume, "Substance Abuse," p. 85; also see Nicoloff and Stiglitz, "Lesbian Alcoholism."

116. Schilit et al., "Social Supports," p. 37.

117. Weinberg, *Gay Men, Drinking, and Alcoholism.*

118. Whitney, "The Ties That Bind."

119. Dana G. Finnegan and Emily B. McNally, "The Lonely Journey: Lesbians and Gay Men Who Are Codependent," *Alcoholism Treatment Quarterly*, Vol. 6, No. 1 (1989), p. 125, copyright 1989, Haworth Press, Binghamton, NY.

120. Hall, "Lesbians and Alcohol: Patterns and Paradoxes in Medical Notions and Lesbians' Beliefs."

121. Whitney, "The Ties That Bind."

122. Nardi, "Alcohol Treatment and the Non-Traditional 'Family' Structures"; also see Cheryl Hetherington, "Dysfunctional Relationship Patterns: Positive Changes for Gay and Lesbian People," *Journal of Gay and Lesbian Social Services*, Vol. 2, No. 1 (1995), pp. 41–55.

123. Anderson and Henderson, "Working with Lesbian Alcoholics," p. 522; also see Deborah J. Bushway, "Chemical Dependency Treatment for Lesbians and Their Families" in Claudia Bepko (Ed.), *Feminism and Addiction* (Binghamton, NY: Haworth, 1991), pp. 161–172.

124. Ubell and Sumberg, "Heterosexual Therapists Treating Homosexual Addicted Clients"; and Dava L. Weinstein, "Application of Family Therapy Concepts in the Treatment of Lesbians and Gay Men," *Journal of Chemical Dependency Treatment*, Vol. 5, No. 1 (1992), pp. 141–155.

125. Barbara P. Rothberg and Deirdre M. Kidder, "Double Trouble: Lesbians Emerging from Alcoholic Families," *Journal of Chemical Dependency Treatment*, Vol. 5, No. 1 (1992), pp. 77–92.

126. Ibid.

127. Personal communication with Louise Warren.

128. Nardi, "Alcohol Treatment and the Non-Traditional 'Family' Structures," p. 87.

129. Ellen Ratner, "A Model for the Treatment of Lesbian and Gay Alcohol Abusers," *Alcoholism Treatment Quarterly*, Vol. 5, No. 1/2 (1988), p. 42.

130. Kus and Smith, "Referrals and Resources for Chemically Dependent Gay and Lesbian Clients."

131. Ziebold, "Alcoholism and Recovery."

132. Ibid.

133. Rosanne Driscoll, "A Gay-Identified Alcohol Treatment Program: A Follow-Up Study," *Journal of Homosexuality*, Vol. 7, No. 4 (1982), pp. 71–80.

134. Israelstam, "Alcoholism and Drug Problems of Gay Males and Lesbians."

135. For a discussion of this issue, see Vourakis, "Homosexuals in Substance Abuse Treatment"; Israelstam, "Alcohol Problems of Gay Males and Lesbians"; and Nicoloff and Stiglitz, "Lesbian Alcoholism."

136. Hawkins, "Lesbianism and Alcoholism," p. 147.

137. Blume, "Substance Abuse."

138. See Diamond-Friedman, "A Multivariant Model of Alcoholism Specific to Gay–Lesbian Populations," p. 112.

139. Vourakis, "Homosexuals in Substance Abuse Treatment."

140. Ratner, "A Model for the Treatment."

141. Driscoll, "A Gay-Identified Alcohol Treatment Program"; and Nicoloff and Stiglitz, "Lesbian Alcoholism."

142. Personal communication with Louise Warren.

143. Tricia A. Zigrang, "Who Should Be Doing What About the Gay Alcoholic?" *Journal of Homosexuality*, Vol. 7, No. 4 (1982), pp. 27–35.

144. Ronald E. Hellman, Michael Stanton, Jacalyn Lee, Alex Tytun, and Ron Vachon, "Treatment of Homosexual Alcoholics in Government-Funded Agencies: Provider Training and Attitudes," *Hospital and Community Psychiatry*, Vol. 40, No. 11 (November 1989), pp. 1163–1168.

145. S. B. Smith and M. A. Schneider, "Treatment of Gays in a Straight Environment," National Drug Abuse Conference, 1978, cited in Israelstam, "Alcohol and Drug Problems of Gay Males and Lesbians."

146. Nicoloff and Stiglitz, "Lesbian Alcoholism," p. 288.

147. Vourakis, "Homosexuals in Substance Abuse Treatment"; also see Freudenberger, "The Gay Addict in a Drug Abuse Therapeutic Community."

148. Blume, "Substance Abuse," p. 83.

149. Vourakis, "Homosexuals in Substance Abuse Treatment."

150. Blume, "Substance Abuse," p. 86; also see Ratner, "A Model for the Treatment."

151. Nicoloff and Stiglitz, "Lesbian Alcoholism."

152. Colcher, "Counseling the Homosexual Alcoholic."

153. Ziebold, "Alcoholism and Recovery."

154. Kus, "Alcoholism and Non-Acceptance of Gay Self."

155. Nicoloff and Stiglitz, "Lesbian Alcoholism."

156. Hall, "Lesbians and Alcohol: Patterns and Paradoxes in Medical Notions and Lesbians' Beliefs," p. 116.

157. Dana G. Finnegan and Emily B. McNally, "The National Association of Lesbian and Gay Alcoholism Professionals (NALGAP): A Retrospective," *Journal of Gay and Lesbian Social Services*, Vol. 2, No. 1 (1995), pp. 83–107.

158. Blume, "Substance Abuse," p. 82.

159. Freudenberger, "The Gay Addict in a Drug and Alcohol Abuse Therapeutic Community"; Finnegan and McNally, "The National Association of Lesbian and Gay Alcoholism Professionals (NALGAP): A Retrospective," and Patricia E. Stevens, "Lesbian Health Care Research: A Review of the Literature from 1970–1990," *Health Care for Women International*, Vol. 13, (1992), pp. 91–120.

160. Glaus, "Alcoholism, Chemical Dependency and the Lesbian Client"; and Freudenberger, "The Gay Addict in a Drug and Alcohol Abuse Therapeutic Community."

161. Finnegan and Cook, "Special Issues"; and Kus and Smith, "Referrals and Resources for Chemically Dependent Gay and Lesbian Clients."

162. Kus, "Alcoholism and Non-Acceptance of Gay Self"; also see Colcher, "Counseling the Homosexual Alcoholic"; and Finnegan and Cook, "Special Issues."

163. Ziebold, "Alcoholism and Recovery."

164. Ubell and Sumberg, "Heterosexual Therapists Treating Homosexual Addicted Clients,"copyright 1992, Haworth Press, Binghamton, NY; also see Hellman, "Dual Diagnosis Issues with Homosexual Persons."

165. Hellman et al., "Treatment of Homosexual Alcoholics."

166. Stephen Israelstam, "Knowledge and Opinions of Alcohol Intervention Workers in Ontario, Canada, Regarding Issues Affecting Male Gays and Lesbians: Parts I and II," *The International Journal of the Addictions*, Vol. 23, No. 3 (1988), pp. 227–252.

167. MacEwan, "Differences in Assessment and Treatment Approaches for Homosexual Clients."

168. Bittle, "Alcoholics Anonymous and the Gay Alcoholic."

169. See, for example, Colcher, "Counseling the Homosexual Alcoholic"; and Robert J. Kus, *Gay Men of Alcoholics Anonymous: First-hand Accounts* (North Liberty, IA: WinterStar Press, 1990).

170. Kominars, "Homophobia: The Heart of Darkness," p. 30, copyright 1995, Haworth Press, Binghamton, NY.

171. Robert J. Kus and Mark A. Latcovich, "Special Interest Groups in Alcoholics Anonymous: A Focus on Gay Men's Groups," *Journal of Gay & Lesbian Social Services*, Vol. 2, No. 1 (1995), pp. 91–107, also published in Kus, *Addiction and Recovery in Gay and Lesbian Persons*, pp. 91–107; Hall, "Lesbians and Alcohol: Patterns and Paradoxes in Medical Notions and Lesbians' Belief."

172. Israelstam, "Alcohol and Drug Problems of Gay Males and Lesbians," p. 447.

173. Kus and Smith, "Referrals and Resources for Chemically Dependent Gay and Lesbian Clients."

174. Hawkins, "Alcoholism and Lesbianism"; also see Saulnier, "Lesbian Alcoholism: Development of a Construct."

175. Colcher, "Counseling the Homosexual Alcoholic"; and Nicoloff and Stiglitz, "Lesbian Alcoholism."

176. Bittle, "Alcoholics Anonymous," p. 81.

177. Also see Hawkins, "Lesbianism and Alcoholism"; and Ubell and Sumberg, "Heterosexual Therapists Treating Homosexual Addicted Clients."

178. Also see Ratner, "A Model for the Treatment."

179. Ziebold, "Alcoholism and Recovery," p. 44.

180. Personal communication with Louise Warren.

181. Christine Flynn Saulnier, "Twelve Steps for Everyone? Lesbians in Al-Anon," in Thomas J. Powell (Ed.), *Understanding the Self-Help Organization* (Thousand Oaks, CA: Sage, 1994), pp. 247–271, quote from pp. 267–268.

182. Bittle, "Alcoholics Anonymous and the Gay Alcoholic."

183. See Kus, "Alcoholism and Non-Acceptance of Gay Self," copyright 1988, Haworth Press, Binghamton, NY; and Robert J. Kus, "Alcoholics Anonymous and Gay American Men," *Journal of Homosexuality*, Vol. 14, Nos. 1–2 (1987), pp. 253–276.

184. Also see Colcher, "Counseling the Homosexual Alcoholic"; and Kus and Latcovich, "Special Interest Groups in Alcoholics Anonymous: A Focus on Gay Men's Groups."

185. Israelstam, "Alcohol and Drug Problems of Gay Males and Lesbians."

186. Colcher, "Counseling the Homosexual Alcoholic."

187. K. A. Jones, J. D. Latham, and M. D. Jenner, "Social Environment within Conventional Alcoholism Treatment Agencies as Perceived by Gay and Non-Gay Recovering Alcoholics: A Preliminary Report" (Seattle: National Council on Alcoholism Convention, 1980), cited in Israelstam, "Alcohol and Drug Problems of Gay Males and Lesbians," p. 448.

188. Kus and Latcovich, "Special Interest Groups in Alcoholics Anonymous: A Focus on Gay Men's Groups."

189. Ibid.

190. Edward J. Saunders, "Homosexual Recovering Alcoholics: A Descriptive Study," *Alcohol Health and Research World* (Winter 1983–84), pp. 18–22.

191. Kus and Latcovich, "Special Interest Groups in Alcoholics Anonymous: A Focus on Gay Men's Groups," p. 72, copyright 1995, Haworth Press, Binghamton, NY.

192. Hall, "Lesbians and Alcohol: Patterns and Paradoxes in Medical Notions and Lesbians' Beliefs," p. 115.

193. Kus, "Alcoholics Anonymous"; and Ratner, "A Model for the Treatment."

194. Kus and Latcovich, "Special Interest Groups in Alcoholics Anonymous: A Focus on Gay Men's Groups."

195. See, for example, Saulnier, "Lesbian Alcoholism: Development of a Construct."

196. Personal communication with Louise Warren.

197. Robert J. Kus, "Spirituality in Everyday Life: Experiences of Gay Men of Alcoholics Anonymous," *Journal of Chemical Dependency Treatment*, Vol. 5, No. 1 (1992), pp. 49–66; quote from pp. 49–50, copyright 1992, Haworth Press, Binghamton, NY.

198. Kus and Smith, "Referrals and Resources for Chemically Dependent Gay and Lesbian Clients"; and Kus and Latcovich, "Special Interest Groups in Alcoholics Anonymous: A Focus on Gay Men's Groups."

199. Kus and Smith, "Referrals and Resources for Chemically Dependent Gay and Lesbian Clients." For a discussion of spiritual issues, see Father Leo Booth, "Spirituality and the Gay Community," *Journal of Gay & Lesbian Social Services*, Vol. 2, No. 1 (1995), pp. 57–65, also published in

Kus, *Addiction and Recovery in Gay and Lesbian Persons*, pp. 57–65.

200. Carter Heyward, "Healing Addiction and Homophobia: Reflections on Empowerment and Liberation," *Journal of Chemical Dependency Treatment*, Vol. 5, No. 1 (1992), pp. 5–18, quote from p. 11, copyright 1992, Haworth Press, Binghamton, NY.

201. Ibid., p. 17, copyright 1992, Haworth Press, Binghamton, NY.

202. Saulnier, "Twelve Steps for Everyone? Lesbians in Al-Anon," p. 267.

203. Rothberg and Kidder, "Double Trouble: Lesbians Emerging from Alcoholic Families."

204. Hall, "Lesbians and Alcohol: Patterns and Paradoxes in Medical Notions and Lesbians' Beliefs."

205. Saulnier, "Lesbian Alcoholism: Development of a Construct."

206. Hall, "Lesbians and Alcohol: Patterns and Paradoxes in Medical Notions and Lesbians' Beliefs."

207. Finnegan and McNally, "The National Association of Lesbian and Gay Alcoholism Professionals (NALGAP): A Retrospective.

208. The rest of this paragraph relies on Emily B. McNally and Dana G. Finnegan, "Working Together: The National Association of Gay Alcoholism Professionals," *Journal of Homosexuality*, Vol. 7, No. 4 (1982), pp. 101–103.

209. The Center for Substance Abuse Prevention produces *Alcohol, Tobacco, and Other Drugs Resource Guide: Lesbians, Gay Men, and Bisexuals* (Rockville, MD: National Clearinghouse for Alcohol and Drug Information, 1996), available on the Internet at: http://www.health.org/pubs/resguide/lgb.htm

13

Compounding the Problem: Substance Abuse and Other Disabilities

Diana M. DiNitto
University of Texas at Austin

Deborah K. Webb
Austin-Travis County Mental Health and Mental Retardation Center

The relatively brief history of professional treatment of substance abuse and dependency has been a time of learning how to improve services to alcoholics and addicts. During this period, substance abusers with other major physical or mental disabilities have apparently been underserved by chemical dependency treatment programs. In its Winter 1980/81 issue of *Alcohol Health & Research World*, the National Institute on Alcohol Abuse and Alcoholism (NIAAA) began to raise the consciousness of chemical dependency professionals about those with multiple disabilities. The professional literature of other health and social service professionals also reflects a growing concern about the combination of substance abuse or dependence and other disabilities, but empirical evidence confirms a lack of recognition of these problems. For example, in a study of 254 vocational rehabilita-

tion clients with various mental or physical disabilities, DiNitto and Schwab found that about one-third who had not been identified as having substance abuse or dependence by their vocational rehabilitation counselor screened positive for these problems.[1] Ingraham and colleagues also found that, on average, rehabilitation counselors substantially underestimated the incidence of alcohol problems among groups of clients with physical trauma (e.g., injuries from auto accidents) and serious mental illness, although they somewhat overestimated it among people with developmental disabilities (e.g., mental retardation) and other physical disabilities (e.g., multiple sclerosis).[2]

Until recently, a good deal of finger pointing occurred between professional groups that come into contact with clients who have multiple disabilities. Those in the chemical dependency field accused professionals in the fields of mental illness and physical disabilities of overlooking or even tacitly condoning alcohol and drug misuse in their clientele.[3] Likewise, chemical dependency specialists were blamed for being uninformed about other disabilities and insensitive to the special treatment needs of clients with multiple disabilities. As late as 1989, Alexander Boros, one of the first to assist chemically dependent persons with additional disabilities, wrote that "persons with physical impairments have not benefited fully from . . . gains achieved in the addiction field. With few exceptions, intensive inpatient treatment programs do not meet the needs of physically impaired clients."[4] Physical barriers prevented acceptance of those with mobility impairments; interpreters for those who are deaf were rarely employed; and few programs had designed or redesigned materials useful to those with visual impairments, brain injury, mental retardation, or other disabilities. Although insufficient funding for chemical dependency services has contributed to the lack of attention to those with multiple disabilities, a greater attitude of cooperation among professionals is emerging along with more cross-training to ensure a knowledgeable cadre of specialists to serve people with multiple disabilites. Debate continues, however, over the incidence of substance abuse problems among those with other disabilities, who should treat the substance abuse problems of individuals with multiple disabilities, the optimum settings for treatment, and the treatment techniques and modalities that might produce the best results. These topics are the concern of this chapter.

Several terms have been used to describe those with more than one disability. NIAAA began by using the term *multidisabled.*[5] The National Institute of Mental Health (NIMH) uses *comorbid,* despite its unpleasant sound.[6] Social workers frequently use *dually diagnosed.*[7] Other terms are *concurrent* or *coexisting disabilities.* All these terms can be confusing because they do not specify the particular disabilities involved. Mental disorders in conjunction with substance disorders have re-

ceived the most attention. Other disabilities on which some literature is available include spinal cord injury, traumatic brain injury, hearing and visual impairments, mental retardation, epilepsy, and diabetes.

Estimates are that nearly 50 million Americans have a physical or mental disability that interferes with performing normal life tasks.[8] One major study found that "alcohol-related [hospital] discharge rates were dramatically higher for the disabled than for the general population."[9] Individuals with some types of disabilities, such as mental disorders, are apparently at greater risk for alcohol and drug problems than the general population.[10]

There is agreement that those with multiple disabilities are likely to need some special services to help them in their recovery from substance abuse. Groups such as the National Association on Alcohol, Drugs and Disability are interested in seeing that those with mental and physical disabilities are treated equitably in receiving substance abuse prevention and treatment services.[11]

Section V of the Rehabilitation Act of 1973 prohibits discrimination against those with disabilities, including alcohol and drug disorders, by health care and other service agencies that receive federal assistance. The Anti-Drug Abuse Act of 1986 drew attention to people with disabilities as a group that may have increased susceptibility to substance abuse.[12] The Americans with Disabilities Act (ADA), which passed with overwhelming congressional and presidential support in 1990, put further pressure on public and private facilities to serve those with disabilities. The act defines a disabled individual as one who has "a physical or mental impairment that substantially limits one or more major life activities, a record of such impairment, or being regarded as having such an impairment."[13] It prohibits health care providers from discriminating against illegal drug users who are otherwise eligible for services. The act's employment discrimination provisions do not protect employees or applicants for employment who are currently using illegal drugs; however, these employment provisions do not exclude individuals with other disabilities if they use or are addicted to drugs. Substance abusers who have been rehabilitated and no longer use illegal drugs may be considered disabled under these employment provisions. De Miranda notes that the controversies over the passage of the ADA reflect ambivalence "about whether to view alcoholism/addiction as a 'real' disability."[14]

Mental Illness and Substance Abuse[15]

Interest in the co-occurence of mental illness and substance abuse or dependence by treatment providers and researchers in the fields of mental health and chemical dependency has surged in recent years.[16] Using criteria found in the *Diagnostic and Statistical Manual of Mental Disorders (DSM),*[17] dual diagnoses experts such as Kathleen Sciacca and Sharon Ekleberry distinguish two large groups of clients who have mental illness and substance disorders.[18]

Persons with mental illness and chemical abuse or addiction (MICAA) are those with severe Axis I mental disorders (such as schizophrenia or bipolar disorder) in addition to Axis I substance abuse or dependence disorders. These individuals are different from those with chemical abuse and mental illness (CAMI) who have no freestanding Axis I disorder of severe mental illness, but who have an Axis I substance abuse or dependency disorder in combination with an Axis II personality disorder.

Prevalence

Just how prevalent is the comorbidity of mental and substance use disorders? In the 1980s, prevalence estimates varied from almost nonexistent to 70 percent, depending on the particular subpopulation being considered, with most estimates falling around 50 percent.[19] The Epidemiologic Catchment Area (ECA) study found that among those with lifetime mental disorders, 22 percent also had

a diagnosis of alcohol abuse or dependence and 15 percent had drug abuse or dependence. ECA results also indicated that "having a lifetime mental disorder is associated with more than twice the risk of having an alcohol disorder and over four times the risk of having another drug abuse disorder."[20] More recently, the National Comorbidity Survey identified even higher rates: "51% of those with a lifetime addictive disorder also had a lifetime mental disorder."[21] The National Longitudinal Alcohol Epidemiologic Survey also identified high rates of comorbidity. For example, "The risk of having a drug use disorder among those with major depression was about seven times . . . as great as among those without major depression."[22] Although mental disorders and substance use disorders may have separate etiologies and courses,[23] evidence from these studies clearly indicates a substantial level of co-occurence.

Substance Vulnerability

Among clinical populations, some of the variation in estimates of comorbidity may be explained by the differences in problem definition and population groups studied. For example, Minkoff believes that any use of particular drugs by those with serious mental disorders should be considered abuse,[24] while others use more restrictive definitions.[25] Since younger rather than older clients are more likely to have experienced substance abuse,[26] those working with young adults with severe mental illness report higher estimates. For many individuals with mental illness, virtually any use of nonprescribed psychoactive drugs, including alcohol, can lead to problems in functioning.[27] Ryglewicz and Pepper refer to such clients as "substance-vulnerable."[28] If criteria for dual diagnoses are modified to include these clients, the number of MICAA individuals increases substantially.

Although helping professionals are generally aware that substance abuse or dependence can exacerbate mental disorders, there is less awareness that many individuals with mental disorders have such fragile brain chemistry that so-called social use can also cause psychotic episodes. Take the case of a young man who had three mental hospital admissions in one year. All his mental health workers assumed it was noncompliance with medications that precipitated his episodes, but none had asked about his alcohol use. Prior to each hospital admission, he had drunk up to a six-pack of beer. When the client independently recognized the association between his drinking and his psychotic episodes, and decided to quit drinking altogether, he was not hospitalized for several years. In another example, a caseworker was asked at a staffing about a female client with whom she had worked closely for three years. The client had had multiple psychiatric hospitalizations. The caseworker gave a long list of observations about the client's daily behaviors, but none indicated intoxication or addiction. Subsequently, the client met with the mental health team and was asked what symptoms she had noticed before her admissions. Much to her caseworker's surprise, the client replied that every time she drank even one beer, the next thing she knew, she was in the hospital. Her use of alcohol was so minimal that it had gone undetected, but its effects were powerful enough to precipitate rehospitalization. These examples demonstrate the need to screen clients with mental disorders for substance use as well as abuse and dependence.

Underdiagnosing

Other difficulties in obtaining accurate diagnoses of those with comorbidity have been the tendencies of mental health professionals to overlook substance use and abuse problems ("everyone drinks" or "they are just self-medicating")[29] and of substance abuse professionals to minimize mental health problems ("they will clear up with sobriety").[30] Making accurate diagnoses, especially during emergencies, can be difficult because the effects produced by some abused drugs appear very similar to the manifestations of psychoses.[31] Administrative rules and regulations, some related to the requirements of different funding

sources, can also prevent accurate reporting. For example, Menicucci and colleagues reported that "many [psychiatric treatment] units are unable to record two primary diagnoses because of computerized systems that allow for the recording of only one major diagnosis."[32] As a result, the number of dual-diagnosis patients in treatment programs may be underreported.

Screening, Assessing, and Making Accurate Diagnoses

Detecting, documenting, and addressing dual disorders are important tasks that are not always done well by mental health or substance abuse treatment providers. Until recently, professionals have specialized in substance abuse or mental health treatment. They were not expected to know how to diagnose or treat both types of illnesses. With greater awareness of dual disorders comes a need for dually qualified staff to routinely screen and assess each client who presents for treatment. In cases of dual disorders, it is preferable for the clients' needs to be simultaneously addressed with one comprehensive plan of services. Positive treatment outcomes for persons with dual disorders have been elusive, in part, because of the lack of comprehensive professional training, treatment planning, and service provision.

Mental health professionals are aided in recognizing substance use, abuse, and dependence through substance abuse prescreening, screening, and assessment instruments (covered in detail in Chapter 5). For example, the easily memorized, four-question CAGE[33] is a useful prescreening questionnaire that any clinician can utilize. Next, any number of standardized, reliable, and valid instruments may be used to detect substance problems over the lifetime. Short instruments such as the Michigan Alcoholism Screening Test (MAST),[34] modified (shorter) versions of the MAST, or the Substance Abuse Subtle Screening Inventory (SASSI)[35] are often selected. Following diagnosis, generally using the *DSM-IV*, mental health professionals may choose to utilize a comprehensive assessment instrument such as the Addiction Severity Index (ASI).[36] As both a clinical tool and an outcome tracking instrument, the ASI may be used to document the presence and severity of substance abuse, family and social problems, and psychological functioning at initial client contact (baseline), periodically during the ongoing rendering of services, at the conclusion of various interventions, and at follow-up visits. Outcomes may also be quickly tracked by use of tools such as Drake and colleagues' Alcohol and/or Drug Use Scales.[37]

Likewise, substance abuse professionals may detect and monitor common mental illnesses such as depression by use of instruments such as the Beck Depression Inventory (BDI).[38] Functional ability may be assessed by periodic use of scales such as the Global Assessment of Functioning (GAF, which is Axis V of the *DSM-IV*)[39] or the Multnomah Community Ability Scale (MCAS).[40] With proper education, substance abuse professionals may also utilize the Brief Psychiatric Rating Scale (BPRS) used to assess the severity of current psychiatric symptoms.[41]

In addressing covert alcohol and other drug use and denial, drug testing in conjunction with gentle, caring confrontation and positive reinforcement may be needed. Nevertheless, many mental health professionals do not utilize drug testing as an assessment or a clinical treatment tool. In contrast, most substance abuse and criminal justice professionals do utilize drug testing.

Patients with substance-induced psychoses may also be misdiagnosed as having an acute exacerbation of a severe mental illness by staff at psychiatric emergency screening units. Urine toxicologies can help to reveal the extent and types of substance use. But again, they are seldom utilized. The treatment regimen used by physicians responding to psychiatric emergencies may differ depending on whether the patient's psychoses was induced by substance abuse, mental illness, or a combination of the two. In many cases, a drug-induced psychosis will clear within a few days following abstinence. However, for those with severe

mental illnesses, abstinence from nonprescribed drugs is often not enough to remedy the situation. Psychotropic medications may be necessary to address symptoms of mental illness. A detailed patient history (see Chapter 5) may be needed to confirm a diagnosis. Clients' self-reports should generally be supplemented by interviews with family members or other collaterals and with close reading of previous inpatient and outpatient treatment records, court records, school records, and so forth, to obtain information that the client may not be able or willing to provide. Identification of any temporal relationships between substance use or abuse and exacerbation of mental illness symptoms is helpful in developing a long-range treatment plan. Mee-Lee suggests using thorough histories to determine whether clients have exhibited mental disorders when not abusing drugs and to determine if mental problems predated drug use whenever possible.[42] However, some children are now using drugs at ages younger than when most mental illnesses may become evident. The rare opportunity to observe a client when totally drug free can be instrumental in determining whether a single diagnosis of substance abuse or dependency is appropriate or if dual diagnoses should be made. However, if the individual's records clearly show beneficial results from psychiatric medication, they are usually prescribed.

Relationships between Abused Drugs and Mental Disorders

The nonprescribed psychoactive drugs chosen by individuals who do have dual disorders may not be random and may be related to their particular mental disorder. For example, Treffert addresses the propensity of persons with paranoid schizophrenia to use marijuana,[43] a phenomenon Khantzian calls nonrandom, self-medication.[44] Schneier and Siris reviewed a number of studies and found that the schizophrenia group's "use of amphetamines and cocaine, cannabis, hallucinogens, inhalants, caffeine, and nicotine was significantly greater than or equal to use by control groups consisting of other psychiatric patients or normal subjects" and that their "use of alcohol, opiates, and sedative hypnotics was significantly less than or equal to use by controls"; they agree that these patterns are selective.[45] McLellan and colleagues report that among psychiatric patients, amphetamines or hallucinogens were preferred by people with paranoid schizophrenia but were less likely to be used by depressed patients, whereas barbiturates were more likely to be preferred by people with depression rather than those with schizophrenia.[46] Furthermore, they found that stimulant and polydrug users showed greater psychiatric symptomatology (especially schizophrenia, psychasthenia, and paranoia) than did other drug abusers, whereas opiate users had less psychiatric symptomatology, except for depression and psychopathy.

The McLellan group considered both self-medication and causative explanations for their findings. The *causative* view suggests that chronic drug use causes mental illness by producing biological changes in the individual. The *self-medication* explanation, which has engendered considerable discussion among mental health and substance abuse professionals,[47] suggests that depressed individuals are drawn to barbiturate, benzodiazepine, and sedative-hypnotic use because these drugs help alleviate distressful symptoms (although over the long run, they may exacerbate depression). The self-medication explanation is less clear as to why people with schizophrenia may use hallucinogens and amphetamines, since these drugs increase dysphoria by exacerbating hallucinations, confusion, and suspiciousness. However, some effects of amphetamines may be pleasing, such as greater awareness, energy, and feelings of power. Additional research is beginning to clarify the relationship between the problems of mental illness and the choice of abused substances. For example, Glassman reviewed evidence suggesting that nicotine may augment the release of dopamine and that this "could be especially appealing to psychiatric patients in whom these systems are defective."[48]

Professionals who treat individuals with psychiatric disorders encourage them to comply with their psychotropic medication regimen. They also educate clients about potential side effects of these prescribed drugs. Education about the potential adverse effects of using alcohol and nonprescribed drugs should be clear and consistent: (1) use or abuse of alcohol, street drugs, and/or other nonprescribed drugs can adversely affect mental stability and (2) the interactions of nonprescribed and prescribed drugs can be harmful or lethal. However, slogans such as "just say no to drugs" and "only sick people use drugs" can confuse some people with mental illness. Treatment staff must continually differentiate between medications (drugs prescribed by the psychiatrist or primary health care physician and used as prescribed) and street drugs, alcohol, and improperly used over-the-counter and prescription drugs.[49]

Treatment

Consensus has not been reached on the optimal psychotherapeutic treatments for clients with mental and substance abuse disorders, but some diagnostic distinctions seem to be important in determining the course of treatment. As mentioned earlier in this chapter, there are two major groups of clients with mental illnesses and substance abuse or dependence. Both groups have substance abuse or dependence, but one group, persons with MICAA, have Axis I severe mental illnesses and the other group, persons with CAMI, have Axis II personality disorders. Providers need to address differences among persons with CAMI and those with MICAA, such as varying sensitivity to confrontation of denial about one or both illnesses. If heavy, more traditional confrontation of denial is utilized, persons with MICAA appear to be at greater risk of decompensating[50] than persons with CAMI.[51] They may regress, withdraw, or become delusional.[52] Thus, many dual diagnoses service providers combine confrontation of denial with a great deal of support. Confrontation with care should always be the rule.

Similarly, Ekleberry has proposed that for persons with CAMI, good practice differs according to the specific personality disorder and functional ability of each client.[53] For example, she considers confrontation to be an appropriate aspect of treatment for persons with antisocial personality disorder, and she finds it useful with high-functioning persons who have borderline or histrionic personality disorders. However, Ekleberry does not use confrontation with people who have borderline personality disorder combined with low global assessment of functioning or with people who have narcissistic or avoidant personality disorders.

There are many MICAA subgroups, as well. People from these subgroups undoubtedly could use better customized services. For example, a man who has schizophrenia (a thought disorder) and who is dependent on crack cocaine might benefit from services that are different from the ones that are most beneficial to a woman with bipolar disorder (a mood disorder) who abuses medications.

Today, programs for those with mental illness or chemical dependency often do not allow for much treatment individualization. When psychopathology is apparent following detoxification, clients with comorbidity may be denied alcohol and drug treatment services for reasons such as "lack of motivation" or "inability to benefit from treatment"—characteristics that are directly related to their mental illnesses. Although some clients may be too fragile or too confused to benefit from substance abuse services,[54] many are capable of understanding the dynamics of substance abuse and recovery. Still, most are simply offered standard mental health services at outpatient clinics,[55] but they may be precluded from participating in other programs designed for people with severe mental illnesses, such as residential and vocational services, due to fears that they will cause disruption or introduce other clients to psychoactive substances. Clients with MICAA or CAMI generally do not fit easily into unmodified traditional treatment settings for chemical abusers or for those with severe mental illness.[56] Most continue to encounter serious gaps in services.[57]

Integrated Treatment. Some initial attempts to treat individuals with dual diagnoses involved joint treatment by a chemical dependency professional and a mental health professional. Another variation has been to treat these patients in psychiatric programs and to invite chemical dependency professionals to provide education and to conduct groups as add-ons to mental health treatments.[58] Newer models are emerging using simultaneous or integrated treatments for mental illness and substance abuse problems administered by dual diagnoses specialists.[59] In these models, mental disorders and substance disorders are generally considered similar or parallel illnesses. Minkoff describes the following similarities between the two disorders: both are primary illnesses, both are chronic, both have multifactor etiology, and both involve denial as well as loss of control.[60] Bricker offers parallels such as, "The risk of relapse in either disease is always high, and will inevitably trigger a relapse in the other."[61] Bakdash emphasizes the cyclical nature of these problems in that substance use or abuse produces mental distress that increases drug use, which in turn creates more mental distress, and so forth.[62] These descriptions suggest a rationale for treating both illnesses simultaneously.

In addition to presenting mental disorders and substance use disorders as similar or parallel types of problems, integrated programs focus on the unique problems of clients who experience both problems concurrently. For example, the cyclical nature and interplay of substance abuse and mental illness are addressed. The treatment modalities used in special programs for dually diagnosed clients are similar to those used in inpatient psychiatric and substance abuse programs and may include education, group therapy, individual therapy, family education, family therapy, and an introduction to self-help programs.

Specialized psychoeducational groups for dually diagnosed individuals have been gaining momentum as important complements to other treatment modalities. Using the analogy of a railroad track, Pepper depicts the "cognitive rail" of treatment as psychoeducation and the "emotional rail" as psychotherapy.[63] Attending an educational, cognitive support group can be a positive experience that evokes little psychological resistance. A number of programs are now using psychoeducational groups for MICAA and CAMI clients.[64] For example, Webb's Good Chemistry Groups combine 45 minutes of group therapy with 15 minutes of psychoeducation. Good Chemistry Groups are being used throughout several states by dually diagnosed individuals as an alternative or supplement to Twelve-Step group attendance.[65] Good Chemistry teaches clients with MICAA to better utilize self-help groups, provides them with an opportunity to discuss both illnesses in a supportive atmosphere, and reinforces the benefits of staying mentally stable (which often includes the need for psychotropic medications) as well as staying sober and clean. (Some Good Chemistry suggestions are found in Table 13.1.) This comprehensive perspective is important for clients with dual diagnoses and helps keep them from becoming confused by some people recovering only from chemical dependency who oppose the use of any medications.

TABLE 13.1 Good Chemistry Dos and Don'ts

1. Don't buy alcohol or drugs for myself or others.
2. Don't "hang out" with people who use or deal.
3. Don't give others my meds.
4. Don't go to liquor stores, bars or places that make me want to use.
5. Do take my medications as prescribed.
6. Do discover my own cues: Recognize and avoid things and situations that make me want to use.
7. Do learn to have "natural highs" and "good chemistry" by socializing and doing fun things without using.
8. Do participate in plenty of healthy activities like going to AA meetings, church, shopping, playing or watching sports, and listening to music (whatever makes me feel good without using).

Source: Copyright 1990 Deborah K. Webb, Ph.D. Reprinted by permission.

Psychoeducation may be most useful when it begins with a definition of substance abuse that clients can understand and appreciate. Based on Atkinson's work, Kofoed and Keys suggest the following brief definition of substance abuse problems for use with clients: "A loss of consistent control over substance use."[66] Another is the use of substances that results in serious life problems, including family, social, psychological, job, and legal problems.[67] These definitions can be used to achieve one of the most important outcomes of treatment—helping mentally ill clients discover a repeated cycle of substance use before mental illness exacerbations occur[68] or a pattern in which increases in psychiatric symptoms (such as may occur when clients take their medication differently than prescribed, refuse to take it at all, or run out of medication) result in the use of nonprescribed, psychoactive drugs. Kofoed and Keys describe the use of their therapy group, the Substance Abuse Group Experience (SAGE), with psychiatric inpatients to help persuade them to "acknowledge their drug addiction and to seek continued substance abuse treatment."[69] SAGE was initiated at a general Veterans Administration hospital for patients who also had drug or alcohol problems. Peer group discussions are used to address denial and to encourage outpatient follow-up after discharge.

Several treatments for clients with dual diagnoses have recently been evaluated using experimental and quasiexperimental research designs. Bond and colleagues compared assertive community treatment (ACT, a type of intensive case management) to group treatment and to standard mental health care.[70] The group treatment and control subjects had fewer hospital admissions than the ACT subjects. There were few differences on other outcomes such as days hospitalized, alcohol use, or life satisfaction. Blankertz and Cnaan compared two types of residential treatment (a psychosocial rehabilitation program and a modified therapeutic community) for clients who were dually diagnosed and homeless.[71] More subjects in the psychosocial program than the therapeutic community successfully completed treatment, although the number of retentions in both groups might be considered less than desirable. A larger number of psychosocial program clients remained abstinent. Jerrell and Ridgely compared Twelve Step recovery, behavioral skills training, and intensive case management. The largest number of positive outcomes was for the behavioral skills group, but differences on many of the outcome variables were not significant.[72]

Lehman and colleagues compared standard mental health treatment with these same services combined with a special group called the Being Sober Group and intensive case management.[73] The experimental group did not do better on the outcome variables (alcohol, drug, and psychiatric functioning and life satisfaction). Burnam and associates studied homeless adults who were dually diagnosed.[74] Clients received either integrated mental health and substance abuse treatment with or without a residential component and were compared to clients who received no special intervention but were free to access other services. Clients in the experimental groups were similar in outcomes to clients in the control group, but improved functioning across groups was noted in the areas of alcohol use, illicit drug use, depression and anxiety, self-esteem, and housing situation, although not on psychotic symptoms, mania, or anger and hostility. Webb and DiNitto compared inpatient chemical dependency treatment and this same treatment combined with Good Chemistry Groups for clients with dual diagnoses.[75] They, too, found few differences in outcomes between the experimental and control groups, but clients in both groups significantly improved in several areas of functioning. In general, the small number of studies conducted to date indicate that client functioning may improve with treatment from baseline, but no particular dual diagnoses treatment model has proven superior. The important factor in client improvement seems to be the willingness of professionals to serve this client population.

Detoxification. Individuals with dual diagnoses may present special management problems in community-based detoxification programs (also see Chapter 6). Unless a patient's history is known at the time of admission, detoxification program staff may be unable to determine whether the client has a severe mental disorder until withdrawal progresses. Many community (social setting) detoxification programs are not designed to assist those with severe mental illnesses. If these problems are detected, the client is likely to be transferred to a psychiatric program. Detoxification in psychiatric hospitals, especially those in which substance abuse and mental disorders are treated simultaneously, may be preferable for many clients with dual diagnoses. More functional clients are undergoing ambulatory detoxification (see Chapter 6), but too many end up detoxifying in jail without proper medical and psychiatric care.

Homeless Shelters. People with dual diagnoses often spend time in public, not-for-profit, or church-sponsored missions and shelters such as the Salvation Army when they have nowhere else to go. There are a growing number of shelters for homeless individuals around the country. Persons who are high on drugs, intoxicated, or currently experiencing serious mental health problems are neither welcomed nor well served in many of these programs because of their unmet medical and mental health needs. The difficulties in serving those who are homeless, mentally ill, and chemically dependent[76] are matched only by their tremendous need for services. Patience and understanding are necessary to engage these individuals in relationships with service providers.

Meeting survival needs consumes most of the energies of these individuals. After helping them obtain food, shelter, and health care, it is possible to encourage them to obtain mental health and substance abuse treatment. This process can begin with therapy groups, such as modified Good Chemistry Groups, held at shelters and soup kitchens.[77] These groups help clients identify the symptoms of mental illness and substance abuse or dependence and encourage them to accept services. The next steps are treatment in detoxification units and substance abuse programs or crisis stabilization units, often followed by involvement in residential programs that promote independent living skills and help the client obtain a regular source of income, and later, assistance in obtaining permanent housing. A smooth transition through a continuum of care promotes the chances of long-term, successful outcomes for homeless individuals with severe mental and substance use disorders.

Inpatient Treatment.   People with dual diagnoses who have private mental health care coverage may soon exhaust their benefits or lose them if they can no longer hold a job. Those without financial means who seek inpatient treatment voluntarily in publicly supported programs usually face long waits, but individuals with severe dual diagnoses may not be able to wait. When inpatient treatment or other supportive living arrangements are not available, clients may be forced onto the streets, where it is almost impossible to maintain abstinence or control symptoms of mental illness. Caton and colleagues emphasize that clients dually diagnosed with mental and substance disorders "cannot be managed on an outpatient or brief inpatient basis. Long-term hospital care is often required."[78]

It may seem that a reasonable approach to inpatient care for individuals with dual diagnoses lies in their attending traditional inpatient substance abuse programs and traditional inpatient psychiatric programs in tandem, but this strategy has not proven very successful.[79] Patients often receive conflicting information about drug use and mental illness when treatment is not integrated. Interactions between clients with dual diagnoses and single diagnoses may also be problematic. Singly diagnosed clients with chemical dependence are often uncomfortable with individuals also struggling to control symptoms of mental illness (such as hallucinations or other thought disorders) and who may need more concrete approaches to substance abuse education and group therapy. As a result, individuals with dual diag-

noses may be inhibited from talking about their psychiatric problems or attempt to deny them. On the other hand, clients with MICAA who are treated in psychiatric programs may succeed at minimizing their drug abuse because other clients are unaware of the need to address this additional problem.

Since programs that offer simultaneous, integrated treatment for mental illness and substance abuse remain scarce, some substance abuse programs are responding to the increase of clients with MICAA on their caseloads by hiring professional staff who are equally qualified to treat both illnesses. Sciacca, however, suggests that these clients are best served in psychiatric settings where the expertise to treat mental health problems with therapeutic interventions, including psychotropic medications, is available.[80] Lawlor implores mental health professionals to stop "passing the buck" and to take responsibility for treating these individuals.[81] Staff in these psychiatric programs must become experts on substance use disorders. However, in many situations, chemical dependency professionals have been more receptive to treating coexisting disorders than mental health professionals.

Supervised Living Arrangements.   As Daley and associates suggest, clients with mental and substance use disorders who lack supportive social networks may find residential treatment programs such as halfway houses particularly beneficial.[82] An increasing number of halfway houses for clients with mental illness accept those who also have substance abuse problems. Residents of these programs typically participate in individual and group therapy, psychiatric services, educational classes, and social and recreational activities geared to promote their social functioning and to develop their independent living skills. Before referring clients with MICAA to these programs, clinicians are wise to ensure that abstinence from alcohol and other nonprescribed drugs is part of the treatment regimen. Other halfway houses are designed for people who are chemically dependent; they may accept individuals with dual diagnoses, especially if their mental illnesses are in remission. Before making referrals to these programs, it is necessary to determine whether clients taking antipsychotic, antidepressant, or antianxiety medications are admitted.

A growing number of residential programs are responding to the special needs of those with coexisting mental and substance disorders. Programs in which length of stay is based on individual need are particularly desirable, since the length of treatment required by clients with MICAA may exceed that needed by people with single diagnoses or permitted by halfway houses that serve individuals with substance abuse or mental illness. In communities without specialized programs, professionals are left with piecing together services for clients with MICAA and CAMI.

Day Treatment. If a client has a "clean" (drug-free) environment in which to live, such as with a supportive and enlightened relative or in a community support residential program, day treatment may be an alternative to traditional inpatient treatment. Sciacca as well as Aliesan and Firth describe model day treatment programs for persons with dual diagnoses that incorporate many of the principles mentioned in this chapter such as non-confrontational approaches and assistance in helping clients identify the relationship between their drug use and their mental illness.[83]

Outpatient Treatment. In many communities, parallel outpatient services for clients with mental illness and services for substance abusers are administered by two separate agencies, complicating coordination of services for people with dual diagnoses. In other communities, the same agency (typically a community mental health center) is responsible for services for individuals singly diagnosed with mental illness or substance abuse, but services to these client groups are provided by separate programs or treatment teams. In this situation, one team may monitor an individual's psychiatric symptoms, psychotropic medications,

side effects, and compliance with medications, while the other team is concerned with her or his sobriety, relapse prevention plan, and participation in self-help programs. Ongoing communication and collaboration between program staff are necessary to successfully assist clients assigned to two programs or treatment teams. But in these programs, which are typically overburdened with large caseloads, the amount of staff contact and the quality of interaction with each client are often far less than desirable. Assessments are often hurried and not comprehensive; treatment plans are not as fleshed out, creative, or individualized as they could be. A better approach is for one fully integrated team with expertise in both areas to provide client services.[84] Many community mental health outpatient centers are developing these teams, but the demand for their services also threatens to limit the time available for interaction with clients. Intensive case management is an important component of such outpatient MICAA treatment and continues to be utilized to help ensure continuity of services.[85]

Developing Independent Living and Social Skills. Although many people with single diagnoses have functioned well in the past, many with dual disorders, especially those who have been living on the streets, need help with independent living skills. These skills are generally taught through training and educational programs that use "showing" and "doing" rather than lecturing. For example, at the Consumer-Operated Drop-in Center of the Austin-Travis County MHMR Center in Austin, Texas, consumer staff members help clients practice social skills in the context of various activities, including Good Chemistry meetings. The only restriction on clients' participation is that they cannot attend if intoxicated or high. These activities model ways to enjoy life without drinking and drugging. Participation in these groups and activities can lead to the development of a network of sober peers. Without sober peers with whom to identify and socialize, many clients find it difficult to stay sober.

Family Involvement. The families of people with single or dual disorders can be the most important allies and resources of a treatment team. Families are often knowledgeable about the most subtle nuances of behavioral changes in the client. They can provide invaluable information for the construction of an accurate social history, and they can be taught to recognize and alert providers to early warning signs of relapse.[86] This sort of partnership with families is particularly vital for individuals with MICAA. Family members who understand and help create treatment goals can also share the task of reinforcing accomplishments. For instance, family members can learn the values of being consistent, practicing "tough love," giving positive reinforcement, shaping and extinguishing behaviors, and not enabling.

Family members often feel alone when facing the mental illness and substance abuse of a loved one. The stigma of these conditions often keeps them from sharing their fears with others. Family support groups, such as Al-Anon for those with alcoholic loved ones and Naranon for those with drug-addicted loved ones, can offer tremendous relief through acceptance, understanding, and fellowship. Support groups and advocacy groups for family members of those with mental illness have been developed through the National Alliance for the Mentally Ill (NAMI). Other groups focus specifically on concerns of families with members who have dual diagnoses.[87] The application of multifamily group technology[88] to the networks of those with dual disorders holds promise.[89]

Self-Help Programs. The term *self-help* denotes programs that are run by and for persons who are recovering from various illnesses. The first Twelve-Step self-help program was Alcoholics Anonymous. Just as many alcoholics benefit from Alcoholics Anonymous, adaptations of AA are now used to help those with other types of problems. For example, some individuals benefit from Emotions Anonymous (EA). Such groups may also serve as useful adjuncts to professional services for those with mental illness and substance abuse. In 1982, professionals and volunteers from Alcoholics Anonymous joined together to start Double Trouble groups in New Jersey.[90] These groups spread throughout Pennsylvania, as well, finally resulting in the Double Trouble Intergroup established in Philadelphia in 1989.[91] Bricker and associates have been using a self-help support group for individuals with schizophrenia and chemical abuse problems since 1984. It is officially called Support Together for Emotional and Mental Serenity and Sobriety (STEMSS).[92] The STEMSS consists of Six Steps adapted by Erickson and Bricker from the original Twelve Steps of AA to include mental illness. In this group, references to a "Higher Power" have been deleted due to the abstract nature of the concept. Meetings are held weekly and focus on chemical dependency and mental illness as parallel disorders. The meetings offer direction and social interaction for those with dual problems. Similar groups continue to develop across the United States. For example, in 1987, the Eisenhower Circle Group, a closed-discussion AA meeting, was started so that "alcoholics and addicts who are also mental health consumers would feel comfortable sharing their experiences and find support in their dual recovery process."[93] Most recently, Hamilton and Samples have published the "blueprint" for Dual Recovery Anonymous and a workbook that can help people with dual disorders successfully work the Twelve Steps.[94]

Good Chemistry Groups[95] (started in Austin, Texas, in 1990) are not self-help groups since they are always professionally cofacilitated. However, since the very first group, individuals who are in dual recovery have served as group coleaders. Webb finds the expertise they bring to these groups to be invaluable. In addition, Good Chemistry II groups are open-discussion, self-help meetings for people who have at least one year of clean, sober, and stable time and who have previously attended Good Chemistry Groups.

Special support groups are often needed for those with mental and substance disorders because some members of traditional self-help groups do not understand severe mental illness. At times, well-meaning but misinformed AA members have told individuals with severe dual disorders to go off medications, which they lump together with all other "drugs." In 1984, at the request of Alcoholics Anonymous World Services, a group of physicians who are members of AA wrote *The AA Member—Medications and Other Drugs.* Good Chemistry Groups utilize this AA pamphlet, often referred to as P11. It includes examples of people who use medications properly as well as improperly and clearly admonishes that "No AA Member Plays Doctor." This message will not reach everyone, but professionals who make referrals to AA and NA can help by preparing clients for the possibility of misguided advice and how to deal with it. Since many communities lack a sufficient number of meetings of special self-help groups in which clients can participate as often as they may need, Minkoff suggests that clients be coached on how to participate in regular AA groups.[97] Professionals can also assist clients in selecting those community AA meetings most appropriate for them.

Mental Retardation

According to PL 103-230, the Developmental Disabilities Assistance and Bill of Rights Act Amendments of 1994, developmental disabilities are physical and mental impairments that are manifest before age 22, that are not likely to remit, and that substantially impair one's functioning, such as the ability to care for oneself, to earn a living, and to live independently. The law indicates that individuals who are developmentally disabled are likely to require an array of services to ensure that they are able to function at the highest level possible. Mental retardation is prominent among these developmental disabilities. The levels of intellectual functioning of people with mental retardation vary from mild (an IQ of 50 to 70) to profound (an IQ of 0 to 20).[98] Chemical dependency treatment providers are concerned primarily with those who fall in the mild range, because they are most likely to reside in the community and have access to alcohol and nonprescribed drugs. Fetal alcohol syndrome (see Chapters 4 and 15) is one of the primary causes of mental retardation, but our interest here is in the drinking and drug-taking behavior of those with mental retardation.

Discussions concerning the drinking habits of people with mental retardation began early in this century.[99] Later, in 1956, Wallin indicated that there did not seem to be an excess of alcoholics among persons with mental retardation,[100] but in the 1960s, Tredgold and Soddy wrote that people with mental retardation had a particular susceptibility to alcohol,[101] and Davies noted a close association between mental retardation and inebriety.[102] During the next two decades, there was "a long silence on this topic."[103] One explanation for this lack of attention was that it seemed unlikely that many people who were mentally retarded would drink alcohol or use illicit drugs. Those who lived in the community were often protected by their families from exposure to psychoactive substances, and many lived in institutions where access to these substances was limited. Deinstitutionalization has changed this. Many individuals with mild mental retardation now live rather independently in the community with less protection from families and professionals. They have greater access to alcohol as well as to nonprescribed psychoactive drugs. Studies indicate that many have used alcohol and, to a lesser extent, other drugs.[104]

Contemporary interest in the problems that individuals with mental retardation might experience when confronted with the use of alcohol or other drugs seems to have been aroused primarily by Wenc and Selan who addressed the isolation of those with mental retardation, their need for socialization, and the possible connection of these factors with substance use and abuse.[105] Many individuals who are mentally retarded recognize that they are different, but they want to fit in with the rest of the community. Wenc indicated that these individuals tend to frequent the same spots—restaurants, stores, and even bars—and to be known by the proprietors.[106] According to Selan, like others who drink, "retarded persons experience that alcohol performs important psychological and social functions."[107] In the words of some of her clients, here is why they drink: "When I am drunk, I am just like everybody else," "It's what everyone else is doing," "The people in the bar are not handicapped," "Bars are always warm and friendly," and "I am less lonely; there is always someone to talk with."[108] And among students in special education classes, Moore and Ford note that they "may find that peer groups which endorse drug use also are the easiest to access."[109]

Selan also reported that her clients became more intellectually and emotionally vulnerable when drinking or intoxicated, and some had terrible experiences such as being physically abused and robbed.[110] These events also occur in the general population, but the cognitive deficits of people with mental retardation may put them at greater risk. According to Sengstock, Vergason, and Sullivan, textbooks stress that those with mental retardation "are easily misled, exploited and abused."[111] However, textbooks on mental retardation ignore substance abuse, and substance abuse texts ignore mental retardation.[112]

Is There a Problem?

There are no good estimates of the number of individuals with mental retardation who have drinking or drug problems. Attempts to extrapolate from general population figures can be misleading, since people with mental retardation may not experience these problems at the same rate as others. Current information has been gleaned from a handful of studies with different types of subjects, different sampling and data gathering techniques, and varying sample sizes.[113] These studies fall into two categories—those that attempt to determine the extent of alcohol and drug use and related problems among people with cognitive disabilities and those that focus on people with cognitive disabilities who have substance abuse problems. The limited available evidence generally suggests that this population is less likely to use alcohol and

drugs and to experience substance abuse problems than the general population.

Among efforts to determine the extent of alcohol consumption among people with mental retardation is Huang's study that compared 190 junior and senior high school students with mental retardation with 187 other students and found less drinking by the students with mental retardation.[114] Some 32 percent of the students with mental retardation reported drinking at least twice during a 12-month period, compared with 59 percent of the other students. However, among those who drank, the students with mental retardation reported that they drank more often than the other students. There was also evidence of greater peer pressure to drink among the students with mental retardation or that they were more easily led to drink.

Using ethnographic techniques, Edgerton studied alcohol and drug use across four different samples of people with mental retardation: (1) 48 "candidates for normalization," (2) 40 adults living independently, (3) 45 inner-city African Americans, and (4) 48 deinstitutionalized adults.[115] Edgerton is vehement that despite ample opportunity to drink and use other drugs, these individuals were less likely to do so and less likely to develop alcohol- and drug-related problems than their families and friends. Few of the subjects who used alcohol or other drugs became dependent on them, and they did not engage in socially inappropriate behavior when using them. Concerns that individuals with cognitive disabilities may be especially susceptible to these substances were not borne out by this investigation despite the many problems they faced, such as social rejection and low socioeconomic status. Reiss found that just 2 percent of 205 individuals with mental retardation participating in community-based day programs had drug or alcohol abuse problems.[116] A study by Halpern involved several hundred adults with mental retardation living semi-independently.[117] Some 56 percent reported some level of alcohol consumption and 3 percent some marijuana use. Halpern's figures are also lower than for the general population and problems related to use appeared to be infrequent.

DiNitto and Krishef used survey methodology and asked staff of Associations for Retarded Citizens and group care facilities to administer a brief instrument to clients to determine whether they drank and the consequences they experienced from drinking.[118] A total of 24 programs assisted and responses were obtained from 214 individuals with mental retardation. Some 52 percent of those respondents had drunk alcohol at some point in their lives, with 7 percent reporting daily drinking, 33 percent drinking at least once a week, and 47 percent drinking at least once a month. About half usually drank in their own homes and about a third in a bar. Some 92 percent of the individuals had a paid job, and of them, one-third said they had been absent from work due to feeling sick after drinking. Four had received substance abuse services (AA, detox, counseling, or services from a church-sponsored program). This study indicates somewhat more cause for concern about drinking among persons with mental retardation.

Myers reported that she did not find evidence of alcohol or drug abuse in a sample of 113 individuals who were developmentally disabled, aged 10 to 21, whom she saw for psychiatric consultation.[119] She speculated on two reasons for this finding: close supervision by parents and the youths' unwillingness to report use. Other reasons have also been offered to explain findings of less substance abuse among those with mental retardation.[120]

1. Individuals who are mentally retarded may not wish to emulate those they know who have alcohol and other drug problems.[121]
2. Parents and professionals have taught people with mental retardation not to drink alcohol and to use prescribed drugs only.[122]
3. Many people who are mentally retarded have limited incomes and the expense of alcohol and other drugs may act as a deterrent.[123]

4. Some belong to religious groups that negatively sanction alcohol and drug use.[124]

In addition, studies that rely on samples of people with mental retardation living in supervised facilities may be biased toward findings of less alcohol and drug use than may be present among those living independently in the community. Supervised programs often prohibit drinking, or they may not accept individuals who use psychoactive substances, especially when problematic use is indicated.[125]

Studies that focus on people with cognitive impairments who have a drinking problem are scarce, but Krishef and DiNitto engaged the participation of Associations for Retarded Citizens (ARCs) and Alcohol Treatment Programs (ATPs) to investigate this subject.[126] The 54 ARCs and 50 ATPs that responded identified 414 clients whom they believed to be dually diagnosed with mental retardation and alcohol abuse or alcoholism; 82 percent were males. The alcohol-related problems that these individuals experienced were quite similar to the problems of those with alcohol abuse or dependency in the general population and included employment problems (e.g., absenteeism) and legal offenses (e.g., public intoxication as well as more serious crimes). Family and social conflicts, including hostile and aggressive behavior, were the most frequently reported problems.

Westermeyer and colleagues also studied substance abuse problems by identifying 40 people with mental retardation who also had diagnoses of substance disorders.[127] These individuals were participating in various types of programs (a chemical dependency treatment program, an AA group for individuals with mental retardation, and residential facilities for those with mental retardation). They matched these subjects with 40 individuals who were mentally retarded but not known to have alcohol or drug problems. As might be expected, the substance abusers began drinking earlier, had more frequent lifetime use of alcohol and other drugs, had more of some childhood acting-out behaviors (but not the most serious types), and were more likely to report substance-related problems (psychological, family, social, and employment). An added note is that during the study, 5 of the comparison group members were also identified as having had substance abuse problems. Like Krishef and DiNitto, Westermeyer and co-workers believe that the substance abuse problems of people with mental retardation are similar to those of the general population. They were also concerned that mentally retarded substance abusers experienced problems at lower doses of alcohol and other drugs than individuals in the general population. Even so, their concluding remarks may seem somewhat paternalistic:

> Licit use (e.g., alcohol) should be at least restricted and monitored. In cases of mentally retarded persons at risk, licit use should be delayed or avoided altogether. Mentally retarded persons (like children, adolescents, prisoners, the mentally ill, and other vulnerable persons) should be protected against any exposure to illicit drugs. Agencies and families serving mentally retarded persons should recognize their special obligation to protect mentally retarded persons against substance abuse.[128]

Russian researchers studied drinking among 122 male youths with mental retardation, most of whom were between 14 and 18 years of age, and found extensive problems.[129] Compared to youths with normal intellectual functioning, those with mental retardation "developed a very unique clinical picture of early alcoholism, the principal symptoms developed more rapidly (three to four times more rapidly) than in the youth population at large, and were accompanied by more marked personality changes."[130] The descriptions of exacerbation of reduced mental functioning among these youths with mental retardation and their conflicts with others were of particular concern. Although it may be risky to make cross-cultural comparisons, the evidence provided by Rychkova lends support to the recommendations expressed

by Westermeyer and colleagues. Associations between substance abuse and learning disabilities and attention deficit and hyperactivity disorder are also mentioned in the literature.[131]

Treating Substance Abusers Who Are Mentally Retarded

What is the most appropriate treatment for people with diagnoses of mental retardation and substance abuse or dependency? The Krishef and DiNitto study indicated that a number of alcoholism treatment programs modified their services to meet the needs of this group of clients.[132] Examples were longer treatment periods, using more supportive and directive techniques and less confrontation, greater emphasis on alcohol education, simplification and more repetition of concepts, use of more concrete goals over shorter time frames, use of more behavioral treatment, working closely with the client's family, being more patient, and use of more individual and less group treatment. Campbell and associates found similar results in another survey of people working in the developmental disabilities or chemical dependency fields.[133]

Lottman obtained information from 19 agencies providing substance abuse services in the Cincinnati area, 12 of which reported that they routinely served people with mental retardation, but even these agencies reported serving few clients with mental retardation and were unsure of how many clients had this diagnosis.[134] The staff of these agencies had no more than minimal education about mental retardation but a number of them expressed an interest in more education. The agencies that did not routinely accept clients with mental retardation were less interested in additional education and reported more difficulty in integrating these clients into their services. None of these agencies accepted Medicaid reimbursement, an important source of assistance for people with mental retardation. The agencies that routinely accepted clients with mental retardation said that the barriers to serving these clients had to do with lack of staff training and the time necessary to serve the clients. Client behavior and communications were not rated as significant barriers to service delivery.

Lottman says that despite an emphasis in the substance abuse field on addressing the needs of particular population groups, people with mental retardation have not been of much interest, perhaps because they are not perceived as being high risk and also because these service providers are besieged with demands for services. Given this situation, Lottman believes that clients who are mentally retarded and who have substance abuse problems will continue to remain the responsibility of the mental retardation service delivery system, even though these providers generally do not have specialized education in substance abuse or dependence. Lottman concludes, "There are reasons to be concerned that the low incidence of clients with MR (mental retardation) in generic chemical dependency programs may be the result of exclusionary referral, assessment, and/or treatment criteria."[135]

For clients who need services from substance abuse, mental retardation, and perhaps other agencies, Wenc recommends use of a multidisciplinary service team to ensure that the client receives comprehensive services.[136] Since detoxification centers are a likely entry point into substance abuse treatment, he also recommends that each center designate a staff liaison to the developmentally disabled community. Lottman also suggests focus groups of community mental retardation service providers and substance abuse service providers to determine what each group needs to know to better serve people who are mentally retarded and have substance abuse problems.[137] Following this, he recommends establishing a "local liaison team . . . to coordinate joint training and service activities" that would also include representatives from the "criminal justice, mental health, and medical communities" to better ensure comprehensive treatment planning for clients with mental retardation who are substance abusers.[138]

A significant aide in assisting this population is *The Maine Approach: A Treatment Model for the Intellectually Limited Substance Abuser.*[139] It is a practical, comprehensive, model program for assisting people with cognitive disabilities who have alcohol and drug problems and it relies heavily on the use of behavioral techniques and contracting. *The Maine Approach* describes assessment interviewing, the treatment process, aftercare, and the administrative arrangements used to establish the program. The manual provides many useful tools such as interviewing formats, informed consent forms, and sample treatment plans. A brief case illustration along with treatment considerations from *The Maine Approach* is reproduced in the accompanying box.

The Maine Approach recommends the use of AA by those who are intellectually capable of participating and encourages assisting clients in locating a sponsor who will actively work with them. Wenc also discusses the use of AA by individuals with mental retardation and emphasized the need for making special efforts to accompany them to group meetings rather than simply referring them.[140] Wenc believes that the socialization aspects of these groups are especially beneficial for people with mental retardation.

Although traditional AA groups are an option, individuals with mental retardation report that they are sometimes uncomfortable in these groups, maybe because they feel that some members are not comfortable with mental retardation.[141] Like other groups with multiple diagnoses, something special seemed to be needed for people with mental retardation who also have alcohol or drug problems. An early publication on this topic was a brief article on Emotions Anonymous (EA), founded by Jim Voytilla in Minnesota.[142] As with some of the other new, self-help groups for individuals with dual diagnoses, professional involvement was an important element in organizing Emotions Anonymous. Voytilla combined elements of Alcoholics Anonymous with education and relaxation techniques to form a long-term approach to outpatient treatment. The term *emotions* is substituted

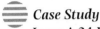

Case Study
Jerry: A 24-Year-Old Client of the Bureau of Mental Retardation

I. History

    A. Mental Retardation—Jerry is diagnosed as having moderate mental retardation (MR). His reported degree of MR, however, is not reflected in his presentation of himself or his conceptual understanding. He is streetwise and relatively high-functioning. Jerry learned at an early age that doing well on his tests would mean that he would "lose his money" [Supplemental Security Income (SSI)].

    B. Family—Mother died when he was very young which left his alcoholic father alone to raise six children. His older brother, Patrick, was the first to introduce Jerry to alcohol and Valium. One sister is a continuous heavy user of Valium and her husband is also an alcoholic. Only one sister has been willing or able to provide a clean, healthy chemical-free living environment. This sister has been supportive of Jerry, but is also very soft-hearted and nonconfrontive. Jerry has taken advantage of this and overrun her household, causing many problems within her family unit.

    C. Medical—Jerry has had many hospital admissions associated with his drinking, both medical and psychiatric. Many times he would feel the need to "dry out" so he would call the ambulance and tell them he had also taken drugs. This ploy was necessary for him to be admitted. Jerry also had been diagnosed as having problems with his "nerves" and was prescribed Valium by a local doctor. Despite all this and his poor eating habits (associated with his drinking) Jerry has maintained relatively good health.

    D. Arrests—His arrests include drunk and disorderly, shoplifting (usually steals vanilla or aftershave when alcohol is not available), and one incident of property damage. Many of his charges (well over twenty) have not been prosecuted or Jerry is released with only a fine to pay, because Jerry will often use his mental retardation to pretend he doesn't understand the police or the judge.

    E. Substance Abuse Treatment—Outpatient: Jerry has had outpatient counseling off and on for the past four years, his sobriety is sporadic. Residential treatment: Jerry has two previous admissions to residential treatment. The information there was at a level which was too high for him, yet he maintained sobriety for six months following treatment. Shelter: He has had numerous admittances, also a halfway house and group home for alcoholics.

        One thing that has been an outstanding problem with Jerry is his manipulative behavior. He knows systems and he knows how to use them—BMR [Bureau of Mental Retardation], alcoholism rehabilitation programs, SSI, hospitals, and the courts.

II. Case Planning

    A. Joint Planning—The Mental Retardation Alcoholism Project became involved with Jerry's case in August 1982. At that time, Jerry was moving back and forth from Aroostook County to Bangor. A team meeting was called to discuss his case. BMR staff from Aroostook County and Bangor, the project coordinator, and Jerry met to plan for his treatment. (Representatives from local substance abuse treatment providers were unable to attend but were informed of the team's decisions.) These meetings have provided an opportunity for the team to discuss case management. It also gave Jerry a chance to get consistent messages from all care providers. Although he has continued at times to try to play one person against another, these manipulation attempts were unsuccessful.

B. **Locate a Supportive Environment**—Jerry was an individual who clearly wanted independence. At the same time, it was just as clear to providers that, in order to maintain sobriety, Jerry would need a supportive and somewhat structured environment. The team decided that a group home for alcoholics would offer him that support (access to AA meetings, his own room, shared transportation and nonmentally retarded peers). Jerry agreed to this plan but stated that he would like to live on his own when things got better. A plan was set up to assist Jerry in getting an apartment if he was able to maintain sobriety on his own for one year.

C. **Integration into AA**—There were two ways that Jerry could become familiar with AA. He attended meetings at the shelter (the staff were very willing to help Jerry become used to the meetings). He also had the support and encouragement to go to meetings at the group home.

D. **Set up a Reward System**—BMR, as representative payee for Jerry, knew that money was very important to him. It became clear to the team that, although Jerry had maintained sobriety for a while, an incentive program was necessary to help him stay that way. Jerry agreed to a plan that would give him extra spending money if he attended his AA and treatment regularly.

E. **Group Therapy**—Jerry was used to dealing with people on the streets and could communicate verbally quite well. Therefore, his participation in group therapy was fairly good. This was supplemented by shelter staff who worked with him individually to deal with the scapegoating by others and to understand the information which was at a level too difficult for him.

F. **Involve in a Meaningful Task**—The team recognized the need for Jerry to become involved in a meaningful task but had difficulty in locating something that was appropriate for his needs. He was too high functioning for sheltered workshops for the mentally retarded and lower-skill jobs were very difficult to come by. Jerry, however, solved this problem on his own and became a volunteer at the halfway house.

III. Follow-Up

Things went relatively smooth for Jerry and he was able to maintain sobriety for nearly eight months. At that time, he began playing his old games and soon after began drinking. The team continued to meet and plan for his case. (Jerry stopped coming to the meetings.) The team decided that an assessment of his "enabling" systems was necessary. The following plan was set up:

A. **Contract**—BMR set up a contract with the client. He would be dealt with in their office only if he came in sober. This included the times when he would come in for his SSI check. Jerry agreed.

B. **Work with the Courts**—Jerry again was being arrested and then given a fine for his actions. This meant very little to him since BMR was his representative payee and, therefore, budgeted his money and helped pay his bills. Since substance abuse treatment providers often dealt with the courts, the shelter agreed to make recommendations to them, including the need for treatment, the next time he got caught.

C. **SSI**—Jerry abuses this system just as he does many others. When Jerry began drinking, his money went for booze, not a place to live or food. Social Security has a rule that, in

(continued)

order to receive benefits, the individual must have a permanent residence. Jerry, who usually lives "on the streets" when he's drinking, was told that SSI would be contacted if he did not have a room.

   D. **The Double Bind**—One problem that we have not been able to solve is a double bind in the system and how Jerry is very wise to this fact. BMR must manage his case to assure that he has money for food and shelter. Jerry knows where he can get free shelter and free food, so his money can be spent on booze. He knows that he will always be taken care of.

We have continued to work with Jerry's case, within our limits. He made considerable progress during his seven and a half months of sobriety, and we have continued to confront his drinking and drinking behavior in hopes that he will again try chemically-free living.

Source: The Maine Approach: A Treatment Model for the Intellectually Limited Substance Abuser (Augusta: The Maine Department of Mental Health and Mental Retardation; and Waterville, ME: The Kennebec Valley Regional Health Agency, 1984), pp. 22–25. Reprinted with permission.

for the word *alcohol* in the Twelve Steps of AA because of the severe anxieties and tensions that people with mental retardation may face. EA members set goals for themselves each week and report back to the group. The behavioral technique of social reinforcement is used to provide ample reward for goal achievement.

Although relatively little has been developed for the treatment of people who are mentally retarded and have substance abuse problems, Paxon describes relapse prevention for these individuals, combining strategies for them with people who have borderline intellectual functioning or are illiterate due to common difficulties such as limited reading and writing skills.[143] Paxon believes that a group format is the preferred approach because it is "versatile and nonthreatening" and it also conserves scarce program resources. Like Selan,[144] Paxon emphasizes the importance of psychotherapy or modified psychotherapy for people with mental retardation, even though many professionals are surprised that these individuals would be able to participate in individual or group psychotherapy as they know it. In addition to directive and structured approaches, Paxon believes that cognitive strategies are best used in relapse prevention with these individuals. They include

(1) self-regulatory training, which helps individuals monitor themselves as well as to anticipate and predict the effects of their behavior, and (2) skills training, which assists individuals in acquiring and gaining proficiency specific to a particular task or situation. These techniques assist clients in evaluating their own relapse behaviors and increases the probability of developing specific skills necessary to avert potential relapses.[145]

Collaboration with special education experts can aid in designing psychoeducational programs that incorporate the learning techniques most suitable to this population.

Mobility Impairments

A British study of clinic outpatients found that 17 percent of people with hypertension, 19 percent of those with diabetes, but 73 percent of those with fractures were heavy drinkers.[146] These numbers indicate the need for screening for alcohol abuse by medical practitioners, especially with regard to accidents. Unfortunately, this often does not happen, perhaps due to time constraints or perhaps because medical personnel are hesitant to ask patients about alcohol or other drug abuse.

One type of injury that is often the result of alcohol- or drug-related accidents is spinal cord injury (SCI).[147] A number of SCI patients abused psychoactive drugs prior to becoming disabled, and alcohol or other drugs may have directly contributed to their accident. Less frequently, psychoactive drug abuse seems to be initiated as a reaction to a spinal cord injury.

Heinemann and Hawkins reviewed studies and found that the relationship between intoxication and head and spinal cord injury varied from 17 to 68 percent of cases.[148] For example, O'Donnell and colleagues studied 47 SCI patients (39 men and 8 women) admitted over a six-month period to a state-operated hospital and found that 62 percent had alcohol- or other drug-related injuries.[149] A total of 41 patients had a prior history of alcohol or drug abuse and 32 apparently resumed use following injury. Heinemann and colleagues found that 43 percent of the 75 SCI patients they studied were intoxicated at the time of injury, including 27 of 49 patients who were identified as having drinking problems before injury, 1 of 4 who developed problems postinjury, and 3 of the 20 who reportedly had no alcohol problem.[150] Drinking behaviors generally declined after SCI, but two-thirds of study participants were drinking 18 months later, with a median frequency of "four drinks one to two times each week." Only 11 percent of the sample had ever received alcohol treatment (7 percent preinjury and 4 percent postinjury). Several individuals who thought they needed treatment immediately following their injury later changed their minds.

In a study of 137 SCI male patients, Frisbie and Tun found that prior to paralysis, 94 were drinkers (i.e., they drank an average of at least one drink per day for at least a year).[151] Of the 94, 39 had been drinking on the day of their injury. Following the injury, 33 of the 137 patients became abstainers, 12 reduced consumption, 8 increased consumption, and 7 became drinkers. In another study, Heinemann and colleagues also found that

the general tendency was a reduction in drinking following SCI.[152] Among the 121 SCI patients they studied, heavy drinking decreased from 55 percent of the sample six months prior to the injury to 20 percent one year after the injury.

Young and associates studied a sample of 123 individuals with SCI living in the community and found that although the prevalence of alcohol and marijuana use were lower than in the general population, the 21 percent prevalence rate of alcohol abuse (as measured by the Short Michigan Alcoholism Screening Test) was higher than in the general population but lower than in other studies of people with SCI.[153] Differences in rates of alcohol abuse in recent studies may be due to a number of factors such as different sampling techniques, different populations studied, and different definitions of alcohol problems. Compared with the nonabusers, the alcohol abusers in Young's study tended to perceive their health as worse and reported more depression and stress. The marijuana users tended to be younger than the nonmarijuana users and they were also younger at the time of injury; they also reported more depression and stress. As in the general population, significantly fewer women than men used alcohol, but this difference was not statistically significant in Young's sample. Approximately equal proportions of men and women used marijuana. About half of those who had abused alcohol in the past reported that they were not currently drinking. Interestingly, neither alcohol use, alcohol abuse, nor marijuana use were related to medical conditions such as level of disability or pain. Psychological factors seemed more important than medical factors in predicting substance use and abuse among this sample. Young provides another call for substance abuse screening among SCI patients and for links between rehabilitation and substance abuse professionals.

Studies of youthful rehabilitation clients and college students with various physical disabilities have produced inconsistent findings about alcohol and drug use. Some suggest higher use and abuse figures than the general population,[154] whereas others indicate little or no differences.[155] Comparisons may be difficult to make due to the confounding effects of various types of disabilities. One study focused on 57 college students with orthopedic impairments who relied on wheelchairs. Of interest were the findings that "abuse of mood-altering drugs, including alcohol, appears to have predated disability for the most problematic cohort in this study. A trauma related disability correlated with greater likelihood of alcohol or other drug abuse during college than did a congenital disability."[156] The authors were particularly concerned about the number of participants who were taking prescription medications but who lacked knowledge about the adverse interactions their medications might have with alcohol or other drugs. The Chemical Dependency/Physical Disability Program at Abbott Northwestern Hospital/Sister Kenny Institute in Minneapolis, Minnesota, reported that 72 of the first 88 clients admitted with onset of disability after their tenth birthday had chemical dependency problems prior to incurring the disability.[157]

There is interest in whether SCI patients, as well as patients who have suffered other injuries such as traumatic brain injury (TBI), have certain personality types. Some SCI patients appear to be thrill seekers who have shunned intellectual interests and pursued behaviors more likely to result in self-destruction.[158] Their inability to pursue previous physical activities seems to increase their frustration during rehabilitation.

There is also considerable interest in the personality traits of substance abusers, although no personality type has been found to typify them. Alston studied "sensation seeking" and drug abuse among individuals with SCI.[159] He received 44 responses (a 70 percent response rate), 28 from men and 16 from women, to his pilot mail survey. A total of 42 subjects reported using at least one substance. Alcohol was reported most often (32 participants), followed by painkillers (28 participants), marijuana (18 participants), tranquilizers (10 participants), cocaine (7 partici-

pants), hallucinogens (1 participant), stimulants (1 participant), heroin (none), and designer drugs (none). Of the 44 respondents, 22 reported using substances one to three times a week, 15 used once every other week, and others used less frequently. There were significant relationships between frequency of use by type of drug (alcohol, recreational, and prescription) and three of the four subscales Alston used to measure sensation seeking. Alston states that study participants "were chronically underaroused and interested in engaging in behaviors to increase stimulus input."[160] Like Young and colleagues, Alston suggests attention to psychological characteristics of people with SCI. He emphasizes the need for early identification of people with a tendency toward sensation seeking as a means of preventing drug abuse, and he recommends psychoeducation to address these tendencies. He also suggests that certain people with disabilities may need assistance in committing to programs of rehabilitation such as job training rather than less stressful and more stimulating activities such as drinking.

SCI patients' expectations about the positive benefits of alcohol use have also been studied. Heinemann and associates found that compared to those who had not drunk problematically before injury, preinjury problem drinkers believed that alcohol would provide greater benefits such as improved mood and social and sexual functioning.[161] The preinjury problem drinkers did report drinking less over time, but their positive expectations about alcohol use continued, although they did diminish somewhat. Furthermore, the preinjury problem drinkers reported that they continued to use more escape-avoidance coping strategies than other study participants who were more likely to use problem-solving strategies. The interest in expectancies and coping styles has gained considerable interest throughout the literature on substance abuse. The Heinemann research team believes that preinjury problem drinking is most telling in patient assessment and that the persistent maladaptive responses of preinjury problem drinkers may signal poorer adjustment to disability as well as a potential to drinking relapse. Both possibilities need further study.

Heinemann and associates have also reported that intoxication at the time of SCI injury was positively related to preinjury drinking levels.[162] The heavier drinkers were also more likely to drink while hospitalized, but it was those who stopped drinking who tended to complete fewer activities independently, a finding warranting further exploration in terms of adjustment of drinkers to SCI.

The crisis caused by SCI or other serious injury can provide a prime opportunity for intervening in a substance abuse problem.[163] Frisbie and Tun noted that those who reduced alcohol consumption or stopped drinking in their study did so primarily for health-related reasons, often in response to advice from loved ones or a physician.[164] But there are barriers to the general rehabilitation of SCI patients. Some SCI patients become comfortable in the institutional setting and fail to make progress because of fears of independent living.[165] Successful rehabilitation may result in a termination of Social Security benefits, public assistance payments, or Veterans Administration benefits. These benefits might exceed what can be earned from employment. Disability payment systems that fail to reward the patient's progress have long been criticized as encouraging dependency.

As the rehabilitation process progresses, patients may resume alcohol and drug use.[166] Family, friends, and even professional caregivers may offer these substances to promote enjoyment and normalcy. Family members may be angry that the individual was responsible for the behavior that caused the injury and that has left everyone overburdened. At the same time, they may be feeling guilty over their resentment toward the person who has the disability. Loved ones are trying to cope with their caregiving responsibilities and wish they could do more. The strains caused by the disability may make opening a beer or rolling a joint for the disabled individual easier than feeling guilty or engaging in hostile encounters.

Many people with physical disabilities take medications to reduce pain, control muscle spasms, prevent infections, and address other medical problems, and serious consequences can ensue when medications such as tranquilizers and pain killers are used with alcohol or street drugs.[167] Among those with SCI (paraplegia and quadriplegia), O'Donnell and colleagues warn of the problems that may arise.[168] For example, depressant drugs exacerbate depressed mood and impede motor activity; lack of movement contributes to other physical problems such as pulmonary, joint, and urinary. In addition, the amount of urine produced by drinking beverages like beer can cause unnecessary dependence on catheterization when bladder control has already been diminished. Clues that SCI patients may be suffering from chemical dependency are lack of attention to health care, nutrition, and hygiene and the development of "severe decubitis ulcers (bed or pressure sores) aggravated by sitting in a wheelchair for days while they are stoned or drunk."[169]

Sores and urinary tract infections can be very painful and debilitating and can impede participation in rehabilitation and employment.[170] In a follow-up study of 71 individuals with SCI, Heinemann and Hawkins found that 30 months after injury, pressure ulcers most often occurred among those who were no longer drinking but had a history of drinking problems.[171] Pressure ulcers were also found more often in those using prescribed medications, and urinary tract infections were associated with illicit drug use. SCI patients must expend considerable energy in self-care in order to avoid medical complications that can become quite serious. Those who were currently abstinent but had preinjury drinking problems also reported more depression and less acceptance of their disability during follow-up. Although concern has centered around SCI patients who are currently drinking, this study also indicates the need to pay attention to former problem drinkers who are currently abstinent. Although this is speculation, current drinkers may be self-medicating or making a better adjustment, while the former problem drinkers who are now abstinent may be experiencing the "dry drunk" syndrome in which they are sober but have not made a good life adjustment. In another study, Heinemann and colleagues also found that greater preinjury drinking among SCI patients was associated with less time spent in productive activities such as rehabilitation.[172]

Some suggestions for screening male SCI patients for substance abuse have emerged in the literature. Rohe and Basford present evidence that the MacAndrew Alcoholism Scale (see Chapter 5) may successfully predict which SCI patients had injuries related to their alcohol use.[173] Earlier detection may promote rehabilitation of those with alcohol abuse and dependency problems and help to deter life-altering SCI accidents. For example, scales such as the MacAndrew may identify young medical patients who have not experienced such serious consequences as SCI but whose alcohol and drug use puts them at risk for such injuries.

One of the first substance abuse treatment programs for SCI patients was developed at the Veterans Administration Spinal Cord Injury Service in Long Beach, California, following drug raids there by federal marshals.[174] It is an integrated service program simultaneously addressing substance abuse and SCI using a therapeutic community model. The Veterans Administration already had treatment programs for alcoholics and addicts, and its SCI units offered the advantages of physical accessibility and the staff and equipment needed for inpatient care. The staff structured the program specifically for this clientele. For example, since it may take a quadriplegic patient two to four hours to accomplish morning hygiene and grooming routines, even with assistance, treatment activities begin later in the day than is the norm in most inpatient chemical dependency programs. The program offers a wide range of services, including education for independent living, assertiveness training, vocational rehabilitation, spiritual awareness, and participation in self-help groups. Clinicians at the program

emphasize the need to avoid providing too much kindness to patients, which often happens when specialized services are not available for them.[175]

Schaschl and Straw describe another type of chemical dependency program that incorporates individuals who have physical impairments (the major physical impairment of clients served by the program is spinal cord injury) with able-bodied patients.[176] There are special group sessions for people with physical impairments to address their unique problems, and special services are also provided to family members. Heinemann and colleagues[177] recommend the "lifestyle assessment and intervention program" which addresses substance use as well as beliefs about use and coping skills.[178]

Traumatic Head and Brain Injury

Like SCI, a link between traumatic head injury or traumatic brain injury (TBI) and substance use, abuse, or dependency seems apparent.[179] Although Miller calls alcohol and other drug disorders "the single greatest risk factor for traumatic brain injury,"[180] the relationship is complex.[181]

According to Sparadeo and Gill, many people believe that an intoxicated individual is more likely to be in an accident, but some also believe that the likelihood of suffering a traumatic injury is reduced, because alcohol is a depressant that relaxes the body.[182] While evidence supports the first of these assumptions, Sparadeo and Gill counter the second. They also report that head trauma patients admitted with a positive blood-alcohol level (BAL), especially those at 0.10 percent or above, experience a more difficult medical course. These patients stayed in the hospital longer, had a longer period of agitation, and had lower cognitive status at the time of discharge. A positive BAL at the time of injury is a problem because "there is an increase in the volume of blood, increasing brain bleeding and agitation."[183] Alcohol also reduces the "ability to marshall an appropriate response to hemorrhage and shock" and "poses a major anesthesia risk for those requiring emergency surgery."[184]

It is not clear, however, whether it is intoxication at the time of injury or a history of alcohol abuse and its related problems that cause a poorer cognitive outcome.[185] A study by Dikmen and associates also raises questions as to whether other variables that may precede or are associated with alcohol abuse, such as lower levels of education and intellectual functioning and poorer neuropsychological functioning, may be a more adequate explanation of poorer outcomes.[186] These researchers did not find that more severe preinjury alcohol problems (as measured using the Short Michigan Alcoholism Screening Test) were associated with poorer postinjury neuropsychological functioning.

An accurate diagnosis is difficult to make immediately following an accident because it may be unclear whether the patient's symptoms are due to intoxication, a head injury, or both.[187] Common symptoms are "lethargy, or agitation, confusion, disorientation, [and] respiratory depression."[188] According to Weinstein and Martin, "After trauma, if alcohol abuse or dependence remains undiagnosed during the evaluation or treatment of TBI, severe neuropsychiatric complications may ensue, including Wernicke-Korsakoff syndrome (if thiamine is not administered prophylactically), seizures, and delirium."[189] Some patients are discharged from the emergency room with diagnoses of intoxication without recognition of having a head injury.[190] Miller says that while both brain injury and psychoactive drug use may result in "poor memory, impaired judgment, fine and gross motor impairments, poor concentration, decreased impulse control, and impaired language," for most people the effects of drug use are largely reversible, whereas the effects from brain injury often are not.[191]

Literature reviews implicate alcohol in more than half of all traumatic head injuries, with 29 to 58 percent of individuals with head injury legally intoxicated at the time the trauma occurred; studies also report that 25 to 68 percent of TBI patients have histories indicative of addiction.[192] Conversely, Hillbom and Holm found that "traumatic head injuries seem to be about two to four times more prevalent in the histories of alcoholics than in the histories of the general population."[193] Alcohol is by far the drug most frequently associated with traumatic brain injury, followed by hashish.[194] Some cocaine use has been reported, although far less frequently; data on other drug use are lacking.[195] The incidence of alcohol use and TBI is greater in men.[196]

As with many other disabilities, substance use or abuse may precede TBI or vice versa. It has been suggested that chemical use following trauma may be prompted by alienation by peers, a change in behavior of family members, a desire to assert independence, or, most often, just plain boredom.[197] However, Kreutzer and associates found that, in general, drinkers curtailed their use of alcohol following traumatic brain injury.[198] According to Sparadeo, the most severely injured do not return to drinking, but of those with moderate or minor injuries, 30 percent and 50 percent, respectively, return to drinking.[199] Head injury professionals believe that substantial numbers of patients do continue to use alcohol and other drugs, and this warrants concern.[200] Alcohol and drug consumption may interfere with cognitive functioning already impaired by the brain trauma. Alcohol use may also be contraindicated due to physical problems and medications taken as a result of brain injury. In addition, there is a high likelihood of a subsequent head injury for those who return to drinking.[201] There may also be an association between substance abuse, antisocial personality (ASP) disorder, and the likelihood of sustaining a traumatic brain injury.[202] Those with ASP tend to act out, and alcohol may contribute to this behavior, resulting in a serious accident. One study indicates that the most frequent postinjury arrests for patients following TBI were alcohol and drug related.[203] Additionally, psychiatric disorders seen in alcoholics and people with TBI include "amnestic states, dementia, mood disorders, personality disorders, and delusional disorders."[204]

Professionals in the head injury field seem to agree that assessment for substance abuse and dependency problems should be routine, but apparently only a portion of programs do this.[205] Since an accurate assessment may be hampered when the patient's memory has been impaired by TBI,[206] Kreutzer and associates recommend the use of multiple assessment tools, including standardized questionnaires, records, and interviews with patients and collaterals in the home setting.[207] They have used three standardized instruments with TBI patients: the Brief MAST (see Chapter 5), the General Health and History Questionnaire (developed by Kreutzer and colleagues), and the Quantity, Frequency, Variability Index (QFVI).[208] Along with neuropsychological and rehabilitation evaluations, Jones recommends the CAGE Questionnaire (also see Chapter 5), because it is brief and minimizes the use of abstract or complex concepts.[209] The CAGE has also been recommended for use with patients who experienced trauma resulting in other types of injuries.[210]

Henry and Jones discuss the behavioral and psychological problems that head injury patients face in recovery.[211] The number and intensity of these problems vary depending on the individual and the injury. Henry notes six problem areas: attention, memory, language, reasoning and judgment, executive functions (abilities of initiation, organization, direction, monitoring, and self-evaluation), and emotion. For example, head injuries may result in a diminution of cause and effect reasoning, of the ability to make inferences, of problem-solving skills, and of determining appropriate behavior. Confabulation to hide memory deficits may be mistaken as intentional dishonesty. Common behaviors among those with TBI such as giggling at inappropriate times (e.g., during group therapy or self-help meetings) or making inappropriate remarks may be misunderstood by others who may then ostracize the person with head injury. In order to help those with head injury, Henry suggests that it is often appropriate for professionals and self-help group sponsors to openly address these behaviors with the individual, discuss specific examples of these behaviors, and give advice gently but firmly for making modifications in behavior.

Similar to those with dual diagnoses of mental and substance disorders, those with TBI or SCI and substance disorders often find that appropriate treatment alternatives are scarce. The refrain has become familiar—rehabilitation centers for those recovering from traumatic brain injury may feel ill equipped to treat problems of chemical dependency, and chemical dependency programs may feel inadequate to respond to the unique aspects of treating those with TBI. Sparadeo and colleagues believe that insurance companies may exacerbate the problem by arguing over which problem should be treated first, or patients find themselves in chemical dependency treatment without comprehensive head injury rehabilitation, because substance abuse treatment is the less costly of the two.[212]

According to Strauss, "We are not dealing with a simple dual diagnosis, but with a truly integrated problem"; therefore, an integrated program of treatment for both the head injury and the substance abuse is recommended.[213] Model programs have been implemented but have yet to be fully evaluated.[214] Behavioral techniques are often used in these programs[215] because deficits experienced by patients with brain injury are likely to make insight-oriented, psychodynamic approaches unsuitable.[216] These behavioral approaches help clients achieve successes by working on long-term goals in small steps.[217] TBI patients with cognitive deficits benefit when material is repeated and presented more slowly than may be done in traditional chemical dependency programs. A longer time period is often needed to engage clients with TBI in overcoming denial, to help them accept a goal of abstinence, and to provide treatment.[218] Miller recommends treatment that is simple, supportive, directive, focused, and concrete.[219] Since the problems of TBI patients vary so widely, individualization of treatment must be the rule. The National Head Injury Foundation located in Washington, DC, is one source of information on the combination of TBI and substance disorders and their treatment.

With regard to self-help groups, concepts used in AA, such as "Higher Power," may be too abstract for those with severe cognitive impairments to grasp.[220] Repetition of the Twelve Steps and making concepts as concrete as possible are suggested.[221] Peterman has reworded the Twelve Steps of Alcoholics Anonymous so that they can be more readily understood by those with head injuries.[222] Regular AA or NA meetings can be followed with sessions for TBI clients so that they can benefit from additional explanation.[223]

Sensory Disabilities

The sensory impairments we discuss are hearing and visual. Although information on these impairments in combination with substance abuse is scarce, the lack of information on visual disabilities is especially striking.

Hearing Impairments

McCrone[224] reports that "the major causes of deafness include premature birth, rubella, meningitis, heredity and Rh incompatibility" and that many deaf clients being treated for substance abuse today have hearing loss as a result of the rubella epidemic ("rubella bubble") of 1964–1965.[225] In one of the few studies of alcohol use among persons who are deaf, Isaacs concluded that "no significant differences were found between the deaf and hearing samples on patterns of drinking or other parameters of alcohol use."[226] His sample was admittedly small, but it was an attempt to bring empirical investigation to this area. Locke and Johnson studied substance use among students at a senior high school for individuals who are deaf.[227] Of the 46 respondents, 26 reported regular alcohol use and 6 reported occasional use. Some drunkenness was reported. Five students had had alcohol-related traffic violations. Fifteen were currently using other drugs and 12 others had tried them. Four re-

spondents had been arrested for disorderly conduct or theft while using drugs. Fulton reported that "one third to one half of the client caseloads in our Counseling and Placement Center at Gallaudet [College] are substance abuse related."[228]

In 1982, McCrone used population estimates of deafness and substance abuse and figured that among persons with deafness, there might be 73,000 alcoholics, 8,500 heroin users, and 14,700 cocaine users.[229] In 1984, Steitler provided estimates of more than 1 million persons with both deafness and substance abuse or dependency.[230] More recent estimates are apparently not available, and it is really not known whether rates of substance use, abuse, or dependency among people who are deaf differ from those of the general population. Dixon expressed surprise that estimates of substance abuse among people who are deaf are not higher, given the misconceptions about deafness and the poor treatment of such people by the public.[231]

The life experiences of those who are prelingually deaf is substantially different from those who became deaf postlingually, and the degree to which individuals with hearing impairments relate to the deaf and hearing communities varies.[232] Families are often overprotective of their deaf members, and the deaf community tends to be close knit and mistrustful of hearing individuals.[233] Within the culture of people who are deaf, substance abuse education, including knowledge about professional treatment resources and self-help groups, is often lacking.[234] As a result, chemical dependency is still often viewed in moralistic terms.[235] According to Boros, members of the deaf community "deny alcoholism among their own, fearful that a dual stigma will be imposed upon them—'deaf and drunk.' "[236] In addition, reports indicate that "the deaf community tends to be very insular, with its own clubs and social life which revolves around alcohol use. An extensive 'grapevine' militates against persons coming forward to discuss and treat their problem."[237] Clients who are deaf often report that a hearing sibling introduced them to drug use.[238]

Assisting substance abusers with hearing impairments requires familiarity with their communication styles. Since the degree of hearing loss varies, some individuals benefit from devices that amplify sound. Among those who are deaf, American Sign Language (ASL) is used most frequently, but it is not the only language: "Variations include spoken English, a mixture of signed and spoken English, manual codes for English, finger-spelled English, unique and privately-developed 'home-signs,' and various regional dialects of American Sign Language."[239] The level of language proficiency also varies. Chemical dependency professionals who rely on "talk therapies" are challenged by gestural languages, since these languages often do not have translations for the jargon of treatment programs and self-help groups.[240] Gestures and other movements used by people who are deaf are often misinterpreted by hearing individuals: "For example, a subtle twitching of the nose signifies 'yeah-I-know,' and a furrowed brow may represent a question"; waving an arm is an attempt to get another's attention, but may be interpreted as abnormal by outsiders and result in misdiagnosis.[241] Determining a client's preferred mode of communication is important, but an appropriate interpreter may not be available. Chemical dependency professionals who can communicate directly with individuals who are hearing impaired are the best choice but are difficult to find. As a result, many hearing impaired substance abusers are underserved.

The first published material on the dual disability of alcoholism and hearing impairment that Boros could find is an article which appeared in *The Grapevine* (AA's newsletter) in December 1968.[242] Special treatment programs did not emerge until the middle of the 1970s. Boros recounts the development of professional services for this population beginning with a program of multiple services (no longer in existence) offered by the Hearing Society of the San Francisco Bay Area. Other programs noted in the literature are the St. Paul-Ramsey Hospital Program for Deaf Alcoholics; the Hurley Medical Center in Flint, Michigan, in conjunction with the area's affiliate of the National Council on Alcoholism and Drug Dependence; and Alcoholism Intervention for the Deaf (AID), which began as a volunteer effort and later became Addiction Intervention with the Disabled.[243]

According to Boros, initial opposition to AID came from the deaf community, which claimed that the program "singled out deaf people from other disabled persons as having drinking problems."[244] Considerable groundwork was done in both the hearing impaired and professional chemical dependency communities to initiate the AID program. In 1979, NIAAA funded a demonstration project for those with deafness and alcoholism at the Cape Cod Alcoholism Intervention and Rehabilitation Unit (CCAIRU) in Massachusetts. This program developed as the result of Paul Rothfeld's friendship with a young man, Stephen Miller, who had dual diagnoses of deafness and substance abuse.[245] No special services for hearing impaired alcoholics were available to Miller. He struggled with his disabilities and eventually took his own life. The facility for CCAIRU clients who are hearing impaired was named for him. More recently, the Center for Substance Abuse Treatment has provided funding for model programs such as the Minnesota Chemical Dependency Program for Deaf and Hard of Hearing Individuals.[246]

The lack of chemical dependency professionals knowledgeable about hearing impairments and the even smaller number who can communicate directly with clients who are deaf results in unresponsiveness toward the deaf community.[247] Professionals can learn to work with an interpreter, but this requires preparation[248] and is not as useful as direct communication. The level of ability of interpreters varies and certified interpreters are usually needed to ensure accurate communication. Professional interpreters subscribe to a code of ethics that includes standards for confidentiality and objectiveness, but clients may still hesitate to reveal confidences with the interpreter present.[249] In crises, interpreters may not be readily available. Family and friends may be able to communicate well with the individual, but the client may not wish to share certain information with them. Another barrier to treatment is the tendency for some people who are hearing impaired to agree passively with professionals rather than express their own opinions.[250] More must be done to foster the participation of people with hearing impairments in substance abuse treatment and to prepare chemical dependency professionals to treat individuals who are hearing impaired. A recent publication of the Substance Abuse Resources and Disability Issues Project is intended to orient substance abuse professionals to deafness and hearing loss.[251]

Many chemical dependency programs use standardized questionnaires and written materials in assessing and treating clients. However, many clients who are deaf do not read at a level that allows them to understand these materials fully.[252] There is a need for validation of diagnostic instruments and development of educational materials for use with these individuals.[253] Some visual aides such as pictorial prevention and treatment materials are available.[254]

With regard to treatment, it has not been determined whether mainstream or separate programs are preferable.[255] However, in mainstream programs, it is not possible to interpret all the interaction for clients with severe hearing impairments.[256] Rothfeld recommends separate programs,[257] whereas the program at the Rochester Institute of Technology brings together members of the hearing and hearing impaired communities to promote mainstreaming of people who are deaf in chemical dependency treatment programs.[258] There is often a need to simplify materials to correspond to clients' reading levels and to slow the pace of presentations since the material is often new to the client.[259] Fatigue may become a factor since the demands of absorbing new material are substantial and gesturing requires additional energy.[260] Longer periods of treatment, especially in inpatient settings, may be needed to compensate for these factors.[261] Although there are some opportunities for inpatient treatment nationwide, outpatient services and aftercare for clients who

are hearing impaired are sorely lacking.[262] Help may not just be a phone call away for the hearing impaired alcoholic.[263] Both treatment programs and clients who are deaf must have Telecommunications Devices for the Deaf (TDD) or at least have access to communication relay services to facilitate calls in times of crisis or at other times when support is needed.[264] There are few halfway houses for substance abusers who are deaf,[265] but this is beginning to change. With the advent of the ADA, more efforts are being made to accommodate individuals with disabilities.

Some self-help groups are conducted in sign language, but the frequency of meetings may be insufficient to adequately assist those who are deaf and chemically dependent.[266] Most self-help groups do not employ interpreters on a regular basis, and bringing one's own interpreter can be expensive and may draw unwanted attention.[267] Interpreting meetings may not be as effective as conducting them entirely in ASL. Few recovering role models who are deaf and alcoholic are available to serve as sponsors.[268] The Stephen Miller House version of the Twelve Steps of Alcoholics Anonymous for persons who are deaf is available from the National Head Injury Foundation.[269] Another version of the steps for individuals who are hearing impaired is found in an article by Hetherington.[270]

A few articles address strategies to assist adolescents who are hearing impaired and who abuse alcohol and other drugs. Reality therapy has been recommended because of its straightforward approach, focus on client strengths, and orientation to the present.[271] Gallaudet College has developed a program for students that incorporates education, prevention, intervention, and treatment and makes use of peer advisors and professionals.[272]

A listing of accessible chemical dependency services is available in national mental health service directories for those with hearing impairments.[273] Sylvester also provides a list of resources,[274] and Alcoholics Anonymous offers literature for hearing impaired alcoholics.[275] Signs of Sobriety (S.O.S.), located in New Jersey, is an advocacy group pressing for legislative reforms in the treatment of deaf chemical abusers.[276]

Visual Impairments

The major cause of vision loss in the United States is diabetes, and diabetes can be aggravated by alcohol or other drug abuse.[277] Other causes of visual problems are cataracts, glaucoma, vascular disease, trauma, and heredity, but the etiology of one-third of the cases is unknown.[278] Approximately 2 million Americans are totally blind or have severe visual impairments.

According to de Miranda, "Without doubt the group of people whose alcohol or other drug problems have been the most ignored . . . are those who are blind or visually impaired."[279] In 1981, Glass described the general course of rehabilitation for individuals with visual handicaps to help acquaint chemical dependency personnel with this process.[280] In 1983, Peterson and Nelipovich published a brief article with basic information about alcohol abuse and alcoholism to assist rehabilitation counselors in identifying these problems among their clientele with visual impairments and in referring them to treatment programs and self-help groups.[281] Recognizing the gap in the literature, Burns and de Miranda[282] and the Addiction Research Foundation[283] developed materials to assist chemical dependency professionals in reaching out to those with visual impairments.

Isolation and unemployment are major problems for those with visual impairments.[284] One study investigated the response of state rehabilitation counselors to their work with visually impaired substance abusers.[285] Of the 32 respondents, half reported no success in helping these clients secure gainful employment and that the client's substance abuse presented a greater obstacle than their visual impairment. The counselors wanted more education in working with clients who have dual disabilities.

To learn more about substance use among individuals with visual impairments, the Wisconsin Bureau of Community Program's Office for Persons with Physical Disabilities and Alcohol and Other Drug Abuse surveyed clients of the state's vocational rehabilitation program and centers for independent living.[286] Of the respondents, 271 were blind or visually impaired. Although the representativeness of the sample is not certain, more of these respondents were heavy drinkers than in the general population (21 percent versus 12 percent, respectively). In addition, drinking was greater among those who lived with other family members than it was among those living alone, suggesting that enabling may play a part in drinking among those with physical disabilities. Also of note was that those who were blind or visually impaired, those with orthopedic impairments, and those with spinal cord injuries were more often heavy drinkers or moderate drinkers than those with other disabilities.

Glass describes two types of problem drinkers among the visually impaired.[287] Type A had a drinking problem prior to the onset of their visual impairment. Glass believes that they lack adequate coping skills and require specific alcoholism treatment. Type B develop alcohol problems after the onset of visual impairments (or another disabling condition). He believes that their chemical abuse may remit following adequate adjustment to the visual disability. In assisting clients, Nelipovich and Buss believe that it is important to recognize which disability came first:[288]

> If the visual impairment is of long standing and if an appropriate level of acceptance of and adjustment to this impairment has been reached before alcohol abuse begins, then treatment should be geared to addressing the alcohol abuse. If the visual impairment has been more recent, then treatment should focus on helping the client to accept and adjust to the visual impairment first, and then on treating the alcohol abuse.

They add that the greatest challenge is to assist those who have accepted neither of their disabilities. To assess the dual disabilities of substance abuse and visual disability, Nelipovich and Buss suggest that professionals employ the ASK approach by determining the client's level of *ac*ceptance of each disability, the client's skills for coping with these disabilities, and the clients *k*nowledge about these disabilities.[289]

Helping professionals are encouraged to remember some basic aspects of interacting with individuals who are visually impaired.[290] For example, communicate directly with the individual rather than deferring to those who might accompany the client to the treatment center. Speak in a normal tone of voice and at a normal speed. Identify yourself to the client and let him or her know when you are entering and leaving the room. Ask individuals how they prefer to acquaint themselves with new surroundings and then help orient them to the physical environment of the treatment setting. In intensive treatment programs, appoint a guide for the first few days to allow the individual time to learn to move about the facility independently. Recreational and social activities might require obtaining Braille playing cards, games, and leisure reading materials.

Treatment facilities can use large-print materials or have magnification devices and other optical aides available so that clients with sufficient vision can utilize educational materials independently without relying on readers. For others, materials in Braille (including admission and consent forms) are useful, but only about 10 percent of those who are blind read Braille. Audiotapes and reading material aloud are also needed. Since most chemical dependency programs are not currently able to provide all the services needed by clients with visual impairments (such as the latest technological equipment), cooperation with agencies that specialize in serving this clientele are needed.[291]

Self-help groups are also recommended for visually impaired substance abusers. It is especially helpful to have a member welcome the newcomer and introduce him or her to others. In addition, members can offer transportation to individuals with visual impairments, especially in communi-

ties where public transportation is lacking. The Big Book and some other AA materials are available in Braille and on audiocassette and can be ordered from AA's General Service Office.

Other Physical Disabilities

Alcohol or drug abuse may be an obvious cause of physically disabling conditions such as liver disease or mental disorders such as organic brain syndrome, but many individuals are unaware of other conditions associated with alcohol abuse. For example, "it is less widely recognized that chronic alcohol abuse may be a predisposing factor of several varieties of arthritis," such as gout.[292] In fact, Wells and colleagues analyzed data from the Epidemiologic Catchment Area study and found that individuals with arthritis were more likely to have had substance, anxiety, and affective disorders than those with no chronic medical conditions.[293]

In many cases, there is a clear indication that use of alcohol or other drugs can exacerbate another disability. For example, although many diabetics are able to accommodate modest amounts of alcohol in their diets, drinking is contraindicated for others.[294] Accurate diagnosis of a diabetic's situation in emergencies can be complicated by the difficulty in distinguishing many of the symptoms of hypoglycemia from those of intoxication.[295] The numbers of individuals who are both diabetic and alcoholic is not thought to be large, but diabetics who drink may incur consequences as severe as brain damage or death.[296]

Although definitive population data are lacking, Wells and colleagues found that lifetime diabetics had no increased propensity over those with no chronic medical condition for substance disorders, although they were more likely to have had anxiety or affective disorders.[297] In a study of 395 patients over age 16 with either insulin-dependent or noninsulin-dependent diabetes mellitus, self-reported problem drinking appeared to be "lower than among other medical outpatient populations" but "in keeping with the prevalence found in community surveys."[298] The gender, ethnic, and age composition of the problem drinkers in this study seemed consistent with that of problem drinkers in general population studies. The problem drinkers were also more likely to smoke. In keeping with the general literature, those identified as having a drinking problem had poorer coping responses to psychological stress and more guilt, hostility, anxiety, and depression than those without drinking problems. The black male patients and the patients with higher negative affects were at greater risk for alcohol problems. The problem drinkers did not perceive their glycemic control as being different than the nonproblem drinkers, and although somewhat surprising due to the negative effects that excessive alcohol consumption can have on people with diabetes, the actual glycemic values of the problem and nonproblem drinkers did not differ.

Gold and Gladstein also found less frequent alcohol and other drug use in a group of 79 campers and counselors, aged 11 to 25, participating in a camp program than in the general population of young people, but scores on a modified version of the MAST indicated that 24 percent had a drinking problem.[299] Those who drank or used drugs tended to have family members who used alcohol or drugs. Most of these 79 young people believed their diabetic control was good to excellent and did not perceive that drinking or drug use would affect diabetic control. Again, there was no relationship between alcohol and drug use and perceived diabetic control, but those identified as problem drinkers were more likely to perceive their diabetic control as poor to fair. The identified problem drinkers were also more likely to believe that alcohol and other drug use altered diabetic control.

In a two-phase study, Glasgow and colleagues first tested 101 young people, aged 12 to 20, attending a diabetes clinic.[300] Like Gold and Gladstein, they were interested in the extent of alcohol and other drug use as well as diabetic control. A total of 26 participants said they had tried alcohol, 19 said they drank occasionally, and 7 reported drinking one or two times a week. Marijuana had been tried by 11 patients, with two reporting occasional use and none reporting weekly use. Other drugs had been tried by 1 to 5 patients, but only in a few instances was occasional use reported, and no one reported weekly use. Self-reported problem alcohol or drug use was lower in this sample, with 10 patients answering yes to at least one of six questions indicating an alcohol or drug problem. Only 1 patient had a urine specimen that tested positive for marijuana, and no other urine samples tested positive for marijuana, cocaine, or PCP. In phase two of the study, 6 patients who had high glycohemoglobin were added to the sample. There was no difference in diabetes control among those who had and had not tried alcohol. Those who reported occasional use of other drugs and those who reported any problem with alcohol or other drugs had higher glycohemoglobin values that were significant at the 0.1 but not at the 0.05 level. Patients reporting that a parent had an alcohol or drug problem also had higher glycohemoglobin values.

These findings should be viewed cautiously due to the small number reporting drug use, but the authors note that although drug use may not cause poor diabetic control, both drug use and poor diabetic control may be associated with risk-taking behavior. These studies support the notion that substance abuse is not any greater among people with diabetes. They also indicate a need for medical personnel to evaluate and educate people with diabetes about alcohol intake and to make referrals to substance abuse treatment when needed. In particular, adolescents who are prone to experiment with alcohol or other drugs need information that will help them avoid a medical emergency.

There is evidence that alcohol can make an individual with epilepsy more prone to seizures.[301] The exact relationship among alcohol consumption, epilepsy, and seizures is a subject of controversy in the medical community, but according to Stoil, "Epileptics who drink to intoxication encounter high risks, in part because of the indirect effects of alcohol consumption on management of their condition."[302] At a minimum, he advises that those with epilepsy be informed of these risks and that patients should be monitored for symptoms of substance abuse to prevent serious negative consequences. Individuals with epilepsy who have not been drinking and not been taking nonprescribed drugs are sometimes mistaken as intoxicated due to the disorientation and lack of coordination that follows a seizure. Likewise, even in the absence of alcohol and other drug use, seizures can be problems for those with mental retardation or traumatic brain injury. Law-enforcement officers working the streets must take care not to make an erroneous arrest for public intoxication or an inappropriate referral to a detoxification center. Medical personnel are certainly aware of the need to make this distinction. It should also be remembered that alcohol and drug abuse can cause seizures in individuals who do not have other disabilities.

In many cases, some of the psychoactive drugs discussed in this book are prescribed to bring relief to an individual suffering a severe injury or illness despite the potential for addiction. For example, individuals with back injuries or other conditions may be prescribed analgesics for pain. More controversial is the experimental use of marijuana to treat various medical conditions, especially now that California and Arizona have laws permitting use for medical purposes, even though these laws conflict with federal statutes. But many individuals use alcohol and other drugs in ways that are not therapeutic and that can result in dependence or cause or aggravate other conditions. Clearly, the interactions of substance abuse and other disabilities can be quite complex—as complex as the individual who has them.

Resources

A number of resources are available to assist those interested in substance disorders and other physi-

cal or mental impairments. Some of those specific to particular disabilities have been referred to earlier in this chapter. Others address a broad range of disabilities. The federal government's National Clearinghouse for Alcohol and Drug Information (NCADI) located in Rockville, Maryland, is one such source of information. The National Center for Youth with Disabilities located in Minneapolis, Minnesota, is also concerned with multiple disabilities. Its newsletter is called *Connections* and it has published a special issue of *CYDLINE Reviews* entitled "Substance Abuse by Youth with Disabilities and Chronic Illnesses."[303] Other resources in the field are the Resource Center on Substance Abuse Prevention and Disability, located in Washington, DC, and Substance Abuse Resources and Disability Issues (SARDI) at Wright State University in Dayton, Ohio, both funded by the U.S. Department of Health and Human Services. The National Association on Alcohol, Drugs and Disability can be reached at 2165 Bunker Hill Drive, San Mateo, CA 94402-3801 (415-578-8047).

Summary

This chapter reviewed information on the combination of psychoactive substance disorders and other disabilities, including the systems that respond to these problems. Any physical or mental disability may coexist with substance abuse. Substance abuse may predate or precipitate another disability, as is often the case with spinal cord injury, traumatic brain injury, or other tragic accidents. Coping with a physical or mental disability may also result in the abuse of alcohol or nonprescribed drugs to diminish psychological anguish or physical pain or to produce euphoric affects. Yet multiple disabilities do not necessarily occur in a cause-effect relationship. An individual's visual impairment, for example, may be unrelated to his or her alcohol or drug abuse.

Those interested in the combination of chemical dependency and other disabilities will continue to investigate and debate statistics on prevalence rates and question the nature of the relationship between substance disorders and other disabilities. For prevention specialists and treatment providers, the most pressing concern is that individuals with multiple disabilities need help now. The combination of disabling conditions presents a challenge to those with multiple diagnoses, their loved ones, and the professionals who work with them. Although there are some helpful suggestions from those in the field, few cookbook-style solutions or tested approaches are available. The development of more innovative programs for substance abusers with other disabilities and studies of their effectiveness would be particularly helpful. Meanwhile, a resourceful professional who is continually willing to be informed remains a tremendous asset to rehabilitation, second only to the tenacity of clients and their loved ones in overcoming these adversities.

Endnotes

1. Diana M. DiNitto and A. James Schwab, "Screening for Undetected Substance Abuse among Vocational Rehabilitation Clients," *American Rehabilitation*, Vol. 19, No. 1 (1993), pp. 12–20.

2. Kirby Ingraham, Steven Kaplan, and Fong Chan, "Rehabilitation Counselors' Awareness of Client Alcohol Abuse Patterns," *Journal of Applied Rehabilitation Counseling*, Vol. 23, No. 3 (1992), pp. 18–22.

3. See, for example, Bobby G. Greer, "Substance Abuse among People with Disabilities: A Problem of Too Much Accessibility," *Journal of Rehabilitation*, Vol. 52, No. 1 (1986), pp. 34–38; and M. Nelipovich and E. Buss, "Investigating Alcohol Abuse among Persons Who Are Blind," *Journal of Visual Impairment and Blindness* (October 1991), pp. 343–345.

4. Alexander Boros, "Facing the Challenge," *Alcohol Health & Research World*, Vol. 13, No. 2 (1989), p. 103.

5. Margaret H. Hindman, "The Multidisabled: Emerging Responses," *Alcohol Health & Research World* (Winter 1980–81), pp. 4–10.

6. "Comorbidity: Mental and Addictive Disorders," *ADAMHA NEWS*, Fifteenth Anniversary Issue (March–April 1989), p. 13; and Frederick K. Goodwin, "From the Alcohol, Drug Abuse, and Mental Health Administration," *Journal of the American Medical Association* (June 23/30, 1989), p. 3517.

7. Lial Kofoed and Alison Keys, "Using Group Therapy to Persuade Dual-Diagnosis Patients to Seek Substance Abuse Treatment," *Hospital and Community Psychiatry*, Vol. 39, No. 11 (1988), pp. 1209–1211.

8. U.S. Bureau of the Census, *Statistical Abstract of the United States: 1996* (Washington, DC: U.S. Government Printing Office, 1996), Table 213, p. 140.

9. Mary C. Dufour, Daryl Bertolucci, Carol Cowell, Frederick S. Stinson, and John Noble, "Alcohol-Related Morbidity among the Disabled, The Medicare Experience, 1985," *Alcohol Health & Research World* (Winter 1989), pp. 158–161.

10. "Comorbidity: Mental and Addictive Disorders"; and Hindman, "The Multidisabled."

11. See John de Miranda, "Join Us in Seeking Equitable Treatment for the Disabled," *Alcoholism and Drug Abuse Weekly*, November 4, 1996.

12. See Dennis Moore and Jo Ann Ford, "Policy Responses to Substance Abuse and Disability," *Journal of Disability Policy Studies*, Vol. 7, No. 1 (1996), pp. 91–106.

13. See "Senate-Passed Bill Prohibits Bias against the Disabled," *Congressional Quarterly Weekly Report*, September 16, 1989, p. 2417.

14. John de Miranda, "The Common Ground: Alcoholism, Addiction and Disability," *Addiction & Recovery* (August 1990), pp. 42–45. For additional information on alcoholism, drug addiction, and the ADA, see Linda R. Shaw, Paula W. MacGillis, and Keith M. Dvorchik, "Alcoholism and the Americans with Disabilities Act: Obligations and Acommodations," *Rehabilitation Counseling Bulletin*, Vol. 38, No. 2 (1994), pp. 108–123.

15. An earlier version of this section appears in Deborah K. Webb and Diana M. DiNitto, "Clinical Practice with Clients Having Dual Diagnoses: Mental Illness and Substance Abuse," in Roberta G. Sands, *Clinical Social Work Practice in Community Mental Health* (New York: Macmillan, 1991), pp. 291–332, by prior agreement.

16. See, for example, Dennis C. Daley, Howard Moss, and Frances Campbell, *Dual Disorders: Counseling Clients with Chemical Dependency and Mental Illness* (Center City, MN: Hazelden Foundation, 1987).

17. American Psychiatric Association, *Diagnostic and Statistical Manual of Mental Disorders*, 4th ed. (Washington, DC: The Association, 1994).

18. Kathleen Sciacca, "An Integrated Approach for Severely Mentally Ill Individuals with Substance Disorders," in Kenneth Minkoff and Robert E. Drake (Eds.), *Dual Diagnosis of Major Illness and Substance Disorder* (San Fransisco: Jossey-Bass, 1991), pp. 69–84; and Sharon C. Ekleberry, "Dual Diagnosis: Addiction and Axis II Personality Disorders," *The Counselor* (March/April 1996), pp. 7–13.

19. Kenneth Minkoff, "Beyond Deinstitutionalization: A New Ideology for the Postinstitutional Era," *Hospital and Community Psychiatry*, Vol. 38, No. 9 (1987), pp. 945–950;

also see Helen E. Ross, Frederick B. Glaser, and Teresa Germanson, "The Prevalence of Psychiatric Disorders in Patients with Alcohol and Other Drug Problems," *Archives of General Psychiatry*, Vol. 45 (1988), pp. 1023–1031.

20. Darrel A. Regier, Mary E. Farmer, Donald S. Rae, Ben Z. Locke, Samuel J. Keith, Lewis L. Judd, and Frederick K. Goodwin, "Comorbidity of Mental Disorders with Alcohol and Other Drug Abuse: Results from the Epidemiologic Catchment Area (ECA) Study," *JAMA*, Vol. 264, No. 19 (November 21, 1990), pp. 2511–2518.

21. Ronald C. Kessler, Christopher B. Nelson, Katherine A. McGonagle et al., "The Epidemiology of Co-occurring Addictive and Mental Disorders: Implications for Prevention and Service Utilization," *American Journal of Orthopsychiatry*, Vol. 66, No. 1 (1996), pp. 17–31, quote from p. 25.

22. Bridget F. Grant, "Comorbidity between DSM-IV Drug Use Disorders and Major Depression: Results of a National Survey of Adults," *Journal of Substance Abuse*, Vol. 7, No. 4 (1995), pp. 481–497, quote from p. 489.

23. Arthur I. Alterman, "Substance Abuse in Psychiatric Patients: Etiological, Developmental, and Treatment Considerations," in Arthur I. Alterman (Ed.), *Substance Abuse and Psychopathology* (New York: Plenum Press, 1985), pp. 121–136.

24. Kenneth Minkoff, "Dual Diagnosis Workshop"; Texas Department of Mental Health and Mental Retardation, Austin, May 1990.

25. Marc Schuckit, "Alcoholic Patients with Secondary Depression," *American Journal of Psychiatry*, Vol. 140, No. 6 (1983), pp. 711–714.

26. Ann Bauer, "Dual Diagnosis Patients: The State of the Problem," *TIE-Lines*, Vol. 14, No. 3 (1987), p. 1; Minkoff, "Beyond Deinstitutionalization"; and Bert Pepper and Hilary Ryglewicz, "Schizophrenia: A Constant Brain Disorder in a Changing World," Presentation at the 140th Annual Meeting of the American Psychiatric Association, Chicago, IL (New City, NY: TIE-Lines, 1987).

27. Minkoff, "Dual Diagnosis Workshop"; and Bert Pepper, "Dual Disorders," presentation, Houston, TX, September 1990.

28. Hilary Ryglewicz and Bert Pepper, *Alcohol, Drugs, and Mental/Emotional Problems: What You Need to Know to Help Your Dual-Disorder Client* (New City, NY: The Information Exchange, 1990), p. 39.

29. Ibid.

30. Roger D. Weiss and Steven M. Mirin, "The Dual Diagnosis Alcoholic: Evaluation and Treatment," *Psychiatric Annals*, Vol. 19, No. 5 (1989), pp. 261–265; Siegfried H. Soika, "Mental Illness and Alcoholism: Implications for Treatment," in David Cook, Christine Fewell, and John Riolo (Eds.), *Social Work Treatment of Alcohol Problems* (Rutgers, NJ: Rutgers Center of Alcohol Studies, 1983), pp. 88–108; William D. Clark, "Alcoholism: Blocks to Diagnosis and Treatment," *The American Journal of Medicine*, Vol. 71 (1981), pp. 275–286; and A. Scott Winter, "Dual Diagnosis = Double Trouble," *The Counselor* (January/February 1991), pp. 9 and 34.

31. Winston M. Turner and Ming T. Tsuang, "Impact of Substance Abuse on the Course and Outcome of Schizophrenia," *Schizophrenia Bulletin*, Vol. 16, No. 1 (1990), pp. 87–95.

32. Linda D. Menicucci, Laurie Wermuth, and James Sorenson, "Treatment Providers' Assessment of Dual-Prognosis Patients: Diagnosis, Treatment, Referral, and Family Involvement," *The International Journal of the Addictions*, Vol. 23, No. 6 (1988), pp. 617–622.

33. John A. Ewing, "Detecting Alcoholism, The CAGE Questionnaire," *Journal of the American Medical Association*, Vol. 252, No. 14 (1984), pp. 1905–1907; and Booker Bush, Sheila Shaw, Paul Cleary, Thomas L. Delbanco, and Mark A. Aronson, "Screening for Alcohol Abuse Using the CAGE Questionnaire," *The American Journal of Medicine*, Vol. 82 (1987), pp. 231–235.

34. Melvin L. Selzer, "The Michigan Alcoholism Screening Test: The Quest for a New Diagnostic Instrument," *American Journal of Psychiatry*, Vol. 127 (1971), pp. 1653–1658.

35. Glenn A. Miller, Franklin J. Miller, James Roberts, Marlene K. Brooks, and Linda E. Lazowski, *The SASSI-3* (Bloomington, IN: Baugh Enterprises, 1977).

36. A. Thomas McLellan, Lester Luborsky, George E. Woody, and Charles P. O'Brien, "An Improved Diagnostic Evaluation Instrument for Substance Abuse Patients: The Addiction Severity Index," *The Journal of Nervous and Mental Diease*, Vol. 168 (1980), pp. 26–33.

37. See Robert E. Drake, Fred C. Osher, Douglas L. Noorsdy, Stephanie C. Hurlbut, Gregory B. Teague, Malcolm S. Beaudett, "Diagnosis of Alcohol Use Disorders in Schizophrenia," *Schizophrenia Bulletin*, Vol. 16 (1990), pp. 57–67.

38. Aaron T. Beck, *Beck Depression Inventory* (San Antonio, TX: The Psychological Corporation, 1978).

39. American Psychiatric Association, *Diagnostic and Statistical Manual of Mental Disorders*, 4th ed.

40. Sela Barker, Nancy Barron, Bentson McFarland, and Douglas Bigelow, *Multnomah Community Ability Scale: User's Manual* (Portland, OR: Western Mental Health Center, Oregon Health Science University, 1993).

41. David Lukoff, Robert Paul Liberman, and Keith H. Neuchterlein, "Symptom Monitoring in Rehabilitation of Schizophrenic Patients," *Schizophrenia Bulletin*, Vol. 12, No. 4 (1986), pp. 578–602.

42. David Mee-Lee, "Diagnostic Dilemmas in Working with Dually Diagnosed Clients," *The Counselor* (January/February 1991), pp. 10–12.

43. Darold A. Treffert, "Marijuana Use in Schizophrenia: A Clear Hazard," *American Journal of Psychiatry*, Vol. 135, No. 10 (1978), pp. 1213–1215.

44. Edward J. Khantzian, "The Self-Medication Hypothesis of Addictive Disorders: Focus on Heroin and Cocaine Dependence," *American Journal of Psychiatry*, Vol. 142, No. 11 (1985), pp. 1259–1264.

45. Franklin R. Schneier and Samuel G. Siris, "A Review of Psychoactive Substance Use and Abuse in Schizophrenia: Patterns of Choice," *The Journal of Nervous and Mental Disease*, Vol. 175, No. 11 (1987), p. 641.

46. A. Thomas McLellan, Anna Rose Childress, and George E. Woody, "Drug Abuse and Psychiatric Disorder: Role of Drug Choice," in Arthur I. Alterman (Ed.), *Substance Abuse and Psychopathology* (New York: Plenum Press, 1985), pp. 137–172.

47. Also see Khantzian, "The Self-Medication Hypothesis"; Schneier and Siris, "A Review of Psychoactive Substance Use"; and Lisa Dixon, Gretchen Haas, Peter J. Weiden, John Sweeney, and Allen J. Frances, "Drug Abuse in Schizophrenic Patients: Clinical Correlates and Reasons for Use," *American Journal of Psychiatry*, Vol. 148, No. 2 (1991), pp. 224–230.

48. Alexander H. Glassman, "Cigarette Smoking: Implications for Psychiatric Illness," *American Journal of Psychiatry*, Vol. 150, No. 4 (1993), pp. 546–553; quote from p. 551.

49. Deborah K. Webb, *Good Chemistry Co-Leader's Manual* (Austin, TX: © Deborah K. Webb 1992, 1995); Michael G. Bricker, *STEMSS, Support Together for Emotional and Mental Serenity and Sobriety* (West Bend, WI: © Michael G. Bricker 1989, 1991); Bricker, *The Twelve Parallels Between Chemical Dependency and Mental Illness* (West Bend, WI: © Michael G. Bricker 1989); also see Kathleen Sciacca, "New Initiatives in the Treatment of the Chronic Patient with Alcohol/Substance Use Problems," *TIE-Lines*, Vol. 4, No. 3 (July 1987), pp. 5–6.

50. Dennis C. Daley, "Relapse Prevention Strategies for Dual Disorders," *The Counselor* (March/April 1996), pp. 26–29.

51. Sciacca, "An Integrated Approach for Severely Mentally Ill Individuals with Substance Disorders"; Ekleberry, "Dual Diagnosis: Addiction and Axis II Personality Disorders."

52. A. Thomas McLellan, Lester Luborsky, George E. Woody, Charles P. O'Brien, and Keith A. Druley, "Predicting Response to Alcohol and Drug Abuse Treatments," *Archives of General Psychiatry*, Vol. 40 (June 1983), pp. 620–625; and Katie Evans and J. Michael Sullivan, *Dual Diagnosis: Counseling the Mentally Ill Substance Abuser* (New York: Guilford Press, 1990).

53. Ekleberry, "Dual Diagnosis: Addiction and Axis II Personality Disorders."

54. Patricia Ann Harrison, Jodi A. Martin, Vincente B. Tuason, and Norman G. Hoffman, "Conjoint Treatment of Dual Disorders," in Alterman, *Substance Abuse and Psychopathology*, pp. 367–390.

55. Phyllis Solomon and Joseph Davis, "The Effects of Alcohol Abuse among the New Chronically Mentally Ill," *Social Work in Health Care*, Vol. 11, No. 3 (1986), pp. 65–74.

56. Ryglewicz and Pepper, *Alcohol, Drugs, and Mental/Emotional Problems*; and Webb and DiNitto, "Clinical Practice with Clients Having Dual Diagnoses: Mental Illness and Substance Abuse."

57. Daley, Moss, and Campbell, *Dual Disorders*.

58. Edward L. Hendrickson, "Treating the Dually Diagnosed (Mental Disorder/Substance Use) Client," *TIE-Lines*, Vol. 5, No. 4 (1988), pp. 1–4.

59. Michael G. Bricker, *STEMSS and 12 Step Recovery Programs: A Comparison* (West Bend, WI: © Michael G. Bricker, 1989); K. Minkoff, "An Integrated Treatment Model for Dual Diagnosis of Psychosis and Addiction," *Hospital and Community Psychiatry*, Vol. 40, No. 10 (1989), pp. 1031–1036; Robert E. Drake, Gregory J. McHugo, and Douglas L. Noordsy, "Treatment of Alcoholism among Schizophrenic Outpatients: 4-Year Outcomes," *American Journal of Psychiatry*, Vol. 150, No. 2 (1993), pp. 328–329; and Stephen J. Bartels and Winfield N. Thomas, "Lessons from a Pilot Residential Treatment Program for People with Dual Diagnoses of Severe Mental Illness and Substance Use Disorder," *Psychosocial Rehabilitation Journal*, Vol. 15, No. 2 (1991), pp. 19–30; Edward L. Hendrickson, Marilyn Strauss Schmal, and Judith Cousins, "Modifying Group Treatment for Seriously Mentally Ill Substance Abusers," *The Counselor* (March/April 1996), pp. 18–23.

60. Minkoff, "An Integrated Treatment Model."

61. Bricker, *The Twelve Parallels between Chemical Dependency and Mental Illness*.

62. Diane P. Bakdash, "Psychiatric/Mental Health Nursing," in Gerald Bennett, Christine Vourakis, and Donna S. Woolf (Eds.), *Substance Abuse: Pharmacologic, Devepmental, and Clinical Perspectives* (New York: John Wiley and Sons, 1983), pp. 223–239.

63. Bert Pepper, "Some Experience with Psychoeducation Groups for Clients with Dual Disorders," *TIE-Lines*, Vol. 8, No. 2 (1991), p. 4.

64. See, for example, Kate Aliesan and Robert C. Firth, "A MICA Program: Outpatient Rehabilitation Services for Individuals with Concurrent Mental Illness and Chemical Abuse Disorders," *Journal of Applied Rehabilitation Counseling*, Vol. 21, No. 3 (1990), pp. 25–29; Kofoed and Keys, "Using Group Therapy"; and Fred C. Osher and Lial L. Kofoed, "Treatment of Patients with Psychiatric and Psychoactive Substance Abuse Disorders," *Hospital and Community Psychiatry*, Vol. 40, No. 10 (1989), pp. 1025–1030.

65. Webb, *Good Chemistry Co-Leader's Manual*.

66. Kofoed and Keys, "Using Group Therapy"; and R. M. Atkinson, "Persuading Alcoholic Patients to Seek Treatment," *Comprehensive Therapy*, Vol. 11 (1985), pp. 16–24.

67. See, for example, Mark Keller, "Alcoholism: Nature and Extent of the Problem," in Seldon D. Bacon (Ed.),

Understanding Alcoholism: Annals of the American Academy of Political and Social Science (Philadelphia: The American Academy of Political and Social Science Society, 1958), pp. 1–11.

68. Sciacca, "New Initiatives"; and Mark Schuckit, "Alcoholism and Other Psychiatric Disorders," *Hospital and Community Psychiatry*, Vol. 34, No. 11 (1983), pp. 1022–1026.

69. Kofoed and Keys, "Using Group Therapy," p. 1210; also see Osher and Kofoed, "Treatment of Patients."

70. Gary R. Bond, Elizabeth C. McDonel, Larry D. Miller, and Michelle Pensec, "Assertive Community Treatment and Reference Groups: An Evaluation of Their Effectiveness for Young Adults with Serious Mental Illness and Substance Abuse Problems," *Psychosocial Rehabilitation Journal*, Vol. 15, No. 2 (1991), pp. 31-43.

71. Laura E. Blankertz and Ram A. Cnaan, "Assessing the Impact of Two Residential Programs for Dually Diagnosed Homeless Individuals," *Social Service Review*, Vol. 68, No. 4 (1994), pp. 536–560.

72. Jeanette M. Jerrell and M. Susan Ridgely, "Comparative Effectiveness of Three Approaches to Serving People with Severe Mental Illness and Substance Abuse Disorders," *Journal of Nervous and Mental Disease*, Vol. 183 (1995), pp. 566–576.

73. Anthony F. Lehman, John D. Herron, Robert P. Schwartz, and C. Patrick Myers, "Rehabilitation for Adults with Severe Mental Illness and Substance Use Disorders: A Clinical Trial," *Journal of Nervous and Mental Disease*, Vol. 14 (1993), pp. 86–90.

74. M. Audrey Burnam, Sally C. Morton, Elizabeth A. McGlynn et al., "An Experimental Evaluation of Residential and Nonresidential Treatment for Dually Diagnosed Homeless Adults," *Journal of Addictive Diseases*, Vol. 14 (1995), pp. 111–134.

75. Deborah K. Webb and Diana M. DiNitto, "Initial Findings from the Effectiveness of Good Chemistry with Dually Diagnosed Consumers: An Experimental Study," Austin, TX: Hogg Foundation for Mental Health, 1997.

76. H. Richard Lamb, "Will We Save the Homeless Mentally Ill?" *American Journal of Psychiatry*, Vol. 147, No. 5 (1990), pp. 649–651.

77. Webb, *Good Chemistry Co-Leader's Manual.*

78. Carol L. M. Caton, Alexander Gralnick, Stephen Bender, and Robert Simon, "Young Chronic Patients and Substance Abuse," *Hospital and Community Psychiatry*, Vol. 40, No. 10 (1989), p. 1039.

79. Osher and Kofoed, "Treatment of Patients with Psychiatric and Psychoactive Substance Abuse Disorders"; M. Susan Ridgely, Fred C. Osher, and John A. Talbott, *Chronic Mentally Ill Young Adults with Substance Abuse Problems: Treatment and Training Issues* (Baltimore: University of Maryland School of Medicine, October 1987); Minkoff, "An Integrated Treatment Model"; and Menicucci et al., "Treatment Providers' Assessment."

80. Sciacca, "New Initiatives."

81. Larry Lawlor, "Re: The 3-D Client: Responsibility Abyss," *TIE-Lines*, Vol. 4, No. 3 (July 1987), p. 7; also see Robert E. Drake, Gregory B. Teague, and S. Reid Warren III, "Dual Diagnosis: The New Hampshire Program," *Addiction and Recovery* (June 1990), pp. 35–39.

82. Daley et al., *Dual Disorders.*

83. Sciacca, "New Initiatives"; and Aliesan and Firth, "A MICA Program."

84. Robert E. Drake, Stephen J. Bartels, Gregory B. Teague, Douglas L. Noordsy, and Robin E. Clark, "Treatment of Substance Abuse in Severely Mentally Ill Patients," *Journal of Nervous and Mental Disease*, Vol. 181, No. 10 (October 1993), pp. 606-611.

85. Leonard I. Stein and Mary Ann Test, "Alternative to Mental Hospital Treatment. I. Conceptual Model, Treatment Program, and Clinical Evaluation," *Archives of General Psychiatry*, Vol. 37 (April 1980), pp. 392–397.

86. Terrence T. Gorski and Merlene Miller, *Staying Sober: A Guide for Relapse Prevention* (Independence, MO: Independence Press, 1986).

87. Kathleen Sciacca, "An Integrated Approach for Severely Mentally Ill Individuals with Substance Disorders."

88. William R. McFarlane, Edward Dunne, Ellen Lukens, Margaret Newmark, Joanne McLaughlin-Toran, Susan Deakins, and Bonnie Horen, "From Research to Clinical Practice: Dissemination of New York State's Family Psychoeducation Project," *Hospital and Community Psychiatry*, Vol. 44, No. 3 (March 1993), pp. 265–270; and Carol M. Anderson, Douglas J. Reiss, and Gerard E. Hogarty, *Schizophrenia and the Family: A Practitioner's Guide to Psychoeducation and Management* (New York: Guilford Press, 1986).

89. Edie Mannion, Kim Mueser, and Phyllis Solomon, "Designing Psychoeducational Services for Spouses of Persons with Serious Mental Illness," *Community Mental Health Journal*, Vol. 30, No. 2 (April 1994), pp. 177–191; and Lisa Dixon, Scott McNary, and Anthony Lehman, "Substance Abuse and Family Relationships of Persons with Severe Mental Illness," *American Journal of Psychiatry*, Vol. 152, No. 3 (March 1995), 456–458.

90. John D. Woods, "Incorporating Services for Chemical Dependency Problems into Clubhouse Model Programs: A Description of Two Programs," *Psychosocial Rehabilitation Journal*, Vol. 15, No. 2 (October 1991), pp. 107–111.

91. Susan Caldwell and Kalma Kartell White, "Co-Creating a Self-Help Recovery Movement," *Psychosocial Rehabilitation Journal*, Vol. 15, No. 2 (October 1991), pp. 91–95; also see Douglas L. Noordsy, Brenda Schwab, Lindy Fox, and Robert E. Drake, "The Role of Self-Help Programs in the Rehabilitation of Persons with Severe Mental Illness and Substance Use Disorders," in Thomas J. Powell (Ed.), *Understanding the Self-Help Organization: Frameworks and Findings* (Thousand Oaks, CA: Sage Publications, 1994), pp. 314–330.

92. Bricker, *STEMSS and 12-Step Recovery Programs;* and Bricker, *STEMSS, Support Together.*

93. Informational materials from the Eisenhower Circle Group of Alcoholics Anonymous (Ypsilanti, MI).

94. Tim Hamilton and Pat Samples, *The Twelve Steps and Dual Disorders: A Framework of Recovery for Those of Us With Addiction and an Emotional or Psychiatric Illness* (Center City, MN: Hazelden Educational Materials, 1994); and Tim Hamilton and Pat Samples, *The Twelve Steps and Dual Disorders Workbook* (Center City, MN: Hazelden Educational Materials, 1995).

95. Webb, *Good Chemistry Co-Leader's Manual.* For more information on Good Chemistry, contact Deborah K. Webb at P.O. Box 3073, Austin, TX 78764-3073.

96. Alcoholics Anonymous World Services, Inc., *The A.A. Member—Medications and Other Drugs* (New York: AA, 1984).

97. Minkoff, "An Integrated Treatment Model."

98. See Herbert J. Grossman (Ed.), *Classification in Mental Retardation* (Washington, DC: American Association on Mental Deficiency, 1983); also see American Association on Mental Retardation, *Mental Retardation: Definition, Classification, and Systems of Support, Workbook* (Washington, DC: The Association, 1992).

99. See Henry Goddard, *The Kallikak Family, A Study in the Heredity of Feeble-Mindedness* (New York: Macmillan, 1912); W. N. East, "Mental Defectiveness and Alcohol and Drug Addiction," *British Journal of Inebriety,* Vol. 29 (1932), pp. 149–168, cited in Joseph Westermeyer, Thithiya Phaobtong, and John Neider, "Substance Use and Abuse among Mentally Retarded Persons: A Comparison of Patients and a Survey Population," *American Journal of Drug and Alcohol Abuse,* Vol. 14, No. 1 (1988), pp. 109–123; and Ruth E. Fairbank, "The Subnormal Child—Seventeen Years After," *Mental Hygiene,* Vol. 17, No. 2 (1933), pp. 177–208.

100. J. E. Wallace Wallin, *Mental Deficiency in Relation to Problems of Genesis, Social Work and Occupational Consequences, Utilization, Control, and Prevention* (Brandon, VT: Journal of Clinic Psychology, 1956).

101. R. F. Tredgold and K. Soddy, *Textbook of Mental Deficiency (Subnormality),* 10th ed. (Baltimore: William and Wilkens, 1963).

102. Stanley Powell Davies, *The Mentally Retarded in Society* (New York: Columbia University Press, 1959).

103. Westermeyer et al., "Substance Use and Abuse among Mentally Retarded Persons"; also see Curtis H. Krishef and Diana M. DiNitto, "Alcohol Abuse among Mentally Retarded Individuals," *Mental Retardation,* Vol. 19, No. 4 (1981), pp. 151–155.

104. Allen M. Huang, "The Drinking Behavior of the Educable Mentally Retarded and the Nonretarded Students," *Journal of Alcohol and Drug Education,* Vol. 26, No. 3 (1981), pp. 41–50; Krishef and DiNitto, "Alcohol Abuse

among Mentally Retarded Individuals"; Robert B. Edgerton, "Alcohol and Drug Use by Mentally Retarded Adults," *American Journal of Mental Deficiency,* Vol. 90, No. 6 (1986), pp. 602–609; and Andrew S. Halpern, Daniel W. Close, and Debra J. Nelson, *On My Own: The Impact of Semi-Independent Living Programs for Adults with Mental Retardation* (Baltimore: Paul H. Brookes, 1986).

105. Frank Wenc, "The Developmentally Disabled Substance Abuser," *Alcohol Health and Research World* (Winter 1980/81), pp. 42–46; and Bella H. Selan, "The Psychological Consequences of Alcohol Use or Abuse by Retarded Persons," paper presented at the American Association on Mental Deficiency, Annual Conference, Detroit, MI, May 26, 1981.

106. Wenc, "The Developmentally Disabled Substance Abuser."

107. Selan, "The Psychological Consequences of Alcohol Use or Abuse by Retarded Persons," p. 6.

108. Ibid., p. 5.

109. Dennis Moore and Jo Ann Ford, "Prevention of Substance Abuse among Persons with Disabilities: A Demonstration Model," *Prevention Forum,* Vol. 11, No. 2 (Winter 1991), pp. 1–3, 7–10.

110. Also see Westermeyer et al., "Substance Use and Abuse among Mentally Retarded Persons."

111. Wayne L. Sengstock, Glenn A. Vergason, and Margaret M. Sullivan, "Considerations and Issues in a Drug Abuse Program for the Mentally Retarded," *Education and Training of the Mentally Retarded,* Vol. 10 (October 1975), pp. 139–143.

112. Dawn Delaney and Alan Poling, "Drug Abuse among Mentally Retarded People: An Overlooked Problem?" *Journal of Alcohol and Drug Education,* Vol. 35, No. 2 (1990), pp. 48–54.

113. Dennis Moore and Lewis Polsgrove, "Disabilities, Developmental Handicaps, and Substance Misuse: A Review," *The International Journal of the Addictions,* Vol. 26, No. 1 (1991), pp. 65–90.

114. Huang, "The Drinking Behavior of the Educable Mentally Retarded."

115. Edgerton, "Alcohol and Drug Use by Mentally Retarded Adults."

116. Steven Reiss, "Prevalence of Dual Diagnosis in Community-Based Day Programs in the Chicago Metropolitan Area," *American Journal on Mental Retardation,* Vol. 94, No. 6, (1990), pp. 578–585.

117. Halpern et al., *On My Own.*

118. Diana M. DiNitto and Curtis H. Krishef, "Drinking Patterns of Mentally Retarded Persons," *Alcohol Health & Research World* (Winter 1983/84), pp. 40–42.

119. Beverly A. Myers, "Psychiatric Problems in Adolescents with Developmental Disabilities," *Journal of the American Academy of Child and Adolescent Psychiatry,* Vol. 26, No. 1 (1987), pp. 74–79.

120. Also see Delaney and Poling, "Drug Abuse among Mentally Retarded People," for a review of this literature on substance abuse and mental retardation.

121. Edgerton, "Alcohol and Drug Use by Mentally Retarded Adults"; also see Halpern et al., *On My Own.*

122. Edgerton, "Alcohol and Drug Use by Mentally Retarded Adults."

123. Ibid.

124. Halpern et al., *On My Own.*

125. Ibid.; and Krishef and DiNitto, "Alcohol Abuse among Mentally Retarded Individuals."

126. Krishef and DiNitto, "Alcohol Abuse among Mentally Retarded Individuals"; and Diana M. DiNitto and Curtis H. Krishef, "Family and Social Problems of Mentally Retarded Alcohol Users," *Social and Behavioral Science Documents,* Vol. 17, No. 1 (1987), p. 31.

127. Westermeyer et al., "Substance Use and Abuse Among Mentally Retarded Persons."

128. Ibid., p. 122.

129. L. S. Rychkova, "Clinical Characteristics of Early Alcoholism in Adolescents with Slight Mental Retardation of Exogenous Etiology," *Soviet Neurology and Psychology* (Fall 1987), pp. 55–63.

130. Ibid., p. 62.

131. See James A. Campbell, Elizabeth Lehr Essex, and Gayle Held, "Issue in Chemical Dependency Treatment and Aftercare for People with Learning Differences," *Health & Social Work,* Vol. 19, No. 1 (1994), pp. 63–69.

132. Krishef and DiNitto, "Alcohol Abuse among Mentally Retarded Individuals."

133. Campbell et al., "Issue in Chemical Dependency Treatment and Aftercare for People with Learning Differences."

134. Thomas J. Lottman, "Access to Generic Substance Abuse Services for Persons with Mental Retardation," *Journal of Alcohol and Drug Education,* Vol. 39, No. 1 (1993), pp. 41–55.

135. Ibid, p. 151.

136. Wenc, "The Developmentally Disabled Substance Abuser."

137. Lottman, "Access to Generic Substance Abuse Services for Persons with Mental Retardation."

138. Ibid., pp. 52–53.

139. *The Maine Approach: A Treatment Model for the Intellectually Limited Substance Abuser* (Augusta: The Maine Department of Mental Health and Mental Retardation, and Waterville, ME: The Kennebec Valley Regional Health Agency, 1984).

140. Wenc, "The Developmentally Disabled Substance Abuser"; also see *The Maine Approach.*

141. John Small, "Emotions Anonymous: Counseling the Mentally Retarded Substance Abuser," *Alcohol Health & Research World* (Winter 1980/81), p. 46.

142. Ibid.

143. JoAnne Elaine Paxon, "Relapse Prevention for Individuals with Developmental Disabilities, Borderline Intellectual Functioning, or Illiteracy," *Journal of Psychoactive Drugs,* Vol. 27, No. 2 (1995), pp. 167–172.

144. Selan, "The Psychological Consequences of Alcohol Use or Abuse by Retarded Persons."

145. Paxon, "Relapse Prevention for Individuals with Developmental Disabilities, Borderline Intellectual Funtioning, or Illiteracy," p. 170.

146. G. Potamianos, D. M. Gorman, S. W. Duffy, and T. J. Peters, "Alcohol Consumption by Patients Attending Outpatient Clinics," *The International Journal of Social Psychiatry,* Vol. 34, No. 2 (1988), pp. 97–101.

147. See, for example, James J. O'Donnell, Jonathan E. Cooper, John E. Gessner, Isabelle Shehan, and Judy Ashley, "Alcohol, Drugs, and Spinal Cord Injury," *Alcohol Health & Research World* (Winter 1981/82), pp. 27–29; James H. Frisbie and Carlos G. Tun, "Drinking and Spinal Cord Injury," *Journal of the American Paraplegia Society,* Vol. 7 (1984), pp. 71–73; and Daniel E. Rohe and Jeffrey R. Basford, "Traumatic Spinal Cord Injury, Alcohol, and the Minnesota Multiphasic Personality Inventory," *Rehabilitation Psychology,* Vol. 34, No. 1 (1989), pp. 25–32.

148. Allen W. Heinemann and Darlene Hawkins, "Substance Abuse and Medical Complications Following Spinal Cord Injury," *Rehabilitation Psychology,* Vol. 40, No. 2 (1995), pp. 125–140.

149. O'Donnell et al., "Alcohol, Drugs, and Spinal Cord Injury"; and Allen W. Heinemann, Matthew Doll, and Sidney Schnoll, "Treatment of Alcohol Abuse in Persons with Recent Spinal Cord Injuries," *Alcohol Health & Research World,* Vol. 13, No. 2 (1989), pp. 110–117.

150. Heinemann et al., "Treatment of Alcohol Abuse in Persons with Recent Spinal Cord Injuries."

151. Frisbie and Tun, "Drinking and Spinal Cord Injury."

152. Allen W. Heinemann, Mary F. Schmidt, and Patrick Semik, "Drinking Patterns, Drinking Expectancies, and Coping after Spinal Cord Injury," *Rehabilitation Counseling Bulletin,* Vol. 38, No. 2 (1994), pp. 134–153.

153. Mary Ellen Young, Diana H. Rintala, Donald Rossi, Karen A. Hart, and Marcus J. Fuhrer, "Alcohol and Marijuana Use in a Community-Based Sample of Persons with Spinal Cord Injury," *Archives of Physical Medicine and Rehabilitation,* Vol. 76 (June 1995,), pp. 525–532.

154. Garry A. Rasmussen and Ronald P. De Boer, "Alcohol and Drug Use among Clients at a Residential Vocational Rehabilitation Facility," *Alcohol Health & Research World* (Winter 1980/81), pp. 48–56.

155. Dennis Moore and Harvey Siegal, "Alcohol and Other Drug Use among Orthopedically Impaired College Students," *Alcohol Health & Research World,* Vol. 13, No. 2 (1989), pp. 118–123.

156. Ibid, p. 123.

157. Sharon Schaschl and Dennis Straw, "Results of a Model Intervention Program for Physically Impaired Persons," *Alcohol Health & Research World*, Vol. 13, No. 2 (1989), pp. 150–153.

158. O'Donnell et al., "Alcohol, Drugs, and Spinal Cord Injury."

159. Reginald J. Alston, "Sensation Seeking as a Psychological Trait of Drug Abuse among Persons with Spinal Cord Injury," *Rehabilitation Counseling Bulletin*, Vol. 38, No. 2 (1994), pp. 154–163.

160. Ibid., p. 160.

161. Heinemann et al., "Drinking Patterns, Drinking Expectancies, and Coping after Spinal Cord Injury."

162. Allen W. Heinemann, Nancy Goranson, Karen Ginsburg, and Sidney Schnoll, "Alcohol Use and Activity Patterns Following Spinal Cord Injury," *Rehabilitation Psychology*, Vol. 34, No. 3 (1989), pp. 191–205.

163. Heinemann et al., "Treatment of Alcohol Abuse in Persons with Recent Spinal Cord Injuries"; and Gregory A. Jones, "Alcohol Abuse and Traumatic Brain Injury," *Alcohol Health & Research World*, Vol. 13, No. 2 (1989), pp. 104–109.

164. Frisbie and Tun, "Drinking and Spinal Cord Injury."

165. Pete Anderson, "Alcoholism and the Spinal Cord Disabled: A Model Program," *Alcohol Health & Research World* (Winter 1980/81), pp. 37–41.

166. Much of this paragraph relies on O'Donnell et al., "Alcohol, Drugs, and Spinal Cord Injury."

167. Moore and Ford, "Prevention of Substance Abuse among Persons with Disabilities: A Demonstration Model."

168. Much of this paragraph relies on O'Donnell et al., "Alcohol, Drugs, and Spinal Cord Injury."; also see Heinemann et al., "Treatment of Alcohol Abuse in Persons with Recent Spinal Cord Injuries"; and Schaschl and Straw, "Results of a Model Intervention Program."

169. Anderson, "Alcoholism and the Spinal Cord Disabled," p. 38.

170. M. Perez and C. Pilsecker, "Group Psychotherapy with Spinal Cord Injured Substance Abusers," *Paraplegia*, Vol. 32 (1994), pp. 188–192.

171. Heinemann and Hawkins, "Substance Abuse and Medical Complications Following Spinal Cord Injury."

172. Heinemann et al., "Alcohol Use and Activity Patterns Following Spinal Cord Injury," pp. 191–206.

173. Rohe and Basford, "Traumatic Spinal Cord Injury, Alcohol, and the Minnesota Multiphasic Personality Inventory."

174. Anderson, "Alcoholism and the Spinal Cord Disabled," p. 38.

175. Perez and Pilsecker, "Group Psychotherapy with Spinal Cord Injured Substance Abusers."

176. Schaschl and Straw, "Results of a Model Intervention Program."

177. Heinemann et al., "Drinking Patterns, Drinking Expectancies, and Coping after Spinal Cord Injury."

178. P. Woll, M. F. Schmidt, and A. W. Heinemann, *Alcohol and Other Drug Abuse Prevention for People with Traumatic Brain and Spinal Cord Injuries* (Chicago, IL: Rehabilitation Institute of Chicago, 1993).

179. See, for example, the review by David D. Weinstein and Peter R. Martin, "Psychiatric Implications of Alcoholism and Traumatic Brain Injury," *The American Journal on Addictions*, Vol. 4, No. 4 (Fall 1995), pp. 285–296.

180. Norman S. Miller, "Alcohol and Drug Disorders," in Jonathan M. Silver, Stuart C. Yudofsky, and Robert E. Hales (Eds.), *Neuropsychiatry of Traumatic Brain Injury* (Washington, DC: American Psychiatric Press), pp. 471–498.

181. Stuart A. Yablon, Maritza Cabrera, Stuart C. Yudofsky, and Jonathan M. Silver, "Prevention," in Silver et al., *Neuropsychiatry of Traumatic Brain Injury*, pp. 805–834.

182. Francis R. Sparadeo and Daryl Gill, "Effects of Prior Alcohol Use on Head Injury Recovery," *Journal of Head Trauma Rehabilitation*, Vol. 4, No. 1 (1989), pp. 75–82.

183. Lisa Terry, "Treating the Head Injured Substance Abuser," *New Jersey Rehab* (no date); also see Weinstein and Martin, "Psychiatric Implications of Alcoholism and Traumatic Brain Injury" for a more medically oriented description of the processes involved when an individual who has chronically consumed alcohol incurs a traumatic brain injury.

184. Judith Mitiguy, "Alcohol and Head Trauma," *Headlines* (Summer 1991), p. 6.

185. Ibid.

186. Sureyya S. Dikmen, Dennis M. Donovan, Tor Lokerg, Joan E. Machamer, and Nancy R. Temkin, "Alcohol Use and Its Effects on Neuropsychological Outcome in Head Injury," *Neuropsychology*, Vol. 7, No. 3 (1993), pp. 296–305.

187. Mitiguy, "Alcohol and Head Trauma"; and James Wasco, "Attacking the Problem Before It Starts," *Headlines* (Summer 1991), p. 20; also see Weinstein and Martin, "Psychiatric Implications of Alcoholism and Traumatic Brain Injury."

188. Miller, "Alcohol and Drug Disorders," p. 475.

189. Weinstein and Martin, "Psychiatric Implications of Alcoholism and Traumatic Brain Injury," p. 291.

190. Miller, "Alcohol and Drug Disorders."

191. Ibid., p. 487.

192. Sparadeo and Gill, "Effects of Prior Alcohol Use"; Francis R. Sparadeo, David Strauss, and Jeffrey T. Barth, "The Incidence, Impact, and Treatment of Substance Abuse in Head Trauma Rehabilitation," *Journal of Head Trauma Rehabilitation*, Vol. 5, No. 3 (1990), pp. 1–8; Weinstein and Martin, "Psychiatric Implications of Alcoholism and Traumatic Brain Injury."

193. Matti Hillbom and Lena Holm, "Contribution of Traumatic Head Injury to Neuropsychological Deficits in

Alcoholics," *Journal of Neurology, Neurosurgery and Psychiatry*, Vol. 49, No. 12 (1986), pp. 1348–1353.

194. D. Gill, M. Stambrook, A. Moore, and L. Peters, "Legal and Illicit Drug Use after Head Injury," presented at the Annual Conference of the Canadian Psychological Association, June 8, 1989, Halifax, Nova Scotia, cited in Sparadeo, Strauss, and Barth, "The Incidence, Impact and Treatment of Substance Abuse."

195. Mitiguy, "Alcohol and Head Trauma"; and Terry, "Treating the Head Injured Substance Abuser."

196. Miller, "Alcohol and Drug Disorders."

197. Sparadeo et al., "The Incidence, Impact, and Treatment of Substance Abuse"; and Suzan Kaitz, "Integrated Treatment: Safety Net for Survival," *Headlines* (Summer 1991), pp. 11–12, 14, 16–17.

198. Jeffrey S. Kreutzer, Kathleen R. Doherty, Jennifer A. Harris, and Nathan D. Zasler, "Alcohol Use among Persons with Traumatic Brain Injury," *Journal of Head Trauma Rehabilitation*, Vol. 5, No. 3 (1990), pp. 9–20; also see J. S. Kreutzer, J. Harris Marwitz, and A. D. Witol, "Interrelationships between Crime, Substance Abuse, and Aggressive Behaviours among Persons with Traumatic Brain Injury," *Brain Injury*, Vol. 9 No. 8 (1995), pp. 757–768.

199. Francis R. Sparadeo, cited in Terry, "Treating the Head Injured Substance Abuser."

200. Sparadeo et al., "The Incidence, Impact, and Treatment of Substance Abuse"; and Kreutzer et al., "Alcohol Use among Persons with Traumatic Brain Injury."

201. Sparadeo et al., "The Incidence, Impact, and Treatment of Substance Abuse"; Mitiguy, "Alcohol and Head Trauma"; and Kaitz, "Integrated Treatment."

202. Paul Malloy, Nora Noel, Richard Longabaugh, and Martha Beattie, "Determinants of Neuropsychological Impairment in Antisocial Substance Abusers," *Addictive Behaviors*, Vol. 15 (1990), pp. 431–438.

203. Jeffrey S. Kreutzer, Paul H. Wehman, Jennifer A. Harris, Cheryl T. Burns, and Harold F. Young, "Substance Abuse and Crime Patterns among Persons with Traumatic Brain Injury Referred for Supported Employment," *Brain Injury*, Vol. 5, No. 2 (1991), pp. 177–187.

204. Weinstein and Martin, "Psychiatric Implications of Alcoholism and Traumatic Brain Injury," p. 291.

205. Sparadeo et al., "The Incidence, Impact, and Treatment of Substance Abuse."

206. Jones, "Alcohol Abuse and Traumatic Brain Injury."

207. Kreutzer et al., "Alcohol Use among Persons with Traumatic Brain Injury."

208. For information on the QFVI, see Don Cahalan and Ira H. Cissin, "American Drinking Practices: Summary of Findings from a National Probability Sample, I. Extent of Drinking by Population Subgroups," *Quarterly Journal of Studies on Alcohol*, Vol. 29 (1968), pp. 130–151.

209. Jones, "Alcohol Abuse and Traumatic Brain Injury."

210. R. Wayne Shipley, Stephen M. Taylor, and Donna R. Falvo, "Concurrent Evaluation and Rehabilitation of Alcohol Abuse and Trauma," *Journal of Applied Rehabilitation Counseling*, Vol. 21, No. 3 (1990), pp. 37–39.

211. Kevin Henry, *A Letter to Sponsors of Chemically Dependent Head Injured Persons* (Washington, DC: National Head Injury Foundation, April 1988); and Jones, "Alcohol Abuse and Traumatic Brain Injury."

212. Sparadeo et al., "The Incidence, Impact, and Treatment of Substance Abuse."

213. David Strauss, quoted in Kaitz, "Integrated Treatment," p. 11; also see *New Medico Head Injury System* (Lynn, NM: New Medico Associates, 1990); and Miller, "Alcohol and Drug Disorders."

214. Sparadeo et al., "The Incidence, Impact, and Treatment of Substance Abuse"; and Miller, "Alcohol and Drug Disorders." For a description of a program and early findings, see W. F. Blackerby and Ann Baumgarten, "A Model Treatment Program for the Head-Injured Substance Abuser: Preliminary Findings," *Journal of Head Trauma Rehabilitation*, Vol. 5, No. 3 (1990), pp. 47–59.

215. Ibid.

216. Jones, "Alcohol Abuse and Traumatic Brain Injury."

217. R. L. Wood, *Brain Injury Rehabilitation: A Neurobehavioral Approach* (Rockville, MD: Aspen Publishers, 1987), cited in Jones, "Alcohol Abuse and Traumatic Brain Injury."

218. David Strauss, cited in Kaitz, "Integrated Treatment"; also see Blackerby and Baumgarten, "A Model Treatment Program for the Head-Injured Substance Abuser: Preliminary Findings."

219. Miller, "Alcohol and Drug Disorders."

220. Kaitz, "Integrated Treatment."

221. Karen Feinberg, "Maintaining Gains through AA," *Headlines* (Summer 1991), p. 16.

222. Bill Peterman, "TBI Explanation [of the original 12 steps of AA]," in Henry, *A Letter to Sponsors of Chemically Dependent Head Injured Persons.*

223. Terry, "Treating the Head Injured Substance Abuser."

224. William P. McCrone, "Serving the Deaf Substance Abuser," *Journal of Psychoactive Drugs*, Vol. 14, No. 3 (1982), p. 199.

225. Also see Rene A. Sylvester, "Treatment of the Deaf Alcoholic: A Review," *Alcoholism Treatment Quarterly*, Vol. 3, No. 4 (1986), pp. 1–23.

226. Morton Isaacs, "Patterns of Drinking among the Deaf," *American Journal of Drug and Alcohol Abuse*, Vol. 6, No. 4 (1979), pp. 463–476, quote from p. 463.

227. Reginald Locke and Shirley Johnson, "A Descriptive Study of Drug Use among the Hearing Impaired in a

Senior High School for the Hearing Impaired," in Arnold J. Schecter (Ed.), *Drug Dependence and Alcoholism, Vol. 2: Social and Behavioral Issues* (New York: Plenum Press, 1981), pp. 833–841.

228. Kay Fulton, "Alcohol and Drug Abuse among the Deaf, Collaborative Programming for the Purposes of Prevention, Intervention and Treatment," in Douglas Watson and Bruce Heller (Eds.), *Mental Health and Deafness: Strategic Perspectives* (Silver Spring, MD: American Deafness and Rehabilitation Association, 1983), p. 367.

229. McCrone, "Serving the Deaf Substance Abuser."

230. Karen A. Steitler, "Substance Abuse and the Deaf Adolescent," in Glenn B. Anderson and Douglas Watson (Eds.), *The Habilitation and Rehabilitation of Deaf Adolescents* (Washington, DC: National Academy of Gallaudet College, 1984), pp. 169–176; also cited in Annie Steinberg, "Issues in Providing Mental Health Services to Hearing Impaired Persons," *Hospital and Community Psychiatry*, Vol. 42, No. 4 (1991), pp. 380–389.

231. Thomas L. Dixon, "Addiction among the Hearing Impaired," *EAP Digest* (January/February 1987), pp. 41–44 and 74.

232. Steinberg, "Issues in Providing Mental Health Services."

233. Sylvester, "Treatment of the Deaf Alcoholic"; and Donald G. Jorgensen and Connie Russert, "An Outpatient Treatment Approach for Hearing-Impaired Alcoholics," *American Annals of the Deaf* (February 1982), pp. 41–44.

234. Alexander Boros, "Activating Solutions to Alcoholism Among the Hearing Impaired," in Schecter, *Drug Dependence and Alcoholism, Vol. 2*, pp. 1007–1014; McCrone, "Serving the Deaf Substance Abuser"; Fulton, "Alcohol and Drug Abuse among the Deaf"; and Debra Guthmann and Katherine A. Sandberg, "Clinical Approches in Substance Abuse Treatment for Use with Deaf and Hard of Hearing Adolescents," *Journal of Child & Adolescent Substance Abuse*, Vol. 4, No. 3 (1995), pp. 69–79.

235. Steinberg, "Issues in Providing Mental Health Services"; Sylvester, "Treatment of the Deaf Alcoholic"; Dixon, "Addiction among the Hearing Impaired"; Boros, "Activating Solutions to Alcoholism"; and Marie Egbert Rendon, "Deaf Culture and Alcohol and Substance Abuse," *Journal of Substance Abuse Treatment*, Vol. 9 (1992) pp. 103–110.

236. Alexander Boros, "Alcoholism Intervention for the Deaf," *Alcohol Health & Research World* (Winter 1980/81), p. 28; also see Boros, "Activating Solutions to Alcoholism."

237. New York State Division of Alcoholism and Alcohol Abuse, "Alcoholism and the Hearing Impaired," *DAAA Focus*, Vol. 3, No. 3 (April 1988), p. 1; also see Fulton, "Alcohol and Drug Use among the Deaf."

238. McCrone, "Serving the Deaf Substance Abuser."

239. Steinberg, "Issues in Providing Mental Health Services," p. 381; also see Dixon, "Addiction among the Hearing Impaired"; Sylvester, "Treatment of the Deaf Alcoholic"; and Isaacs, "Patterns of Drinking among the Deaf."

240. Jorgensen and Russert, "An Outpatient Treatment Approach."

241. Steinberg, "Issues in Providing Mental Health Services," p. 381.

242. See Boros, "Alcoholism Intervention for the Deaf."

243. Ibid.

244. Ibid., p. 29.

245. Paul Rothfeld, "Alcoholism Treatment for the Deaf: Specialized Services for Special People," *Journal of Rehabilitation of the Deaf*, Vol. 14, No. 4 (1981), pp. 14–17.

246. Guthmann and Sandberg, "Clinical Approaches in Substance Abuse Treatment for Use with Deaf and Hard of Hearing Adolescents."

247. Fulton, "Alcohol and Drug Abuse among the Deaf"; Janet E. Dick, "Serving Hearing-Impaired Alcoholics," *Social Work* (November 1989), pp. 555–556; and Mary Ann Kelin and Pedro Acevedo, "Self-Help Groups for Deaf Adolescents: Problems of Drug and Alcohol Abuse," in Glenn B. Anderson and Douglas Watson (Eds.), *Innovations in the Habilitation and Rehabilitation of Deaf Adolescents* (Little Rock, AR: University of Arkansas Press, 1987), pp. 325–330; Boros, "Activating Solutions to Alcoholism."

248. Boros, "Alcoholism Intervention for the Deaf"; and Steinberg, "Issues in Providing Mental Health Services."

249. Steinberg, "Issues in Providing Mental Health Services."

250. Thomas N. Grant, Carol A. Kramer, and Karen Nash, "Working with Deaf Alcoholics in a Vocational Training Program," *Journal of Rehabilitation of the Deaf*, Vol. 15, No. 4 (1982), pp. 14–20.

251. Jo Ann Ford, Dennis Moore, and Jean Modry (Eds.), *Orientation to Deafness and Hearing Loss: Identity, Culture, and Resiliency* (Dayton, OH: Wright State University, 1996).

252. Dixon, "Addiction among the Hearing-Impaired"; New York State Division of Alcoholism and Alcohol Abuse (NYSDAAA), "Alcoholism and the Hearing-Impaired"; and Steinberg, "Issues in Providing Mental Health Services."

253. Sylvester, "Treatment of the Deaf Alcoholic."

254. *Addiction Intervention with the Disabled*. Kent, OH: Kent State University.

255. Boros, "Alcoholism Intervention for the Deaf"; and Sylvester, "Treatment of the Deaf Alcoholic."

256. Ibid.; Rothfeld, "Alcoholism Treatment for the Deaf"; William Dore, "An Open Letter to Chemical Dependency Counselors," *The Counselor* (May/June 1989), p. 26; Jorgensen and Russert, "An Outpatient Treatment Approach"; and Dick, "Serving Hearing Impaired Alcoholics."

257. Rothfeld, "Alcoholism Treatment for the Deaf."

258. Dixon, "Addiction among the Hearing Impaired."

259. Boros, "Alcoholism Intervention for the Deaf."

260. Ibid.; and Gladys A. Kearns, "Hearing-Impaired Alcoholics—An Underserved Community," *Alcohol Health & Research World,* Vol. 13, No. 2 (1989), pp. 162–166.

261. NYSDAAA, "Alcoholism and the Hearing-Impaired"; and Sylvester, "Treatment of the Deaf Alcoholic."

262. Steinberg, "Issues in Providing Mental Health Services."

263. Rothfeld, "Alcoholism Treatment for the Deaf."

264. Ibid.; and McCrone, "Serving the Deaf Substance Abuser."

265. NIAAA, "Alcoholism and the Hearing-Impaired."

266. Boros, "Alcoholism Intervention for the Deaf"; and Dick, "Serving Hearing-Impaired Alcoholics."

267. Steinberg, "Issues in Providing Mental Health Services."

268. Sylvester, "Treatment of the Deaf Alcoholic"; and NYSDAAA, "Alcoholism and the Hearing-Impaired."

269. See Stephen Miller House Version [of the Twelve Steps of Alcoholics Anonymous for the deaf] in Henry, *A Letter to Sponsors.*

270. Richard G. Hetherington, "Deafness and Alcoholism," *Journal of Rehabilitation of the Deaf,* Vol. 12, No. 4 (1979), pp. 9–12.

271. Jerry Edelwich and Pat Arre, "Reality Therapy as an Intervention for Deaf Adolescents Involved in Alcohol and Drug Use and Abuse," in Anderson and Watson, *Innovations in the Habilitation and Rehabilitation of Deaf Adolescents,* pp. 344–349. Reality therapy was developed by William Glasser; see his book *Reality Therapy* (New York: Harper Colophon, 1965).

272. John Mihall, Emily Smith, and Melanie Wilding, "Gallaudet's Student Development Approach to Substance Abuse Education and Identification/Treatment," in Anderson and Watson, *Innovations in the Habilitation and Rehabilitation of Deaf Adolescents,* pp. 331–343.

273. Steinberg, "Issues in Providing Mental Health Services."

274. Sylvester, "Treatment of the Deaf Alcoholic."

275. Alcoholics Anonymous World Services, New York, New York.

276. John L. Hulick, "S.O.S.," *The Counselor* (May/June 1989), p. 25.

277. Leonard F. Burns and John de Miranda, *Blindness and Visual Impairment: Drug and Alcohol Abuse Prevention & Treatment* (San Mateo, CA: Peninsula Health Concepts, August 1991).

278. The remainder of this paragraph relies on *A Look at Alcohol and Other Drug Abuse Prevention and . . . Blindness and Visual Impairments* (Washington, DC: Resource Center on Substance Abuse Prevention and Disability, no date).

279. John de Miranda, *California Alcohol, Drug and Disability Study: Literature Review and Bibliography* (San Mateo, CA: Institute on Alcohol, Drugs and Disability, 1990), p. 9; also see M. Nelipovich and E. Buss, "Investigating Alcohol Abuse among Persons Who are Blind," *Journal of Visual Impairment and Blindness* (October, 1991), pp. 343–345.

280. Edward J. Glass, "Problem Drinking among the Blind and Visually Impaired," *Alcohol Health & Research World* (Winter 1980/81), pp. 20–25.

281. James Peterson and Michael Nelipovich, "Alcoholism and the Visually Impaired Client," *Journal of Visual Impairment and Blindness,* Vol. 77 (1983), pp. 345–348.

282. Burns and de Miranda, *Blindness and Visual Impairment.*

283. *Working with People with Visual Impairments* (Toronto: Addiction Research Foundation, no date).

284. Burns and de Miranda, *Blindness and Visual Impairment.*

285. Michael Nelipovich and Randy Parker, "The Visually Impaired Substance Abuser," *Journal of Visual Impairment and Blindness* (September 1981), p. 305.

286. Nelipovich and Buss, "Investigating Alcohol Abuse among Persons Who Are Blind."

287. Glass, "Problem Drinking among the Blind and Visually Impaired."

288. Michael Nelipovich and Elmer Buss, "Alcohol Abuse and Persons Who Are Blind, Treatment Considerations," *Alcohol Health & Research World,* Vol. 13, No. 2 (1989), p. 129.

289. Nelipovich and Buss, "Investigating Alcohol Abuse among Persons Who Are Blind."

290. The remainder of this section relies primarily on Nelipovich and Buss, "Alcohol Abuse and Persons Who Are Blind"; also see *Working with People with Visual Impairments;* and *A Look at Alcohol and Other Drug Abuse Prevention and . . . Blindness and Visual Impairment.*

291. Burns and de Miranda, *Blindness and Visual Impairment.*

292. David J. Nashel, "Arthritic Disease and Alcohol Abuse," *Alcohol Health and Research World,* Vol. 13, No. 2 (1989), pp. 124–125.

293. Kenneth B. Wells, Jacqueline M. Golding, and M. Audrey Burnam, "Affective, Substance Use, and Anxiety Disorders in Persons with Arthritis, Diabetes, Heart Disease, High Blood Pressure, or Chronic Lung Condition," *General Hospital Psychiatry,* Vol. 11 (1989), pp. 320–327.

294. Ronald A. Arky, "Alcohol Use and the Diabetic Patient," *Alcohol Health & Research World,* Vol. 8, No. 2 (1983/84), pp. 8–13.

295. Keith Ryan, "Alcohol and Blood Sugar Disorders, An Overview," *Alcohol Health & Research World,* Vol. 8, No. 2 (1983/84), pp. 3–7 and 15.

296. Ryan, "Alcohol and Blood Sugar Disorders, An Overview." also see Arky, "Alcohol Use and the Diabetic Patient."

297. Wells et al., "Affective, Substance Use, and Anxiety Disorders in Persons with Arthritis, Diabetes, Heart Disease, High Blood Pressure, or Chronic Lung Condition."

298. John G. Spangler, Joseph C. Konen, and K. Patricia McGann, "Prevalence and Predictors of Problem Drinking among Primary Care Diabetic Patients," *The Journal of Family Practice*, Vol. 37, No. 4 (1993), pp. 370–375.

299. Melanie A. Gold and Jack Gladstein, "Substance Use among Adolescents with Diabetes Mellitus: Preliminary Findings," *Journal of Adolescent Health*, Vol. 14 (1993), pp. 80–84.

300. Helen M. Glasgow et al., "Alcohol and Drug Use in Teenagers with Diabetes Mellitus," *Journal of Adolescent Health*, Vol. 12 (1991), pp. 11–14.

301. For a discussion of this issue, see Ruth E. Little and James L. Gayle, "Epilepsy and Alcoholism," *Alcohol Health & Research World* (Winter 1980/81), pp. 31–36.

302. Michael J. Stoil, "Epilepsy, Seizures, and Alcohol," *Alcohol Health & Research World*, Vol. 13, No. 2 (1989), p. 141.

303. National Center for Youth with Disabilities, *CYDLINE Reviews: Substance Use by Youth with Disabilities and Chronic Illnesses* (Minneapolis: The Center, May 1990). The Center's web site is http://www.cyfc.umn.edu/youth/ncyd.html/

14

Alcohol and Drug Use among the Elderly

Linda Vinton
Florida State University

Kathryn G. Wambach
University of Texas at Austin

Although age demarcation does vary, *elderly* generally refers to people at least 60 or 65 years of age. Among the elderly are the only people in the United States today who were alive at the time of the Eighteenth Amendment to the Constitution, which brought about Prohibition in 1920, as well as when it was repealed with the Twenty-First Amendment in 1933. Gilliland and James[1] state that from a social perspective, such legislation had much to say about what U.S. society believed to be good or evil, and as young people during this time, the elderly cut their eye-teeth on these messages.

This chapter focuses primarily on the elderly and their abuse of one particular substance—alcohol. Much more information is available on their use of alcohol than their use of illicit drugs. Whenever the population of interest is the elderly, writers begin by telling the demographic story. This is because the United States, like most other nations in the world, is aging. Life expectancy in the United States has increased from 47.3 years in 1900 to 75.8 years in 1995, and the oldest age

segment is growing most rapidly. There were 33.5 million people aged 65 and over in the United States in 1995 (12.8 percent of the population), and this number is expected to increase to 69.4 million in the year 2030. The cohort aged 85 and over increased by 2,900 percent between 1900 and 1995, and Census Bureau projections indicate that this trend is expected to continue.[2]

A growing elderly population has gone hand in hand with a growing interest in alcohol abuse among older people. Graham[3] believes this concern stems from both humanitarian and economic interests. She asks, on the one hand, to what extent does alcohol abuse undermine elders' quality of life and, on the other hand, how much does alcohol use and abuse among the elderly contribute to growing health care costs?

Prevalence and Patterns

No standardized methods have been utilized for estimating the prevalence of alcohol abuse among the elderly, and the domains typically included in alcohol abuse questionnaires are problematic in terms of older respondents.[4] For example, elders with memory loss may have difficulty remembering recent alcohol consumption, and a number of authors have suggested that denial of alcohol abuse and symptoms of drunkenness or dependence are greater among the elderly than other age groups. Another problem with using consumption as a measure is that studies at the National Institute on Aging have shown that the elderly have a decreased tolerance for alcohol and its effects.[5]

Measures have routinely been standardized on nonelderly men; thus, they also lack recognition of the particular alcohol-related health, social, and legal problems of male and female elderly. Perhaps an even more fundamental issue with respect to the validity of the research in this area is that alcohol abuse has been variously defined and the concepts of alcohol abuse, alcohol dependence, problem drinking, heavy drinking, and alcoholism (chronic and acute) have been used and operationalized differently.

Keeping in mind these methodological limitations, there appears to be general agreement among researchers that prevalence rates are higher among younger than older persons and that elderly men abuse alcohol more often than do elderly women.[6] The variations among racial and ethnic groups typical of younger cohorts are not evident in the elderly population; for example, alcohol consumption among elderly Native Americans mirrors use among elders in other racial and ethnic groups.[7] Overall, prevalency rates for alcohol abuse by the aged (also variously defined) have ranged anywhere from 4 to 14 percent.[8] Allowing for these variations, Bienenfeld[9] states that most surveys agree that at least 10 percent of persons aged 65 and over have some kind of drinking problem and that 8 percent in this same age group are alcohol dependent.

When *DSM-III-R*[10] criteria for alcoholism have been utilized, as in the case of the Epidemiologic Catchment Area (ECA) program, rates of alcohol abuse and dependence were seen to differ from most other prevalency studies. The ECA project was a combination of five interrelated epidemiologic research studies conducted in New Haven (Connecticut), Baltimore, St. Louis, Los Angeles, and Durham (North Carolina), and the surrounding counties. An instrument to collect information covering three diagnostic systems, including *DSM-III-R*, was specially designed for these studies. For men aged 65 and over, the lifetime prevalence rate of alcohol abuse was 14 percent, whereas for women in this same age group, the rate was 1.5 percent. Remission rates were seen to rise consistently with increasing age.[11]

Reasons for the low rate of alcohol abuse among older people, when compared to rates for younger persons, include the fact that alcohol abusers have shorter life expectancies. Although alcoholics can and do survive to old age, an undetermined number die earlier as a result of alcohol-related medical complications. A higher percentage of surviving alcoholics may live in institutional settings due to medical complications, and consequently be unrepresented in community surveys. Other explanations are that older Americans were influenced early in their lives by the Prohibition Era mentality, and thus the drinking mores of the older generation may be responsible for lower rates. Finally, some individuals who abuse alcohol may reduce their consumption because of disabilities or increased effects related to the ingestion of alcohol.[12]

As with younger populations, certain groups of older people have higher rates of alcoholism than the general population of elderly. Bearing in mind that clinical diagnoses of alcoholism tend to be underdiagnosed when compared with prevalency rates determined by population surveys, estimates for the prevalence of alcoholism in the general medical population of elderly range from 25 to 50 percent. Even higher rates—50 to 75 percent—have been reported for general psychiatric populations.[13] Relying on structured interviews for case definition, Joseph and associates[14] found that 49 percent of those entering a Veterans Administration nursing home met the *DSM-III-R* definition criteria for lifetime alcohol abuse or dependence, and 18 percent were active alcoholics. Staff providing community-based services to the elderly estimated that one-fourth (25.9 percent) had alcohol abuse problems.[15] Others noted a high rate of alcoholism among the homeless population. Butler, Lewis, and Sunderland[16] caution, however, that only about 5 percent of alcoholics fit the stereotypic caricature of the inebriated individual who is seen sleeping on a sidewalk or doorstep. In a study conducted by one of the authors of this chapter, competent yet self-neglectful elders were also seen to have a higher rate of alcohol abuse (15 percent) when compared with elders who were either abused or neglected by others (4 percent).[17]

In terms of duration, alcoholism among the elderly is of two types: early onset (Type I) and late-life onset (Type II, also labeled reactive or geriatric alcoholism). It is estimated that half of elderly alcoholics began drinking heavily prior to age 40 and about two-thirds began before age 60.[18] Reviewing a number of studies regarding the occurrence of late-life onset alcoholism among populations under treatment, Liberto and Oslin[19] note wide variation but conclude that a significant number of older alcoholics began drinking abusively in later life. Although it may change in the future due to higher use among young females, elderly women are more likely than elderly men to fall in the late-life-onset category.[20] This leaves a smaller but still sizable number of older persons who started to abuse alcohol late in life.

Antecedents and Correlates

Although each has its shortcomings, both conceptually and empirically, each of the models of addiction described in Chapter 2 suggests certain causations of alcoholism, which, in turn, relate to treatment approaches. Not all these models have received much attention in the literature on alcoholism among the aged, but a wide range of antecedent factors have been suggested. The determinants of alcohol abuse among the elderly that have been examined most extensively have been either sociocultural or psychologic/psychosocial in nature.

Sociocultural Models

Minnis[21] has proposed a sociological perspective for studying the determinants of alcoholism. Social control theory, as formulated by Hirschi,[22] assumes that deviance (e.g., alcoholism) results when an individual's bond with society is weak or broken. Based on this theory, Minnis has stated four hypotheses to explain alcohol abuse:

1. The greater the attachment to conventional others, the less likely is the elderly person to engage in alcohol abuse.
2. The greater the commitment to conventional goals or aspirations, the less likely is the elderly person to engage in alcohol abuse.
3. The greater the involvement in conventional activities, the less likely is the older person to engage in alcohol abuse.
4. The greater the beliefs in the moral validity of conventional norms, the less likely is the elderly person to engage in alcohol abuse.

To these authors' knowledge, this model of alcohol abuse remains untested. Perhaps this is due to the difficulty that would be encountered in measuring some of the concepts employed in the hypotheses (e.g., attachment, commitment, involvement, moral validity, conventional activities, and norms).

The ECA project looked at sociodemographic factors such as age, sex, race, marital status, education, employment, and study site as correlates of alcohol abuse or dependence. Being younger, male, separated or divorced, and poor, and having less than a high school education were all found to be associated with a higher prevalence of alcoholism, regardless of age. Site, race, and employment status were not found, however, to have a relationship to the prevalence of alcoholism in the study sample.[23]

Gurnack and Thomas[24] state that little research exists that specifically focuses on late-onset alcohol abuse. They further question the validity of the term *late onset*. It appears, however, that a considerable number of studies exist that have contrasted the characteristics of early- and late-onset elderly alcoholics. It could be argued that there has actually been a disproportionate interest shown in the sociocultural and psychological determinants of late-onset alcoholism, since estimates indicate that only one-third of elderly alcohol abusers fall into this group. However, Liberto and Oslin[25] disagree, concluding that the clinical differences between these two groups affect the natural course of the disease as well as treatment outcomes.

Psychologic and Psychosocial Models

Psychological factors are particularly problematic to investigate, although several authors have concluded that alcohol abuse in old age is less likely to be associated with deep-seated psychological problems or personality factors than excessive drinking among young persons.[26] Royce[27] more explicitly states that persons who began to drink at a late age were reported as having no evidence of severe antisocial behaviors or psychiatric problems and as having fewer life-style disruptions. In an empirical study by Atkinson, Tolson, and Turner[28] conducted at a Veterans Administration geriatric alcoholism outpatient program, late-onset problems were determined to be "milder" and more circumscribed than early-onset problems and, further, were associated with less family alcoholism and greater overall psychological stability.

The psychosocial model of addiction proposes that an interrelated constellation of personal, environmental, behavioral, and health care system factors influence the onset, continuation, and termination of alcohol abuse.[20] Although the model is a popular one due to its holistic approach, it is also difficult to test empirically because of its complex and multivariable nature. Most researchers view the psychosocial model as one of stress and coping or adaptation and use it to explain late-onset rather than early-onset alcoholism among elders. Accordingly, loneliness, losses, physical or emotional separation from children, poor health, and lack of purposeful activity can precipitate alcohol abuse.[30] Such factors are viewed as causing the elder to become less attached to or isolated from sources of social support such as his or her family, community, society, or peers, and he or she must rely on past coping skills to deal with feelings of grief, low self-esteem, and low status.

In a recent survey of elderly Canadians,[31] strong associations were noted between the reasons for drinking and the extent of problems associated with alcohol consumption. Roughly one-fourth of those who reported social reasons for using alcohol also indicated two or more problems due to their drinking. In contrast, all of those who indicated that their motivation for drinking was to block out loneliness reported two or more drinking-related problems. Among those indicating other nonsocial motivations (e.g., to cheer up, to help sleep, to relax and relieve pain, to relieve tension, to pass time), at least three-fourths had experienced two or more serious problems with their drinking.

In a study conducted at the Mayo Clinic between 1972 and 1983, researchers found little difference in terms of demographics between early- and late-onset alcoholics.[32] The sample consisted of 216 primarily middle-class men and women aged 65 and older who were patients at the clinic. The outstanding finding was that the majority of patients had a favorable social status despite their alcoholism (67 percent lived at home with a spouse, and many continued to be active in their jobs). In this particular study, early-onset alcoholism was present in 59 percent of the men and 51 percent of the women, and late-onset was seen in 39 percent of the men and 46 percent of the women (undetermined for the rest).

A number of earlier studies suggest that retirement has the potential to be a serious life crisis for many aging persons, especially for elderly men. According to this body of research, retirement is associated with loss—loss of roles, status, income, and mobility, thus leading to loss of stability and self-worth. In a study conducted by Rosin and Glatt,[33] retirement was found to be a precipitating factor of excessive drinking among male professionals versus working-class men in the sample. Retirement was also seen as an antecedent of drinking problems among older Californians.[34] In a recent Canadian survey,[35] poorer well-being, greater alcohol problems, and greater tranquilizer use were noted for younger cohorts of elders (aged 60 to 65), particularly males, apparently associated with stresses related to the transition between work and retirement.

Although their study examined alcohol use rather than abuse, Alexander and Duff[36] surveyed 260 residents aged 57 to 97 at three retirement communities. Their results showed that regular drinking was more common in these communities and the rate of abstinence was lower than in the general population of elders. These researchers argue that drinking was associated with social activity and that it was an integral part of the leisure subculture found in such communities.

More recent findings have also cast doubt on viewing retirement as a possible determinant of late-onset alcohol abuse. For example, Vejnoska[38] found that drinking decreased among rural Arizonians soon after retirement. Along the same lines, in a study by Gomberg,[38] men reported that they drank heavily in response to the stresses and frustrations associated with work and that when they retired, they moderated their consumption.

Ekerdt and associates[39] studied changes in drinking behaviors with retirement in 100 men aged 55 and over who had retired and 316 age-matched men who were employed. These researchers found no evidence that retirement was associated with shifts in alcohol consumption or drinking behaviors. What they did find, though, was that retirees were more likely to report the onset of periodic heavier drinking and problems with drinking than the controls.

In a study of Mayo Clinic patients being treated for alcoholism, researchers found that patients with a late onset of the problem reported an association between a life event and problem drinking more frequently than the early-onset patients (81 versus 45 percent; $p < .001$).[40] Perhaps more notable is the fact that the groups did not differ in terms of all the other stressors that were examined, including retirement, death of a spouse or close relative, family conflict, physical health problems, employment stress, psychologic symptoms, and financial problems. Similarly, in their study of 1,410 elders in two retirement and two age-heterogeneous communities, LaGreca and associates[41] found no support for their hypothesis that higher frequency, greater quantity, or problem drinking occurs in response to significant life events. If anything, these authors point out, drinking appeared to decrease with the experience of life events.

Early research in the area suggested that declining health and accompanying anxiety are factors associated with alcohol abuse among the elderly. Giordano and Beckham[42] point out that physical health or the individual's perceived health status plays a role in determining older people's energies and adaptive capacities. The flaw in much of this research, however, is that matched controls were not used nor were early- and late-onset alcohol abusers compared. Rather, alcoholic elderly people were asked if they had a medical or health problem, and the resulting percentage was deemed to be large.

Studies conducted during the 1980s disputed some of the earlier findings in terms of the relationship between health and alcohol abuse. Bainton[43] found there was a greater likelihood of drinking among older people in good health and Barnes[44] found poor health was associated with a decrease in drinking.

Loneliness, alienation, and boredom have been proposed as variables that are related to abuse of alcohol by the elderly. The disengagement theory of aging posits that older people become less engaged over time and become isolated from others. As a result of this separation from the mainstream of society and activity, an individual may drink to cope with or to dull the feelings associated with disengagement. In a survey of 200 elders, Leigh[45] discovered that 50 percent of the women and 25 percent of the men cited loneliness as the reason for their use of alcohol and medication. When asked how they coped with feelings of loneliness and depression, 13 percent said they had a drink and 2 percent turned to drugs and alcohol.

As Gurnack and Thomas[46] point out, and is evidenced in the preceding discussion, the relationship between life stressors and the onset of alcohol abuse is still not clearly defined. There is also considerable disagreement about cause and effect when looking at factors purported to explain addiction. One can easily inquire as to which are the antecedents and which are the consequences of alcohol abuse among elders.

Alcohol and Drug Abuse

The elderly are the largest users of legal drugs. On average, they take three prescription drugs and seven over-the-counter drugs on a regular basis.[47] There is little wonder that the major problem with drug abuse among the elderly is with licit rather than illicit drugs. The ECA study estimated that the lifetime prevalence rates for illicit drug dependence in the 60-plus age group was less than 1 percent, as contrasted with 17 percent for the 18- to 29-year age group. Among the individuals in the sample who did not meet the *DSM-III-R* criteria for alcohol dependence, 3.5 percent received a diagnosis of illicit drug dependence. For those with a diagnosis of alcohol dependence, however, the rate was much greater (18 percent).[48]

The South Carolina Commission on Alcohol and Drug Abuse (SCCADA) also examined the prevalency and nature of alcohol and drug abuse by collecting data from its alcohol programs throughout the 45 counties of the state. Client records were reviewed for the 1976 year to determine primary, secondary, and tertiary substances of concern. Of the 28,836 clients in the total population, 5,500 were aged 55 and over. Among this older group, 96 percent mentioned alcohol as a problem substance, but only 2.7 percent reported a second substance as being problematic. Sedatives led the list of both secondary and tertiary problem substances (0.8 percent and 0.3 percent, respectively).[49]

Mixing alcohol and prescription drugs is probably more common than the SCCADA study indicates, though, since clients were asked to self-report on their problems at the time of intake. In the study conducted at the Mayo Clinic on elderly inpatients who were receiving treatment for their alcoholism, 14 percent were assessed by the medical team as part of a comprehensive workup as having a drug abuse or dependence problem.[50] The Established Populations for Epidemiologic Studies of the Elderly[51] found concurrent prescription drug and alcohol use to be common among a large sample of elderly people living in geographically diverse communities. In that study, alcohol users were as likely as abstainers to be taking prescription medications.

Abrams and Alexopoulos[52] state that provider-initiated misuse or the failure of the prescription-writer to take into account the physiological (as well as psychosocial) aspects of aging, along with the elderly consumer's belief that over-the-counter drugs are not harmful, "may contribute to patterns of abuse or dependence." Approximately 80 percent of the elderly who take over-the-counter drugs regularly also use alcohol and/or prescription medications. Allergy, cold, and sleep medications, which are sold without prescriptions, contain antihistamines and anticholinergic drugs that can enhance the anticholinergic effects of antipsychotic and tricyclic antidepressant medications. Some nonprescription preparations also contain amounts of alcohol and caffeine, which can lead to oversedation and a reduction in the therapeutic effects of commonly prescribed antihypertensive, antiarrhythmic, and anxiolytic medications. Lamy[53] reports that of the

100 most frequently prescribed drugs, one-half interact with alcohol. Further, all of the 10 most frequently prescribed drugs can interact with alcohol. Clearly, the interactive effects of alcohol and drugs pose a risk of harm for older persons or can even be life threatening.

It is interesting to note that in a study by Folkman and colleagues[54] over a six-month period of 141 community-dwelling people aged 65 to 74, misuse of substances (alcohol and prescription and over-the-counter drugs) was not found to be linked to low self-esteem or a low sense of mastery over the environment. The antecedent personality variables that were studied did not correlate with misuse as hypothesized. Instead, these authors suggest that misuse was related in part to the inadequate attention given to the patients' total patterns of drug and alcohol use by all those involved—physicians, pharmacists, and patients themselves.

In hearings before the House of Representatives Select Committee on Aging,[55] it was pointed out that fewer than 2 percent of U.S. medical students were required to take courses in geriatrics and most took only one course in pharmacology. Hence, many physicians have only minimal knowledge about the aging process and how it affects drug tolerance and dependence. Other factors that were cited as contributing to the abuse and misuse of medication among the elderly included patient noncompliance (over one-half of the elderly have been found not to comply with their daily drug regimen), the high cost of prescription drugs, and the lack of formal Food and Drug Administration guidelines for premarket clinical testing of drugs for elderly consumers.

Assessment and Biopsychosocial Effects

Assessment Strategies and Problems

There are numerous diagnostic instruments for the detection of alcoholism in clinical settings that relate to risk factors and biopsychosocial symptoms of alcoholism. As noted elsewhere, these can include the *DSM-IV,* the Michigan Alcoholism Screening Test (MAST), CAGE questions, the Quantitative Inventory of Alcohol Disorders (QIAD), and the Structured Addictions Assessment Interview for Selecting Treatment (SAAST).[56] The newly developed Geriatric Version of the MAST (MAST-G)[57], a 24-item screening measure with a reported sensitivity of 93.9 percent and specificity of 78.1 percent, was designed specifically to identify alcoholism among older adults. Physicians also use medical tests such as lean body mass and amount of alcohol consumed, but these measures are confounded by age effects, making them less useful in assessing alcoholism among the elderly. Bienenfeld[58] concludes that a person may even begin to experience alcohol-induced problems without changing the amount of alcohol consumed, simply by becoming older.

Most health professionals would likely agree that assessment of alcohol abuse needs to be comprehensive, interdisciplinary, and age and gender relevant. Along these lines, Graham[59] suggests that five overlapping areas need to be included in screening for alcohol abuse among the elderly: (1) quantity and frequency of alcohol consumption, (2) alcohol-related social and legal problems (e.g., housing problems, falls or accidents, poor nutrition, inadequate self- and home-care, lack of exercise, and social isolation), (3) alcohol-related health problems, (4) symptoms of drunkenness or dependence, and (5) self-recognition of alcohol-related problems. Beresford and colleagues[60] add that a series of neuropsychological tests should also be executed as a protocol. Measures of concept formation and abstraction; short- and long-term memory; motor strength, speed, and dexterity; visual-motor coordination; attention, concentration, and vigilance; novel problem solving; language functions; and perceptual integrity need to be included.

Graham, Beresford, and co-workers, along with others, have noted particular difficulties in assessing elders for alcohol abuse using existing measures.[61] Self-report of alcohol consumption and dependence or drunkenness may be unreliable for several reasons. Denial, sense of stigma, social desirability effects, and memory loss can affect accurate recollection or admission of an alcohol problem among the elderly. Also, physical and cognitive changes, due to aging itself or a disease process, confound consumption measures. The health problems and cognitive impairment that are related to alcohol abuse that have been used as markers have not been standardized for general elderly populations, and therefore are questionable when used to distinguish the elderly alcohol abuser.

Effects

What are the effects or consequences of alcohol abuse among the elderly? The problem with temporal ordering needs to be mentioned here again because determining which factors are antecedent and which are the effects of alcohol abuse is not a straightforward exercise. Nevertheless, it is generally agreed that there are interrelated biopsychosocial effects associated with alcoholism, some of which are age specific and some of which are not.

Medical Complications

Miller and Gold[62] categorize the physiological effects from alcohol and drugs as cardiovascular, gastrointestinal, metabolic, and cerebrovascular. Alcohol itself can lead to such things as hypertension, myocardial infarction, cardiac arrhythmias, stroke, peptic ulcer disease, immunosuppression, accidents, dehydration, and electrolyte abnormalities, among others.[63]

Looking specifically at the effect of aging and alcohol on the liver, Scott and Mitchell[64] state that alcohol competes with other drugs for metabolic enzymes in the liver and impairs drug clearance if acutely ingested. Conversely, if chronically ingested, alcohol induces additional metabolic enzymes, which can lead to increased drug clearance. These medical researchers conclude by saying that

although routine liver tests change little with age, there may be less biochemical and metabolic reserve capacity in the older person's liver if it is stressed by diminished blood flow, infections, or exogenous drugs and toxins. As discussed earlier in the section on alcohol and drug abuse and misuse, reiterated by Scott and Mitchell, drug-alcohol and aging interactions are particularly complex and can lead to unpredictable medical problems.

Cognitive Impairment

Beresford and colleagues[65] state, "It is misleading and even irresponsible to examine a patient on a very difficult measure, obtain errors or slowness, and then label such a patient as 'brain damaged.'" They go on to note that this has been the case when looking at elderly alcoholic patients. These authors recommend that the issues of test coverage and difficulty level be examined and that age norms be considered, since there is increasing evidence that decrements in test scores produced by chronic alcoholism and by abnormal aging are separate and additive at most.

Alcohol-related dementia has been described in the literature as a global cognitive impairment that mimics Alzheimer's disease but does not progress after the cessation of drinking. It has been estimated that at least 10 percent of people presenting with dementia actually have alcohol-related brain disease. Although this appears to be a consequence of alcohol abuse, it might also be suggested that excessive drinking occurs in response to the emotional symptoms of dementia or impaired mental functioning.[66] Studies of alcohol-related dementia have found that as age increases, there is a more severe decline in intellect among older alcoholics. Such findings have been confirmed with brain scans that reveal significant cerebral atrophy among alcoholics, especially older alcoholics.[67]

In a study that used older and younger and nonalcoholic control groups, and was therefore able to tease out the effects of alcohol abuse and aging, it was found that tactile discrimination accuracy for nonverbal information was disrupted by aging, but that alcoholism alone does not have this effect. The researchers also reported that the combined effects of aging and alcohol abuse were seen only on tactile tasks that required identification of verbal items.[68]

Goldman[69] states there is reason for some optimism, however, in regard to cognitive impairment in chronic alcoholics. He reports that although many alcoholics continue to show impairment of cognitive functioning on both neuropsychological and intelligence tests (e.g., deficits in visual perception, learning, and memory and in problem solving), studies have shown that a considerable recovery of cognitive functioning can occur immediately after drinking ceases and slower improvements can be made thereafter.

Depression and Suicide

Do older persons drink because they are depressed, or drink and become depressed, or both? Depression is often referred to as the most common psychiatric problem seen in the elderly population and is viewed as a response to loss.[70] Normally, the aging process involves losses—loss of a spouse or loved one, loss of health, loss of job and income, loss of social roles, and loss of status. All people grieve their losses, but depression can set in when they get stuck in the grieving process.

Depression is characterized by physical, emotional, cognitive, behavioral, and social disturbances. An individual suffering from depression might encounter somatic difficulties; experience moods characterized by feelings of sadness, despondency, and hopelessness; have thoughts of death and feelings of worthlessness and self-reproach; be unable to experience pleasure; suffer changes in appetite, sleep habits, and level of energy; and lose interest in usual social and sexual activities.[71]

Alcohol itself is a depressant, and alcohol abuse and depression have long been associated. Although some authors contend that virtually all alcoholics are depressed, the comparison of reported prevalence rates of depression in elderly alcoholics is difficult due to problems with distinguishing depressive symptoms that are common in alcohol abusers and evidence of a primary affective disorder. In looking at major depression in particular, however, using *DSM-III-R* criteria, Mayo Clinic researchers gave 8.3 percent of the alcoholics in their sample this diagnosis.[72] They contrasted this figure with a 3.7 percent rate determined in a study of a general elderly population in North Carolina and the 0.8 to 1.8 percent rates for the lifetime prevalence of major depressive episodes reported by Robins and associates.[73]

Alcohol abuse is considered a risk factor in suicide among the elderly.[74] Suicides in the older population represent a disproportionate amount of successful suicides when compared with the total population. Rich and colleagues[75] determined that overall for the population, males had a rate of 18.2 suicides per 100,000 and females had a rate of 7.9. For persons aged 65 and over, these rates jumped to 31.9 for males and 15.9 for females. Pfeiffer[76] has further noted that suicide rates steadily increase with age and a peak is reached at the age group of 80–84, where the suicide rate for white males (who have higher rates at all ages than women and nonwhites) is 51.4 per 100,000. Rates of suicide for elderly alcohol abusers are suggested to be even higher than rates in the general population.[77]

Case Finding and Treatment

There is consensus that alcohol abuse among the elderly is a hidden problem; therefore, case finding is a critical step that needs to be examined before issues of treatment can be discussed. Dupree[78] looked at the effectiveness of three case-finding strategies employed in Florida to locate elderly alcohol abusers. These approaches employed formal caregivers, the general public, and community health clinics. The author concludes that there was a general hesitancy among formal caregivers and community health clinic staff to label older persons as alcoholic, and that periodic, consistent contact and on-site visits were needed to enhance and sustain the referral flow that was indicated at these sites. At the same time, referrals resulting from a public awareness campaign remained constant.

Graham and Romaniec[79] likewise report that case finding presented ethical dilemmas among outreach agency personnel. Outreach workers expressed concern for the elderly alcoholic client's right to privacy and felt that intervention could intrude on that privacy. In summary, they believed that no intervention should be attempted in cases of milder alcohol problems and that intervention was warranted only when drinking interfered with the client's health or medical treatment. At the same time, the severity of adverse clinical outcomes resulting from interactions between alcohol and prescription drugs led Adams[80] to suggest that educating patients about the risks should be a routine part of health care visits.

In a nationwide examination of alcoholism treatment programs serving 2,600 people aged 21 and over, Janik and Dunham[81] found few age-related differences among alcoholics in treatment. These authors concluded that specialized alcoholism treatment programs for the elderly were perhaps unnecessary. This conclusion appears premature if one accepts Beresford and colleagues' statement, "If we know little about screening elderly populations with respect to alcoholism, we know considerably less about specific treatment strategies appropriate to this age group."[82] These authors go on to say that from a clinical perspective, complete abstinence from alcohol is the only practical treatment goal in light of the profound physical, psychological, and social effects older people experience when they abuse alcohol.

As social workers rather than physicians, Rathbone-McCuan and Hashimi are also careful to include the client's wants and desires in treatment planning and delivery, which also may help to avoid some of the dilemmas cited earlier with respect to case finding. They believe that a framework to guide interventions "should explicate how alcohol abuse interferes with what older men and women are required, expected, or prefer to do in their daily lives."[83] According to this perspective, it is important to consider environmental, physical, and social behavioral factors from a causal and interventive point of view. Goals of treatment might include either total abstinence or controlled drinking, depending on what is most appropriate and attainable for individual elders, based on their history and circumstances.

Although there are disproportionately few elderly persons receiving mental health services (which some believe reflects ageist attitudes whereby people believe that older persons cannot be helped given their age and declining health), there is evidence that older alcohol abusers are more likely to complete a treatment program.[84] Several authors have further reported that as a group, later-life-onset alcohol abusers were the most responsive to treatment.[85] Atkinson and associates[86] found, though, that treatment program variables were better predictors of compliance than age of onset in their study conducted at a Veterans Administration geriatric alcoholism outpatient program.

Traditional treatment approaches to alcoholism have used multiple modalities such as detoxification; Alcoholics Anonymous; behavior modification; individual, family, or group therapy; and aversion therapy (hypoaversion, disulfiram/ antabuse, condition reflex treatment). These approaches have been variously utilized and found to be effective with groups of elderly alcohol abusers. Mellor and associates[87] have suggested that residential detoxification should be utilized routinely with elders because of increased likelihood of serious complications during the process. Carstensen and colleagues[88] have indicated some success with a behavioral inpatient program that consisted of medical attention, individual counseling, alcohol education class, training in self-management and problem solving, vocational assistance, and marital therapy when appropriate. Participants aged 60 and over at time of treatment were contacted two to four years after discharge and results indicated that beneficial effects were maintained for 50 percent of the sample. An additional 12 percent reported significant modification of their drinking at follow-up.

In a study conducted at a Veterans Administration hospital of 24 male alcoholics treated in a mixed-age outpatient group (mean age = 58.8 years) and 25 male and female alcoholics treated in special peer groups (mean age = 60.2 years), Kofoed and colleagues[89] found that peer-group patients remained in treatment significantly longer and were more likely to complete treatment than were mixed-age controls. These authors describe treatment as consisting of group therapy that tended to be active and to emphasize expression of feelings. Peer and staff confrontation was fairly frequent and policies regarding alcohol use (breathalyzer tests were given) and attendance were strictly enforced for the two groups.

As reported on by Felker,[90] a peer-group approach was also utilized in Madison, Wisconsin, by a geriatric nurse practitioner and social worker who named their endeavor Elderly Recovery Group. The program had minimal norms, rules, and structures, and the first 30 minutes of each weekly 90-minute meeting was devoted to informal socializing. Next, an inquiry was made about members who were not present, and members gave information about persons with whom they had had contact. A Thought and Meditation for the Day was then read by a member and discussion ensued either about the thought or members' current problems or experiences. Expression of feelings were reinforced and the group facilitators provided on-the-spot planning for dealing with age- and health-related issues. Two-thirds of the members were attending Alcoholics Anonymous at the same time they attended the Elderly Recovery Group. In terms of treatment effectiveness, of the 15 members of the group who were active during the year being reported on, 12, or 80 percent, remained sober and three continued to abuse alcohol.

Blake[91] emphasizes that sociopsychological approaches to alcoholism in the elderly relate more to the stress of aging than do traditional alco-holism treatment programs. He cites the work of Zimberg,[92] Mishara and Kastenbaum,[93] and the National Institute on Alcohol Abuse and Alcoholism,[94] which all recommend such sociotherapeutic approaches and consider "senior services and home care treatment to be proper directions for treatment to follow." The National Institute on Alcohol Abuse and Alcoholism has further urged that the range of services employed in community-based approaches to alcohol abuse among the elderly be coordinated.

Keeping in mind that sociotherapy typically consists of building informal social support networks, Alcoholics Anonymous, peer groups, and involvement with other self-help organizations,[95] along with the physical health and nutritional needs of the elderly, Rathbone-McCuan and Hashimi[96] have proposed an ideal treatment model for older alcoholics. They state that such a model would have both health and social components that would differ from day treatment for younger alcoholics. Under the health component, activities would include regular health screening, physical and occupational rehabilitation, linkages to nursing homes or other inpatient settings for short-term admissions along with accessible hospital-based services, and nutrition and pharmacy input. On the social side, individuals would be involved in Alcoholics Anonymous and be encouraged to participate in social activities not focused on recovery. Participants in the program would receive intensive case management to coordinate needed housing, legal and transportation services, and employment and recreational activities counseling. Older recovering alcoholics would also be included on the treatment team and would have extensive outreach functions both in the community as well as within the program.

Schonfeld and Dupree[97] recently reviewed the literature regarding the various components needed in the continuum of care and outlined specific strategies to make programs effectively age-specific for the elderly. For example, the confrontational approach typical of Alcoholics Anonymous groups should be modified to a more supportive approach for effective intervention with the elderly.

Participation in traditional, community-based programs may be problematic both for individuals with physical or cognitive impairments and for those residing in nursing homes. Schaschl and Straw[98] developed an intervention program to accommodate persons with physical disabilities. Horton and Howe[99] report success using behavioral modification with a nursing home resident who had cognitive impairments. Programs emphasizing peer-group socialization have been modified for nursing home settings for residents who are more cognitively intact.[100]

Summary

In the future, those who work in the medical and aging fields are likely to see an increasing number of female and male elderly alcoholics.[101] It is hoped that these individuals will have at their disposal a growing body of information on the problem, its sufferers, and which outreach and treatment approaches seem to work with the older population and special groups of elders. This means that the research and practice literature, along with the practitioner's own experiences, will serve as funds of knowledge for working in this area. One of the most recent developments in terms of disseminating such knowledge is the Gerontological Society of America Elderly Alcohol/Drug Interest Group home page on the Internet. The only way practitioners can continue to draw from these wells is to continuously fill them with new scientific findings, along with personal insights derived from practice.

Endnotes

1. Burt E. Gilliland and Richard K. James, *Crisis Intervention Strategies* (Pacific Grove, CA: Brooks/Cole, 1988), p. 276.

2. Administration on Aging, *A Profile of Older Americans, 1996* (http://www.aoa.dhhs.gov/aoa/pages/profil96.html), updated February 25, 1997.

3. Kathryn Graham, "Identifying and Measuring Alcohol Abuse among the Elderly: Serious Problems with Existing Instrumentation," *Journal of Studies on Alcohol*, Vol. 47, No. 4 (1986), pp. 322–326.

4. Dan G. Blazer and Margaret R. Pennybacker, "Epidemiology of Alcoholism in the Elderly," in James T. Hartford and T. Samorajski (Eds.), *Alcoholism in the Elderly: Social and Biomedical Issues*, Aging Series Volume 25 (New York: Raven Press, 1984), pp. 25–33; and Graham, "Identifying and Measuring Alcohol Abuse among the Elderly," p. 325.

5. Robert N. Butler, Myra Lewis, and Trey Sunderland, *Aging and Mental Health: Positive Psychosocial and Biomedical Approaches*, 4th ed. (New York: Macmillan, 1991), pp. 210–211.

6. Nancy J. Osgood, Helen E. Wood, and Iris A. Parham, *Alcoholism and Aging: An Annotated Bibliography and Review* (Westport, CT: Greenwood Press, 1995).

7. Judith C. Barker and B. Josea Kramer, "Alcohol Consumption among Older Urban American Indians," *Journal of Studies on Alcohol* (March 1996), pp. 119–124.

8. Eloise Rathbone-McCuan and Joan Hashimi, *Isolated Elders* (Rockville, MD: Aspen Publishers, 1982), p. 212; and George J. Warheit and Joanne B. Auth, "The Mental Health and Social Correlates of Alcohol Use among Differing Life Cycle Groups," in George Maddox, Lee N. Robins, and Nathan Rosenberg (Eds), *Nature and Extent of Alcohol Problems among the Elderly* (New York: Springer, 1986), pp. 29–82.

9. David Bienenfeld, "Alcoholism in the Elderly," *American Family Physician*, Vol. 36, No. 2 (1987), pp. 163–169.

10. American Psychiatric Association, *Diagnostic and Statistical Manual of Mental Disorders*, 3rd ed. (rev.) (Washington, DC: Author, 1987).

11. Lee N. Robins, John E. Helzer, T. R. Przybeck, and D. A. Regier, "Alcohol Disorders in the Community: A Report from the Epidemiologic Catchment Area," in *Alcoholism: Origins and Outcomes* (New York: Raven Press, 1988).

12. Bienenfeld, "Alcoholism in the Elderly," pp. 164–165; and Graham, "Identifying and Measuring Alcohol Abuse in the Elderly," p. 322.

13. J. Randall Curtis, Gail Geller, Emma J. Stokes, David M. Levine, and R. D. Moore, "Characteristics, Diagnosis and Treatment of Alcoholism in Elderly Patients," *Journal of the American Geriatrics Society*, Vol. 37 (1989), pp. 310–316; and Mark A. Schuckit, "A Clinical Review of Alcohol, Alcoholism, and the Elderly Patient," *Journal of Clinical Psychiatry*, Vol. 43 (1983), pp. 396–399.

14. Carol L. Joseph, Roland M. Atkinson, and Linda Ganzini, "Problem Drinking among Residents of a VA Nursing Home," *International Journal of Geriatric Psychiatry*, Vol. 10, No. 3 (March 1995), pp. 243–248.

15. Lawrence Schonfeld, Glenn E. Rohrer, Marge Zima, and Terri Spiegel, "Alcohol Abuse and Medication Misuse in Older Adults as Estimated by Service Providers," *Journal of Gerontological Social Work*, Vol. 21, Nos. 1/2 (1993), pp. 113–125.

16. Butler, Lewis, and Sutherland, *Aging and Mental Health*, p. 211.

17. Linda Vinton, "An Exploratory Study of Self-Neglectful Elderly," *Journal of Gerontological Social Work*, Vol. 18, No. 1/2 (1991), pp. 55–67.

18. Roland Atkinson, John A. Turner, Lial L. Kofoed, and Robert L. Tolson, "Early versus Late Onset Alcoholism in Older Persons: Preliminary Findings," *Alcoholism*, Vol. 9 (1985), pp. 513–515.

19. Joseph G. Liberto and David W. Oslin, "Early versus Late Onset of Alcoholism in the Elderly," *International Journal of the Addictions*, Vol. 30, No. 13 & 14 (1995), pp. 1799–1818.

20. Charles E. Holzer, Jerome K. Myers, Myrna W. Weissman, Gary L. Tischler, Philip J. Leaf, James Anthony, and Philip B. Bednarski, "Antecedents and Correlates of Alcohol Abuse and Dependence in the Elderly," in George Maddox, Lee N. Robins, and Nathan Rosenberg (Eds.), *Nature and Extent of Alcohol Problems among the Elderly* (New York: Springer, 1986), pp. 217–244.

21. John R. Minnis, "Toward an Understanding of Alcohol Abuse among the Elderly: A Sociological Perspective," *Journal of Alcohol and Drug Education*, Vol. 33, No. 3 (1988), pp. 32–40.

22. Travis Hirschi, *Causes of Delinquency* (Berkeley: University of California Press, 1969).

23. Holzer et al., "Antecedents and Correlates," pp. 217–244.

24. Anne M. Burnack and Jeanne L. Thomas, "Behavioral Factors Related to Elderly Alcohol Abuse: Research and Policy Issues," *The International Journal of the Addictions*, Vol. 24, No. 7 (1989), pp. 641–654.

25. Liberto and Oslin, "Early versus Late Onset of Alcoholism in the Elderly," pp. 1812–1813.

26. U.S. Department of Health and Human Services, "Nature and Extent of Alcohol Problems among the Elderly," *Research Monograph 14* DHHS Pub. No. ADM 84–1321 (Washington, DC: U.S. Government Printing Office, 1984); and Meyer D. Glantz, "Predictions of Elderly Drug Abuse," *Journal of Psychoactive Drugs*, Vol. 13, No. 2 (1981), pp. 117–126.

27. James E. Royce, *Alcohol Problems and Alcoholism: A Comprehensive Survey* (New York: The Free Press, 1981).

28. Roland M. Atkinson, Robert L. Tolson, and John A. Turner, "Late versus Early Onset Problem Drinking in Older Men," *Alcoholism Clinical and Experimental Research*, Vol. 14, No. 4 (July-August, 1990), pp. 574–579.

29. Gilliland and James, *Crisis Intervention Strategies*, p. 282.

30. Jeffrey A. Giordano and Kathryn Beckham, "Alcohol Use and Abuse in Old Age: An Examination of Type II Alcoholism," *Journal of Gerontological Social Work*, Vol. 9, No. 1 (1985), pp. 65–83.

31. Edward M. Adlaf and Reginald G. Smart, "Alcohol Use, Drug Use, and Well-Being in Older Adults in Toronto," *International Journal of the Addictions*, Vol. 30, Nos. 13 & 14 (1995), pp. 1985–2016.

32. Richard E. Finlayson, Richard D. Hurt, Leo J. Davis, and Robert M. Morse, "Alcoholism in Elderly Persons: A Study of the Psychiatric and Psychosocial Features of 216 Inpatients," *Mayo Clinic Proceedings*, Vol. 63, pp. 761–768.

33. Arnold J. Rosin and M. M. Glatt, "The Older Alcoholic and the Family," *Quarterly Journal of Studies on Alcohol*, Vol. 32 (1971), pp. 53–59.

34. R. A. M. Downing, "Alcoholism and the Elderly: A Comparative Study of Coping Strategies Utilized by Alcoholics and Non-Alcoholic," unpublished thesis, California State University, Los Angeles, 1979.

35. Adlaf and Smart, "Alcohol Use, Drug, Use, and Well-Being," pp. 2009–2010.

36. Francesca Alexander and Robert W. Duff, "Social Interaction and Alcohol Use in Retirement Communities," *The Gerontologist*, Vol. 28, No. 5 (1988), pp. 632–636.

37. J. Vejnoska, "Arizona Group Studies Drinking of Elderly," *National Institute of Alcohol Abuse and Alcoholism Information and Feature Service*, 1982.

38. Edith L. Gomberg, "Alcohol Use and Alcohol Problems among the Elderly," in National Institute on Alcohol Abuse and Alcoholism, *Alcohol and Health Monograph 4, Special Population Issues*, DHHS Pub. No. ADM 82-1193 (Washington, DC: U.S. Government Printing Office, 1982).

39. David J. Ekerdt, Lorraine O. deLabry, Robert J. Glynn, and Richard W. Davis, "Change in Drinking Behaviors with Retirement: Findings from the Normative Aging Study," *Journal of Studies on Alcohol*, Vol. 50, No. 4 (July 1989), pp. 347–353.

40. Finlayson et al., "Alcoholism in Elderly Patients," pp. 761–768.

41. Anthony J. LeGreca, Ronald L. Akers, and Jeffrey W. Dwyer, "Life Events and Alcohol Behavior among Older Adults," *The Gerontologist*, Vol. 28, No. 4 (1988), pp. 552–558.

42. Giordano and Beckham, "Alcohol Use and Abuse in Old Age," p. 72.

43. Barry R. Bainton, "Drinking Patterns of the Rural Aged," in Christine L. Fry (Ed.), *Dimensions: Aging, Culture, and Health* (Brooklyn, NY: J. F. Bergin, 1981).

44. Grace M. Barnes, "Alcohol Use among Older Persons: Findings from a Western New York State General Population Survey," *Journal of the American Geriatrics Society*, Vol. 27, No. 6 (1979), pp. 244–250.

45. D. H. Leigh, "Prevention Work among the Elderly: A Workable Model," paper presented at the Annual Forum of the National Council on Alcoholism, Seattle, WA, 1980.

46. Gurnack and Thomas, "Behavioral Factors," p. 649.

47. F. T. Crews, "Factors Predisposing to Alcohol and Medication Abuse in the Elderly," part of handout from University of Florida Geriatric Education Center teleconference; and Patricia Bandy and Patricia A. President, "Recent Literature on Drug Abuse Prevention and Mass Media: Focusing on Youth, Parents, Women and the Elderly," *Journal of Drug Education*, Vol. 13, No. 3 (1983), pp. 255–271.

48. Robins et al., "Alcohol Disorders in the Community."

49. Larry G. Peppers and Ronald G. Stover, "The Elderly Abuser: A Challenge for the Future," *Journal of Drug Issues*, Vol. 9, No. 1 (1979), pp. 73–83.

50. Finlayson et al., "Alcoholism in Elderly Persons," p. 761.

51. Elizabeth A. Crischilles, David J. Foley, Robert B. Wallace, Jon H. Lemke et al., "Use of Medications by Persons 65 and Over: Data from the Established Populations for Epidemiologic Studies of the Elderly," *Journal of Gerontology*, Vol. 47, No. 5 (September 1992), pp. M137–M144.

52. Robert C. Abrams and George S. Alexopoulos, "Substance Abuse in the Elderly: Over-the-Counter and Illegal Drugs," *Hospital and Community Psychiatry*, Vol. 39, No. 8 (August 1988), pp. 822–823.

53. Peter P. Lamy, "Alcohol Misuse and Abuse among the Elderly," *Drug Intelligence in Clinical Pharmacology*, Vol. 18 (1984), p. 649.

54. Susan Folkman, Linda Berstein, and Richard S. Lazarus, "Stress Processes and the Misuse of Drugs in Older Adults," *Psychology and Aging*, Vol. 2, No. 4 (1987), pp. 366–374.

55. Hearing Before the House of Representatives Select Committee on Aging, *Drug Use and Misuse among the Elderly* (Washington, DC: U.S. Government Printing Office, June 23, 1989).

56. Thomas P. Beresford, Frederic C. Blow, Kirk J. Brower, Kenneth M. Adams, and Richard C. W. Hall, "Alcoholism and Aging in the General Hospital," *Psychosomatics*, Vol. 29, No. 1 (Winter 1988), pp. 61–72; and Graham, "Identifying and Measuring," p. 323.

57. F. C. Blow, K. J. Brower, J. E. Schulenberg, L. M. Demo-Dananberg, K. J. Young, and T. P. Beresford, "The Michigan Alcoholism Screening Test: Geriatric Version (MAST-G): A New Elderly-Specific Screening Instrument," *Alcoholism: Clinical and Experimental Research*, Vol. 16 (1992), p. 172.

58. Bienenfeld, "Alcoholism in the Elderly," pp. 164–165.

59. Graham, "Identifying and Measuring," p. 323–325.

60. Beresford et al., "Alcoholism and Aging," p. 69.

61. Graham, "Identifying and Measuring, p. 325; Beresford et al., "Alcoholism and Aging," p. 69; Rathbone-McCuan and Hashimi, *Isolated Elders*, pp. 220–223; and Sara S. DeHart and Norman G. Hoffman, "Screening and Diagnosis of 'Alcohol Abuse and Dependence' in Older Adults," *International Journal of the Addictions*, Vol. 30, Nos. 13 & 14 (1995), pp. 1717–1747.

62. Norman S. Miller and Mark S. Gold, *Alcohol* (New York: Plenum Press, 1991), p. 242.

63. James T. Hartford and T. Samorajski, "Alcoholism in the Geriatric Population," *Journal of the American Geriatrics Society*, Vol. 30 (1982), p. 18; and James W. Smith, "Medical Manifestations of Alcoholism in the Elderly," *International Journal of the Addictions*, Vol. 30, Nos. 13 & 14 (1995), pp. 1749–1798.

64. Robert B. Scott and Mack C. Mitchell, "Aging, Alcoholism, and the Liver," *Journal of the American Geriatrics Society*, Vol. 35, No. 3 (1988), pp. 255–265.

65. Beresford et al., "Alcoholism and Aging," p. 69.

66. Richard M. Atkinson (Ed.), *Alcohol and Drug Abuse in Old Age* (Washington, DC: American Psychiatric Press, 1984); and Ole J. Thienhaus and James T. Hartford, "Alcoholism in the Elderly," *Psychiatric Medicine*, Vol. 2, No. 1 (March 1984), pp. 27–41.

67. Harford and Samorajski, "Alcoholism in the Geriatric Population," p. 18.

68. Marlene Oscar-Berman, Amy Weinstein, and Diane Wysocki, "Bimanual Tactual Discrimination in Aging Alcoholics," *Alcoholism Clinical and Experimental Research*, Vol. 7, No. 4 (Fall 1983), pp. 398–403.

69. Mark S. Goldman, "Cognitive Impairment in Chronic Alcoholics: Some Cause for Optimism," *American Psychologist*, Vol. 38, No. 10 (October 1983), pp. 1045–1054.

70. Butler, Lewis, and Sunderland, *Aging and Mental Health*, p. 125.

71. Rathbone-McCuan and Hashimi, *Isolated Elders*, p. 218; and Gerald K. Klerman and Myrna M. Weissman, "Depressions among Women: Their Nature and Causes," in M. Guttentag, S. Salasin, and D. Belle (Eds.), *The Mental Health of Women* (New York: Academic Press, 1980), pp. 57–92.

72. Finlayson et al., "Alcoholism in Elderly Persons," p. 766.

73. Dan Blazer and Candyce D. Williams, "Epidemiology of Dysphoria and Depression in an Elderly Population," *American Journal of Psychiatry*, Vol. 137 (1980), pp. 439–444; and Lee N. Robins, John E. Helzer, Myrna M. Weissman, H. Orvaschel, Ernest Gruenberg, Jack D. Burke, and Darrel A. Regier, "Lifetime Prevalence of Specific Psychiatric Disorders in Three Sites," *Archives of General Psychiatry*, Vol. 41 (1984), pp. 949–958.

74. Joseph Richman, *Suicide in the Elderly* (New York: Springer, 1992).

75. Charles L. Rich, Deborah Young, and Richard C. Fowler, "San Diego Suicide Study," *Archives of General Psychiatry*, Vol. 43 (1986), pp. 577–582.

76. Eric Pfeiffer, "Psychopathology and Social Pathology," in J. E. Birren and K. Warner Schaie (Eds.), *Handbook of Psychology and Aging* (New York: Van Nostrand Reinhold, 1977).

77. Atkinson, Turner, Kofoed, and Tolson, "Early versus Late Onset Alcoholism," pp. 513–515; and Hartford and Samorajski, "Alcoholism in the Geriatric Population," pp. 18–24.

78. Larry W. Dupree, "Comparison of Three Case-Finding Strategies Relative to Elderly Alcohol Abusers," *Journal of Applied Gerontology*, Vol. 8, No. 4 (December 1989), pp. 502–511.

79. Kathryn Graham and Jadzia Romaniec, "Case-Finding vs. Right to Privacy: A General Dilemma Emerging from a Study of the Elderly," *Journal of Drug Issues*, Vol. 16, No. 3 (Summer 1986), pp. 391–395.

80. Wendy L. Adams, "Interactions between Alcohol and Other Drugs," *International Journal of the Addictions*, Vol. 30, Nos. 13 & 14 (1995), pp. 1903–1923.

81. Stephen W. Janik and Roger G. Dunham, "A Nation-wide Examination of the Need for Specific Alcoholism Treatment Programs for the Elderly," *Journal of Studies on Alcohol*, Vol. 44, No. 2 (March 1983), pp. 307–317.

82. Beresford et al., "Alcoholism and Aging," p. 70.

83. Rathbone-McCuan and Hashimi, *Isolated Elders*, p. 223.

84. Laura L. Carstensen Robert G. Rychtarik, and Donald M. Prue, "Behavioral Treatment of the Geriatric Alcohol Abuser: A Long-Term Follow-Up Study," *Addictive Behaviors*, Vol. 10 (1985), pp. 307–311; and Mark A. Shuckit, "Geriatric Alcoholism and Drug Abuse," *The Gerontologist*, Vol. 17 (1977), pp. 168–174.

85. Roger G. Dunham, "Aging and Changing Patterns of Alcohol Use," *Journal of Psychoactive Drugs*, Vol. 13 (1981), pp. 143–151; and Larry N. Dupree, Helen Broskowski, and Lawrence I. Schonfeld, "The Gerontology Alcohol Project: A Behavioral Treatment Program for Elderly Alcohol Abusers," *The Gerontologist*, Vol. 24, No. 5 (1984), pp. 510–516.

86. Atkinson, Tolson, and Turner, "Late versus Early Onset Problem Drinking in Older Men," pp. 574–579.

87. M. Joanna Mellor, Alfredo Garcia, Ellen Kenny, June Lazarus, Judi Matiz Conway, Lorraine Rivers, Nalini Viswanathan, and Joan Zimmerman, "Alcohol and Aging," *Journal of Gerontological Social Work*, Vol. 25, No. 1/2 (1996), pp. 71–89.

88. Carstensen, Rychtarik, and Prue, "Behavioral Treatment of the Geriatric Alcohol Abuser," p. 307.

89. Lial L. Kofoed, Robert L. Tolson, Roland M. Atkinson, Rodger L. Toth, and John A. Turner, "Treatment Compliance of Older Alcoholics: An Elder-Specific Approach Is Superior to 'Mainstreaming,' " *Journal of Studies on Alcohol*, Vol. 48, No. 1 (1987), pp. 47–51.

90. Margaret P. Felker, "A Recovery Group for Elderly Alcoholics," *Geriatric Nursing* (March/April 1988), pp. 110–113.

91. Richard Blake, "Mental Health Counseling and Older Problem Drinkers," *Journal of Mental Health Counseling*, Vol. 12, No. 3 (July 1990), pp. 354–367.

92. Sheldon Zimberg, "Diagnosis and Treatment of Elderly Alcoholics," *Alcoholism: Clinical and Experimental Research*, Vol. 2, No. 1 (1978), pp. 27–29.

93. Brian L. Mishara and Robert Kastenbaum, *Alcoholism and Old Age* (Orlando, FL: Grune & Stratton, 1980).

94. National Institute on Alcohol Abuse and Alcoholism, *A Guide to Planning Alcoholism Treatment Programs*, DHHS Pub. No. ADM 86-1430 (Washington, DC: U.S. Government Printing Office, 1986).

95. Edith J. Gomberg, "Alcohol Use and Alcohol Problems among the Elderly," in National Institute on Alcohol Abuse and Alcoholism, *Alcohol and Health Monograph No. 4, Special Population Issues* (Washington, DC: U.S. Government Printing Office), pp. 263–289; and "Patterns of Alcohol Use and Abuse among the Elderly," in National Institute on Alcohol Abuse and Alcoholism, *Alcohol and Health Monograph No. 4*, Special Population Issues, DHHS Pub. No. ADM 82-1193 (Rockville, MD: U.S. Department of Health and Human Services, 1982).

96. Rathbone-McCuan and Hashimi, *Isolated Elders*, p. 233.

97. Lawrence Schonfeld and Larry W. Dupree, "Treatment Approaches for Older Problem Drinkers," *International Journal of the Addictions*, Vol. 30, Nos. 13 & 14 (1995), pp. 1819–1840.

98. S. Schaschl and D. Straw, "Results of a Model Intervention Program for Physically Impaired Persons," *Alcohol Health Research World*, Vol. 13 (1989), pp. 150–153.

99. A. Horton, Jr. and N. Howe, "Behavior Therapy with an Aged Alcoholic: A Case Study," *International Journal of Behavioral Geriatrics*, Vol. 1 (1982), pp. 17–18.

100. Carol L. Joseph, "Alcohol and Drug Misuse in the Nursing Home," *International Journal of the Addictions*, Vol. 30, Nos. 13 & 14 (1995), pp. 1953–1984.

101. Wendy L. Adams and Narra Smith Cox, "Epidemiology of Problem Drinking among Elderly People," *International Journal of the Addictions*, Vol. 30, Nos. 13 & 14 (1995), pp. 1693–1716.

15

Gender and Drugs: Fact, Fiction, and Unanswered Questions

Diane R. Davis
Eastern Washington University

Diana M. DiNitto
University of Texas at Austin

en and women operate in many of the same social systems, but these systems view substance disorders from a different perspective when the person using alcohol or drugs is a woman rather than a man. Chemically dependent women are typically considered more sick or deviant than men who abuse alcohol or other drugs in the same way.[1] Test this difference for yourself. Think of one of the hundreds of "drunk jokes" or one of the many cartoons that feature a male alcoholic (for example, the character Thirsty in the syndicated cartoon "Hi and Lois" by Greg and Brian Walker). Substitute a female alcoholic and the joke isn't so funny. The social systems of the family, the courts, the medical establishment, and so forth continue to treat male and female drug abusers differently. These differences and other social, physiological, and psychological factors that distinguish the psychoactive drug problems of men and women are the subjects of this chapter. More important, the implications of these differences for prevention and

recovery are addressed. We begin with a woman's story that illustrates many of these issues.

Susan's Story*

Looking good was something Susan always knew how to do. She was a cheerleader, an honor student, and part of the "in crowd" all through junior high and high school, when those kinds of things really count. Even in college, she was active in lots of extracurricular activities and kept a 3.0 grade-point average. Only if you looked very carefully would you see the cracks in her outwardly perfect facade: wine mixed in her grape juice after school in junior high, bourbon from her dad's liquor cabinet mysteriously missing on a regular basis, the real reason she often stayed out all night during

---

*Susan's story is based on the accounts of many alcoholic women in recovery, especially one woman who is well known to both authors,

high school (she kept getting drunk and was afraid to come home), the time she showed up "blasted" at her Economics 301 final, the blackouts, her reputation for being able to hold her liquor, the time she woke up in the woods as her date was trying to take off her clothes. As with most women beginning their addiction to alcohol, nobody really noticed. Or if they did, they explained her behavior as feisty, a little rebellious, or going through a phase. As Susan herself said, "It's no big deal."

Susan wasn't looking very closely at herself either. When she looked at her family, she saw a mother whose life revolved around her husband, and she saw a father whose life revolved around his job—wasn't everybody like that? When she saw her dad drinking every night and her mother covering up the many times he "had a few too many," it didn't even occur to her there might be a problem; after all, he always had a job of some kind and put food on the table for the family. When she looked at her older brother, she saw the one source of affection she had felt in her family; 20 years later, she remembered the sexual abuse. Most of the time, she didn't look at all.

Susan's first marriage started before she finished college because she got pregnant, but then that wasn't all that unusual. A second child soon after gave Susan the illusion that she had settled down with a family, just like she thought she was supposed to do. Her drinking became more episodic, because she was very busy with two small children and her husband did not really like to drink as she did. At age 23, however, she went overboard at her husband's company party. All the hidden anguish of her life erupted in a rage. She stomped out of the party and tried to hitch a ride, anywhere! She has no memory of how she got home the next day or what happened to her. Her husband made her go to an Alcoholics Anonymous meeting. It was perfectly clear to Susan that this was not the place for her. She was not an alcoholic. Besides, when she finally mentioned having blackouts to her physician, he said it was normal and she should "cut down a little."

Susan became more careful with her drinking. When she and her husband divorced, drinking was not the issue (she thought). She saw nothing unusual in buying a bottle of Scotch her first day in her new apartment and drinking it until she passed out. She spent many nights drinking Scotch, always waiting until the kids were in bed to start drinking and always "falling asleep" on the couch. Her new job kept her busy during the day. It was only after the kids were asleep and things got quiet that she would "reward herself." After all, it's a tough job being a single parent.

Soon, the nights were taken up with a new acquaintance who liked to drink just as Susan did. He also had access to other drugs that she had never tried. The next year was spent experimenting with the finest: clearlight acid from San Francisco, peyote from Mexico, and hashish, marijuana, and cocaine from the connection of a prominent businessman in town. A whole new world of "beautiful people" opened up and Susan felt like she'd walked through the looking glass, far away from the straight middle-class world where she had always felt like an outsider. Even so, she didn't quit her job or quite lose track of her children. Her lover became her new husband. When he tapered off drugs and switched to martinis, she did too. Like many women substance abusers, Susan's use mirrored her husband's.

Most of the time, they didn't start drinking until 5 P.M. They always had lots to celebrate, or sometimes just a need to "take the edge off." Susan's job was becoming more stressful, and her husband's work was either feast or famine. The arguments seemed unfortunate, but they continued to forgive each other for having "a few too many." Even when he hit her, she understood. One time, she threw an end table across the room at him and cut his face. Neither one remembered why the next day. The kids seemed to have grown up into lives of their own—they were teenagers and were gone a lot. Susan rarely saw any friends who didn't like to drink. Although she couldn't control her drinking anymore around her family, no one told her she had a problem. She once was advised by her mother to "cut down a little," and her dad told her to quit drinking brandy after dinner. The hangovers were becoming almost unendurable, but she forced herself to show up at work, even when she had the shakes. As the humiliations of covering for both herself and her husband piled up, Susan became more and more isolated (except from people who drank just as she did).

One day, a drinking buddy of Susan's told her she had joined AA. Susan was stunned! Why would she want to do that? She drinks just like I do, she thought. A few months later, when Susan had moved out of the house after a particularly abusive episode with her husband, this friend gave her a copy of the Big Book of Alcoholics Anonymous. "Have a nice life," was the way the friend inscribed the front page. Susan read the book, drinking martinis the whole time. Three years later, she sobered up. During those three years, "I tried everything to control my drinking—except quitting drinking." She tried marriage counseling, drinking only wine, individual therapy, vitamins, willpower, AA, self-help books, leaving her husband, reconciling with her husband, and all she could put together was a few weeks of abstinence. It never occurred to her to enter "treatment," partly because no one suggested it and partly because she didn't have the money or insurance to cover it. At least once, she celebrated her sobriety with a pitcher of martinis. Like other substance abusers, she was on an endless cycle of "I'll do better tomorrow" and of course she was always drunk again by 9 o'clock that night. Her husband continued to drink because he thought Susan was the one with the problem.

How did Susan finally get sober? Was it because she "hit bottom" and got "sick and tired of being sick and tired" as they say in AA? The answer according to Susan is a spiritual one—but for the grace of God and her AA woman friend, she would still be drinking or dead. Academics, researchers, and practitioners want more concrete answers. Yet, given the high rates of relapse from substance abuse, the road to recovery is still elusive.

Susan's story doesn't end with sobriety. She is now "recovering from recovery," a long, painful process of facing the reality of her past alcohol abuse and lost dreams, and learning to live sober "one day at a time." She divorced her husband and started her recovery with no job and no place to live. She now has a new job that she loves, but the salary is much lower. She is slowly repairing the relationship with her children. One of her children has already gone through her own addiction to drugs and into recovery. Susan goes to AA regularly and sponsors other women. She has been in therapy for a number of years, dealing with her own shame and guilt, depression, family-of-origin issues, sexual abuse, and trying to find out what's "normal." Many times when Susan has disclosed to another person that she is a recovering alcoholic, they don't believe her. Her favorite response is, "Baby, this is what an alcoholic looks like!" She still knows how to look good.

An Equality Women Don't Want

Within every age group in the United States there are more men than women who drink alcohol, and within every age group, more men than women are classified as heavy drinkers. For instance, in 1993, 9.5 percent of men were reported to be heavy drinkers, compared with 1.5 percent of women.[2] The number of "heavy" drinkers among women may be underestimated, however. Definitions of heavy drinking differ among studies, but a typical definition includes five or more drinks at one sitting[3] or consumption of one ounce or more of pure alcohol per day.[4] These definitions often fail to consider gender differences. For example, body weight, as well as water and fat content in the body, affect the metabolism of alcohol. When consumed, alcohol is dispersed or diluted throughout the water in the body. The concentration of alcohol is relative to the total amount of body water. On the average, women weigh less than men, and they have more body fat in relation to water content. Generally speaking, a

140-pound woman will have a higher blood-alcohol level after ingesting the same amount of alcohol over the same time period than a 140-pound man, and she will almost certainly have a higher blood-alcohol level than a 180-pound man. Yet studies of drinking behavior do not usually take these well-known facts into account. If adjustments for physiological factors are made, and measures of heavy drinking were adjusted accordingly, the percentage of women classified as heavy drinkers might increase substantially.

Although heavy drinking can be detrimental, it is not necessarily the same as alcohol abuse or dependence. In addition to estimates of heavy drinkers, researchers are also interested in differences in estimates of men and women in the population who abuse or are dependent on alcohol. In recent years, estimates of the ratio of men to women with problems of alcohol abuse and dependence have changed. Edith Lisansky Gomberg, one of the earliest researchers on women and alcoholism, reviewed literature on this subject and reported that rates varied depending on the populations studied, such as rural versus urban or clinical samples versus general population samples.[5] In the 1950s, estimates indicated that there were as many as 5 or 6 male alcoholics for every 1 female. In the 1960s and 1970s, estimates were about 4 to 1. More recent reports indicate that within the past year, approximately 11 percent of U.S. men and 4.1 percent of U.S. women meet the diagnostic criteria for alcohol abuse or dependence, a ratio of 2.7 to 1.[6]

The United States and other Western cultures are not alone in reports that men are at higher risk for alcohol disorders than women. Figures for Eastern countries such as Korea and Taiwan paint a more dramatic picture of gender differences. Helzer and colleagues conducted a cross-national study in St. Louis, Missouri; Edmonton, Canada; Puerto Rico; Taipei City, Taiwan; and South Korea.[7] The lifetime prevalence rates for alcoholism (i.e., anyone who at any time in his or her life had the symptoms of alcoholism) varied considerably across countries but were substan-

tially higher for men than for women at all sites. Edmonton had the smallest current male to female ratio at 4:1, whereas Taiwan had the largest difference at a ratio of 18:1. South Korea had a ratio of 16:1 and for Puerto Rico it was 12:1. In St. Louis, the ratio was 7:1. The bad news for women is that as lifetime prevalence rates for the general population increased over the years in each of the countries, the prevalence rate for women not only rose but it rose disproportionately. The authors of the study conclude that the general acceptance of alcohol in a society appears to influence rates of alcoholism among women. The exception to this trend was Korea, where alcoholism among women remained very low. The authors suggest that male domination and strictly defined sex roles in Korea continue to mitigate against women's drinking.

In addition to alcohol, men are also more likely to report the use of virtually all types of illicit drugs (marijuana, cocaine, crack, inhalants, hallucinogens, tranquilizers, stimulants, analgesics, and sedatives).[8] However, patterns of use vary by age group. For example, the 1994 National Household Survey on Drug Abuse conducted in the United States indicates that women in the 12- to 17-year age bracket were somewhat more likely to have used cocaine, crack, inhalants, analgesics, and stimulants during their lifetimes and in the past year than young men, whereas in older age groups, men generally used more.[9] However, because the percentages of people having used many of the types of drugs is small, and because there is a margin of error in these population estimates, these differences should be interpreted cautiously. When diagnoses of all psychoactive substance disorders (including alcohol) are considered, 18 percent of women and 35 percent of men have had such diagnoses in their lifetimes, and 7 percent of women and 16 percent of men had these diagnoses in the past year.[10] Although women generally report less alcohol and other drug use and are less often diagnosed with psychoactive substance disorders, one danger of making these comparisons is that their alcohol and drug use will continue to be minimized, resulting in less attention to their needs.

Will rates of chemical abuse and dependence for men and women someday be equal in the United States? The evidence varies. The National Household Survey shows more similarities among young men and women in their drinking and drug use, which may portend more problems for women. Other investigations, such as the cross-cultural study of Helzer and co-workers, also suggest that this may eventually happen. Gaps in rates of alcohol disorders and age of onset for men and women seemed to be narrowing at the same time that rates were increasing for both genders.[11] The Wilsnacks and their colleagues, however, conducted a study that focused on women and found no evidence of a major increase in rates of alcohol consumption by women from 1971 to 1981.[12] Consistent with previous surveys, women remained predominantly abstainers (39 percent) or light drinkers (38 percent), with increasing abstinence in the age groups over 50. The percentage of drinkers increased among middle-aged women (35–64) and heavy drinking increased in the 35- to 49-year-old group. The proportion of heavy drinkers remained relatively low (6 percent). The Wilsnack's follow-up longitudinal study conducted between 1981 and 1991 showed a modest decline in most measures of drinking behaviors (frequency, days felt drunk, problem consequences, and dependence symptoms).[13] The proportion of women who were classified as heavy drinkers also declined from 6 percent to 3 percent, with younger women having higher rates than older women. Others have reported increased heavy drinking among younger women,[14] yet, given the public's historical intolerance of female alcoholism,[15] it may be that male to female ratios will not converge completely, at least not in the near future.

Erickson and Watson provide an interesting analysis of convergence with respect to the use of illicit drugs among men and women in younger age groups.[16] Their research review indicates that in the early 1970s, when drug use was on the rise, men's and women's usage rates were becoming more similar due to increases in women's drug use. More recently, they report that rates are converging slightly because men's illicit drug use has declined, making them more similar to women.

A number of women—among them chemical dependency professionals and recovering alcoholics and addicts—think that the rates of chemical dependency problems have already converged.[17] Many feel certain that women are equal to men when it comes to the incidence of chemical dependency problems but that the research has failed to uncover this fact.[18] Although their concerns could be dismissed as unscientific, the methodological problems in the literature on gender differences warrant attention in a later section of this chapter. This review of research issues points to the need for healthy skepticism about the literature on substance disorders and gender differences. In the meantime, we will now focus on some of the differences that have been studied, because regardless of who has higher rates of abuse and dependence, the more important issue is how to advance knowledge of psychoactive substance disorders among women and among men so that the quality of life of both groups is improved.[19]

Biological Differences

The biological differences among male and female substance abusers that concern chemical abuse fall into three categories. First is genetic factors that may influence the etiology of substance abuse in men and women. Second is a number of physiological differences, especially in the metabolism of alcohol and in the consequences of alcohol consumption and alcoholism for men and women. Third is sexual dysfunction, including the gynecological and obstetrical problems that chemically dependent women face.

Genetics and Etiology

The interplay of the effects of heredity and environment have been given considerable attention in the search for the etiology of alcoholism and other drug problems. Chapter 2 covered etiological theories at length. Family, adoption, and twin studies, molecular studies, biological marker studies, and animal studies demonstrate that the vulnerability for alcohol dependence is partly genetic.[20] However, as in other areas of addiction research, studies on the genetic basis for developing alcoholism have overwhelmingly used male subjects or have failed to differentiate between males and females in the analysis of the data.[21] According to Kendler, "Compared to what has been learned from studies of alcoholism in men, our knowledge of the role of genetic factors in the etiology of alcoholism in women is sparse and contradictory."[22] Here we focus on what is known about the genetic factors that play a role in the etiology of alcoholism in women.

Family studies (that focus on the rates of alcoholism in male and female relatives) have demonstrated that alcoholism certainly runs in families, but these studies generally do not control for factors in the environment that may influence drinking behavior, such as gender socialization. Overall, these studies suggest that the risk for alcoholism is 4 to 7 times greater in relatives of alcoholics, compared with relatives of nonalcoholics.[23] A recent review of the literature found only seven family studies that addressed the rate of alcoholism in female and male relatives of both female and male alcoholics.[24] In general, these family studies did not find a significant gender difference in the genetic influence on alcoholism.[25]

Adoption studies are particularly useful because adopted-away children of alcoholic parents can be compared with adopted-away children of nonalcoholic parents, thus distinguishing between the effects of heredity and environment. In one of the most influential adoption studies, Cloninger, Bohman, and associates identified two types of alcoholics from studies of Swedish adoptees.[26] They studied individuals adopted early in life to differentiate genetic and environmental influences. Child welfare records and records of other governmental agencies were used to collect the data. The more common and milder type of alcoholism found in the adoptees was labeled *milieu limited* (or Type I) by the researchers, and it occurs in both men and women. Type I alcoholism is associated with the presence of *two* conditions: mild, untreated, adult-onset alcohol abuse in either the biological mother or father *and* low socioeconomic status of the adoptive father. Those with only one risk factor had no greater chance of becoming alcoholic than the rest of the population. The adoptive father's low socioeconomic status was the only environmental (milieu) factor that influenced the development of Type I alcoholism. Alcoholism in the adoptive parents did not lead to a greater occurrence of alcoholism among their children.

The other type of alcoholism they found is called *male limited* (Type II). It is the more severe form and accounted for 25 percent of alcoholism cases among men. Type II is associated with severe alcoholism in the biological father (but not the biological mother). These fathers developed alcoholism early in life and had several episodes of treatment. They were also more likely to have a history of criminal involvement. No factors in the adoptive home appeared to prevent the development of male-limited alcoholism, although many of the male adoptees had less severe alcoholism problems than their biological fathers. Daughters tended not to develop this type of alcoholism, but daughters of fathers with severe alcoholism had a greater frequency of medically unexplained complaints of pain or discomfort.

Although the Swedish adoption studies as well as similar findings in the United States by Gilligan and colleagues[27] indicate that daughters of alcoholics are far less susceptible to the more severe form of alcoholism, genetics does appear to play a substantial role in the development of alcoholism in both men and women.[28] But the fact that women are less susceptible to the more severe form remains an interesting issue. The Gilligan group suggests that the expression of alcoholism may also be related to personality characteristics and psychopathology, factors that may also be influenced by heredity and may be gender related. Gender socialization (i.e., environmental factors) may also continue to account for some of the difference, and it will be interesting to note the prevalence of these forms of alcoholism if gender norms continue to converge in the United States.

Finally, twin studies have generally produced consistent results on the heritability of alcoholism, but again the data for males is more definitive. A recent population-based study by Kendler and associates using 1,030 female twin pairs from the Virginia Twin Registry, found the heritability of liability to alcoholism in women in the range of 50 to 60 percent.[29] Environmental factors did not seem to play a role, and the role of mothers and fathers in genetic transmission was equal. This study is significant for several reasons: (1) it is contrary to the findings of most previous adoption and twin studies that have produced mixed results for women; (2) it is the only such study in which subjects were recruited from the general population instead of alcoholism treatment centers, thus adding to the generalizability of the findings; (3) the size of the sample is considerably greater than samples contained in previous studies; and (4) twin studies are powerful methods for detecting genetic effects because they can compare the concordance (agreement) of alcoholism between pairs of genetically identical twins living in the same environment and pairs of fraternal twins who are genetically different but also live in the same environment.

The results of the Kendler twin study strongly suggest that women should be fully represented in future research that investigates the role of genetic factors in alcoholism. Results of that research have critical implications for understanding risk factors that influence the prevention and treatment of alcohol disorders in women.

Is Biology Destiny?

At the beginning of this chapter, we noted that women generally reach higher blood-alcohol levels (BAL) or concentrations (BAC) than men of the same weight after drinking the same amount of alcohol. Men can also more consistently predict their blood-alcohol levels than women, because the menstrual cycle, which changes the balance of hormones in a women's body, may affect alcohol metabolism; women seem to achieve the highest blood-alcohol levels in the days just before the menstrual flow begins.[30] In addition, oral contraceptives may inhibit alcohol metabolism,[31] so that women taking birth control pills are likely to become intoxicated faster and remain intoxicated longer than those not on birth control pills.[32] Although McKim notes that women appear to eliminate alcohol faster than men,[33] Frezza and colleagues' work indicates that less efficient alcohol metabolism in women results in their achieving higher BACs more quickly than men, even after controlling for differences in size.[34]

There are some practical lessons to be learned from what is known about alcohol metabolism. First, women who try to keep up with men when drinking are likely to become more intoxicated, and therefore more impaired than their male counterparts. Second, the blood-alcohol charts that help people to approximate their level of intoxication by checking the number of drinks consumed and the amount of time elapsed are only approximations. A woman's BAL may be higher than what is suggested, also putting her at greater risk for alcohol-related traffic accidents or other mishaps.

Differences in alcohol metabolism may help to explain what is called the *telescoping effect* in which women apparently develop alcoholism more quickly than men once serious drinking is initiated.[35] It may also help to explain many of the physiological risks from drinking that appear to be greater for women than they are for men.[36] Women reportedly experience greater physiological impairment earlier in their drinking careers than men, even though they may consume less alcohol.[37] Hill, for example, summarizes the evidence on liver disease:

> The female alcoholic appears to run a greater risk for developing liver disease at an earlier age, following a shorter duration of heavy drinking, and presumably in association with a lower level of consumption than males. Once the liver has sustained injury, women appear to have the added

risk of increased mortality over that of their male counterparts.[38]

Women alcoholics also have higher rates of other alcohol-related health problems such as accidents and circulatory disorders,[39] and there is evidence of increased risk for alcoholic pancreatitis.[40] In a 20-year follow-up study of alcoholics admitted to treatment, men who were either divorced or separated at intake had the highest mortality rate, whereas the presence of delirium tremens at intake was a stronger predictor of mortality in women.[41]

There is confusion over whether women experience higher alcohol-related death rates than men.[42] Some of the confusion is due to whether alcoholic women are compared to women in the general population or to male alcoholics. Male alcoholics appear to have death rates at least twice as high as those reported for men in the general population, and alcoholic women are reported to have death rates that are nearly three times as high as women in the general population. If death rates for female and male alcoholics are compared, women alcoholics do not appear to have greater mortality than male alcoholics. But Hill has argued that female alcoholics should be compared with women in the general population and male alcoholics with men in the general population. If this is done, then women alcoholics experience higher mortality rates than do alcoholic men. In considering gender differences in mortality of a very large sample of patients at the Northern California Kaiser Permanente Medical Program over an eight-year period, Klatsky and colleagues found a 160 percent higher mortality risk for women who consumed six or more drinks a day, compared with those who drank more than one drink a month but less than one drink a day; the comparable risk for men was 40 percent.[43]

Corrigan suggests that women are also likely to "run a higher risk of alcohol and other drug overdoses at a lower level of consumption" than are men.[44] Data from the Drug Abuse Warning Network (DAWN) gathered from emergency-room admissions show that about one-fourth of men and one-half of women attributed their drug over-

dose to an intent to commit suicide, whereas men's drug dependence was twice as likely to have caused the emergency-room visit.[45]

Death rates associated with drug-related emergency-room visits were low for both men and women (0.4 and 0.3 percent, respectively). Confusion over whether suicide rates are higher among substance-abusing women also occurs because of the comparison group used, but Hill concludes that even using the more conservative estimates, women alcoholics die from suicide at a rate at least equal to alcoholic men.[46]

Sexual Dysfunction

Among nonalcoholics, the effects of alcohol consumption on the sexual performance of men is probably better recognized than it is among women. Despite alcohol's disinhibiting effects, many men can attest to difficulty in achieving an erection during an episode of heavy drinking. Women may also experience negative effects such as difficulty achieving orgasm.[47] Even moderate drinking has been linked with decreased sexual responsiveness in women because of decreased vaginal blood flow or orgasmic intensity.[48] Perhaps Shakespeare said it best: "Alcohol provoketh the desire but taketh away the performance."[49]

Problems of sexual dysfunction are frequently experienced by male and female alcoholics. Loss of sexual interest, difficulty achieving erections, impotence, and premature ejaculation are found among male alcoholics,[50] and female alcoholics may become anorgasmic.[51] Wilsnack notes that "rates of sexual inhibition, reduced sexual responsiveness, and orgasmic dysfunction in 13 samples of alcoholic women ranged from 28 to 100 percent."[52] In a longitudinal study, Wilsnack and associates found sexual dysfunction to be the strongest predictor of chronic problem drinking in women.[53]

There is hope, however, that these patterns of dysfunction may not be fixed or permanent, and will change when substance abusers begin to recover from their addictions. In a study of 61 recovering alcoholic women, Apter-Marsh reported that the rate of orgasm achieved with a partner and through masturbation increased over time.[54] Of interest is that prior to addiction, the subjects reported being orgasmic 47 percent of the time; during addiction, they achieved orgasm 55 percent of the time, but following sobriety (a mean of 4.2 years for the sample), they were orgasmic 70 percent of the time. The lowest frequency of sexual activity and orgasm occurred during the fragile period of the first three months of sobriety, when many of the women temporarily ceased sexual activity with both self and partners.

The effects of barbiturate use in sexual functioning are reported to be similar to alcohol since both fall into the class of sedative-hypnotic drugs.[55] Both male and female narcotics addicts are reported to have low levels of sexual desire and difficulty in achieving orgasm.[56] In the case of lower levels of cocaine use, sexual desire, excitement, and orgasm reportedly are enhanced, but high doses may result in impotence in men and may also take a toll on orgasms, especially in women.[57] Reports of pleasurable sexual responsiveness among cocaine users may be due to subjective expectations.[58] With amphetamine use, desire is reportedly enhanced at low doses and diminished with high doses; the effects on orgasm are similar to that of cocaine use.[59] There is evidence of sexual performance problems associated with benzodiazepine use in high doses.[60] Marijuana reportedly enhances sexual feelings, but regular use may result in erectile difficulties in men and may also reduce their testosterone levels and affect sperm production, including impaired fertility.[61] A drug most popular in enhancing sexual pleasure among gay men is amyl nitrite, known as "poppers" or "snappers."

Although there may be a direct cause-and-effect relationship in which alcohol and other drug abuse results in sexual dysfunction, the relationship between these two factors may be reciprocal or circular, such that "heavy drinking becomes both cause and consequence of sexual dysfunction."[62] This relationship may also reflect psychological and social issues.[63] For example, men and women may drink excessively as a means of coping with the psychological and sexual difficulties they experience. Wilsnack points out that a particularly high-risk subgroup for the development of both sexual dysfunction and alcoholism appears to be women who have experienced sexual abuse and rape, including those with histories of incest.[64] Klassen and Wilsnack found that many women who drink, especially those classified as heavy drinkers, believe that alcohol not only reduces their sexual inhibitions but also increases their feelings of closeness to others.[65] Substance abuse, however, generally diminishes the ability to engage in healthy and satisfying emotional and sexual relationships, since it clouds one's ability to make rational judgments and to act in a manner consistent with one's feelings. Alcoholic women have also reported more guilt related to sexual activity than nonalcoholic women,[66] and women frequently become the targets of others' sexual aggression as a result of one or both parties' drinking.[67]

Gynecological and Reproductive Problems

Alcoholic women report gynecological and reproductive disorders more frequently than nonalcoholic women, including dysmenorrhea, irregular periods, hysterectomies, infertility, spontaneous abortions, stillbirth, premature birth, and birth defects.[68] Women who are chronic marijuana users may have abnormal periods and may not ovulate.[69] Cocaine can also suppress female hormones and affect the menstrual cycle.[70]

Research findings that link alcohol use and premenstrual dysphoria are interesting but remain inconclusive. In a prospective design with 14 women, Mello and colleagues reported increased alcohol use in the premenstrual phase of women who scored high on premenstrual syndrome (PMS) symptoms.[71] Tobin and associates also found greater alcohol use by women with PMS than comparison subjects, but they did not find a specific link between the increased alcohol use and the premenstrum phase.[72] Streett notes that low levels of serotonin have been identified in alcoholics (even those abstinent for some time) and that serotonin levels may fall even further during the premenstrum, compounding distress for women alcoholics.[73]

It is still unclear whether gynecological problems precede chemical abuse and are causative factors in the development of alcoholism or other drug abuse or whether gynecological problems are the results of excessive drinking and drug use.[74] However, since PMS symptoms (irritability, anger, and depression) mimic the symptoms that frequently precede relapse, some clinicians are advocating more attention to the prevalence of PMS in their female clients and that more efforts be made to educate female clients to this potential trigger to relapse, including teaching practices that can relieve PMS symptoms.[75]

The topics of fetal alcohol syndrome (FAS) and fetal alcohol effects (FAE) have received considerable attention in the *Special Report to the U.S. Congress on Alcohol and Health.* Almost every society has had some folk wisdom regarding alcohol use and pregnancy (see, for example, *The Old Testament,* "The Book of Judges," Chapter 13). Alcohol is a well-known teratogen (a substance that produces abnormal formations). FAS was first described in the American literature in 1973 by Jones and colleagues.[76] It is defined as:

> a distinct pattern of abnormalities found in children born to alcohol-abusing mothers. Criteria for defining FAS were standardized by the Fetal Alcohol Study Group of the Research Society on Alcoholism in 1980. The criteria include: prenatal and/or postnatal growth retardation; impairment of the central nervous system (neurological abnormalities, developmental delays, behavioral dysfunction, intellectual impairment, and skull or brain malformations); and facial abnormalities such as small eye openings, a thin upper lip, and an unusually long, flattened midface.[77]

Postnatal growth retardation may result from a poor sucking response in infants exposed to alcohol prenatally.[78]

The 11 children originally studied by Jones and colleagues were followed up 10 years later.[79] Two of the children had died and one was lost to follow-up, but in the remaining eight cases, many of the symptoms of the syndrome were permanent. Facial deformities had improved somewhat, and stable home environments had helped with social and emotional development, but some additional abnormalities (hearing, dental, and vision problems) had also become apparent.

Streissguth and colleagues studied 48 adolescents and 18 adults ranging in age from 12 to 40 years old, 70 percent of whom had FAS and 30 percent of whom had fewer symptoms, known as fetal alcoholic effects (FAE).[80] Their facial features had become less distinctive over time but they tended to remain shorter and to be microcephalic. They had a wide variation in IQ scores, with some functioning at a level that might preclude them from receiving special services after leaving school. Average academic functioning was at a second- to fourth-grade level. Arithmetic deficits were most common. Superficial verbal skills were often much better. Maladaptive behaviors (poor judgment, attention deficits, and difficulty perceiving social cues) seemed to be the greatest challenge for these individuals. Some also had conduct problems. Behavior problems seemed to be more pervasive than among people with Down's syndrome. Most had spent their lives in unstable environments (perhaps environment is also a factor in outcomes[81]), and none was "independent in terms of both housing and income." Despite the small study sample, the researchers were especially concerned about the poor outcomes of these individuals, regardless of their level of intellectual functioning, implicating the involvement of prenatal brain damage.

FAS is a leading cause of mental retardation. The exact rate of FAS is not known because it is difficult to make an early diagnosis, resulting in underidentification and underreporting.[82] Estimates of the incidence have varied. Abel and Sokol originally estimated 1.9 cases of FAS per 1,000 live births.[83] More recently, they have developed a more conservative estimate of 0.33 case per 1,000 live births, but estimates must be viewed with caution, given the problems in detection.[84] Estimates of FAE (now also called "alcohol-related birth defects"[85]) are thought to be about three times higher than FAS in the general population.[86] FAS is generally associated with heavy drinking, but no one yet knows if there is a level of alcohol consumption at which no such effects will be produced. Clarren and associates state, "It is probable that there is no *single* dose-response relationship for ethanol teratogenesis, but rather that each abnormal outcome in brain structure or function, morphology, and growth has its own dose-response and gestational timing parameters."[87] In 1981, the Surgeon General encouraged women who are planning on conceiving or who know they are pregnant to abstain totally.[88] Many women apparently automatically reduce their alcohol consumption while pregnant. Alcohol may be less appealing during this time, probably because of nausea or other effects of pregnancy. As of late 1989, alcoholic beverage containers must contain warnings of alcohol's potential to cause birth defects (look carefully for the small print).

Sandmaier, in a pamphlet directed to pregnant women, describes the way in which alcohol affects the fetus:

> When a pregnant women takes a drink, the alcohol readily crosses the placenta to the fetus. Moreover, the alcohol travels through the baby's bloodstream in the same concentration as that of the mother. So if the expectant mother becomes drunk at a party, her unborn baby becomes drunk as well. But, of course, the tiny, developing system of the fetus is not nearly as equipped to handle alcohol as the system of its adult mother. Among other things, the undeveloped liver of the unborn baby can burn up alcohol at less than half the rate of an adult liver, which means that alcohol remains in the fetal system longer than in the adult system.[89]

Since not all women who drink or who drink abusively during pregnancy give birth to children with FAE or FAS, it is important for researchers to isolate those factors, such as genetic or biological or environmental, that contribute to the development of these problems and those that mitigate against them.[90]

The rate of FAS seems to vary among different population groups. African Americans[91] and some Native American tribes[92] have been found to be at greater risk than the general population. A study by May and colleagues of three Native American tribes indicated that the Pueblo and the Navajo had rates similar to the rest of the population, but the Plains Indians had the highest rate ever reported—almost 1 case in every 100 births.[93] The authors suggest that social and cultural customs are possible explanations for the variance in rates: Although abusive drinking by women is not condoned among any of the tribes, the Plains Indians apparently demonstrate greater tolerance of women drinkers, whereas the Pueblos and Navajo more strongly ostracize them.

In addition to alcohol, infants who have been exposed to other drugs in utero are also of concern. Chasnoff estimated that 375,000 babies (11 percent of all births) are born each year to mothers who had used an illicit drug.[94] The drugs used include crack, heroin, methadone, cocaine, amphetamines, PCP, and marijuana. More recently, data collected from 1992 to 1993 for a NIDA study indicate that "an estimated 5.5 percent, or 221,000 women, used an illicit drug at least once during pregnancy."[95]

Although a number of negative outcomes for drug-exposed infants have been reported, such as premature birth, hypertension, visual abnormalities, and an abnormal brain, the findings are inconsistent.[96] The effects of drug use have not been differentiated from other physical, social (including environmental), and psychological factors during pregnancy.[97]

According to NIDA, poor inner-city neighborhoods report the highest rates of infants born to drug-using mothers, as high as 50 percent,[98] but the issue of whether hospitals, particularly private hospitals in more affluent areas, underdetect and underreport the incidence of chemically exposed infants remains to be addressed.[99] An exploratory study of hospital providers indicates several disincentives to developing adequate detection and response policies, including the reluctance of obstetricians, limited resources for successful treatment, potential discharge delays of infants, and increased personnel costs.[100] The authors suggest that the best hope for mitigating some of these barriers is to use the leverage of federal funding to develop a uniform set of policies with which hospitals must comply.

Currently, there is good news and bad news with respect to assisting women whose pregnancies are threatened due to alcohol or other drug exposure. The good news is that some researchers and service providers believe that pregnancy may motivate women to receive treatment for chemical dependency.[101] The bad news is that attempts at criminal prosecutions of women who have used illicit drugs during pregnancy and the modification of state child abuse and neglect statutes to allow termination of parental rights of these women act as a barrier for both prenatal care and drug treatment.[102] Although the courts have dismissed cases or have not upheld the criminal convictions of pregnant women on charges such as child abuse or delivery of drugs to a minor, the use of civil child neglect and abuse statutes following birth have been more successful.[103] Gustavsson notes:

> The war on drugs has become a war on pregnant women, particularly poor women of color. As attempts to reduce both the supply and demand for mood-altering chemicals by instituting harsh criminal sanctions fail, attention is being redirected toward a group that is easy to identify, dislike, and control. Pregnant women who use chemicals and give birth to infants suffering from a variety of health problems fit these three criteria.[104]

Of particular concern to those interested in helping women who are chemically addicted and pregnant is that many treatment programs will not admit pregnant women. Despite greater attention to the needs of these women by the Substance Abuse and Mental Health Services Administration and the development of some special treatment programs for pregnant women and women with young children, residential treatment slots are especially scarce. The need is for compassionate interventions that will help prevent the use or continued use of harmful substances. As Blank suggests, "The provision of universal prenatal and preconception care . . . , along with adequate counseling and substance abuse treatment programs, is essential and would drastically reduce the problems leading to unhealthy maternal behavior."[105]

Dealing with maternal substance abuse in a positive, rather than punitive, manner is at the heart of the matter for many social workers. Ferguson and Kaplan recommend adopting a harm-reduction, normalization policy toward drug misuse similar to the approach used in the Netherlands, instead of the current war on drugs approach.[106] Others call for the development of nurturing environments for mothers and for their children who were exposed to drugs prenatally, such as treatment programs that will reunite mothers and children in a therapeutic milieu and provide coordinated, comprehensive, and family-centered care during treatment.[107]

Although the outcomes of pregnancy are ideally a concern of both parents, the affects of fathers' drug use on pregnancy and on other aspects of child development have not received the attention they perhaps deserve. Few programs are like the family-oriented program in Australia, described by Magor-Blatch, that accepts pregnant women, single mothers and fathers with children, and couples with or without children, although there are separate therapy groups for men and women.[108]

Social Differences

In addition to experiencing more physical deterioration than men, women alcoholics are often reported to have more personally destructive drinking careers and to have suffered greater social and psychological deterioration prior to entering treatment.[109] Female narcotics addicts appear similar to their male counterparts in many aspects of their patterns of use and relapse, but both women alcoholics and addicts reportedly have shorter drinking and drug careers before entering treatment than men.[110] Some of the social differences between men and women reported in the literature are not surprising. For example, alcoholic women suffer more economic disadvantage than alcoholic men,[111] which is consistent with the financial disadvantages (such as employment in low-status jobs and more dependency on welfare) of women, compared to men in the general population. Additional social issues deserve attention in the consideration of women with chemical dependency problems. These include negative attitudes toward them, lack of social supports, and drug-related criminal activity.

Falling from the Pedestal

Until the 1970s, alcoholism and drug addiction were viewed almost exclusively as problems of men. The women substance abusers who were noticed were considered particularly deviant, and they tended to be scorned as unfeminine and promiscuous. In 1974, Gomberg noted that the "universality of this attitude is such that both sexes and all social classes show the same negative attitude."[112] This picture has not changed substantially. Films such as *Thelma and Louise*, for example, continue to reinforce a link between women's intoxication and seduction or rape.[113] Kagle refers to alcoholic women as a "discredited social group."[114] They seem to suffer from the "double whammy" of societal bias against alcoholics and against women. Broom has called this phenomenon the "double bind,"[115] and Crawford and Elliott call it "doubly disadvantaged."[116] There is likely to be a "triple whammy" or "triple bind" if the woman is also a member of an oppressed ethnic group.

Ridlon believes that in spite of efforts to establish equality in social and economic spheres, women are expected to remain on a pedestal—above the problems of chemical abuse and dependency—due to their responsibilities as primary child rearers and as the keepers of marital and other familial relationships.[117] Women's chemically induced behavior has historically been excused or ra-

tionalized. For example, women stopped for drunk driving were more likely to be escorted home by police, whereas men were more often arrested for driving while intoxicated.[118] Women's depression may be explained as mental illness rather than a result of alcoholism or drug addiction. This "status insularity" has impeded the recognition of psychoactive drug problems in women.[119]

Social Supports

Alcohol use varies by marital status.[120] Among women, widows are most likely to be abstainers, followed by those who are married. Divorced, separated, and never-married women are less likely to abstain, and cohabiting women are the least likely to abstain. Conversely, cohabiting women are most likely to be heavy drinkers, followed by married, divorced, or separated women. Widows are least likely to be heavy drinkers. Married men are more likely to abstain than are those who are divorced, separated, or never married, and divorced or separated men report more heavy drinking than married or never-married men.

Male partners apparently play a significant role in women's chemical dependency. A consistent finding in the research on social factors is that women frequently engage in excessive drinking and drug use as a result of their relationships with male partners who are alcoholics or addicts rather than the other way around. Some researchers contend that a relationship with an addicted male is the greatest factor predisposing a woman's addiction.[121] In a series of studies of men and women in methadone maintenance programs, Hser and colleagues found that:

> it was much more likely that a woman's partner was an addict than a man's partner. For many women, spouses' or partners' use was the major reason for their own first addiction to and/or increased use of narcotics. As a related matter, the heroin habits of many women were often supported by others (including a spouse or partner).[122]

Amaro and colleagues also found that the most significant factor in an adolescent mother's own drug use was her male partner's use.[123] Evidence from other countries also supports this conclusion.[124]

Women alcoholics are reportedly less likely to be married than men alcoholics when they enter treatment.[125] Additional reports also suggest that alcoholic women have greater marital instability than alcoholic men,[126] but perhaps not more than women in the general population since they also experience high rates of divorce and separation.[127] But based on a longitudinal study of 143 problem drinking women and 157 nonproblem drinking women, Wilsnack and colleagues suggest that divorce and separation may actually be more of a "remedy" than a "risk."[128] Among the women problem drinkers identified in the early part of their study, those that became divorced or separated during the study period had lower levels of subsequent alcohol dependence.

Although women are more likely than men to become alcohol or drug dependent as a result of having a partner who has these problems, once in treatment, they are likely to have less social support than men. Lindbeck suggests that this may be due to the husband's especially strong denial of his wife's drinking[129] (which may result from his own excessive use of alcohol or other drugs). In addition, professionals may have "excused" men from participation in their wives' treatment, because these husbands have been considered exceptional for staying with their alcohol or drug dependent wives.[130] Today's treatment programs are more likely to expect equal participation by both husbands and wives of alcoholics and addicts.

Not only do chemically dependent women receive less support for entering treatment, according to Beckman and Amaro, but they are also more likely to encounter opposition to entering treatment from family and friends.[131] Such opposition is almost unheard of among the families and friends of men. When women do get this support, it reportedly is more likely to come from children and parents, whereas men are more likely to be motivated to enter treatment by their spouses.[132] Robinson concurs that families rarely played a part in women's referrals to treatment and were often an actual barrier to treatment.[133] Saunders

and associates also found that women were less likely than their male counterparts to have been advised to stop or reduce their drinking by family members.[134] In a comparison of black and white women entering treatment, Amaro and colleagues found that more black (68 percent) than white (49 percent) women had family or friends who suggested treatment, and fewer black (8 percent) than white (25 percent) women faced opposition from significant others to their entering treatment.[135]

Two examples from alcoholic women in recovery who were respondents in an exploratory study illustrate families' opposition to seeking help:

> My parents didn't see that I had any drinking problem. Part of it was that they just didn't see a lot. They'd say, "if your husband would give you some money, you'd be O.K."

> The rest of my family was just vaguely aware of what was going on, and they were counter-supportive. They talked about A.A. in a derogatory way.[136]

Another study confirms the weak social support structure and isolation of alcoholic women in treatment, compared to nonalcoholic female controls.[137] The alcoholic women had significantly fewer friends and no close women friends, felt lonely some or most of the time, had more poor relationships with others, were more resentful toward their parents, and received less emotional support from them.

A qualitative study in Finland reveals the complexities of social control of women's drinking.[138] On the one hand, women who had lost control over their drinking wanted more help from their partners and families in controlling their behavior and avoiding the loss of dignity and shame. On the other hand, the partners' and relatives' own drinking made control attempts (nagging, threatening, not letting them go out, quarreling) seem fake and aroused the women's suspicions.

Following treatment, interpersonal and marital conflict[139] and the lack of family support[140] also seem to increase the risk of relapse. However, being married is more likely to be associated with posttreatment abstinence among men than it is women.[141]

Mothers, even those with alcohol and other drug problems, are more likely to be the caregivers of their children than fathers. Although these mothers are probably aware that chemical dependency treatment will benefit their children, the inability to secure safe child care can impede their entering treatment. Conversely, access to child care at chemical dependency programs encourages participation in treatment.[142]

In addition to the treatment system, evidence is that other social systems such as health care and criminal justice systems are less likely to address the chemical dependency problems of women. Saunders and associates compared men and women with alcohol-related liver disease and found that even in these life-threatening cases, women were still somewhat less likely to have been advised by a physician to curtail drinking or to have been referred to a hospital for alcoholism treatment; they were also less likely to have been convicted for alcohol-related offenses.[143] Although women in this study more often received psychiatric treatment for nonalcoholic-related problems, few of the men or women were referred to alcoholism counseling or to Alcoholics Anonymous.

Crime

The relationship between drug use and crime is known to almost everyone (see Chapter 8). In an effort to determine the level of drug use among arrestees, the National Institute of Justice implemented the Drug Use Forecasting (DUF) program. In 1995, 23 cities reported on adult male booked arrestees and 21 on females.[144] From 51 to 83 percent of the men at each site tested positive for at least one drug; among women, the figures were comparable (41 to 84 percent with only one site reporting less than 50 percent). The primary drugs used were cocaine and marijuana. Other research suggests that women in prison may actually be more likely than male inmates to have used heroin.[145] Rough estimates of the number of women incarcerated due to alcohol or other drug-related offenses are as high as 90 percent,[146] yet the hard evidence on this subject is inadequate to justify drug use as a primary, causative factor in the rise in the number of incarcerated women.

Like female alcoholics and addicts, female offenders are typically seen as more abnormal than their male counterparts. The criminal activity of men has been described as motivated by economics, status, or a need for acceptance,[147] but female offenders are often characterized as the victims of biological, psychological, or personal imbalance.[148] In their extensive review of the literature on this topic, Erickson and Watson found that female addicts have most often been linked to the crime of prostitution, with the assumption that they became prostitutes to support their drug habit, or they became addicts to cope with the stress of prostitution.[149] They add that this simplistic and narrow view of the behavior of female drug users is the result of a lack of research on women by criminologists and addiction specialists, and the perception that addiction and crime are primarily male activities. In addition, prior to the criminalization of narcotics use, opiate addiction was greater for women than for men; following criminalization, the pattern was reversed, with male opiate addicts now outnumbering females.[150] Although previous studies have reported less criminal involvement for women addicts,[151] Hser and colleagues found support for the position that many women turn to illegal activities just as men do after addiction to narcotics.[152] The major gender difference these researchers noted was the type of crime committed—both men and women reported theft; men reported burglary or robbery more than women, and women reported forgery and prostitution more often. Erickson and Watson report that the most common crimes of women drug users are drug offenses (especially drug dealing), whereas prostitution is the primary offense for a smaller group of women who use drugs (primarily narcotics addicts).[153]

Erickson and Watson do not deny an association between drug use and prostitution among women, but their review raises questions about the assumption that the need to support a drug habit is the factor that precedes prostitution. For example, the Special Committee on Pornography and Prostitution in Canada noted that many prostitutes do not use drugs and alcohol because of the dangers they face and the need to be alert; instead, prostitution results from the need to meet their everyday economic needs.[154] However, among female addicts, prostitution is common, and one study indicated an increase in the frequency of these offenses for some women. Inciardi and Pottieger compared 153 women heroin users studied in 1977 and 1978 with 133 similar women studied in 1983 and 1984.[155] While the percentage involved in prostitution decreased from 71 to 54 percent, the incidence of this offense increased from 38 percent of their total crimes to 54 percent. The later cohort also reverted more often to prostitution and drug sales than property offenses.

Past stereotypes that made illicit drug use by women synonymous with prostitution no longer seem adequate. More recent research suggests that female addicts engage in prostitution less frequently and engage in a greater variety of other criminal activities than was formerly assumed.[156] Criminology researchers are suggesting that gender-based theories of crime alone are inadequate to explain differences in criminal activity. The interaction of gender and class must be considered, since differences in level of criminal activity between the genders become less apparent as socioeconomic status declines.[157] For example, Fagan interviewed 311 New York City women from neighborhoods with high concentrations of crack use and selling.[158] These inner-city neighborhoods are characterized by the erosion of informal social controls, the growth of female-headed households, and a decline in male status due to unemployment, high death rates, criminal activity, and incarceration. As the size and activity of current crack markets escalated in these areas, Fagan found that women were able to increase their participation in drug selling in higher-income markets. According to Fagan, "Higher in-

come from drug selling reduced the likelihood of prostitution, while more frequent crack use increased prostitution rates."[159] The emergence of women as high-income drug entrepreneurs may be helpful in avoiding prostitution, but it is perhaps another example of an equality that women do not really want.

Psychological Differences

Psychological issues that chemically dependent individuals face have also received considerable attention in the literature. They include a variety of symptoms often attributed not only to substance abusers but also to women in the general population, such as low self-esteem and depression. The high incidence of physical and sexual abuse reported by women substance abusers may also be a substantial factor contributing to their psychological distress.

Psychological Distress

The relationship between alcohol use and stress has garnered considerable attention, and research on the topic demonstrates gender differences. Cooper and associates found that stress due to recent negative life events predicted alcohol use and alcohol-related problems among men who have strong beliefs about alcohol's positive effects or among those who use avoidant, emotion-focused coping strategies.[160] However, stressors were negatively associated with alcohol and alcohol-related problems among men whose positive expectancies about drinking are low or who have low avoidant, emotion-focused coping scores. Among women, alcohol use and related problems were not associated with their drinking expectancies or coping styles. Similarly, Pohorecky's review of the subject indicates that although more study would be useful, "stress does not appear to play a significant role in alcohol ingestion by women."[161] Since just about everyone deals with stress, the interesting questions these authors raise are What accounts for the gender differences? and What means do women use to cope with stress?

Other symptoms of psychological distress, such as depression[162] and low self-esteem,[163] as well as passivity, aggression, conflict,[164] and anxiety,[165] are mentioned as especially problematic for alcoholic and alcohol-abusing women, whereas male alcoholics are more often reported to have sociopathy[166] and antisocial personality disorders.[167] There is some similar evidence for male and female cocaine abusers.[168] Since women in the general population are also described as having more psychological problems, it is unclear to what extent gender, substance abuse, or an interaction between these two factors explains psychopathology in chemically dependent women.[169]

Drinking alcohol excessively is often cited as a means of coping with depression or self-medicating, especially in the drinking behavior of women. However, in the first longitudinal study to analyze the relationship between depressive symptoms and drinking behavior, Shutte and colleagues found no support for a positive relationship between the two factors in 621 late middle-aged women and 951 late middle-aged men; higher levels of depression did not lead to higher alcohol consumption.[170] They did find that alcohol consumption in women was associated with a reduction of depressive symptoms over time (one to three years), giving some support to the self-medication hypothesis for women.

DeSoto and colleagues studied 163 men and 149 women members of Alcoholics Anonymous with varying lengths of abstinence and found no differences in symptomatology using raw scores, but when these scores were normed for gender, men were *more* symptomatic with respect to depression, anxiety, and phobic anxiety, and they also scored higher on overall symptomatology or pathology.[171] A follow-up study four years later with 233 of these same subjects showed the same course of recovery from severity of symptoms or pathology for both abstinent alcoholic men and women.[172] In the first six months of abstinence, there typically was considerable distress (depression, obsessive-compulsive behavior, and interpersonal sensitivity), comparable

to that seen in psychiatric inpatients. These symptoms dramatically decreased after three years of abstinence, with continuing improvement after 10 or more years of abstinence, at which time symptomatology approached the norm for the general population. The *Seventh Special Report to the U.S. Congress on Alcohol and Health* cites a number of studies showing the decrease of depressive symptoms, anxiety, and cognitive impairment as alcoholics progress from drinking to abstinence, although an important etiological question remains unanswered: Which comes first—the psychological distress or the substance abuse?[173]

In spite of indications that both men and women can recover from the psychological impairment associated with substance abuse, there is some evidence that women may experience a more difficult (or at least different) road in the recovery process because of additional psychological stressors they face. For example, alcoholic women are reported to have had more disruption in their families of origin than alcoholic men, such as mentally ill and alcoholic parents,[174] and they report more isolation and unhappiness in early life than nonalcoholic women.[175] More recently, the often devastating effects of the physical and sexual abuse of women substance abusers are being acknowledged.

Physical and Sexual Abuse

Connections between physical abuse and alcoholism have become clearer in recent decades. For example, in a study of incarcerated substance abusers, Sheridan found significant correlations between parental substance abuse, low family competence, and the experience of physical and sexual abuse as a child and adult.[176] In addition, all of these factors were significantly associated with the respondents' own substance abuse in adult life.

Research on battered women indicates a high degree of drinking problems in their battering husbands or partners. Lehmann and Krupp reported that of 1,500 calls about spouse abuse to a community hotline, 828 women callers (55 percent) reported that their husbands were abusive while drinking.[177] Since many alcoholic women have husbands and partners who also drink heavily, it may be reasonable to assume that a great many alcoholic women are physically abused. Additional research could help to determine whether there is a difference in the risk of women (and men) being battered if both partners are dependent on alcohol or other drugs or if one partner is chemically dependent and the other is not. For example, a man (whether or not he is chemically dependent) may strike out at his wife, but if she is chemically dependent, she may be less able to defend herself from physical or psychological abuse. Given concerns about the incidence of alcohol and other drug problems reported among gay men and lesbians (see Chapter 12), similar studies of partners of the same gender would also be useful.

Women alcoholics apparently suffer from a high degree of sexual trauma in addition to other types of abuse. Wilsnack reports several studies that found a high incidence of incest and other sexual abuse, including rape, among alcoholic women.[178] For example, Covington found that rates appear higher than in the general population, ranging from 12 to 53 percent for incest or other childhood sexual abuse and as high as 74 percent for all types of sexual trauma combined.[179] Other reports indicate that the combined rates of incest, battering, child sexual abuse, and sexual assault for women in alcoholism treatment in various studies range from 40 to 74 percent[180] and that as many as 29 to 54 percent of women alcoholics in treatment have been raped at some point in their lives.[181] Covington notes that for the majority of women alcoholics, "this [abuse] has been part of their life experience, and it is part of the same guilt and degradation that contributes, along with the stigma of alcoholism, to their lower-self esteem."[182]

In a comparison of women in several types of social service settings, Miller and Downs found that significantly higher rates of severe violence from either parent were reported by women in alcoholism treatment programs (65 percent) and shelters (64 percent) than by women in mental health centers (55 percent), drinking and driving classes (33 percent), and randomly selected households (38 percent).[183] The highest rates of any type of childhood sexual abuse were also reported by women in alcoholism treatment programs (66 percent), and 41 percent of the women in treatment reported severe violence from their pretreatment partners (surpassed only by the 93 percent rate of partner violence reported by women in shelters). Needless to say, the authors feel that the recognition of repeated victimization of women and the possibility of violent intergenerational patterns setting the stage for alcoholism in women have not been given the attention they deserve. Gomberg has commented on the "internalized shame factor" (lack of self-worth and self-hatred; also see Chapter 10) "as an important, even necessary, condition" to alcoholism for women, although she concludes that it is not sufficient to explain chemical dependency in women.[184]

Women, Treatment, and Recovery

Vannicelli[185] traced the idea that female substance abusers are "sicker" than male substance abusers to Benjamin Karpman, who in 1948 suggested that these women had to be more abnormal than their male counterparts in order to violate the more restrictive social barriers against women developing alcoholism.[186] Assertions such as these led to a belief that women alcoholics were not only sicker than male alcoholics but that they were also more difficult to treat. Vanicelli investigated whether this was true by reviewing 23 studies that reported gender-related treatment outcomes.[187] Of the total studies, 18 showed no significant difference in treatment outcomes between male and female alcoholics; 4 studies showed better outcomes for women, and 1 showed better outcomes for men. Hser and associates[188] and the Institute of Medicine[189] also agree that recovery rates following treatment are similar for men and women.

Interpretations of existing treatment effectiveness studies are often confounded due to high relapse rates for both men and women, lack of study of gender differences among treatment dropouts, and failure to study those lost to follow-up.[190] Each of these problems makes it difficult to discern just what aspects of treatment promote recovery and whether there are gender-related differences in the recovery process.[191] DeSoto and associates found that the course of recovery as measured by severity of psychological symptoms, work history, and probability of relapse was essentially the same for men and women.[192] The combined relapse rates for men and women were highest in the first six months of abstinence (46 percent). Between six months and two years, the percentage of relapse dropped to 24 percent. Relapse rates for both men and women tended to flatten to almost zero after the first five years of abstinence. Schneider and colleagues also found no significant gender differences in relapse rates or in efforts made toward recovery (self-help group attendance, receiving therapy), though they did find some differences in recovery patterns; psychological impairment was more strongly related to relapse for women than for men, and marriage was more of a protective factor for men than for women.[193]

Treatment Matching

Do similarities in patterns of relapse and recovery for men and women imply that the treatments offered to them should be the same, or could treatment outcomes be improved by matching clients to treatment based on gender? Given that Anglin and colleagues found that female addicts were more motivated for treatment than men, they were surprised to find that women did not surpass men in positive treatment outcomes.[194] Like many others, they believe that women's outcomes might be better if treatment addressed their specific needs. Few studies have examined topics such as whether various treatment modalities (individual, family, or group) or various theoretical perspectives (psychodynamic, behavioral, etc.) are superior for women, whether women do better in women's-only or coed treatment programs, or whether having a male or female therapist makes a difference.[195] Annis char-

acterized the literature on these subjects as "dominated by rhetoric and speculation" as well as by "myth" and "cliches,"[196] and Braiker described the research as being "riddled with methodological problems, yielding equivocal and frequently contradictory results."[197] There remains a critical need for more systematic studies designed to evaluate the response of female and male substance abusers to various types of treatment in order to close the gap between untested beliefs and facts about women-sensitive treatment.[198]

In one of the few research studies designed to address the question of whether coed treatment is better than all-women's treatment, Swedish researchers Dalhgren and Willander suggest that an all-women's treatment approach offers more positive results.[199] Their two-year follow-up study involved 200 alcohol-dependent women who were randomly assigned to either a specialized female outpatient unit or a mixed male and female unit. Women treated in the specialized female unit had significantly better social adjustment and consumed less alcohol following treatment. Some 67 percent of the female unit clients showed improvement after the first year and 59 percent after the second year, compared with 45 percent and 48 percent of the controls, respectively.

Dalhgren and Willander report that the unique treatment components of the all-women's unit included assistance for mothers from a child psychiatrist, an individualized treatment program for each client, relatives' involvement in the treatment, and a focus on women's problems, including the women's exchange of experiences with each other. These components are consistent with the clinical literature that indicates that factors such as attention to children's needs and a safe environment in which to discuss gender issues are important considerations in women's chemical dependency treatment. Unfortunately, many studies fail to describe adequately the treatment rendered to clients, making it difficult to replicate treatments.

Despite efforts to describe the unique needs of women, there is little hard research evidence about the effectiveness of particular treatment approaches.[200] Project MATCH (a major NIAAA-funded research study) researchers found no gender-related outcome differences after applying three treatment approaches to a large number of male and female subjects with alcohol abuse and dependence problems (also see Chapter 6).[201] Yet it remains important to remember that women cannot be lumped together purely because of their gender. There is some evidence to indicate that treatment strategies should reflect the varying characteristics of women such as ethnic differences. The results of at least one study show that black and white women in alcoholism treatment differed on several dimensions that may have important implications for treatment.[202] Black women had more limited financial resources and less insurance coverage, and were significantly younger. Ethnic differences that may require differential treatment methods are explored further in Chapter 11.

Evidence also indicates that women of different generations may need different types of treatment that reflect their life experiences. The findings of Harrison and Belille, based on a sample of 1,776 adult women in chemical dependency treatment, show substantial differences between women who grew up in the 1940s and 1950s and those born later.[203] These differences were apparent with respect to substance abuse patterns, education and employment patterns, familial alcohol and other drug abuse, familial violence, and psychosocial dysfunction. Similar to prevalence studies done by NIDA, younger women were four to six times more likely to report marijuana, hallucinogen, and cocaine or other stimulant use, whereas the older women were twice as likely to report only alcohol use. Younger women were more likely to use in the company of others; older women tended to report solitary use. Older women were more often homemakers, and younger women more often reported poorer sociovocational functioning, including higher unemployment. Younger women were more likely to be high school dropouts and to have greater dependence on welfare. They also reported more drug use and more violence in their family of origin and in their present family constellation.

Rather than age or maturational level, Harrison and Belille think these differences reflect cohort or societal changes. This seems reasonable, given that women who became teenagers in the late 1960s and in the 1970s were more likely to have been exposed to drug use other than alcohol and are more likely to come from nonintact families. These findings raise concerns that patterns of polydrug use and more impaired psychosocial functioning among today's young women may present even greater challenges in treatment and recovery. Gomberg also suggests a life span or developmental approach since substance abuse risk factors vary at each stage of the life cycle.[204] Few services have yet been developed to meet the needs of older women (also see Chapter 14). The results of one innovative program, located in San Francisco's Tenderloin District, indicate that the ingredients of success for this often difficult to reach and isolated group include specialized outreach services (instead of expecting the women to come to community centers for the elderly), an emphasis on building self-esteem and support networks, and defining success as reduced alcohol or drug misuse instead of total abstinence.[205]

There are also promising developments in treatment modalities for addicted pregnant women and women with children. Several residential therapeutic communities (TCs) for women and children have been funded in the recent federal push to make mental and physical disorders in women a service and research priority. In contrast to what has been termed the "tear down, build up" philosophy of the earlier prototypes of TCs such as Synanon in the 1960s, the newer approach is more to "support, educate, and guide."[206] The protected environment and length of stay (15 to 18 months) provides a therapeutic milieu for addressing trauma (such as sexual and physical abuse) that is typically associated with women's substance abuse, as well as an opportunity for strengthening parenting skills, life skills, and abilities in an atmosphere of acceptance.

Programs funded by NIDA and the Center for Substance Abuse Treatment in Arizona and Florida report positive preliminary outcomes for treatment completers such as decreased alcohol and drug use, decreased criminal activities, improved parent/child relations, and higher employment rates.[207] Case management approaches have also provided some promising results with this population.[208] For example, in a study of 225 pregnant substance abusers, Laken and Ager found case management using a team of two social workers, a nurse, and a paraprofessional to be a significant factor in retaining these clients in substance abuse treatment.[209] Provision of transportation was also important.

Attention should also be paid to women who have diagnoses in addition to substance abuse or dependence (also see Chapter 13). Given the rates of depression among women and other diagnoses such as eating disorders,[210] treatment approaches must simultaneously address these serious risks to physical and psychological functioning.

Are women getting a fair shake in treatment programs, at least in terms of their representation in the client population? Early in this chapter, we mentioned that using 1991 data, 16 percent of men and 7 percent of women in the United States had some type of psychoactive substance disorder in the past year, a ratio of 2.3 to 1. In that same year, the National Drug and Alcoholism Treatment Utilization Survey (NDATUS) reported that 72 percent of clients were men and 28 percent were women, a ratio of 2.6 to 1,[211] indicating that women are somewhat underrepresented in substance abuse treatment programs, but not to the extent that some people might believe. Since then, the percentage of women clients reported in this national survey has increased slightly to 30 percent in 1994.[212]

This is one way to view the situation. However, studies on alcoholism treatment only paint a picture of serious gaps in the number of women receiving services. In 1990, Weisner and associates studied treatment utilization using a probability sample of 1,150 households.[213] Alcohol problems were assessed based on dependence symptoms and on the social consequences of drinking. Respondents were asked if they had ever received any type

of help for a drinking problem; if the response was yes, they were asked about the type(s) of help they had received. The data were compared with earlier samples from 1979 and 1984. Since few women in the general population have received alcoholism treatment, the data must be interpreted carefully; nonetheless, the results with respect to women are a concern. Although there were significant increases in the percentage of men receiving treatment in several types of settings, there was not a significant increase for women in any of the categories. Particularly disturbing is that "the male-to-female ratio in specialized alcohol programs enlarged from 2.5:1 to 8:1 during the period."[214] For the measure of seeking any type of help (including Alcoholics Anonymous), the ratio enlarged from 2.2:1 to 3.1:1.

Previously, we reported that the male to female ratio for current rates of alcohol abuse or dependence is approximately 2.7:1. The Weisner study data, therefore, indicate a substantial gap in services for women, especially with regard to specialized, professional alcohol treatment. Also at about the same time, the Institute of Medicine reported the treatment ratio for alcohol disorders at about 4 men for every 1 woman.[215] Although women may be more underserved, both men and women face a service gap, for only a fraction of both groups receive the services they might need. In 1991, about half of the programs responding to the NDATUS reported having specialized programming for women.[216]

Self-Help Groups

Women used to be as rare in AA as they were in treatment programs, but this fact has changed. In 1996, women under age 30 comprised an estimated 40 percent of all members in this age group, and women in general comprised an estimated 33 percent of members compared to 30 percent in 1983 and 22 percent in 1968.[217] The participation of women in AA is reflected in the growth of all-women's AA groups (men are also holding meetings of their own); women are featured in many more of the recovery stories in the Big Book of Alcoholics Anonymous; women are routinely invited as guest speakers at local meetings and at state and national AA conventions; and at some of the thousands of meetings held daily around the world, women are starting the "Lord's Prayer" with "Our Father and Mother."

The Twelve Steps of Alcoholics Anonymous have helped many men and women recover, but even with the emergence of AA groups for women only, not everyone has been satisfied with the program's gender sensitivity. Kasl claims that since "the steps were formulated by a white, middle-class male in the 1930s, not surprisingly, they work to break down an overinflated ego, and put reliance on an all-powerful male God."[218] She believes that most women need just the opposite—to strengthen their sense of self and affirm their own inner wisdom. Earlier, Jean Kirkpatrick expressed similar sentiments about women's identity. In 1975, she introduced a self-help program called Women for Sobriety (WFS).[219] Kirkpatrick says that AA may be more effective in early sobriety, "if you can get 90 meetings in 90 days,"[220] but this is often difficult for women, given their many responsibilities. She believes that WFS can successfully be used alone or as a complement to AA or other programs.[221] Groups operate in the community as well as in treatment programs.[222]

Rather than the Twelve Steps of AA (see Chapter 6), WFS uses Thirteen Statements of Acceptance. For example, "I am a competent woman and have much to give life."[223] At the heart of WFS is its New Life Program. Kaskutas identifies four major themes of WFS: no drinking, positive thinking, believing one is competent, and growing spiritually and emotionally.[224] WFS meetings are led by certified moderators. During meetings, members focus on what happened to them during the previous week and on current topics posed for discussion. But unlike AA, members are discouraged from telling the stories of their drinking and from introducing themselves as alcoholics or addicts, because these are considered examples of negative rather than positive thinking. Kaskutas

describes the WFS program as far less directive than AA. For example, members are not told to "keep coming back," to get a sponsor, or to work the steps. She also says the program is highly accepting, with much more "cross-talk" than in AA. Kaskutas maintains that:

> Sobriety is inside the mind for the WFS members; thus, their decision to affirm sobriety. Sobriety is outside the self for AA members; thus their reliance on meetings, on 12th-step activities, and on a power greater than themselves. In AA, members admit to a loss of control (surrender); in WFS, members strive to regain control (take charge).[225]

Others, of course, take exception to her description of AA and offer an alternative understanding that AA, like other self-help groups, can be viewed as a "narrative community," not an alternative treatment model; and the people who join AA are not clients, but story-tellers who transform their lives through listening and sharing their "experience, strength, and hope."[226] Understanding AA implies a conceptual shift from a rational (service delivery) model to a metaphorical (spiritual understanding). Thus, "powerlessness" can be understood like a Buddhist koan: "giving in is the greatest form of control,"[227] or in the Christian tradition of "to gain your life you must lose it." Brown calls this a "power from within model" instead of a "power over" model.[228] This is very different from the meanings of powerlessness associated with contemporary social and behavioral sciences, such as alienation, anomie, victimization, oppression, discrimination, and poverty.[229]

Although the philosophies of AA and WFS apparently differ, some women take what they need from each program and make good use of both. A survey of 600 WFS members revealed that approximately one-third are also current members of AA, primarily for "insurance" against relapse, for wider availability of meetings, and for sharing, fellowship, and support.[230] Kirkpatrick emphasizes proper nutrition for WFS members and advises limiting coffee intake, smoking, and candy.[231] Although not as prevalent as AA groups, Women for

Sobriety and other self-help groups are options for women seeking recovery.

Kasl has also offered an alternative set of steps to AA that she says emphasize "empowerment."[232] An example is: "We became willing to let go of our shame, guilt, and other behavior that prevents us from taking control of our lives and loving ourselves."

Murky Methodological Waters

Our review of the literature on women with alcohol and other drug problems leaves important questions unanswered. Have incidence and prevalence studies captured the true rates of alcohol and other drug problems among women? Can the rates of reported problems be expected to converge at some point in the future? Is the etiology of chemical abuse and dependence in women different from that for men? Is the course of treatment and recovery the same? Would women benefit from different treatment methods than men? There are several explanations for why there is inadequate research on these and other questions.

The Feminist Critique

Early feminist criticisms of social science research addressed two areas that are also particularly vulnerable in substance abuse studies: (1) the lack of research on women and (2) the inaccurate research "findings" that were produced. Speculation about men's drinking and findings from studies using only male subjects were often generalized to women, or dubious conclusions were drawn about women based on research interest in men. It is likely that even the research community (largely composed of male researchers), dedicated to objectivity, has been affected by the "status insularity" of women substance abusers previously described in this chapter. No doubt, this has contributed to an underrepresentation of women in the chemical dependency research literature. A brief history of some of the literature illustrates this point.[233]

In 1960, McCord and McCord attempted to explain the cause of alcoholism.[234] At the risk of oversimplifying their research, they used dependency theory to suggest that alcoholism develops in men as a result of their inability to express or fulfill dependency needs in society. Women were not included in their study, but it was suggested that women were protected from excessive drinking because of society's acceptance of their dependence. The McCords suggested that "role confusion" rather than "dependency conflict" might better explain women's alcoholism and that due to women's changing role in society, alcoholism rates among women would likely increase (as they have). In 1972, in *The Drinking Man*, McClelland and colleagues attributed part of the variance in men's drinking to their need to increase feelings of power.[235] As the study's title implies, women were not included, and the authors suggested that the power theory may not be applicable to them. Others commented that women's lower rates of alcoholism might be partially explained by their lack of interest in power. In the 1970s, Wilsnack explored the possibility that problems with sex-role identification may help to explain alcoholism in women.[236] She attempted to test dependency, power, and sex-role identification theories. Her findings did not support the power or dependency explanations, but she did find that drinking resulted in women feeling more feminine.

Meanwhile, the women's and feminist movements have changed many ideas about masculine and feminine characteristics and the appropriate behaviors of men and women. Scida and Vanicelli, for example, proposed a broader sex conflict explanation of women's drinking that was not limited to the need to enhance feelings of femininity.[237] Wilsnack[238] wrote that female alcoholics had not adequately integrated masculine and feminine characteristics, and Colman[239] also found that women who were problem drinkers or at risk for such problems lack flexibility in being both assertive and expressive. Integrating these ideas, Henderson and Boyd suggest a model of addiction in which:

substance use is a choice that people often make in an attempt to integrate the polarities represented by the metaphors of masculine/feminine. For instance, individuals often describe their drug experience as supplying them with the qualities they believe they lack. These may be characteristics that are stereotypically labeled masculine or feminine such as feelings of warmth, sensuality, power, dependence, affiliation, peace, etc.[240]

Henderson and Boyd pose an interesting hypothesis, and additional studies in this area may improve understanding of the causes of substance abuse in men and women.

Emrick's 1974 analysis of 271 treatment evaluation studies revealed that only 4 (1.5 percent) solely involved women.[241] Vannicelli's 1984 review of 259 studies (which picks up after Emrick's review) found that only 6 studies (2.3 percent) focused solely on women.[242] In many cases, female and male subjects were combined in data analyses as if this would make no difference. Even after a congressional mandate in the 1970s for increased attention to women's alcoholism problems, only 8 percent of research subjects in treatment outcome studies from 1972 to 1980 were women.[243] We know of no more current report that has evaluated the inclusion of women in research studies, but as we read the literature, we believe that a substantial increase has likely occurred.

Alcohol, Drugs, and Measurement

Lack of agreement on what constitutes alcoholism and other drug problems and lack of standard measures for assessing these problems continues to plague the substance abuse literature on both men and women. Many researchers in the United States are using the American Psychiatric Association's *Diagnostic and Statistical Manual of Mental Disorders* (see Chapter 5) to achieve comparability across studies, but issues such as how to define and measure the concept of heavy drinking among men and women and whether different standards should be applied have not been addressed as well.

Polydrug abuse is thought to be quite common among alcoholics and addicts, yet many studies investigate alcohol or other drug use, but not both. The establishment of two separate federal agencies in the 1970s, the National Institute on Alcohol Abuse and Alcoholism (NIAAA) and the National Institute on Drug Abuse (NIDA), has contributed to a pattern of funding studies on alcohol *or* on other drugs. This may obscure the patterns of substance use, abuse, and dependence in men and women. Corrigan's review of the epidemiological and survey evidence suggests that the higher rates of abuse of prescription and over-the-counter drugs by females needs to be considered in determining the dynamics of substance abuse among this group.[244]

In describing the differences between male and female substance abusers, little effort has been made to determine whether the problems they face are due to gender, substance abuse, or an interaction between the two. Davis and DiNitto tried to clarify differences between male and female vocational rehabilitation clients who showed evidence of substance abuse problems by comparing them with clients who did not report substance abuse.[245] They found that the vast majority of the problems these individuals reported were associated with gender *or* substance abuse, but not an interaction between the two. Women, regardless of whether or not they were substance abusers, felt more bothered by family problems, had more current medical problems, and made more suicide attempts. Men did not score higher than women on any problem area. The substance abusers, regardless of their gender, had more current family problems, anxiety, and problems controlling violence. There was only one problem for which the interaction of substance abuse and gender was associated with more problems: women substance abusers had more psychiatric hospitalizations. According to these findings, women substance abusers are the more seriously disadvantaged group because they share the problems of both the women in the study and the substance abusers in the study.

As noted earlier, methodological problems are also pervasive in studies of the substance abuse treatment process and of treatment outcomes. In attempts to find better ways for investigating these phenomena, those concerned about psychoactive drug problems in women hope that researchers will be mindful of possible gender differences. Wilke calls for more qualitative research based on women's unique experiences "to learn how women become aware of and decide that they have a problem with alcohol, how they experience the treatment process, and their meaning of recovery."[246] Recent examples include Woodhouse's use of a life history approach with women in treatment to explore the themes of violence (rape and incest), abuse, male dominance, dependence, motherhood issues, and depression that typically emerged in these women's lives[247]; and Davis's use of in-depth open-ended interviews with women in recovery to uncover barriers in using all-women's support groups and the nature of economic difficulties they faced on the road to recovery.[248]

Emerging from Invisibility

Part of the unequal treatment of women in the substance abuse literature exists because men have long outnumbered women in treatment programs, especially public programs. A great deal of valuable research has been conducted on substance abusers treated at Veterans Administration hospitals and other public facilities where, to date, few patients have been women. The proportion of women treated in private programs may be higher, but these programs have been involved in few of the large-scale research studies supported by NIAAA and NIDA. Studies of both tiers (public and private) of the chemical dependency treatment system are needed, because the sociodemographic characteristics of clients served in these programs, and perhaps other treatment factors, differ.

In considering the research that has been done on male alcoholics, Braiker cautions against "throwing the baby out with the bathwater—simply because the baby is a boy rather than girl."[249] However, the field is far from making a determination about the extent to which gender should be considered in prevention and treatment services, and without solid research, it is unlikely that the answers to these questions will be discovered. Now that women are 30 percent of the treatment population, there are many more opportunities to include them in research studies.

Susan's Story Revisited

Methodological problems of research studies and the lack of research on all-women's treatment programs have sustained the controversy on whether there are real differences between male and female substance abusers. The argument continues to be made that "an alcoholic is an alcoholic is an alcoholic." However, this chapter describes many differences in the lives of substance-abusing women that a reasonable person would expect to impact recovery. Susan's story illustrates some of these differences:[250]

- The reluctance of women to identify their alcohol or other drug problems due to the social stigma involved and instead to seek help for health, psychiatric, emotional, or family problems
- The propensity of health care professionals and the criminal justice system to fail to detect and address alcohol and other drug problems in women
- The higher incidence of substance disorders and psychiatric disorders in the families of origin of female alcoholics
- The alarming estimates of incest, child sexual abuse, and sexual assault in the histories of women with chemical dependency
- The influence of having a male partner who is an alcoholic or drug addict
- The greater child care responsibilities of women and the lack of child care services that would allow women to seek treatment
- The social isolation of chemically dependent women and the opposition of family and friends to women's entering treatment

- The higher rate of affective disorders in women
- The high rate of marital instability
- The lack of financial resources

Fortunately for Susan, she did not experience some of the physiological problems such as liver disease or the gynecological problems for which alcoholic women also have a greater propensity.

Where Do We Go from Here?

Identification

The telescoping effect of alcohol and other drug use among women makes it critical that their chemical abuse problems be recognized early. Unfortunately, many women effectively hide their problems, and, even when their work performance is poor[251] or when they have serious health problems,[252] women are less likely than men to be confronted about their substance abuse. Duckert recommends routine screening for substance abuse during a woman's regular gynecological and prenatal care,[253] and Turnbull suggests further training of medical, mental health, and social service professionals so they can recognize the signs of substance use disorders in women.[254]

Most of the commonly used alcoholism screening instruments were developed using primarily male samples. Some screening instruments that are more sensitive to detecting possible alcohol problems in women have recently been developed. For example, the TWEAK test was developed from items on the MAST and CAGE tests (see Chapter 5) and from the T-ACE (another gender-sensitive instrument) in order to better screen for risk drinking during pregnancy.[255] Russell notes that the adaptations helped the TWEAK to outperform the widely used MAST and CAGE with a group of pregnant African American women in the Detroit area.[256] Although simple wording changes seemed to make a substantial difference in detecting alcohol problems in this group of women, replication studies with other populations will further help to determine its utility.[257] Instruments that screen for other drug problems are also needed. Perhaps a most important step in breaking the chain of shame and denial that surrounds women's substance abuse is the education of their families, friends, and co-workers (i.e., the American public).

Treatment

A major report by the Institute of Medicine recommends attention to several factors in treatment programs that may improve women's chances of recovery. These include:

- Offering child care options
- Assessment and treatment of psychiatric and medical disorders
- Assertiveness and other skills training and methods of building self-esteem
- Making staff available to educate and treat family and friends and to encourage their support
- Teaching coping strategies for dealing with stress[258]

Changing the funding base for services from a problem-centered approach that separates the issues of chemical dependency, sexual abuse, poverty, and parenting skills to a family-centered approach that views the woman holistically and in relationship to others and her community is also recommended. Morgain notes, however, the continuing difficulties in trying to take a holistic, feminist, or "communal (and thus political)" approach to women's chemical dependency problems.[259] Some believe that a shift in thinking is particularly important for treating women with children. As Finkelstein points out,

> The attitude that recovery must come first and that women need their own space to recover and cannot concentrate on their recovery with children present reflects a lack of understanding of access issues, of maternal and child health issues, and of the fact that true recovery for a mother usually works only when it includes her children.[260]

The high number of clients mutually seen by domestic-violence agencies and substance abuse treatment staff suggests more attention to networking and developing creative ways to solve differences between these two fields.[261]

A number of clinicians have advocated all-women's groups in all phases of the recovery process, particularly in dealing with problems related to sexual abuse.[262] Although the effectiveness of all-women's programs has yet to be validated empirically in the United States, there is a compelling reason for treating women separately: The overwhelming majority of sexual abuse survivors are women and most perpetrators are men.[263] In addition, women in mixed groups tend to be supportive of the male members and may neglect their own issues. For example, the results of a study by Aries suggested that in mixed groups, the women had minimal interactions with other female members and allowed men to dominate the discussions.[264] The need for long-term aftercare and the development of a sober support network is also important to women who often have less social support and may be more isolated than men.[265] For example, the need for and benefits of social support was demonstrated in a study of older women using an innovative approach in a San Francisco community.[266]

The Big Picture

Of prime importance is the continuing need to challenge the gaps in knowledge and communication among researchers, policymakers, service providers, and the general public.[267] During the 1970s, NIAAA sponsored an initiative to increase the responsiveness of treatment programs to women. A number of programs were funded across the country to develop services especially for this population. Emphasis was more on increasing services than on rigorous process and outcome evaluations. NIAAA was also concerned that women were underrepresented as referrals to employee assistance programs (EAPs). In the 1980s, it funded several research projects to increase the number of women with substance abuse problems assisted through EAPS. These studies identified little in the way of especially promising techniques to assist women at work, although many interventions were tried, including special supervisory training, lunch-time education, and information included with paychecks.[268]

During the 1990s, the federal government made mental and physical disorders in women a service and research priority.[269] Efforts were made to consider gender in Project MATCH; a 10-year follow-up study of problem drinking in women was funded along with increased research on maternal and fetal effects of alcohol; and the National Longitudinal Alcohol Epidemiological Survey was designed to include information on arrests and barriers to treatment services, particularly among women. NIDA adopted a similar emphasis that included studies of drug abuse effects on reproduction, comprehensive demonstration projects aimed at women of childbearing age, along with services to their children and other family members, clinical research on the pharmacotherapy of cocaine abuse in women, and AIDS outreach programs targeting specific subgroups of women. In addition, the Office for Women's Services was established in 1992 under the Substance Abuse and Mental Health Services Administration (SAMHSA). The office is concerned with mental health and substance abuse services for women, including mothers who are substance abusers and women from various cultural backgrounds. It collects data on mental health and substance abuse problems among women, identifies service gaps, and recommends policy to promote better treatment of women.[270] It is hoped that the twenty-first century will take the field much further in the development of knowledge about women and chemical abuse and dependency.

Summary

The literature indicates a number of differences in substance problems among men and women. Men use alcohol and drugs more than women, and they have higher rates of alcohol and drug problems than women, although evidence indicates that these gender gaps have narrowed. Women metabolize alcohol and drugs differently than men, and they are especially susceptible to a number of alcohol-related physical problems as a result of excessive alcohol use. Women with substance abuse problems seem to lack some of the social supports that men have, and women often become involved with alcohol and other drugs as a result of involvement with a male partner who is an alcoholic or addict. Health, mental health, and criminal justice systems have been more reluctant to address alcohol and drug problems in women than men, although this has begun to change. Historically, women substance abusers have been described as psychologically more impaired than male substance abusers, but whether this is true is questionable, given that the patterns of relapse and recovery are similar for men and women with alcohol and drug problems.

Many other questions regarding gender and substance abuse remain unanswered—such as whether alcohol and drug problems among men and women will converge and how treatment matching by gender can substantially improve treatment outcomes. Greater attention to research with alcohol- and drug-abusing women may well lead to answers to these questions, and the federal government now seems more committed to addressing these issues. In the meantime, chemical dependency treatment providers must continue to reach out to women in all sociodemographic categories who are affected by alcohol and drug problems to assure that they receive the services that are currently available. Until definitive studies are completed, the authors join other clinicians and researchers in recommending that practical steps be taken to attend to some of the issues that can be reasonably expected to impact the recovery process of women.

Endnotes

1. See, for example, Jeanne C. Marsh, Mary Ellen Colten, and M. Belinda Tucker, "Women's Use of Drugs and Alcohol: New Perspectives," *Journal of Social Issues,* Vol. 38, No. 2 (1982) pp. 1–8; and Jill Doner Kagle, "Women Who Drink: Changing Images, Changing Realities," *Journal of Social Work Education,* Vol. 23, No. 3 (1987), pp. 21–28.

2. Substance Abuse and Mental Health Services Administration, *National Household Survey on Drug Abuse: Main Findings 1993* (Rockville, MD: SAMHSA, 1995), p. 107, DHHS Pub. No. (SMA) 95-3020.

3. See, for example, Don Cahalan and Ira H. Cisin, "American Drinking Practices: Summary of Findings from a National Probability Sample," *Journal of Studies on Alcohol,* Vol. 29 (1968), pp. 130–151.

4. See National Institute on Alcohol Abuse and Alcoholism, *Eighth Special Report to the U. S. Congress on Alcohol and Health* (Rockville, MD: NIAAA, 1993), pp. 3 and 5, NIH Pub. No. 94-3699.

5. Edith S. Gomberg, "The Female Alcoholic," in Ralph E. Tarter and A. Arthur Sugerman (Eds.), *Alcoholism: Interdisciplinary Approaches to an Enduring Problem* (Reading, MA: Addison-Wesley, 1976), pp. 605–607.

6. These data from the National Longitudinal Alcohol Epidemiologic Survey for 1992 are reported in National Institute on Alcohol Abuse and Alcoholism, *Ninth Special Report to the U. S. Congress on Alcohol and Health* (Rockville, MD: NIAAA, 1997), see p. 19.

7. John E. Helzer, Glorisa J. Canino, Eng-Kung Yeh, Roger C. Bland, Chung Kyoon Lee, Hai-Gwo Hwu, and Stephen Newman, "Alcoholism—North America and Asia," *Archives of General Psychiatry,* Vol. 47 (April 1990), pp. 313–319.

8. Substance Abuse and Mental Health Services Administration, *National Household Survey on Drug Abuse: Population Estimates 1994* (Rockville, MD: SAMHSA, 1995), DHHS Pub. No. (SMA) 95-3063.

9. Ibid.

10. Ronald C. Kessler, "Lifetime and 12-Month Prevalence of DSM-III-R Psychiatric Disorders in the U.S.," *Archives of General Psychiatry,* Vol. 51 (1994), pp. 8–19.

11. Lee N. Robins, John E. Helzer, Thomas R. Przybeck, and Darrell A. Regier, "Alcohol Disorders in the Community: A Report from the Epidemiologic Catchment Area," in Robert M. Rose and James E. Barrett (Eds.), *Alcoholism: Origins and Outcome* (New York: Raven Press, 1988), pp. 15–29.

12. Richard W. Wilsnack, Sharon C. Wilsnack, and Albert D. Klassen, "Women's Drinking and Drinking Problems: Patterns from a 1981 National Survey," *American Journal of Public Health,* Vol. 74 (1984), pp. 1231–1238; and Sharon C. Wilsnack, Richard W. Wilsnack, and Albert D. Klassen, "Drinking and Drinking Problems among Women in a U.S. National Survey," *Alcohol Health & Research World,* Vol. 9, No. 2 (1985), pp. 3–13.

13. Sharon C. Wilsnack, Richard W. Wilsnack, and Susanne Hiller-Sturmhöfel, "Epidemiology of Women's Drinking and Problem Drinking," *Alcohol Health & Research World,* Vol. 18, No. 3 (1994), pp. 173–181.

14. Kaye Middleton Fillmore, "When Angels Fall: Women's Drinking as Cultural Preoccupation and as Reality," in Sharon C. Wilsnack and Linda J. Beckman (Eds.), *Alcohol Problems in Women: Antecedents, Consequences, and Intervention* (New York: Guilford Press, 1984), pp. 7–36; and Michael E. Hilton, "Trends in U.S. Drinking Patterns: Further Evidence from the Past 20 Years," *British Journal of Addiction,* Vol. 83 (1988), pp. 269–278.

15. Edith S. Lisansky Gomberg, "Historical and Political Perspective: Women and Drug Use," *Journal of Social Issues,* Vol. 38, No. 2 (1982), pp. 9–23.

16. See Patricia G. Erickson and Valerie A. Watson, "Women, Illicit Drugs, and Crime," in Lynn T. Kozlowski et al. (Eds.), *Research Advances in Alcohol and Drug Problems,* Volume 10 (New York: Plenum Press, 1990), pp. 251–272; this analysis refers primarily to L. D. Johnston, P. M. O'Malley, and J. G. Bachman, *National Trends in Drug Use and Related Factors among American High School Students and Young Adults, 1975–1986* (Rockville, MD: National Institute on Drug Abuse, 1987).

17. See, for example, Jean Kirkpatrick, *Turnabout: Help for a New Life* (Garden City, NY: Doubleday, 1978), p. 162.

18. See Alex Wodak, "She Who Pays the Piper Calls the Tune," *Drug and Alcohol Review,* Vol. 11 (1992), pp. 107–109.

19. Also see Dorothy H. Broom (Ed.), *Double Bind: Women Affected by Alcohol and Other Drugs* (St. Leonards, NSW, Australia: Allen & Unwin, 1994), Introduction and Chapter 15; and Dorothy H. Broom, "Rethinking Gender and Drugs," *Drug and Alcohol Review,* Vol. 14 (1995), pp. 411–415.

20. National Institute on Alcohol Abuse and Alcoholism, *Eighth Special Report to the U.S. Congress on Alcohol and Health,* pp. 61–83.

21. Dace S. Svikis, Martha L. Velez, and Roy W. Pickens, "Genetic Aspects of Alcohol Use and Alcoholism in Women," *Alcohol Health & Research World,* Vol. 18, No. 3 (1994), pp. 193–196.

22. Kenneth S. Kendler, Andrew C. Heath, Michael C. Neale, Ronald C. Kessler, and Lindon J. Eaves, "A Population-Based Twin Study of Alcoholism in Women," *Journal of the American Medical Association,* Vol. 268, No. 14 (1992), pp. 1877–1882, quote from p. 1877.

23. National Institute on Alcohol Abuse and Alcoholism, *Eighth Special Report to the U.S. Congress on Alcohol and Health;* and Svikis et al. "Genetic Aspects of Alcohol Use and Alcoholism in Women."

24. M. McGue and W. Slutske, "The Inheritance of Alcoholism in Women," paper presented at the National Institute on Alcohol Abuse and Alcoholism Working Group for Prevention Research on Women and Alcohol, Bethesda, MD, 1993, cited in Svikis et al., "Genetic Aspects of Alcohol Use and Alcoholism in Women."

25. Svikis et al., "Genetic Aspects of Alcohol Use and Alcoholism in Women."

26. C. Robert Cloninger, Michael Bohman, and Sören Sigvardsson, "Inheritance of Alcohol Abuse," *Archives of General Psychiatry,* Vol. 38 (August 1981), pp. 861–868; C. Robert Cloninger, "Genetic and Environmental Factors in the Development of Alcoholism," *Journal of Psychiatric Treatment and Evaluation,* Vol. 5 (1983), pp. 487–496; Michael Bohman, C. Robert Cloninger, Anne-Liis von Knorring, and Sören Sigvardsson, "An Adoption Study of Somatoform Disorders," *Archives of General Psychiatry,* Vol. 41 (September 1984), pp. 872–878; and Michael Bohman, Sören Sigvardsson, and C. Robert Cloninger, "Maternal Inheritance of Alcohol Abuse," *Archives of General Psychiatry,* Vol. 38 (1981), pp. 965–969. Also see National Institute on Alcohol Abuse and Alcoholism, *Sixth Special Report to the U.S. Congress on Alcohol and Health* (Rockville, MD: NIAAA, 1987), Chapter II, for a review of this literature.

27. Sheila B. Gilligan, Theodore Reich, and C. Robert Cloninger, "Alcohol-related Symptoms in Heterogeneous Families of Hospitalized Alcoholics," *Alcoholism: Clinical and Experimental Research,* Vol. 12, No. 5 (1988), pp. 671–678.

28. Also see Kendler et al., "A Population-Based Twin Study of Alcoholism in Women."

29. Kendler et al., "A Population-Based Twin Study of Alcoholism in Women"; and Kenneth S. Kendler et al., "A Twin–Family Study of Alcoholism in Women," *American Journal of Psychiatry,* Vol. 151, No. 5 (1994), pp. 707–715.

30. Ben Morgan Jones and Marilyn K. Jones, "Alcohol Effects in Women during the Menstrual Cycle," *Annals of the New York Academy of Sciences,* Vol. 273 (1976), pp. 576–587.

31. Ben Morgan Jones and Marilyn K. Jones, "Women and Alcohol: Intoxication, Metabolism and the Menstrual Cycle," in Milton Greenblatt and Marc A. Schuckit (Eds.), *Alcoholism Problems in Women and Children* (New York: Grune & Stratton, 1976), pp. 103–136.

32. Also see James H. Winchester, "The Special Problems of Women Alcoholics," *The Reader's Digest* (March 1978), reprint.

33. William A. McKim, *Drugs and Behavior: An Introduction to Behavioral Pharmacology,* 2nd ed. (Englewood Cliffs, NJ: Prentice-Hall, 1991), p. 92.

34. Mario Frezza et al., "High Blood Alcohol Levels in Women: The Role of Decreased Gastric Alcohol Dehydrogenase Activity and First-Pass Metabolism," *The New England Journal of Medicine,* Vol. 322, No. 2 (1990), pp. 95–99.

35. Steven J. Wolin, "Introduction: The Psychosocial Consequences," in National Institute on Alcohol Abuse and Alcoholism, Research Monograph 1, *Alcoholism and Alcohol Abuse among Women: Research Issues,* DHEW Pub. No. (ADM) 80-835 (Rockville, MD: U. S. Department of Health, Education, and Welfare, 1980), pp. 63–72; and Camberwell Council on Alcoholism, *Women and Alcohol* (London: Tavistock Publications, 1980).

36. Frezza et al., "High Blood Alcohol Levels in Women: The Role of Decreased Gastric Alcohol Dehydrogenase Activity and First-Pass Metabolism."

37. Paul M. Roman, *Women and Alcohol Use: A Review of the Research Literature* (Rockville, MD: U.S. Department of Health and Human Services, Public Health Service/Alcohol, Drug Abuse, and Mental Health Administration, 1988).

38. Shirley Y. Hill, "Introduction: The Biological Consequences," in NIAAA, *Alcoholism and Alcohol Abuse among Women*, p. 50; Shirley Y. Hill, "Biological Consequences of Alcoholism and Alcohol-Related Problems among Women," in National Institute on Alcohol Abuse and Alcoholism, *Alcohol and Health Monograph 4, Special Population Issues*, DHHS Pub. No. (ADM) 82-1193 (Rockville, MD: U.S. Department of Health and Human Services, 1982), p. 53; also see Institute of Medicine, *Broadening the Base of Treatment for Alcohol Problems* (Washington, DC: National Academy Press, 1990).

39. Hill, "Biological Consequences of Alcoholism and Alcohol-Related Problems among Women," pp. 44–48.

40. See National Institute on Alcohol Abuse and Alcoholism, *Eighth Special Report to the U.S. Congress on Alcohol and Health*.

41. Collins E. Lewis, Elizabeth Smith, Carmen Kercher, and Edward Spitznagel, "Assessing Gender Interactions in the Prediction of Mortality in Alcoholic Men and Women: A 20-Year Follow-Up Study," *Alcoholism: Clinical and Experimental Research*, Vol. 19, No. 5 (1995), pp. 1162–1172.

42. Much of this paragraph relies on Hill, "Biological Consequences of Alcoholism and Alcohol-Related Problems among Women."

43. Arthur L. Klatsky, Mary Anne Armstrong, and Gary D. Friedman, "Alcohol and Mortality," *Annals of Internal Medicine*, Vol. 117 (1992), pp. 646–654.

44. Eileen M. Corrigan, "Gender Differences in Alcohol and Other Drug Use," *Addictive Behaviors*, Vol. 10 (1985), p. 315.

45. Substance Abuse and Mental Health Services Administration, *Annual Emergency Room Data 1991*, Data from the Drug Abuse Warning Network (Rockville, MD: U.S. Department of Health and Human Services, 1994), DHHS Pub. No. (SMA) 94-2080.

46. See Hill, "Biological Consequences of Alcoholism and Alcohol-Related Problems among Women" for a discussion.

47. William H. Masters, Virginia E. Johnson, and Robert C. Kolodny, *Masters and Johnson on Sex and Human Loving* (Boston: Little, Brown, 1986), p. 521.

48. Jeanette Norris, "Alcohol and Female Sexuality," *Alcohol Health & Research World*, Vol. 18, No. 3 (1994), pp. 197–201.

49. William Shakespeare, *The Tragedy of Macbeth* (New York: Washington Square Press, 1959), p. 29, Act 2, scene 3, line 34.

50. Masters, Johnson, and Kolodny, *Masters and Johnson on Sex and Human Loving*, p. 519; Helen Singer Kaplan, *Disorders of Sexual Desire* (New York: Simon & Schuster, 1979), p. 203; also see National Institute on Alcohol Abuse and Alcoholism, *Eighth Special Report to the U.S. Congress on Alcohol and Health*, p. 178.

51. M. J. Sholty, *Female Sexual Experience and Satisfaction as Related to Alcohol Consumption* (Baltimore: University of Maryland, Alcohol and Drug Abuse Program, 1979), cited in Roman, *Women and Alcohol Use: A Review of the Research Literature*.

52. Sharon C. Wilsnack, "Alcohol Abuse and Alcoholism in Women," in E. Mansell Pattison and Edward Kaufman (Eds.), *Encyclopedic Handbook of Alcoholism* (New York: Gardner Press, 1982), p. 724.

53. Sharon C. Wilsnack, Albert D. Klassen, Brett E. Shur, and Richard W. Wilsnack, "Predicting Onset and Chronicity of Women's Problem Drinking: A Five-Year Longitudinal Analysis, *American Journal of Public Health*, Vol. 81, No. 3, (1991), pp. 305–318.

54. Mildred Apter-Marsh, "The Sexual Behavior of Alcoholic Women While Drinking and During Sobriety," *Alcoholism Treatment Quarterly*, Vol. 1, No. 3 (1984), pp. 35–48; also see Mark S. Gold, "Alcohol, Drugs, and Sexual Dysfunction," *Alcoholism and Addiction* (December 1988), p. 13.

55. Kaplan, *Disorders of Sexual Desire*, p. 203.

56. Masters, Johnson, and Kolodny, *Masters and Johnson on Sex and Human Loving*, pp. 521–522; also see Kaplan, *Disorders of Sexual Desire*, p. 204.

57. Ibid.

58. Masters, Johnson, and Kolodny, *Masters and Johnson on Sex and Human Loving*, p. 522; also see Mark S. Gold, "Sexual Dysfunction Challenges Today's Addiction Clinicians," *Alcoholism and Addiction* (July–August 1987), p. 11.

59. Ibid.; also see Mark S. Gold, "Alcohol, Drugs, and Sexual Dysfunction."

60. Kaplan, *Disorders of Sexual Desire*, p. 203.

61. Ronald C. Bloodworth, "Medical Problems Associated with Marijuana Abuse," *Psychiatric Medicine*, Vol. 3, No. 3 (1987), pp. 173–184.

62. Wilsnack et al., "Predicting Onset and Chronicity of Women's Problem Drinking: A Five-Year Longitudinal Analysis."

63. Albert D. Klassen and Sharon C. Wilsnack, "Sexual Experience and Drinking among Women in a U.S. National Survey," *Archives of Sexual Behavior*, Vol. 15, No. 5 (1986), pp. 363–392; also see Paul M. Roman, "Biological Features of Women's Alcohol Use: A Review," *Public Health Reports*, Vol. 103, No. 6 (November–December 1988), pp. 628–637.

64. Sharon C. Wilsnack, "Drinking, Sexuality, and Sexual Dysfunction in Women," in Sharon C. Wilsnack and Linda J. Beckman (Eds.), *Alcohol Problems in Women* (New York: Guilford Press, 1984), Chapter 7, pp. 189–227.

65. Klassen and Wilsnack, "Sexual Experience and Drinking among Women in a U.S. National Survey."

66. Valerie Pinhas, "Sex Guilt and Sexual Control in Women Alcoholics in Early Sobriety," *Sexuality and Disability* (Winter 1980), pp. 256–272.

67. Klassen and Wilsnack, "Sexual Experience and Drinking among Women in a U.S. National Survey."

68. Wilsnack, "Alcohol Abuse and Alcoholism in Women"; Gomberg, "The Female Alcoholic"; Roman, "Biological Features of Women's Alcohol Use: A Review"; and National Institute on Alcohol Abuse and Alcoholism, *Eighth Special Report to the U.S. Congress on Alcohol and Health*, p. 179.

69. See Bloodworth, "Medical Problems Associated with Marijuana Abuse."

70. *ADAMHA News Supplement* (July–August 1991), p. 3.

71. Nancy K. Mello, Jack H. Mendelson, and Barbara W. Lex, "Alcohol Use and Premenstrual Symptoms in Social Drinkers," *Psychopharmacology*, Vol. 101, No. 4 (1990), pp. 448–455.

72. Marie B. Tobin, Peter J. Schmidt, and David R. Rubinow, "Reported Alcohol Use in Women with Premenstrual Syndrome," *American Journal of Psychiatry*, Vol. 151, No. 10 (1994), pp. 1503–1504.

73. Betty Streett, "Chemically Dependent Women and Premenstrual Syndrome," *The Counselor* (May/June 1993), pp. 18–20.

74. Gomberg, "The Female Alcoholic"; Marc A. Schuckit and Jane Duby, "Alcoholism in Women," in Benjamin Kissin and Henri Begleiter (Eds.), *The Biology of Alcoholism, Volume 6, The Pathogensis of Alcoholism, Psychosocial Factors* (New York: Plenum Press, 1983), pp. 215–241; Roman, *Women and Alcohol Use: A Review of the Research Literature;* Wilsnack, "Alcohol Abuse and Alcoholism in Women"; and Mello, "Drug Use Patterns and Premenstural Dysphoria."

75. Streett, "Chemically Dependent Women and Premenstrual Syndrome."

76. Kenneth L. Jones and David W. Smith, "Recognition of the Fetal Alcohol Syndrome in Early Infancy," *The Lancet*, Vol. 11, No. 7836 (November 3, 1973), pp. 999–1001; and Kenneth L. Jones, David W. Smith, Christy N. Ulleland, and Ann P. Streissguth, "Pattern of Malformation in Offspring of Chronic Alcoholic Mothers," *The Lancet*, Vol. 1, No. 7815 (June 9, 1973), pp. 1267–1271.

77. *ADAMHA News*, Vol. 17, No. 5 (September–October 1991), p. 9.

78. See National Institute on Alcohol Abuse and Alcoholism, *Eighth Special Report to the U.S. Congress on Alcohol and Health*, p. 213.

79. Ann Pytkowicz Streissguth, Sterling Keith Clarren, and Kenneth Lyons Jones, "Natural History of the Fetal Alcohol Syndrome: A 10-Year Follow-Up of Eleven Patients," *The Lancet*, Vol. 11, No. 8446 (July 13, 1985), pp. 85–91.

80. Ann Pytkowicz Streissguth, "Fetal Alcohol Syndrome in Adolescents and Adults," *Journal of the American Medical Association*, Vol. 265, No. 15 (1991), pp. 1961–1967.

81. See National Institute on Alcohol Abuse and Alcoholism, *Eighth Special Report to the U.S. Congress on Alcohol and Health*, Chapter 9.

82. Ibid.

83. Ernest L. Abel and Robert J. Sokol, "Incidence of Fetal Alcohol Syndrome and Economic Impact of FAS-Related Anomalies," *Drug and Alcohol Dependence*, Vol. 19 (1987), pp. 51–70.

84. Ernest L. Abel and Robert J. Sokol, "A Revised Conservative Estimate of the Incidence of FAS and Its Economic Impact," *Alcoholism: Clinical and Experimental Research*, Vol. 15, No. 3 (1991), pp. 514–524.

85. Sterling K. Clarren, Douglas M. Bowden, and Susan J. Astley, "Pregnancy Outcomes After Weekly Oral Administration of Ethanol During Gestation in the Pig-Tailed Macaque (Macaca nemestrina)," *Teratology*, Vol. 35 (1987), pp. 345–354.

86. Ernest L. Abel, *Fetal Alcohol Syndrome and Fetal Alcohol Effects* (New York: Plenum Press, 1984), see Chapter 6.

87. Clarren et al., "Pregnancy Outcomes after Weekly Oral Administration of Ethanol," p. 345.

88. National Institute on Alcohol Abuse and Alcoholism, *Seventh Special Report to the U.S. Congress on Alcohol and Health* (Rockville, MD: Department of Health and Human Services, 1990), Chapter VI.

89. Marian Sandmaier, *Alcohol and Your Unborn Baby*, a pamphlet distributed by The Texas Commission on Alcoholism, Austin, TX, no date.

90. NIAAA, *Eighth Special Report to the U.S. Congress on Alcohol and Health*; and Robert J. Sokol, Joel Ager, Susan Martier, Sara Debanne, Claire Ernhart, Jan Kuzma, and Sheldon I. Miller, "Significant Determinants of Susceptibility to Alcohol Teratogenicity," *Annals of the New York Academy of Sciences*, Vol. 477 (1986), pp. 87–102.

91. Sokol et al., "Significant Determinants of Susceptibility"; and Abel and Sokol, "A Revised Conservative Estimate of the Incidence of FAS and Its Economic Impact."

92. Philip A. May, Karen J. Hymbaugh, John M. Aase, and Jonathan M. Samet, "Epidemiology of Fetal Alcohol Syndrome among American Indians of the Southwest," *Social Biology*, Vol. 30, No. 4 (1983), pp. 374–387.

93. Ibid.

94. Ira Chasnoff, "Drug Use and Women: Establishing a Standard of Care," in Donald E. Hutchings (Ed.), *Parental Abuse of Licit and Illicit Drugs* (New York: New York Academy of Sciences, 1989), pp. 208–210; see also Nora S. Gustavsson, "Pregnant Chemically Dependent Women: The New Criminals," *Affilia*, Vol. 6, No. 2 (Summer 1991), pp. 61–73.

95. National Institute on Drug Abuse, *National Pregnancy & Health Survey: Drug Use among Women Delivering Live Births: 1992* (Rockville, MD: NIDA, 1996), p. xxi.

96. Samuel Granick, "Psychological Functioning of Children Exposed to Cocaine Prenatally," *Journal of Child & Adolescent Substance Abuse*, Vol. 4, No. 3 (1995), pp. 1–14.

97. Gustavsson, "Pregnant Chemically Dependent Women: The New Criminals"; also see Maureen A. Norton Hawk, "How Social Policies Make Matters Worse: The Case of Maternal Substance Abuse," *Journal of Drug Issues*, Vol. 24, No. 3 (1994), pp. 517–526

98. "Prenatal Substance Abuse," *New Voices* (Newsletter of the Texas Commission on Alcohol and Drug Abuse), Vol. 1, No. 5 (May 1991), p. 1.

99. Gustavsson, "Pregnant Chemically Dependent Women: The New Criminals"; also see Gail L. Zellman, Peter D. Jacobson, Helen DuPlessis, and M. Robin DiMatteo, "Detecting Prenatal Substance Exposure: An Exploratory Analysis and Policy Discussion," *Journal of Drug Issues*, Vol. 23, No. 3 (1993), pp. 375–387.

100. Zellman et al., "Detecting Prenatal Substance Exposure: An Exploratory Analysis and Policy Discussion."

101. *ADAMHA News*, Vol. 17, No. 5, p. 2.

102. Victoria J. Swenson and Cheryl Crabbe, "Pregnant Substance Abusers: A Problem That Won't Go Away," *St. Mary's Law Journal*, Vol. 25, No. 2 (1994), pp. 623–673; also see Robert H. Blank, "Maternal–Fetal Relationship: The Courts and Social Policy," *The Journal of Legal Medicine*, Vol. 14, No. 1 (1993), pp. 73–92; and Norma Finkelstein, "Treatment Issues for Alcohol- and Drug-Dependent Pregnant and Parenting Women," *Health and Social Work*, Vol. 18–19 (1993–1994), pp. 7–13.

103. Swenson and Crabbe, "Pregnant Substance Abusers: A Problem That Won't Go Away."

104. Gustavsson, "Pregnant Chemically Dependent Women: The New Criminals," p. 61.

105. Blank, "Maternal-Fetal Relationship: The Courts and Social Policy," p. 91.

106. Sandra K. Ferguson and Mark S. Kaplan, "Women and Drug Policy: Implications of Normalization," *Affilia*, Vol. 9, No. 2 (1994), pp. 129–144.

107. Center for Substance Abuse Treatment, *Practical Approaches in the Treatment of Women Who Abuse Alcohol and Other Drugs* (Rockville, MD: Department of Health and Human Services, Public Health Service, 1994), p. 126, DHHS Pub. No. (SMA) 94-3006; Granick, "Psychological Functioning of Children Exposed to Cocaine Prenatally"; and Finkelstein, "Treatment Issues for Alcohol- and Drug-Dependent Pregnant and Parenting Women."

108. Lynne Magor-Blatch, "Women in Therapeutic Communities: A Family Approach to Treatment," in Broom, *Double Bind: Women Affected by Alcohol and Other Drugs*, pp. 183–193.

109. See Joan Curlee, "A Comparison of Male and Female Patients at an Alcoholism Treatment Center," *Journal of Psychology*, Vol. 74 (1970), pp. 239–247; Genevieve Knupfer, "Problems Associated with Drunkenness in Women: Some Research Issues," in NIAAA, *Alcohol and Health Monograph 4, Special Population Issues*, pp. 3–39; also see Wilsnack, "Alcohol Abuse and Alcoholism in Women," for a discussion.

110. Yih-Ing Hser, M. Douglas Anglin, and Mary W. Booth, "Sex Differences in Addict Careers. 3. Addiction," *American Journal of Drug and Alcohol Abuse*, Vol. 13, No. 3 (1987), pp. 231–251; and M. Douglas Anglin, Yih-Ing Hser, and Mary W. Booth, "Sex Differences in Addict Careers. 4. Treatment," *American Journal of Drug and Alcohol Abuse*, Vol. 13, No. 3 (1987), pp. 253–280.

111. Linda J. Beckman and Hortensia Amaro, "Personal and Social Difficulties Faced by Women and Men Entering Alcoholism Treatment," *Journal of Studies on Alcohol*, Vol. 47 (1986), pp. 135–145.

112. Edith S. Gomberg, "Women and Alcoholism," in Violet Franks and Vasanti Burtle (Eds.), *Women in Therapy* (New York: Brunner/Mazel, 1974), p. 170.

113. Barbara C. Leigh, "A Thing So Fallen, and So Vile: Images of Drinking and Sexuality in Women," *Contemporary Drug Problems*, Vol. 22 (Fall 1995), pp. 415–434.

114. Kagle, "Women Who Drink: Changing Images, Changing Realities."

115. Broom, *Double Bind: Women Affected by Alcohol and Other Drugs*.

116. Phyl Crawford and Kathleen V. Elliott, "A National Survey of Services for Women with Alcohol and Other Drug-Related Problems," in Broom, *Double Bind: Women Affected by Alcohol and Other Drugs*, pp. 141–154.

117. Florence V. Ridlon, *A Fallen Angel: The Status Insularity of the Female Alcoholic* (London: Associated University Presses, 1988).

118. Sheila Blume, "Women and Alcohol: A Review," *Journal of the American Medical Association*, Vol. 256 (1986), pp. 1467–1470.

119. Ridlon, *A Fallen Angel: The Status Insularity of the Female Alcoholic*.

120. Wilsnack et al., "Drinking and Drinking Problems among Women in a U.S. National Survey"; also see Wilsnack et al., "How Women Drink: Epidemiology of Women's Drinking and Problem Drinking."

121. *ADAMHA News Supplement*, July–August, 1991; also see Walter R. Cuskey, Lisa H. Berger, and Judianne Densen-Gerber, "Issues in the Treatment of Female Addiction: A Review and Critique of the Literature," in Elizabeth Howell and Marjorie Bayes (Eds.), *Women and Mental Health* (New York: Basic Books, 1981), pp. 269–295.

122. Hser, Anglin, and Booth, "Sex Differences in Addict Careers. 3. Addiction," p. 249.

123. Hortensia Amaro, Barry Zuckerman, and Howard Cabral, "Drug Use among Adolescent Mothers: Profile of Risk," *Pediatrics*, Vol. 84 (1989), pp. 144–151.

124. Torild Hammer and Per Vaglum, "The Increase in Alcohol Consumption among Women: A Phenomenon Related to Accessibility or Stress? A General Population Study," *British Journal of Addiction*, Vol. 84 (1989), pp. 767–775.

125. Curlee, "A Comparison of Male and Female Patients at an Alcoholism Treatment Center"; and Gomberg, "The Female Alcoholic."

126. Jack R. Cornelius et al., "Gender Effects on the Clinical Presentation of Alcoholics at a Psychiatric Hospital," *Comprehensive Psychiatry*, Vol. 36, No. 6 (1995), pp. 435–440.

127. Geraldine Youcha, *Women and Alcohol* (New York: Crown Publishers, 1986).

128. Wilsnack et al., "Predicting Onset and Chronicity of Women's Problem Drinking: A Five-Year Longitudinal Analysis."

129. Vera L. Lindbeck, "The Woman Alcoholic: A Review of the Literature," *The International Journal of the Addictions*, Vol. 7, No. 3 (1972), pp. 567–580.

130. Ibid.

131. Beckman and Amaro, "Personal and Social Difficulties Faced by Women and Men Entering Alcoholism Treatment."

132. Ibid.

133. Sue Dobbs Robinson, "Women and Alcohol Abuse Factors Involved in Successful Interventions," *International Journal of the Addictions*, Vol. 19, No. 6 (1984), pp. 601–611.

134. John B. Saunders, A. D. Wodak, and Roger Williams, "Past Experience of Advice and Treatment for Drinking Problems of Patients with Alcoholic Liver Disease," *British Journal of Addiction*, Vol. 80 (1985), pp. 51–56.

135. Hortensia Amaro, Linda J. Beckman, and Vickie M. Mays, "A Comparison of Black and White Women Entering Alcoholism Treatment," *Journal of Studies on Alcohol*, Vol. 48, No. 3 (1987), pp. 220–228.

136. Diane R. Davis, "Women Healing from Alcoholism: A Qualitative Study," *Contemporary Drug Problems*, Vol. 24, No. 1(1997), pp. 147–177.

137. Rebecca Schilit and Edith Lisansky Gomberg, "Social Support Structures of Women in Treatment for Alcoholism," *Health and Social Work* (Summer 1987), pp. 187–195.

138. Marja Holmila, "Social Control Experienced by Heavily Drinking Women," *Contemporary Drug Problems*, Vol. 18, No. 4 (1991), pp. 547–571.

139. Rudolf H. Moos and Bernice S. Moos, "The Process of Recovery from Alcoholism: III. Comparing Functioning in Families of Alcoholics and Matched Control Families," *Journal of Studies on Alcohol*, Vol. 45, No. 2 (1984), pp. 111–118.

140. Andrew G. Billings and Rudolf H. Moos, "Social Support and Functioning among Community and Clinical Groups: A Panel Model," *Journal of Behavioral Medicine*, Vol. 5, No. 3 (1982), pp. 295–311.

141. Kathleen M. Schneider, Frederick J. Kviz, Miriam L. Isola, and William J. Filstead, "Evaluating Multiple Outcomes and Gender Differences in Alcoholism Treatment," *Addictive Behaviors*, Vol. 20, No. 1 (l995), pp. 1–21.

142. Linda J. Beckman and Katherine M. Kocel, "The Treatment-Delivery System and Alcohol Abuse in Women: Social Policy Implications," *Journal of Social Issues*, Vol. 38, No. 2 (1982), pp. 139–151.

143. Saunders et al., "Past Experience of Advice."

144. National Institute of Justice, *1995 Drug Use Forecasting: Annual Report on Adult and Juvenile Arrestees* (Washington, DC: U.S. Department of Justice, 1996).

145. Joseph J. Senna and Larry J. Siegel, *Introduction to Criminal Justice*, 5th ed. (St. Paul, MN: West, 1990), p. 562.

146. Elaine DeCostanzo and Helen Scholes, "Women Behind Bars, Their Numbers Increase," *Corrections Today* (June 1988), pp. 104–108.

147. Erickson and Watson, "Women, Illicit Drugs, and Crime."

148. Douglas A. Smith and Raymond Paternoster, "The Gender Gap in Theories of Deviance," *Journal of Research in Crime and Delinquency*, Vol. 24, No. 2 (May 1987), pp. 140–171.

149. Much of this section relies on Erickson and Watson, "Women, Illicit Drugs, and Crime"; see their work for the list of studies on which their conclusions are based.

150. See ibid. for a discussion of the analyses reported in W. R. Cuskey, T. Premkumar, and L. Sigel, "Survey of Opiate Addiction among Females in the United States between 1850 and 1970," *Public Health Review*, Vol. 1 (1972), pp. 5–39; and R. G. Ferrence and P. C. Whitehead, "Sex Differences in Psychoactive Drug Use: Recent Epidemiology," in O. J. Kalant (Ed.), *Alcohol and Drug Problems in Women* (New York: Plenum Press, 1980), pp. 125–201.

151. M. R. Burt, T. J. Glynn, and B. J. Sowder, *Psychosocial Characteristics of Drug-Abusing Women*, NIDA, Services Research Monograph Series (Bethesda, MD: Burt Associates, 1979), cited in Hser, Anglin, and Booth, "Sex Differences in Addict Careers. 3. Addiction"; also see Yih-Ing Hser, M. Douglas Anglin, and Chih-Ping Chou, "Narcotics Use and Crime among Addicted Women: Longitudinal Patterns and Effects of Social Interventions," in Thomas Mieczkowski (Ed.), *Drugs, Crime, and Social Policy: Research, Issues, and Concerns* (Boston: Allyn and Bacon, 1992), pp. 197–221.

152. Hser et al., "Sex Differences in Addict Careers. 3. Addiction."

153. Erickson and Watson, "Women, Illicit Drugs, and Crime."

154. Special Committee on Pornography and Prostitution, *Pornography and Prostitution in Canada* (Ottawa: Department of Supply and Services, 1985), cited in Erickson and Watson, "Women, Illicit Drugs, and Crime."

155. James A. Inciardi and Anne E. Pottieger, "Drug Use and Crime among Two Cohorts of Women Narcotics Users: An Empirical Assessment," *Journal of Drug Issues*, Vol. 16, No. 1 (1986), pp. 61–106. See National Institute of Justice, *1995 Drug Use Forecasting: Annual Report on Adult and Juvenile Arrestees* for data on drug use by women who were arrested for prostitution and other crimes.

156. Erickson and Watson, "Women, Illicit Drugs, and Crime."

157. John Hagan, A. R. Gillis, and John Simpson, "The Class Structure of Gender and Delinquency: Toward a Power-Control Theory of Common Delinquent Behavior," *American Journal of Sociology*, Vol. 90, No. 6 (1985), pp. 1151–1178.

158. Jeffrey Fagan, "Women and Drugs Revisited: Female Participation in the Cocaine Economy," *The Journal of Drug Issues*, Vol. 24, No. 2 (1994), pp. 179–225.

159. Ibid., p. 206.

160. M. Lynne Cooper, "Stress and Alcohol Use: Moderating Effects of Gender, Coping, and Alcohol Expectancies," *Journal of Abnormal Psychology*, Vol. 101, No. 1 (1992), pp. 139–152.

161. Larissa A. Pohorecky, "Stress and Alcohol Interaction: An Update of Human Research," *Alcoholism: Clinical and Experimental Research*, Vol. 15, No. 3 (1991), pp. 438–459.

162. See, for example, Beckman and Amaro, "Personal and Social Difficulties Faced by Women and Men Entering Alcoholism Treatment"; Hope R. Conte, Robert Plutchik, Susan Picard, Marc Galanter, and Jacob Jacoby, "Sex Differences in Personality Traits and Coping Styles of Hospitalized Alcoholics," *Journal of Studies on Alcohol*, Vol. 52, No. 1 (1991), pp. 26–32; and Joanne E. Turnbull and Edith S. L. Gomberg, "Impact of Depressive Symptomatology on Alcohol Problems in Women," *Alcoholism: Clinical and Experimental Research*, Vol. 12, No. 3 (May–June 1988), pp. 374–381.

163. See, for example, Roman, *Women and Alcohol Use: A Review of the Research Literature*; Linda J. Beckman, "Treatment Needs of Women Alcoholics," *Alcoholism Treatment Quarterly*, Vol. 1, No. 2 (Summer 1984), pp. 101–114; and Cornelius et al., "Gender Effects on the Clinical Presentation of Alcoholics at a Psychiatric Hospital."

164. Conte et al., "Sex Differences in Personality Traits and Coping Styles of Hospitalized Alcoholics."

165. Cornelius et al., "Gender Effects on the Clinical Presentation of Alcoholics at a Psychiatric Hospital."

166. Marc A. Schuckit and Elizabeth R. Morrissey, "Alcoholism in Women: Some Clinical and Social Perspectives with an Emphasis on Possible Subtypes," in Greenblatt and Schuckit (Eds.), *Alcoholism Problems in Women and Children*, pp. 5–35; and Wilsnack, "Alcohol Abuse and Alcoholism in Women."

167. Helen E. Ross, "Alcohol and Drug Abuse in Treated Alcoholics: A Comparison of Men and Women," *Alcoholism: Clinical and Experimental Research*, Vol. 13, No. 6 (1989), pp. 810–816; Michie N. Hesselbrock, Roger E. Meyer, and Janet J. Keener, "Psychopathology in Hospitalized Alcoholics," *Archives of General Psychiatry*, Vol. 42 (November 1985), pp. 1050–1055; Cornelius et al., "Gender Effects on the Clinical Presentation of Alcoholics at a Psychiatric Hospital."

168. Margaret L. Griffin, Roger D. Weiss, Steven M. Mirin, and Ulrike Lange, "A Comparison of Male and Female Cocaine Abusers," *Archives of General Psychiatry*, Vol. 46 (February 1989), pp. 122–126.

169. Roman, *Women and Alcohol Use: A Review of the Research Literature*; and Elizabeth R. Morrissey and Marc A. Schuckit, "Stressful Life Events and Alcohol Problems among Women Seen at a Detoxification Center," *Journal of Studies on Alcohol*, Vol. 39, No. 9 (1978), pp. 1559–1576.

170. Kathleen K. Shutte, Rudolf J. Moos, and Penny L. Brennan, "Depression and Drinking Behavior among Women and Men: A Three-Wave Longitudinal Study of Older Adults," *Journal of Consulting and Clinical Psychology*, Vol. 63, No. 5 (1995), pp. 810–822.

171. Clinton B. De Soto, William E. O'Donnell, Linda J. Allred, and Cheryl E. Lopes, "Symptomatology in Alcoholics at Various Stages of Abstinence," *Alcoholism: Clinical and Experimental Research*, Vol. 9, No. 6 (1985), pp. 505–512.

172. Clinton B. De Soto, William E. O'Donnell, and Janet L. De Soto, "Long-Term Recovery in Alcoholics," *Alcoholism: Clinical and Experimental Research*, Vol. 13, No. 2 (1989), pp. 693–697.

173. National Intitute on Alcohol Abuse and Alcoholism, *Seventh Special Report to the U. S. Congress on Alcohol and Health*.

174. Curlee, "A Comparison of Male and Female Patients at an Alcoholism Treatment Center"; and Susan Wagner Glenn and Oscar A. Parsons, "Alcohol Abuse and Familial Alcoholism: Psychosocial Correlates in Men and Women," *Journal of Studies on Alcohol*, Vol. 50, No. 2 (1989), pp. 116–127.

175. Schilit and Gomberg, "Social Support Structures of Women in Treatment for Alcoholism."

176. Michael J. Sheridan, "A Proposed Intergenerational Model of Substance Abuse, Family Functioning, and Abuse/Neglect," *Child Abuse & Neglect*, Vol. 19, No. 5 (1995), pp. 519–530.

177. Nannette Lehmann and Steven L. Krupp, "Incidence of Alcohol-Related Domestic Violence," *Alcohol Health and Research World* (Winter 1983/84), pp. 23–27 and 39.

178. Sharon C. Wilsnack, "Drinking, Sexuality, and Sexual Dysfunction in Women," in Wilsnack and Beckman, *Alcohol Problems in Women*, pp. 189–227; also see Dorothy L. Hurley, "Women, Alcohol and Incest: An Analytical

Review," *Journal of Studies on Alcohol*, Vol. 52, No. 3 (1991), pp. 253–268.

179. S. S. Covington, "Sexual Experience, Dysfunction and Abuse: A Comparative Study of Alcoholic and Non-Alcoholic Women," doctoral dissertation, Union Graduate School, 1982, cited in Wilsnack, "Drinking, Sexuality, and Sexual Dysfunction in Women.

180. S. Covington, "Sex and Violence: The Unmentionable in Alcoholism Treatment," paper presented at the National Alcoholism Forum, Washington, DC, 1982, cited in Brenda L. Underhill, "Issues Relevant to Aftercare Programs for Women," *Alcohol Health & Research World* (Fall 1986), p. 46.

181. Roman, *Women and Alcohol Use.*

182. Covington, "Sex and Violence," cited in Underhill, "Issues Relevant to Aftercare," pp. 46–47.

183. Brenda A. Miller and William R. Downs, "The Impact of Family Violence on the Use of Alcohol by Women," *Alcohol Health and Research World*, Vol. 17, No. 2 (1993), pp. 137–143.

184. Edith S. Lisansky Gomberg, "Shame and Guilt Issues among Women Alcoholics," *Alcoholism Treatment Quarterly*, Vol. 4, No. 2 (1987), pp. 139–155.

185. Marsha Vannicelli, "Treatment Outcome of Alcoholic Women: The State of the Art in Relation to Sex Bias and Expectancy Effects," in Wilsnack and Beckman, *Alcohol Problems in Women*, Chapter 13, pp. 369–412, see especially p. 376.

186. Benjamin M. Karpman, *The Woman Alcoholic: Case Studies in the Psychodynamics of Alcoholism* (Washington, DC: Linacre, 1948).

187. Vannicelli, "Treatment Outcome of Alcoholic Women: The State of the Art in Relation to Sex Bias and Expectancy Effects."

188. Hser, Anglin, and Booth, "Sex Differences in Addict Careers. 3. Addiction."

189. Institute of Medicine, *Broadening the Base of Treatment for Alcohol Problems*, p. 356; also see Helen M. Annis and Carolyn B. Liban, "Alcoholism in Women: Treatment Modalities and Outcomes," in Oriana Josseau Kalant (Ed.), *Alcohol and Drug Problems in Women: Research Advances in Alcohol and Drug Problems*, Volume 5 (New York: Plenum Press, 1980), pp. 385–422.

190. Institute of Medicine, *Broadening the Base of Treatment for Alcoholism.*

191. Richard Longabaugh and David C. Lewis, "Key Issues in Treatment Outcome Studies," *Alcohol Health and Research World*, Vol. 12, No. 3 (1988), pp. 168–175.

192. De Soto, O'Donnell, and DeSoto, "Long-Term Recovery in Alcoholics."

193. Schneider et al., "Evaluating Multiple Outcomes and Gender Differences in Alcoholism Treatment."

194. Anglin et al., "Sex Differences in Addict Careers. 4. Treatment."

195. Vannicelli, "Treatment Outcome of Alcoholic Women: The State of the Art in Relation to Sex Bias and Expectancy Effects"; also see Institute of Medicine, *Broadening the Base of Treatment for Alcoholism.*

196. Helen M. Annis, "Treatment of Alcoholic Women," in Griffith Edwards and Marcus Grant (Eds.), *Alcoholism Treatment in Transition* (London: Croom Helm, 1980), Chapter 8, p. 128.

197. Harriet B. Braiker, "Therapeutic Issues in the Treatment of Alcoholic Women," in Wilsnack and Beckman, *Alcohol Problems in Women*, Ch. 12, pp. 349–368, especially p. 349.

198. Linda J. Beckman, "Treatment Needs of Women with Alcohol Problems," *Alcohol Health & Research World*, Vol. 18, No. 3 (1994), pp. 206–210.

199. Lena Dahlgren and Anders Willander, "Are Special Treatment Facilities for Female Alcoholics Needed? A Controlled 2-Year Follow-up Study from a Specialized Female Unit (EWA) versus a Mixed Male/Female Treatment Facility," *Alcoholism: Clinical and Experimental Research*, Vol. 13, No. 4 (July/August 1989), pp. 499–504.

200. National Institute on Alcohol Abuse and Alcoholism, *Eighth Special Report to the U.S. Congress on Alcohol and Health.*

201. Project MATCH Research Group, "Matching Alcoholism Treatments to Client Heterogeneity: Project MATCH Posttreatment Drinking Outcomes," *Journal of Studies on Alcohol*, Vol. 58 (1997), pp. 7–29.

202. Amaro, Beckman, and Mays, "A Comparison of Black and White Women Entering Alcoholism Treatment."

203. Patricia Ann Harrison and Carol A. Belille, "Women in Treatment: Beyond the Stereotype," *Journal of Studies on Alcohol*, Vol. 48, No. 6 (1987), pp. 574–578.

204. Edith S. Lisansky Gomberg, "Risk Factors for Drinking Over a Woman's Life Span," *Alcohol Health & Research World*, Vol. 18, No. 3 (1994), pp. 220–227.

205. Karen I. Fredricksen, "North of Market: Older Women's Alcohol Outreach Program," *The Gerontologist*, Vol. 32, No. 2 (1992), pp. 270–272.

206. Shirley D. Coletti et al., "Par Village for Chemically Dependent Women," *Journal of Substance Abuse Treatment*, Vol. 12, No. 4 (1995), pp. 289–296; also see Sally J. Stevens and Naya Arbiter, "A Therapeutic Community for Substance-Abusing Pregnant Women and Women with Children: Process and Outcome," *Journal of Psychoactive Drugs*, Vol. 27, No. 1 (1995), pp. 49–56.

207. Coletti et al., "PAR Village for Chemically Dependent Women,"

208. Various models of case management are discussed in Rebecca Sager Ashery (Ed.), *Progress and Issues in Case Management* (Rockville, MD: National Institute on Drug Abuse, 1992), DHHS Publication No. (ADM) 92-1946.

209. Marilyn Poland Laken and Joel W. Ager, "Effects of Case Management on Retention in Prenatal Substance

Abuse Treatment," *American Journal of Drug and Alcohol Abuse,* Vol. 22, No. 3 (1996), pp. 439–448.

210. Carlos M. Grilo et al., "Eating Disorders in Female Inpatients with versus without Substance Use Disorders," *Addictive Behavior,* Vol. 20, No. 2 (1995) pp. 255–260; and Ruth H. Striegel-Moore and Edward S. Huydic, "Problem Drinking and Symptoms of Disordered Eating in Female High School Students," *International Journal of Eating Disorders,* Vol. 14, No. 4 (1993), pp. 417–425.

211. Substance Abuse and Mental Health Services Administration, *National Drug and Alcoholism Treatment Unit Survey (NDATUS): 1991 Main Findings Report* (Rockville, MD: U.S. Department of Health and Human Services, 1993), DHHS Pub. No. (SMA) 93-2007.

212. Substance Abuse and Mental Health Services Administration, *National Drug and Alcoholism Treatment Unit Survey (NDATUS): Data for 1994 and 1980–1994 Main Findings Report,* Advance Report Number 13 (Rockville, MD: U.S. Department of Health and Human Services, June 1996).

213. Constance Weisner, Thomas Greenfield, and Robin Room, "Trends in the Treatment of Alcohol Problems in the US General Population, 1979 through 1990," *American Journal of Public Health,* Vol. 85, No. 1 (1995), pp. 55–60.

214. Ibid., p. 57.

215. See Institute of Medicine, *Broadening the Base of Treatment for Alcohol Problems,* p. 365.

216. Substance Abuse and Mental Health Services Administration, *National Drug and Alcoholism Treatment Unit Survey (NDATUS): 1991 Main Findings Report.*

217. Alcoholics Anonymous World Services, *Alcoholics Anonymous Membership Survey* (New York: Alcoholics Anonymous World Services, 1989 and 1997); also see Chad D. Emrick, "Alcoholics Anonymous: Affiliation Processes and Effectiveness as Treatment," *Alcoholism: Clinical and Experimental Research,* Vol. 11, No. 5 (September/October 1987), pp. 416–423.

218. Charlotte Davis Kasl, "The Twelve Step Controversy," *Ms. Magazine* (November/December 1990), pp. 30–31; and Charlotte Davis Kasl, *Many Roads, One Journey, Moving Beyond the Twelve Steps* (New York: Harper Perennial, 1992).

219. Kirkpatrick, *Turnabout: Help for a New Life.*

220. J. S. Rudolf, "Jean Kirkpatrick," *Sober Times* (October 1990).

221. Women for Sobriety, "Who We Are" (Quakertown, PA: Author, 1976).

222. Women for Sobriety may be reached at P. O. Box 618, Quakertown, PA 18951-0618, (215) 536-8026. WFS's e-mail address is WFSobriety@aol.com and its Internet address is http://www.mediapulse.com/wfs/

223. Women for Sobriety, "Overview" (Quakertown, PA: Author, 1989).

224. The remainder of this paragraph relies on Lee Kaskutas, "Women for Sobriety: A Qualitative Analysis," *Contemporary Drug Problems* (Summer 1989), pp. 177–200; also see Kirkpatrick, *Turnabout,* for a discussion of Women for Sobriety.

225. Kaskutas, "Women for Sobriety," p. 195.

226. Julian Rappaport, "Narrative Studies, Personal Stories, and Identity Transformation in the Mutual Help Context," *Journal of Applied Behavioral Science,* Vol. 29, No. 2 (1993), pp. 239–256.

227. Insoo Kim Berg and Scott D. Miller, *Working with the Problem Drinker: A Solution-Focused Approach* (New York: W. W. Norton and Co., 1992).

228. Stephanie D. Brown, "Alcoholics Anonymous: An Interpretation of Its Spiritual Foundation," *Behavioral Health Management,* Vol. 14, No. 1 (1994), pp. 25–27, adapted from Barbara S. McCrady and William Miller (Eds.), *Research on Alcoholics Anonymous: Opportunities and Alternatives* (New Brunswick, NJ: Rutgers Center of Alcohol Studies, 1993).

229. Thomasina Borkman, "Alcoholics Anonymous: The Stories," *Social Policy,* Vol. 19, No. 4 (1989), pp. 58–63.

230. Lee Ann Kaskutas, "What Do Women Get Out of Self-Help? Their Reasons for Attending Women for Sobriety and Alcoholics Anonymous," *Journal of Substance Abuse Treatment,* Vol. 11, No. 3 (1994), pp. 184–195.

231. Jean Kirkpatrick, "A Self-Help Program for Women Alcoholics," *Alcohol Health & Research World* (Summer 1982), reprint.

232. Kasl, "The Twelve Step Controversy," p. 31.

233. This history is also recounted in Sharon C. Wilsnack, "The Impact of Sex Roles on Women's Alcohol Use and Abuse," in Greenblatt and Schuckit, *Alcoholism Problems in Women and Children,* pp. 37–63, and in Dorothy Henderson and Carol Boyd, "Masculinity, Femininity, and Addiction," in Mieczkowski, *Drugs, Crime, and Social Policy: Research, Issues and Concerns,* pp. 153–166.

234. William McCord and Joan McCord, *Origins of Alcoholism* (Stanford, CA: Stanford University Press, 1960), see especially pp. 162–164.

235. David C. McClelland, William N. Davis, Rudolf Kalin, and Eric Wanner, *The Drinking Man* (New York: The Free Press, 1972).

236. Sharon C. Wilsnack, "Sex Role Identity in Female Alcoholism," *Journal of Abnormal Psychology,* Vol. 82, No. 2 (1973), pp. 253–261; and Sharon C. Wilsnack, "Femininity by the Bottle," in Cristen C. Eddy and John L. Ford (Eds.), *Alcoholism in Women* (Dubuque, IA: Kendall/Hunt, 1980), pp. 16–24.

237. Joan Scida and Marsha Vannicelli, "Sex-Role Conflict and Women's Drinking," *Journal of Studies on Alcohol,* Vol. 40, No. 1 (1979), pp. 28–44.

238. Wilsnack, "The Impact of Sex Roles on Women's Alcohol Use and Abuse."

239. C. J. Colman, "Problem Drinking Women: Aspects of Their Marital Interaction and Sex Role Style," unpublished doctoral dissertation, Howard University, 1975, cited in Wilsnack, "The Impact of Sex Roles on Women's

Alcohol Use and Abuse," and in Henderson and Boyd, "Masculinity, Feminity, and Addiction."

240. This paragraph relies on Henderson and Boyd, "Masculinity, Feminity, and Addiction," quote from p. 159.

241. These four studies were part of the original pool of studies discussed in Chad D. Emrick, "A Review of Psychologically Oriented Treatment of Alcoholism," *Quarterly Journal of Studies on Alcohol*, Vol. 35 (1974), pp. 523–549. Emrick did not discuss gender differences but made the data available to Marsha Vannicelli, who discussed them in her article "Treatment Outcome of Alcoholic Women: The State of the Art in Relation to Sex Bias and Expectancy Effects," in Wilsnack and Beckman, *Alcohol Problems in Women*, pp. 369–412.

242. Vannicelli, "Treatment Outcome of Alcoholic Women: The State of the Art in Relation to Sex Bias and Expectancy Effects."

243. Ibid.

244. Corrigan, "Gender Differences in Alcohol and Other Drug Use."

245. Diane R. Davis and Diana M. DiNitto, "Gender Differences in Social and Psychological Problems of Substance Abusers: A Comparison to Non-Substance Abusers, *Journal of Psychoactive Drugs*, Vol. 28, No. 2 (1995), pp. 135–145.

246. Dina Wilke, "Women and Alcoholism: How a Male-as-Norm Bias Affects Research, Assessment, and Treatment," *Health & Social Work*, Vol. 19, No. 1 (1994), pp. 29–35, quote from p. 33.

247. Lynn D. Woodhouse, "Women with Jagged Edges: Voices from a Culture of Substance Abuse," *Qualitative Health Research*, Vol. 2, No. 3 (1992), pp. 262–281.

248. Diane R. Davis, "Women Healing from Alcoholism: A Qualitative Study," *Contemporary Drug Problems*, in press.

249. Braiker, "Therapeutic Issues in the Treatment of Alcoholic Women," especially p. 350.

250. Also see Institute of Medicine, *Broadening the Base of Treatment for Alcoholism*, p. 357.

251. Susan D. Solomon, "Women in the Workplace: An Overview of NIAAA's Occupational Alcoholism Demonstration Project," *Alcohol Health & Research World*, Vol. 7, No. 3 (Spring 1983), Special Focus: Women in the Workplace, pp. 3–5.

252. Saunders et al., "Past Experience of Advice and Treatment for Drinking Problems of Patients with Alcoholic Liver Disease."

253. F. Ducker, "Recruitment into Treatment and Effects of Treatment for Female Problem Drinkers," *Addictive Behaviors*, Vol. 12 (1987), pp. 137–150.

254. Joanne E. Turnbull, "Treatment Issues for Alcoholic Women," *Social Casework*, Vol. 70, No. 6 (1989), pp. 364–369.

255. See Marcia Russell, "New Assessment Tools for Risk Drinking during Pregnancy," *Alcohol Health & Research World*, Vol. 18, No. 1 (1994), pp. 55–61; also see NIAAA, *Eighth Special Report to the U.S. Congress on Alcohol and Health*.

256. Russell, "New Assessment Tools for Risk Drinking during Pregnancy."

257. Also see Arthur W. K. Chan, Edward A. Pristach, John W. Welte, and Marcia Russell, "Use of the TWEAK Test in Screening for Alcoholism/Heavy Drinking in Three Populations," *Alcoholism: Clinical and Experimental Research*, Vol. 17, No. 6 (1993), pp. 1188–1192.

258. Institute of Medicine, *Broadening the Base of Treatment for Alcoholism*; also see Linda J. Beckman, "Treatment Needs of Women with Alcohol Problems," *Alcohol Health and Research World*, Vol. 18, No. 3 (1994), pp. 206–211.

259. Lyn Morgain, "Women's Addiction Recovery Service: A Community Development Model," in Broom, *Double Bind: Women Affected by Alcohol and Other Drugs*, pp. 171–181.

260. Finkelstein, "Treatment Issues for Alcohol- and Drug-Dependent Pregnant and Parenting Women," p. 9.

261. Larry Bennett and Marie Lawson, "Barriers to Cooperation between Domestic-Violence and Substance-Abuse Programs," *Families in Society: The Journal of Contemporary Human Services*, Vol. 75, No. 5 (1994), pp. 277–286.

262. Underhill, "Issues Relevant to Aftercare Programs for Women."

263. Ibid.

264. Elizabeth Aries, "Interaction Patterns and Themes of Male, Female, and Mixed Groups," *Small Group Behavior*, Vol. 7, No. 1, (February 1976) pp. 7–18.

265. Underhill, "Issues Relevant to Aftercare Programs for Women."

266. Fredricksen, "North of Market: Older Women's Alcohol Outreach Program."

267. Jan Waterson and Betsy Ettorre, "Providing Services for Women with Difficulties with Alcohol or Other Drugs: The Current U.K. Situation as Seen by Women Practitioners, Researchers and Policy Makers in the Field," *Drug and Alcohol Dependence*, Vol. 24 (1989), p. 124.

268. See *Alcohol Health & Research World*, Vol. 7, No. 3 (Spring 1983), Special Focus: Women in the Workplace.

269. *ADMAHA News*, Vol. 17, No. 4 (July–August 1991).

270. "New Offices to Track Special Issues," *ADAMHA News*, Vol. 18, No. 4 (September–October 1992), p. 7.

PART FOUR

Summary and Conclusions

16

Chemical Dependency:
Current Issues and Future Prospects

Paul R. Raffoul
University of Houston

A great deal is known about the phenomenon of drug use and abuse; unfortunately, much of that knowledge simply is not utilized in developing public policy and planning programs. One reason is that this is a highly charged emotional issue for many individuals and many politically powerful groups. For example, the legalization (or decriminalization) of any illicit drug faces a steep uphill battle as long as it is opposed by organized church groups and large factions of both major political parties. Nevertheless, it seems to us that the following observations should be made in this concluding chapter:

- *There have always been some people in just about every society who use drugs excessively.* The type of drugs used may vary, as well as the proportion of individuals using them, but drug use is one of the more common historical phenomena. This is not likely to change.
- *Society cannot prevent all drug use; at most, it may control or regulate it.* Various efforts to prohibit drug use, especially in a civil rights–oriented democracy such as the United States,

are doomed to failure. Furthermore, the side effects of prohibition efforts may be worse than the direct effects of drug use. Prohibition of alcohol and the current "war on drugs" are examples of these policy failures.

- *Societal decisions about which drugs to allow or prohibit are essentially political decisions.* Some drugs with minimal (or nonexistent) benefits are frequently allowed and regulated, while others with comparatively safe risk levels are illegal. For example, facts pertaining to the dangers of both alcohol and tobacco have been discussed in this book.
- *Other drugs many come and go, but alcohol is the one great historical constant in drug use.* Undoubtedly, alcohol's popularity is related to its status as the only legal psychoactive drug that most people can use to get high.
- *New drugs that are even more addicting than the current popular drugs will become major problems in the next century.* Only a decade ago, almost no one had heard of the drug ice. In some communities today, it rivals crack cocaine in popularity. As society advances in its

445

technological capacity, the chemists who invent new psychoactive drugs will continue refining and improving their products.

- *Society does not know how to effectively treat many drug abuse problems.* As explained in Chapter 6, treatment programs for alcohol and drug abuse have had mixed results. Many people who are chemically dependent are just as likely to recover without treatment as they are with treatment, and relapse rates for those who do "recover" are quite high.

- *Drug abuse is not a unitary phenomenon.* People who use drugs are from a diverse population in terms of age and developmental level, drugs of abuse and reasons for use, presence of co-morbidity, family composition and dynamics, ethnicity, gender, and socioeconomic status. Current research shows that understanding this behavior requires contextual knowledge about the individual, the substance(s), and the environment(s). "The middle-class 14-year-old academic underachiever using alcohol and marijuana once every other week is worlds apart from the 17-year-old high school dropout living in poverty, involved in the juvenile justice system, and smoking marijuana every day. And the daily lives of these two youths are quite different from that of the adult cocaine addict."[1]

- *Insurers and other organizations who finance treatment programs are demanding more for their money.* Despite some evidence that inpatient programs sometimes may be more effective than outpatient treatment programs, they are much more expensive. When they are used, insurance companies are insisting on shorter stays.

Based on these observations, several courses of action regarding research, policy change, and the delivery of treatment services are outlined in the paragraphs that follow.

Research

Despite several excellent recent studies of treatment effectiveness, the state of knowledge in this field is still in its infancy. Experts know that most treatment programs seem to have little or no effect, and that there is a moderately strong relationship between length of treatment and treatment effectiveness. It is still unclear why most treatment is ineffective, but the most obvious reason is that the research methodologies used in evaluating treatment programs are simply not designed to answer this question. We strongly suspect that one of the reasons for this is that experts are still ignorant about the etiology of alcohol and drug problems.

It is now recognized that drug abuse and drug addiction are not identical phenomena. The relationship of different treatment contexts and the interaction of different patient population characteristics and cultures are important variables to consider in treatment effectiveness. Current research has begun to focus more specifically on questions such as: "What kinds of therapy delivered by what kinds of therapists are effective in the short term and the long term, reflected by what breadth of changes, with what kinds of people suffering from what kinds of disorders, and how do those changes come about?"[2]

Furthermore, there is increasing concern about the appropriateness of viewing alcoholism or drug addiction as phenomena amenable to the medical model. There are, of course, many justifications for this point of view. First, it is much easier to find ways to finance treatment if chemical dependency is a medical problem. Second, many of the physiological consequences of alcohol or heroin use are undeniably appropriate for medical treatment.

> The current treatment consensus indicates that opiate addicts who remain in methadone maintenance treatment for 1 year or more show reductions in use of opiates and other drugs, and reduced involvement in illegal activity. Moreover, recent evidence indicates that methadone in conjunction with counseling and psychotherapy shows the best outcomes. Family treatment of opiate-addiction in the absence of long-term, higher dose methadone maintenance would not represent current state-of-the-science treatment.[3]

However, except for medical detoxification of alcohol and heroin users, most drug treatment protocols consist of talk therapies and self-help programs.

Too much of the research on drug and alcohol abuse and treatment has been narrowly focused on specific subpopulations that may behave quite differently from other groups. At the risk of overgeneralizing, white male alcoholics have received a great deal more attention than most other groups. Women alcoholics and drug users have been underrepresented in chemical dependency research. Research on illicit drugs, especially opiates, has been conducted primarily on those who have been arrested and have become involved in the criminal justice system. Research on noncriminal substance abusers has concentrated on low-income groups and special populations such as Veterans Administration clients.

One area of research that has been largely ignored is the study of those individuals who are dually diagnosed (i.e., having a drug problem along with a clinical diagnosis such as conduct disorder, affective disorders, antisocial behavior, or depression). Given estimates ranging from 40 to 60 percent of adults with mental illness who also have a substance abuse problem, the lack of research information about comorbidity in the literature prevents an accurate and complete description of the population and the extent of the problem.

Another avenue of research that has been ignored is the study of those people who have recovered from chemical dependency without treatment. One recent study of 101 opiate addicts who recovered without the help of any formal treatment discovered a potentially useful pattern of recovery among these individuals, rather than a "spontaneous remission." This pattern included forming a resolve, becoming abstinent, creating an alternative, dealing with the craving problem, and becoming "ordinary."[4] More research is needed on similar groups of people dependent on other drugs, especially alcohol.

Another promising line of research involves the application of the concept of self-efficacy to addictive behaviors, as outlined by DiClemente.[5] Originally conceptualized by Bandura as an individual's perception of competence in his or her environment, and related to Julian Rotter's concept of internal-external locus of control, the application of self-efficacy to addictive behaviors and the relapse process began with nicotine addiction, then eating disorders and alcoholics.[6] DiClemente and associates stress that application of self-efficacy requires practitioners to view addictive behaviors from a biopsychosocial perspective. Prochaska and DiClemente conceptualized a typology of planned behavior change from (1) precontemplation, (2) contemplation, (3) action, and (4) maintenance common to smokers, drug abusers, people with eating disorders, and alcoholics.[7] A scale to measure alcohol abstinence self-efficacy[8] was developed and promising research efforts are now underway to expand the utility of this cognitive concept to relapse prevention in alcohol and substance abuse programs. No one can deny that new, innovative treatment methods are sorely needed. However, it *does* seem prudent to begin on a small scale and thoroughly evaluate the impact of new methods before allowing them to proliferate. Law-enforcement and treatment professionals are so desperate for ways to deal with the growing problems of abuse and addiction that it is understandable why they might be willing to use nontraditional methods. After all, the more traditional approaches have been successful with relatively few clients.

Policy Change

We proposed a number of policy changes in Chapter 8 that we will not repeat here. We will remind the reader, however, that we believe the national drug policy should be guided by the overall philosophy of minimizing risks both to the user and to the larger society. This does not necessarily mean that the government should legalize or decriminalize illicit drugs, although that option certainly should be given serious consideration. It does mean that the nation should do things such as expand methadone maintenance clinics and needle/syringe exchange programs. The AIDS crisis alone is enough to justify this change. On a less controversial level, why not require brewers and distillers to add vitamins and minerals to alcoholic beverages in order to prevent some of the nutritional problems associated with alcohol abuse?

Decriminalization should be seriously considered for another very practical reason. Americans run the risk of bankrupting the nation if drug offenders are continued to be incarcerated at the present rate. Current estimates of this country's war on drugs are as high as *$15 billion* a year, with two-thirds of these funds spent on criminal justice and interdiction and only one-third on treatment and prevention.[9] (For example, at the current rate of increase in drug-related prison admissions in Florida, everyone in the state will be incarcerated by the year 2021!) Not only is this an immense financial problem but it is also responsible for an overall increase in criminality and disrespect for society and its institutions. It is estimated that more that 1.5 million of U. S. citizens are incarcerated in state and federal prisons and local jails and more than 3 million more are court supervised. In 1994, one out of three black men between the ages of 20 and 29 were incarcerated or under court supervision, and drug-related offenses make up about 60 percent of all federal prisoners.[10] Cocaine users who spend a year or two in prison are much more likely to become involved in other criminal activity once they are returned to the community. In many states, people convicted of murder, armed robbery, and rape are being released from prison early to make room for the dramatic increase in drug offenders.

While so many people are being imprisoned for illicit drug use, the federal government continues to provide subsidies and price supports to tobacco farmers and to benefit from tax revenues on both tobacco and alcohol sales. Remember that tobacco alone kills more people each year than all illicit drugs combined! It is no surprise that many people fail to see any rationality or fairness in current policies.

Providing Services

Chemical dependency treatment services, especially those public programs available to low-income individuals, are woefully inadequate. The private tier of services are so expensive that they are generally unavailable to anyone except the wealthy or those fortunate enough to have adequate insurance. Current estimates indicate that as many as half of all Americans either have no health insurance or are seriously underinsured.[11] There does seem to be a widespread recognition that something must be done about the cost of services. One approach is to provide *managed care.* To see how this concept evolved, however, a review of the development of third-party coverage for chemical dependency is needed.

Third-Party Coverage

Early in its existence, the National Institute on Alcohol Abuse and Alcoholism (NIAAA) decided that health insurance for alcoholism was the best way to assure a stable funding base for treatment. State alcoholism agencies joined the effort, and by 1981, 33 states had mandated that group health insurance providers had to offer optional coverage for treatment. The federal Health Maintenance Organization Act of 1973 required all health maintenance organizations to provide alcoholism treatment services to qualify for federal subsidies.[12] By 1988, about 140 million Americans had specifically defined coverage for drug treatment in their health insurance plans. About 74 percent of full-time employees of medium-sized and large firms had this type of insurance coverage, as well as 94 percent of public employees.[13] By 1990, similar initiatives regarding drug abuse treatment had resulted in mandatory coverage laws in 18 states and the District of Columbia.[14] Growing numbers of employee assistance programs provided chemical dependency services.

In recent years, however, the high cost and the relative ineffectiveness of treatment for both alcohol and drug abuse have prompted insurers of all types to reconsider. It appears that the movement toward universal coverage of chemical dependency has leveled off or perhaps lost ground. Private coverage is likely to be optional, expensive, and more difficult to obtain. When private coverage is available, insurers are insisting on more effective and cheaper methods of treatment. Some third-party payers have strongly questioned the value of treatment, and there is a movement to view drug and alcohol treatment as part of the nonmedical/surgical fringe of health coverage that may be differentially limited to trim increasing overall costs.[15]

Managed Care

During the 1980s, there were serious attempts by managed-care companies to cut the costs of treating drug and alcohol abuse. Stimulated by the work of Miller and Hester[16] and Saxe and co-workers,[17] these companies attempted to direct all drug clients away from hospital-based inpatient programs toward outpatient services. The primary motivation for this movement was the evidence regarding the relative ineffectiveness and the greater expense of inpatient programs (see Chapter 6).

An important current trend is the merging of public and private sector care, with the collapsing of boundaries between public, not-for-profit, and for-profit agencies.[18] Managed care is generally provided in the context of a health maintenance organization (HMO), preferred provider organization (PPO), or independent practice association (IPA). Whatever the setting, the essence of managed care is attention to health care delivery and health care costs.[19]

The objective of managed-care strategies is to accumulate information about accepted clinical practices, their costs, and their appropriateness as treatment strategies. They attempt to generate knowledge to be used as protocols for permitting or disallowing reimbursement for particular services. Managed care uses strategies such as prospective certification or preadmission review of hospital stays, utilization review during or after discharge, the use of preferred providers who cooperate on "planned treatment" approaches, and specialized case management directed at cost containment.[20] It is thought that if managed-care strategies for drug and alcohol treatment are supported by adequate research on treatment effectiveness, they can ensure access to appropriate treatment while containing the costs.[21]

There are obviously many tensions between managed-care organizations and insurers, on the one hand, and residential treatment organizations (especially hospital-based programs), on the other. As discussed earlier, there is some evidence that treatment outcomes are related to length of treatment, and there is agreement that some clients need lengthy, inpatient services.[22] Legislation regarding managed care has focused primarily on cost containment and has not adequately dealt with its potential to compromise the quality of treatment.[23] Still, until service providers have evidence that the more expensive methods produce better outcomes, the cost-containment philosophies of managed-care organizations will be difficult to refute.

Summary and Concluding Thoughts

The stakes in the nation's war on drugs are enormously high. Generations of young people are at risk, not just for addiction, but for all the associated problems that go hand in hand with drug and alcohol abuse under current policies: AIDS, domestic violence, incarceration, and the inability to function economically and socially as normal citizens.

The current approaches to treating chemical dependency and substance abuse have not served the people well. We believe that a large part of the problem is that a systemic perspective in planning treatment strategies has not been used. Too frequently, drug or alcohol abuse has been considered an individual problem amenable to a clinical solution. Even the use of family therapy models is much too narrow a perspective for a problem of such magnitude. In many instances, symptoms of drug-taking behavior have been treated rather than the underlying causes of such behavior. If the United States has the most widespread abuse of alcohol and other drugs of any modern industrial society, it seems likely to be related to factors at the societal level. Realistic solutions must be planned and executed at the same level.

The country must start by shifting the emphasis from curing the disease of addiction to building personal capacities and increasing opportunities for alternatives in the workplace, in social relationships, within families and entire communities. As Elliott Currie said,

> When we fail to deal with the underlying social issues of inadequate work, poor housing, abusive families, and poor health care that shape most addicts' lives, we virtually ensure that drug treatment will become a revolving door. And what is truly expensive is cycling drug abusers from treatment to shattered and dismal lives and back again.[24]

The problems of drug abuse and dependency are of such a magnitude that new, dramatic intervention strategies are essential. The new strategies must use a systemic approach in dealing with these problems at the level of the client, the community, and the nation. The United States has reached the point where program failure is no longer acceptable. No new approach should be rejected without careful examination. The future of this nation is at stake.

Endnotes

1. H. A. Liddle and G. A. Dakof, "Efficacy of Family Therapy for Drug Abuse: Promising but Not definitive," *Journal of Marital and Family Therapy*, Vol. 21 (1995), p. 522.

2. T. D. Borkovec, "Psychotherapy Outcome Research," in L. Onken and J. Blaine (Eds.), *Psychotherapy and Counseling in the Treatment of Drug Abuse.* NIDA Research Monograph 104 (Washington, DC: U. S. Government Printing Office, 1990), p. 65.

3. Liddle and Dakof, "Efficacy of Family Therapy for Drug Abuse," p. 521.

4. Patrick Biernacki, *Recovery from Opiate Addiction without Treatment: A Summary.* Research Monograph 98 (Washington, DC: National Institute on Drug Abuse, 1990).

5. Carlo C. DiClemente. "Self-Efficacy and the Addictive Behaviors." *Journal of Social and Clinical Psychology*, Vol. 4 (1986), pp. 302–315.

6. C. C. DiClemente, S. K. Fairhurst, and N. A. Piotrowski, "The Role of Self-Efficacy in the Addictive Behaviors" in James Maddus (Ed.), *Self-Efficacy, Adaptation, and Adjustment: Theory, Research, and Application* (New York, Plenum Press, 1995).

7. J. O. Prochaska and C. C. DiClemente, "Stages of Change in the Modification of Problem Behaviors" in M. Hersen, R. M. Eisler, and P. M. Miller (Eds.), *Progress in Behavior Modification* (Sycamore, IL: Sycamore Publishing Company, 1992).

8. C. C. DiClemente, J. P. Carbonari, P. G. Rosario, and S. O. Hughes, "The Alcohol Abstinence Self-Efficacy Scale." *Journal of Studies on Alcohol*, Vol. 55 (1994), pp. 141–148.

9. Kurt Schmoke, Mayor, City of Baltimore, "Save Money, Cut Crime, Get Real," *Playboy* (January 1997), p. 128.

10. M. Joycelyn Elders, Former U. S. Surgeon General, *Ibid*, pp. 128, 191.

11. Speech by former Surgeon General C. Everett Koop at Florida State University, Tallahassee, FL, November 19, 1991.

12. Constance Weisner and Robin Room, "Financing and Ideology in Alcohol Treatment," in Maureen E. Kelleher, Bruce K. MacMurray, and Thomas M. Shapiro (Eds.), *Drugs and Society: A Critical Reader,* 2nd ed. (Dubuque, IA: Kendall/Hunt, 1988), pp. 360–378.

13. Dean R. Gerstein and Henrick R. Harwood (Eds.), *Treating Drug Problems,* Volume 1 (Washington, DC: National Academy Press, 1990).

14. *Ibid.*, p. 289.

15. *Ibid.*, p. 294.

16. William R. Miller and Reid K. Hester, "Inpatient Alcoholism Treatment: Who Benefits?" *American Psychologist*, Vol. 41 (1986), pp. 794–805.

17. Leonard M. Saxe, Denise M. Dougherty, K. Esty, and Michelle Fine, *The Effectiveness and Costs of Alcoholism Treatment*, Health Technology Case Study 22 (Washington, DC: Office of Technology Assessment, 1983).

18. Robert I. Paulson, "Swimming with the Sharks or Walking in the Garden of Eden," in Paul R. Raffoul and C. Aaron McNeece (Eds.), *Future Issues for Social Work Practice* (Boston: Allyn and Bacon, 1996), pp. 85–96.

19. Linda M. Richardson and Carol S. Austad, "Realities of Mental Health Practice in Managed-Care Settings," *Professional Psychology: Research and Practice*, Vol. 22, No. 1 (1991), pp. 52–59.

20. Lloyd I. Sederer and R. Lawrence St. Clair, "Quality Assurance and Managed Health Care," *Psychiatric Clinics of North America*, Vol. 13, No. 1 (March 1990), pp. 89–97.

21. Gerstein and Harwood, *Treating Drug Problems*, p. 286.

22. *Ibid.*, p. 135.

23. Russ Newman and Patricia M. Bricklin, "Parameters of Managed Mental Health Care: Legal, Ethical, and Professional Guidelines," *Professional Psychology Research and Practice*, Vol. 22, No. 1 (February 1991), pp. 26–35.

24. Elliott Currie, *Reckoning, Drugs, the Cities, and the American Future* (New York: Hill and Wang, 1993), p. 279.

Index

Abstainers, 10, 11, 13, 30, 260, 273, 274, 282–283, 291, 294, 367, 396, 410, 418

Abstinence (*also see* Sobriety), 6, 9, 30, 36, 40, 47, 48, 50, 58, 61, 83, 88, 112, 113, 115, 117, 118, 120, 126, 128, 129, 131, 132, 135, 136, 137, 140, 146–148, 150, 155, 205–206, 208, 209, 220, 221, 229, 230, 245, 274, 287, 325, 335, 351, 355, 356, 369, 372, 395, 400, 408, 410, 420, 422, 424, 425, 447

Abuse of alcohol and drugs, 1, 5–7, 65, 71, 72, 79, 221–222, 370, 373, 376, 377, 379, 391, 392, 393, 394, 395, 396–397, 399

Acculturation, 258–259, 282, 284–285, 289, 293–294, 300–301

Acetaldehyde, 27, 46, 154, 294

Acid (*also see* Lysergic acid diethylamide), 14, 59, 407

Acquired immune deficiency syndrome (AIDS) (*also see* Human Immunodeficiency Virus) 19, 57, 60, 149, 165, 172, 177, 182, 215, 275, 288, 322, 432, 447, 449

Acupuncture, 148–150

Addiction (*see* Chemical dependence)

Addiction Intervention with the Disabled, 374

Addiction Research Foundation, 376

Addiction Severity Index (ASI), 82, 83

Adolescents (*see* Youth)

Adult Children of Alcoholics (ACOAS), 197, 211, 230, 231, 235–237, 238–239

Advertising, 173–177, 280

Africa, 167, 260, 265, 269, 270

African Americans, 10, 11, 14, 19, 124, 150, 167, 182, 192, 198, 202, 255, 269–281, 284, 291, 326

    alcohol and drug use, 271–272, 274–275

    alcohol-related problems, 272, 275

    churches, 277

    cirrhosis, 270, 271

    demographic characteristics, 9–14, 375

    explanations of chemical abuse, 270–271

    and fetal alcohol syndrome, 415–416

    history of alcohol use, 269–270

    men, 14, 270, 271, 448

    prevention, 280

    self-help groups, 279, 280

    treatment, 275–276, 280

    women, 270, 272, 416, 431

    youth, 270, 277, 280, 284

African Methodist Episcopal (AME) Church, 277

Aging (*see* Elderly)

Al-Anon, 91, 99, 113, 156, 225, 230, 242, 244, 249, 288, 358

Alaskan Natives (*see also* Native Americans), 258, 259, 263

Alateen, 156, 216

Alatot, 138, 156, 216

Alcohol, 3, 4, 5, 6, 7, 8, 16, 18, 23, 36, 54, 58, 59, 62, 88, 133, 146, 148, 156, 167, 171, 172, 181, 182, 183, 195, 199, 204, 245, 284, 291, 349, 364, 368, 370, 371, 378, 391, 394, 396, 397, 398, 409, 445–446, 447

    abuse, 4, 5–7, 23, 26, 71, 79, 81, 165

    advertising, 173–177, 184–185

    behavioral effects, 45–51, 289

    cardiovascular system, 48

    cognitive impairment, 398–399, 422

    consumption, 3, 8, 11, 13, 26, 47, 48, 50, 77, 133, 155, 173, 176, 177, 185–189, 392, 394, 395, 397, 410, 416, 422

    and crime, 194–202, 288

    by demographic characteristics, 9–14

    dependence, 5, 6, 7, 23, 24, 25, 37, 79, 259

    digestive system, 47–48

    and domestic violence, 196, 197, 199–200, 264, 422–423, 430, 431

    endocrine system, 48–49

    epidemiology, 8–14

    ethyl (ethanol), 4, 27, 32, 39, 46

    fermentation, 4

    history of, 8–9

    inherited (heredity), 27, 28, 29

    metabolism, 46, 131, 259, 294, 408, 410, 412, 432

    methyl (methanol), 4

    minimum age of purchase, 184, 185–187, 191

    negative reinforcement, 25

    neurological effects, 49–50

Alcohol (continued)
  open container laws, 188
  physiological effects, 45–51, 172,
    398, 412–413
  and pregnancy (also see Fetal
    alcohol effects; Fetal alcohol
    syndrome), 61, 175–176,
    415–417
  prevention of use, 168–170
  pricing, 176, 177, 184, 185
  psychological effects, 172
  psychosis, 184, 266
  regulation, 68, 167–173
  reinforcement, 25
  related automobile accidents,
    184–190, 187–189, 265,
    370, 412
  related deaths, 3, 10, 170,
    174–176, 184, 188, 189,
    191, 194, 204, 205, 261,
    262, 271, 413
  related dementia, 398–399
  related economic problems, 3
  related health problems, 3, 44–50,
    184, 350, 392, 398
  related social problems, 3, 255,
    397
  religious use of, 181, 299
  reproductive system, 48–49
  taxes, 166, 176, 177, 181, 182,
    185, 186
  in television programming, 174,
    175
  tolerance, 6, 7, 31, 37, 43, 46, 47,
    392, 397
  and violence, 195–199, 269, 289
  withdrawal, 24, 25, 47, 78, 105,
    106, 107, 109
  and youth, 166, 170, 261, 262,
    267, 283, 299, 301
Alcohol dehydrogenase, 46
Alcohol Treatment Programs (ATP),
  361
Alcohol Use Disorders Identification
  Test (AUDIT), 70, 71, 72, 75
Alcoholic hallucinosis, 47, 49
Alcoholics (also see Alcoholism), 3, 6,
  7, 31, 37, 59, 131, 134, 135,
  150, 447
  children of, 7, 27, 156, 229, 230,
    231, 235, 237–238, 250,
    289, 364, 371, 373, 375,
    377
  recovering, 95, 106
Alcoholics Anonymous (AA), 6, 7,
  27, 37, 71, 99, 106, 107,
  113, 115, 116, 118, 128,
  137, 141, 149, 151–156,
  170, 217, 221, 224, 225,
  230, 244, 245, 263, 267,

  279, 288, 296, 301, 361,
  363, 373, 374, 375, 377,
  401, 407–408, 419, 420,
  422, 426–428
Alcoholics Together, 156, 304, 307,
  335, 339
Alcoholism (also see Chemical
  dependence), 1, 3, 4, 5, 8, 19,
  36, 39, 43, 120, 135, 174,
  175, 184, 215, 255, 257,
  259, 261, 294–300, 318,
  349, 361, 362, 373, 376,
  392, 393
  behavioral effects, 45–51
  etiology, 23–35, 410–412
  and gynecological problems, 412
  phases, 33, 35, 39
  physiological consequences, 45–51
  types, 28–29, 393, 411
  unitary concept, 32
Alcoholism Intervention for the Deaf
  (AID), 374
Aldehyde dehydrogenase (ALDH),
  294
Alkali Lake Indians, 263
Alpha alcoholics, 5
Alzheimer's disease, 398
American Association for Marriage
  and Family Therapy, 208
American Civil Liberties Union, 267
American Indians (see Native
  Americans)
American Medical Association
  (AMA), 267
American Psychiatric Association
  (APA) 6, 78–82, 318, 429
American Psychological Association,
  318
American Sign Language (ASL), 374,
  375
American Society of Addiction
  Medicine, 125
Americans with Disabilities Act
  (ADA) of 1990, 212, 348,
  349, 375
Amphetamines (also see Central
  nervous system, stimulants),
  17, 52, 53–55, 56, 119, 201,
  297, 351–352, 416
  and alcohol use, 54
  behavioral effects, 53–54
  and pregnancy, 62, 373, 416
  psychosis, 53, 54
  and violence, 196
  withdrawal, 54
Amylnitrite ("snappers," "poppers"),
  60, 321, 414
Anadarko Indians, 260
Analgesics, 47, 379, 409
Anglos (see Whites)

Antabuse (disulfiram), 123, 124,
  131–132, 133, 134, 135,
  172, 400
Anticholinergic drugs, 396
Antidepressant drugs, 357, 396
Anti-Drug Abuse Act, 204, 263
Antihistamines, 396
Antipsychotic drugs, 357, 396
Anti-Saloon League, 9
Antislavery Movement, 269
Antisocial personality disorder (see
  Personality disorders)
Anxiety, 4, 17, 25, 42, 47, 49, 53,
  54, 79, 121, 134, 214, 247,
  259, 321, 355, 366, 377,
  395, 422, 429
Apnea, 56
Arabs, 19, 181
Arrests (see Crime)
Arthritis, 377
Asia (see also China; Japan), 10, 55,
  156, 181, 201, 255, 283,
  290, 294
Asian Americans, 11, 145, 240,
  290–292
  alcohol and drug use, 291–292
  flushing response, 294
  men, 291–292
  self-help, 295
  sociocultural influences, 290,
    293–294
  treatment, 295–296
  women, 272, 291
  youth, 292
Asian Indians, 290
Aspirin, 59, 132
Assessment, 67, 69, 70, 78, 82–90,
  96, 98, 99, 100, 105, 110,
  121, 138, 146, 213, 248,
  256, 375, 377
  biopsychosocial approach, 70,
    82–90, 397–399
  of elderly persons, 397–399
  family, 230
  of those with mental illness, 239,
    244, 350, 357
  of those with mental retardation,
    363
  of those with traumatic head
    injury, 222, 372
  of youth, 214, 216
Association for Retarded Citizens
  (ARC), 361
Asthma, 59
Australia, 417
Aversion treatment, 141, 142

Barbiturates, 4, 17, 18, 54, 56–57,
  58, 245, 292, 294, 352, 414
  and alcohol use, 56

and pregnancy, 62
  withdrawal, 56–57, 107
Basin Indian Tribe, 262
Beer, 171, 174, 181, 187, 188, 242, 257, 369
  taxes on (*also see* Alcohol, taxes), 183
Benzedrine inhaler, 17
Benzodiazepines, 4, 18, 98, 352, 414
  and pregnancy, 62
Beta alcoholics, 5, 6
Bible, 61, 257, 415
Binge drinking, 11, 12, 107, 229
  and Native Americans, 257, 259, 260
Biofeedback, 148, 150
Bipolar disorder, 75, 79, 82, 353, 399
Blackouts, 37, 38, 87, 407
Blacks (*see* African Americans)
Blood alcohol concentration (BAC) or blood alcohol levels (BAL), 46, 47, 49, 87, 135, 146, 187, 188, 409, 412
Boerhaave's syndrome, 47
Bolivia, 285
Braille, 377
Brain disorders, 27, 49–50, 370–373, 398
Breathalyzer, 87, 189, 401
Brief MAST, 71, 76, 372
Brief Psychiatric Rating Scale (BPRS), 351
Britain (England), 18, 117, 148, 176, 181, 183, 191, 199, 255
British Road Safety Act of 1967, 188
  Dangerous Drug Act, 193
Buprenorphine, 134, 135
Bureau of Indian Affairs, 264–265
Bush, George, 185, 190

Caddo Indians, 260
Caffeine, 4, 17, 181, 183, 351, 396
  and pregnancy, 62
CAGE Questionnaire, 70–71, 76, 335, 350, 372, 398, 431
California Civil Addict Program, 203
Canada, 117, 148, 156, 201, 367, 409, 421
Cancer, 47, 50, 51, 180, 271, 338
Cannabis (*see* Marijuana)
Cardiovascular disease, 45, 48, 398
Cardiovascular system, 48
Care management (*see* Case management)
Caribbean, 253
Case management, 116, 138–139, 226, 355, 357, 364, 400, 401, 425, 449
Caucasians (*see* Whites)
Centers for Disease Control, 60

Central America, 253, 260
Central nervous system (CNS), 4, 7, 19, 42, 46, 49, 57, 61, 415
  depressants (sedatives), 4 17, 45, 47, 54, 56, 57, 60, 88, 107, 196, 352, 396, 409, 414
  stimulants, 4, 17–18, 19, 52–56, 255, 352, 409, 414, 425
Chemical dependence, 1, 5, 6, 7, 20, 27, 32, 36–44, 45–66, 104, 182, 196, 214, 215, 222, 230, 255–256, 271, 284, 287, 295–298, 300–302, 392, 393, 397, 410, 428, 447, 449–450
  behavioral effects, 45–66
  definitions, 4–8, 20, 23, 24, 67, 354
  diagnosis, 4, 6, 69, 77–82, 88, 100, 138, 243, 246, 267, 350, 371
  and other disabilities, 347–380
  disease model, 1, 4, 5, 6, 7, 8, 20, 27, 31, 36, 39, 43, 201, 216, 230, 231, 318, 449
  drift, 37, 40, 43
  among the elderly, 391, 405
  epidemiology, 8–19
  among ethnic groups, 255–317
  etiology, 1, 23–35, 213, 214, 446
  and the family, 229–284
  among gay men and lesbians, 318–346
  physiological effects, 40, 41, 45–66, 67, 398
  prevention of, 166–170
  process of becoming chemically dependent, 36–44
  psychological effects, 1, 40, 41, 45–66, 67
  public health model, 32
  screening for, 70–75
  systems perspective, 25, 95, 138, 139, 197
  treatment, 104–165, 266, 275–276
  unitary concept, 83
  among women, 406–442
  among youth, 213–228, 267
Cherokee Indians, 260
Cheyenne-Arapaho Indians, 260
Chickasaw Indians, 260
Child abuse and neglect, 89, 97, 98, 196, 200, 239, 264, 417
Child Protective Services (CPS), 98
Children (*see* Youth)
Children of alcoholics (COAs), 7, 27, 156, 229, 230, 235, 237–238, 250, 281, 289
Children of Alcoholics Foundation, 229

China, 8, 19, 290–291
Chinese, 51, 148, 201, 290–291, 297
Chinese Americans, 11, 290, 291–294
"Chipping," 146
Church (*see* Religion)
Cigarettes (*see* Nicotine)
Cirrhosis, 7, 10, 11, 47, 176, 181, 255, 260, 262, 269, 271, 292
Civil commitment, 108, 203
Client Oriented Data Acquisition Process (CODAP), 261
Clinton, Bill, 191
Coalcoholic (*see* Codependency)
Coastal Salish Indians, 267
Coca (*also see* Cocaine), 16, 48, 52, 182, 191
Coca-Cola Company, 17, 173, 182
Cocaine, 4, 15, 16–17, 19, 36, 39, 41, 43, 45, 52, 53, 54, 55, 56, 59, 78, 124, 126, 133, 134, 149, 150, 151, 181, 183, 187, 188, 189, 190, 191–195, 198, 199, 201, 202, 245, 271, 274, 283–284, 351, 371, 373, 378, 407, 409, 414, 422, 425, 432, 445, 446, 448
  behavioral effects, 52, 53
  and crime, 182, 195–197
  and gynecological problems, 412, 414–417, 431
  physiological effects, 52–53
  and pregnancy, 53, 62, 416
  withdrawal, 52
Cocaine Abuse Assessment Profile (CAAP), 91
Cocaine Anonymous, 156
Codeine, 4, 19, 57, 235–237
Codependency, 113, 197, 211, 230, 235–239, 249, 250, 287, 331
Co-dependents Anonymous (CODA), 231
Coffee (*see* Caffeine)
Colombia, 176, 202
Commonwealth of Independent States (CIS), 181, 186, 255
Community Oriented Program Environments Scale, 118
Comorbidity (*see* Dual diagnosis)
Comprehensive Alcohol Abuse and Alcoholism Prevention, Treatment and Rehabilitation Act of 1970, 105, 262
Confidentiality, 67, 70, 77, 96–98, 111, 374
Confrontation, 92, 93–96, 118, 130, 248, 351, 352, 358, 362

Confucianism, 290, 293
Congeners, 4, 27
Controlled drinking, 146–148, 400
Cork Institute on Black Alcohol and
    Drug Abuse, 279
Crack (also see Cocaine), 17, 43, 52, 53,
    55, 62, 147–148, 149, 150,
    182, 199, 201, 202, 271,
    274, 283, 353, 409, 421, 445
    and pregnancy, 416
Crank, 54
Cravings, 40, 134, 135, 149, 447
Creek Indians, 245
Crime, 143, 166, 180, 192–205,
    255, 271, 287, 364, 373,
    420–421, 448
    organized, 184–201, 202
    Uniform Crime Reports, 197
    victims, 199
Crisis lines, 91, 108
Cuba, 281–283
Cuban Americans, 281–283, 285
Culture, 4, 11, 24, 29–33, 37, 58,
    71, 89, 107, 167, 181, 193,
    196, 197, 204, 205, 231,
    255–317, 432
Cyclazocine, 172

Danshukai (a version of AA), 296
D.A.R.E., 68
Darvon, 3
Date-rape drug, 19, 56–57
Day Top Village, 118
Day treatment, 114–115, 124, 357,
    401
Decompensating, 352
Decriminalization (also see
    Legalization), 8, 67
    of illicit drug use, 191, 193, 445,
    447, 448
    of public intoxication, 105
Defense mechanisms (also see Denial),
    90–91
Deinstitutionalization, 89, 359, 360
Delirium tremens, 47, 56, 69, 87,
    106, 108, 131
Delta alcoholics, 5
Dementia, 6, 50, 398
Denial, 39, 40, 67, 70, 75, 90–92,
    100, 118, 236, 240, 246,
    247, 248, 328, 339, 351,
    352, 353, 372, 392, 397,
    419, 431
Department of Justice, 154
Department of Veteran Affairs, 143
Depression, 10, 17, 39, 40, 42, 49,
    52, 53, 54, 55, 60, 75, 79,
    108, 121, 134, 150, 271,
    283–284, 349, 351, 352,
    355, 367, 369, 396, 399,

408, 415, 418, 421, 422,
    426, 430, 447
Detoxification, 27, 67, 87, 104–109,
    111, 117, 126–127, 131,
    132, 144, 148, 149, 150,
    243, 248, 355, 361, 400, 446
    inpatient, 104, 105–108
    outpatient, 104, 105, 108
Detoxification centers, 89, 104–109,
    146, 276, 363, 379, 446
    funding, 120
    using acupuncture, 148, 150
Developmental Disabilities Assistance
    and Bill of Rights Act
    Amendments of 1994, 359
Diabetes, 39, 50, 58, 86, 131, 348,
    366, 376, 377, 378
Diagnosis, 4, 24, 67, 69, 70, 77–82,
    88, 100, 110, 111, 128, 138,
    243, 246, 350, 371, 392,
    396, 399
    American Psychiatric Association,
        78–81
    and cultural issues, 242
    National Council on Alcoholism
        and Drug Dependence, 78–79
    of Native Americans, 247
    primary, 79, 82
    secondary, 79, 82
    World Health Organization, 78–81
    of youth, 213, 222, 224
Diagnostic and Statistical Manual of
    Mental Disorders, 6, 7, 10, 24,
    26, 78–81, 82, 217, 221,
    318, 349, 351, 392, 393,
    396, 397, 399, 429
Diazepam (see Benzodiazepines)
Diet pills (also see Central nervous
    system, stimulants), 17
Digestive system, 46, 47–48, 58
Dilaudin, 57
Dipipanone, 4
Distilled spirits, 181, 187, 255
Disulfiram, 131–132, 135, 136, 154
Domestic violence, 87, 196, 199,
    200, 264, 422–423, 430,
    431, 449
Domiciliaries, 119, 351
Dominicans, 284
Dopamine, 28, 352
Double Trouble, 358
Dramshop laws, 189, 190
Drinamyl, 17
Driving under the influence (DUI)
    (also see Drunk driving), 71,
    86, 87, 138, 150, 154, 159,
    160, 187, 272, 254
Driving while intoxicated (DWI) (also
    see Drunk driving), 86, 87,
    122, 138, 149, 188, 300, 418

Drug Abuse Reporting Program,
    (DARP), 125
Drug Abuse Resistance Education
    (D.A.R.E.), 68
Drug Abuse Screening Test (DAST),
    70, 71
Drug Abuse Warning Network
    (DAWN), 413
Drug testing (also see Urinalysis),
    180, 188, 189, 196, 202,
    203, 351
Drug Use Forecasting (DUF) program,
    420
Drug Use Screening Inventory-
    Revised (DUSI-R), 82
Drugs (also see drugs by specific
    names; Abuse of alcohol and
    drugs; Chemical dependence
    overdose, 413
    patterns of use, 182
Drunk driving (also see Driving under
    the influence; Driving while
    intoxicated), 160, 173–177,
    183, 257
Dual diagnosis, 71, 79, 86, 88, 100,
    105, 156, 214, 217, 223,
    347–390, 447
    diagnosis of, 349
    hearing impairments and
        substance abuse, 348,
        373–376
    mental illness and substance
        abuse, 328, 348, 349–359
    mobility impairments and
        substance abuse, 348,
        366–370
    other physical impairments and
        substance abuse, 377–379
    self-help groups, 334, 358–359,
        363, 375
    traumatic brain/head injury and
        substance abuse, 348,
        370–373
    treatment of, 352–359, 362–363
    visual impairments and substance
        abuse, 348, 376–377
Dual Recovery Anonymous, 358
Dutch, 9, 193
Dysphoria, 352

Ecstasy, 55
Ego defenses (also see Denial), 90–91
Egypt, 8, 41
Eisenhower Circle Group, 358
Elderly, 10, 11, 198, 391–405
    abuse of, 97
    alcohol and drug use, 352–355,
        391–393, 396–397, 399
    alcoholism, onset of, 393–396,
        400

assessment of, 397, 399
case finding, 399–400
life expectancy, 212
losses of, 394, 399
marijuana use, 14
men, 392, 393, 394–395, 399,
    401, 402
models of alcohol abuse among,
    393–396
psychologic/psychosocial
    problems, 212, 394–396
retirement, 394
socioculture, 393–394
suicide, 399
treatment, 400, 402
women, 392, 393, 394, 399, 401,
    402
Emotional abuse, 89
Emotions Anonymous (EA), 358,
    363, 366
Employee assistance programs
    (EAPs), 85, 115, 121, 191,
    254, 432, 448
Employment discrimination, 348
Empowerment, 221, 224, 226, 257
Enabling, 94, 98, 235, 243, 358,
    365, 376
Endocrine system, 48–49, 58
Endorphins, 30, 134, 148
Epidemiologic Catchment Area (ECA)
    program, 271–272, 278,
    349, 377, 392, 393
Epidemiology, 8–19
Epilepsy, 59, 62, 86, 131, 378, 379
Epsilon alcoholics, 5, 348
Eskimos, 271
Ethnicity (also see culture-specific
    ethnic groups), 76, 89, 152,
    192, 193, 197, 201, 202,
    211, 255–317, 328
Etiology of chemical dependence, 8,
    23–35, 67, 79, 141, 157,
    163, 214, 229–239, 230
    alternative explanations, 31–32
    biologic theories, 27–29, 215
        biochemical, 27
        brain dysfunction, 27
        enzymes, 28
        genetic, 27–28, 244, 269,
            270–271, 276, 410–412
        vitamin deficiencies, 28
    culture-specific, 30–31
    environment, 28, 31, 41
    family dynamics, 229–239
    moral model, 1, 24, 32, 230, 262
    multicausal model, 1, 32
    among Native Americans, 244
    psychologic theories, 24–27
        cognitive-behavioral, 24–25
        learning, 25

personality, 26–27
psychodynamic, 25–26
sociocultural theories (see also
    Culture; Ethnicity) 29–31, 33
subcultural, 31, 196, 197
supracultural, 30
Europe, 10, 15, 16, 19, 156, 181,
    255, 281

Family, 5, 28, 37, 88–90, 113, 120,
    197, 214, 215, 218–220,
    221, 285–286, 302, 446,
    449
    assessment, 222, 229–254
    behavioral model, 229, 231
    education, 216, 219, 240
    psychoeducation, 243, 247
    rituals and routines, 232–233,
        238, 243
    roles, 235
    rules, 235
    shame, 234–235
    treatment, 100, 123, 137,
        221–222, 223–226,
        229–254
        behavioral, 231, 240–241, 250
        family therapy perspective,
            242–244, 250
        stress-coping model, 221, 229,
            231–232, 242, 280
        systems theory, 211, 221, 229,
            232–235, 242, 250
    violence, 87, 196–197, 199, 200
Fermentation, 4
Fetal alcohol effects (FAE), 48, 274,
    415–416
Fetal alcohol syndrome (FAS), 48, 61,
    268, 359, 415–416
    among African Americans, 416
    among Native Americans, 262
        416
Filipino Americans, 9, 290–293
Filipinos, 290–291
Finland, 164, 170, 419
    Alcohol Act of 1969, 170
Flashbacks, 59, 60
Flushing response, 131, 270–271
Fly agaric, 59
Food and Drug Administration, 17,
    132, 133, 134, 397
France, 30, 61
Freebasing, 52, 53
French, 30, 47, 255
Freud, Sigmund, 17, 25

Gallaudet College, 373, 375
Gamma alcoholics, 147
Gangs, 201, 202
Gastritis, 47, 86, 103
Gay adult children of alcoholics, 331

Gay Al-Anon, 301
Gay Alcoholics Anonymous, 156,
    334–337
Gay men, 197, 318–346, 423
    alcohol and drug use, 318–323
    explanations of, 323–327
    prevention of alcohol abuse, 327
    rights of, 212
    and self-help groups, 99, 134, 152,
        301, 335–338
    and treatment, 121, 122, 212,
        328–333
    youth, 297
Gayellow Pages, 338
Gender (also see Men; Women), 10,
    31, 198, 406–442, 446
    bias, 232, 237, 397
    and codependency, 222
    and crime, 198, 199, 420–421
    and prevention of drug abuse, 168
    and treatment, 122
General Health and History
    Questionnaire, 372
Genetics, 27, 29, 32, 51, 92, 259,
    301, 410–412
Genitourinary system, 58
German Americans, 11, 256
Germany, 53, 181, 255
Gestalt therapy, 141
Glaucoma, 376
Good Chemistry Groups, 354, 355,
    357, 358, 359
Gout, 377
Greece, 8
Group Against Smoking Pollution
    (GASP), 166

Haitians, 188
Halfway houses, 92, 107, 115, 117,
    119, 120
Hallucinations, 25, 51, 52, 57, 60,
    79, 87, 352, 356
Hallucinogens, 14, 58–60, 108, 242,
    257, 274, 283–284, 321,
    351, 352, 368, 409, 425
    and pregnancy, 62
    and religious use, 164
Harrison Act, 17, 19, 155, 182, 191,
    192
Hashish (also see Marijuana), 41, 51,
    371, 407
Hawaiians, 11, 41, 268–269, 292
Health Maintenance Organization
    Act of 1973, 448
Health maintenance organizations
    (HMOs), 99, 109, 110–112,
    121, 143, 448–449
Hearing impairments, 373–376
Hepatic dysfunction (also see
    Cirrhosis; Liver), 45

Hepatitis, 47, 50, 53, 57, 149, 182
Heroin, 4, 19, 29, 30, 31, 36–37,
    40–41, 43, 51, 53, 56, 57,
    118, 132, 133, 134, 135,
    146, 148, 150, 181, 182,
    183, 193, 194, 198, 199,
    246, 256, 261, 271, 282,
    368, 373, 420, 421, 446
  and crime, 183–185, 198–199,
    201
  and pregnancy, 61, 416
  "rush," 57
  withdrawal, 25, 40–41, 56, 107
Hispanic Americans (also see Cuban
    Americans; Mexican
    Americans; Puerto Rican
    Americans), 11, 145, 182,
    201, 202, 255–256,
    273–275, 280, 281–285,
    287–289, 290, 326
  alcohol and drug problems,
    281–284
  education, 287
  men, 263, 281, 286
  prevention, 287–288
  and self-help groups, 99
  treatment, 262, 264–266
  women, 273, 282, 286, 289
  youth, 265, 266, 274, 281
Holocaust, 297, 301
Homelessness, 85, 108, 119, 120,
    139, 354, 355, 356, 393
Homicide, 3, 11, 271
Homosexuals (also see Gay men;
    Lesbians), 60, 79, 318–346
Hong Kong, 201, 290
Hopi Indians, 245, 260
Hormones, 48, 412, 414
Hughes Act, 105, 262
Human immunodeficiency virus
    (HIV) (also see Acquired
    immune deficiency
    syndrome), 19, 53, 139, 214,
    288, 298, 319, 327
Hypertension, 48, 52, 54, 366, 398
Hypoglycemia, 49, 50, 58, 377

"Ice" (crystal methamphetamine),
    17–18, 55, 445
  and violence, 200
Immune system, 50, 51, 55, 60, 398
Incas, 16
Index of Drug Involvement, 71
India, 8, 19, 41, 181–183, 255
Indian Health Services (IHS),
    262–263, 268
Indians, American (see Native
    Americans)
Indonesia, 267

Inhalants, 4, 31, 60, 173, 261, 284,
    351, 409
  and pregnancy, 62
Institute on Black Chemical Abuse,
    259
Institute of Medicine, 132, 423, 426
Insurance coverage, 90, 99, 106,
    109, 113, 121, 143–145,
    176, 217–218, 223, 372,
    425, 446, 448
Integument, 58
International Classification of
    Diseases (ICD), 79–81
Internet, 402
Intervention, 240, 248, 302
  implications, 211
Intoxication, 6, 7, 46, 49, 56,
    126–127, 229, 231, 269,
    377, 379, 412
Intravenous drug use, 133, 139,
    160, 172, 173, 177, 181,
    182, 215, 293
Ireland, 181
Irish, 30–31, 255
Irish Americans, 11, 300
Isobutyl nitrite, 60, 321, 414
Israel, 297–298
Israeli Department of Prevention and
    Treatment of Alcoholism, 298
Israeli Society for the Prevention of
    Alcoholism, 298
Italian Americans, 11
Italians, 30, 255, 300, 275

JACS Foundation, 301
Jamaica, 183
Jamaicans, 201
Japan, 53, 201, 267
Japanese Americans, 290–291, 293,
    294
Jellinek, E. M., 5, 6, 10, 37–39, 40,
    79, 215
Jewish Americans, 255, 299–300
  alcohol and drug use, 299–300
  explanations of drinking and drug
    taking, 274–275
  prevention, 275–276
  self-help programs, 276
  treatment, 275–276
  women, 274
Jews, 11, 30–31, 255, 297–301
Juvenile delinquency, 197, 205, 219,
    223

Kant, Immanuel, 297, 299
Kaposi's sarcoma, 60
Keller's law, 26
Khat, 4
Koran, 16

Korea, 409
Korean Americans, 11, 291, 296
Korsakoff's psychosis, 7, 49, 50
Ku Klux Klan, 269

LAAM, 133, 135
Latin America, 16, 201
Latinos (see Hispanic Americans)
Laudanum, 19, 57
Law enforcement, 148, 188–189,
    190, 205, 447
Legalization (see also
    Decriminalization), 180–181,
    191–195, 398, 445, 447
Lesbians, 197, 318–346, 423
  alcohol and drug use, 318–323
  explanations of, 323–327
  oppression, 211
  prevention of substance abuse,
    327
  rights of, 212
  and self-help groups, 99, 152,
    331–333, 335–338
  and treatment, 122, 328–335
  youth, 326
Levo-alpha-acetylmethadol,
    (LAAM), 133, 135
Librium, 107
Liver (also see Cirrhosis), 46, 47, 51,
    54, 398, 416
Liver disease, 48, 60, 261, 377, 412,
    420, 430
LSD (see Lysergic acid diethylamide)
Lysergic acid diethylamide (LSD), 4,
    14, 18, 27, 30, 407
  and pregnancy, 59–60, 62

MacAndrew Alcoholism Scale, 75,
    77, 370
"Machismo," 175, 286–287
MADD, 166, 188
Malaysia, 30, 267
Mallory-Weiss syndrome, 47
Managed care (also see Insurance
    coverage), 68, 109, 110–112,
    143, 217, 218, 448, 449
Mandrax, 18
Mann, Marty, 37
Marijuana, 4, 14, 15, 16, 24, 41–43,
    51, 52, 55, 56, 146, 181,
    191, 192, 193, 195, 199,
    201, 205, 219, 245, 261,
    274, 283, 290, 297–298,
    316, 321, 351, 360, 378,
    379, 407, 409, 414, 420,
    425
  ceremonial use of, 181
  and gynecological problems, 414
  legalization of, 181, 193, 194

physiological effects, 51–52
and pregnancy, 62, 416
price of, 176–177
psychological effects, 51–52
regulation of, 173
withdrawal, 41–42
Marijuana Tax Act, 159, 173, 177,
    183
Mayas, 15
Medicaid, 99, 143–145, 362
Medicare, 99, 143
Mediterranean, 255
Men, 9–10, 12, 20, 189, 276,
    406–442, 447
  alcohol-related deaths, 413
  alcohol use, 29, 31
  cardiovascular disease, 48
  cirrhosis, 47
  and crime, 183–184, 420–421
  endocrine problems, 48
  etiology of alcoholism, 410–412
  hallucinogens, 14
  heroin use, 19
  marijuana use, 14
  nicotine use, 16
  osteoporosis, 50
  and recovery, 379, 422, 423
  research, 382, 447
  sedative use, 18
  and self-help groups, 99, 152, 155
  sexual dysfunction, 52, 413–414
  stimulant use, 18
  suicide, 399, 413
  treatment of, 230
Menninger, Karl, 248
Mental illness (disorders), 8, 18, 51,
    71, 75, 79, 88, 89, 98, 105,
    106, 108, 110, 114, 119,
    127, 131, 140, 156, 197,
    212, 214, 216, 220, 237,
    271, 349, 394, 399, 418,
    422, 429, 430, 447
Mental retardation, 61, 156, 347,
    359–366, 379, 415
Mescaline, 4, 14, 59
Metabolism, 27, 39
  of alcohol, 46, 131, 408, 410,
    412, 433
Methadone (also see Treatment), 4,
    18, 107, 124, 132–133, 134,
    135, 139, 150–151, 154
  methamphetamines (also see
    "Ice"), 4, 54, 55–56
  and pregnancy, 416
Methaqualone, 18, 56
  withdrawal, 56
Methylphenidate, 18
Mexican Americans, 11, 122, 256,
    281, 282–286, 289

Mexicans, 281
Mexico, 14, 59, 201, 255, 260, 407
Michigan Alcoholism Screening Test
    (MAST), 70–72, 75, 293,
    350, 355, 378, 431
Michigan Alcoholism Screening Test-
    Geriatric Version (MAST-G),
    397
Middle East, 19, 181
Minnesota model intensive treatment
    programs, 113, 114, 248,
    266
Minnesota Multiphasic Personality
    Inventory (MMPI), 26, 75
Minorities (see Culture; Ethnicity)
Missions, 108, 119–120
Moderated drinking, 146–148, 400
Moderation Management, 148
Morphine, 19, 29, 57–58
Mothers Against Drunk Driving
    (MADD), 166, 188
Mythology, 8, 257

Naloxone, 134, 172
Naltrexone, 134, 135, 136, 141, 172
Naranon, 99, 113, 156, 358
Narcotic antagonists, 154
Narcotics (also see Opiates), 18, 19,
    32, 46, 47, 57–58, 61, 122,
    132, 133, 134, 146, 182,
    193, 287, 290–291, 414,
    420
Narcotics Anonymous (NA), 99, 116,
    119, 151, 156, 336, 373
National Academy of Sciences, 26
National Acupuncture Detoxification
    Association, 149
National Alcohol Survey, 272, 281
National Alliance for the Mentally Ill
    (NAMI), 358
National Association on Alcohol,
    Drugs and Disability, 379
National Association of Broadcasters,
    175
National Association for Children of
    Alcoholics, 216
National Association of Lesbian and
    Gay Alcoholism Professionals
    (NALGAP), 306, 307
National Center for American Indian
    and Alaska Native Mental
    Health Research, 263
National Center for Health Statistics,
    291–292
National Center for Youth with
    Disabilities, 379
National Clearinghouse for Alcohol
    and Drug Information
    (NCADI), 379

National Council on Alcoholism and
    Drug Abuse (NCADD), 6,
    78–79, 82
National Council on Crime and
    Delinquency, 202
National Drug and Alcoholism
    Treatment Utilization Survey,
    276, 426
National Head Injury Foundation,
    372, 375
National Health Interview Survey,
    10, 291
National Household Survey on Drug
    Abuse, 15, 17, 273–274,
    283, 409, 410
National Institute on Aging, 392
National Institute on Alcohol Abuse
    and Alcoholism (NIAAA), 10,
    75, 98, 114, 124, 125, 128,
    137, 141, 146, 147, 260,
    262, 347, 348, 374, 401,
    425, 429, 430, 432, 448
National Institute on Drug Abuse
    (NIDA), 14, 18, 19, 98, 139,
    416, 425, 429, 430, 432
National Institute of Justice, 420
National Institute of Mental Health
    (NIMH) (see Epidemiologic
    Catchment Area program)
National Lesbian and Gay Health
    Foundation, 338
National Longitudinal Alcohol
    Epidemiological Survey, 10,
    349, 432
Native American Church (NAC), 29,
    164, 266
Native Americans (also see specific
    tribes), 11, 14, 15, 29, 145,
    181, 255–268, 271, 272,
    283, 285, 288, 296, 392,
    416
  alcohol-related mortality, 260, 301
  alcohol-related problems,
    257–279
  etiology of substance abuse, 257
  fetal alcohol syndrome, 61, 262,
    415–416
  firewater myth, 257
  history of alcohol and drug use,
    257–258
  liver disease, 11, 260–261
  men, 261
  prevention, 260
  and self-help groups, 266
  treatment, 246–249, 262–267
  women, 246
  youth, 243, 246, 247, 249, 262,
    301
Navajo Indians, 261, 262, 416

Needle exchange program, 447
Netherlands, 191, 193, 255, 417
Neuritis, 131
Neurologic system, 49–50
Neurotransmitters (*also see* specific
  neurotransmitters), 27, 42, 49
Nicotine, 3, 4, 7, 14, 16, 36, 43, 154,
  181, 183, 191, 194, 204,
  256, 284, 297, 351, 352,
  445, 447, 448
  advertising, 173, 176
  minimum age of purchase, 165,
    175
  and pregnancy, 61, 175
  prevention of use, 166–177, 184
  pricing, 176
  taxes, 176, 177
Nixon, Richard, 192
Norway, 148, 181
Nutrition (and malnutrition), 47, 50,
  54, 105, 106, 177, 200, 201,
  401, 447, 448

Odyssey House, 118
Opiates (*also see* Opium; specific
  opiate drugs), 4, 19, 43, 59,
  57–58, 132, 134, 135, 172,
  190, 191, 203, 297, 316,
  352, 375, 420, 446, 447
  and crime, 185
  and pregnancy, 61
  regulation of, 173
  withdrawal, 58, 134, 172
Opium, 3, 19, 57, 182, 191, 267,
  290
Organic brain syndrome, 377
Over-the-counter (OTC) drugs, 3, 86,
  113, 396, 397, 429

Pacific Islanders, 290
Pakistan, 187
Pancreatitis, 7, 47, 48, 69, 413
Paraldehyde, 181
Paranoia, 352
Paregoric, 57
Partial hospitalization, 114
PCP ("angel dust"), 14, 196, 261,
  378
  and pregnancy, 416
  and violence, 181
Personality disorders, 26, 28, 75, 79,
  88, 127, 200, 349, 352, 353,
  371, 422
Personality factors and drug use,
  26–27
Peru, 16, 201, 285
Pethidine, 4
Peyote, 14, 29, 59, 164, 181, 257,
  266, 407

Phencyclidine, 14
Phenobarbital, 57, 107
Physical abuse, 89, 121, 360,
  421–422, 425
Physical disabilities (*also see* specific
  disabilities), 86, 98, 197
Plains Indians, 262, 416
Polydrug use, 149, 156, 199, 352,
  425, 429
Pregnancy, 60–62, 131
  and alcohol use, 61, 158,
    415–417
  and drug use, 61–62, 416–417
Preludin, 4
Prevention, 67, 145, 163, 166–179,
  184, 185–193, 198, 218
  and adults, 168
  among African Americans, 259
  demand reduction, 168
  early drug education, 219
  economic measures, 68, 168,
    176–177
  among ethnic groups, 256
  among gay men and lesbians, 298
  harm-reduction approach, 167,
    177, 191
  among Hispanic Americans,
    265–266
  implications, 211
  legislative and regulatory
    measures, 68, 167, 173–176
  among Native Americans, 249
  public health model, 167
  public information and education,
    68, 168–170, 177
  service measures, 68, 170–171
  technologic measures, 68, 167,
    171–173
  and youth, 166–170, 203, 205,
    218–221, 375
  zero tolerance approach, 167, 190
Pride Institute, 332, 338
Privileged communication, 97
Probation and parole, 86, 92, 100,
  106, 108, 132, 171, 188,
  202–204
Problem drinking, 5, 9, 10, 29–31,
  368, 378, 392
Prohibition Amendment of 1917
  (18th Amendment), 9, 167,
  173, 176, 230, 257, 391,
  392, 445
Prostitution, 264, 420–421
Psilocybin ("magic mushrooms"), 4,
  14, 59
Psychasthenia, 352
Psychedelic drugs (*see* Hallucinogens)
Psychiatric problems (*see* Mental
  illness)

Psychoactive substance abuse
  disorders (*also see* Alcohol;
  drugs by name), 6, 409, 410,
  426
Psychopathy, 352
Psychosis, 131, 271, 350, 351, 355
  alcoholic, 184, 266
  amphetamine, 53–55
  and "ice," 55
Psychotherapy, 141, 142, 146, 151,
  446
Psychotropic medications, 351, 352,
  354, 356, 357
Public information, 68
Public intoxication, 87, 105, 361,
  379
Public policy (*see* Regulation of
  alcohol and other drugs)
Pueblo Indians, 246, 416
Puerto Rican Americans, 260–261,
  264, 265
Puerto Ricans, 282, 284
Puerto Rico, 409

Quaaludes, 18, 56
Quantitative Inventory of Alcohol
  Disorders (QIAD), 397
Quantity, Frequency, Variability Index
  (QFVI), 372
Quinlan, Karen Ann, 18

Race (*also see* Culture; Ethnicity),
  165, 257, 277
Racism, 189, 252, 253, 257, 271
Rand Corporation, 146
Rational behavioral therapy, 141
Rational emotive therapy, 141, 156
Rational Recovery, 156
Reagan, Nancy, 205
Reagan, Ronald, 190
Reality therapy, 118, 141, 375
Recovery (*also see* Treatment), 78, 83,
  89, 93–96, 100, 106, 125,
  126–127, 131, 136, 154,
  157, 237, 239, 242, 245,
  248, 250, 276, 324,
  335–338, 401, 406, 407,
  422, 423, 424, 427, 428,
  430, 447
Referrals, 67, 69, 85, 86, 87, 88, 90,
  98–100, 105, 106, 121, 138,
  146, 203
Regulation of alcohol and other
  drugs, 68, 180–204, 445
  advertising, 173–176, 186
  and alcohol consumption,
    182–187
  civil penalties, 191
  decriminalization, 68

distribution, 186, 187
insurance laws, 189, 190
legislation, 68
liability laws, 189
minimum age of purchase, 166,
    173, 177, 184, 187
open container laws, 188, 191
pricing, 185, 186, 188
sociocultural influences on public
    policy, 68
taxes, 175, 176, 183, 185, 186,
    204
Rehabilitation Act of 1973, 153, 313
Relapse, 42, 88, 111, 113, 117, 125,
    126, 127, 134, 135,
    136–137, 141, 148, 157,
    167, 210, 225, 241, 353,
    357, 358, 366, 369, 407,
    415, 417, 419, 423, 424,
    433, 446, 447
Relaxation techniques, 21, 136, 150,
    363
Religion, 7, 8, 30, 31, 33, 89, 90,
    115, 119, 152, 181, 241,
    277, 325
  Buddhism, 290
  Catholic, 9, 11, 16, 30, 288, 293,
    298
  Christian, 276, 298
  Jewish, 11, 31, 297–301
  Metropolitan Community Church,
    303
  Moslem, 51, 269, 290, 293
  Muslim, 16, 19, 181
  and Native Americans, 248–249
  Protestant, 9, 11, 298
Reproductive system (also see
    Pregnancy)
  and alcohol use, 48–49
  and marijuana use, 51
Research Society on Alcoholism, 372
Residential treatment and treatment
    communities, 217, 218, 223
Resource Center on Substance Abuse
    Prevention and Disability, 379
Ritalin, 4, 18
Rohypnol, 19
Routes of drug administration, 17,
    19, 52, 53, 54, 57, 182, 183
Rush, Benjamin, 16
Russia (also see Commonwealth of
    Independent States), 164, 362

SADD, 166, 172
Saki, 266
Salsolinol, 27
Salvation Army, 108, 119, 120, 125,
    355
Saudi Arabia, 181

Scandinavia, 159, 255
Schizophrenia, 54, 55, 79, 88, 349,
    351, 352, 353, 358
Screening, 67, 69–75, 100, 138,
    154, 315
  reliability, 71, 75–77
  sensitivity, 76
  specificity, 76
  validity, 71, 75–77
Seconal, 56
Secular Organization for Sobriety
    (S.O.S.), 156
Sedative-hypnotic drugs (see Central
    nervous system, depressants)
Seizures, 25, 47, 53, 57, 69, 86, 87,
    106, 108, 371, 378, 379
Self-help groups (also see specific
    groups by name), 67, 69, 92,
    99–100, 101, 106, 113, 136,
    148, 151–156, 157, 203,
    219, 221, 231, 278,
    288–289, 295, 301, 353,
    354, 355, 370, 377, 447
  for families, 208
  for gay men and lesbians, 99, 331,
    332, 335–339
  for those with hearing
    impairments, 375
  for those with mental illness and
    substance disorders, 357,
    358–359
  for those with mental retardation
    and substance disorders, 363
  for those with traumatic
    brain/head injury, 373
  for women, 99, 426–428
  for youth, 203, 204, 205, 206,
    215, 217, 219–222
Self-report instruments, 70–77
Seminole Indians, 260
Serotonin, 27, 55, 414
Serum GGT, 71
Server training, 190
Sex (see Gender)
Sexual abuse, 89, 117, 121, 138,
    407, 408, 414, 421,
    422–423, 425, 430, 431,
    432
Sexual assault, 183, 430
Sexual function (dysfunction), 121,
    410, 413–414
  and alcohol use, 413–414
  and alcoholism, 48, 413–414
  and amphetamine use, 54, 414
  and antabuse, 131
  and barbiturate use, 414
  and benzodiazepine use, 414
  and cocaine use, 52, 414
  and MDMA, 55

and narcotic use, 414
Sexually transmitted disease, 57, 58,
    138, 327
Shakespeare, William, 413
Shame, 238, 243, 294, 323, 408,
    419, 423, 428, 431
Shame-bound families, 232,
    234–235, 237, 238
Shintoism, 290
Short MAST (SMAST), 71, 367, 371
Signs of Sobriety (SOS), 375
Sioux, 258, 262, 265
Skid row, 85, 260
Smoking (see Nicotine)
Sobriety, 85, 88, 91, 107, 113, 118,
    121, 122, 137, 141, 151,
    153, 154, 226, 233, 234,
    240, 248, 250, 263, 276,
    323, 335, 357, 364, 365,
    408, 414, 427
Social history, 69, 83–90, 358
Social Security, 369
Socioeconomic status, 31, 106, 108,
    109, 181, 182, 196, 197,
    200, 256, 323, 421, 446
Solvents (see Inhalants)
Sopor, 18
South America, 15, 182, 270, 281
South Korea, 409
Soviet Union, 181, 186, 255
Spain, 281, 290
Special Office for Drug Abuse
    Prevention, (SODAP), 169
"Speed" (also see Central nervous
    system, stimulants), 17, 36
Speedballs, 53
Spinal cord injuries (SCI), 348,
    367–370, 372, 376, 379
Spirituality, 90, 119, 152, 221, 266,
    278, 288, 305
Stephen Miller House, 375
Stimulants (see Central nervous
    system, stimulants)
STP, 59
Stress, 25, 90, 113, 114, 121, 136,
    142, 150, 169, 236, 239,
    258, 270, 295, 367, 378,
    394, 401, 421, 431
Structured Addictions Assessment
    Interview for Selecting
    Treatment (SAAST), 397
Students Against Driving Drunk
    (SADD), 166, 172
Substance abuse (see Abuse of
    alcohol and drugs;
    Alcoholism; Chemical
    dependence)
Substance Abuse Group Experience
    (SAGE), 354

Substance Abuse and Mental Health
Services Administration
(SAMHSA), 145, 261, 263,
417, 432
Substance Abuse Resources and
Disabilities Project, 375, 379
Substance Abuse Subtle Screening
Inventory (SASSI), 70, 73, 74,
75, 77, 350
Suicide, 3, 11, 18, 54, 56, 75, 88,
97, 108, 109, 270, 276, 299,
319, 374, 399, 413, 429
Supplemental Security Income (SSI),
364, 365
Support Together for Emotional and
Mental Serenity and Sobriety
(STEMSS), 358
Sweden, 61, 164
Synanon, 118, 425
Syphilis, 53

Taiwan, 409
Taoism, 290, 293
Task Force on Black and Minority
Health, 271, 279
Teenagers (see Youth)
Telecommunications Devices for the
Deaf (TDD), 375
Television programming, 174–175
Temperance Movement, 9, 184, 185,
230, 269
Temperance Union, 16
Teton Dakota Indians, 264
Tetrahydrosioquinolines, 27
Therapeutic communities (see
Treatment)
Tobacco (see Nicotine)
Tolerance, 6, 7, 11, 33, 37, 40, 41,
42, 43, 46, 47, 52, 54, 55, 57,
58, 62, 78, 87, 196, 392, 397
Torah, 297
"Tracks," 58
Tranquilizers (minor) (also see
Benzodiazepines), 18, 19, 86,
98, 274, 369, 409
Transactional analysis, 141
Traumatic brain injury (TBI), 368,
370–373, 379
Treasury Department, 166
Treatment, 8, 67–68, 69, 70, 88, 90,
92, 97–98, 100, 104–165,
171, 180, 194, 198, 200,
214, 216–217, 230, 256,
364, 372, 409, 423–426,
431–432, 445–447, 448,
449, 450
    acupuncture, 148–150, 398, 400
    adjunctive services, 104, 127,
    138–139

of African Americans, 275–279,
280
aftercare, 67, 104, 129, 136–137,
198, 203, 363
alternatives, 217, 222
amount and intensity of services,
139–140
Antabuse, 121–132, 133, 134,
135, 172, 400
art therapy, 208
of Asian Americans, 11, 295–297
aversion, 141, 142, 400
behavioral, 136, 240–241, 355,
362, 363, 372, 400
behavioral marital and family
therapy, 141, 142
behavioral self-control training,
141, 142, 146
biofeedback, 148, 150
biopsychosocial approach, 104,
110, 121, 127, 139, 449
brief interventions, 124, 131, 140,
142
buprenophrine, 134, 135
case management, 110, 138, 226,
355, 357, 364, 401, 425,
449
and client characteristics, 140
clonidine, 134
cognitive, 241, 366, 447
cognitive-behavioral, 141
community reinforcement, 123,
124, 131, 141, 142
conjoint, 112, 123, 124, 136,
216, 230–231
continuum of care, 104, 115, 111,
136, 138, 356, 401
controlled drinking, 146–148, 400
coping skills training, 141
couple, 120, 123
cue exposure therapy, 141
culturally appropriate, 197, 242,
255–317
day treatment, 114, 115, 124
detoxification, 67, 100, 104–109,
117, 120, 126–127, 146,
151, 232, 243, 248, 400
domiciliaries, 119, 351
dropouts, 118, 122, 133, 149,
150, 424
education, 67, 92, 104, 106, 113,
137–138, 146, 207, 216,
219, 220, 240, 353, 354,
355, 356, 362, 363, 370,
375, 400
effectiveness, 67, 76, 104,
108–109, 114–115,
117–118, 120, 124–131,
133, 134–136, 137,

139–145, 149–150,
154–156, 159, 203, 423,
424–426, 446, 449
of elderly alcoholics, 400, 402
ethics, 148, 208, 210, 400
family, 113, 114, 120, 123, 124,
148, 203, 217, 221–222,
223–226, 229–254, 296,
353, 362, 400, 424, 446,
449
funding, 142, 143–146, 190, 191,
226, 326
for gay men, 122, 328–333
gender issues, 122
group, 113, 114, 115, 116, 119,
120, 121–123, 124, 138,
153, 224, 231, 331–333,
353, 354, 355, 356, 362,
365, 366, 400, 401, 424
halfway houses, 92, 115–118,
120, 356, 357, 364, 365,
375
of Hispanic Americans, 287–290
individual, 113, 114, 116, 118,
120, 121, 128, 242, 353,
356, 362, 400, 408, 424
inpatient, 89, 96, 100, 104, 105,
108, 109–113, 114, 115,
123, 125, 134, 140, 144,
155, 207–208, 211, 217,
218, 221, 222–223, 348,
356, 400, 446, 449
integrated, 82, 198, 353–355,
356, 370
intensive, 67, 89, 100, 104, 105,
109–115, 118, 120, 125,
136, 137, 313, 319–320,
401
in jail, 203
of Jewish Americans, 300–301
length of, 139, 140, 190, 446,
449
for lesbians, 111, 326, 334, 335
levo-alpha-acetylmethadol
(LAAM), 133, 135
maintenance, 67, 104, 137
marital, 123, 124, 215, 216,
230–231, 242, 243, 244,
249, 400
matching, 104, 125–130, 140,
141, 142, 157, 180,
424–426
of men, 230
of mentally ill substance abusers,
352–359
of mentally retarded substance
abusers, 361, 363–366
methadone maintenance,
132–133, 134, 135, 139,

143, 149, 172, 191, 203, 418, 446, 447
missions, 108, 119–120
motivation, 116, 121, 142, 204
motivation interviewing, 141
motivational enhancement therapy (MET), 128–129
multidimensional approach, 83, 124, 138, 139
naltrexone, 134, 135, 136, 141
of Native Americans, 262–263, 266–267
nontraditional, 104, 146–151, 497
outpatient, 67, 89, 91, 100, 104, 105, 108, 111, 113–114, 115, 120–124, 129, 131, 134, 136, 137, 139, 140, 143, 144, 145, 148, 155, 190, 217–220, 223, 245, 248, 353, 357, 364, 394, 399, 446, 449
pharmacotherapy, 67, 104, 128, 131–136
planning, 82, 114, 399, 400
psychoeducation, 104, 137–138, 209, 243, 287–288, 354, 366, 368
psychotherapy, 141, 142, 146, 230, 354, 366
relapse prevention, 141
residential, 67, 104, 111, 114, 115–120, 121, 136, 142, 143, 217, 218, 223, 353, 354, 356, 357, 361, 364, 417, 425, 449
team approach, 133
theoretical perspectives, 141–142, 204, 239–244, 424
therapeutic communities, 92, 115, 118–119, 124, 139, 170, 217, 223, 287, 370, 425
therapist characteristics, 140–141, 424
twelve-step facilitation therapy (TSF), 128
"two-tier system," 143–146, 430, 448
unidimensional approach, 83
voluntary and involuntary (mandatory), 91–92, 105, 108, 177, 203, 204
women, 296, 417, 419–420, 423–426
youth, 213–228
Treatment Alternatives to Street Crime (TASC), 203
Treatment Outcome Perspective Study (TOPS), 125

"Tripping," 59
TWEAK, 59
Twelve-step programs (see Self-help groups)
Twenty-First Amendment to the U.S. Constitution (repeal of Prohibition), 185, 391
Twenty-Sixth Amendment to the U.S. Constitution, 172

Ulcers, 58, 355, 359
United States:
    Department of Justice, 172
    Drug Enforcement Administration, 187
    military, 53, 186
    Office of Drug Control Policy, 192
    Supreme Court, 267
    Treasury Department, 182
Urinalysis, 87, 114, 118, 133, 149, 150, 172, 220, 351

Valium, 3, 18, 56, 364
Venereal disease, 57, 58, 327
Veterans Administration, 86, 99, 119, 354, 369, 370, 392, 393, 394, 401, 430, 447
Vietnam War, 19
Vietnamese Americans, 290
Violence, 198–200, 429, 430
Virginia Twin Registry, 412
Visual impairments, 376–377
Vocational rehabilitation, 85, 98, 116, 117, 140, 223, 347, 353, 400, 429
Volstead Act (see Prohibition Amendment of 1917)

Walden House, 114
War on drugs (see also Regulation of alcohol and other drugs), 68, 192, 202, 204, 417, 445, 447, 449
Wernicke-Korsakoff syndrome (also see Korsakoff's psychosis, Wernicke's syndrome), 50
Wernicke's syndrome, 49, 50
West Indies, 270
Western Region Indian Alcoholism Training Center, 263
Whites, 10, 11, 14, 19, 145, 202, 255–257, 258–259, 262, 264, 269–271, 273–279, 281, 283, 286–287, 291, 292, 294, 295
Whitman-Walker Clinic, 306
Wine, 170, 173, 174, 177, 181, 185, 255, 257, 283
Witchita Indians, 260

Withdrawal, 6, 7, 25, 33, 39–41, 43, 52, 57, 86, 87, 105–109, 124, 125–127, 352, 355
    alcohol, 25, 47, 123
    amphetamine, 54–55
    cocaine, 52
    heroine, 25, 40, 41, 57, 107
    marijuana, 41, 42
    opiate, 58, 134, 154
Women, 9, 10, 11, 12, 14, 89, 198, 230–231, 301, 406–442, 447
    African American, 14, 272–275, 416, 431
    and Alcoholics Anonymous, 134, 152, 156
    alcohol use, 31, 254–255, 408–410
    alcohol-related deaths, 413
    alcohol-related health problems, 412–413
    Asian American, 297
    attitudes towards, 418
    biological issues, 410–417
    cardiovascular disease, 48
    cirrhosis, 47, 262
    and codependency, 235–237
    and crime, 198, 199, 287, 418, 420–421
    domestic violence, 196, 199, 200, 422–423, 430, 431
    drug use, 409–410
    genetics, 410–412
    gynecological and reproductive problems, 10, 48, 412, 414–417, 431
    heroin use, 19, 418, 420, 421
    Hispanic American, 286–287
    Jewish American, 297
    lesbian, 318–327, 329–330, 423
    marijuana use, 14
    Native American, 86, 416
    nicotine use, 16
    obstetrical problems, 10
    physical abuse, 421–422, 425
    and pregnancy, 60–62, 133, 139, 415–417, 431
    premenstrual syndrome, 414–415
    psychological, 421–423
    recovery, 422, 423, 424
    research, 428–430, 432, 447
    sedative use, 18
    and self-help groups, 99, 152, 426–428
    sexual abuse, 89, 421, 422–423, 425, 430, 431, 432
    sexual dysfunction, 52, 413–414
    social issues, 417–421
    special needs, 212

Women *(continued)*
    stimulant use, 18
    suicide, 399, 413
    treatment, 295, 409, 417,
        419–420, 423–426,
        431–432
Women for Sobriety (WFS), 156,
    337, 427–428
World Health Organization (WHO),
    5, 6, 8, 32, 71, 78, 79–81,
    82, 131
World War II, 17, 53, 170, 260, 271

Youth *(also see Family)*, 1, 11, 24, 37,
    75, 82, 139, 166, 189, 190,
    192, 195, 198, 213–228
    African American, 11, 217,
        274–275, 284, 416
    alcohol use, 11, 197, 211
    chemical dependence among,
        213

cocaine use, 274
crack use, 274
crime, 195, 196, 205
developmental approach to
    assessment, 214–216, 222
diagnosis, 199, 207, 224
drug use, 211, 274
education, 138, 203–205, 207,
    216, 219
ethnic, 302
gangs, 147–148, 187–188
gay and lesbian, 326
hallucinogen use, 14, 274
heroin use, 19, 134
Hispanic, 283–284
inhalant use, 31, 274
levo-alpha-acetylmethadol
    (LAAM), 133
marijuana use, 14, 197, 208, 211,
    274
meanings of drug use, 215–216

mentally retarded, 361, 362
Native American, 31, 262–263,
    267
nicotine use, 16, 176
offenders, 172
peer influences, 168, 169, 216,
    219, 224–225, 268, 275
prevention of alcohol and drug
    problems, 166–168, 218–219
screening for substance abuse, 77
sedative use, 18
self-help programs, 152, 205–206,
    207, 215, 319–322
sexual activity, 215
skills training, 205, 215, 220
stimulant use, 18, 274
suicide, 217, 222
surveys of youth, 211
tranquilizer use, 274
treatment of, 213–228